CLEAR WRITING

CLEAR WRITING
READINGS IN EXPOSITORY PROSE

edited by
MARJORIE MATHER AND BRETT MCLENITHAN

broadview press

Library and Archives Canada Cataloguing in Publication

Clear writing : readings in expository prose / edited by Marjorie Mather and Brett McLenithan.

Includes bibliographical references and index.
ISBN-13: 978-1-55111-824-6
ISBN-10: 1-55111-824-6

1. College readers.   2. Exposition (Rhetoric).   3. English language (Rhetoric).
I. Mather, Marjorie.   II. McLenithan, Brett

PE1122.C54 2006   808'.0427   C2006-905151-8

Broadview Press is an independent, international publishing house, incorporated in 1985. Broadview believes in shared ownership, both with its employees and with the general public; since the year 2000 Broadview shares have traded publicly on the Toronto Venture Exchange under the symbol BDP.

We welcome comments and suggestions regarding any aspect of our publications – please feel free to contact us at the addresses below or at broadview@broadviewpress.com.

North America
Post Office Box 1243, Peterborough, Ontario, Canada K9J 7H5
3576 California Road, Orchard Park, NY, USA 14127
Tel: (705) 743-8990; Fax: (705) 743-8353;
e-mail: customerservice@broadviewpress.com

UK, Ireland, and continental Europe
NBN International, Estover Road, Plymouth, UK PL6 7PY
Tel: 44 (0) 1752 202300; Fax: 44 (0) 1752 202330
email: enquiries@nbninternational.com

Australia and New Zealand
UNIREPS, University of New South Wales
Sydney, NSW, Australia 2052
Tel: 61 2 9664 0999; Fax: 61 2 9664 5420
email: info.press@unsw.edu.au

www.broadviewpress.com

Broadview Press gratefully acknowledges the financial support of the Ministry of Canadian Heritage through the Book Publishing Industry Development Program.

Typesetting and assembly: True to Type Inc., Mississauga, Canada.

PRINTED IN CANADA

808.
042
MAT

CONTENTS

Law and Politics

History

Science and Technology

Human Nature

Languages and Culture

Literature and Other Arts

INDEX
RHETORICAL MODES

Definition

Description

Narration

Persuasion and Argument

Analysis

Classification

Example and Illustration

PREFACE

One cannot spend the better part of a work day around books—producing them, discussing them, and, of course, reading them—without developing an appreciation for clarity and conciseness in writing. *Clear Writing: Readings in Expository Prose* is fundamentally just this: a collection of examples of clear writing, from a variety of disciplines, modes (academic, popular, journalistic), rhetorical practices, and cultural perspectives.

A student can successfully produce effective writing only after waking to the subtle elements that contribute to a "good read." To this end, we have chosen varied pieces of writing with an eye toward generating curiosity or provoking discussion or reflection. Along with such classics as Jonathan Swift's "A Modest Proposal," Henry David Thoreau's "Civil Disobedience," George Orwell's "Shooting an Elephant," and Ernest Hemingway's "Pamplona in July," we have included a broad selection of works by such contemporary writers as Malcolm Gladwell, Amy Tan, Barbara Ehrenreich, and Douglas Coupland, among many others.

Jonathan Swift wrote of "proper words in proper places"; for many undergraduates, what is and what is not proper is still a matter for investigation and discovery. In this spirit, we hope that this collection provides models that are enjoyable, as well as exemplary, for students and general readers alike.

We are very grateful to Laura Cardiff, Joelle Dunne, Judith Earnshaw, Julia Gaunce, Craig Lawson, Don LePan, Jennifer McCue, Mical Moser, Amy Nimegeer, Indrani Roy, and Tania Therien for their help with this project. We would also like to thank those academics who provided valuable comments and suggestions towards the shaping of the book.

Marjorie Mather and Brett McLenithan

Personal Experiences

E.B. WHITE

Once More to the Lake

(1941)

Though perhaps better known as the author of the renowned children's books Stuart Little *(1945) and* Charlotte's Web *(1952), E.B. White (1899-1985) spent most of his writing time as a journalist and essayist, and was a regular contributor to* The New Yorker.

In this essay, White describes the experience of returning with his son to the lake in Maine where he spent his childhood summers.

One summer, along about 1904, my father rented a camp on a lake in Maine and took us all there for the month of August. We all got ringworm from some kittens and had to rub Pond's Extract on our arms and legs night and morning, and my father rolled over in a canoe with all his clothes on; but outside of that the vacation was a success and from then on none of us ever thought there was any place in the world like that lake in Maine. We returned summer after summer—always on August 1st for one month. I have since become a salt-water man, but sometimes in summer there are days when the restlessness of the tides and the fearful cold of the sea water and the incessant wind that blows across the afternoon and into the evening make me wish for the placidity of a lake in the woods. A few weeks ago this feeling got so strong I bought myself a couple of bass hooks and a spinner and returned to the lake where we used to go, for a week's fishing and to revisit old haunts.

I took along my son, who had never had any fresh water up his nose and who had seen lily pads only from train windows. On the journey over to the lake I began to wonder what it would be like. I wondered how time would have marred this unique, this holy spot—the coves and streams, the hills that the sun set behind, the camps and the paths behind the camps. I was sure that the tarred road would have found it out and I wondered in what other ways it would be desolated. It is strange how much you can remember about places like that once you allow your mind to return into the grooves which lead back. You remember one thing, and that suddenly reminds you of another thing. I guess I remembered clearest of all the early mornings, when the lake was cool and motionless, remembered how the bedroom smelled of the lumber it was made of and of the wet woods whose scent entered through the screen. The partitions in the camp were thin and did not extend clear to the top of the rooms, and as I was always the first up I would dress softly so as not to wake the others, and sneak out into the sweet outdoors and start out in the canoe, keeping close along the shore in the long shadows of the pines. I remembered being very careful never to rub my paddle against the gunwale for fear of disturbing the stillness of the cathedral.

The lake had never been what you would call a wild lake. There were cottages sprinkled around the shores, and it was in farming country although the shores of the lake were quite heavily wooded. Some of the cottages were owned by nearby farmers, and you would live at the shore and eat your meals at the farmhouse. That's what our family did. But although it wasn't wild, it was a fairly large and undisturbed lake and there were places in it which, to a child at least, seemed infinitely remote and primeval.

I was right about the tar: it led to within half a mile of the shore. But when I got back there, with my boy, and we settled into a camp near a farmhouse and into the kind of summertime I had known, I could tell that it was going to be pretty much the same as it had been before—I knew it, lying in bed the first morning, smelling the bedroom, and hearing the boy sneak quietly out and go off along the shore in a boat. I began to sustain the illusion that he was I, and therefore, by simple transposition, that I was my father. This sensation persisted, kept cropping up all the time we were there. It was not an entirely new feeling, but in this setting it grew much stronger. I seemed to be living a dual existence. I would be in the middle of some simple act, I would be picking up a bait box or laying down a table fork, or I would be saying something, and suddenly it would be not I but my father who was saying the words or making the gesture. It gave me a creepy sensation.

5   We went fishing the first morning. I felt the same damp moss covering the worms in the bait can, and saw the dragonfly alight on the tip of my rod as it hovered a few inches from the surface of the water. It was the arrival of this fly that convinced me beyond any doubt that everything was as it always had been, that the years were a mirage and there had been no years. The small waves were the same, chucking the rowboat under the chin as we fished at anchor, and the boat was the same boat, the same color green and the ribs broken in the same places, and under the floor-boards the same fresh-water leavings and debris—the dead helgramite, the wisps of moss,

the rusty discarded fishhook, the dried blood from yesterday's catch. We stared silently at the tips of our rods, at the dragonflies that came and went. I lowered the tip of mine into the water, tentatively, pensively dislodging the fly, which darted two feet away, poised, darted two feet back, and came to rest again a little farther up the rod. There had been no years between the ducking of this dragonfly and the other one—the one that was part of memory. I looked at the boy, who was silently watching his fly, and it was my hands that held his rod, my eyes watching. I felt dizzy and didn't know which rod I was at the end of.

We caught two bass, hauling them in briskly as though they were mackerel, pulling them over the side of the boat in a businesslike manner without any landing net, and stunning them with a blow on the back of the head. When we got back for a swim before lunch, the lake was exactly where we had left it, the same number of inches from the dock, and there was only the merest suggestion of a breeze. This seemed an utterly enchanted sea, this lake you could leave to its own devices for a few hours and come back to, and find that it had not stirred, this constant and trustworthy body of water. In the shallows, the dark, water-soaked sticks and twigs, smooth and old, were undulating in clusters on the bottom against the clean ribbed sand, and the track of the mussel was plain. A school of minnows swam by, each minnow with its small individual shadow, doubling the attendance, so clear and sharp in the sunlight. Some of the other campers were in swimming, along the shore, one of them with a cake of soap, and the water felt thin and clear and unsubstantial. Over the years there had been this person with the cake of soap, this cultist, and here he was. There had been no years.

Up to the farmhouse to dinner through the teeming, dusty field, the road under our sneakers was only a two-track road. The middle track was missing, the one with the marks of the hooves and the splotches of dried, flaky manure. There had always been three tracks to choose from in choosing which track to walk in; now the choice was narrowed down to two. For a moment I missed terribly the middle alternative. But the way led past the tennis court, and something about the way it lay there in the sun reassured me; the tape had loosened along the backline, the alleys were green with plantains and other weeds, and the net (installed in June and removed in September) sagged in the dry noon, and the whole place steamed with midday heat and hunger and emptiness. There was a choice of pie for dessert, and one was blueberry and one was apple, and the waitresses were the same country girls, there having been no passage of time, only the illusion of it as in a dropped curtain—the waitresses were still fifteen; their hair had been washed, that was the only difference—they had been to the movies and seen the pretty girls with the clean hair.

Summertime, oh, summertime, pattern of life indelible, with fadeproof lake, the wood unshatterable, the pasture with the sweetfern and the juniper forever and ever, summer without end; this was the background, and the life along the shore was the design, the cottages with their innocent and tranquil design, their tiny docks with the flagpole and the American flag floating against the white clouds in the blue sky, the little paths over the roots of trees leading from camp to camp and the paths leading back to the outhouses and the can of lime for sprinkling, and at the souvenir counters at the store the miniature birch-bark canoes and the postcards that showed things looking a little better than they looked. This was the American family at play, escaping the city heat, wondering whether the newcomers in the camp at the head of the cove were "common" or "nice," wondering whether it was true that the people who drove up for Sunday dinner at the farmhouse were turned away because there wasn't enough chicken.

It seemed to me, as I kept remembering all this, that those times and those summers had been infinitely precious and worth saving. There had been jollity and peace and goodness. The arriving (at the beginning of August) had been so big a business in itself, at the railway station the farm wagon drawn up, the first smell of the pine-laden air, the first glimpse of the smiling farmer, and the great importance of the trunks and your father's enormous authority in such matters, and the feel of the wagon under you for the long ten-mile haul, and at the top of the last long hill catching the first view of the lake after eleven months of not seeing this cherished body of water. The shouts and cries of the other campers when they saw you, and the trunks to be unpacked, to give up their rich burden. (Arriving was less exciting nowadays, when you sneaked up in your car and parked it under a tree near the camp and took out the bags and in five minutes it was all over, no fuss, no loud wonderful fuss about the trunks.)

10   Peace and goodness and jollity. The only thing that was wrong now, really, was the sound of the place, an unfamiliar nervous sound of the outboard motors. This was the note that jarred, the one thing that would sometimes break the illusion and set the years moving. In those other summertimes all motors were inboard; and when they were at a little distance, the noise they made was a sedative, an ingredient of summer sleep. They were one-cylinder and two-cylinder engines, and some were make-and-break and some were jump-spark, but they all made a sleepy sound across the lake. The one-lungers throbbed and fluttered, and the twin-cylinder ones purred and purred, and that was a quiet sound, too. But now the campers all had outboards. In the daytime, in the hot mornings, these motors made a petulant, irritable sound; at night in the still evening when the afterglow lit the water, they whined about one's ears like mosquitoes. My boy loved our rented outboard, and his great desire was to achieve single-handed mastery over it, and authority, and he soon learned the trick of choking it a little (but not too much), and the adjustment of the needle valve. Watching him I would

remember the things you could do with the old one-cylinder engine with the heavy flywheel, how you could have it eating out of your hand if you got really close to it spiritually. Motor boats in those days didn't have clutches, and you would make a landing by shutting off the motor at the proper time and coasting in with a dead rudder. But there was a way of reversing them, if you learned the trick, by cutting the switch and putting it on again exactly on the final dying revolution of the flywheel, so that it would kick back against compression and begin reversing. Approaching a dock in a strong following breeze, it was difficult to slow up sufficiently by the ordinary coasting method, and if a boy felt he had complete mastery over his motor, he was tempted to keep it running beyond its time and then reverse it a few feet from the dock. It took a cool nerve, because if you threw the switch a twentieth of a second too soon you would catch the flywheel when it still had speed enough to go up past center, and the boat would leap ahead, charging bull-fashion at the dock.

We had a good week at the camp. The bass were biting well and the sun shone endlessly, day after day. We would be tired at night and lie down in the accumulated heat of the little bedrooms after the long hot day and the breeze would stir almost imperceptibly outside and the smell of the swamp drift in through the rusty screens. Sleep would come easily and in the morning the red squirrel would be on the roof, tapping out his gay routine. I kept remembering everything, lying in bed in the mornings—the small steamboat that had a long rounded stern like the lip of a Ubangi, and how quietly she ran on the moonlight sails, when the older boys played their mandolins and the girls sang and we ate doughnuts dipped in sugar, and how sweet the music was on the water in the shining night, and what it had felt like to think about girls then. After breakfast we would go up to the store and the things were in the same place—the minnows in a bottle, the plugs and spinners disarranged and pawed over by the youngsters from the boys' camp, the fig newtons and the Beeman's gum. Outside, the road was tarred and cars stood in front of the store. Inside, all was just as it had always been, except there was more Coca-Cola and not so much Moxie and root beer and birch beer and sarsaparilla. We would walk out with a bottle of pop apiece and sometimes the pop would backfire up our noses and hurt. We explored the streams, quietly, where the turtles slid off the sunny logs and dug their way into the soft bottom; and we lay on the town wharf and fed worms to the tame bass. Everywhere we went I had trouble making out which was I, the one walking at my side, the one walking in my pants.

One afternoon while we were there at that lake a thunderstorm came up. It was like the revival of an old melodrama that I had seen long ago with childish awe. The second-act climax of the drama of the electrical disturbance over a lake in America had not changed in any important respect. This was the big scene, still the big scene. The whole thing was so familiar, the first feeling of oppression and heat and a general air around camp of not wanting to go very far away. In midafternoon (it was all the same) a curious darkening of the sky, and a lull in everything that had made life tick; and then the way the boats suddenly swung the other way at their moorings with the coming breeze out of the new quarter, and the premonitory rumble. Then the kettle drum, then the snare, then the bass drum and cymbals, then crackling light against the dark, and the gods grinning and licking their chops in the hills. Afterward the calm, the rain steadily rustling in the calm lake, the return of light and hope and spirits, and the campers running out in joy and relief to go swimming in the rain, their bright cries perpetuating the deathless joke about how they were getting simply drenched, and the children screaming with delight at the new sensation of bathing in the rain, and the joke about getting drenched linking the generations in a strong indestructible chain. And the comedian who waded in carrying an umbrella.

When the others went swimming my son said he was going in too. He pulled his dripping trunks from the line where they had hung all through the shower, and wrung them out. Languidly, and with no thought of going in, I watched him, his hard little body, skinny and bare, saw him wince slightly as he pulled up around his vitals the small, soggy, icy garment. As he buckled the swollen belt suddenly my groin felt the chill of death.

Questions

1. White never refers to his son by name, and in such a deeply personal, autobiographical essay, one might expect precisely the opposite. Why might White have decided to do this?
2. White's essay, although in essence the narration of an extended memory, does not proceed chronologically. Speculate as to why White chose to arrange his essay topic thematically rather than sequentially.
3. At what point in the essay does White first acknowledge a significant change between his experience of the lake as a child and later as an adult? Trace his attitude from that point to the concluding paragraph. What, finally, is White trying to communicate?

JAMES BALDWIN

Notes of a Native Son

(1963)

James Baldwin (1924–87) was a writer of short stories, novels, and essays, many of which focused on mid twentieth-century racial and sexual issues. His major works include the novel Go Tell It on the Mountain *(1953), and two essay collections:* Notes of a Native Son *(1955) and* Nobody Knows My Name *(1961).*

In the following passage from Notes of a Native Son, *Baldwin combines personal narrative with an analysis of systemic racism.*

On the 29th of July, in 1943, my father died. On the same day, a few hours later, his last child was born. Over a month before this, while all our energies were concentrated in waiting for these events, there had been, in Detroit, one of the bloodiest race riots of the century. A few hours after my father's funeral, while he lay in state in the undertaker's chapel, a race riot broke out in Harlem. On the morning of the 3rd of August, we drove my father to the graveyard through a wilderness of smashed plate glass.

The day of my father's funeral had also been my nineteenth birthday. As we drove him to the graveyard, the spoils of injustice, anarchy, discontent, and hatred were all around us. It seemed to me that God himself had devised, to mark my father's end, the most sustained and brutally dissonant of codas. And it seemed to me, too, that the violence which rose all about us as my father left the world had been devised as a corrective for the pride of his eldest son. I had declined to believe in that apocalypse which had been central to my father's vision; very well, life seemed to be saying, here is something that will certainly pass for an apocalypse until the real thing comes along. I had inclined to be contemptuous of my father for the conditions of his life, for the conditions of our lives. When his life had ended I began to wonder about that life and also, in a new way, to be apprehensive about my own.

I had not known my father very well. We had got on badly, partly because we shared, in our different fashions, the vice of stubborn pride. When he was dead I realized that I had hardly ever spoken to him. When he had been dead a long time I began to wish I had. It seems to be typical of life in America, where opportunities, real and fancied, are thicker than anywhere else on the globe, that the second generation has no time to talk to the first.

No one, including my father, seems to have known exactly how old he was, but his mother had been born during slavery. He was of the first generation of free men. He, along with thousands of other Negroes, came North after 1919 and I was part of that generation which had never seen the landscape of what Negroes sometimes call the Old Country.

He had been born in New Orleans and had been a quite young man there during the time that Louis Armstrong, a boy, was running errands for the dives and honkytonks of what was always presented to me as one of the most wicked of cities—to this day, whenever I think of New Orleans, I also helplessly think of Sodom and Gomorrah. My father never mentioned Louis Armstrong, except to forbid us to play his records; but there was a picture of him on our wall for a long time. One of my father's strong-willed female relatives had placed it there and forbade my father to take it down. He never did, but he eventually maneuvered her out of the house and when, some years later, she was in trouble and near death, he refused to do anything to help her.

5   He was, I think, very handsome. I gather this from photographs and from my own memories of him, dressed in his Sunday best and on his way to preach a sermon somewhere, when I was little. Handsome, proud, and ingrown, "like a toe-nail," somebody said. But he looked to me, as I grew older, like pictures I had seen of African tribal chieftains: he really should have been naked, with war-paint on and barbaric mementos, standing among spears. He could be chilling in the pulpit and indescribably cruel in his personal life and he was certainly the most bitter man I have ever met; yet it must be said that there was something else in him, buried in him, which lent him his tremendous power and, even, a rather crushing charm. It had something to do with his blackness, I think—he was very black—with his blackness and his beauty, and with the fact that he knew that he was black but did not know that he was beautiful. He claimed to be proud of his blackness but it had also been the cause of much humiliation and it had fixed bleak boundaries to his life. He was not a young man when we were growing up and he had already suffered many kinds of ruin; in his outrageously demanding and protective way he loved his children, who were black like him and menaced, like him; and all these things sometimes showed in his face when he tried, never to my knowledge with any success, to establish contact with any of us. When he took one of his children on his knee to play, the child always became fretful and began to cry; when he tried to help one of us with our homework the absolutely unabating tension which emanated from him caused our minds and our tongues to become paralyzed, so that he, scarcely knowing why, flew into a rage and the child, not knowing why, was punished. If it ever entered his head to bring a surprise home for his children, it was, almost unfailingly, the wrong surprise and even the big watermelons he often brought home on his back in the summertime led to the most appalling scenes. I do not remember, in all

those years, that one of his children was ever glad to see him come home. From what I was able to gather of his early life, it seemed that this inability to establish contact with other people had always marked him and had been one of the things which had driven him out of New Orleans. There was something in him, therefore, groping and tentative, which was never expressed and which was buried with him. One saw it most clearly when he was facing new people and hoping to impress them. But he never did, not for long. We went from church to smaller and more improbable church, he found himself in less and less demand as a minister, and by the time he died none of his friends had come to see him for a long time. He had lived and died in an intolerable bitterness of spirit and it frightened me, as we drove him to the graveyard through those unquiet, ruined streets, to see how powerful and overflowing this bitterness could be and to realize that this bitterness now was mine.

When he died I had been away from home for a little over a year. In that year I had had time to become aware of the meaning of all my father's bitter warnings, had discovered the secret of his proudly pursed lips and rigid carriage: I had discovered the weight of white people in the world. I saw that this had been for my ancestors and now would be for me an awful thing to live with and that the bitterness which had helped to kill my father could also kill me.

He had been ill a long time—in the mind, as we now realized, reliving instances of his fantastic intransigence in the new light of his affliction and endeavoring to feel a sorrow for him which never, quite, came true. We had not known that he was being eaten up by paranoia, and the discovery that his cruelty, to our bodies and our minds, had been one of the symptoms of his illness was not, then, enough to enable us to forgive him. The younger children felt, quite simply, relief that he would not be coming home any more. My mother's observation that it was he, after all, who had kept them alive all these years meant nothing because the problems of keeping children alive are not real for children. The older children felt, with my father gone, that they could invite their friends to the house without fear that their friends would be insulted or, as had sometimes happened with me, being told that their friends were in league with the devil and intended to rob our family of everything we owned. (I didn't fail to wonder, and it made me hate him, what on earth we owned that anybody else would want.)

His illness was beyond all hope of healing before anyone realized that he was ill. He had always been so strange and had lived, like a prophet, in such unimaginably close communion with the Lord that his long silences which were punctuated by moans and hallelujahs and snatches of old songs while he sat at the living-room window never seemed odd to us. It was not until he refused to eat because, he said, his family was trying to poison him that my mother was forced to accept as a fact what had, until then, been only an unwilling suspicion. When he was committed, it was discovered that he had tuberculosis and, as it turned out, the disease of his mind allowed the disease of his body to destroy him. For the doctors could not force him to eat, either, and, though he was fed intravenously, it was clear from the beginning that there was no hope for him.

In my mind's eye I could see him, sitting at the window, locked up in his terrors; hating and fearing every living soul including his children who had betrayed him, too, by reaching toward the world which had despised him. There were nine of us. I began to wonder what it could have felt like for such a man to have had nine children whom he could barely feed. He used to make little jokes about our poverty, which never, of course, seemed very funny to us; they could not have seemed very funny to him, either, or else our all too feeble response to them would never have caused such rages. He spent great energy and achieved, to our chagrin, no small amount of success in keeping us away from the people who surrounded us, people who had all-night rent parties to which we listened when we should have been sleeping, people who cursed and drank and flashed razor blades on Lenox Avenue. He could not understand why, if they had so much energy to spare, they could not use it to make their lives better. He treated almost everybody on our block with a most uncharitable asperity and neither they, nor, of course, their children were slow to reciprocate.

10   The only white people who came to our house were welfare workers and bill collectors. It was almost always my mother who dealt with them, for my father's temper, which was at the mercy of his pride, was never to be trusted. It was clear that he felt their very presence in his home to be a violation: this was conveyed by his carriage, almost ludicrously stiff, and by his voice, harsh and vindictively polite. When I was around nine or ten I wrote a play which was directed by a young, white schoolteacher, a woman, who then took an interest in me, and gave me books to read and, in order to corroborate my theatrical bent, decided to take me to see what she somewhat tactlessly referred to as "real" plays. Theatergoing was forbidden in our house, but, with the really cruel intuitiveness of a child, I suspected that the color of this woman's skin would carry the day for me. When, at school, she suggested taking me to the theater, I did not, as I might have done if she had been a Negro, find a way of discouraging her, but agreed that she should pick me up at my house one evening. I then, very cleverly, left all the rest to my mother, who suggested to my father, as I knew she would, that it would not be very nice to let such a kind woman make the trip for nothing. Also, since it was a schoolteacher, I imagine that my mother countered the idea of sin with the idea of "education," which word, even with my father, carried a kind of bitter weight.

Before the teacher came my father took me aside to ask *why* she was coming, what *interest* she could possibly have in our house, in a boy like me. I said I didn't know but I, too, suggested that it had something to do with education. And I understood that my father was waiting for me to say something—I didn't quite know what; perhaps that I wanted his protection against this teacher and her "education." I said none of these things and the teacher came and we went out. It was clear, during the brief interview in our living room, that my father was agreeing very much against his will and that he would have refused permission if he had dared. The fact that he did not dare caused me to despise him: I had no way of knowing that he was facing in that living room a wholly unprecedented and frightening situation.

Later, when my father had been laid off from his job, this woman became very important to us. She was really a very sweet and generous woman and went to a great deal of trouble to be of help to us, particularly during one awful winter. My mother called her by the highest name she knew: she said she was a "christian." My father could scarcely disagree but during the four or five years of our relatively close association he never trusted her and was always trying to surprise in her open, Midwestern face the genuine, cunningly hidden, and hideous motivation. In later years, particularly when it began to be clear that this "education" of mine was going to lead me to perdition, he became more explicit and warned me that my white friends in high school were not really my friends and that I would see, when I was older, how white people would do anything to keep a Negro down. Some of them could be nice, he admitted, but none of them were to be trusted and most of them were not even nice. The best thing was to have as little to do with them as possible. I did not feel this way and I was certain, in my innocence, that I never would.

But the year which preceded my father's death had made a great change in my life. I had been living in New Jersey, working in defense plants, working and living among southerners, white and black. I knew about the south, of course, and about how southerners treated Negroes and how they expected them to behave, but it had never entered my mind that anyone would look at me and expect *me* to behave that way. I learned in New Jersey that to be a Negro meant, precisely, that one was never looked at but was simply at the mercy of the reflexes the color of one's skin caused in other people. I acted in New Jersey as I had always acted, that is as though I thought a great deal of myself—I had to *act* that way— with results that were, simply, unbelievable. I had scarcely arrived before I had earned the enmity, which was extraordinarily ingenious, of all my superiors and nearly all my co-workers. In the beginning, to make matters worse, I simply did not know what was happening. I did not know what I had done, and I shortly began to wonder what *anyone* could possibly do, to bring about such unanimous, active, and unbearably vocal hostility. I knew about jim-crow[1] but I had never experienced it. I went to the same

---

1 *jim-crow* Euphemism for racial segregation, in reference to a series of segregation laws enacted in the later nineteenth century in the United States, which became known as Jim Crow laws.

self-service restaurant three times and stood with all the Princeton boys before the counter, waiting for a hamburger and coffee; it was always an extraordinarily long time before anything was set before me; but it was not until the fourth visit that I learned that, in fact, nothing had ever been set before me: I had simply picked something up. Negroes were not served there, I was told, and they had been waiting for me to realize that I was always the only Negro present. Once I was told this, I determined to go there all the time. But now they were ready for me and, though some dreadful scenes were subsequently enacted in that restaurant, I never ate there again.

It was the same story all over New Jersey, in bars, bowling alleys, diners, places to live. I was always being forced to leave, silently, or with mutual imprecations. I very shortly became notorious and children giggled behind me when I passed and their elders whispered or shouted—they really believed that I was mad. And it did begin to work on my mind, of course; I began to be afraid to go anywhere and to compensate for this I went places to which I really should not have gone and where, God knows, I had no desire to be. My reputation in town naturally enhanced my reputation at work and my working day became one long series of acrobatics designed to keep me out of trouble. I cannot say that these acrobatics succeeded. It began to seem that the machinery of the organization I worked for was turning over, day and night, with but one aim: to eject me. I was fired once, and contrived, with the aid of a friend from New York, to get back on the payroll; was fired again, and bounced back again. It took a while to fire me for the third time, but the third time took. There were no loopholes anywhere. There was not even any way of getting back inside the gates.

15   That year in New Jersey lives in my mind as though it were the year during which, having an unsuspected predilection for it, I first contracted some dread, chronic disease, the unfailing symptom of which is a kind of blind fever, a pounding in the skull and fire in the bowels. Once this disease is contracted, one can never be really carefree again, for the fever, without an instant's warning, can recur at any moment. It can wreck more important things than race relations. There is not a Negro alive who does not have this rage in his blood—one has the choice, merely, of living with it consciously or surrendering to it. As for me, this fever has recurred in me, and does, and will until the day I die.

My last night in New Jersey, a white friend from New York took me to the nearest big town, Trenton, to go to the movies and have a few drinks. As it turned out, he also saved me from, at the very least, a violent whipping. Almost every detail of that night stands out very clearly in my memory. I even remember the name of the movie we saw because its title impressed me as being so patly ironical. It was a movie about the German occupation of France, starring Maureen O'Hara and Charles Laughton and called *This*

Land Is Mine. I remember the name of the diner we walked into when the movie ended: it was the "American Diner." When we walked in the counterman asked what we wanted and I remember answering with the casual sharpness which had become my habit: "We want a hamburger and a cup of coffee, what do you think we want?" I do not know why, after a year of such rebuffs, I so completely failed to anticipate his answer, which was, of course, "We don't serve Negroes here." This reply failed to discompose me, at least for the moment. I made some sardonic comment about the name of the diner and we walked out into the streets.

This was the time of what was called the "brownout," when the lights in all American cities were very dim. When we re-entered the streets something happened to me which had the force of an optical illusion, or a nightmare. The streets were very crowded and I was facing north. People were moving in every direction but it seemed to me, in that instant, that all of the people I could see, and many more than that, were moving toward me, against me, and that everyone was white. I remember how their faces gleamed. And I felt, like a physical sensation, a *click* at the nape of my neck as though some interior string connecting my head to my body had been cut. I began to walk. I heard my friend call after me, but I ignored him. Heaven only knows what was going on in his mind, but he had the good sense not to touch me—I don't know what would have happened if he had—and to keep me in sight. I don't know what was going on in my mind, either; I certainly had no conscious plan. I wanted to do something to crush these white faces, which were crushing me. I walked for perhaps a block or two until I came to an enormous, glittering, and fashionable restaurant in which I knew not even the intercession of the Virgin would cause me to be served. I pushed through the doors and took the first vacant seat I saw, at a table for two, and waited.

I do not know how long I waited and I rather wonder, until today, what I could possibly have looked like. Whatever I looked like, I frightened the waitress who shortly appeared, and the moment she appeared all of my fury flowed toward her. I hated her for her white face, and for her great, astounded, frightened eyes. I felt that if she found a black man so frightening I would make her fright worth-while.

She did not ask me what I wanted, but repeated, as though she had learned it somewhere, "We don't serve Negroes here." She did not say it with the blunt, derisive hostility to which I had grown so accustomed, but, rather, with a note of apology in her voice, and fear. This made me colder and more murderous than ever. I felt I had to do something with my hands. I wanted her to come close enough for me to get her neck between my hands.

So I pretended not to have understood her, hoping to draw her closer. And she did step a very short step closer, with her pencil poised incongru- 20 ously over her pad, and repeated the formula: "... don't serve Negroes here."

Somehow, with the repetition of that phrase, which was already ringing in my head like a thousand bells of a nightmare, I realized that she would never come any closer and that I would have to strike from a distance. There was nothing on the table but an ordinary water-mug half full of water, and I picked this up and hurled it with all my strength at her. She ducked and it missed her and shattered against the mirror behind the bar. And, with that sound, my frozen blood abruptly thawed, I returned from wherever I had been, I *saw*, for the first time, the restaurant, the people with their mouths open, already, as it seemed to me, rising as one man, and I realized what I had done, and where I was, and I was frightened. I rose and began running for the door. A round, potbellied man grabbed me by the nape of the neck just as I reached the doors and began to beat me about the face. I kicked him and got loose and ran into the streets. My friend whispered, "*Run!*" and I ran.

My friend stayed outside the restaurant long enough to misdirect my pursuers and the police, who arrived, he told me, at once. I do not know what I said to him when he came to my room that night. I could not have said much. I felt, in the oddest, most awful way, that I had somehow betrayed him. I lived it over and over and over again, the way one relives an automobile accident after it has happened and one finds oneself alone and safe. I could not get over two facts, both equally difficult for the imagination to grasp, and one was that I could have been murdered. But the other was that I had been ready to commit murder. I saw nothing very clearly but I did see this: that my life, my *real* life, was in danger, and not from anything other people might do but from the hatred I carried in my own heart.

Questions

1. Baldwin's essay sets up an intricate series of relationships: between Baldwin and his father, between his father and society, and between Baldwin and society. Discuss how these relationships are themselves related to each other.
2. In the first paragraph of the essay, Baldwin lists three important events that take place within a period of a few days: a birth, a death, and a riot. What effect does Baldwin achieve by discussing these events together?
3. Baldwin wrote this essay in 1963, at the peak of the civil rights movement in the United States. To whom is it addressed?

ANNIE DILLARD

Terwilliger Bunts One

(1987)

Annie Dillard (1945–) is an American essayist, poet, and novelist. Her book Pilgrim at Tinker Creek *(1974) won the Pulitzer Prize. Dillard's other works include a collection of narrative essays,* Teaching a Stone to Talk *(1982), and a book of poetry,* Mornings Like This: Found Poems *(1995).*

This chapter from Dillard's memoir, An American Childhood *(1987), focuses primarily on recollections of her mother.*

One Sunday afternoon Mother wandered through our kitchen, where Father was making a sandwich and listening to the ball game. The Pirates were playing the New York Giants at Forbes Field. In those days, the Giants had a utility infielder named Wayne Terwilliger. Just as Mother passed through, the radio announcer cried—with undue drama—"Terwilliger bunts one!"

"Terwilliger bunts one?" Mother cried back, stopped short. She turned. "Is that English?"

"The player's name is Terwilliger," Father said. "He bunted."

"That's marvelous," Mother said. "'Terwilliger bunts one.' No wonder you listen to baseball. 'Terwilliger bunts one.'"

For the next seven or eight years, Mother made this surprising string of syllables her own. Testing a microphone, she repeated, "Terwilliger bunts one"; testing a pen or a typewriter, she wrote it. If, as happened surprisingly often in the course of various improvised gags, she pretended to whisper something else in my ear, she actually whispered, "Terwilliger bunts one." Whenever someone used a French phrase, or a Latin one, she answered solemnly, "Terwilliger bunts one." If Mother had had, like Andrew Carnegie, the opportunity to cook up a motto for a coat of arms, hers would have read simply and tellingly, "Terwilliger bunts one." (Carnegie's was "Death to Privilege.")

She served us with other words and phrases. On a Florida trip, she repeated tremulously, "That ... is a royal poinciana." I don't remember the tree; I remember the thrill in her voice. She pronounced it carefully, and spelled it. She also liked to say "portulaca."

5

The drama of the words "Tamiami Trail" stirred her, we learned on the same Florida trip. People built Tampa on one coast, and they built Miami on another. Then—the height of visionary ambition and folly—they piled a slow, tremendous road through the terrible Everglades to connect them. To build the road, men stood sunk in muck to their armpits. They fought off cottonmouth moccasins and six-foot alligators. They slept in boats, wet. They blasted muck with dynamite, cut jungle with machetes; they laid logs, dragged drilling machines, hauled dredges, heaped limestone. The road took fourteen years to build up by the shovelful, a Panama Canal in reverse, and cost hundreds of lives from tropical, mosquito-carried diseases. Then, capping it all, some genius thought of the word Tamiami: they called the road from Tampa to Miami, this very road under our spinning wheels, the Tamiami Trail. Some called it Alligator Alley. Anyone could drive over this road without a thought.

Hearing this, moved, I thought all the suffering of road building was worth it (it wasn't my suffering), now that we had this new thing to hang these new words on—Alligator Alley for those who liked things cute, and, for connoisseurs like Mother, for lovers of the human drama in all its boldness and terror, the Tamiami Trail.

Back home, Mother cut clips from reels of talk, as it were, and played them back at leisure. She noticed that many Pittsburghers confuse "leave" and "let." One kind relative brightened our morning by mentioning why she'd brought her son to visit: "He wanted to come with me, so I left him." Mother filled in Amy and me on locutions we missed. "I can't do it on Friday," her pretty sister told a crowded dinner party, "because Friday's the day I lay in the stores."

10 (All unconsciously, though, we ourselves used some pure Pittsburghisms. We said "tele pole," pronounced "telly pole," for that splintery sidewalk post I loved to climb. We said "slippy"—the sidewalks are "slippy." We said, "That's all the farther I could go." And we said, as Pittsburghers do say, "This glass needs washed," or "The dog needs walked"—a usage our father eschewed; he knew it was not standard English, nor even comprehensible English, but he never let on.)

"Spell 'poinsettia,'" Mother would throw out at me, smiling with pleasure. "Spell 'sherbet.'" The idea was not to make us whizzes, but, quite the contrary, to remind us—and I, especially, needed reminding—that we didn't know it all just yet.

"There's a deer standing in the front hall," she told me one quiet evening in the country.

"Really?"

"No, I just wanted to tell you something once without your saying, 'I know.'"

15 Supermarkets in the middle 1950s began luring, or bothering, customers by giving out Top Value Stamps or Green Stamps. Where, shopping with Moth-

er, we got to the head of the checkout line, the checker, always a young man, asked, "Save stamps?"

"No," Mother replied genially, week after week, "I build model airplanes." I believe she originated this line. It took me years to determine where the joke lay.

Anyone who met her verbal challenges she adored. She had surgery on one of her eyes. On the operating table, just before she conked out, she appealed feelingly to the surgeon, saying, as she had been planning to say for weeks, "Will I be able to play the piano?" "Not on me," the surgeon said. "You won't pull that old one on me."

It was, indeed, an old one. The surgeon was supposed to answer, "Yes, my dear, brave woman, you will be able to play the piano after this operation," to which Mother intended to reply, "Oh, good, I've always wanted to play the piano." This pat scenario bored her; she loved having it interrupted. It must have galled her that usually her acquaintances were so predictably unalert; it must have galled her that, for the length of her life, she could surprise everyone so continually, so easily, when she had been the same all along. At any rate, she loved anyone who, as she put it, saw it coming, and called her on it.

She regarded the instructions on bureaucratic forms as straight lines. "Do you advocate the overthrow of the United States government by force or violence?" After some thought she wrote, "Force." She regarded children, even babies, as straight men. When Molly learned to crawl, Mother delighted in buying her gowns with drawstrings at the bottom, like Swee'-pea's, because, as she explained energetically, you could easily step on the drawstring without the baby's noticing, so that she crawled and crawled and crawled and never got anywhere except into a small ball at the gown's top.

When we children were young, she mothered us tenderly and dependably; as we got older, she resumed her career of anarchism. She collared us into her gags. If she answered the phone on a wrong number, she told the caller, "Just a minute," and dragged the receiver to Amy or me, saying, "Here, take this, your name is Cecile," or, worse, just, "It's for you." You had to think on your feet. But did you want to perform well as Cecile, or did you want to take pity on the wretched caller?

During a family trip to the Highland Park Zoo, Mother and I were alone for a minute. She approached a young couple holding hands on a bench by the seals, and addressed the young man in dripping tones: "Where have you been? Still got those baby blue eyes; always did slay me. And this"—a swift nod at the dumbstruck young woman, who had removed her hand from the man's— "must be the one you were telling me about. She's not so bad, really, as you used to make out. But listen, you know how I miss you, you know where to reach me, same old place. And there's Ann over there— see how she's grown? See the blue eyes?"

And off she sashayed, taking me firmly by the hand, and leading us

20

around briskly past the monkey house and away. She cocked an ear back, and both of us heard the desperate man begin, in a high-pitched wail, "I swear, I never saw her before in my life...."

On a long, sloping beach by the ocean, she lay stretched out sunning with Father and friends, until the conversation gradually grew tedious, when without forethought she gave a little push with her heel and rolled away. People were stunned. She rolled deadpan and apparently effortlessly, arms and legs extended and tidy, down the beach to the distant water's edge, where she lay at ease just as she had been, but half in the surf, and well out of earshot.

She dearly loved to fluster people by throwing out a game's rules at whim—when she was getting bored, losing in a dull sort of way, and when everybody else was taking it too seriously. If you turned your back, she moved the checkers around on the board. When you got them all straightened out, she denied she'd touched them; the next time you turned your back, she lined them up on the rug or hid them under your chair. In a betting rummy game called Michigan, she routinely played out of turn, or called out a card she didn't hold, or counted backward, simply to amuse herself by causing an uproar and watching the rest of us do double takes and have fits. (Much later, when serious suitors came to call, Mother subjected them to this fast card game as a trial by ordeal; she used it as an intelligence test and a measure of spirit. If the poor man could stay a round without breaking down or running out, he got to marry one of us, if he still wanted to.)

25   She excelled at bridge, playing fast and boldly, but when the stakes were low and the hands dull, she bid slams for the devilment of it, or raised her opponents' suit to bug them, or showed her hand, or tossed her cards in a handful behind her back in a characteristic swift motion accompanied by a vibrantly innocent look. It drove our stolid father crazy. The hand was over before it began, and the guests were appalled. How do you score it, who deals now, what do you do with a crazy person who is having so much fun? Or they were down seven, and the guests were appalled. "Pam!" "Dammit, Pam!" He groaned. What ails such people? What on earth possesses them? He rubbed his face.

She was an unstoppable force; she never let go. When we moved across town, she persuaded the U.S. Post Office to let her keep her old address— forever—because she'd had stationery printed. I don't know how she did it. Every new post office worker, over decades, needed to learn that although the Doaks' mail is addressed to here, it is delivered to there.

Mother's energy and intelligence suited her for a greater role in a larger arena—mayor of New York, say—than the one she had. She followed American politics closely; she had been known to vote for Democrats. She saw how things should be run, but she had nothing to run but our household. Even there, small minds bugged her, she was smarter than the people who designed the things she had to use all day for the length of her life.

"Look," she said. "Whoever designed this corkscrew never used one. Why would anyone sell it without trying it out?" So she invented a better one. She showed me a drawing of it. The spirit of American enterprise never faded in Mother. If capitalizing and tooling up had been as interesting as theorizing and thinking up, she would have fired up a new factory every week, and chaired several hundred corporations.

"It grieves me," she would say, "it grieves my heart," that the company that made one superior product packaged it poorly, or took the wrong tack in its advertising. She knew, as she held the thing mournfully in her two hands, that she'd never find another. She was right. We children wholly sympathized, and so did Father; what could she do, what could anyone do, about it? She was Samson in chains. She paced.

She didn't like the taste of stamps so she didn't lick stamps, she licked the corner of the envelope instead. She glued sandpaper to the sides of kitchen drawers, and under kitchen cabinets, so she always had a handy place to strike a match. She designed, and hounded workmen to build against all norms, doubly wide kitchen counters and elevated bathroom sinks. To splint a finger, she stuck it in a lightweight cigar tube. Conversely, to protect a pack of cigarettes, she carried it in a Band-Aid box. She drew plans for an over-the-finger toothbrush for babies, an oven rack that slid up and down, and—the family favorite—Lendalarm. Lendalarm was a beeper you attached to books (or tools) you loaned friends. After ten days, the beeper sounded. Only the rightful owner could silence it. 30

She repeatedly reminded us of P.T. Barnum's dictum: You could sell anything to anybody if you marketed it right. The adman who thought of making Americans believe they needed underarm deodorant was a visionary. So, too, was the hero who made a success of a new product, Ivory soap. The executives were horrified, Mother told me, that a cake of this stuff floated. Soap wasn't supposed to float. Anyone would be able to tell it was mostly whipped-up air. Then some inspired adman made a leap: Advertise that it floats. Flaunt it. The rest is history.

She respected the rare few who broke through to new ways. "Look," she'd say, "here's an intelligent apron." She called upon us to admire intelligent control knobs and intelligent pan handles, intelligent andirons and picture frames and knife sharpeners. She questioned everything, every pair of scissors, every knitting needle, gardening glove, tape dispenser. Hers was a restless mental vigor that just about ignited the dumb household objects with its force.

Torpid conformity was a kind of sin; it was stupidity itself, the mighty stream against which Mother would never cease to struggle. If you held no minority opinions, or if you failed to risk total ostracism for them daily, the world would be a better place without you.

Always I heard Mother's emotional voice asking Amy and me the same few questions: Is that your own idea? Or somebody else's? "*Giant* is a good movie," I pronounced to the family at dinner. "Oh, really?" Mother warmed to these occasions. She all but rolled up her sleeves. She knew I hadn't seen it. "Is that your considered opinion?"

35   She herself held many unpopular, even fantastic, positions. She was scathingly sarcastic about the McCarthy hearings while they took place, right on our living-room television; she frantically opposed Father's wait-and-see calm. "We don't know enough about it," he said. "I do," she said. "I know all I need to know."

She asserted, against all opposition, that people who lived in trailer parks were not bad but simply poor, and had as much right to settle on beautiful land, such as rural Ligonier, Pennsylvania, as did the oldest of families in the finest of hidden houses. Therefore, the people who owned trailer parks, and sought zoning changes to permit trailer parks, needed our help. Her profound belief that the country-club pool sweeper was a person, and that the department-store saleslady, the bus driver, telephone operator, and housepainter were people, and even in groups the steelworkers who carried pickets and the Christmas shoppers who clogged intersections were people—this was a conviction common enough in democratic Pittsburgh, but not altogether common among our friends' parents, or even, perhaps, among our parents' friends.

Opposition emboldened Mother, and she would take on anybody on any issue—the chairman of the board, at a cocktail party, on the current strike; she would fly at him in a flurry of passion, as a songbird selflessly attacks a big hawk.

"Eisenhower's going to win," I announced after school. She lowered her magazine and looked me in the eyes: "How do you know?" I was doomed. It was fatal to say, "Everyone says so." We all knew well what happened. "Do you consult this Everyone before you make your decisions? What if Everyone decided to round up all the Jews?" Mother knew there was no danger of cowing me. She simply tried to keep us all awake. And in fact it was always clear to Amy and me, and to Molly when she grew old enough to listen, that if our classmates came to cruelty, just as much as if the neighborhood or the nation came to madness, we were expected to take, and would be each separately capable of taking, a stand.

Questions

1. Why does Dillard's mother think that the phrase "Terwilliger bunts one" is "marvellous"?
2. How exactly is her mother, as Dillard observes, a "connoisseur" (paragraph 8)?
3. In what ways does the style of Dillard's writing complement its subject? What is the effect of its accumulated anecdotes?
4. What role does Dillard's father play in this piece?

LUCY GREALY

Pony Party

(1994)

Lucy Grealy (1963–2002) was a poet who received many awards for her work, including the Harper's National Magazine award, two Academy of American Poets Prizes, and the Whiting Writer's Award. Grealy documented her childhood struggle with illness and its after-effects in the non-fiction prose work Autobiography of a Face *(1994).*

In this chapter from Autobiography of a Face, *Grealy recollects her first childhood job.*

My friend Stephen and I used to do pony parties together. The festivities took place on the well-tended lawns of the vast suburban communities that had sprung up around Diamond D Stables in the rural acres of Rockland County. Mrs. Daniels, the owner of Diamond D, took advantage of the opportunity and readily dispatched a couple of ponies for birthday parties. In the early years Mrs. Daniels used to attend the parties with us, something Stephen and I dreaded. She fancied herself a sort of Mrs. Roy Rogers and dressed in embarrassing accordance: fringed shirts, oversized belt buckles, ramshackle hats. I'd stand there holding a pony, cringing inwardly with mortification as if she were my own mother. But as we got older and Stephen got his driver's license, and as Diamond D itself slowly sank into a somewhat surreal, muddy, and orphaned state of anarchy, we worked the parties by ourselves, which I relished.

We were invariably late for the birthday party, a result of loading the ponies at the last minute, combined with our truly remarkable propensity for getting lost. I never really minded, though. I enjoyed the drive through those precisely planned streets as the summer air swirled through the cab of the pickup, rustling the crepe-paper ribbons temporarily draped over the rear-view mirror. When we finally found our destination, we'd clip the ribbons into the ponies' manes and tails in a rather sad attempt to imbue a festive air. The neighborhoods were varied, from close, tree-laden streets crammed with ranch-style houses to more spacious boulevards dotted with outsized Tudors. Still, all the communities seemed to share a certain carbon-copy quality: house after house looked exactly like the one next to it, save for the occasional cement deer or sculpted shrub. A dog would always appear and chase the trailer for a set number of lawns—some mysterious canine demarcation of territory—before suddenly dropping away, to be replaced by another dog running and barking behind us a few lawns later.

I liked those dogs, liked their sense of purpose and enjoyment and responsibility. I especially liked being lost, tooling through strange neighborhoods with Stephen. As we drove by the houses, I gazed into the windows, imagining what the families inside were like. My ideas were loosely based on what I had learned from TV and films. I pictured a father in a reclining chair next to a lamp, its shade trimmed with small white tassels. Somewhere nearby a wife in a coordinated outfit chatted on the phone with friends while their children set the dinner table. As they ate their home-cooked food, passing assorted white serving dishes, they'd casually ask each other about the day. Perhaps someone would mention the unusual sight of a horse trailer going past the house that day. Certain that these families were nothing like my own, a certainty wrought with a sense of vague superiority and even vaguer longing, I took pride and pleasure in knowing that I was the person in that strangely surreal trailer with the kicking ponies and angry muffler, that I had driven by their house that day, that I had brushed against their lives, and past them, like that.

Once we reached the party, there was a great rush of excitement. The children, realizing that the ponies had arrived, would come running from the back yard in their silly hats; their now forgotten balloons, bobbing colorfully behind them, would fly off in search of some tree or telephone wire. The ponies, reacting to the excitement of new sounds and smells, would promptly take a crap in the driveway, to a chorus of disgusted groans.

5   My pleasure at the sight of the children didn't last long, however. I knew what was coming. As soon as they got over the thrill of being near the ponies, they'd notice me. Half my jaw was missing, which gave my face a strange triangular shape, accentuated by the fact that I was unable to keep my mouth completely closed. When I first started doing pony parties, my hair was still short and wispy, still growing in from the chemo. But as it grew I made things worse by continuously bowing my head and hiding behind the curtain of hair, furtively peering out at the world like some nervous actor. Unlike the actor, though, I didn't secretly relish my audience, and if it were possible I would have stood behind that curtain forever, my head bent in an eternal act of deference. I was, however, dependent upon my audience. Their approval or disapproval defined everything for me, and I believed with every cell in my body that approval wasn't written into my particular script. I was fourteen years old.

"*I hate* this, why am I doing this?" I'd ask myself each time, but I had no choice if I wanted to keep my job at the stable. Everyone who worked at Diamond D had to do pony parties—no exceptions. Years later a friend remarked how odd it was that an adult would even think to send a disfigured child to work at a kid's party, but at the time it was never an issue. If my presence in these back yards was something of an anomaly, it wasn't just because of my face. In fact, my physical oddness seemed somehow to fit in with the general oddness and failings of Diamond D.

The stable was a small place near the bottom of a gently sloping hill. Each spring the melting snow left behind ankle-deep mud that wouldn't dry up completely until midsummer. Mrs. Daniels possessed a number of peculiar traits that made life at Diamond D unpredictable. When she wasn't trying to save our souls, or treating Stephen's rumored homosexuality by unexpectedly exposing her breasts to him, she was taking us on shoplifting sprees, dropping criminal hints like some Artful Dodger.

No one at Diamond D knew how to properly care for horses. Most of the animals were kept outside in three small, grassless corrals. The barn was on the verge of collapse; our every entry was accompanied by the fluttering sounds of startled rats. The "staff" consisted of a bunch of junior high and high school kids willing to work in exchange for riding privileges. And the main source of income, apart from pony parties, was hacking—renting out the horses for ten dollars an hour to anyone willing to pay. Mrs. Daniels bought the horses at an auction whose main customer was the meat dealer for a dog-food company; Diamond D, more often than not, was merely a way station. The general air of neglect surrounding the stable was the result more of ignorance than of apathy. It's not as if we didn't care about the horses—we simply didn't know any better. And for most of us, especially me, Diamond D was a haven. Though I had to suffer through the pony parties, I was more willing to do so to spend time alone with the horses. I considered animals bearers of higher truth, and I wanted to align myself with their knowledge. I thought animals were the only beings capable of understanding me.

I had finished chemotherapy only a few months before I started looking in the Yellow Pages for stables where I might work. Just fourteen and still unclear about the exact details of my surgery, I made my way down the listings. It was the July Fourth weekend, and Mrs. Daniels, typically overbooked, said I had called at exactly the right moment. Overjoyed, I went into the kitchen to tell my mother I had a job at a stable. She looked at me dubiously.

"Did you tell them about yourself?"

I hesitated, and lied. "Yes, of course I did."

"Are you sure they know you were sick? Will you be up for this?"

"Of *course* I am," I replied in my most petulant adolescent tone.

In actuality it hadn't even occurred to me to mention cancer, or my face,

10

to Mrs. Daniels. I was still blissfully unaware, somehow believing that the only reason people stared at me was because my hair was still growing in. So my mother obligingly drove all sixty-odd pounds of me down to Diamond D, where my pale and misshapen face seemed to surprise all of us. They let me water a few horses, imagining I wouldn't last more than a day. I stayed for four years.

15   That first day I walked a small pinto in circle after circle, practically drunk with the aroma of the horses. But with each circle, each new child lifted into the tiny saddle, I became more and more uncomfortable, and with each circuit my head dropped just a little bit further in shame. With time I became adept at handling the horses, and even more adept at avoiding the direct stares of the children.

When our trailer pulled into the driveway for a pony party, I would briefly remember my own excitement at being around ponies for the first time. But I also knew that these children lived apart from me. Through them I learned the language of paranoia: every whisper I heard was a comment about the way I looked, every laugh a joke at my expense.

Partly I was honing my self-consciousness into a torture device, sharp and efficient enough to last me the rest of my life. Partly I was right: they *were* staring at me, laughing at me. The cruelty of children is immense, almost startling in its precision. The kids at the parties were fairly young and, surrounded by adults, they rarely made cruel remarks outright. But their open, uncensored stares were more painful than the deliberate taunts of my peers at school, where insecurities drove everything and everyone like some looming, evil presence in a haunted machine. But in those back yards, where the grass was mown so short and sharp it would have hurt to walk on it, there was only the fact of me, my face, my ugliness.

This singularity of meaning—I *was* my face, I *was* ugliness—though sometimes unbearable, also offered a possible point of escape. It became the launching pad from which to lift off, the one immediately recognizable place to point to when asked what was wrong with my life. Everything led to it, everything receded from it—my face as personal vanishing point. The pain these children brought with their stares engulfed every other pain in my life. Yet occasionally, just as that vast ocean threatened to swallow me whole, some greater force would lift me out and enable me to walk among them easily and carelessly, as alien as the pony that trotted beside me, his tail held high in excitement, his nostrils wide in anticipation of a brief encounter with a world beyond his comprehension.

The parents would trail behind the kids, iced drinks clinking, making their own, more practical comments about the fresh horse manure in their driveway. If Stephen and I liked their looks (all our judgments were instantaneous), we'd shovel it up; if not, we'd tell them cleanup wasn't included in the fee. Stephen came from a large, all-American family, but for me these grownups provided a secret fascination. The mothers had frosted lipstick and long bright fingernails; the fathers sported gold watches and smelled of too much aftershave.

This was the late seventies, and a number of corporate headquarters had sprung up across the border in New Jersey. Complete with duck ponds and fountains, these "industrial parks" looked more like fancy hotels than office buildings. The newly planted suburban lawns I found myself parading ponies on were a direct result of their proliferation.

My feelings of being an outsider were strengthened by the reminder of what my own family didn't have: money. We *should* have had money: this was true in practical terms, for my father was a successful journalist, and it was also true within my family mythology, which conjured up images of Fallen Aristocracy. We were displaced foreigners, Europeans newly arrived in an alien landscape. If we had had the money we felt entitled to, we would never have spent it on anything as mundane as a house in Spring Valley or as silly and trivial as a pony party.

Unfortunately, the mythologically endowed money didn't materialize. Despite my father's good job with a major television network, we were barraged by collection agencies, and our house was falling apart around us. Either unwilling or unable, I'm not sure which, to spend money on plumbers and electricians and general handymen, my father kept our house barely together by a complex system of odd bits of wire, duct tape, and putty, which he applied rather haphazardly and good-naturedly on weekend afternoons. He sang when he worked. Bits of opera, slapped together jauntily with the current top forty and ancient ditties from his childhood, were periodically interrupted as he patiently explained his work to the dog, who always listened attentively.

Anything my father fixed usually did not stay fixed for more than a few months. Flushing our toilets when it rained required coaxing with a Zenlike ritual of jiggles to avoid spilling the entire contents of the septic tank onto the basement floor. One walked by the oven door with a sense of near reverence, lest it fall open with an operatic crash. Pantheism ruled.

Similarly, when dealing with my mother, one always had to act in a delicate and prescribed way, though the exact rules of protocol seemed to shift frequently and without advance notice. One day, running out of milk was a problem easily dealt with, but on the next it was a symbol of her children's selfishness, our father's failure, and her tragic, wasted life. Lack of money, it was driven into us, was the root of all our unhappiness. So as Stephen and I drove through those "bourgeois" suburbs (my radical older brothers had taught me to identify them as such), I genuinely believed that if our family were as well-off as those families, the extra carton of milk would not have been an issue, and my mother would have been more than delighted to buy gallon after gallon until the house fairly spilled over with fresh milk.

20

25   Though our whole family shared the burden of my mother's anger, in my heart I suspected that part of it was my fault and my fault alone. Cancer is an obscenely expensive illness; I saw the bills, I heard their fights. There was no doubt that I was personally responsible for a great deal of my family's money problems: ergo, I was responsible for my mother's unhappy life. During my parents' many fights over money, I would sit in the kitchen in silence, unable to move even after my brothers and sisters had fled to their bedrooms. I sat listening as some kind of penance.

     The parents who presided over the pony parties never fought, or at least not about anything significant, of this I felt sure. Resentment made me scorn them, their gauche houses, their spoiled children. These feelings might have been purely political, like those of my left-wing brothers (whose philosophies I understood very little of), if it weren't for the painfully personal detail of my face.

     "What's wrong with her face?"

     The mothers bent down to hear this question and, still bent over, they'd look over at me, their glances refracting away as quickly and predictably as light through a prism. I couldn't always hear their response, but I knew from experience that vague pleas for politeness would hardly satisfy a child's curiosity.

     While the eyes of these perfectly formed children swiftly and deftly bored into the deepest part of me, the glances from their parents provided me with an exotic sense of power as I watched them inexpertly pretend not to notice me. After I passed the swing sets and looped around to pick up the next child waiting near the picnic table littered with cake plates, juice bottles, and party favors, I'd pause confrontationally, like some Dickensian ghost, imagining that my presence served as an uneasy reminder of what might be. What had happened to me was any parent's nightmare, and I allowed myself to believe that I was dangerous to them. The parents obliged me in this: they brushed past me, around me, sometimes even smiled at me. But not once in the three or so years that I worked pony parties did anyone ask me directly what had happened.

30   They were uncomfortable because of my face. I ignored the deep hurt by allowing the side of me that was desperate for any kind of definition to staunchly act out, if not exactly relish, this macabre status.

Zoom lenses, fancy flash systems, perfect focus—these cameras probably were worth more than the ponies instigating the pictures. A physical sense of dread came over me as soon as I spotted the thickly padded case, heard the sound of the zipper, noted the ridiculous, almost surgical protection provided by the fitted foam compartment. I'd automatically hold the pony's halter, careful to keep his head tight and high in case he suddenly decided to pull down for a bite of lawn. I'd expertly turn my own head away, pretending I was only just then aware of something more important off to the side. I'd tilt away at exactly the same angle each time, my hair falling in a perfect sheet of camouflage between me and the camera.

I stood there perfectly still, just as I had sat for countless medical photographs: full face, turn to the left, the right, now a three-quarter shot to the left. I took a certain pride in knowing the routine so well. I've even seen some of these medical photographs in publications. Curiously, those sterile, bright photos are easy for me to look at. For one thing, I know that only doctors look at them, and perhaps I'm even slightly proud that I'm such an interesting case, worthy of documentation. Or maybe I do not really think it is me sitting there, *Case* 3, *figure 6-A*.

Once, when my doctor left me waiting too long in his examining room, I leafed through my file, which I knew was strictly off-limits. I was thrilled to find a whole section of slides housed in a clear plastic folder. Removing one, I lifted it up to the fluorescent light, stared for a moment, then carefully, calmly replaced it. It was a photograph taken of me on the operating table. Most of the skin of the right side of my face had been pulled over and back, exposing something with the general shape of a face and neck but with the color and consistency of raw steak. A clamp gleamed off to the side, holding something unidentifiable in place. I wasn't particularly bothered; I've always had a fascination with gore, and had it been someone else I'd have stared endlessly. But I simply put the slide in its slot and made a mental note not to look at slides from my file again, ever.

With the same numbed yet cavalier stance, I waited for a father to click the shutter. At least these were photographs I'd never have to see, though to this day I fantasize about meeting someone who eventually shows me their photo album and there, inexplicably, in the middle of a page, is me holding a pony. I have seen one pony party photo of me. In it I'm holding on to a small dark bay pony whose name I don't remember. I look frail and thin and certainly peculiar, but I don't look anywhere near as repulsive as I then believed I did. There's a gaggle of children around me, waiting for their turn on the pony. My stomach was always in knots then, surrounded by so many children, but I can tell by my expression that I'm convincing myself I don't care as I point to the back of the line. The children look older than most of the kids at the backyard parties: some of them are even older than nine, the age I was when I got sick. I'm probably thinking about this, too, as I order them into line.

I can still hear the rubbery, metallic thud of hooves on the trailer's ramp as we loaded the ponies back into the hot and smelly box for the ride back to Diamond D. Fifteen years later, when I see that photo, I am filled with questions I rarely allow myself, such as, how do we go about turning into the people we are meant to be? What relation do the human beings in that picture have to the people they are now? How is it that all of us were caught

35

together in that brief moment of time, me standing there pretending I was-n't hurt by a single thing in this world while they lined up for their turn on the pony, some of them excited and some of them scared, but all of them neatly, at my insistence, one in front of the other, like all the days ahead.

Questions

1. How would you describe Grealy's attitude towards her fourteen-year-old self? Find specific passages in the essay that support your description.
2. The last part of the essay consists of anecdotes about both photographs and the experience of being photographed. Why might Grealy have chosen to end this way?

DAVID SEDARIS

Old Faithful

(2004)

David Sedaris (1956–) is an American humorist, writer, and radio commentator. He has written numerous essays, books, and plays. His essay collections include Me Talk Pretty One Day *(2000) and* Dress Your Family in Corduroy and Denim *(2004).*

In this essay, Sedaris uses a personal experience to discuss the benefits and drawbacks of a long-term, committed relationship.

Out of nowhere I developed this lump. I think it was a cyst or a boil, one of those words you associate with trolls, and it was right on my tailbone, like a peach pit. That's what it felt like, anyway. I was afraid to look. At first it was just this insignificant knot, but as it grew larger it started to hurt. Sitting became difficult, and forget about lying on my back or bending over. By day five my tailbone was throbbing and I told myself, just as I had the day before, that if this kept up I was going to see a doctor. "I mean it," I said. I even went so far as to pull out the phone book and turn my back on it, hoping that the boil would know that I meant business and go away on its own. But of course it didn't.

All of this took place in London, which is cruelly, insanely expensive. My boyfriend, Hugh, and I went to the movies one night, and our tickets cost a total of forty dollars, this after spending sixty dollars on pizzas. And these were mini-pizzas, not much bigger than pancakes. Given the price of a simple evening out, I figured that a doctor's visit would cost about the same as a customized van. More than the money, though, I was afraid of the diagnosis. "Lower-back cancer," the doctor would say. "It looks like we'll have to remove your entire bottom."

Actually, this being England, he'd probably have said "bum," a word I have never really cottoned to. The sad thing is that they could remove my ass and most people wouldn't even notice. It's so insubstantial that the boil was actually an improvement, something like a bustle but filled with poison. The only real drawback was the pain.

For the first few days I kept my discomfort to myself, thinking all the while of what a good example I was setting. When Hugh feels bad, you hear about it immediately. A tiny splinter works itself into his palm and he claims to know exactly how Jesus must have felt on the Cross. He demands sympathy for insect bites and paper cuts, while I have to lose at least a quart of blood before I get so much as a pat on the hand.

5   One time in France we were lucky enough to catch an identical stomach virus. It was a twenty-four-hour bug, the kind that completely empties you out and takes away your will to live. You'd get a glass of water, but that would involve standing, and so instead you just sort of stare toward the kitchen, hoping that maybe one of the pipes will burst, and the water will come to you. We had the exact same symptoms, yet he insisted that his virus was much more powerful than mine. I suspected the same thing, so there we were, competing over who was the sickest.

"You can at least move your hands," he said.

"No," I told him, "it was the wind that moved them. I have no muscle control whatsoever."

"Liar."

"Well, that's a nice thing to say to someone who'll probably die during the night. Thanks a lot, pal."

10   At such times you have to wonder how things got to this point. You meet someone and fall in love, then thirteen years later you're lying on the floor in a foreign country, promising, hoping, as a matter of principle, that you'll be dead by sunrise. "I'll show you," I moaned, and then I must have fallen back to sleep.

When Hugh and I bicker over who is in the most pain, I think back to my first boyfriend, whom I met while I was in my late twenties. Something about our combination was rotten, and as a result we competed over everything, no matter how petty. When someone laughed at one of his jokes, I would need to make that person laugh harder. If I found something at a yard sale, he would have to find something better—and so on. My boyfriend's mother was a handful, and every year, just before Christmas, she would schedule a mammogram, knowing she would not get the results until after the holidays. The remote possibility of cancer was something to hang over her children's heads, just out of reach, like mistletoe, and she took great pleasure in arranging it. The family would gather and she'd tear up, saying, "I don't want to spoil your happiness, but this may well be our last Christmas together." Other times, if somebody had something going on—a wedding, a graduation—she'd go in for exploratory surgery, anything to capture and hold attention. By the time I finally met her, she did not have a single organ that had not been touched by human hands. "Oh, my God," I thought, watching her cry on our living-room sofa, "my boyfriend's family is more fucked up than my own." I mean, this actually bothered me.

We were together for six years, and when we finally broke up I felt like a failure, a divorced person. I now had what the self-help books called relationship baggage, which I would carry around for the rest of my life. The trick was to meet someone with similar baggage, and form a matching set, but how would one go about finding such a person? Bars were out; I knew that much. I'd met my first boyfriend at a place called the Man Hole—not the sort of name that suggests fidelity. It was like meeting someone at Fisticuffs and then complaining when he turned out to be violent. To be fair, he had never actually promised to be monogamous. That was my idea, and I tried my hardest to convert him, but the allure of other people was just too great.

Almost all of the gay couples I knew at that time had some sort of an arrangement. Boyfriend A could sleep with someone else as long as he didn't bring him home—or as long as he *did* bring him home. And boyfriend B was free to do the same. It was a good setup for those who enjoyed variety and the thrill of the hunt, but to me it was just scary, and way too much work—like having one job while applying for another. One boyfriend was all I could handle, all I wanted to handle, really, and while I found this to be perfectly natural, my friends saw it as a form of repression and came to view me as something of a puritan. Am I? I wondered. But there were buckles to polish, and stones to kneel upon, and so I put the question out of my mind.

I needed a boyfriend as conventional as I was, and luckily I found one—just met him one evening through a mutual friend. I was thirty-three and Hugh had just turned thirty. Like me, he had recently broken up with someone, and had moved to New York to start over. His former boyfriend had been a lot like mine, and we spent our first few weeks comparing notes. "Did he ever say he was going out for a hamburger and then—"

"—hook up with someone he'd met that afternoon on a bus? Yes!"

We had a few practical things in common as well, but what really brought Hugh and me together was our mutual fear of abandonment and group sex. It was a foundation, and we built on it, adding our fears of AIDS and pierced nipples, of commitment ceremonies and the loss of self-control. In dreams sometimes I'll discover a handsome stranger waiting in my hotel room. He's usually someone I've seen earlier that day, on the street or in a television commercial, and now he's naked and beckoning me toward the bed. I look at my key, convinced that I have the wrong room, and when he springs forward and reaches for my zipper I run for the door, which is inevitably made of snakes or hot tar, one of those maddening, hard-to-clean building materials so often used in dreams. The handle moves this way and that, and while struggling to grab it I stammer an explanation as to why I can't go through with this. "I have a boyfriend, see, and, well, the thing is that he'd kill me if he ever found out I'd been, you know, unfaithful or anything."

15

Really, though, it's not the fear of Hugh's punishment that stops me. I remember once riding in the car with my dad. I was twelve, and it was just the two of us, coming home from the bank. We'd been silent for blocks, when out of nowhere he turned to me and said, "I want you to know that I've never once cheated on your mother."

"Um. O.K.," I said. And then he turned on the radio and listened to a football game.

Years later, I mentioned this incident to a friend, who speculated that my father had said this specifically because he *had* been unfaithful. "That was a guilty conscience talking," she said, but I knew that she was wrong. More likely my father was having some problem at work and needed to remind himself that he was not completely worthless. It sounds like something you'd read on a movie poster, but sometimes the sins you haven't committed are all you have to hold on to. If you're really desperate, you might find yourself groping, saying, for example, "I've never killed anyone *with a hammer*" or "I've never stolen from anyone *who didn't deserve it.*" But, whatever his faults, my dad did not have to stoop quite that low.

20   I have never cheated on a boyfriend, and, as with my father, it's become part of my idea of myself. In my foiled wet dreams I can glimpse at what my life would be like without my perfect record, of how lost I'd feel without this scrap of integrity, and the fear is enough to wake me up. Once I'm awake, though, I tend to lie there, wondering if I've made a terrible mistake.

In books and movies infidelity always looks so compelling, so right. Here are people who defy petty convention and are rewarded with only the tastiest bits of human experience. Never do they grow old or suffer the crippling panic I feel whenever Hugh gets spontaneous and suggests we go to a restaurant.

"A restaurant? But what will we talk about?"

"I don't know," he'll say. "What does it matter?"

Alone together, I enjoy our companionable silence, but it creeps me out to sit in public, propped in our chairs like a pair of mummies. At a nearby table there's always a couple in their late seventies, blinking at their menus from behind thick glasses.

25   "Soup's a good thing," the wife will say, and the man will nod or grunt or fool with the stem of his wineglass. Eventually he'll look my way, and I'll catch in his eyes a look of grim recognition. "We are your future," he seems to say. "Get used to it."

I'm so afraid that Hugh and I won't have anything to talk about that now, before leaving home, I'll comb the papers and jot down a half dozen topics that might keep a conversation going at least through the entrées. The last time we ate out, I prepared by reading both the *Herald Tribune* and the *Animal Finders' Guide,* a publication devoted to exotic pets and the nuts who keep them. The waiter took our orders, and as he walked away I turned to

Hugh, saying, "So, anyway, I hear that monkeys can really become surly once they reach breeding age."

"Well, I could have told you that," he said. "It happened with my own monkey."

I tried to draw him out, but it saddens Hugh to discuss his childhood monkey. "Oh, Maxwell," he'll sigh, and within a minute he'll have started crying. Next on my list were the five warning signs of depression among captive camels, but I couldn't read my handwriting, and the topic crashed and burned after sign No. 2: an unwillingness to cush. At a nearby table an elderly woman arranged and rearranged the napkin in her lap. Her husband stared at a potted plant, and I resorted to the *Herald Tribune.* "Did you hear about those three Indian women who were burned as witches?"

"What?"

"Neighbors accused them of casting spells and burned them alive."   30

"Well, that's horrible," he said, slightly accusatory, as if I myself had had a hand in it. "You can't go around burning people alive, not in this day and age."

"I know it, but—"

"It's sick is what it is. I remember once when I was living in Somalia there was this woman ..."

"Yes!" I whispered, and then I looked over at the elderly couple, thinking, See, we're talking about witch burnings! It's work, though, and it's always *my* work. If left up to Hugh, we'd just sit there acting like what we are: two people so familiar with one another they could scream. Sometimes, when I find it hard to sleep, I'll think of when we first met, of the newness of each other's body, and my impatience to know everything about this person. Looking back, I should have taken it more slowly, measured him out over the course of fifty years rather than cramming him in so quickly. By the end of our first month together, he'd been so thoroughly interrogated that all I had left was breaking news—what little had happened in the few hours since I'd last seen him. Were he a cop or an emergency-room doctor, there might have been a lot to catch up on, but, like me, Hugh works alone, so there was never much to report. "I ate some potato chips," he might say, to which I'd reply, "What kind?" or "That's funny, so did I!" More often than not we'd just breathe into our separate receivers.

"Are you still there?"   35

"I'm here."

"Good. Don't hang up."

"I won't."

In New York we slept on a futon. I took the left side and would lie awake at night, looking at the closet door. In Paris we got a real bed in a room just big enough to contain it. Hugh would fall asleep immediately, the way he's always done, and I'd stare at the blank wall, wondering about all the people who had slept in this room before us. The building dated from the seventeenth century, and I envisioned musketeers in tall, soft boots, pleasuring the sorts of women who wouldn't complain when sword tips tore the sheets. I saw gentlemen in top hats and sleeping caps, women in bonnets and berets and beaded headbands, a swarm of phantom copulators all looking down and comparing my life with theirs.

40   After Paris came London, and a bedroom on the sixth floor with windows looking onto neat rows of Edwardian chimney tops. A friend characterized it as "a Peter Pan view," and now I can't see it any other way. I lie awake thinking of someone with a hook for a hand, and then, inevitably, of youth, and whether I have wasted it. Twenty-five years ago I was twenty-two, a young man with his whole sexual life ahead of him. How had nine thousand one hundred and twenty-five relatively uneventful days passed so quickly, and how might I slow the days ahead? In another twenty-five years I'll be seventy-two, and twenty-five years after that I'll be one of the figures haunting my Paris bedroom. Is it morally permissible, I wonder, to cheat after death? Is it even called cheating at that point? What are the rules? Do I have to wait a certain amount of time, or can I just jump or, as the case may be, seep right in?

During the period that I had my boil, these questions seemed particularly relevant. The pain was always greater after dark, and by the sixth night I was fairly certain that I was dying. Hugh had gone to sleep hours earlier, and it startled me to hear his voice. "What do you say we lance that thing?" he said.

It's the sort of question that takes you off guard. "Did you just use the verb 'to lance'?" I asked.

He turned on the lights.

"Since when did you learn to lance boils?"

45   "I didn't," he said. "But I bet I could teach myself."

With anyone else I'd put up a fight, but Hugh can do just about anything he sets his mind to. This is a person who welded the plumbing pipes at his house in Normandy, then went into the cellar to make his own cheese. There's no one I trust more than him, and so I limped to the bathroom, that theatre of home surgery, where I lowered my pajama bottoms and braced myself against the towel rack, waiting as he sterilized the needle.

"This is hurting me a lot more than it's hurting you," he said. It was his standard line, but I knew that this time he was right. Worse than the boil was the stuff that came out of it. What got to me, and got to him even worse, was the stench, which was unbearable, and unlike anything I had come across before. It was, I thought, what evil must smell like—not an evil person but the wicked ideas that have made him that way. How could a person continue to live with something so rotten inside? And so much of it! "How are you doing back there?" I asked, but he was dry-heaving and couldn't answer.

When my boil was empty, he doused it with alcohol and put a bandage on it, as if it had been a minor injury, a shaving cut, a skinned knee, something normal he hadn't milked like a dead cow. And this, to me, was worth at least a hundred of the hundred and twenty nights of Sodom.[1] Back in bed I referred to him as Sir Lance-A-Lot.

"Once is not a lot," he said.

This was true, but Sir Lance Occasionally lacks a certain ring. "Besides,"   50
I said, "I know you'll do it again if I need you to. We're an elderly monogamous couple, and this is all part of the bargain."

The thought of this kept Hugh awake that night, and still does. We go to bed and he stares toward the window as I sleep soundly beside him, my bandaged boil silently weeping onto the sheets.

Questions

1. Choose three or four sentences in this essay that you found funny. Why exactly are these moments funny?
2. How do the story of the boil and Sedaris's commentary on human relationships work together?
3. Discuss Sedaris's technique of combining humor with more serious observations about human nature. Is this technique effective? Why or why not? (Give examples.)

---

1   *hundred and twenty nights of Sodom* A reference to *The 120 Days of Sodom* (1785), a notoriously sexually explicit work by the Marquis de Sade.

TEMPLE GRANDIN

My Story

(2005)

Diagnosed with autism when she was three years old, Temple Grandin (1947–) holds a PhD in animal science from the University of Illinois and is an Associate Professor at Colorado State University. Grandin has innovated livestock equipment designed to minimize animal suffering, and she is the author of several books on both autism and animal management.

In this passage from her book Animals in Translation *(2005), Grandin relates some of her childhood experience with animals.*

People who aren't autistic always ask me about the moment I realized I could understand the way animals think. They think I must have had an epiphany.

But it wasn't like that. It took me a long time to figure out that I see things about animals other people don't. And it wasn't until I was in my forties that I finally realized I had one big advantage over the feedlot owners who were hiring me to manage their animals: being autistic. Autism made school and social life hard, but it made animals easy.

I had no idea I had a special connection to animals when I was little. I liked animals, but I had enough problems just trying to figure out things like why a really small dog isn't a cat. That was a big crisis in my life. All the dogs I knew were pretty big, and I used to sort them by size. Then the neighbors bought a dachshund, and I was totally confused. I kept saying, "How can it be a dog?" I studied and studied that dachshund, trying to figure it out. Finally I realized that the dachshund had the same kind of nose my golden retriever did, and I got it. Dogs have dog noses.

That was pretty much the extent of my expertise when I was five.

5   I started to fall in love with animals in high school when my mother sent me to a special boarding school for gifted children with emotional problems. Back then they called everything "emotional problems." Mother had to find a place for me because I got kicked out of high school for fighting. I got in fights because kids teased me. They'd call me names, like "Retard," or "Tape recorder."

They called me Tape Recorder because I'd stored up a lot of phrases in my memory and I used them over and over again in every conversation. Plus there were only a few conversations I liked to have, so that amplified the effect. I especially liked to talk about the rotor ride at the carnival. I would go up to somebody and say, "I went to Nantasket Park and I went on the rotor and I really liked the way it pushed me up against the wall." Then I would say stuff like, "How did you like it?" and they'd say how they liked it, and then I'd tell the story all over again, start to finish. It was like a loop inside my head, it just ran over and over again. So the kids called me Tape Recorder.

Teasing hurts. The kids would tease me, so I'd get mad and smack 'em. That simple. They always started it, they liked to see me react.

My new school solved that problem. The school had a stable and horses for the kids to ride, and the teachers took away horseback riding privileges if I smacked somebody. After I lost privileges enough times I learned just to cry when somebody did something bad to me. I'd cry, and that would take away the aggression. I still cry when people are mean to me.

Nothing ever happened to the kids who were teasing.

The funny thing about the school was, the horses had emotional prob- 10 lems, too. They had emotional problems because in order to save money the headmaster was buying cheap horses. They'd been marked down because they had gigantic behavior problems. They were pretty, their legs were fine, but emotionally they were a mess. The school had nine horses altogether, and two of them couldn't be ridden at all. Half the horses in that barn had serious psychological problems. But I didn't understand that as a fourteen-year-old.

So there we all were up at boarding school, a bunch of emotionally disturbed teenagers living with a bunch of emotionally disturbed animals. There was one horse, Lady, who was a good horse when you rode her in the ring, but on the trail she would go berserk. She would rear, and constantly jump around and prance; you had to hold her back with the bridle or she'd bolt to the barn.

Then there was Beauty. You could ride Beauty, but he had very nasty habits like kicking and biting while you were in the saddle. He would swing his foot up and kick you in the leg or foot, or turn his head around and bite your knee. You had to watch out. Whenever you tried to mount Beauty he kicked *and* bit—you had both ends coming at you at the same time.

But that was nothing compared to Goldie, who reared and plunged whenever anyone tried to sit on her back. There was no way to ride that horse; it was all you could do just to stay in the saddle. If you did ride her, Goldie would work herself up into an absolute sweat. In five minutes she'd be drenched, dripping wet. It was flop sweat. Pure fear. She was terrified of being ridden.

Goldie was a beautiful horse, though; light brown with a golden mane and tail. She was built like an Arab horse, slender and fine, and had perfect ground manners. You could walk her on a lead, you could groom her, you could do anything you liked and she was perfectly behaved just so long as you didn't try to ride her. That sounds like an obvious problem for any nervous horse to have, but it can go the other way, too. I've known horses where people say, "Yeah you can ride them, but that's all you can do with them." That kind of horse is fine with people in the saddle, and nasty to people on the ground.

15   All the horses at the school had been abused. The lady they bought Goldie from had used a nasty, sharp bit and jerked on it as hard as she could, so Goldie's tongue was all twisted and deformed. Beauty had been kept locked in a dairy stanchion all day long. I don't know why. These were badly abused animals; they were very, very messed up.

But I had no understanding of this as a girl. I was never mean to the horses at the school (other kids were sometimes), but I wasn't any horse-whispering autistic savant, either. I just loved the horses.

I was so wrapped up in them that I spent every spare moment working the barns. I was dedicated to keeping the barn clean, making sure the horses were groomed. One of the high points of my high school career was the day my mom bought me a really nice English bridle and saddle. That was a huge event in my life, because it was mine, but also because the saddles at school were so crummy. We rode on old McClellands, which were honest-to-god cavalry saddles first used in the Civil War. The school's saddles probably went back to World War II when they still had some horse units in the army. The McClelland was designed with a slot down the center of it to spare the horse's back. The slot was good for the horse but horrible for the rider. I don't think there's ever been a more uncomfortable saddle on earth, though I have to say that when I read about the Northern Alliance soldiers in Afghanistan riding on saddles made out of wood, that sounded worse.

Boy did I take care of that saddle. I loved it so much I didn't even leave it in the tack room where it belonged. I brought it up to my dorm room every day and kept it with me. I bought special saddle soap and leather conditioner from the saddle shop, and I spent hours washing and polishing it.

As happy as I was with the horses at school, my high school years were hard. When I reached adolescence I was hit by a tidal wave of anxiety that never stopped. It was the same level of anxiety I felt later on when I was defending my dissertation in front of my thesis committee, only I felt that way all day long and all night, too. Nothing bad happened to make me so anxious all of a sudden; I think it was just one of my autism genes kicking into high gear. Autism has a lot in common with obsessive-compulsive disorder, which is listed as an anxiety disorder in the *Diagnostic and Statistical Manual.*

Animals saved me. One summer when I was visiting my aunt, who had a   20
dude ranch in Arizona, I saw a herd of cattle being put through the *squeeze*
chute at a neighboring ranch. A squeeze chute is an apparatus vets use to
hold cattle still for their shots by squeezing them so tight they can't move.
The squeeze chute looks like a big V made out of metal bars hinged together at the bottom. When a cow walks into the chute an air compressor closes up the V, which squeezes the cow's body in place. The rancher has plenty of space for his hands and the hypodermic needle between the metal
bars. You can find pictures of them on the Web if you want to see what they
look like.

As soon as I caught sight of that thing I made my aunt stop the car so I
could get out and watch. I was riveted by the sight of those big animals
inside that squeezing machine. You might think cattle would get really
scared when all of a sudden this big metal structure clamps together on
their bodies, but it's exactly the opposite. They get really calm. When you
think about it, it makes sense, because deep pressure is a calming sensation
for just about everyone. That's one of the reasons a massage feels so good—
it's the deep pressure. The squeeze chute probably gives cattle a feeling like
the soothing sensation newborns have when they're swaddled, or scuba
divers have underwater. They like it.

Watching those cattle calm down, I knew I needed a squeeze chute of my
own. When I got back to school that fall, my high school teacher helped me
build my own squeeze chute, the size of a human being down on all fours.
I bought my own air compressor, and I used plywood boards for the V. It
worked beautifully. Whenever I put myself inside my squeeze machine, I felt
calmer. I still use it today.

I got through my teenage years thanks to my squeeze machine and my
horses. Animals kept me going. I spent every waking minute that I didn't
have to be studying or going to school with those horses. I even rode Lady
at a show. It's hard to imagine today, a school keeping a stable of emotionally disturbed and dangerous horses for its underaged students to ride.
These days you can't even play dodgeball in gym class because somebody
might get hurt. But that's the way it was. A lot of us got nipped or stepped
on or thrown at that school, but no one was ever seriously hurt, at least not
while I was there. So it worked out.

I wish more kids could ride horses today. People and animals are supposed to be together. We spent quite a long time evolving together, and we
used to be partners. Now people are cut off from animals unless they have
a dog or a cat.

Horses are especially good for teenagers. I have a psychiatrist friend in   25
Massachusetts who has a lot of teenage patients, and he has a whole different set of expectations for the ones who ride horses. He says that if you take
two kids who have the same problem to the same degree of severity, and

one of them rides a horse regularly and the other one doesn't, the rider will end up doing better than the nonrider. For one thing, a horse is a huge responsibility, so any teenage kid who's looking after a horse is developing good character. But for another, riding a horse isn't what it looks like: it isn't a person sitting in a saddle telling the horse what to do by yanking on the reins. Real riding is a lot like ballroom dancing or maybe figure skating in pairs. It's a relationship.

I remember looking down to make sure my horse was on the right lead. When a horse is cantering around the ring one of his front hooves has to thrust out farther forward than the other one, and the rider has to help him do that. If I leaned my body just the right way, it helped my horse get on the right lead. My sense of balance was so bad I could never learn to parallel ski no matter how hard I tried, though I did reach the advanced snowplow stage. Yet there I was, moving my body in sync with the horse's body to help him run right.

Horseback riding was joyous for me. I can remember being on a horse sometimes and we'd gallop in the pasture and that was such a big thrill. Of course it's not good for horses to run them all the time, but once in a while we'd get to have a little run, and I'd feel exhilarated. Or we'd be out on a trail riding, and do a really fast gallop down the road. I remember what it looked like, the trees whizzing by; I remember that really well to this day.

Riding becomes instinctual after a while; a good rider and his horse are a team. It's not a one-way relationship, either; it's not just the human relating to the horse and telling him what to do. Horses are super-sensitive to their riders and are constantly responding to the riders' needs even without being asked. School horses—the horses a stable uses to teach people how to ride—will actually stop trotting when they feel their rider start to lose his balance. That's why learning to ride a horse is completely different from learning to ride a bicycle. The horses make sure nobody gets hurt.

The love a teenager gets from a horse is good for him, and so is the teamwork. For years people always said you needed to send difficult kids to military school or the army. A lot of times that works because those places are so highly structured. But it would work a lot better if military schools still had horses.

Questions

1. What assumptions, if any, did you make when you read the first paragraph of "My Story"? Were those assumptions challenged by the rest of the essay?
2. In this essay Grandin writes in a conversational tone and draws conclusions based on her own personal experience. What are the advantages of such an approach? The disadvantages?

Global Media

SAMUEL JOHNSON

On Advertising

(1759)

Samuel Johnson (1709–84) was an English writer, lexicographer, and publisher of the periodicals The Rambler *(1750–52) and* The Idler *(1758–60). Johnson's other major contributions to eighteenth-century literature include his* Dictionary of the English Language *(1755) and* The Lives of the English Poets *(1781).*

In this essay published in The Idler *on 20 January 1759, Johnson discusses eighteenth-century advertisers.*

The practice of appending to the narratives of publick transactions more minute and domestick intelligence, and filling the newspapers with advertisements, has grown up by slow degrees to its present state.

Genius is shown only by invention. The man who first took advantage of the general curiosity that was excited by a siege or battle, to betray the readers of news into the knowledge of the shop where the best puffs and powder were to be sold, was undoubtedly a man of great sagacity, and profound skill in the nature of man. But when he had once shown the way, it was easy to follow him; and every man now knows a ready method of informing the publick of all that he desires to buy or sell; whether his wares be material or intellectual; whether he makes clothes, or teaches the mathematicks; whether he be a tutor that wants a pupil, or a pupil that wants a tutor.

Whatever is common is despised. Advertisements are now so numerous that they are very negligently perused, and it is, therefore, become necessary to gain attention by magnificence of promises, and by eloquence sometimes sublime and sometimes pathetick.

Promise, large promise, is the soul of an advertisement. I remember a *wash-ball*[1] that had a quality truly wonderful—it gave *an exquisite edge to the*

---

1   *wash-ball* Ball of soap used for shaving or washing the face and hands.

razor. And there are now to be sold, *for ready money only,* some *duvets for bed coverings, of down, beyond comparison superior to what is called otter-down,* and indeed such, that its *many excellencies cannot be here set forth.* With one excellence we are made acquainted—*it is warmer than four or five blankets, and lighter than one.*

5   There are some, however, that know the prejudice of mankind in favour of modest sincerity. The vender of the *beautifying fluid* sells a lotion that repels pimples, washes away freckles, smooths the skin, and plumps the flesh; and yet, with a generous abhorrence of ostentation, confesses, that it will not *restore the bloom of fifteen to a lady of fifty.*

The true pathos of advertisements must have sunk deep into the heart of every man that remembers the zeal shown by the seller of the *anodyne*[1] *necklace,* for the ease and safety *of poor teething infants,* and the affection with which he warned every mother, that *she would never forgive herself,* if her infant should perish without a necklace.

I cannot but remark to the celebrated author who gave, in his notifications of the camel and dromedary,[2] so many specimens of the genuine sublime, that there is now arrived another subject yet more worthy of his pen. *A famous Mohawk Indian warrior,*[3] *who took* Dieskaw[4] *the French general prisoner, dressed in the same manner with the native Indians when they go to war, with his face and body painted, with his scalping-knife, tom-axe, and all other implements of war! a sight worthy the curiosity of every true Briton!* This is a very powerful description; but a critick of great refinement would say, that it conveys rather *horrour* than *terrour.* An Indian, dressed as he goes to war, may bring company together; but if he carries the scalping-knife and tom-axe, there are many true Britons that will never be persuaded to see him but through a grate.

It has been remarked by the severer judges, that the salutary sorrow of tragick scenes is too soon effaced by the merriment of the epilogue; the same inconvenience arises from the improper disposition of advertisements. The noblest objects may be so associated as to be made ridiculous. The camel and dromedary themselves might have lost much of their dignity between *the true flower of mustard* and the *original Daffy's elixir;*[5] and I could not but feel some indignation when I found this illustrious Indian warrior immediately succeeded by *a fresh parcel of Dublin butter.*

---

1   *anodyne* Having pain-relieving qualities.
2   *notifications ... dromedary* Johnson refers to past notices about London exhibitions of exotic animals.
3   *A famous ... warrior* Johnson refers to a contemporary advertisement describing the exhibition of a Mohawk warrior at a London coffee house.
4   *Dieskaw* Baron Jean-Armand Dieskau (1701–67), French general during the French and Indian War; Dieskau was captured by Sir William Johnson at the Battle of Lake George in 1755.
5   *Daffy's elixir* Gin.

The trade of advertising is now so near to perfection, that it is not easy to propose any improvement. But as every art ought to be exercised in due subordination to the publick good, I cannot but propose it as a moral question to these masters of the publick ear, Whether they do not sometimes play too wantonly with our passions, as when the registrar of lottery-tickets invites us to his shop by an account of the prize which he sold last year; and whether the advertising controvertists do not indulge asperity of language without any adequate provocation; as in the dispute about *straps for razors*, now happily subsided, and in the altercation which at present subsists concerning *eau de luce?*[1]

In an advertisement it is allowed to every man to speak well of himself, but I know not why he should assume the privilege of censuring his neighbour. He may proclaim his own virtue or skill, but ought not to exclude others from the same pretensions.   10

Every man that advertises his own excellence should write with some consciousness of a character which dares to call the attention of the publick. He should remember that his name is to stand in the same paper with those of the king of Prussia and the emperour of Germany, and endeavour to make himself worthy of such association.

Some regard is likewise to be paid to posterity. There are men of diligence and curiosity who treasure up the papers of the day merely because others neglect them, and in time they will be scarce. When these collections shall be read in another century, how will numberless contradictions be reconciled? and how shall fame be possibly distributed among the tailors and bodice-makers of the present age?

Surely these things deserve consideration. It is enough for me to have hinted my desire that these abuses may be rectified; but such is the state of nature, that what all have the right of doing, many will attempt without sufficient care or due qualifications.

Questions

1. Do you see similarities between the advertisements that Johnson highlights and the advertisements of today? Have advertising practices changed dramatically?
2. Describe specific rhetorical techniques that Johnson uses in the course of his critique of advertising, citing passages from the text.

---

1 *eau de luce* Smelling salts, consisting of alcohol, ammonia, and oil of amber.

NAOMI KLEIN

The Swoosh

(2000)

Naomi Klein (1970–) is a Canadian journalist whose work has appeared in such magazines as The Village Voice, The Nation, *and* Ms. *She is the author of the books* No Logo: Taking Aim at the Brand Bullies (2000) *and* Fences and Windows: Dispatches from the Front Lines of the Globalization Debate (2002).

In this excerpt from No Logo, *Klein discusses "the most inflated of all the balloon brands."*

Nike CEO Phil Knight has long been a hero of the business schools. Prestigious academic publications such as *The Harvard Business Review* have lauded his pioneering marketing techniques, his understanding of branding and his early use of outsourcing. Countless MBA candidates and other students of marketing and communications have studied the Nike formula of "brands, not products." So when Phil Knight was invited to be a guest speaker at the Stanford University Business School—Knight's own alma mater—in May 1997, the visit was expected to be one in a long line of Nike love-ins. Instead, Knight was greeted by a crowd of picketing students, and when he approached the microphone he was taunted with chants of "Hey Phil, off the stage. Pay your workers a living wage." The Nike honeymoon had come to a grinding halt.

No story illustrates the growing distrust of the culture of corporate branding more than the international anti-Nike movement—the most publicized and tenacious of the brand-based campaigns. Nike's sweatshop scandals have been the subject of over 1,500 news articles and opinion columns. Its Asian factories have been probed by cameras from nearly every major media organization, from CBS to Disney's sports station, ESPN. On top of all that, it has been the subject of a series of Doonesbury cartoon strips and the butt of Michael Moore's documentary *The Big One*. As a result, several people in Nike's PR department work full time dealing with the sweatshop controversy—fielding complaints, meeting with local groups and developing Nike's response—and the company has created a new executive position: vice president for corporate responsibility. Nike has received hun-

dreds and thousands of letters of protest, faced hundreds of both small and   5
large groups of demonstrators, and is the target of a dozen critical Web
sites.

For the last two years, anti-Nike forces in North America and Europe
have attempted to focus all the scattered swoosh bashing on a single day.
Every six months they have declared an International Nike Day of Action,
and brought their demands for fair wages and independent monitoring
directly to Nike's customers, shoppers at flagship Nike Towns in urban centers or the less glamorous Foot Locker outlets in suburban malls. According to Campaign for Labor Rights, the largest anti-Nike event so far took
place on October 18, 1997: eighty-five cities in thirteen countries participated. Not all the protests have attracted large crowds, but since the movement is so decentralized, the sheer number of individual anti-Nike events
has left the company's public-relations department scrambling to get its
spin onto dozens of local newscasts. Though you'd never know it from its
branding ubiquity, even Nike can't be everywhere at once.

Since so many of the stores that sell Nike products are located in malls,
protests often end with a security guard escorting participants into the parking lot. Jeff Smith, an activist from Grand Rapids, Michigan, reported that
"when we asked if private property rights ruled over free speech rights, the
[security] officer hesitated and then emphatically said YES!" (Though in
the economically depressed city of St. John's, Newfoundland, anti-Nike
campaigners reported that after being thrown out of a mall, "they were
approached by a security guard who asked to sign their petition."[1]) But
there's plenty that can be done on the sidewalk or in the mall parking lot.
Campaigners have dramatized Nike's labor practices through what they call
"sweatshop fashion shows," and "The Transnational Capital Auction: A
Game of Survival" (the lowest bidder wins), and a global economy treadmill
(run fast, stay in the same place). In Australia, anti-Nike protestors have
been known to parade around in calico bags painted with the slogan
"Rather wear a bag than Nike." Students at the University of Colorado in
Boulder dramatized the difference between the legal minimum wage and a
living wage by holding a fundraising run in which "participants pay an
entrance fee of $1.60 (daily wages for a Nike worker in Vietnam) and the
winner will receive $2.10 (the price of three square meals in Vietnam)."[2]
Meanwhile, activists in Austin, Texas, made a giant papier-mâché Nike
sneaker piñata, and a protest outside a Regina, Saskatchewan, shopping
center featured a deface-the-swoosh booth. The last stunt is something of a

1   Memo, 4 May 1998, from Maquila Solidarity Network, "Nike Day of Action
    Canada Report & Task Force Update." [Unless otherwise noted, all notes to
    this essay are by the author.]
2   "Nike protest update," *Labour Alerts*, 18 October 1997.

running theme in all the anti-Nike actions: Nike's logo and slogan have been jammed so many times—on T-shirts, stickers, placards, banners and pins—that the semiotic bruises have turned them black and blue.

5   Tellingly, the anti-Nike movement is at its strongest inside the company's home state of Oregon, even though the area has reaped substantial economic benefits from Nike's success (Nike is the largest employer in Portland and a significant local philanthropist). Phil Knight's neighbors, nonetheless, have not all rushed to his defense in his hour of need. In fact, since the *Life* magazine soccer-ball story[1] broke, many Oregonians have been out for blood. The demonstrations outside the Portland Nike Town are among the largest and most militant in the country, sometimes sporting a menacing giant Phil Knight puppet with dollar signs for eyes or a twelve-foot Nike swoosh dragged by small children (to dramatize child labor). And in contravention of the principles of nonviolence that govern the anti-Nike movement, one protest in Eugene, Oregon, led to acts of vandalism including the tearing-down of a fence surrounding the construction of a new Nike Town, gear pulled off shelves at an existing Nike store and, according to one eyewitness, "an entire rack of clothes ... dumped off a balcony into a fountain below."[2]

Local papers in Oregon have aggressively (sometimes gleefully) followed Knight's sweatshop scandals, and the daily paper *The Oregonian* sent a reporter to Southeast Asia to do its own lengthy investigation of the factories. Mark Zusman, editor of the Oregon newspaper *The Willamette Week*, publicly admonished Knight in a 1996 "memo": "Frankly, Phil, it's time to get a little more sophisticated about this media orgy ... Oregonians already have suffered through the shame of Tonya Harding, Bob Packwood and Wes Cooley. Spare us the added humiliation of being known as the home of the most exploitative capitalist in the free world."[3]

Even Nike's charitable donations have become controversial. In the midst of a critical fundraising drive to try to address a $15 million shortfall, the Portland School Board was torn apart by a debate about whether to accept Nike's gift of $500,000 in cash and swooshed athletic gear. The board ended up accepting the donation, but not before looking their gift horse publicly in the mouth. "I asked myself," school board trustee Joseph Tam told *The Oregonian*, "Nike contributed this money so my children can have a better education, but at whose expense? At the expense of children who work for six cents an hour? ... As an immigrant and as an Asian I have to face this moral and ethical dilemma."[4]

---

1   *soccer-ball story* In 1996 *Life* magazine published a story about Nike's use of child labour in soccer ball production in Pakistan.
2   "Nike Mobilization: Local Reports," *Labor Alerts*, Campaign for Labor Rights, 26 October 1998.
3   Mark L. Zusman, "Editor's Notebook," *Willamette Week*, 12 June 1996.
4   *Oregonian*, 16 June 1996.

Nike's sponsorship scandals have reached far beyond the company's home state. In Edmonton, Alberta, teachers, parents and some students tried to block Nike from sponsoring a children's street hockey program because "a company which profits from child labor in Pakistan ought not to be held up as a hero to Edmonton children."[1] At least one school involved in the city-wide program sent back its swooshed equipment to Nike headquarters. And when Nike approached the City of Ottawa Council in March 1998 to suggest building one of its swooshed gymnasium floors in a local community center, it faced questions about "blood money." Nike withdrew its offer and gave the court to a more grateful center, run by the Boys and Girls Clubs. The dilemma of accepting Nike sponsorship money has also exploded on university campuses.

At first, much of the outrage stemmed from the fact that when the sweatshop scandal hit the papers, Nike wasn't really acting all that sorry about it. While Kathie Lee Gifford and the Gap had at least displayed contrition when they got caught with their sweatshops showing, Phil Knight had practically stonewalled: denying responsibility, attacking journalists, blaming rogue contractors and sending out flacks to speak for the company. While Kathie Lee was crying on TV, Michael Jordan was shrugging his shoulders and saying that his job was to shoot hoop, not play politics. And while the Gap agreed to allow a particularly controversial factory in El Salvador to be monitored by local human-rights groups, Nike was paying lip service to a code of conduct that its Asian workers, when interviewed, had never heard of.

But there was a critical difference between Nike and the Gap at this stage.   10
Nike didn't panic when its scandals hit the middle-American mall, because the mall, while it is indeed where most Nike products are sold, is not where Nike's image was made. Unlike the Gap, Nike has drawn on the inner cities, merging, as we've seen, with the styles of poor black and Latino youth to load up on imagery and attitude. Nike's branding power is thoroughly intertwined with the African-American heroes who have endorsed its products since the mid-eighties: Michael Jordan, Charles Barkley, Scottie Pippen, Michael Johnson, Spike Lee, Tiger Woods, Bo Jackson—not to mention the rappers who wear Nike gear on stage. While hip-hop style was the major influence at the mall, Phil Knight must have known that as long as Nike was King Brand with Jordan fans in Compton and the Bronx, he could be stirred but not shaken. Sure, their parents, teachers and church leaders might be tut-tutting over sweatshops, but as far as Nike's core demographic of thirteen- to seventeen-year-old kids was concerned, the swoosh was still made of Teflon.

---

1 Campaign for Labor Rights Web site, regional reports.

By 1997, it had become clear to Nike's critics that if they were serious about taking on the swoosh in an image war, they would have to get at the source of the brand's cachet—and as Nick Alexander of the multicultural *Third Force* magazine wrote in the summer of that year, they weren't even close. "Nobody has figured out how to make Nike break down and cry. The reason is that nobody has engaged African Americans in the fight.... To gain significant support from communities of color, corporate campaigns need to make connections between Nike's overseas operations and conditions here at home."[1]

The connections were there to be made. It is the cruelest irony of Nike's "brands, not products" formula that the people who have done the most to infuse the swoosh with cutting-edge meaning are the very people most hurt by the company's pumped-up prices and nonexistent manufacturing base. It is inner-city youth who have most directly felt the impact of Nike's decision to manufacture its products outside the U.S., both in high unemployment rates and in the erosion of the community tax base (which sets the stage for the deterioration of local public schools).

Instead of jobs for their parents, what the inner-city kids get from Nike is the occasional visit from its marketers and designers on "bro-ing" pilgrimages. "Hey, bro, what do you think of these new Jordans—are they fresh or what?" The effect of high-priced cool hunters whipping up brand frenzy on the cracked asphalt basketball courts of Harlem, the Bronx and Compton has already been discussed: kids incorporate the brands into gang-wear uniforms; some want the gear so badly they are willing to sell drugs, steal, mug, even kill for it. Jessie Collins, executive director of the Edenwald-Gun Hill Neighborhood Center in the northeast Bronx, tells me that it's sometimes drug or gang money, but more often it's the mothers' minimum-wage salary or welfare checks that are spent on disposable status wear. When I asked her about the media reports of kids stabbing each other for their $150 Air Jordans she said dryly, "It's enough to beat up on your mother for ... $150 is a hell of a lot of money."[2]

Shoe-store owners like Steven Roth of Essex House of Fashion are often uncomfortable with the way so-called street fashions play out for real on the postindustrial streets of Newark, New Jersey, where his store is located:

> I do get weary and worn down from it all. I'm always forced to face the fact that I make my money from poor people. A lot of them are on welfare. Sometimes a mother will come in here with a kid, and the kid is dirty and poorly dressed. But the kid wants a hundred-twenty-buck pair of shoes and that stupid mother buys them for him. I can feel that kid's

---

1   Nick Alexander, "Sweatshop Activism: Missing Pieces," *Z Magazine*, September 1997, 14–17.
2   Personal interview, 6 October 1997.

inner need—this desire to own these things and have the feelings that go with them—but it hurts me that this is the way things are.[1]

It's easy to blame the parents for giving in, but that "deep inner need" for   15
designer gear has grown so intense that it has confounded everyone from community leaders to the police. Everyone pretty much agrees that brands like Nike are playing a powerful surrogate role in the ghetto, subbing for everything from self-esteem to African-American cultural history to political power. What they are far less sure about is how to fill that need with empowerment and a sense of self-worth that does not necessarily come with a logo attached. Even broaching the subject of brand fetishism to these kids is risky. With so much emotion invested in celebrity consumer goods, many kids take criticism of Nike or Tommy as a personal attack, as grave a transgression as insulting someone's mother to his face.

Not surprisingly, Nike sees its appeal among disadvantaged kids differently. By supporting sports programs in Boys and Girls Clubs, by paying to repave urban basketball courts and by turning high-performance sports gear into street fashions, the company claims it is sending out the inspirational message that even poor kids can "Just Do It." In its press material and ads, there is an almost messianic quality to Nike's portrayal of its role in the inner cities: troubled kids will have higher self-esteem, fewer unwanted pregnancies and more ambition—all because at Nike "We see them as athletes." For Nike, its $150 Air Jordans are not a shoe but a kind of talisman with which poor kids can run out of the ghetto and better their lives. Nike's magic slippers will help them fly—just as they made Michael Jordan fly.

A remarkable, subversive accomplishment? Maybe. But one can't help thinking that one of the main reasons black urban youth can get out of the ghetto only by rapping or shooting hoops is that Nike and the other multinationals are reinforcing stereotypical images of black youth and simultaneously taking all the jobs away. As U.S. Congressman Bernie Sanders and Congresswoman Marcy Kaptur stated in a letter to the company, Nike has played a pivotal part in the industrial exodus from urban centers. "Nike has led the way in abandoning the manufacturing workers of the United States and their families.... Apparently, Nike believes that workers in the United States are good enough to purchase your shoe products, but are no longer worthy enough to manufacture them."[2]

And when the company's urban branding strategy is taken in conjunction with this employment record, Nike ceases to be the savior of the inner city and turns into the guy who steals your job, then sells you a pair of overpriced sneakers and yells, "Run like hell!" Hey, it's the only way out of the ghetto, kid. Just do it.

---

1 Katz, *Just Do It*, 271.
2 Letter dated 24 October 1997.

That's what Mike Gitelson thought, anyway. A social worker at the Bronx's Edenwald-Gun Hill Neighborhood Center, he was unimpressed with the swoosh's powers as a self-help guru in the projects and "sick of seeing kids wearing sneakers they couldn't afford and which their parents couldn't afford."[1] Nike's critics on college campuses and in the labor movement may be fueled largely by moral outrage, but Mike Gitelson and his colleagues simply feel ripped off. So rather than lecturing the kids on the virtues of frugality, they began telling them about how Nike made the shoes that they wanted so badly. Gitelson told them about the workers in Indonesia who earned $2 a day, he told them that it cost Nike only $5 to make the shoes they bought for between $100 and $180, and he told them about how Nike didn't make any of its shoes in the U.S.—which was part of the reason their parents had such a tough time finding work. "We got really angry," says Gitelson, "because they were taking so much money from us here and then going to other countries and exploiting people even worse.... We want our kids to see how it affects them here on the streets, but also how here on the streets affects people in Southeast Asia." His colleague at the center, youth worker Leo Johnson, lays out the issue using the kids' own lingo. "Yo, dude," he tells his preteen audiences, "you're being suckered if you pay $100 for a sneaker that costs $5 to make. If somebody did that to you on the block, you know where it's going."[2]

20   The kids at the center were upset to learn about the sweatshops but they were clearly most pissed off that Phil Knight and Michael Jordan were playing them for chumps. They sent Phil Knight a hundred letters about how much money they had spent on Nike gear over the years—and how, the way they figured it, Nike owed them big time. "I just bought a pair of Nikes for $100," one kid wrote. "It's not right what you're doing. A fair price would have been $30. Could you please send me back $70?" When the company answered the kids with a form letter, "That's when we got really angry and started putting together the protest," Gitelson says.

They decided the protest would take the form of a "shoe-in" at the Nike Town at Fifth Avenue and Fifty-seventh Street. Since most of the kids at the center are full-fledged swooshaholics, their closets are jam-packed with old Air Jordans and Air Carnivores that they would no longer even consider wearing. To put the obsolete shoes to practical use, they decided to gather them together in garbage bags and dump them on the doorstep of Nike Town.

When Nike executives got wind that a bunch of black and Latino kids from the Bronx were planning to publicly diss their company, the form letters

---

1   Personal interview.
2   David Gonzalez, "Youthful Foes Go Toe to Toe with Nike," *New York Times*, 27 September 1997, B1.

came to an abrupt halt. Up to that point, Nike had met most criticism by attacking its critics as members of "fringe groups," but this was different: if a backlash took root in the inner cities, it could sink the brand at the mall. As Gitelson puts it, "Our kids are exactly who Nike depends upon to set the trends for them so that the rest of the country buys their sneakers. White middle-class adults who are fighting them, well, it's almost okay. But when youth of color start speaking out against Nike, they start getting scared."[1]

The executives in Oregon also knew, no doubt, that Edenwald was only the tip of the iceberg. For the past couple of years, debates have been raging in hip-hop scenes about rappers "label whoring for Nike and Tommy" instead of supporting black-owned clothing companies like FUBU (For Us By Us). And rapper KRS-One planned to launch the Temple of Hip Hop, a project that promised to wrest the culture of African-American youth away from white record and clothing labels and return it to the communities that built it. It was against this backdrop that, on September 10, 1997—two weeks before the shoe-in protest was scheduled to take place—Nike's chief of public relations, Vada Manager, made the unprecedented move of flying in from Oregon with a colleague to try to convince the center that the swoosh was a friend of the projects.

"He was working overtime to put the spins on us," says Gitelson. It didn't work. At the meeting, the center laid out three very concrete demands:

1. Those who work for Nike overseas should be paid a living wage, with independent monitoring to ensure that it is happening.
2. Nike sneakers should be sold less expensively here in America with no concessions to American workforce (i.e. no downsizing, or loss of benefits).
3. Nike should seriously re-invest in the inner city in America, especially New York City since we have been the subject of much of their advertising.[2]

Gitelson may have recognized that Nike was scared—but not *that* scared. Once it became clear that the two parties were at an impasse, the meeting turned into a scolding session as the two Nike executives were required to listen to Edenwald director Jessie Collins comparing the company's Asian sweatshops with her experience as a young girl picking cotton in the sharecropping South. Back in Alabama, she told Manager, she earned $2 a day, just like the Indonesians. "And maybe a lot of Americans can't identify with those workers' situation, but I certainly can."[3]

25

---

1 Personal interview.
2 Minutes from 10 September meeting between Nike executives and the Edenwald-Gun Hill Neighborhood Center.
3 Personal interview.

Vada Manager returned to Oregon defeated and the protest went off as planned, with two hundred participants from eleven community centers around New York. The kids—most of whom were between eleven and thirteen years old—hooted and hollered and dumped several clear garbage bags of smelly old Nikes at the feet of a line of security guards who had been brought in on special assignment to protect the sacred Nike premises. Vada Manager again flew to New York to run damage control, but there was little he could do. Local TV crews covered the event, as did an ABC news team and *The New York Times*.

In a harsh bit of bad timing for the company, the *Times* piece ran on a page facing another story about Nike. Graphically underlining the urgency of the protest, this story reported that a fourteen-year-old boy from Crown Heights had just been murdered by a fifteen-year-old boy who beat him and left him on the subway tracks with a train approaching. "Police Say Teenager Died for His Sneakers and Beeper," the headline read. And the brand of his sneakers? Air Jordans. The article quoted the killer's mother saying that her son had got mixed up with gangs because he wanted to "have nice things." A friend of the victim explained that wearing designer clothes and carrying a beeper had become a way for poor kids to "feel important."

The African-American and Latino kids outside Nike Town on Fifth Avenue—the ones swarmed by cameras and surrounded by curious onlookers—were feeling pretty important, too. Taking on Nike "toe to toe," as they said, turned out to be even more fun than wearing Nikes. With the Fox News camera pointed in his face, one of the young activists—a thirteen-year-old boy from the Bronx—stared into the lens and delivered a message to Phil Knight: "Nike, we made you. We can break you."

What is perhaps most remarkable about the Nike backlash is its durability. After four solid years in the public eye, the Nike story still has legs (so too, of course, does the Nike brand). Still, most corporate scandals are successfully faced down with a statement of "regret" and a few glossy ads of children playing happily under the offending logo. Not with Nike. The news reports, labor studies and academic research documenting the sweat behind the swoosh have yet to slow down, and Nike critics remain tireless at dissecting the steady stream of materials churned out by Nike's PR machine. They were unmoved by Phil Knight's presence on the White House Task Force on Sweatshops—despite his priceless photo op standing beside President Clinton at the Rose Garden press conference. They sliced and diced the report Nike commissioned from civil-rights leader Andrew Young, pointing out that Young completely dodged the question of whether Nike's factory wages are inhumanely exploitative, and attacking him for relying on translators provided by Nike itself when he visited the factories in Indonesia and Vietnam. As for Nike's other study-for-hire—this one by a group of Dartmouth business students who concluded that workers in Vietnam were living the good life on less than $2 a day—well, everyone pretty much ignored that one altogether.

Finally, in May 1998, Phil Knight stepped out from behind the curtain of spin doctors and called a press conference in Washington to address his critics directly. Knight began by saying that he had been painted as a "corporate crook, the perfect corporate villain for these times." He acknowledged that his shoes "have become synonymous with slave wages, forced overtime and arbitrary abuse." Then, to much fanfare, he unveiled a plan to improve working conditions in Asia. It contained some tough new regulations on factory air quality and the use of petroleum-based chemicals. It promised to provide classes inside some Indonesian factories and promised not to hire anyone under eighteen years old in the shoe factories. But there was still nothing substantial in the plan about allowing independent outside monitors to inspect the factories, and there were no wage raises for the workers. Knight did promise, however, that Nike's contractors would no longer be permitted to appeal to the Indonesian government for a waiver on the minimum wage.

It wasn't enough. That September the San Francisco human-rights group Global Exchange, one of the company's harshest critics, released an alarming report on the status of Nike's Indonesian workers in the midst of the country's economic and political crisis. "While workers producing Nike shoes were low paid before their currency, the rupiah, began plummeting in late 1997, the dollar value of their wages has dropped from $2.47/day in 1997 to 80 cents/day in 1998." Meanwhile, the report noted that with soaring commodity prices, workers "estimated that their cost of living had gone up anywhere from 100 to 300 per cent."[1] Global Exchange called on Nike to double the wages of its Indonesian workforce, an exercise that would cost it $20 million a year—exactly what Michael Jordan is paid annually to endorse the company.

Not surprisingly, Nike did not double the wages, but it did, three weeks later, give 30 percent of the Indonesian workforce a 25 percent raise.[2] That, too, failed to silence the crowds outside the superstores, and five months later Nike came forward again, this time with what vice president of corporate responsibility Maria Eitel called "an aggressive corporate responsibility agenda at Nike."[3] As of April 1, 1999, workers would get another 6 percent raise. The company had also opened up a Vietnamese factory near Ho Chi Minh City to outside health and safety monitors, who found conditions

1 "Wages and Living Expense for Nike Workers in Indonesia," report released by Global Exchange, 23 September 1998.
2 "Nike Raises Wages for Indonesian Workers," *Oregonian*, 16 October 1998.
3 "Nike to Improve Minimum Monthly Wage Package for Indonesian Workers," Nike press release, 19 March 1999.

much improved. Dara O'Rourke of the University of California at Berkeley reported that the factory had "implemented important changes over the past 18 months which appear to have significantly reduced worker exposures to toxic solvents, adhesives and other chemicals." What made the report all the more remarkable was that O'Rourke's inspection was a genuinely independent one: in fact, less than two years earlier, he had enraged the company by leaking a report conducted by Ernst & Young that showed that Nike was ignoring widespread violations at that same factory.

O'Rourke's findings weren't all glowing. There were still persistent problems with air quality, factory overheating and safety gear—and he had visited only the one factory.[1] As well, Nike's much-heralded 6 percent pay raise for Indonesian workers still left much to be desired; it amounted to an increase of one cent an hour and, with inflation and currency fluctuation, only brought wages to about half of what Nike paychecks were worth before the economic crisis. Even so, these were significant gestures coming from a company that two years earlier was playing the role of the powerless global shopper, claiming that contractors alone had the authority to set wages and make the rules.

The resilience of the Nike campaign in the face of the public-relations onslaught is persuasive evidence that invasive marketing, coupled with worker abandonment, strikes a wide range of people from different walks of life as grossly unfair and unsustainable. Moreover, many of those people are not interested in letting Nike off the hook simply because this formula has become the standard one for capitalism-as-usual. On the contrary, there seems to be a part of the public psyche that likes kicking the most macho and extreme of all the sporting-goods companies in the shins—I mean *really* likes it. Nike's critics have shown that they don't want this story to be brushed under the rug with a reassuring bit of corporate PR; they want it out in the open, where they can keep a close eye on it.

35   In large part, this is because Nike's critics know the company's sweatshop scandals are not the result of a series of freak accidents: they know that the criticisms leveled at Nike apply to all the brand-based shoe companies contracting out to a global maze of firms. But rather than this serving as a justification, Nike—as the market leader—has become a lightning rod for this broader resentment. It has been latched on to as the essential story of the extremes of the current global economy: the disparities between those who profit from Nike's success and those who are exploited by it are so gaping that a child could understand what is wrong with this picture and indeed it is children and teenagers who most readily do.

---

1   Steven Greenhouse, "Nike Critic Praises Gains in Air Quality at Vietnam Factory," *New York Times*, 12 March 1999.

So, when does the total boycott of Nike products begin? Not soon, apparently. A cursory glance around any city in the world shows that the swoosh is still ubiquitous; some athletes still tattoo it on their navels, and plenty of high-school students still deck themselves out in the coveted gear. But at the same time, there can be little doubt that the millions of dollars that Nike has saved in labor costs over the years are beginning to bite back, and take a toll on its bottom line. "We didn't think that the Nike situation would be as bad as it seems to be," said Nikko stock analyst Tim Finucane in *The Wall Street Journal* in March 1998.[1] Wall Street really had no choice but to turn on the company that had been its darling for so many years. Despite the fact that Asia's plummeting currencies meant that Nike's labor costs in Indonesia, for instance, were a quarter of what they were before the crash, the company was still suffering. Nike's profits were down, orders were down, stock prices were *way* down, and after an average annual growth of 34 percent since 1995, quarterly earnings were suddenly down by 70 percent. By the third quarter, which ended in February 1999, Nike's profits were once again up 70 percent—but by the company's own account, the recovery was not the result of rebounding sales but rather of Nike's decision to cut jobs and contracts. In fact, Nike's revenues and future orders were down in 1999 for the second year in a row.[2]

Nike has blamed its financial problems on everything *but* the human-rights campaign. The Asian currency crisis was the reason Nikes weren't selling well in Japan and South Korea; or it was because Americans were buying "brown shoes" (walking shoes and hiking boots) as opposed to big white sneakers. But the brown-shoe excuse rang hollow. Nike makes plenty of brown shoes—it has a line of hiking boots, and it owns Cole Haan (and recently saved millions by closing down the Cole Haan factory in Portland, Maine, and moving production to Mexico and Brazil).[3] More to the point, Adidas staged a massive comeback during the very year that Nike was free-falling. In the quarter when Nike nose-dived, Adidas sales were up 42 percent, its net income was up 48 percent, to $255 million, and its stock price had tripled in two years. The German company, as we have seen, turned its fortunes around by copying Nike's production structure and all but Xeroxing its approach to marketing and sponsorships. In 1997–98, Adidas even redesigned its basketball shoes so they looked just like Nikes: big, white and ultra high tech. But unlike Nikes, they sold briskly. So much for the brown-shoe theory.

1   Shanthi Kalathil, "Being Tied to Nike Affects Share Price of Yue Yuen," *Wall Street Journal*, 25 March 1998.
2   "Third quarter brings 70 percent increase in net income for sneaker giant," Associated Press, 19 March 1999.
3   "Cole Haan Joins Ranks of Shoe Companies Leaving Maine," Associated Press, 23 April 1999.

Over the years Nike has tried dozens of tactics to silence the cries of its critics, but the most ironic by far has been the company's desperate attempt to hide behind its product. "We're not political activists. We are a footwear manufacturer," said Nike spokeswoman Donna Gibbs, when the sweatshop scandal first began to erupt.[1] A footwear manufacturer? This from the company that made a concerted decision in the mid-eighties not to be about boring corporeal stuff like footwear—and certainly nothing as crass as manufacturing. Nike wanted to be about sports, Knight told us, it wanted to be about the idea of sports, then the idea of transcendence through sports; then it wanted to be about self-empowerment, women's rights, racial equality. It wanted its stores to be temples, its ads a religion, its customers a nation, its workers a tribe. After taking us all on such a branded ride, to turn around and say, "Don't look at us, we just make shoes" rings laughably hollow.

Nike was the most inflated of all the balloon brands, and the bigger it grew, the louder it popped.

Questions

1. What is a "balloon brand" (paragraph 39)?
2. In Klein's view, why is it particularly pernicious for Nike to have drawn on the ethos of black inner-city culture in shaping the image of its brand?
3. Compare the style and tone of Klein's writing here with a non-editorial newspaper report. Evaluate the similarities and differences in terms of types of sources, audiences, aims, and possible effects.

---

1   Zusman, "Editor's Notebook."

DOUGLAS COUPLAND

Cigs

(2002)

Douglas Coupland (1961–) studied art and design at the Emily Carr Institute, and has published many novels and short story collections. His novels include Generation X: Tales for an Accelerated Culture *(1991), the book that popularized the term "generation X," and* Eleanor Rigby *(2005).*

Coupland has also published two volumes of short non-fiction works, Souvenir of Canada *(2002), from which this piece is taken, and* Souvenir of Canada 2 *(2004).*

One sunny afternoon in the 1990s, Canada's prime minister was wearing Ray-Ban sunglasses. This was in Ottawa, on Parliament Hill, and he was walking from wherever to wherever, accompanied by a scrum of a crowd. During this walk, he was pestered one too many times by a persistent heckler who'd been on his case for a long time. The prime minister snapped, and a photo of him strangling the heckler went out on the wire services. The day it appeared in newspapers, I got three e-mails from Americans saying, "Wow! It's so great that you have a prime minister who wears Ray-Bans and strangles people. I wish we had a president like that." I mention this story to introduce the fact that strange causes can have even stranger effects on people. For example: *cigarette packaging.*

If you smoke in Canada, every time you reach for your pack you encounter a huge, screaming black-and-white statement that reads: CIGA-RETTES CAUSE CANCER. That simple. Or something equally frightening. As an added bonus, there are countless grotesque photos of diseased you-name-its appended to the words. These warnings have been growing in size for years, and they now remind me of avant-garde art from New York in the 1980s. They're backwards hip. I quit smoking in 1988, but these new packages are so cool looking that, human nature being as perverse as it is, they almost make me want to start up again. And as of recently, cigarette manu-facturers are no longer going to be able to use the words "mild" or "light" on their boxes—Emphysema Lite, Cancer Mild.

Visit the U.S. where they pussyfoot like mad about tobacco (THE SUR-GEON GENERAL THINKS SMOKING MIGHT NOT BE THE BEST IDEA,

BUT THAT'S ONLY ONE PERSON'S OPINION), or Europe, where they don't bother with anything at all, and it makes me kind of proud that Canada's telling the truth. It'll be a decade before we know if the new tactic works. I suppose these Canadian cigarette packs will only become more and more collectible as the years pass, joining Victorian dental tools and 1960s gerbil toys as a beloved collecting category.

Questions

1. Compare the reaction of Coupland's American friends to the incident involving the Canadian Prime Minister to Coupland's reaction to Canadian cigarette packaging. What is the effect of Coupland's juxtaposition of these?
2. What is "backwards hip," and what does this suggest about human nature as Coupland sees it? In what ways does Coupland's writing itself exhibit aspects of "backwards hip"?
3. Compare and contrast the three approaches to cigarette packaging (Canadian, American, European) as described by Coupland to Samuel Johnson's characterizations of advertising.

Model Citizens

(2005)

Nancy Franklin is the television critic at The New Yorker.

This is a review of the television show America's Next Top Model, *in which participants face elimination each week as they compete for the opportunity of a modelling career.*

If you watched the first episode of the fourth installment of UPN's "America's Next Top Model" last week, you may have noticed that I was not one of the contestants competing for the hundred-thousand-dollar contract with Cover Girl cosmetics, the model-management contract with Ford Models, and the spread in *Elle*, even though I fulfilled many of the show's stated eligibility requirements: I am not currently a candidate for public office; I am not shorter than five feet seven; my age is between eighteen and twenty-seven if you divide it by any number between 1.778 and 2.667; and, to the best of my recollection, I have not had previous experience as a model in a national campaign within the past five years. As for the stipulation that applicants must "exhibit.... a willingness to share their most private thoughts in an open forum of strangers," is there anyone left on the planet who doesn't fit into this category? Also, I can totally work it, bring it, feel it, slam it, serve it, and own it—to use the terms that the fashion photographers, advisers, and judges fall back on when coaching the contestants or explaining their decision to keep them on the show or boot them.

The reason I'm not on the show is that I didn't want a tarantula crawling on my face; I'm funny that way. In a photo shoot for a jewelry ad in the third installment of "A.N.T.M.," last fall, the models had to pose with a tarantula, either on or near their face. In one shot, the huge beast adjusts itself so that one leg is on the girl's eyelid and another is in the corner of her mouth. Another girl—the one with the most assertive personality—freaks out and cries, because she's terrified of spiders and so much rides on her being able to act like a pro. The contestants all regularly comment on one another to the camera, and one of them says during this scene, "Eva's really stressing. She's worried that her inability to perform with the spider on her face is going to send her home, so I don't think that she really is cut out to be America's Next Top Model." Since I, too, have an inability to perform with spiders on my face, I thought I wasn't cut out for it, either. But Eva was able to pull herself together, and she looked gorgeous in her picture with Spidey—*and* she went on to win the entire competition. So I guess I should have gone ahead and sent in an application, arachnophobia be damned.

The supermodel Tyra Banks created "America's Next Top Model," and she is also the host and one of the show's executive producers. The aspiring models view her both as the bearer of a magic ticket out of poverty, obscurity, stripping, or waitressing and as a comforting, maternal, Oprah-like figure. Even while she is pondering which chick will be thrown out of the nest each week, Banks dispenses plentiful hugs to her charges, at one point getting down on a bathroom floor to console a distressed girl. During each episode, she makes sure the contestants understand the hardships of the modelling life—facing rejection, working in countries where they don't speak the language, putting makeup on in a moving limousine—and gives them the kind of challenges they would face as pros, such as wearing stiletto heels while posing in a bikini on volcanic rock along the coast of Jamaica. Oh, my God—now *I'm* crying.

One refreshing aspect of "A.N.T.M." is that there is more diversity among the contestants than one usually sees in reality shows. In the last series, or "cycle," there was an Indian woman, and all the cycles have featured several black semi-finalists, as well as a couple of plus-size hopefuls. (The show has not, however, stepped up—to use another of its recurring exhortatory phrases—when it comes to Asian and Latino women. Not that United Nations-style casting guarantees loftiness or anything. The Indian woman believed that she was "setting a goal for Indians: They're either engineers or doctors. But we can go outside of that. We can use our intelligence in this industry.") Banks, who has healthy, womanly curves, has included cautionary tales relating to the body-image problems that occur in the modelling business; the last cycle had a finalist who was a half inch under six feet tall and weighed a hundred and fifteen pounds, and another confessed to having problems with food, though she balked at the label "bulimic," because she didn't throw up after every single meal. Comments about the tall drink of water were left to the girls, who all live together for eight weeks and have the usual fights and dish the usual dirt on one another; for the model who was avowedly obsessed with thinness, Banks brought in a nutritionist, but the young woman resisted help—an accurate illustration of the difficulty that even experts often have in treating such disorders. It's hard not to think, though, that it was a little unfair to the extreme cases to let them get so far along in the competition, since they didn't have the remotest chance of winning; they're there, it seems, mainly to short-circuit potential complaints from viewers who may consider the modelling profession itself partly responsible for the fact that so many young women hate their bodies.

Much as Banks wants to come across as a hey-girlfriend confidante to the   5
contestants, she in fact heightens the atmosphere of anxiety, by drawing out the elimination at the end of each episode for as long as possible, and by emphasizing that the loser will have to leave "immediately." For some contestants, immediately may not be soon enough. One girl from Oklahoma, after living in a gigantic suite at the Waldorf-Astoria for a while, had simply had it. "In Oklahoma, people look at me," she said. "I don't feel like people are looking at me here. I'm not having that much fun." While the opportunity these women are angling for is real, and even has benefits for the losers—two of whom appeared on UPN sitcoms last week—you can't help wondering why they want it so much, when success in the world they're trying to enter seems to hinge on how much of themselves they can make disappear. In this week's episode, Banks says to the girls, "Part of being a top model is about being a blank palette." And the stylist for the photo shoots, Jay Manuel, says after a session, "My concern with Toccara is that she allows too much of her personality to get in the way." At one point during a shoot, when a model strikes a less than erect pose, she is rewarded with this evaluation: "I love the broken-down-doll look." In the third cycle, the girls have to walk into a room wearing high heels that are two sizes too small and a dress that is too tight—the point being that a model has to smile through all kinds of discomfort. Nolé Marin, the fashion director of a magazine for gay men, and one of the arbiters of style who sit in judgment at the end of each episode—the others are Banks, a photographer named Nigel Barker, and the former supermodel Janice Dickinson—says to one of the less graceful girls, "You look like the broken Tin Man. You needed a major oil job." Sometimes looking broken is good; sometimes it's not. It's all so confusing! This is actually among the most humane comments heard during the series from Marin, who is—and let's ourselves be fashion judges for a moment here—a chubby little bespectacled bald man with an unattractive soul patch. None of the judges offer much in the way of constructive criticism; it's always either "I'm loving the look, honey. I'm *loving* the look" or "Lose the pearls! Ugh! This is a model contest, not a secretary contest." (And yet—one more schmatte[1] in the bundle of contradictions that is the fashion world—Mikimoto pearls are given out as a reward to a couple of the models.) Dickinson is a stun gun in human form, zealously zapping the girls as they parade before her. Referring to a picture of the bulimic woman, who is five feet ten, weighs a hundred and thirty pounds, and has a flat stomach, she says, "You look about two months pregnant there."

"America's Next Top Model" is fascinating, if you like trying to figure out

---

1   *schmatte* A rag; an old or ragged garment; a worthless thing (Yiddish).

life's little mysteries, such as how it could possibly be that someone has "wanted to model since I was three years old," and why models are trained to walk like people who have hip dysplasia. If you already think that models are vacuous, apparently you are not alone: even models themselves make that assumption. As one of the contestants, who is surprised (and shouldn't be) by how much Banks has on the ball, says, "I mean, you see Tyra, and you think boobs and lingerie. And she's got a brain—I mean, who woulda thought?"

Questions

1. Overall, is this a positive or negative review? Provide evidence from the text.
2. What is the function of Franklin's observation that she could have or should have applied to be a contestant?
3. Choose a newspaper article written in a journalistic style that is different than Franklin's style in this review. Discuss in detail how these styles (and their effects) differ.

MALCOLM GLADWELL

Brain Candy

(2005)

Malcolm Gladwell (1963–) was a reporter at The Washington Post *from 1987 to 1996, and has been a staff writer for* The New Yorker *magazine since 1996. He is the author of* Tipping Point: How Little Things Can Make a Big Difference *(2000) and* Blink: The Power of Thinking without Thinking *(2005).*

In this review of Steven Johnson's book Everything Bad is Good for You, *Gladwell examines the assumptions underlying North American conceptions of intelligence.*

Twenty years ago, a political philosopher named James Flynn uncovered a curious fact. Americans—at least, as measured by I.Q. tests—were getting smarter. This fact had been obscured for years, because the people who give I.Q. tests continually recalibrate the scoring system to keep the average at 100. But if you took out the recalibration, Flynn found, I.Q. scores showed a steady upward trajectory, rising by about three points per decade, which means that a person whose I.Q. placed him in the top ten per cent of the American population in 1920 would today fall in the bottom third. Some of that effect, no doubt, is a simple by-product of economic progress: in the surge of prosperity during the middle part of the last century, people in the West became better fed, better educated, and more familiar with things like I.Q. tests. But, even as that wave of change has subsided, test scores have continued to rise—not just in America but all over the developed world. What's more, the increases have not been confined to children who go to enriched day-care centers and private schools. The middle part of the curve—the people who have supposedly been suffering from a deteriorating public-school system and a steady diet of lowest-common-denominator television and mindless pop music—has increased just as much. What on earth is happening? In the wonderfully entertaining "Everything Bad Is Good for You" (Riverhead; $23.95), Steven Johnson proposes that what is making us smarter is precisely what we thought was making us dumber: popular culture.

Johnson is the former editor of the online magazine *Feed* and the author of a number of books on science and technology. There is a pleasing eclecticism to his thinking. He is as happy analyzing "Finding Nemo" as he is dissecting the intricacies of a piece of software, and he's perfectly capable of using Nietzsche's notion of eternal recurrence[1] to discuss the new creative rules of television shows. Johnson wants to understand popular culture—not in the postmodern, academic sense of wondering what "The Dukes of Hazzard" tells us about Southern male alienation but in the very practical sense of wondering what watching something like "The Dukes of Hazzard" does to the way our minds work.

As Johnson points out, television is very different now from what it was thirty years ago. It's *harder*. A typical episode of "Starsky and Hutch," in the nineteen-seventies, followed an essentially linear path: two characters, engaged in a single story line, moving toward a decisive conclusion. To watch an episode of "Dallas" today is to be stunned by its glacial pace—by the arduous attempts to establish social relationships, by the excruciating simplicity of the plotline, by how *obvious* it was. A single episode of "The Sopranos," by contrast, might follow five narrative threads, involving a dozen characters who weave in and out of the plot. Modern television also requires the viewer to do a lot of what Johnson calls "filling in," as in a "Seinfeld" episode that subtly parodies the Kennedy assassination conspiracists, or a typical "Simpsons" episode, which may contain numerous allusions to politics or cinema or pop culture. The extraordinary amount of money now being made in the television aftermarket—DVD sales and syndication—means that the creators of television shows now have an incentive to make programming that can sustain two or three or four viewings. Even reality shows like "Survivor," Johnson argues, engage the viewer in a way that television rarely has in the past:

> When we watch these shows, the part of our brain that monitors the emotional lives of the people around us—the part that tracks subtle shifts in intonation and gesture and facial expression—scrutinizes the action on the screen, looking for clues.... The phrase "Monday-morning quarterbacking" was coined to describe the engaged feeling spectators have in relation to games as opposed to stories. We absorb stories, but we second-guess games. Reality programming has brought that second-guessing to prime time, only the game in question revolves around social dexterity rather than the physical kind.

How can the greater cognitive demands that television makes on us now, he wonders, not *matter*?

5   Johnson develops the same argument about video games. Most of the people who denounce video games, he says, haven't actually played them—

---

1   *eternal recurrence* German philosopher Friedrich Wilhelm Nietzsche
(1844–1900) suggested in several texts that one's life will recur infinitely.

at least, not recently. Twenty years ago, games like Tetris or Pac-Man were ⁵ simple exercises in motor coördination and pattern recognition. Today's games belong to another realm. Johnson points out that one of the "walk-throughs" for "Grand Theft Auto III"—that is, the informal guides that break down the games and help players navigate their complexities—is fifty-three thousand words long, about the length of his book. The contemporary video game involves a fully realized imaginary world, dense with detail and levels of complexity.

Indeed, video games are not games in the sense of those pastimes—like Monopoly or gin rummy or chess—which most of us grew up with. They don't have a set of unambiguous rules that have to be learned and then followed during the course of play. This is why many of us find modern video games baffling: we're not used to being in a situation where we have to figure out what to do. We think we only have to learn how to press the buttons faster. But these games withhold critical information from the player. Players have to explore and sort through hypotheses in order to make sense of the game's environment, which is why a modern video game can take forty hours to complete. Far from being engines of instant gratification, as they are often described, video games are actually, Johnson writes, "all about delayed gratification—sometimes so long delayed that you wonder if the gratification is ever going to show."

At the same time, players are required to manage a dizzying array of information and options. The game presents the player with a series of puzzles, and you can't succeed at the game simply by solving the puzzles one at a time. You have to craft a longer-term strategy, in order to juggle and coördinate competing interests. In denigrating the video game, Johnson argues, we have confused it with other phenomena in teen-age life, like multitask-ing—simultaneously e-mailing and listening to music and talking on the telephone and surfing the Internet. Playing a video game is, in fact, an exercise in "constructing the proper hierarchy of tasks and moving through the tasks in the correct sequence," he writes. "It's about finding order and meaning in the world, and making decisions that help create that order."

It doesn't seem right, of course, that watching "24" or playing a video game could be as important cognitively as reading a book. Isn't the extra-ordinary success of the "Harry Potter" novels better news for the culture than the equivalent success of "Grand Theft Auto III"? Johnson's response is to imagine what cultural critics might have said had video games been invented hundreds of years ago, and only recently had something called the book been marketed aggressively to children:

> Reading books chronically understimulates the senses. Unlike the long-standing tradition of gameplaying—which engages the child in a vivid, three-dimensional world filled with moving images and musical sound-

scapes, navigated and controlled with complex muscular movements—books are simply a barren string of words on the page....

Books are also tragically isolating. While games have for many years engaged the young in complex social relationships with their peers, building and exploring worlds together, books force the child to sequester him or herself in a quiet space, shut off from interaction with other children....

But perhaps the most dangerous property of these books is the fact that they follow a fixed linear path. You can't control their narratives in any fashion—you simply sit back and have the story dictated to you.... This risks instilling a general passivity in our children, making them feel as though they're powerless to change their circumstances. Reading is not an active, participatory process; it's a submissive one.

He's joking, of course, but only in part. The point is that books and video games represent two very different kinds of learning. When you read a biology textbook, the content of what you read is what matters. Reading is a form of explicit learning. When you play a video game, the value is in how it makes you think. Video games are an example of collateral learning, which is no less important.

10   Being "smart" involves facility in both kinds of thinking—the kind of fluid problem solving that matters in things like video games and I.Q. tests, but also the kind of crystallized knowledge that comes from explicit learning. If Johnson's book has a flaw, it is that he sometimes speaks of our culture being "smarter" when he's really referring just to that fluid problem-solving facility. When it comes to the other kind of intelligence, it is not clear at all what kind of progress we are making, as anyone who has read, say, the Gettysburg Address[1] alongside any Presidential speech from the past twenty years can attest. The real question is what the right balance of these two forms of intelligence might look like. "Everything Bad Is Good for You" doesn't answer that question. But Johnson does something nearly as important, which is to remind us that we shouldn't fall into the trap of thinking that explicit learning is the only kind of learning that matters.

In recent years, for example, a number of elementary schools have phased out or reduced recess and replaced it with extra math or English instruction. This is the triumph of the explicit over the collateral. After all, recess is "play" for a ten-year-old in precisely the sense that Johnson describes video games as play for an adolescent: an unstructured environment that requires the child actively to intervene, to look for the hidden logic, to find order and meaning in chaos.

---

1   *Gettysburg Address* Speech by Abraham Lincoln given on 19 November 1863 (see p. 170).

One of the ongoing debates in the educational community, similarly, is over the value of homework. Meta-analysis[1] of hundreds of studies done on the effects of homework shows that the evidence supporting the practice is, at best, modest. Homework seems to be most useful in high school and for subjects like math. At the elementary-school level, homework seems to be of marginal or no academic value. Its effect on discipline and personal responsibility is unproved. And the causal relation between high-school homework and achievement is unclear: it hasn't been firmly established whether spending more time on homework in high school makes you a better student or whether better students, finding homework more pleasurable, spend more time doing it. So why, as a society, are we so enamored of homework? Perhaps because we have so little faith in the value of the things that children would otherwise be doing with their time. They could go out for a walk, and get some exercise; they could spend time with their peers, and reap the rewards of friendship. Or, Johnson suggests, they could be playing a video game, and giving their minds a rigorous workout.

Questions

1. How, according to Gladwell's reading of Steven Johnson, is popular culture actually making us smarter? Do you agree or disagree?
2. Using evidence from the text, explain what particular aspects of Gladwell's writing are engaging.
3. In what ways does Gladwell's essay fulfill the conventions of a book review? In what ways is it unconventional?

---

1   *Meta-analysis* The analysis of data from separate but related studies in order to determine trends.

❧ *Nature and the Environment* ❧

VIRGINIA WOOLF

The Death of the Moth

(1942)

Virginia Woolf (1882–1941) *was an influential English writer whose novels include* Mrs. Dalloway *(1925),* To the Lighthouse *(1927), and* The Waves *(1931). She was also a literary critic and an early advocate of feminism, most notably in her book* A Room of One's Own *(1929).*

In the following essay, Woolf's observations of the final living moments of a moth lead her to reflect upon the nature of life and the inevitability of death.

Moths that fly by day are not properly to be called moths; they do not excite that pleasant sense of dark autumn nights and ivy-blossom which the commonest yellow underwing asleep in the shadow of the curtain never fails to rouse in us. They are hybrid creatures, neither gay like butterflies nor sombre like their own species. Nevertheless the present specimen, with his narrow hay-coloured wings, fringed with a tassel of the same colour, seemed to be content with life. It was a pleasant morning, mid-September, mild, benignant, yet with a keener breath than that of the summer months. The plough was already scoring the field opposite the window, and where the share had been, the earth was pressed flat and gleamed with moisture. Such vigour came rolling in from the fields and the down beyond that it was difficult to keep the eyes strictly turned upon the book. The rooks too were keeping one of their annual festivities; soaring round the tree-tops until it looked as if a vast net with thousands of black knots in it has been cast up into the air; which, after a few moments sank slowly down upon the trees until every twig seemed to have a knot at the end of it. Then, suddenly, the net would be thrown into the air again in a wider circle this time, with the utmost clamour and vociferation, as though to be thrown into the air and settle slowly down upon the tree-tops were a tremendously exciting experience.

The same energy which inspired the rooks, the ploughmen, the horses, and even, it seemed, the lean bare-backed downs, sent the moth fluttering from side to side of his square of the window-pane. One could not help watching him. One was, indeed, conscious of a queer feeling of pity for him. The possibilities of pleasure seemed that morning so enormous and so various that to have only a moth's part in life, and a day moth's at that, appeared a hard fate, and his zest in enjoying his meagre opportunities to the full, pathetic. He flew vigorously to one corner of his compartment, and, after waiting there for a second, flew across to the other. What remained for him but to fly to a third corner and then to a fourth? That was all he could do, in spite of the size of the downs, the width of the sky, the far-off smoke of houses, and the romantic voice, now and then, of a steamer out at sea. What he could do he did. Watching him, it seemed as if a fibre, very thin but pure, of the enormous energy of the world had been thrust into his frail and diminutive body. As often as he crossed the pane, I could fancy that a thread of vital light became visible. He was little or nothing but life.

Yet, because he was so small, and so simple a form of the energy that was rolling in at the open window and driving its way through so many narrow and intricate corridors in my own brain and in those of other human beings, there was something marvellous as well as pathetic about him. It was as if someone had taken a tiny bead of pure life and decking it as lightly as possible with down and feathers, had set it dancing and zigzagging to show us the true nature of life. Thus displayed one could not get over the strangeness of it. One is apt to forget all about life, seeing it humped and bossed and garnished and cumbered so that it has to move with the greatest circumspection and dignity. Again, the thought of all that life might have been had he been born in any other shape caused one to view his simple activities with a kind of pity.

After a time, tired by his dancing apparently, he settled on the window ledge in the sun, and the queer spectacle being at an end, I forgot about him. Then, looking up, my eye was caught by him. He was trying to resume his dancing, but seemed either so stiff or so awkward that he could only flutter to the bottom of the window-pane; and when he tried to fly across it he failed. Being intent on other matters I watched these futile attempts for a time without thinking, unconsciously waiting for him to resume his flight, as one waits for a machine, that has stopped momentarily, to start again without considering the reason for its failure. After perhaps a seventh attempt he slipped from the wooden ledge and fell, fluttering his wings, on to his back on the window-sill. The helplessness of his attitude roused me. It flashed upon me that he was in difficulties; he could no longer raise himself; his legs struggled vainly. But, as I stretched out a pencil, meaning to help him to right himself, it came over me that the failure and awkwardness were the approach of death. I laid the pencil down again.

The legs agitated themselves once more. I looked as if for the enemy against which he struggled. I looked out of doors. What had happened there? Presumably it was midday, and work in the fields had stopped. Stillness and quiet had replaced the previous animation. The birds had taken themselves off to feed in the brooks. The horses stood still. Yet the power was there all the same, massed outside indifferent, impersonal, not attending to anything in particular. Somehow it was opposed to the little hay-coloured moth. It was useless to try to do anything. One could only watch the extraordinary efforts made by those tiny legs against an oncoming doom which could, had it chosen, have submerged an entire city, not merely a city, but masses of human beings; nothing, I knew, had any chance against death. Nevertheless after a pause of exhaustion the legs fluttered again. It was superb this last protest, and so frantic that he succeeded at last in righting himself. One's sympathies, of course, were all on the side of life. Also, when there was nobody to care or to know, this gigantic effort on the part of an insignificant little moth, against a power of such magnitude, to retain what no one else valued or desired to keep, moved one strangely. Again, somehow, one saw life, a pure bead. I lifted the pencil again, useless though I knew it to be. But even as I did so, the unmistakable tokens of death showed themselves. The body relaxed, and instantly grew stiff. The struggle was over. The insignificant little creature now knew death. As I looked at the dead moth, this minute wayside triumph of so great a force over so mean an antagonist filled me with wonder. Just as life had been strange a few minutes before, so death was now as strange. The moth having righted himself now lay most decently and uncomplainingly composed. O yes, he seemed to say, death is stronger than I am.

Questions

1. Woolf writes, "there was something marvellous as well as pathetic" about the moth (paragraph 3). What about the moth's life leads her to describe it in this way?
2. What is Woolf's attitude toward the moth? Citing specific examples, explain how she informs the reader of this attitude.
3. Assess those aspects of Woolf's writing style that help make "The Death of the Moth" a poignant allegory.

EDWARD HOAGLAND

The Courage of Turtles

(1968)

Edward Hoagland (1932–) is an American essayist and novelist best known for his nature and travel writing. Born in New York City, Hoagland moved to rural Connecticut as a young boy where he developed his love for wildlife and wild places. His nearly twenty books include African Calliope: A Journey to the Sudan *(1979),* Balancing Acts *(1992),* Cat Man *(1956),* Compass Points (2001), *The Courage of Turtles (1970), and* Walking the Dead Diamond River *(1973).*

In this essay, Hoagland recounts his life-long interest in turtles, while raising questions about the compatibility of human and natural environments.

Turtles are a kind of bird with the governor turned low. With the same attitude of removal, they cock a glance at what is going on, as if they need only to fly away. Until recently they were also a case of virtue rewarded, at least in the town where I grew up, because, being humble creatures, there were plenty of them. Even when we still had a few bobcats in the woods the local snapping turtles, growing up to forty pounds, were the largest carnivores. You would see them through the amber water, as big as greeny wash basins at the bottom of the pond, until they faded into the inscrutable mud as if they hadn't existed at all.

When I was ten I went to Dr. Green's Pond, a two-acre pond across the road. When I was twelve I walked a mile or so to Taggart's Pond, which was lusher, had big water snakes and a waterfall; and shortly after that I was bicycling way up to the adventuresome vastness of Mud Pond, a lake-sized body of water in the reservoir system of a Connecticut city, possessed of cat-backed little islands and empty shacks and a forest of pines and hardwoods along the shore. Otters, foxes and mink left their prints on the bank; there were pike and perch. As I got older, the estates and forgotten back lots in town were parceled out and sold for nice prices, yet, though the woods had shrunk, it seemed that fewer people walked in the woods. The new residents didn't know how to find them. Eventually, exploring, they did find them; and it required some ingenuity and doubling around on my part to go for eight miles without meeting someone. I was grown by now, I lived in New York, and that's what I wanted on the occasional weekends when I came out.

Since Mud Pond contained drinking water I had felt confident nothing untoward would happen there. For a long while the developers stayed away, until the drought of the mid-1960s. This event, squeezing the edges in, convinced the local water company that the pond really wasn't a necessity as a catch basin, however; so they bulldozed a hole in the earthen dam, bulldozed the banks to fill in the bottom, and landscaped the flow of water that remained to wind like an English brook and provide a domestic view for the houses which were planned. Most of the painted turtles of Mud Pond, who had been inaccessible as they sunned on their rocks, wound up in boxes in boys' closets within a matter of days. Their footsteps in the dry leaves gave them away as they wandered forlornly. The snappers and the little musk turtles, neither of whom leave the water except once a year to lay their eggs, dug into the drying mud for another siege of hot weather, which they were accustomed to doing whenever the pond got low. But this time it was low for good; the mud baked over them and slowly entombed them. As for the ducks, I couldn't stroll in the woods and not feel guilty, because they were crouched beside every stagnant pothole, or were slinking between the bushes with their heads tucked into their shoulders so that I wouldn't see them. If they decided I had, they beat their way up through the screen of trees, striking their wings dangerously, and wheeled about with that headlong, magnificent velocity to locate another poor puddle.

I used to catch possums and black snakes as well as turtles, and I kept dogs and goats. Some summers I worked in a menagerie with the big personalities of the animal kingdom, like elephants and rhinoceroses. I was twenty before these enthusiasms began to wane, and it was then that I picked turtles as the particular animal I wanted to keep in touch with. I was allergic to fur, for one thing, and turtles need minimal care and not much in the way of quarters. They're personable beasts. They see the same colors we do and they seem to see just as well, as one discovers in trying to sneak up on them. In the laboratory they unravel the twists of a maze with the hot-blooded rapidity of a mammal. Though they can't run as fast as a rat, they improve on their errors just as quickly, pausing at each crossroads to look left and right. And they rock rhythmically in place, as we often do, although they are hatched from eggs, not the womb. (A common explanation psychologists give for our pleasure in rocking quietly is that it recapitulates our mother's heartbeat *in utero*.)[1]

5   Snakes, by contrast, are dryly silent and priapic. They are smooth movers, legalistic, unblinking, and they afford the humor which the humorless do. But they make challenging captives; sometimes they don't eat for months on a point of order—if the light isn't right, for instance. Alligators are sticklers too. They're like war-horses, or German shepherds, and with their bar-shaped, vertical pupils adding emphasis, they have the *idée fixe*[2] of eating, eating, even when they choose to refuse all food and stubbornly die. They

---

1   *in utero* In the womb.
2   *idée fixe* Obsession.

delight in tossing a salamander up towards the sky and grabbing him in their long mouths as he comes down. They're so eager that they get the jitters, and they're too much of a proposition for a casual aquarium like mine. Frogs are depressingly defenseless: that moist, extensive back, with the bones almost sticking through. Hold a frog and you're holding its skeleton. Frogs' tasty legs are the staff of life[1] to many animals—herons, raccoons, ribbon snakes—though they themselves are hard to feed. It's not an enviable role to be the staff of life, and after frogs you descend down the evolutionary ladder a big step to fish.

Turtles cough, burp, whistle, grunt and hiss, and produce social judgments. They put their heads together amicably enough, but then one drives the other back with the suddenness of two dogs who have been conversing in tones too low for an onlooker to hear. They pee in fear when they're first caught, but exercise both pluck and optimism in trying to escape, walking for hundreds of yards within the confines of their pen, carrying the weight of that cumbersome box on legs which are cruelly positioned for walking. They don't feel that the contest is unfair; they keep plugging, rolling like sailorly souls—a bobbing, infirm gait, a brave, sea-legged momentum—stopping occasionally to study the lay of the land. For me, anyway, they manage to contain the rest of the animal world. They can stretch out their necks like a giraffe, or loom underwater like an apocryphal hippo. They browse on lettuce thrown on the water like a cow moose which is partly submerged. They have a penguin's alertness, combined with a build like a Brontosaurus when they rise up on tiptoe. Then they hunch and ponderously lunge like a grizzly going forward.

Baby turtles in a turtle bowl are a puzzle in geometrics. They're as decorative as pansy petals, but they are also self-directed building blocks, propping themselves on one another in different arrangements, before upending the tower. The timid individuals turn fearless, or vice versa. If one gets a bit arrogant he will push the others off the rock and afterwards climb down into the water and cling to the back of one of those he has bullied, tickling him with his hind feet until he bucks like a bronco. On the other hand, when this same milder-mannered fellow isn't exerting himself, he will stare right into the face of the sun for hours. What could be more lionlike? And he's at home in or out of the water and does lots of metaphysical tilting.[2] He sinks and rises, with an infinity of levels to choose from; or, elongating himself, he climbs out on the land again to perambulate, sits boxed in his box, and finally slides back in the water, submerging into dreams.

I have five of these babies in a kidney-shaped bowl. The hatchling, who is a painted turtle, is not as large as the top joint of my thumb. He eats chick-

---

1   *staff of life* Staple food.
2   *metaphysical tilting* Reference to *Don Quixote* (1605, 1615) by Miguel de Cervantes (1547-1616); "tilting at windmills" means confronting an imaginary opponent.

en gladly. Other foods he will attempt to eat but not with sufficient perse-
verance to succeed because he's so little. The yellow-bellied terrapin is
probably a yearling, and he eats salad voraciously, but no meat, fish or fowl.
The Cumberland terrapin won't touch salad or chicken but eats fish and all
of the meats except for bacon. The little snapper, with a black crenelated
shell, feasts on any kind of meat, but rejects greens and fish. The fifth of the
turtles is African. I acquired him only recently and don't know him well. A
mottled brown, he unnerves the green turtles, dragging their food off to his
lairs. He doesn't seem to want to be green—he bites the algae off his shell,
hanging meanwhile at daring, steep, head-first angles.

The snapper was a Ferdinand[1] until I provided him with deeper water. Now
he snaps at my pencil with his downturned and fearsome mouth, his swollen
face like a napalm[2] victim's. The Cumberland has an elliptical red mark on
the side of his green-and-yellow head. He is benign by nature and ought to
be as elegant as his scientific name (*Pseudemys scripta elegans*), except he has
contracted a disease of the air bladder which has permanently inflated it; he
floats high in the water at an undignified slant and can't go under. There may
have been internal bleeding, too, because his carapace is stained along its
ridge. Unfortunately, like flowers, baby turtles often die. Their mouths fill up
with a white fungus and their lungs with pneumonia. Their organs clog up
from the rust in the water, or diet troubles, and, like a dying man's, their eyes
and heads become too prominent. Toward the end, the edge of the shell
becomes flabby as felt and folds around them like a shroud.

10   While they live they're like puppies. Although they're vivacious, they
would be a bore to be with all the time, so I also have an adult wood turtle
about six inches long. Her shell is the equal of any seashell for sculpturing,
even a Cellini[3] shell; it's like an old, dusty, richly engraved medallion dug out
of a hillside. Her legs are salmon-orange bordered with black and protected
by canted, heroic scales. Her plastron—the bottom shell—is splotched like
a margay cat's[4] coat, with black ocelli[5] on a yellow background. It is convex
to make room for the female organs inside, whereas a male's would be con-
cave to help him fit tightly on top of her. Altogether, she exhibits every camouflage color on her limbs and shells. She has a turtleneck neck, a tail like
an elephant's, wise old pachydermous hind legs and the face of a turkey—
except that when I carry her she gazes at the passing ground with a hawk's
eyes and mouth. Her feet fit to the fingers of my hand, one to each one, and

---

1 *Ferdinand* Reference to the 1936 children's book *The Story of Ferdinand* by
   Munro Leaf, in which the Spanish bull, Ferdinand, prefers smelling flowers to
   fighting in the ring.
2 *napalm* A form of jellied petroleum used as an incendiary weapon in war.
3 *Cellini* Benvenuto Cellini (1500–71), Italian sculptor and metalsmith who regularly included shells in his work.
4 *margay cat* Central and South American tree cat with brownish-black spots and
   yellow fur.
5 *ocelli* Eyelike spots.

she rides looking down. She can walk on the floor in perfect silence, but usually she lets her shell knock portentously, like a footstep, so that she resembles some grand, concise, slow-moving id. But if an earthworm is presented, she jerks swiftly ahead, poises above it and strikes like a mongoose, consuming it with wild vigor. Yet she will climb on my lap to eat bread or boiled eggs.

If put into a creek, she swims like a cutter,[1] nosing forward to intercept a strange turtle and smell him. She drifts with the current to go downstream, maneuvering behind a rock when she wants to take stock, or sinking to the nether levels, while bubbles float up. Getting out, choosing her path, she will proceed a distance and dig into a pile of humus, thrusting herself to the coolest layer at the bottom. The hole closes over her until it's as small as a mouse's hole. She's not as aquatic as a musk turtle, not quite as terrestrial as the box turtles in the same woods, but because of her versatility she's marvelous, she's everywhere. And though she breathes the way we breathe, with scarcely perceptible movements of her chest, sometimes instead she pumps her throat ruminatively, like a pipe smoker sucking and puffing. She waits and blinks, pumping her throat, turning her head, then sets off like a loping tiger in slow motion, hurdling the jungly lumber, the pea vine and twigs. She estimates angles so well that when she rides over the rocks, sliding down a drop-off with her rugged front legs extended, she has the grace of a rodeo mare.

But she's well off to be with me rather than at Mud Pond. The other turtles have fled—those that aren't baked into the bottom. Creeping up the brooks to sad, constricted marshes, burdened as they are with that box on their backs, they're walking into a setup where all their enemies move thirty times faster than they. It's like the nightmare most of us have whimpered through, where we are weighted down disastrously while trying to flee; fleeing our home ground, we try to run.

I've seen turtles in still worse straits. On Broadway, in New York, there is a penny arcade which used to sell baby terrapins that were scrawled with bon mots[2] in enamel paint, such as KISS ME BABY. The manager turned out to be a wholesaler as well, and once I asked him whether he had any larger turtles to sell. He took me upstairs to a loft room devoted to the turtle business. There were desks for the paper work and a series of racks that held shallow tin bins atop one another, each with several hundred babies crawling around in it. He was a smudgy-complexioned, serious fellow and he did have a few adult terrapins, but I was going to school and wasn't actually planning to buy; I'd only wanted to see them. They were aquatic turtles, but here they went without water, presumably for weeks, lurching about in those dry bins like handicapped citizens, living on gumption. An easel where the artist worked stood in the middle of the floor. She had a palette and a clip attachment for fastening the babies in place. She wore a smock

---

1   *cutter* Small boat, with oars and sails, used for carrying supplies and passengers.
2   *bon mots* Witty sayings.

and a beret, and was homely, short and eccentric-looking, with funny black hair, like some of the ladies who show their paintings in Washington Square in May. She had a cold, she was smoking, and her hand wasn't very steady, although she worked quickly enough. The smile that she produced for me would have looked giddy if she had been happier, or drunk. Of course the turtles' doom was sealed when she painted them, because their bodies inside would continue to grow but their shells would not. Gradually, invisibly, they would be crushed. Around us their bellies—two thousand belly shells—rubbed on the bins with a mournful, momentous hiss.

Somehow there were so many of them I didn't rescue one. Years later, however, I was walking on First Avenue when I noticed a basket of living turtles in front of a fish store. They were as dry as a heap of old bones in the sun; nevertheless, they were creeping over one another gimpily, doing their best to escape. I looked and was touched to discover that they appeared to be wood turtles, my favorites, so I bought one. In my apartment I looked closer and realized that in fact this was a diamond-back terrapin, which was bad news. Diamondbacks are tidewater turtles from brackish estuaries, and I had no sea water to keep him in. He spent his days thumping interminably against the baseboards, pushing for an opening through the wall. He drank thirstily but would not eat and had none of the hearty, accepting qualities of wood turtles. He was morose, paler in color, sleeker and more Oriental in the carved ridges and rings that formed his shell. Though I felt sorry for him, finally I found his unrelenting presence exasperating. I carried him, struggling in a paper bag, across town to the Morton Street Pier on the Hudson. It was August but gray and windy. He was very surprised when I tossed him in; for the first time in our association, I think, he was afraid. He looked afraid as he bobbed about on top of the water, looking up at me from ten feet below. Though we were both accustomed to his resistance and rigidity, seeing him still pitiful, I recognized that I must have done the wrong thing. At least the river was salty, but it was also bottomless; the waves were too rough for him, and the tide was coming in, bumping him against the pilings underneath the pier. Too late, I realized that he wouldn't be able to swim to a peaceful inlet in New Jersey, even if he could figure out which way to swim. But since, short of diving in after him, there was nothing I could do, I walked away.

Questions

1. Why do you think that, in describing his turtles, Hoagland compares them to such a wide variety of other animals? What effect do these comparisons have on the reader?
2. Hoagland uses the word "courage" in the title of the essay, but never in the essay itself. How does the title affect your understanding of the essay?

BARRY LOPEZ

The Passing Wisdom of Birds

(1982)

Barry Lopez (1945-) is a writer of fiction, non-fiction, and poetry. His work is often concerned with ecological issues, such as the delicate relationship between humans and animals, as well as issues of ethics and identity. His books include Arctic Dreams (1986), Crossing Open Ground *(1989), and* About This Life *(1998).*

In this essay, Lopez examines aspects of the relationship between ecology and colonialism.

On the eighth of November, 1519, Hernando Cortés[1] and four hundred Spanish soldiers marched self-consciously out of the city of Iztapalapa, Mexico, and started across the great Iztapalapan Causeway separating the lakes of Xochimilco and Chalco. They had been received the afternoon before in Iztapalapa as demigods; but they stared now in disbelief at what lay before them. Reflecting brilliantly on the vast plain of dark water like a landscape of sunlit chalk, its lines sharp as cut stone in the dustless air at 7200 feet, was the Aztec Byzantium[2]—Tenochtitlán. Mexico City.

It is impossible to know what was in the facile, highly charged mind of Cortés that morning, anticipating his first meeting with the reluctant Montezuma;[3] but Bernal Díaz,[4] who was present, tells us what was on the minds of the soldiers. They asked each other was it real—gleaming Iztapalapa behind them, the smooth causeway beneath their feet, imposing Tenochtitlán ahead? The Spanish had been in the New World for twenty-seven years, but what they discovered in the Valley of Mexico that fall "had never been heard of or seen before, nor even dreamed about" in their world. What astounded them was not, solely, the extent and sophistication of the engi-

---

1 *Hernando Cortés* (1485–1547) Spanish conquistador who lead the conquest of Mexico for Spain.

2 *Byzantium* Ancient Greek prosperous city-state that is now the location of the Turkish capital Istanbul.

3 *Montezuma* (1480–1520) Aztec ruler at the time of the Spanish arrival in Mexico.

4 *Bernal Díaz* Bernal Díaz del Castillo (1492–1581), a Spanish conquistador who wrote an eyewitness account of Cortés's invasion of Mexico.

neering that divided and encompassed the lakes surrounding Tenochtitlán; nor the evidence that a separate culture, utterly different from their own, pursued a complex life in this huge city. It was the depth and pervasiveness of the natural beauty before their senses.

The day before, they had strolled the spotless streets of Iztapalapa through plots of full-blossomed flowers, arranged in patterns and in colors pleasing to the eye; through irrigated fruit orchards; and into still groves of aromatic trees, like cedar. They sat in the shade of bright cotton awnings in quiet stone patios and marveled at the well-tended orderliness of the vegetable gardens around them. Roses glowed against the lime-washed walls of the houses like garnets and alexandrites.[1] In the hour before sunset, the cool, fragrant air was filled with the whir and flutter of birds, and lit with birdsong.

That had been Iztapalapa. Mexico City, they thought, even as their leader dismounted that morning with solemn deliberation from that magical creature, the horse, to meet an advancing Montezuma ornately caparisoned in gold and silver and bird feathers—Mexico City, they thought as they approached, could only outdo Iztapalapa. And it did. With Montezuma's tentative welcome they were free to wander in its various precincts. Mexico City confirmed the image of a people gardening with meticulous care and with exquisite attention to line and detail at the edge of nature.

5   It is clear from Díaz's historical account that the soldiers were stunned by the physical beauty of Tenochtitlán. Venice came to their minds in comparison, because of its canals; but Venice was not as intensely fresh, as well lit as Mexico City. And there was not to be found in Venice, or in Salamanca or Paris for that matter, anything like the great aviaries[2] where thousands of birds—white egrets, energetic wrens and thrushes, fierce accipiters, brilliantly colored parrots—were housed and tended. They were as captivating, as fabulous, as the displays of flowers: vermilion flycatchers, copper-tailed trogons, green jays, blue-throated hummingbirds, and summer tanagers. Great blue herons, brooding condors.

And throughout the city wild birds nested.

Even Cortés, intensely preoccupied with politics, with guiding a diplomacy of conquest in the region, noticed the birds. He was struck, too, by the affinity of the Mexican people for their gardens and for the measured and intricate flow of water through their city. He took time to write Charles V in Spain, describing it all.

Cortés's men, says Díaz, never seemed to tire of the arboretums, gardens, and aviaries in the months following their entry into the city. By June 1520, however, Cortés's psychological manipulation of Montezuma and a concomitant arrogance, greed, and disrespect on the part of the Spanish mili-

---

1   *alexandrites* Yellowish-green gems.
2   *aviaries* Enclosures for holding captive birds.

tary force had become too much for the Mexicans, and they drove them out. Cortés, relentless and vengeful, returned to the Valley of Mexico eleven months later with a larger army and laid siege to the city. Canal by canal, garden by garden, home by home, he destroyed what he had described to Charles V as "the most beautiful city in the world." On June 16, in a move calculated to humiliate and frighten the Mexican people, Cortés set fire to the aviaries.

The grotesqueness and unmitigated violence of Cortés's act has come back to me repeatedly in reading of early European encounters with the landscapes of the New World, like a kind of darkness. The siege of Mexico City was fought barbarously on both sides; and the breathtaking parks and beautiful gardens of Mexico City, of course, stood hard by temples in which human life was regularly offered up to Aztec gods, by priests whose hair was matted with human gore and blood. No human culture has ever existed apart from its dark side. But what Cortés did, even under conditions of war, flies wildly in the face of a desire to find a dignified and honorable relationship with nature. It is an ambitious and vague longing, but one that has been with us for centuries, I think, and which today is a voice heard clearly from many different quarters—political science, anthropology, biology, philosophy. The desire is that, our colonial conquests of the human and natural world finally at an end, we will find our way back to a more equitable set of relationships with all we have subjugated. I say back because the early cultures from which Western civilization evolved, such as the Magdalenian phase of Cro-Magnon[1] culture in Europe, apparently had a less contentious arrangement with nature before the development of agriculture in northern Mesopotamia, and the rise of cities.

The image of Cortés burning the aviaries is not simply for me an image   10
of a kind of destructive madness that lies at the heart of imperialistic conquest; it is also a symbol of a long-term failure of Western civilization to recognize the intrinsic worth of the American landscape, and its potential value to human societies that have since come to be at odds with the natural world. While English, French, and Spanish explorers were cruising the eastern shores of America, dreaming of feudal fiefdoms, gold, and political advantage, the continent itself was, already, occupied in a complex way by more than five hundred different cultures, each of which regarded itself as living in some kind of enlightened intimacy with the land. A chance to rediscover the original wisdom inherent in the myriad sorts of human relationships possible with the nonhuman world, of course, was not of concern to us in the sixteenth century, as it is now, particularly to geographers, philosophers, historians, and ecologists. It would not in fact become clear for centuries that the metaphysics we had thrown out thousands of years

---

1   *Cro-Magnon* A group of homo sapiens who lived in Europe 40,000 years ago.

before was still intact in tribal America. America offered us the opportunity to deliberate with historical perspective, to see if we wished to reclaim that metaphysics.

The need to reexamine our experience in the New World is, increasingly, a practical need. Contemporary American culture, founded on the original material wealth of the continent, on its timber, ores, and furs, has become a culture that devours the earth. Minerals, fresh water, darkness, tribal peoples, everything the land produces we now consume in prodigious amounts. There are at least two schools of thought on how to rectify this high rate of consumption, which most Western thinkers agree is unsustainable and likely wrongheaded if not disastrous. First, there are technical approaches. No matter how sophisticated or innovative these may be, however, they finally seem only clever or artful adjustments, not solutions. Secondly, we can consider a change in attitude toward nature, adopting a fundamentally different way of thinking about it than we have previously had, perhaps ever had as human beings. The insights of aboriginal peoples are of inestimable value here in rethinking our relationships with the natural world (i.e., in figuring out how to get ourselves back *into* it); but the solution to our plight, I think, is likely to be something no other culture has ever thought of, something over which !Kung,[1] Inuit,[2] Navajo,[3] Walbiri,[4] and the other traditions we have turned to for wisdom in the twentieth century will marvel at as well.

The question before us is how do we find a viable natural philosophy, one that places us again within the elements of our natural history. The answer, I believe, lies with wild animals.

II

Over the past ten years it has been my privilege to spend time in the field in North America with biologists studying several different kinds of animals, including wolves, polar bears, mountain lions, seals, and whales. Of all that could be said about this exercise, about people watching animals, I would like to restrict myself to but one or two things. First, although such studies are scientific they are conducted by human beings whose individual speculations may take them out beyond the bounds of scientific inquiry. The animals they scrutinize may draw them back into an older, more intimate and less rational association with the local landscape. In this frame of mind, they may privately begin to question the methodology of Western science, especially its purported objectivity and its troublesome lack of heart. It may

1   *!Kung* Indigenous people in isolated areas of Botswana, Angola, and Namibia.
2   *Inuit* Indigenous people in Arctic Canada.
3   *Navajo* Indigenous people in Southwestern US.
4   *Walbiri* Indigenous people in Australia.

seem to them incapable of addressing questions they intuit are crucial. Even as they perceive its flaws, however, scientists continue to offer such studies as a dependable source of reliable information—and they are. Science's flaws as a tool of inquiry are relatively minor, and it is further saved by its strengths.

Science's strength lies with its rigor and objectivity, and it is undoubtedly as rigorous as any system available to us. Even with its flaws (its failure, for example, to address disorderly or idiosyncratic behavior) field biology is as strong and reliable in its way as the collective wisdom of a hunting people actively involved with the land. The highest order of field work being done in biology today, then, from an elucidation of the way polar bears hunt ringed seals to working out the ecology of night-flying moths pollinating agaves in the Mojave Desert, forms part of the foundation for a modern realignment with the natural world. (The other parts of the foundation would include work done by anthropologists among hunter-gatherer people and studies by natural geographers; philosophical work in the tradition of Aldo Leopold[1] and Rachel Carson;[2] and the nearly indispensable element of personal experience.)

I often search out scientific reports to read; many are based on years of research and have been patiently thought through. Despite my regard, however, I read with caution, for I cannot rid myself of the thought that, even though it is the best theoretical approach we have, the process is not perfect. I have participated in some of this type of work and know that innocent mistakes are occasionally made in the data. I understand how influential a misleading coincidence can become in the overall collection of data; how unconsciously the human mind can follow a teasing parallel. I am cautious, too, for even more fundamental reasons. It is hard to say exactly what any animal is *doing*. It is impossible to know when or where an event in an animal's life begins or ends. And our human senses confine us to realms that may contain only a small part of the information produced in an event. Something critical could be missing and we would not know. And as far as the experiments themselves are concerned, although we can design and carry out thousands of them, no animal can ever be described as the sum of these experiments. And, finally, though it is possible to write precisely about something, this does not automatically mean one is accurate.

The scientific approach is flawed, therefore, by its imposition of a subjective framework around animal behavior; but it only fails, really, because it is incomplete. We would be rash, using this approach exclusively, to claim to understand any one animal, let alone the environment in which that ani-

1 *Aldo Leopold* (1887–1948) American ecologist, environmentalist, and forester.
2 *Rachel Carson* (1907–64) American zoologist, biologist, and author of *Silent Spring* (1962), an influential book credited with starting the global environmental movement.

mal is evolving. Two remedies to this dilemma of the partially perceived animal suggest themselves. One, obviously, is to turn to the long-term field observations of non-Western cultural traditions. These non-Aristotelian,[1] non-Cartesian,[2] non-Baconian[3] views of wild animals are stimulating, challenging, and, like a good bibliography, heuristic,[4] pointing one toward discovery. (They are also problematic in that, for example, they do not take sufficiently into account the full range of behavior of migratory animals and they have a highly nonlinear [though ultimately, possibly, more correct] understanding of population biology.)

A second, much less practiced remedy is to cultivate within ourselves a sense of mystery—to see that the possibilities for an expression of life in any environment, or in any single animal, are larger than we can predict or understand, and that this is all right. Biology should borrow here from quantum physics, which accepts the premise that, under certain circumstances, the observer can be deceived. Quantum physics, with its ambiguous particles and ten-dimensional universes, is a branch of science that has in fact returned us to a state of awe with nature, without threatening our intellectual capacity to analyze complex events.

If it is true that modern people desire a new relationship with the natural world, one that is not condescending, manipulative, and purely utilitarian; and if the foundation upon which the relationship is to be built is as I suggest—a natural history growing largely out of science and the insights of native peoples—then a staggering task lies before us.

The initial steps to be taken seem obvious. First, we must identify and protect those regions where landscapes largely undisturbed by human technology remain intact. Within these ecosystems lie blueprints for the different patterns of life that have matured outside the pervasive influence of myriad Western technologies (though no place on earth has escaped their influence entirely). We can contemplate and study endlessly the natural associations here, and draw from these smaller universes a sophisticated wisdom about process and event, and about evolution. Second, we need to subscribe a great public support to the discipline of field biology. Third, we need to seek an introduction to the reservoirs of intelligence that native cultures have preserved in both oral tradition and in their personal experi-

---

1 *Aristotelian* Relating to the Greek philosopher Aristotle, who valued knowledge gained from the senses.

2 *Cartesian* Relating to the French philosopher and mathematician René Descartes, whose work was influential in the development of analytic geometry, calculus, and cartography.

3 *Baconian* Relating to the English philosopher Francis Bacon (1561–1626); this describes a method of procedures used to isolate the cause of a phenomenon.

4 *heuristic* Use of experimentation, evaluation, and trial-and-error methods to solve problems.

ence with the land, the highly complex detail of a way of life not yet torn entirely from the fabric of nature.

We must, too, look out after the repositories of our own long-term cul- 20 tural wisdom more keenly. Our libraries, which preserve the best of what we have to say about ourselves and nature, are under siege in an age of cost-benefit analysis. We need to immerse ourselves thoughtfully, too, in what is being written and produced on tape and film, so that we become able to distinguish again between truthful expression and mere entertainment. We need, to do this not only for our own sake but so that our children, who too often have only the half-eclipsed lives of zoo animals or the contrived dramas of television wildlife adventure before them, will know that this heritage is disappearing and what we are apt to lose with it.

What disappears with a debasement of wild landscapes is more than genetic diversity, more than a homeland for Henry Beston's "other nations,"[1] more, to be perfectly selfish, than a source of future medical cures for human illness or a chance for personal revitalization on a wilderness trip. We stand to lose the focus of our ideals. We stand to lose our sense of dignity, of compassion, even our sense of what we call God. The philosophy of nature we set aside eight thousand years ago in the Fertile Crescent[2] we can, I think, locate again and greatly refine in North America. The New World is a landscape still overwhelming in the vigor of its animals and plants, resonant with mystery. It encourages, still, an enlightened response toward indigenous cultures that differ from our own, whether Aztecan, Lakotan, lupine, avian, or invertebrate. By broadening our sense of the intrinsic worth of life and by cultivating respect for other ways of moving toward perfection, we may find a sense of resolution we have been looking for, I think, for centuries.

Two practical steps occur to me. Each by itself is so small I hesitate to set it forth; but to say nothing would be cowardly, and both appear to me to be reasonable, a beginning. They also acknowledge an obvious impediment: to bridge the chasm between a colonial attitude toward the land and a more filial relationship with it takes time. The task has always been, and must be, carried into the next generation.

The first thought I would offer is that each university and college in the country establish the position of university naturalist, a position to be held by a student in his or her senior year and passed on at the end of the year to another student. The university naturalist would be responsible for estab-

1 *"other nations"* Cf. Henry Beston's (1888–1968) *The Outermost House* (1928), pg. 25: "They [animals] are not brethren, they are not underlings; they are other nations, caught with ourselves in the net of life and time, fellow prisoners of the splendor and travail of the earth."
2 *Fertile Crescent* Crescent-shaped area of fertile land that includes parts of Iraq, Syria, Lebanon, Israel, and Jordan.

lishing and maintaining a natural history of the campus, would confer with architects and grounds keepers, escort guests, and otherwise look out after the nonhuman elements of the campus, their relationships to human beings, and the preservation of this knowledge. Though the position itself might be honorary and unsalaried, the student would receive substantial academic credit for his or her work and would be provided with a budget to conduct research, maintain a library, and produce an occasional paper. Depending on his or her gifts and personality, the university naturalist might elect to teach a course or to speak at some point during the academic year. In concert with the university archivist and university historian, the university naturalist would seek to protect the relationships-in-time that define a culture's growth and ideals.

A second suggestion is more difficult to implement, but no less important than a system of university naturalists. In recent years several American and British publishers have developed plans to reprint in an extended series classic works of natural history. These plans should be pursued; the list of books should include not only works of contemporary natural history but early works by such people as Thomas Nuttal[1] and William Bartram,[2] so that the project has historical depth. It should also include books by nonscientists who have immersed themselves "beyond reason" in the world occupied by animals and who have emerged with stunning reports, such as J.A. Baker's *The Peregrine*.[3] And books that offer us a resounding and affecting vision of the landscape, such as John Van Dyke's *The Desert*.[4] It should also include the writing of anthropologists who have worked, or are working, with the native peoples of North America to define an indigenous natural history, such as Richard Nelson's *Make Prayers to the Raven*.[5] And a special effort should be made to unearth those voices that once spoke eloquently for parts of the country the natural history of which is now too often overlooked, or overshadowed, by a focus on western or northern North American ecosystems: the pine barrens of New Jersey, the Connecticut River Valley, the White Mountains of New Hampshire, the remnant hardwood forests of Indiana and Ohio, the Outer Banks, the

1   *Thomas Nuttal* (1786–1859) English botanist and zoologist who primarily studied plant life in the United States.
2   *William Bartram* (1739–1823) American naturalist who studied the flora, fauna, and indigenous people of the southern areas of colonial United States.
3   *The Peregrine* Published in 1967, Baker's text describes six months in the lives of two peregrine falcons in Essex, England.
4   *The Desert* Published in 1901, this book changed the perception of deserts as dead and empty land by describing the rich plant and animal life as well as the extraordinary beauty of deserts.
5   *Make Prayers to the Raven* Published in 1983, this book details the year that Nelson spent living among the Koyukon people of western Alaska and describes the Koyukon's relationship with the land and animals.

relictual prairies of Texas, and the mangrove swamps and the piney woods of Georgia.

Such a collection, it seems to me, should be assembled with several   25
thoughts in mind. It should be inexpensive so that the books can fall easily into the hands of young people. It should document the extraordinary variety of natural ecosystems in North America, and reflect the great range of dignified and legitimate human response to them. And it should make clear that human beings belong in these landscapes, that they, too, are a part of the earth's natural history.

III

The image I carry of Cortés setting fire to the aviaries in Mexico City that June day in 1521 is an image I cannot rid myself of. It stands, in my mind, for a fundamental lapse of wisdom in the European conquest of America, an underlying trouble in which political conquest, personal greed, revenge, and national pride outweigh what is innocent, beautiful, serene, and defenseless—the birds. The incineration of these creatures 450 years ago is not something that can be rectified today. Indeed, one could argue, the same oblivious irreverence is still with us, among those who would ravage and poison the earth to sustain the economic growth of Western societies. But Cortés's act can be transcended. It is possible to fix in the mind that heedless violence, the hysterical cry of the birds, the stench of death, to look it square in the face and say that there is more to us than this, this will not forever distinguish us from among the other cultures. It is possible to imagine that on the far side of the Renaissance and the Enlightenment we can recover the threads of an earlier wisdom.

Again I think of the animals, because of the myriad ways in which they have helped us since we first regarded each other differently. They offered us early models of rectitude and determination in adversity, which we put in stories. The grace of a moving animal, in some ineluctable way, kindles still in us a sense of imitation. They continue to produce for us a sense of the Other: to encounter a truly wild animal on its own ground is to know the defeat of thought, to feel reason overpowered. The animals have fed us; and the cultures of the great hunters particularly—the bears, the dogs, and the cats—have provided the central metaphors by which we have taken satisfaction in our ways and explained ourselves to strangers.

Cortés's soldiers, on their walks through the gleaming gardens of Tenochtitlán, would have been as struck by the flight paths of songbirds as we are today. In neither a horizontal nor a vertical dimension do these pathways match the line and scale of human creation, within which the birds dwell. The corridors they travel are curved around some other universe. When the birds passed over them, moving across the grain of sunlight, the soldiers must have stopped occasionally to watch, as we do. It is the birds' independence from predictable patterns of human design that draws us to them. In the birds' separate but related universe we are able to sense hope for ourselves. Against a background of the familiar, we recognize with astonishment a new pattern.

In such a moment, pausing to take in the flight of a flock of birds passing through sunshine and banking gracefully into a grove of trees, it is possible to move beyond a moment in the Valley of Mexico when we behaved as though we were insane.

Questions

1. Lopez begins and ends his essay with an anecdote about Cortés burning the Mexican aviaries. How does this story set up his article and the themes he develops? Why do you think he focuses on the suffering of animals, rather than that of human beings?
2. Lopez's prose is filled with descriptive adjectives and active verbs. What is the effect of such rich description? How does it aid or hinder his thesis?
3. What is the significance of the essay's title?

PETER SINGER

Speciesism

(1990)

Peter Singer (1946–) is a professor of philosophy, specializing in applied ethics, at both Princeton University and University of Melbourne. His many books include Animal Liberation *(1975),* Practical Ethics *(1979), and* Pushing Time Away: My Grandfather and the Tragedy of Jewish Vienna *(2003).*

In these excerpts from Animal Liberation *(updated in 1990), Singer discusses the notion of "speciesism" and challenges readers to examine their relationships to other species.*

Speciesism—the word is not an attractive one, but I can think of no better term—is a prejudice or attitude of bias in favor of the interests of members of one's own species and against those of members of other species. It should be obvious that the fundamental objections to racism and sexism made by Thomas Jefferson and Sojourner Truth apply equally to speciesism. If possessing a higher degree of intelligence does not entitle one human to use another for his or her own ends, how can it entitle humans to exploit nonhumans for the same purpose?[1]

Many philosophers and other writers have proposed the principle of equal consideration of interests, in some form or other, as a basic moral principle; but not many of them have recognized that this principle applies to members of other species as well as to our own. Jeremy Bentham was one of the few who did realize this. In a forward-looking passage written at a time when black slaves had been freed by the French but in the British dominions were still being treated in the way we now treat animals, Bentham wrote:

> The day *may* come when the rest of the animal creation may acquire those rights which never could have been withholden from them but by

---

1 I owe the term "speciesism" to Richard Ryder. It has become accepted in general use since the first edition of this book, and now appears in *The Oxford English Dictionary*, second edition (Oxford: Clarendon Press, 1989). [Unless otherwise stated, notes are by the author.]

the hand of tyranny. The French have already discovered that the blackness of the skin is no reason why a human being should be abandoned without redress to the caprice of a tormentor. It may one day come to be recognized that the number of the legs, the villosity of the skin, or the termination of the *os sacrum* are reasons equally insufficient for abandoning a sensitive being to the same fate. What else is it that should trace the insuperable line? Is it the faculty of reason, or perhaps the faculty of discourse? But a full-grown horse or dog is beyond comparison a more rational, as well as a more conversable animal, than an infant of a day or a week or even a month, old. But suppose they were otherwise, what would it avail? The question is not, Can they *reason?* nor Can they *talk?* but, Can they *suffer?*[1]

In this passage Bentham points to the capacity for suffering as the vital characteristic that gives a being the right to equal consideration. The capacity for suffering—or more strictly, for suffering and/or enjoyment or happiness—is not just another characteristic like the capacity for language or higher mathematics. Bentham is not saying that those who try to mark "the insuperable line" that determines whether the interests of a being should be considered happen to have chosen the wrong characteristic. By saying that we must consider the interests of all beings with the capacity for suffering or enjoyment Bentham does not arbitrarily exclude from consideration any interests at all—as those who draw the line with reference to the possession of reason or language do. The capacity for suffering and enjoyment is *a prerequisite for having interests at all,* a condition that must be satisfied before we can speak of interests in a meaningful way. It would be nonsense to say that it was not in the interests of a stone to be kicked along the road by a schoolboy. A stone does not have interests because it cannot suffer. Nothing that we can do to it could possibly make any difference to its welfare. The capacity for suffering and enjoyment is, however, not only necessary, but also sufficient for us to say that a being has interests—at an absolute minimum, an interest in not suffering. A mouse, for example, does have an interest in not being kicked along the road, because it will suffer if it is.

If a being suffers there can be no moral justification for refusing to take that suffering into consideration. No matter what the nature of the being, the principle of equality requires that its suffering be counted equally with the like suffering—insofar as rough comparisons can be made—of any other being. If a being is not capable of suffering, or of experiencing enjoyment or happiness, there is nothing to be taken into account. So the limit of sentience (using the term as a convenient if not strictly accurate shorthand for the capacity to suffer and/or experience enjoyment) is the only defensible

---

1   *Introduction to the Principles of Morals and Legislation,* chapter 17.

boundary of concern for the interests of others. To mark this boundary by some other characteristic like intelligence or rationality would be to mark it in an arbitrary manner. Why not choose some other characteristic, like skin color?

Racists violate the principle of equality by giving greater weight to the   5
interests of members of their own race when there is a clash between their interests and the interests of those of another race. Sexists violate the principle of equality by favoring the interests of their own sex. Similarly, speciesists allow the interests of their own species to override the greater interests of members of other species. The pattern is identical in each case.

Down on the Factory Farm

For most human beings, especially those in modern urban and suburban communities, the most direct form of contact with nonhuman animals is at mealtime: we eat them. This simple fact is the key to our attitudes to other animals, and also the key to what each one of us can do about changing these attitudes. The use and abuse of animals raised for food far exceeds, in sheer numbers of animals affected, any other kind of mistreatment. Over 100 million cows, pigs, and sheep are raised and slaughtered in the United States alone each year; and for poultry the figure is a staggering 5 billion. (That means that about eight thousand birds—mostly chickens—will have been slaughtered in the time it takes you to read this page.) It is here, on our dinner table and in our neighborhood supermarket or butcher's shop, that we are brought into direct touch with the most extensive exploitation of other species that has ever existed.

In general, we are ignorant of the abuse of living creatures that lies behind the food we eat. Buying food in a store or restaurant is the culmination of a long process, of which all but the end product is delicately screened from our eyes. We buy our meat and poultry in neat plastic packages. It hardly bleeds. There is no reason to associate this package with a living, breathing, walking, suffering animal. The very words we use conceal its origins: we eat beef, not bull, steer, or cow, and pork, not pig—although for some reason we seem to find it easier to face the true nature of a leg of lamb. The term "meat" is itself deceptive. It originally meant any solid food, not necessarily the flesh of animals. This usage still lingers in an expression like "nut meat," which seems to imply a substitute for "flesh meat" but actually has an equally good claim to be called "meat" in its own right. By using the more general "meat" we avoid facing the fact that what we are eating is really flesh.

These verbal disguises are merely the top layer of a much deeper ignorance of the origin of our food. Consider the images conjured up by the word "farm": a house; a barn; a flock of hens, overseen by a strutting rooster, scratching around the farmyard; a herd of cows being brought in from the fields for milking; and perhaps a sow rooting around in the orchard with a litter of squealing piglets running excitedly behind her.

Very few farms were ever as idyllic as that traditional image would have us believe. Yet we still think of a farm as a pleasant place, far removed from our own industrial, profit-conscious city life. Of those few who think about the lives of animals on farms, not many know much about modern methods of animal raising. Some people wonder whether animals are slaughtered painlessly, and anyone who has followed a truckload of cattle on the road will probably know that farm animals are transported in extremely crowded conditions; but not many suspect that transportation and slaughter are anything more than the brief and inevitable conclusion of a life of ease and contentment, a life that contains the natural pleasures of animal existence without the hardships that wild animals must endure in their struggle for survival.

10   These comfortable assumptions bear little relation to the realities of modern farming. For a start, farming is no longer controlled by simple country folk. During the last fifty years, large corporations and assembly-line methods of production have turned agriculture into agribusiness. The process began when big companies gained control of poultry production, once the preserve of the farmer's wife. Today, fifty large corporations virtually control all poultry production in the United States. In the field of egg production, where fifty years ago a big producer might have had three thousand laying hens, today many producers have more than 500,000 layers, and the largest have over 10 million. The remaining small producers have had to adopt the methods of the giants or else go out of business. Companies that had no connection with agriculture have become farmers on a huge scale in order to gain tax concessions or to diversify profits. Greyhound Corporation now produces turkeys, and your roast beef may have come from John Hancock Mutual Life Insurance or from one of a dozen oil companies that have invested in cattle feeding, building feedlots that hold 100,000 or more cattle.[1]

The big corporations and those who must compete with them are not concerned with a sense of harmony among plants, animals, and nature. Farming is competitive and the methods adopted are those that cut costs and increase production. So farming is now "factory farming." Animals are treated like machines that convert low-priced fodder into high-priced flesh, and any innovation will be used if it results in a cheaper "conversion ratio." ... [My] point is not that the people who do these things to the animals are

---

1   *The Washington Post*, October 3, 1971; see also the testimony during September and October 1971, before the Subcommittee on Monopoly of the Select Committee on Small Business of the U.S. Senate, in the Hearings on the Role of Giant Corporations, especially the testimony of Jim Hightower of the Agribusiness Accountability Project. For the size of egg producers, see *Poultry Tribune*, June 1987, p. 27.

cruel and wicked. On the contrary, the attitudes of the consumers and the producers are not fundamentally different.

Of all the forms of intensive farming now practiced, the veal industry ranks as the most morally repugnant. The essence of veal raising is the feeding of a high-protein food to confined, anemic calves in a manner that will produce a tender, pale-colored flesh that will be served to the patrons of expensive restaurants. Fortunately this industry does not compare in size with poultry, beef, or pig production; nevertheless it is worth our attention because it represents an extreme, both in the degree of exploitation to which it subjects the animals and in its absurd inefficiency as a method of providing people with nourishment.

Veal is the flesh of a young calf. The term was originally reserved for calves killed before they had been weaned from their mothers. The flesh of these very young animals was paler and more tender than that of a calf who had begun to eat grass; but there was not much of it, since calves begin to eat grass when they are a few weeks old and still very small. The small amount available came from the unwanted male calves produced by the dairy industry. A day or two after being born they were trucked to market where, hungry and frightened by the strange surroundings and the absence of their mothers, they were sold for immediate delivery to the slaughterhouse.

Then in the 1950s veal producers in Holland found a way to keep the calf alive longer without the flesh becoming red or less tender. The trick depends on keeping the calf in highly unnatural conditions. If calves were left to grow up outside they would romp around the fields, developing muscles that would toughen their flesh and burning up calories that the producer must replace with costly feed. At the same time they would eat grass, and their flesh would lose the pale color that the flesh of newborn calves has. So the specialist veal producers take their calves straight from the auction ring to a confinement unit. Here, in a converted barn or specially built shed, they have rows of wooden stalls, each 1 foot 10 inches wide by 4 feet 6 inches long. It has a slatted wooden floor, raised above the concrete floor of the shed. The calves are tethered by a chain around the neck to prevent them from turning in their stalls when they are small. (The chain may be removed when the calves grow too big to turn around in such narrow stalls.) The stall has no straw or other bedding, since the calves might eat it, spoiling the paleness of their flesh. They leave their stalls only to be taken out to slaughter. They are fed a totally liquid diet, based on nonfat milk powder with vitamins, minerals, and growth-promoting drugs added. Thus the calves live for the next sixteen weeks. The beauty of the system, from the producers' point of view, is that at this age the veal calf may weigh as much as four hundred pounds, instead of the ninety-odd pounds that newborn calves weigh; and since veal fetches a premium price, rearing veal calves in this manner is a profitable occupation.

15   This method of raising calves was introduced to the United States in 1962 by Provimi, Inc., a feed manufacturer based in Watertown, Wisconsin. Its name comes from the "proteins, vitamins, and minerals" of which its feeds are composed—ingredients that, one might think, could be put to better use than veal raising. Provimi, according to its own boast, created this "new and complete concept in veal raising" and it is still by far the largest company in the business, controlling 50 to 75 percent of the domestic market. Its interest in promoting veal production lies in developing a market for its feed. Describing what it considered "optimum veal production," Provimi's now defunct newssheet, *The Stall Street Journal*, gives us an insight into the nature of the industry, which in the United States and some European countries has remained essentially unchanged since its introduction:

> The dual aims of veal production are firstly, to produce a calf of the greatest weight in the shortest possible time and secondly, to keep its meat as light colored as possible to fulfill the consumer's requirement. All at a profit commensurate to the risk and investment involved.[1]

The narrow stalls and their slatted wooden floors are a serious source of discomfort to the calves. When the calves grow larger, they cannot even stand up and lie down without difficulty. As a report from a research group headed by Professor John Webster of the animal husbandry unit at the School of Veterinary Science, University of Bristol, in England, noted:

> Veal calves in crates 750 mm wide cannot, of course, lie flat with their legs extended.... Calves may lie like this when they feel warm and wish to lose heat.... Well-grown veal calves at air temperatures above 20 degrees C [68 degrees F] may be uncomfortably hot. Denying them the opportunity to adopt a position designed to maximise heat loss only makes things worse.... Veal calves in boxes over the age of 10 weeks were unable to adopt a normal sleeping position with their heads tucked into their sides. We conclude that denying veal calves the opportunity to adopt a normal sleeping posture is a significant insult to welfare. To overcome this, the crates would need to be at least 900 mm wide.[2]

---

1   *The Stall Street Journal*, July 1972.
2   J. Webster, C. Saville, and D. Welchman, "Improved Husbandry Systems for Veal Calves," Animal Health Trust and Farm Animal Care Trust, no date, p. 5; see also Webster et al., "The Effect of Different Rearing Systems on the Development of Calf Behavior," and "Some Effects of Different Rearing Systems on Health, Cleanliness and Injury in Calves," *British Veterinary Journal* 1141: 249 and 472 (1985).

American readers should note that 750 millimeters is equivalent to 2 feet 6 inches, and 900 millimeters to 3 feet, both considerably more than standard 1 foot 10 inch crates used in the United States.

The crates are also too narrow to permit the calf to turn around. This is another source of frustration. In addition, a stall too narrow to turn around in is also too narrow to groom comfortably in; and calves have an innate desire to twist their heads around and groom themselves with their tongues. As the University of Bristol researchers said:

> Because veal calves grow so fast and produce so much heat they tend to shed their coats at about 10 weeks of age. During this time they have a great urge to groom themselves. They are also particularly prone to infestation with external parasites, especially in mild, humid conditions. Veal calves in crates cannot reach much of their body. We conclude that denying the veal calf the opportunity to groom itself thoroughly is an unacceptable insult to welfare whether this is achieved by constraining its freedom of movement or, worse, by the use of a muzzle.[1]

A slatted wooden floor without any bedding is hard and uncomfortable; it is rough on the calves' knees as they get up and lie down. In addition, animals with hooves are uncomfortable on slatted floors. A slatted floor is like a cattle grid, which cattle always avoid, except that the slats are closer together. The spaces, however, must still be large enough to allow most of the manure to fall or be washed through, and this means that they are large enough to make the calves uncomfortable on them. The Bristol team described the young calves as "for some days insecure and reluctant to change position."

The young calves sorely miss their mothers. They also miss something to   20
suck on. The urge to suck is strong in a baby calf, as it is in a baby human. These calves have no teat to suck on, nor do they have any substitute. From their first day in confinement—which may well be only the third or fourth day of their lives—they drink from a plastic bucket. Attempts have been made to feed calves through artificial teats, but the task of keeping the teats clean and sterile is apparently not worth the producer's trouble. It is common to see calves frantically trying to suck some part of their stalls, although there is usually nothing suitable; and if you offer a veal calf your finger you will find that he immediately begins to suck on it, as human babies suck their thumbs.

Later the calf develops a need to ruminate—that is, to take in roughage and chew the cud. But roughage is strictly forbidden because it contains iron and will darken the flesh, so, again, the calf may resort to vain attempts

---

1 J. Webster, C. Saville, and D. Welchman, "Improved Husbandry Systems for Veal Calves," p. 6.

to chew the sides of his stall. Digestive disorders, including stomach ulcers, are common in veal calves. So is chronic diarrhea. To quote the Bristol study once again:

> The calves are deprived of dry feed. This completely distorts the normal development of the rumen and encourages the development of hair balls which may also lead to chronic indigestion.[1]

As if this were not enough, the calf is deliberately kept anemic. Provimi's *Stall Street Journal* explains why:

> Color of veal is one of the primary factors involved in obtaining "top-dollar" returns from the fancy veal markets.... "Light color" veal is a premium item much in demand at better clubs, hotels and restaurants. "Light color" or pink veal is partly associated with the amount of iron in the muscle of the calves.[2]

So Provimi's feeds, like those of other manufacturers of veal feeds, are deliberately kept low in iron. A normal calf would obtain iron from grass and other forms of roughage, but since veal calves are not allowed this, they become anemic. Pale pink flesh is in fact anemic flesh. The demand for flesh of this color is a matter of snob appeal. The color does not affect the taste and it certainly does not make the flesh more nourishing—it just means that it lacks iron.

The anemia is, of course, controlled. Without any iron at all the calves would drop dead. With a normal intake their flesh will not fetch as much per pound. So a balance is struck which keeps the flesh pale and the calves—or most of them—on their feet long enough for them to reach market weight. The calves, however, are unhealthy and anemic animals. Kept deliberately short of iron, they develop a craving for it and will lick any iron fittings in their stalls. This explains the use of wooden stalls. As Provimi tells its customers:

> The main reason for using hardwood instead of metal boxstalls is that metal may affect the light veal color.... Keep all iron out of reach of your calves.[3]

25   And again:

---

1   J. Webster, C. Saville, and D. Welchman, "Improved Husbandry Systems for Veal Calves," p. 2.
2   *The Stall Street Journal*, November 1973.
3   *The Stall Street Journal*, April 1973.

It is also necessary that calves do not have access to a continuous source of iron. (Water supplied should be checked. If a high level of iron [excess of 0.5 ppm] is present an iron filter should be considered.) Calf crates should be constructed so calves have no access to rusty metal.[1]

The anemic calf's insatiable craving for iron is one of the reasons the producer is anxious to prevent him turning around in his stall. Although calves, like pigs, normally prefer not to go near their own urine or manure, urine does contain some iron. The desire for iron is strong enough to overcome the natural repugnance, and the anemic calves will lick the slats that are saturated with urine. The producer does not like this, because it gives calves a little iron and because in licking the slats the calves may pick up infections from their manure, which falls on the same spot as their urine.

We have seen that in the view of Provimi, Inc., the twin aims of veal production are producing a calf of the greatest possible weight in the shortest possible time and keeping the meat as light in color as possible. We have seen what is done to achieve the second of these aims, but there is more to be said about the techniques used to achieve fast growth.

To make animals grow quickly they must take in as much food as possible, and they must use up as little of this food as possible in their daily life. To see that the veal calf takes in as much as possible, most calves are given no water. Their only source of liquid is their food—the rich milk replacer based on powdered milk and added fat. Since the buildings in which they are housed are kept warm, the thirsty animals take in more of their food than they would do if they could drink water. A common result of this overeating is that the calves break out in a sweat, rather like, it has been said, an executive who has had too much to eat too quickly.[2] In sweating, the calf loses moisture, which makes him thirsty, so that he overeats again next time. By most standards this process is an unhealthy one, but by the standards of the veal producer aiming at producing the heaviest calf in the shortest possible time, the long-term health of the animal is irrelevant, so long as he survives to be taken to market; and so Provimi advises that sweating is a sign that "the calf is healthy and growing at capacity."[3]

Getting the calf to overeat is half the battle; the other half is ensuring that as much as possible of what has been eaten goes toward putting on weight. Confining the calf so that he cannot exercise is one requirement for achieving this aim. Keeping the barn warm also contributes to it, since a cold calf burns calories just to keep warm. Even warm calves in their stalls are apt to

---

1 *The Stall Street Journal,* November 1973.
2 *Farmer and Stockbreeder,* September 13, 1960, quoted by Ruth Harrison, *Animal Machines,* p. 70.
3 *The Stall Street Journal,* April 1973.

become restless, however, for they have nothing to do all day except at their two mealtimes. A Dutch researcher has written:

> Veal calves suffer from the inability to do something.... The food-intake of a veal calf takes only 20 minutes a day! Besides that there is nothing the animal can do.... One can observe teeth grinding, tail wagging, tongue swaying and other stereotype behavior.... Such stereotype movements can be regarded as a reaction to a lack of occupation.[1]

30   To reduce the restlessness of their bored calves, many veal producers leave the animals in the dark at all times, except when they are being fed. Since the veal sheds are normally windowless, this simply means turning off the lights. Thus the calves, already missing most of the affection, activity, and stimulation that their natures require, are deprived of visual stimulation and of contact with other calves for more than twenty-two hours out of every twenty-four. Illnesses have been found to be more persistent in dark sheds.[2]

Calves kept in this manner are unhappy and unhealthy animals. Despite the fact that the veal producer selects only the strongest, healthiest calves to begin with, uses a medicated feed as a routine measure, and gives additional injections at the slightest sign of illness, digestive, respiratory, and infectious diseases are widespread. It is common for a veal producer to find that one in ten of a batch of calves do not survive the fifteen weeks of confinement. Between 10 and 15 percent mortality over such a short period would be disastrous for anyone raising calves for beef, but veal producers can tolerate this loss because the high-priced restaurants are prepared to pay well for their products.

Given the cozy relationship that normally exists between veterinarians working with farm animals and intensive producers (it is, after all, the owners, not the animals, who pay the bills), it gives us some indication of the extreme conditions under which veal calves are kept to learn that this is one aspect of animal production that has strained relations between veterinarians and producers. A 1982 issue of *The Vealer* reports:

> Besides waiting too long to call veterinarians for a really sick calf, vets do not look favorable [sic] on relations with veal growers because they have long defied accepted agricultural methods. The feeding of long hay to

---

1   G. van Putten, "Some General Remarks Concerning Farm Animal Welfare in Intensive Farming Systems," unpublished paper from the Research Institute for Animal Husbandry, "Schoonoord," Driebergseweg, Zeist, The Netherlands, p. 2.

2   G. van Putten, "Some General Remarks Concerning Farm Animal Welfare in Intensive Farming Systems," p. 3.

livestock, in order to maintain a proper digestive system, has been considered a sound practice for years.[1]

The one bright spot in this sorry tale is that the conditions created by the veal crates are so appalling for animal welfare that British government regulations now require that a calf must be able to turn around without difficulty, must be fed a daily diet containing "sufficient iron to maintain it in full health and vigour," and must receive enough fiber to allow normal development of the rumen.[2] These are minimal welfare requirements, and still fall well short of satisfying the needs of calves; but they are violated by almost all the veal units in the United States and by many in Europe.

If the reader will recall that this whole laborious, wasteful, and painful process of veal raising exists for the sole purpose of pandering to people who insist on pale, soft veal, no further comment should be needed.

Questions

1. What is the characteristic, according to Singer, that makes a being worthy of moral consideration? What makes this, in his view, the defining characteristic?
2. What examples does Singer present of deceptive and euphemistic words for animal flesh? Why are these examples important to his larger argument?

---

1   *The Vealer*, March/April 1982.
2   U.K. Ministry of Agriculture, Fisheries and Food, Welfare of Calves Regulations, 1987 (London: Her Majesty's Stationery Office, 1987).

DON GAYTON

A Cautionary Tale

(2003)

Don Gayton (1946–) is a writer and ecosystem management specialist who lives in Nelson, British Columbia.

This article examines an instance of human intervention in nature.

There was a morning, back in time, when this region of British Columbia they call the Kootenays changed from ice and rock to land and water, from Pleistocene[1] to Holocene.[2] This morning can be described neatly in multiples of ten; at the beginning of the morning, some ten millennia ago, the glaciers lay across the landscape a thousand metres thick. At the end of the postglacial morning, a thousand years later, the continental glaciers were gone.

One of the very first inhabitants of the region, arriving literally on the melt-waters of receding glaciers, is a fish. This fish is an extravagant gift from the Pacific Ocean to the interior. It is an elusive flash of molten silver, a lustful reproductive torrent of fire-engine red, a marvel of adaptation, an icon of regional culture, and a pawn of industry. Its name has cycled through various cultures as kukeni, redfish, kickininee, silver, *Oncorhynchus nerka*, kokanee. These cultures have depended on it, studied it, even brought it close to annihilation, but none has ever completely possessed it.

In the early 1960s, the diminutive kokanee of Kootenay Lake began a radical transformation. Once herring-sized, kokanee were now achieving lengths up to 45 centimetres and weights of 3.5 kilograms, nearly as large as their saltwater cousins, the sockeye salmon. The kokanee's fine red flesh and sportiness made them a welcome addition to the creels of both local and visiting anglers, who now could chase the bulked-up kokanee as well as fish for the world-class Gerrard rainbow trout.

This transformation was attributed to the work of biologist Peter Larkin of the BC government's Game Commission. He felt that the fishery at

1 *Pleistocene* Geological period of climatic changes, including ice ages, from about 1.8 million years ago to 10,000 years ago.
2 *Holocene* Geological period of earth's warming following the end of the Ice Age from 10,000 years ago to present period.

Kootenay Lake, in southeastern British Columbia, was not reaching its full potential, and he had an idea how to enhance it.

In the spring of 1949, Larkin made a trip to Waterton Lake, Alberta.   5
Using a fine-meshed net, he trawled the bottom of Waterton Lake and captured a small population of a tiny crustacean called Mysis. This organism was found in Waterton and other lakes east of the Rockies, but not in BC lakes. Larkin's idea was that Mysis (also known as the "opossum shrimp," for its nocturnal habits) would be an ideal food source for the Gerrard rainbow trout.

The Gerrards fed on plankton when they were fry, then switched to a diet of kokanee once they were mature. Larkin felt that the crustacean might become an intermediate food source that would help the growing rainbows as they moved from juvenile to adult food. Accordingly, he released Mysis into Kootenay Lake in 1949, and again in 1950.

As the newcomer slowly worked its way into the lake's ecology, biologists duly included it in their periodic monitoring regime. Kootenay Lake is remarkable in many ways, but one of the unique aspects of this rather remote mountain lake is its lengthy legacy of monitoring. Beginning as early as the 1930s, scientists from as far away as Ontario have made the trek to the lake with their sample bottles and trawling nets, making the time-consuming and often tedious measurements that form the basis of limnology, the scientific study of inland waters.

For the first several years, Larkin's species introduction was written off as a failure since the monitoring found Mysis in only vanishingly small quantities. This was not unexpected. In the lengthy history of aquatic introductions around North America, certain species caught on and others didn't, and it was hard to predict outcomes in advance.

Far off in the East Kootenay community of Kimberley, another interference was taking place. In 1953, Cominco's massive Sullivan lead-zinc mine began producing phosphate fertilizer as a by-product.

In the industrial style of the day, the fertilizer plant was a messy opera-   10
tion, producing large quantities of phosphorous-laced wastewater, which was dumped unceremoniously into the adjacent Saint Mary River. Tumbling down the rapids of the Saint Mary and into the Kootenay River system, this concentrated pulse of phosphorous acted like an ecological steroid. Quickly snapped up by ravening algae and spiralled upward into Kootenay Lake's food chain, Cominco's phosphorous boosted kokanee numbers as well as their size at maturity.

By 1962, fertilizer production was in full swing. Phosphorous fertilizer tonnage, as well as phosphorous pollution, increased steadily to a peak in 1967. Around Kootenay Lake, people noticed a decrease in the renowned clarity of the lake's water, and during hot summers, floating algae mats appeared, which no one could remember seeing before.

Meanwhile, the Mysis had been biding its time in the lake, slowly adapting to the conditions of its new home. In the early 1960s it began to show up in the monthly monitoring reports, and scientists belatedly realized that the Mysis transplant had indeed been successful.

Peter Larkin was belatedly applauded for his pioneering Mysis work. The media picked up the story, and soon Mysis was the instant solution for overfished and unproductive lakes. Based on the Kootenay Lake example, Mysis introductions were made in Okanagan Lake, the Arrow Lakes and several other lakes in BC, the United States and even Scandinavia.

By the early 70s, however, the Mysis data began to set off alarm bells in the scientific community. The shrimp were now multiplying rapidly and feeding on Daphnia, the primary food of the kokanee, yet very few Mysis were showing up in the guts of either rainbows or kokanee. The normal algae to Daphnia to kokanee to rainbow food chain was being disrupted by what the biologists dubbed "the Mysis shunt," which was algae to Daphnia to Mysis, period.

15   In other words, the Mysis were happily consuming, but rarely being consumed. Exploring further, the scientists stumbled onto a fundamental problem: the daily migrations of the light-shy Mysis were completely out of phase with the daily migrations of both kokanee and rainbows. The cagey, opossum-like shrimp would rise at nightfall to feed and then migrate back down to the bottom to avoid predation during the day. The fish, in their turn, carried out the opposite diurnal migration, feeding in the surface layers in the mornings and moving to intermediate depths later in the day and at night. Because of the great depth of the lake, the Mysis were able to avoid being eaten by either kokanee or rainbow.

As the biologists pored over their reams of lake and fish data, a new and disturbing picture emerged. They realized the Mysis was actually not responsible for the overall enhancement of the fishery. Cominco's phosphorous pollution was in fact the main engine behind the increase, and the Mysis introduction was actually a tragic mistake.

Not long after Mysis and Cominco, a further interference was added to this already complex and volatile mix. In 1972, Libby Dam was installed across the Kootenay River near the bottom of its southward loop into Montana. This dam administered the *coup de grace*[1] for the artificially inflated kokanee fishery. The long stretch of dead water created behind the Libby Dam, euphemistically named "Lake Koocanusa," caused virtually all the nutrients to settle out, not only those from the Cominco plant, but the naturally occurring ones as well.

In a final and ironic twist to the story, settling ponds were finally installed at the Cominco fertilizer plant in 1969, removing most of the phosphorous from the wastewater, and in 1987 the fertilizer plant was shut down alto-

---

1   *coup de grace* Literally a "blow of mercy"—the blow which brings death to end suffering or brings about the end of something.

gether. Cut off from its phosphorous supply and disrupted by the Mysis, the lake's food chain started into freefall. Kokanee populations dropped dramatically. The kokanee-dependent Gerrard rainbows, the trophy fish of Kootenay Lake, suffered much the same fate. Fishing success rates were pathetic. The same charter, tackle, moorage, food and accommodation businesses that had done so well during the phosphorous pollution years were now either out of business or complaining loudly. What happened to the vaunted Mysis solution? Why wasn't it working? they asked.

The scientists who had worked on the lake over the years were called in and began poring over data on nutrient loading,[1] temperature gradients, zooplankton,[2] Mysis and fish reproduction, looking for a solution. One unique proposal that came out of this process, and which was actually seriously considered, was to install a string of swimming pool lights along the bottom of the lake. The light would drive the Mysis back up toward the surface, where they could be eaten by fish.

Another blue-sky proposal was to install a giant circular air bubbler on the bottom, creating an upward current that would sweep helpless Mysis into the waiting jaws of kokanee and juvenile Gerrards. However, one of the mathematically inclined scientists pulled out a calculator and showed that a bubbler of a scale large enough to bring shrimp to the surface would also create a huge downward vortex powerful enough to suck in canoes and water-skiers.

Ken Ashley, a bright young fisheries scientist from UBC, proposed the radical solution of fertilizing the lake. With support from the fledgling Columbia Basin Fish and Wildlife Compensation Program, the Fish and Wildlife Branch approved a five-year pilot fertilization experiment. It was to be the largest lake-fertilization project ever undertaken anywhere. A pair of huge fertilizer tanks were mounted on a barge with a pusher tug behind it, and beginning in April 1992, this bizarre craft, with a mixture of dissolved phosphorous and nitrogen in its tanks, made a weekly ten-kilometre run down the middle of the North Arm of Kootenay Lake, dribbling the mixture overboard at a predetermined rate. The scientific community held its collective breath and waited for the results. Contrary to expectations, the kokanee did respond positively to fertilization.

Arriving in Nelson just as the Kootenay Lake fertilization program was being proposed, I was deeply offended by it. Knowing nothing of the local situation, but having had my fill of decades of industrial solutions to ecological problems (problems largely caused by industrial development to begin with), I went storming into the Fish and Wildlife office, demanding to talk to a fisheries person. Jay Hammond, the regional fisheries biologist,

20

---

1 *nutrient loading* The introduction of excessive amounts of nutrients such as nitrogen or phosphorous from fertilizers into the soil or water.

2 *zooplankton* Small, usually microscopic animals found in lakes and reservoirs.

received me and patiently walked me through the basics of the phosphorous history of Kootenay Lake. An hour later I had the picture and remember making the comment, "So there's really only three options here. Either
you let the fishery die, you blow up Libby Dam or you fertilize."

The Kootenay Lake phosphorous story, as well as the Libby Dam experience, are ecological moral tales, modern fables. They show that once we
touch a system, it seems we have to keep on touching it. When we have damaged an ecosystem (a river, for instance) with technology (a dam), we may
have to use more technology (fertilization) to repair it. This runs counter
to a strong current in contemporary thinking, which is that the best way to
manage or repair an ecosystem is to leave it alone. The Kootenay Lake
experience suggests a different, more interventionist paradigm.

The Mysis tale is a parallel one, teaching us a history lesson. It is easy to
condemn Peter Larkin for an unwise and destructive biological introduction, to write him off as an unthinking ecological cowboy. It is more difficult, but more instructive, to recognize that Larkin was a well-respected scientist at the time; that he was following a lengthy tradition of purposeful
alien biological introductions; and that his example was eagerly copied by
his peers across North America and elsewhere. As Tom Northcote, another
early Game Commission biologist admitted, they were looking for a "quick
fix," and the Mysis seemed to be it.

25 Noted fisheries scientist Carl Walters feels that Larkin's idea of filling a
perceived gap in the food chain was innovative and imaginative. The problem, Walters says, was that scientists were focused on "first-order" impacts
on ecosystems and had no understanding of second-order, indirect effects.
Walters does fault Larkin for not asking the obvious question about Mysis
while it was still confined to Waterton, its home lake: if this shrimp is such
perfect fish food, how come it is so rarely eaten?

Folktales and children's stories help ease young people into the complex
and ambiguous world of adult life. Perhaps these ecological moral tales of
fish and shrimp can help ease us adults into the complex and ambiguous
world of living with nature, rather than in spite of it. They help us understand
that ecosystems are complex, our actions upon them are far-reaching, human
arrogance comes at a price, and that we are not god-like in our wisdom.

Questions

1. Gayton sets up his article as a fable: it begins with the heightened
   imagery of a fairy tale and ends with a moral. What are the effects of this
   strategy?

2. How does Gayton's article complicate the debate for or against human
   intervention in nature?

❧ *Social Issues* ❧

JONATHAN SWIFT

A Modest Proposal

For Preventing the Children of Poor People in Ireland
From Being a Burden to their Parents or Country,
and for Making Them Beneficial to the Public
(1729)

Jonathan Swift (1667-1745) was an Irish poet, fiction writer, essayist, and political pamphleteer, best known for his satire aimed at political hypocrisy, literary pretension, and the folly of human society. Among his major works are Tale of a Tub *(1704) and* Gulliver's Travels *(1726).*

In this satirical pamphlet, Swift provides an ironic solution to the poverty and squalid living conditions of Catholics in early eighteenth-century Ireland.

It is a melancholy object to those who walk through this great town[1] or travel in the country, when they see the streets, the roads, and cabin doors, crowded with beggars of the female sex, followed by three, four, or six children, all in rags and importuning every passenger for an alms. These mothers, instead of being able to work for their honest livelihood, are forced to employ all their time in strolling to beg sustenance for their helpless infants; who, as they grow up, either turn thieves for want of work, or leave their dear native country to fight for the Pretender[2] in Spain, or sell themselves to the Barbadoes.[3]

---

1   *town* Dublin.
2   *the Pretender* James Francis Edward Stuart, son of James II, who had been over-thrown in 1688 in the English revolution, was known as "the old pretender." Many Irish-Catholics supported him.
3   *the Barbadoes* It was common at the time for poverty-stricken Irish citizens to go into debt in order to pay for passage to the West Indies, where they would then pay off the debt through labor.

I think it is agreed by all parties that this prodigious number of children in the arms, or on the backs, or at the heels of their mothers, and frequently of their fathers, is, in the present deplorable state of the kingdom, a very great additional grievance; and, therefore, whoever could find out a fair, cheap, and easy method of making these children sound, useful members of the commonwealth, would deserve so well of the public, as to have his statue set up for a preserver of the nation.

But my intention is very far from being confined to provide only for the children of professed beggars; it is of a much greater extent, and shall take in the whole number of infants at a certain age, who are born of parents in effect as little able to support them, as those who demand our charity in the streets.

As to my own part, having turned my thoughts for many years upon this important subject, and maturely weighed the several schemes of our projectors,[1] I have always found them grossly mistaken in their computation. It is true, a child, just dropped from its dam, may be supported by her milk for a solar year, with little other nourishment; at most, not above the value of two shillings, which the mother may certainly get, or the value in scraps, by her lawful occupation of begging; and it is exactly at one year old that I propose to provide for them in such a manner, as, instead of being a charge upon their parents, or the parish, or wanting food and raiment for the rest of their lives, they shall, on the contrary, contribute to the feeding, and partly to the clothing, of many thousands.

5   There is likewise another great advantage in my scheme, that it will prevent those voluntary abortions, and that horrid practice of women murdering their bastard children, alas, too frequent among us! sacrificing the poor innocent babes, I doubt,[2] more to avoid the expense than the shame, which would move tears and pity in the most savage and in-human breast.

The number of souls in this kingdom being usually reckoned one million and a half, of these I calculate there may be about two hundred thousand couple whose wives are breeders; from which number I subtract thirty thousand couple, who are able to maintain their own children, (although I apprehend there cannot be so many, under the present distresses of the kingdom;) but this being granted, there will remain a hundred and seventy thousand breeders. I again subtract fifty thousand, for those women who miscarry, or whose children die by accident or disease within the year. There only remain a hundred and twenty thousand children of poor parents annually born. The question therefore is, How this number shall be reared and provided for? which, as I have already said, under the present situation of affairs, is utterly impossible by all the methods hitherto proposed. For we can neither employ them in handicraft or agriculture; we neither build houses (I mean in the country,) nor cultivate land: they can

---

1   *projectors* People who put forward schemes or projects.

2   *doubt* Suspect.

very seldom pick up a livelihood by stealing, till they arrive at six years old, except where they are of towardly parts; although I confess they learn the rudiments much earlier; during which time they can, however, be properly looked upon only as probationers; as I have been informed by a principal gentleman in the county of Cavan, who protested to me, that he never knew above one or two instances under the age of six, even in a part of the kingdom so renowned for the quickest proficiency in that art.

I am assured by our merchants, that a boy or a girl before twelve years old is no saleable commodity; and even when they come to this age they will not yield above three pounds, or three pounds and half-a-crown at most on the exchange; which cannot turn to account either to the parents or kingdom, the charge of nutriment and rags having been at least four times that value.

I shall now, therefore, humbly propose my own thoughts, which I hope will not be liable to the least objection.

I have been assured by a very knowing American of my acquaintance in London, that a young healthy child, well nursed is, at a year old, a most delicious, nourishing, and wholesome food, whether stewed, roasted, baked, or boiled; and I make no doubt that it will equally serve in a fricassee or a ragout.

I do therefore humbly offer it to public consideration, that of the hundred and twenty thousand children already computed, twenty thousand may be reserved for breed, whereof only one-fourth part to be males; which is more than we allow to sheep, black cattle, or swine; and my reason is, that these children are seldom the fruits of marriage, a circumstance not much regarded by our savages, therefore one male will be sufficient to serve four females. That the remaining hundred thousand may, at a year old, be offered in sale to the persons of quality and fortune through the kingdom; always advising the mother to let them suck plentifully in the last month, so as to render them plump and fat for a good table. A child will make two dishes at an entertainment for friends; and when the family dines alone, the fore or hind quarter will make a reasonable dish, and, seasoned with a little pepper or salt, will be very good boiled on the fourth day, especially in winter.

I have reckoned, upon a medium, that a child just born will weigh twelve pounds, and in a solar year, if tolerably nursed, will increase to twenty-eight pounds.

I grant this food will be somewhat dear, and therefore very proper for landlords, who, as they have already devoured most of the parents, seem to have the best title to the children.

Infants' flesh will be in season throughout the year, but more plentiful in March, and a little before and after: for we are told by a grave author,[1]

---

1   *grave author* Rabelais.

an eminent French physician, that fish being a prolific diet, there are more children born in Roman Catholic countries about nine months after Lent, than at any other season; therefore, reckoning a year after Lent, the markets will be more glutted than usual, because the number of Popish infants is at least three to one in this kingdom: and therefore it will have one other collateral advantage, by lessening the number of Papists among us.

I have already computed the charge of nursing a beggar's child (in which list I reckon all cottagers, labourers, and four-fifths of the farmers) to be about two shillings per annum, rags included; and I believe no gentleman would repine to give ten shillings for the carcass of a good fat child, which, as I have said, will make four dishes of excellent nutritive meat, when he has only some particular friend or his own family, to dine with him. Thus the squire will learn to be a good landlord, and grow popular among his tenants; the mother will have eight shillings net profit, and be fit for work till she produces another child.

15   Those who are more thrifty (as I must confess the times require) may flay the carcass; the skin of which, artificially[1] dressed, will make admirable gloves for ladies, and summer boots for fine gentlemen.

As to our city of Dublin, shambles may be appointed for this purpose in the most convenient parts of it, and butchers, we may be assured, will not be wanting; although I rather recommend buying the children alive, and dressing them hot from the knife as we do roasting pigs.

A very worthy person, a true lover of his country, and whose virtues I highly esteem, was lately pleased in discoursing on this matter, to offer a refinement upon my scheme. He said, that many gentlemen of this kingdom, having of late destroyed their deer, he conceived that the want of venison might be well supplied by the bodies of young lads and maidens, not exceeding fourteen years of age, nor under twelve; so great a number of both sexes in every county being now ready to starve for want of work and service; and these to be disposed of by their parents, if alive, or otherwise by their nearest relations. But, with due deference to so excellent a friend, and so deserving a patriot, I cannot be altogether in his sentiments; for as to the males, my American acquaintance assured me, from frequent experience, that their flesh was generally tough and lean, like that of our schoolboys, by continual exercise, and their taste disagreeable; and to fatten them would not answer the charge. Then as to the females, it would, I think, with humble submission, be a loss to the public, because they soon would become breeders themselves: and besides, it is not improbable that some scrupulous people might be apt to censure such a practice, (although indeed very unjustly,) as a little bordering upon cruelty; which, I confess, has always been with me the strongest objection against any project, how well soever intended.

---

1 *artificially* With artifice or skill.

But in order to justify my friend, he confessed that this expedient was put into his head by the famous Psalmanazar,[1] a native of the island Formosa, who came from thence to London above twenty years ago; and in conversation told my friend, that in his country when any young person happened to be put to death, the executioner sold the carcass to persons of quality as a prime dainty; and that in his time the body of a plump girl of fifteen, who was crucified for an attempt to poison the emperor, was sold to his imperial majesty's prime minister of state, and other great mandarins of the court, in joints from the gibbet, at four hundred crowns. Neither indeed can I deny, that if the same use were made of several plump young girls in this town, who, without one single groat to their fortunes, cannot stir abroad without a chair,[2] and appear at playhouse and assemblies in foreign fineries which they never will pay for, the kingdom would not be the worse.

Some persons of a desponding spirit are in great concern about that vast number of poor people, who are aged, diseased, or maimed; and I have been desired to employ my thoughts, what course may be taken to ease the nation of so grievous an encumbrance. But I am not in the least pain upon that matter, because it is very well known, that they are every day dying, and rotting, by cold and famine, and filth and vermin, as fast as can be reasonably expected. And as to the young labourers, they are now in almost as hopeful a condition: they cannot get work, and consequently pine away for want of nourishment, to a degree, that if at any time they are accidentally hired to common labour, they have not strength to perform it; and thus the country and themselves are delivered from the evils to come.

I have too long digressed, and therefore shall return to my subject. I think the advantages by the proposal, which I have made, are obvious and many, as well as of the highest importance. 20

For first, as I have already observed, it would greatly lessen the number of Papists, with whom we are yearly over-run, being the principal breeders of the nation, as well as our most dangerous enemies; and who stay at home on purpose to deliver the kingdom to the Pretender, hoping to take their advantage by the absence of so many good Protestants, who have chosen rather to leave their country than stay at home and pay tithes against their conscience to an Episcopal curate.

Secondly, The poor tenants will have something valuable of their own, which by law may be made liable to distress, and help to pay their landlord's rent; their corn and cattle being already seized, and money a thing unknown.

---

1   *Psalmanazar* Under the false name "George Psalmanazar," a French citizen published in 1704 a popular book about Formosa (now Taiwan) where he claims to have been born; he was later exposed as an impostor.

2   *chair* Sedan chair.

Thirdly, Whereas the maintenance of a hundred thousand children, from two years old and upward, cannot be computed at less than ten shillings apiece per annum, the nation's stock will be thereby increased fifty thousand pounds per annum, beside the profit of a new dish introduced to the tables of all gentlemen of fortune in the kingdom who have any refinement in taste. And the money will circulate among ourselves, the goods being entirely of our own growth and manufacture.

Fourthly, The constant breeders, beside the gain of eight shillings sterling per annum by the sale of their children, will be rid of the charge of maintaining them after the first year.

25   Fifthly, This food would likewise bring great custom to taverns; where the vintners will certainly be so prudent as to procure the best receipts[1] for dressing it to perfection, and, consequently, have their houses frequented by all the fine gentlemen, who justly value themselves upon their knowledge in good eating: and a skilful cook, who understands how to oblige his guests, will contrive to make it as expensive as they please.

Sixthly, This would be a great inducement to marriage, which all wise nations have either encouraged by rewards, or enforced by laws and penalties. It would increase the care and tenderness of mothers toward their children, when they were sure of a settlement for life to the poor babes, provided in some sort by the public, to their annual profit instead of expense. We should see an honest emulation among the married women, which of them could bring the fattest child to the market. Men would become as fond of their wives during the time of their pregnancy as they are now of their mares in foal, their cows in calf, their sows when they are ready to farrow; nor offer to beat or kick them (as is too frequent a practice) for fear of a miscarriage.

Many other advantages might be enumerated. For instance, the addition of some thousand carcasses in our exportation of barrelled beef; the propagation of swine's flesh, and improvement in the art of making good bacon, so much wanted among us by the great destruction of pigs, too frequent at our table; which are no way comparable in taste or magnificence to a well-grown, fat, yearling child, which, roasted whole, will make a considerable figure at a lord mayor's feast, or any other public entertainment. But this, and many others, I omit, being studious of brevity.

Supposing that one thousand families in this city would be constant customers for infants' flesh, beside others who might have it at merry-meetings, particularly at weddings and christenings, I compute that Dublin would take off annually about twenty thousand carcasses; and the rest of the kingdom (where probably they will be sold somewhat cheaper) the remaining eighty thousand.

---

1   *receipts* Recipes.

I can think of no one objection, that will possibly be raised against this proposal, unless it should be urged, that the number of people will be thereby much lessened in the kingdom. This I freely own, and it was indeed one principal design in offering it to the world. I desire the reader will observe, that I calculate my remedy for this one individual kingdom of Ireland, and for no other that ever was, is, or I think ever can be, upon earth. Therefore let no man talk to me of other expedients: of taxing our absentees at five shillings a pound: of using neither clothes, nor household furniture, except what is our own growth and manufacture: of utterly rejecting the materials and instruments that promote foreign luxury: of curing the expensiveness of pride, vanity, idleness, and gaming in our women: of introducing a vein of parsimony, prudence, and temperance: of learning to love our country, in the want of which we differ even from LAP-LANDERS, and the inhabitants of TOPINAMBOO:[1] of quitting our animosities and factions, nor acting any longer like the Jews,[2] who were murdering one another at the very moment their city was taken: of being a little cautious not to sell our country and conscience for nothing: of teaching landlords to have at least one degree of mercy toward their tenants: lastly, of putting a spirit of honesty, industry, and skill into our shopkeepers; who, if a resolution could now be taken to buy only our negative goods, would immediately unite to cheat and exact upon us in the price, the measure, and the goodness, nor could ever yet be brought to make one fair proposal of just dealing, though often and earnestly invited to it.

Therefore I repeat, let no man talk to me of these and the like expedients, till he has at least some glimpse of hope, that there will be ever some hearty and sincere attempt to put them in practice.

But, as to myself, having been wearied out for many years with offering vain, idle, visionary thoughts, and at length utterly despairing of success, I fortunately fell upon this proposal; which, as it is wholly new, so it has something solid and real, of no expense and little trouble, full in our own power, and whereby we can incur no danger in disobliging ENGLAND. For this kind of commodity will not bear exportation, the flesh being of too tender a consistence to admit a long continuance in salt, although perhaps I could name a country, which would be glad to eat up our whole nation without it.

After all, I am not so violently bent upon my own opinion as to reject any offer proposed by wise men, which shall be found equally innocent, cheap, easy, and effectual. But before something of that kind shall be advanced in contradiction to my scheme, and offering a better, I desire the author, or

30

---

1 *Topinamboo* Name given in the eighteenth century to what is now coastal and central Brazil.
2 *like the Jews* Anti-Semitic, biblical reference whose source is unclear, but possible references include II Kings 24, II Chronicles 37.

authors, will be pleased maturely to consider two points. First, as things now stand, how they will be able to find food and raiment for a hundred thousand useless mouths and backs. And, secondly, there being a round million of creatures in human figure throughout this kingdom, whose whole subsistence put into a common stock would leave them in debt two millions of pounds sterling, adding those who are beggars by profession, to the bulk of farmers, cottagers, and labourers, with the wives and children who are beggars in effect; I desire those politicians who dislike my overture, and may perhaps be so bold as to attempt an answer, that they will first ask the parents of these mortals, whether they would not at this day think it a great happiness to have been sold for food at a year old, in the manner I prescribe, and thereby have avoided such a perpetual scene of misfortunes, as they have since gone through, by the oppression of landlords, the impossibility of paying rent without money or trade, the want of common sustenance, with neither house nor clothes to cover them from the inclemencies of the weather, and the most inevitable prospect of entailing the like, or greater miseries, upon their breed for ever.

I profess, in the sincerity of my heart, that I have not the least personal interest in endeavouring to promote this necessary work, having no other motive than the public good of my country, by advancing our trade, providing for infants, relieving the poor, and giving some pleasure to the rich. I have no children by which I can propose to get a single penny; the youngest being nine years old, and my wife past child-bearing.

Questions

1. At what point does the reader realize that this is a satire? Discuss the effect of this delay.
2. What is it possible to infer about the character of the narrator?
3. What is the purpose of the long list of other "expedients" provided in paragraph 29?
4. Comment on Swift's diction, in particular on the use of such terms as "dam" (paragraph 4), "breeders" (paragraphs 6, 17, 21, and 24), and "yearling child" (paragraph 27), among others.

W.E.B. DU BOIS

A Mild Suggestion

(1912)

W.E.B. Du Bois (1868–1963) was a writer, educator, historian, and a founder of the National Association for the Advancement of Colored People. His autobiographical, sociological, and historical works include The Souls of Black Folks *(1903)*, John Brown *(1909)*, The Negro *(1915), and* Dusk of Dawn *(1940).*

This short piece, first published in the activist magazine Crisis *(which Du Bois edited for twenty-five years) is one of his most famous works.*

They were sitting on the leeward deck of the vessel and the colored man was there with his usual look of unconcern. Before the seasickness his presence aboard had caused some upheaval. The Woman, for instance, glancing at the Southerner, had refused point blank to sit beside him at meals, so she had changed places with the Little Old Lady. The Westerner, who sat opposite, said he did not care a ———, then he looked at the Little Old Lady, and added in a lower voice to the New Yorker that there was no accounting for tastes. The Southerner from the other table broadened his back and tried to express with his shoulders both ancestors and hauteur. All this, however, was half forgotten during the seasickness, and the Woman sat beside the colored man for a full half hour before she noticed it, and then was glad to realize that the Southerner was too sick to see. Now again with sunshine and smiling weather, they all quite naturally reverted (did the Southerner suggest it?) to the Negro problem. The usual solutions had been suggested: education, work, emigration, etc.

They had not noticed the back of the colored man, until the thoughtless Westerner turned toward him and said breezily: "Well, now, what do you say? I guess you are rather interested." The colored man was leaning over the rail and about to light his cigarette—he had several such bad habits, as the Little Old Lady noticed. The Southerner simply stared. Over the face of the colored man went the shadow of several expressions; some the New Yorker could interpret, others he could not.

"I have," said the colored man, with deliberation, "a perfect solution." The Southerner selected a look of disdain from his repertoire, and assumed it. The Woman moved nearer, but partly turned her back. The Westerner and the Little Old Lady sat down. "Yes," repeated the colored man, "I have a perfect solution. The trouble with most of the solutions which are generally suggested is that they aggravate the disease." The Southerner could not help looking interested. "For instance," proceeded the colored man, airily waving his hand, "take education; education means ambition, dissatisfaction and revolt. You cannot both educate people and hold them down."

"Then stop educating them," growled the Southerner aside.

5   "Or," continued the colored man, "if the black man works, he must come into competition with whites——"

"He sure will, and it ought to be stopped," returned the Westerner. "It brings down wages."

"Precisely," said the speaker, "and if by underselling the labor market he develops a few millionaires, how now would you protect your residential districts or your select social circles or—your daughters?"

The Southerner started angrily, but the colored man was continuing placidly with a far-off look in his eyes. "Now, migration is both costly and inhuman; the transportation would be the smallest matter. You must buy up perhaps a thousand millions' worth of Negro property; you must furnish some capital for the masses of poor; you must get some place for them to go; you must protect them there, and here you must pay not only higher wages to white men, but still higher on account of the labor scarcity. Meantime, the Negroes suddenly removed from one climate and social system to another climate and utterly new conditions would die in droves—it would be simply prolonged murder at enormous cost.

"Very well," continued the colored man, seating himself and throwing away his cigarette, "listen to my plan," looking almost quizzically at the Little Old Lady; "you must not be alarmed at its severity—it may seem radical, but really it is—it is—well, it is quite the only practical thing and it has surely one advantage: it settles the problem once, suddenly, and forever. My plan is this: You now outnumber us nearly ten to one. I propose that on a certain date, shall we say next Christmas, or possibly Easter, 1912? No, come to think of it, the first of January, 1913, would, for historical reasons, probably be best. Well, then, on the first of January, 1913, let each person who has a colored friend invite him to dinner. This would take care of a few; among such friends might be included the black mammies and faithful old servants of the South; in this way we could get together quite a number. Then those who have not the pleasure of black friends might arrange for meetings, especially in "white" churches and Young Men's and Young Women's Christian Associations, where Negroes are not expected. At such meetings, contrary to custom, the black people should not be seated by themselves, but distributed very carefully among the whites. The remaining Negroes who could not be flattered or attracted by these invitations should be induced to assemble among themselves at their own churches or at little parties and house warmings.

10   "The few stragglers, vagrants and wanderers could be put under careful

watch and ward. Now, then, we have the thing in shape. First, the hosts of those invited to dine should provide themselves with a sufficient quantity of cyanide of potassium, placing it carefully in the proper cups, and being careful not to mix the cups. Those at church and prayer meeting could choose between long sharp stilettoes and pistols—I should recommend the former as less noisy. Those who guard the colored assemblies and the stragglers without should carefully surround the groups and use Winchesters. Then, at a given signal, let the colored folk of the United States be quietly dispatched; the signal might be a church bell or the singing of the national hymn; probably the bell would be best, for the diners would be eating."

By this time the auditors of the colored man were staring; the Southerner had forgotten to pose; the Woman had forgotten to watch the Southerner; the Westerner was staring with admiration; there were tears in the eyes of the Little Old Lady, while the New Yorker was smiling; but the colored man held up a deprecating hand: "Now don't prejudge my plan," he urged. "The next morning there would be ten million funerals, and therefore no Negro problem. Think how quietly the thing would be settled; no more bother, no more argument; the whole country united and happy. Even the Negroes would be a great deal happier than they are at present. Instead of being made heirs to hope by education, or ambitious by wealth, or exiled invalids on the fever coast, they would all be happily ensconced in Heaven. Of course, I admit that at first the plan may seem a little abrupt and cruel, and yet is it more cruel than present conditions, and would it not be well to be a little more abrupt in our social solutions? At any rate think it over," and the colored man dropped lazily into his steamer chair and felt for another cigarette.

The crowd slowly dispersed; the Southerner chose the Woman, but was heard to say something about fools. The Westerner turned to the New Yorker and said: "Now, what in hell do you suppose that darky meant?" But the Little Old Lady went silently to her cabin.

Questions

1. This essay is similar in several respects to "A Modest Proposal" by Jonathan Swift. What are some of these similarities? Are there also significant differences between the two essays in tone and approach?
2. What are the implications of the author's use of unnamed characters in this work?
3. Comment on the tone and diction of Du Bois's prose in this piece, using evidence from the text.

RICHARD RODRIGUEZ

Profession

(1982)

Richard Rodriguez (1944–) is the author of the books Hunger of Memory: The Education of Richard Rodriguez *(1982),* Mexico's Children *(1990), and* Days of Obligation: An Argument with My Mexican Father *(1992). He has also published widely in periodicals such as* Harper's Magazine, The Wall Street Journal, The New Republic, *and* Time.

This excerpt from Hunger of Memory *explains Rodriguez's objections to the system of affirmative action.*

Minority student—that was the label I bore in college at Stanford, then in graduate school at Columbia and Berkeley: a nonwhite reader of Spenser and Milton and Austen.[1]

In the late 1960s nonwhite Americans clamored for access to higher education, and I became a principal beneficiary of the academy's response, its programs of affirmative action. My presence was noted each fall by the campus press office in its proud tally of Hispanic-American students enrolled; my progress was followed by HEW[2] statisticians. One of the lucky ones. Rewarded. Advanced for belonging to a racial group "underrepresented" in American institutional life. When I sought admission to graduate schools, when I applied for fellowships and summer study grants, when I needed a teaching assistantship, my Spanish surname or the dark mark in the space indicating my race—"check one"—nearly always got me whatever I asked for. When the time came for me to look for a college teaching job (the end of my years as a scholarship boy), potential employers came looking for me—a minority student.

Fittingly, it falls to me, as someone who so awkwardly carried the label, to question it now, its juxtaposition of terms—minority, student. For me

---

1 *Spenser* Edmund Spenser (c. 1552–99), English poet, author of *The Faerie Queen; Milton* John Milton (1608–74) English poet, author of *Paradise Lost; Austen* Jane Austen (1775–1817) English writer, author of *Pride and Prejudice.*
2 *HEW* United States Department of Health, Education, and Welfare, founded in 1953 and revamped in 1979 when a separate Department of Education was created.

there is no way to say it with grace. I say it rather with irony sharpened by self-pity. I say it with anger. It is a term that should never have been foisted on me. One I was wrong to accept.

In college one day a professor of English returned my term paper with this comment penciled just under the grade: "Maybe the reason you feel Dickens's[1] sense of alienation so acutely is because you are a minority student." *Minority student.* It was the first time I had seen the expression; I remember sensing that it somehow referred to my race. Never before had a teacher suggested that my academic performance was linked to my racial identity. After class I reread the remark several times. Around me other students were talking and leaving. The professor remained in front of the room, collecting his papers and books. I was about to go up and question his note. But I didn't. I let the comment pass; thus became implicated in the strange reform movement that followed.

The year was 1967. And what I did not realize was that my life would be rad-   5
ically changed by deceptively distant events. In 1967, their campaign against southern segregation laws successful at last, black civil rights leaders were turning their attention to the North, a North they no longer saw in contrast to the South. What they realized was that although no official restrictions denied blacks access to northern institutions of advancement and power, for most blacks this freedom was only theoretical. (The obstacle was "institutional racism.") Activists made their case against institutions of higher education. Schools like Wisconsin and Princeton long had been open to blacks. But the tiny number of nonwhite students and faculty members at such schools suggested that there was more than the issue of access to consider. Most blacks simply couldn't afford tuition for higher education. And, because the primary and secondary schooling blacks received was usually poor, few qualified for admission. Many were so culturally alienated that they never thought to apply; they couldn't even imagine themselves going to college.

I think—as I thought in 1967—that the black civil rights leaders were correct: Higher education was not, nor is it yet, accessible to many black Americans. I think now, however, that the activists tragically limited the impact of their movement with the reforms they proposed. Seeing the problem solely in racial terms (as a case of *de facto*[2] segregation), they pressured universities and colleges to admit more black students and hire more black faculty members. There were demands for financial aid programs. And tutoring help. And more aggressive student recruitment. But this was all. The aim was to integrate higher education in the North. So no one seemed troubled by the fact that those who were in the best position

---

1   *Dickens* Charles Dickens (1812–70), English writer, author of *Great Expectations* and other works.
2   *de facto* Actual (Latin for "in fact" or "in practice").

to benefit from such reforms were those blacks least victimized by racism or any other social oppression—those culturally, if not always economically, of the middle class.

The lead established, other civil rights groups followed. Soon Hispanic-American activists began to complain that there were too few Hispanics in colleges. They concluded that this was the result of racism. They offered racial solutions. They demanded that Hispanic-American professors be hired. And that students with Spanish surnames be admitted in greater numbers to colleges. Shortly after, I was "recognized" on campus: an Hispanic-American, a "Latino," a Mexican-American, a "Chicano." No longer would people ask me, as I had been asked before, if I were a foreign student. (From India? Peru?) All of a sudden everyone seemed to know—as the professor of English had known—that I was a minority student.

I became a highly rewarded minority student. For campus officials came first to students like me with their numerous offers of aid. And why not? Administrators met their angriest critics' demands by promoting any plausible Hispanic on hand. They were able, moreover, to use the presence of conventionally qualified nonwhite students like me to prove that they were meeting the goals of their critics.

In 1969, the assassination of Dr. Martin Luther King, Jr., prompted many academic officials to commit themselves publicly to the goal of integrating their institutions. One day I watched the nationally televised funeral; a week later I received invitations to teach at community colleges. There were opportunities to travel to foreign countries with contingents of "minority group scholars." And I went to the financial aid office on campus and was handed special forms for minority student applicants. I was a minority student, wasn't I? the lady behind the counter asked me rhetorically. Yes, I said. Carelessly said. I completed the application. Was later awarded.

10   In a way, it was true. I was a minority. The word, as popularly used, did describe me. In the sixties, *minority* became a synonym for socially disadvantaged Americans—but it was primarily a numerical designation. The word referred to entire races and nationalities of Americans, those numerically underrepresented in institutional life. (Thus, without contradiction, one could speak of "minority groups.") And who were they exactly? Blacks—all blacks—most obviously were minorities. And Hispanic-Americans. And American Indians. And some others. (It was left to federal statisticians, using elaborate surveys and charts, to determine which others precisely.)

I was a minority.

I believed it. For the first several years, I accepted the label. I certainly supported the racial civil rights movement; supported the goal of broadening access to higher education. But there was a problem: One day I listened approvingly to a government official defend affirmative action; the next day *I* realized the benefits of the program. I was the minority student the political activists shouted about at noontime rallies. Against their rhetoric, I stood out in relief, unrelieved. *Knowing:* I was not really more socially disadvantaged than the white graduate students in my classes. *Knowing:* I was not disadvantaged like many of the new nonwhite students who were entering college, lacking good early schooling.

Nineteen sixty-nine. 1970. 1971. Slowly, slowly, the term *minority* became a source of unease. It would remind me of those boyhood years when I had felt myself alienated from public (majority) society—*los gringos*.[1] *Minority. Minorities. Minority groups.* The terms sounded in public to remind me in private of the truth: I was not—in a *cultural* sense—a minority, an alien from public life. (Not like *los pobres*[2] I had encountered during my recent laboring summer.) The truth was summarized in the sense of irony I'd feel at hearing myself called a minority student: The reason I was no longer a minority was because I had become a student.

Minority student!

In conversations with faculty members I began to worry the issue, only to be told that my unease was unfounded. A dean said he was certain that after I graduated I would be able to work among "my people." A senior faculty member expressed his confidence that, though I was unrepresentative of lower-class Hispanics, I would serve as a role model for others of my race. Another faculty member was sure that I would be a valued counselor to incoming minority students. (He assumed that, because of my race, I retained a special capacity for communicating with nonwhite students.) I also heard academic officials say that minority students would someday form a leadership class in America. (From our probable positions of power, we would be able to lobby for reforms to benefit others of our race.) 15

In 1973 I wrote and had published two essays in which I said that I had been educated away from the culture of my mother and father. In 1974 I published an essay admitting unease over becoming the beneficiary of affirmative action. There was another article against affirmative action in 1977. One more soon after. At times, I proposed contrary ideas; consistent always was the admission that I was no longer like socially disadvantaged Hispanic-Americans. But this admission, made in national magazines, only brought me a greater degree of success. A published minority student, I won a kind of celebrity. In my mail were admiring letters from right-wing politicians. There were also invitations to address conferences of college administrators or government officials.

My essays served as my "authority" to speak at the Marriott Something or the Sheraton Somewhere. To stand at a ballroom podium and hear my surprised echo sound from a microphone. I spoke. I started getting angry

---

1   *los gringos* Spanish derogatory term for English speakers.
2   *los pobres* Spanish: the poor.

letters from activists. One wrote to say that I was becoming the *gringos'* fawning pet. What "they" want all Hispanics to be. I remembered the remark when I was introduced to an all-white audience and heard their applause so loud. I remembered the remark when I stood in a university auditorium and saw an audience of brown and black faces watching me. I publicly wondered whether a person like me should really be termed a minority. But some members of the audience thought I was denying racial pride, trying somehow to deny my racial identity. They rose to protest. One Mexican-American said I was a minority whether I wanted to be or not. And he said that the reason I was a beneficiary of affirmative action was simple: I was a Chicano. (Wasn't I?) It was only an issue of race.

It is important now to remember that the early leaders of the northern civil rights movement were from the South. (The civil rights movement in the North depended upon an understanding of racism derived from the South.) Here was the source of the mistaken strategy—the reason why activists could so easily ignore class and could consider race alone a sufficient measure of social oppression. In the South, where racism had been legally enforced, all blacks suffered discrimination uniformly. The black businessman and the black maid were undifferentiated by the law that forced them to the rear of the bus. Thus, when segregation laws were challenged and finally defeated, the benefit to one became a benefit for all; the integration of an institution by a single black implied an advance for the entire race.

From the experience of southern blacks, a generation of Americans came to realize with new force that there are forms of oppression that touch all levels of a society. This was the crucial lesson that survived the turbulence in the South of the fifties and sixties. The southern movement gave impetus initially to the civil rights drives of nonwhite Americans in the North. Later, the black movement's vitality extended to animate the liberation movements of women, the elderly, the physically disabled, and the homosexual. Leaders of these groups described the oppression they suffered by analogy to that suffered by blacks. Thus one heard of sexism— that echo of racism, and something called gray power. People in wheelchairs gave the black-power salute. And homosexuals termed themselves "America's last niggers." As racism rhetorically replaced poverty as the key social oppression, Americans learned to look beyond class in considering social oppression. The public conscience was enlarged. Americans were able to take seriously, say, the woman business executive's claim to be the victim of social oppression. But with this advance there was a danger. It became easy to underestimate, even to ignore altogether, the importance of *class.* Easy to forget that those whose lives are shaped by poverty and poor education (cultural minorities) are least able to defend themselves against social oppression, whatever its form.

In the era of affirmative action it became more and more difficult to distinguish the middle-class victim of social oppression from the lower-class victim. In fact, it became hard to say when a person ever *stops* being disadvantaged. Quite apart from poverty, the variety of social oppressions that most concerned Americans involved unchangeable conditions. (One does not ever stop being a woman; one does not stop being aged—short of death; one does not stop being a quadriplegic.) The commonplace heard in the sixties was precisely this: A black never stops being black. (The assertion became a kind of justification for affirmative action.)

For my part I believe the black lawyer who tells me that there is never a day in his life when he forgets he is black. I believe the black business executive who says that, although he drives an expensive foreign car, he must be especially wary when a policeman stops him for speeding. I do not doubt that middle-class blacks need to remain watchful when they look for jobs or try to rent or when they travel to unfamiliar towns. "You can't know what it is like for us," a black woman shouted at me one day from an audience somewhere. Like a white liberal, I was awed, shaken by her rage; I gave her the point. But now I must insist, must risk presumption to say that I do not think that all blacks are equally "black." Surely those uneducated and poor will remain most vulnerable to racism. It was not coincidence that the leadership of the southern civil rights movement was drawn mainly from a well-educated black middle class. Even in the South of the 1950s, all blacks were not equally black.

All Mexican-Americans certainly are not equally Mexican-Americans. The policy of affirmative action, however, was never able to distinguish someone like me (a graduate student of English, ambitious for a college teaching career) from a slightly educated Mexican-American who lived in a barrio[1] and worked as a menial laborer, never expecting a future improved. Worse, affirmative action made me the beneficiary of his condition. Such was the foolish logic of this program of social reform: Because many Hispanics were absent from higher education, I became with my matriculation an exception, a numerical minority. Because I was not a cultural minority, I was extremely well placed to enjoy the advantages of affirmative action. I was groomed for a position in the multiversity's leadership class.

Remarkably, affirmative action passed as a program of the Left. In fact, its supporters ignored the most fundamental assumptions of the classical Left by disregarding the importance of class and by assuming that the disadvantages of the lower class would necessarily be ameliorated by the creation of an elite society. The movement that began so nobly in the South, in the North came to parody social reform. Those least disadvantaged were helped first, advanced because many others of their race were more dis-

---

1   *barrio* Spanish: neighborhood, used to describe Spanish-speaking districts of cities in the United States.

advantaged. The strategy of affirmative action, finally, did not take seriously the educational dilemma of disadvantaged students. They need good early schooling! Activists pushed to get more nonwhite students into colleges. Meritocratic standards were dismissed as exclusionary. But activists should have asked why so many minority students could not meet those standards; why so many more would never be in a position to apply. The revolutionary demand would have called for a reform of primary and secondary schools.

To improve the education of disadvantaged students requires social changes which educational institutions alone cannot make, of course. Parents of such students need jobs and good housing; the students themselves need to grow up with three meals a day, in safe neighborhoods. But disadvantaged students also require good teachers. Good teachers—not fancy electronic gadgets—to teach them to read and to write. Teachers who are not overwhelmed; teachers with sufficient time to devote to individual students; to inspire. In the late sixties, civil rights activists might have harnessed the great idealism that the southern movement inspired in Americans. They might have called on teachers, might have demanded some kind of national literacy campaign for children of the poor—white and nonwhite—at the earliest levels of learning.

25   But the opportunity passed. The guardians of institutional America in Washington were able to ignore the need for fundamental social changes. College and university administrators could proudly claim that their institutions had yielded, were open to minority groups. (There was proof in a handful of numbers computed each fall.) So less thought had to be given to the procession of teenagers who leave ghetto high schools disadvantaged, badly taught, unable to find decent jobs.

I wish as I write these things that I could be angry at those who mislabeled me. I wish I could enjoy the luxury of self-pity and cast myself as a kind of "invisible man."[1] But guilt is not disposed of so easily. The fact is that I complied with affirmative action. I permitted myself to be prized. Even after publicly voicing objections to affirmative action, I accepted its benefits. I continued to indicate my race on applications for financial aid. (It didn't occur to me to leave the question unanswered.) I'd apply for prestigious national fellowships and tell friends that the reason I won was because I was a minority. (This by way of accepting the fellowship money.) I published essays admitting that I was not a minority—saw my by-line in magazines and journals which once had seemed very remote from my life. It was a scholarship boy's dream come true. I enjoyed being—not being— a minority student, the featured speaker. I was invited to lecture at schools

---

1   *invisible man* Cf. Ralph Ellison's *Invisible Man* (1952), which tells the story of an unnamed African-American man dealing with racism and intolerance in the United States.

that only a few years before would have rejected my application for graduate study. My life was unlike that of any other graduate student I knew. On weekends I flew cross country to say—through a microphone—that I was not a minority.

Someone told me this: A senior faculty member in the English department at Berkeley smirked when my name came up in a conversation. Someone at the sherry party had wondered if the professor had seen my latest article on affirmative action. The professor replied with arch politeness, "And what does Mr. Rodriguez have to complain about?"

You who read this act of contrition should know that by writing it I seek a kind of forgiveness—not yours. The forgiveness, rather, of those many persons whose absence from higher education permitted me to be classed a minority student. I wish that they would read this. I doubt they ever will.

Questions

1. Describe Rodriguez's objections to affirmative action. Do you agree or disagree? Why?
2. Comment on Rodriguez's use of varied sentence structure. What are the effects of the extremely short sentences in the essay?
3. Discuss how the last paragraph of this piece frames (or re-frames) the writing that precedes it.

GLORIA STEINEM

Supremacy Crimes

(1999)

Gloria Steinem (1934–) is a pioneering journalist and feminist activist. She was one of the co-founders of the feminist magazine Ms. *and has also worked as a staff writer for* The New Yorker.

This essay was written in response to the shootings at Columbine High School on 20 April 1999.

You've seen the ocean of television coverage, you've read the headlines: "How to Spot a Troubled Kid," "Twisted Teens," "When Teens Fall Apart."

After the slaughter in Colorado that inspired those phrases, dozens of copycat threats were reported in the same generalized way: "Junior high students charged with conspiracy to kill students and teachers" (in Texas); "Five honor students overheard planning a June graduation bombing" (in New York); "More than 100 minor threats reported statewide" (in Pennsylvania). In response, the White House held an emergency strategy session titled "Children, Violence, and Responsibility." Nonetheless, another attack was soon reported: "Youth With 2 Guns Shoots 6 at Georgia School."

I don't know about you, but I've been talking back to the television set, waiting for someone to tell us the obvious: it's not "youth," "our children," or "our teens." It's our sons—and "our" can usually be read as "white," "middle class," and "heterosexual."

We know that hate crimes, violent and otherwise, are overwhelmingly committed by white men who are apparently straight. The same is true for an even higher percentage of impersonal, resentment-driven, mass killings like those in Colorado; the sort committed for no economic or rational gain except the need to say, "I'm superior because I can kill." Think of Charles Starkweather, who reported feeling powerful and serene after murdering ten women and men in the 1950s; or the shooter who climbed the University of Texas Tower in 1966, raining down death to gain celebrity. Think of the engineering student at the University of Montreal who resented females' ability to study that subject, and so shot to death 14 women students in 1989, while saying, "I'm against feminism." Think of nearly all those who have killed impersonally in the workplace, the post office, McDonald's.

White males—usually intelligent, middle class, and heterosexual, or try- 5
ing desperately to appear so—also account for virtually all the serial, sexually motivated, sadistic killings, those characterized by stalking, imprison-
ing, torturing, and, "owning" victims in death. Think of Edmund Kemper,
who began by killing animals, then murdered his grandparents, yet was
released to sexually torture and dismember college students and other
young women until he himself decided he "didn't want to kill *all* the coeds
in the world." Or David Berkowitz, the Son of Sam, who murdered *some*
women in order to feel in control of *all* women. Or consider Ted Bundy,
the charming, snobbish young would-be lawyer who tortured and murdered as many as 40 women, usually beautiful students who were symbols
of the economic class he longed to join. As for John Wayne Gacy, he was
obsessed with maintaining the public mask of masculinity, and so hid his
homosexuality by killing and burying men and boys with whom he had had
sex.

These "senseless" killings begin to seem less mysterious when you consider that they were committed disproportionately by white, non-poor
males, the group most likely to become hooked on the drug of superiority. It's a drug pushed by a male-dominant culture that presents dominance
as a natural right; a racist hierarchy that falsely elevates whiteness; a mate-
rialist society that equates superiority with possessions, and a homophobic
one that empowers only one form of sexuality.

As Elliott Leyton reports in *Hunting Humans: The Rise of the Modern Multiple Murderer*, these killers see their behavior as "an appropriate—even
'manly'—response to the frustrations and disappointments that are a normal part of life." In other words, it's not their life experiences that are the
problem, it's the impossible expectation of dominance to which they've
become addicted.

This is not about blame. This is about causation. If anything, ending the
massive cultural cover-up of supremacy crimes should make heroes out of
boys and men who reject violence, especially those who reject the notion
of superiority altogether. Even if one believes in a biogenetic component
of male aggression, the very existence of gentle men proves that socialization can override it.

Nor is this about attributing such crimes to a single cause. Addiction to
the drug of supremacy is not their only root, just the deepest and most
ignored one. Additional reasons why this country has such a high rate of
violence include the plentiful guns that make killing seem as unreal as a
video game; male violence in the media that desensitizes viewers in much
the same way that combat killers are desensitized in training; affluence
that allows maximum access to violence-as-entertainment; a national history of genocide and slavery; the romanticizing of frontier violence and organized crime; not to mention extremes of wealth and poverty and the illusion that both are deserved.

10   But it is truly remarkable, given the relative reasons for anger at injustice in this country, that white, non-poor men have a near-monopoly on multiple killings of strangers, whether serial and sadistic or mass and random. How can we ignore this obvious fact? Others may kill to improve their own condition—in self-defense, or for money or drugs; to eliminate enemies; to declare turf in drive-by shootings; even for a jacket or a pair of sneakers—but white males addicted to supremacy kill even when it worsens their condition or ends in suicide.

Men of color and females are capable of serial and mass killing, and commit just enough to prove it. Think of Colin Ferguson, the crazed black man on the Long Island Railroad, or Wayne Williams, the young black man in Atlanta who kidnapped and killed black boys, apparently to conceal his homosexuality. Think of Aileen Carol Wuornos, the white prostitute in Florida who killed abusive johns "in self-defense," or Waneta Hoyt, the upstate New York woman who strangled her five infant children between 1965 and 1971, disguising their cause of death as sudden infant death syndrome. Such crimes are rare enough to leave a haunting refrain of disbelief as evoked in Pat Parker's poem "Jonestown": "Black folks do not / Black folks do not / Black folks do not commit suicide." And yet they did.

Nonetheless, the proportion of serial killings that are not committed by white males is about the same as the proportion of anorexics who are not female. Yet we discuss the gender, race, and class components of anorexia, but not the role of the same factors in producing epidemics among the powerful.

The reasons are buried deep in the culture, so invisible that only by reversing our assumptions can we reveal them.

Suppose, for instance, that young black males—or any other men of color—had carried out the slaughter in Colorado. Would the media reports be so willing to describe the murderers as "our children"? Would there be so little discussion about the boys' race? Would experts be calling the motive a mystery, or condemning the high school cliques for making those young men feel like "outsiders"? Would there be the same empathy for parents who gave the murderers luxurious homes, expensive cars, even rescued them from brushes with the law? Would there be as much attention to generalized causes, such as the dangers of violent video games and recipes for bombs on the Internet?

15   As for the victims, if racial identities had been reversed, would racism remain so little discussed? In fact, the killers themselves said they were targeting blacks and athletes. They used a racial epithet, shot a black male student in the head, and then laughed over the fact that they could see his brain. What if *that* had been reversed?

What if these two young murderers, who were called "fags" by some of the jocks at Columbine High School, actually had been gay? Would they have got the same sympathy for being gay-baited? What if they had been lovers? Would we hear as little about their sexuality as we now do, even though only their own homophobia could have given the word "fag" such power to humiliate them?

Take one more leap of the imagination: suppose these killings had been planned and executed by young women—of any race, sexuality, or class. Would the media still be so disinterested in the role played by gender-conditioning? Would journalists assume that female murderers had suffered from being shut out of access to power in high school, so much so that they were pushed beyond their limits? What if dozens, even hundreds of young women around the country had made imitative threats—as young men have done—expressing admiration for a well-planned massacre and promising to do the same? Would we be discussing their youth more than their gender, as is the case so far with these male killers?

I think we begin to see that our national self-examination is ignoring something fundamental, precisely because it's like the air we breathe: the white male factor, the middle-class and heterosexual one, and the promise of superiority it carries. Yet this denial is self-defeating—to say the least. We will never reduce the number of violent Americans, from bullies to killers, without challenging the assumptions on which masculinity is based: that males are superior to females, that they must find a place in a male hierarchy, and that the ability to dominate *someone* is so important that even a mere insult can justify lethal revenge. There are plenty of studies to support this view. As Dr. James Gilligan concluded in *Violence: Reflections on a National Epidemic*, "If humanity is to evolve beyond the propensity toward violence ... then it can only do so by recognizing the extent to which the patriarchal code of honor and shame generates and obligates male violence."

I think the way out can only be found through a deeper reversal: just as we as a society have begun to raise our daughters more like our sons— more like whole people—we must begin to raise our sons more like our daughters—that is, to value empathy as well as hierarchy; to measure success by other people's welfare as well as their own.

But first, we have to admit and name the truth about supremacy crimes.   20

Questions

1. What is Steinem's thesis?
2. What specific rhetorical techniques does Steinem employ in making her argument? What evidence does she provide, from where, and how exactly does she present it? Is her argument effective? Why or why not?

It's Not Like Falling Asleep

(2000)

Robert Murray (1964–) and his brother Roger were sentenced to death in 1992 for the first-degree murders of Dean Morrison and Jackie Appelhans. Robert Murray received notice of his order of execution in 1999. He is the author of the book Life on Death Row *(2004), which examines the lives of death row prisoners held in Florence, Arizona.*

In this essay, published in 2000 in Harper's Magazine, *Murray explains that a death-row inmate is given a choice of execution methods.*

The idea of death and dying is never far from my mind. Before coming to death row, I hadn't given much thought to my own demise. I've come very close to death a couple of times, but they were mere moments.

Now not only does the state of Arizona intend to kill me; they want me to participate in the process by deciding the method they will use. It's a strange form of polite behavior. For years, state officials have determined every aspect of my existence. Now, in a sudden burst of good manners, they want to add a bit of civility to my death by offering me a choice.

They've given me two methods to consider: lethal injection and lethal gas. I often imagine myself in the gas chamber and try to guess at the difference between dying there and dying by lethal injection. But I just keep coming back to the outcome. I wanted to ask someone's advice about which method I should choose, but dead is dead, and the handful of people I might have consulted are testaments to this finality.

Lethal injection is now paraded about as the easy way to die. Most of the public is under the impression that since lethal injection seems simple and painless it somehow makes killing more acceptable. Witnesses to injection executions come away with the illusory perception that a patient has fallen asleep. Typical witness testimony goes something like this:

5 "Well, he just seemed to fall asleep."

"Could you better describe the event?"

"We were standing there, and suddenly the curtain opened and there he was, just lying there."

"What happened next?"

"Well, like I said, he was just lying there looking at the ceiling. His lips were moving a little, and he ... well, you know, he just closed his eyes and went to sleep. I wasn't expecting it to be so easy and fast. He just went to sleep."

Easy as going to sleep. I have thought about this for literally hundreds of   10
hours. Easy as falling asleep. I guess everybody wants to die as easily as they fall asleep.

The state of Arizona has given me a description of the two methods of execution from which I am allowed to choose:

One (1) pound of sodium cyanide is placed in a container underneath the gas chamber chair. The chair is made of perforated metal which allows the cyanide gas to pass through and fill the chamber. A bowl below the chair contains sulfuric acid and distilled water. A lever is pulled and the sodium cyanide falls into the solution, releasing the gas. It takes the prisoner several minutes to die. After the execution, the excess gas is released through an exhaust pipe which extends about 50 feet above the Death House.

Inmates executed by lethal injection are brought into the injection room a few minutes prior to the appointed time of execution. He/she is then strapped to a gurney-type bed and two (2) sets of intravenous tubes are inserted, one (1) in each arm. The three (3) drugs used include: Sodium Pentothal (a sedative intended to put the inmate to sleep); Pavulon (stops breathing and paralyzes the muscular system); and Potassium Chloride (causes the heart to stop). Death by lethal injection is not painful and the inmate goes to sleep prior to the fatal effects of the Pavulon and Potassium Chloride.

These descriptions do not begin to illustrate the overall reality of an execution. The claim "Death by lethal injection is not painful ..." is far from accurate, and "going to sleep" with an overdose of sodium pentothal isn't all it's cracked up to be. It's death by any definition. The pain lies in the years, months, days, hours, minutes, and seconds leading up to the moment of execution. The pain lies in choosing your own method of execution. Going to sleep while strapped to a table is the least of it; in fact, it ends a great deal of pain—the terror, nightmares, and constant internal struggles.

The gas chamber was introduced to Arizona in the 1930s. Before that, the state hanged people. Nooses from every execution were saved and displayed in glass cases on the walls of the witness chamber of the death house. Hanging was discontinued after a woman was accidentally decapitated in 1930.

On April 6, 1992, at 12:18 A.M., Donald Harding was pronounced dead after spending a full eleven minutes in the state's gas chamber. It was Arizona's first execution in twenty-nine years, and state officials were somewhat out of practice. The spectacle of Harding gasping in the execution chamber was a little too hard for people to handle. In response, a movement grew to make executions more "humane."

15   Suddenly there was a new political crisis. People were outraged. Politicians took to the stump. State execution was cruel, ghastly, horrid. It took a prisoner eleven minutes to cough up his life to the gas. Of course, if executions could be made to seem more humane, that was something else altogether.

It was a wonderful political banner to wave come election time: Arizona would continue to execute people, but they would be *nice* executions. The politicians went about their task with glee. They preserved their right to kill people by coming up with a new way to kill people. Lethal injection was their new champion, and champion it they did.

Seven months after Harding's execution, a new law was born: "Any person sentenced to death prior to November 23, 1992, is afforded a choice of execution by either lethal gas or lethal injection. Inmates receiving death after November 23, 1992, are to be executed by lethal injection."

As it happened, my brother Roger and I were sentenced to death on October 26, 1992. We were among the lucky few who were given a Hobson's choice[1] about how we should die.

Offering prisoners a "humane" execution seems to be the latest strategy to keep capital punishment alive. But the notion that any execution could be humane eludes me. People today seem generally happy with the idea of lethal injection, as long as it is done in a neat, sanitary, easy-to-watch fashion. I'm not sure what this says about our society. However, I am sure most people don't grasp the reality of the "sleeping" death of which they so widely approve. Indeed, many witnesses leave an execution with a serene look on their faces, as if they'd just seen a somewhat pleasant movie. To my mind, it's actually the witnesses who are falling asleep at injection killings, lulled by the calmness of it all.

20   As I see it, death by injection is very like being tossed out of an airplane. Suppose I'm told that on November 3, someone will escort me from my cell, take me up in an airplane, and, at three o'clock in the afternoon, toss me out without a parachute. After a few minutes, my body will hit a target area, killing me immediately. It's an easy, instant, painless death. The impact of hitting the ground after falling several thousand feet will kill me as instantly and effectively as lethal injection.

---

1 *Hobson's choice* An apparent choice with no true alternatives. Named for Thomas Hobson (1544–1631) who kept a stable and insisted customers take the horse nearest the stable door, or none at all.

Killing inmates by tossing them out of airplanes would of course be unacceptable to the public. But why? It's as fast and effective as lethal injection. The terror of falling two minutes isn't all that different from the terror of lying strapped to a table; and neither is physically painful. There's a similar waiting process before each execution. If an airplane is used, you wait for the time it takes the aircraft to take off and reach the target area at the proper altitude. For lethal injection, you wait in the death house until everything's ready and all possibility of a stay of execution has been exhausted. In an airplane, a cargo door is opened; in the death house, a curtain across the viewing window is drawn back. In an airplane, you are thrown to an absolute death and witnesses watch your body fall. In the death house, you are strapped to a gurney and witnesses watch state officials inject you with sodium pentothal. In both cases, death is sudden and final.

To me they are the same. I will feel the same powerful emotions and chaotic anxiety either way. But the public would never describe my death by falling from an aircraft as "simply falling asleep." They would be outraged. Politicians would rush to give speeches about giving prisoners a "choice," and the law would be changed.

The public would cry out, not because the prisoner died an agonizing and painful death but because most people feel that the anxiety of being tossed from an aircraft without a parachute would be too terrible for an inmate to bear, and the spectacle of death would be too terrible for observers to bear. In this case, the public would be forced to understand the emotions an inmate feels before execution; when lethal injection is used, all such emotions are hidden behind a veil that is not drawn aside until the moment before death.

This airplane analogy is as close as I can come to illustrating the fallacy of the humane execution. There is much more to death by injection than just falling asleep, beginning with the long wait on death row (where execution is a constant presence), the terror of being taken to the death house, the helpless panic of being strapped to a table, and finally the sense of utter loss as the curtain is opened. All of the fear and anxiety of falling from an aircraft is present when the injection begins. Both are horrible by any measure. And neither is anything like falling asleep.

Questions

1. What exactly is Murray's argument?
2. Murray characterizes the choice given to him by state officials as "a strange form of polite behavior" (paragraph 2). Is this characterization justified or not, in your view?
3. Do you agree that "the airplane method" is essentially the same as lethal injection?
4. Does Murray's identity (a death-row prisoner, who maintains his innocence) strengthen or weaken his argument, or do neither? Why?

BARBARA EHRENREICH

Maid to Order

The Politics of Other Women's Work
(2000)

A social critic, feminist, journalist, and essayist, Barbara Ehrenreich (1941–) has contributed to publications such as The New York Times, Harper's, Time, Mother Jones, *and* The Atlantic Monthly. *She has written thirteen books, including the bestseller* Nickel and Dimed *(2001) in which she describes her attempt to live on low-wage jobs for one year.*

In this essay, Ehrenreich describes her experience working as a domestic cleaner and analyzes Americans' reliance on house-cleaning services.

In line with growing class polarization, the classic posture of submission is making a stealthy comeback. "We scrub your floors the old-fashioned way," boasts the brochure from Merry Maids, the largest of the residential-cleaning services that have sprung up in the last two decades, "on our hands and knees." This is not a posture that independent "cleaning ladies" willingly assume—preferring, like most people who clean their own homes, the sponge mop wielded from a standing position. In her comprehensive 1999 guide to homemaking, *Home Comforts,* Cheryl Mendelson warns: "Never ask hired housecleaners to clean your floors on their hands and knees; the request is likely to be regarded as degrading." But in a society in which 40 percent of the wealth is owned by 1 percent of households while the bottom 20 percent reports negative assets, the degradation of others is readily purchased. Kneepads entered American political discourse as a tool of the sexually subservient, but employees of Merry Maids, The Maids International, and other corporate cleaning services spend hours every day on these kinky devices, wiping up the drippings of the affluent.

I spent three weeks in September 1999 as an employee of The Maids International in Portland, Maine, cleaning, along with my fellow team members, approximately sixty houses containing a total of about 250 scrubbable floors—bathrooms, kitchens, and entryways requiring the hands-and-knees treatment. It's a different world down there below knee level, one that few adults voluntarily enter. Here you find elaborate dust structures held together by a scaffolding of dog hair; dried bits of pasta glued to the floor by their sauce; the congealed remains of gravies, jellies, contraceptive creams, vomit, and urine. Sometimes, too, you encounter some fragment of a human being: a child's legs, stamping by in disgust because the maids are still present when he gets home from school; more commonly, the Joan & David[1]-clad feet and electrolyzed calves of the female homeowner. Look up and you may find this person staring at you, arms folded, in anticipation of an overlooked stain. In rare instances she may try to help in some vague, symbolic way, by moving the cockatoo's cage, for example, or apologizing for the leaves shed by a miniature indoor tree. Mostly, though, she will not see you at all and may even sit down with her mail at a table in the very room you are cleaning, where she would remain completely unaware of your existence unless you were to crawl under that table and start gnawing away at her ankles.

Housework, as you may recall from the feminist theories of the Sixties and Seventies, was supposed to be the great equalizer of women. Whatever else women did—jobs, school, child care—we also did housework, and if there were some women who hired others to do it for them, they seemed too privileged and rare to include in the theoretical calculus. All women were workers, and the home was their workplace—unpaid and unsupervised, to be sure, but a workplace no less than the offices and factories men repaired to every morning. If men thought of the home as a site of leisure and recreation—a "haven in a heartless world"—this was to ignore the invisible female proletariat that kept it cozy and humming. We were on the march now, or so we imagined, united against a society that devalued our labor even as it waxed mawkish over "the family" and "the home." Shoulder to shoulder and arm in arm, women were finally getting up off the floor.

In the most eye-catching elaboration of the home-as-workplace theme, Marxist feminists Maria Rosa Dallacosta and Selma James proposed in 1972 that the home was in fact an economically productive and significant workplace, an extension of the actual factory, since housework served to "reproduce the labor power" of others, particularly men. The male worker would hardly be in shape to punch in for his shift, after all, if some woman had not fed him, laundered his clothes, and cared for the children who were his contribution to the next generation of workers. If the home was a quasi-industrial workplace staffed by women for the ultimate benefit of the capitalists, then it followed that "wages for housework" was the obvious demand.

But when most American feminists, Marxist or otherwise, asked the   5

1 *Joan & David* Upscale brand of American women's footwear.

Marxist question *cui bono?*[1] they tended to come up with a far simpler answer—men. If women were the domestic proletariat, then men made up the class of domestic exploiters, free to lounge while their mates scrubbed. In consciousness-raising groups, we railed against husbands and boyfriends who refused to pick up after themselves, who were unaware of housework at all, unless of course it hadn't been done. The "dropped socks," left by a man for a woman to gather up and launder, joined lipstick and spike heels as emblems of gender oppression. And if, somewhere, a man had actually dropped a sock in the calm expectation that his wife would retrieve it, it was a sock heard round the world. Wherever second-wave feminism took root, battles broke out between lovers and spouses over sticky countertops, piled-up laundry, and whose turn it was to do the dishes.

The radical new idea was that housework was not only a relationship between a woman and a dust bunny or an unmade bed; it also defined a relationship between human beings, typically husbands and wives. This represented a marked departure from the more conservative Betty Friedan, who, in *The Feminine Mystique,* had never thought to enter the male sex into the equation, as either part of the housework problem or part of an eventual solution. She raged against a society that consigned its educated women to what she saw as essentially janitorial chores, beneath "the abilities of a woman of average or normal human intelligence," and, according to unidentified studies she cited, "peculiarly suited to the capacities of feeble-minded girls." But men are virtually exempt from housework in *The Feminine Mystique*—why drag them down too? At one point she even disparages a "Mrs. G.," who "somehow couldn't get her housework done before her husband came home at night and was so tired then that he had to do it." Educated women would just have to become more efficient so that housework could no longer "expand to fill the time available."

Or they could hire other women to do it—an option approved by Friedan in *The Feminine Mystique* as well as by the National Organization for Women, which she had helped launch. At the 1973 congressional hearings on whether to extend the Fair Labor Standards Act to household workers, NOW testified on the affirmative side, arguing that improved wages and working conditions would attract more women to the field, and offering the seemingly self-contradictory prediction that "the demand for household help inside the home will continue to increase as more women seek occupations outside the home." One NOW member added, on a personal note: "Like many young women today, I am in school in order to develop a rewarding career for myself. I also have a home to run and can fully conceive of the need for household help as my free time at home becomes

---

1   *cui bono* "Who benefits?" (Latin). Adage meaning the person who commits a crime is often the one who has something to gain from it.

more and more restricted. Women know [that] housework is dirty, tedious work, and they are willing to pay to have it done...." On the aspirations of the women paid to do it, assuming that at least some of them were bright enough to entertain a few, neither Friedan nor these members of NOW had, at the time, a word to say.

So the insight that distinguished the more radical, post-Friedan cohort of feminists was that when we talk about housework, we are really talking, yet again, about power. Housework was not degrading because it was manual labor, as Friedan thought, but because it was embedded in degrading relationships and inevitably served to reinforce them. To make a mess that another person will have to deal with—the dropped socks, the toothpaste sprayed on the bathroom mirror, the dirty dishes left from a late-night snack—is to exert domination in one of its more silent and intimate forms. One person's arrogance—or indifference, or hurry—becomes another person's occasion for toil. And when the person who is cleaned up after is consistently male, while the person who cleans up is consistently female, you have a formula for reproducing male domination from one generation to the next.

Hence the feminist perception of housework as one more way by which men exploit women or, more neutrally stated, as "a symbolic enactment of gender relations." An early German women's liberation cartoon depicted a woman scrubbing on her hands and knees while her husband, apparently excited by this pose, approaches from behind, unzipping his fly. Hence, too, the second-wave feminists' revulsion at the hiring of maids, especially when they were women of color: At a feminist conference I attended in 1980, poet Audre Lorde[1] chose to insult the all too-white audience by accusing them of being present only because they had black housekeepers to look after their children at home. She had the wrong crowd; most of the assembled radical feminists would no sooner have employed a black maid than they would have attached Confederate flag stickers to the rear windows of their cars. But accusations like hers, repeated in countless conferences and meetings, reinforced our rejection of the servant option. There already were at least two able-bodied adults in the average home—a man and a woman—and the hope was that, after a few initial skirmishes, they would learn to share the housework graciously.

A couple of decades later, however, the average household still falls far short of that goal. True, women do less housework than they did before the feminist revolution and the rise of the two-income family: down from an average of 30 hours per week in 1965 to 17.5 hours in 1995, according to a July 1999 study by the University of Maryland. Some of that decline reflects a relaxation of standards rather than a redistribution of chores; women still do two thirds of whatever housework—including bill paying,

10

---

1   *Audre Lorde* (1934–92) Influential black lesbian poet and activist.

pet care, tidying, and lawn care—gets done. The inequity is sharpest for the most despised of household chores, cleaning: in the thirty years between 1965 and 1995, men increased the time they spent scrubbing, vacuuming, and sweeping by 240 percent—all the way up to 1.7 hours per week—while women decreased their cleaning time by only 7 percent, to 6.7 hours per week. The averages conceal a variety of arrangements, of course, from minutely negotiated sharing to the most clichéd division of labour, as described by one woman to the *Washington Post*: "I take care of the inside, he takes care of the outside." But perhaps the most disturbing finding is that almost the entire increase in male participation took place between the 1970s and the mid-1980s. Fifteen years after the apparent cessation of hostilities, it is probably not to soon to announce the score: in the "chore wars" of the Seventies and Eighties, women gained a little ground, but overall, and after a few strategic concessions, men won.

Enter then, the cleaning lady as *dea ex machina*,[1] restoring tranquility as well as order to the home. Marriage counselors recommend her as an alternative to squabbling, as do many within the cleaning industry itself. A Chicago cleaning woman quotes one of her clients as saying that if she gives up the service, "my husband and I will be divorced in six months." When the trend toward hiring out was just beginning to take off, in 1988, the owner of a Merry Maids franchise in Arlington, Massachusetts, told the *Christian Science Monitor*, "I kid some women. I say, 'We even save marriages. In this new eighties period you expect more from the male partner, but very often you don't get the cooperation you would like to have. The alternative is to pay somebody to come in....'" Another Merry Maids franchise owner has learned to capitalize more directly on housework-related spats; he closes between 30 and 35 percent of his sales by making follow-up calls Saturday mornings, which is "prime time for arguing over the fact that the house is a mess." The micro-defeat of feminism in the household opened a new door for women, only this time it was the servants' entrance.

In 1999, somewhere between 14 and 18 percent of households employed an outsider to do the cleaning, and the numbers have been rising dramatically. Mediamark Research reports a 53 percent increase, between 1995 and 1999, in the number of households using a hired cleaner or service once a month or more, and Maritz Marketing finds that 30 percent of the people who hired help in 1999 did so for the first time that year. Among my middle-class, professional women friends and acquaintances, including some who made important contributions to the early feminist analysis of housework, the employment of a maid is now nearly universal. This sudden emergence of a servant class is consistent with what

1   *dea ex machina* "Goddess from a machine," a play on the standard reference "deus ex machina" (Latin), which describes a miraculous turn of events in a literary work, usually an outside force intervening to resolve the plot.

some economists have called the "Brazilianization" of the American economy: We are dividing along the lines of traditional Latin American societies—into a tiny overclass and a huge underclass, with the latter available to perform intimate household services for the former. Or, to put it another way, the home, or at least the affluent home, is finally becoming what radical feminists in the Seventies only imagined it was—a true "workplace" for women and a tiny, though increasingly visible, part of the capitalist economy. And the question is: As the home becomes a workplace for someone else, is it still a place where you would want to live?

Strangely, or perhaps not so strangely at all, no one talks about the "politics of housework" anymore. The demand for "wages for housework" has sunk to the status of a curio, along with the consciousness-raising groups in which women once rallied support in their struggles with messy men. In the academy, according to the feminist sociologists I interviewed, housework has lost much of its former cachet—in part, I suspect, because fewer sociologists actually do it. Most Americans, over 80 percent, still clean their homes, but the minority who do not include a sizable fraction of the nation's opinion-makers and culture-producers—professors, writers, editors, politicians, talking heads, and celebrities of all sorts. In their homes, the politics of housework is becoming a politics not only of gender but of race and class—and these are subjects that the opinion-making elite, if not most Americans, generally prefer to avoid.

Even the number of paid houseworkers is hard to pin down. The Census Bureau reports that there were 549,000 domestic workers in 1998, up 9 percent since 1996, but this may be a considerable underestimate, since so much of the servant economy is still underground. In 1995, two years after Zoe Baird lost her chance to be attorney general for paying her undocumented nanny off the books, the *Los Angeles Times* reported that fewer than 10 percent of those Americans who paid a housecleaner reported those payments to the IRS. Sociologist Mary Romero, one of the few academics who retain an active interest in housework and the women who do it for pay, offers an example of how severe the undercounting can be: the 1980 Census found only 1,063 "private household workers" in El Paso, Texas, though the city estimated their numbers at 13,400 and local bus drivers estimated that half of the 28,300 daily bus trips were taken by maids going to and from work. The honesty of employers has increased since the Baird scandal, but most experts believe that household workers remain, in large part, uncounted and invisible to the larger economy.

One thing you can say with certainty about the population of household workers is that they are disproportionately women of color: "lower" kinds of people for a "lower" kind of work. Of the "private household cleaners and servants" it managed to locate in 1998, the Bureau of Labor Statistics

15

reports that 36.8 percent were Hispanic, 15.8 percent black, and 2.7 percent "other." Certainly the association between housecleaning and minority status is well established in the psyches of the white employing class. When my daughter, Rosa, was introduced to the wealthy father of a Harvard classmate, he ventured that she must have been named for a favorite maid. And Audre Lorde can perhaps be forgiven for her intemperate accusation at the feminist conference mentioned above when we consider an experience she had in 1967: "I wheel my two-year-old daughter in a shopping cart through a supermarket ... and a little white girl riding past in her mother's cart calls out excitedly, 'Oh look, Mommy, a baby maid.'" But the composition of the household workforce is hardly fixed and has changed with the life chances of the different ethnic groups. In the late nineteenth century, Irish and German immigrants served the northern upper and middle classes, then left for the factories as soon as they could. Black women replaced them, accounting for 60 percent of all domestics in the 1940s, and dominated the field until other occupations began to open up to them. Similarly, West Coast maids were disproportionately Japanese American until that group, too, found more congenial options. Today, the color of the hand that pushes the sponge varies from region to region: Chicanas in the Southwest, Caribbeans in New York, native Hawaiians in Hawaii, whites, many of recent rural extraction, in Maine.

The great majority—though again, no one knows exact numbers—of paid housekeepers are freelancers, or "independents," who find their clients through agencies or networks of already employed friends and relatives. To my acquaintances in the employing class, the freelance housekeeper seems to be a fairly privileged and prosperous type of worker, a veritable aristocrat of labor—sometimes paid $15 an hour or more and usually said to be viewed as a friend or even treated as "one of the family." But the shifting ethnic composition of the workforce tells another story: this is a kind of work that many have been trapped in—by racism, imperfect English skills, immigration status, or lack of education—but few have happily chosen. Interviews with independent maids collected by Romero and by sociologist Judith Rollins, who herself worked as a maid in the Boston area in the early Eighties, confirm that the work is undesirable to those who perform it. Even when the pay is deemed acceptable, the hours may be long and unpredictable; there are usually no health benefits, no job security, and, if the employer has failed to pay Social Security taxes (in some cases because the maid herself prefers to be paid off the books), no retirement benefits. And the pay is often far from acceptable. The BLS found full-time "private household cleaners and servants" earning a median annual income of $12,220 in 1998, which is $1,092 below the poverty level for a family of three. Recall that in 1993 Zoe Baird paid her undocumented household workers about $5 an hour out of her earnings of $507,000 a year.

At the most lurid extreme there is slavery. A few cases of forced labor pop up in the press every year, most recently—in some nightmare version of globalization—of undocumented women held in servitude by high-ranking staff members of the United Nations, the World Bank, and the International Monetary Fund. Consider the suit brought by Elizabeth Senghor, a Senegalese woman who alleged that she was forced to work fourteen-hour days for her employers in Manhattan, without any regular pay, and was given no accommodations beyond a pull-out bed in her employers' living room. Hers is not a particularly startling instance of domestic slavery; no beatings or sexual assaults were charged, and Ms. Senghor was apparently fed. What gives this case a certain rueful poignancy is that her employer, former U.N. employee Marie Angelique Savane, is one of Senegal's leading women's rights advocates and had told *The Christian Science Monitor* in 1986 about her efforts to get the Senegalese to "realize that being a woman can mean other things than simply having children, taking care of the house."

Mostly, though, independent maids—and sometimes the women who employ them—complain about the peculiar intimacy of the employer-employee relationship. Domestic service is an occupation that predates the refreshing impersonality of capitalism by several thousand years, conditions of work being still largely defined by the idiosyncrasies of the employers. Some of them seek friendship and even what their maids describe as "therapy," though they are usually quick to redraw the lines once the maid is perceived as overstepping. Others demand deference bordering on servility, while a growing fraction of the nouveau riche is simply out of control. In August 1999, the *New York Times* reported on the growing problem of dinner parties being disrupted by hostesses screaming at their help. To the verbal abuse add published reports of sexual and physical assaults—a young teenage boy, for example, kicking a live-in nanny for refusing to make sandwiches for him and his friends after school.

But for better or worse, capitalist rationality is finally making some headway into this weird preindustrial backwater. Corporate cleaning services now control 25 to 30 percent of the $1.4 billion housecleaning business, and perhaps their greatest innovation has been to abolish the mistress-maid relationship, with all its quirks and dependencies. The customer hires the service, not the maid, who has been replaced anyway by a team of two to four uniformed people, only one of whom—the team leader—is usually authorized to speak to the customer about the work at hand. The maids' wages, their Social Security taxes, their green cards, backaches, and child-care problems—all these are the sole concern of the company, meaning the local franchise owner. If there are complaints on either side, they are addressed to the franchise owner; the customer and the actual workers need never interact. Since the franchise owner is usually a middle-class white person, cleaning services are the ideal solution for anyone still sensitive enough to find the traditional employer-maid relationship morally vexing.

20   In a 1997 article about Merry Maids, *Franchise Times* reported tersely that the "category is booming, [the] niche is hot, too, as Americans look to outsource work even at home." Not all cleaning services do well, and there is a high rate of failure among informal, mom-and-pop services. The "boom" is concentrated among the national and international chains—outfits like Merry Maids, Molly Maids, Mini Maids, Maid Brigade, and The Maids International—all named, curiously enough, to highlight the more antique aspects of the industry, though the "maid" may occasionally be male. Merry Maids claimed to be growing at 15 to 20 percent a year in 1996, and spokesmen for both Molly Maids and The Maids International told me that their firms' sales are growing by 25 percent a year; local franchisers are equally bullish. Dan Libby, my boss at The Maids, confided to me that he could double his business overnight if only he could find enough reliable employees. To this end, The Maids offers a week's paid vacation, health insurance after ninety days, and a free breakfast every morning consisting—at least where I worked—of coffee, doughnuts, bagels, and bananas. Some franchises have dealt with the tight labor market by participating in welfare-to-work projects that not only funnel employees to them but often subsidize their paychecks with public money, at least for the first few months of work (which doesn't mean the newly minted maid earns more, only that the company has to pay her less). The Merry Maids franchise in the city where I worked is conveniently located a block away from the city's welfare office.

Among the women I worked with at The Maids, only one said she had previously worked as an independent, and she professed to be pleased with her new status as a cleaning-service employee. She no longer needed a car to get her from house to house and could take a day off—unpaid of course—to stay home with a sick child without risking the loss of a customer. I myself could see the advantage of not having to deal directly with the customers, who were sometimes at home while we worked and eager to make use of their supervisory skills: criticisms of our methods, and demands that we perform unscheduled tasks, could simply be referred to the franchise owner.

But there are inevitable losses for the workers as any industry moves from the entrepreneurial to the industrial phase, probably most strikingly, in this case, in the matter of pay. At Merry Maids, I was promised $200 for a forty-hour week, the manager hastening to add that "you can't calculate it in dollars per hour" since the forty hours include all the time spent traveling from house to house—up to five houses a day—which is unpaid. The Maids International, with its straightforward starting rate of $6.63 an hour, seemed preferable, though this rate was conditional on perfect attendance. Miss one day and your wage dropped to $6 an hour for two weeks, a rule that weighed particularly heavily on those who had young children. In addition, I soon learned that management had ways of shaving off nearly an hour's worth of wages a day. We were told to arrive at 7:30 in the morning, but our billable hours began only after we had been teamed up, given our list of houses for the day, and packed off in the company car at about 8:00 A.M. At the end of the day, we were no longer paid from the moment we left the car, though as much as fifteen minutes of work—refilling cleaning-fluid bottles, etc.—remained to be done. So for a standard nine-hour day, the actual pay amounted to about $6.10 an hour, unless you were still being punished for an absence, in which case it came out to $5.50 an hour.

Nor are cleaning-service employees likely to receive any of the perks or tips familiar to independents—free lunches and coffee, cast-off clothing, or a Christmas gift of cash. When I asked, only one of my coworkers could recall ever receiving a tip, and that was a voucher for a free meal at a downtown restaurant owned by a customer. The customers of cleaning services are probably no stingier than the employers of independents; they just don't know their cleaning people and probably wouldn't even recognize them on the street. Plus, customers probably assume that the fee they pay the service—$25 per person-hour in the case of The Maids franchise I worked for—goes largely to the workers who do the actual cleaning.

But the most interesting feature of the cleaning-service chains, at least from an abstract, historical perspective, is that they are finally transforming the home into a fully capitalist-style workplace, and in ways that the old wages-for-housework advocates could never have imagined. A house is an innately difficult workplace to control, especially a house with ten or more rooms like so many of those we cleaned; workers may remain out of one another's sight for as much as an hour at a time. For independents, the ungovernable nature of the home-as-workplace means a certain amount of autonomy. They can take breaks (though this is probably ill-advised if the homeowner is on the premises); they can ease the monotony by listening to the radio or TV while they work. But cleaning services lay down rules meant to enforce a factorylike—or even conventlike—discipline on their far-flung employees. At The Maids, there were no breaks except for a daily ten-minute stop at a convenience store for coffee or "lunch"—meaning something like a slice of pizza. Otherwise, the time spent driving between houses was considered our "break" and the only chance to eat, drink, or (although this was also officially forbidden) smoke a cigarette. When the houses were spaced well apart, I could eat my sandwich in one sitting; otherwise it would have to be divided into as many as three separate, hasty snacks.

Within a customer's house, nothing was to touch our lips at all, not even water—a rule that, on hot days, I sometimes broke by drinking from a   25 bathroom faucet. TVs and radios were off-limits, and we were never, ever, to curse out loud, even in an ostensibly deserted house. There might be a homeowner secreted in some locked room, we were told, ear pressed to the door, or, more likely, a tape recorder or video camera running. At the time, I dismissed this as a scare story, but I have since come across ads for devices like the Tech-7 "incredible coin-sized camera" designed to "get a visual record of your babysitter's actions" and "watch employees to prevent theft." It was the threat or rumor of hidden recording devices that provided the final capitalist-industrial touch—supervision.

What makes the work most factorylike, though, is the intense Taylorization[1] imposed by the companies. An independent, or a person cleaning his or her own home, chooses where she will start and, within each room, probably tackles the most egregious dirt first. Or she may plan her work more or less ergonomically, first doing whatever can be done from a standing position and then squatting or crouching to reach the lower levels. But with the special "systems" devised by the cleaning services and imparted to employees via training videos, there are no such decisions to make. In The Maids' "healthy touch" system, which is similar to what I saw of the Merry Maids' system on the training tape I was shown during my interview, all cleaning is divided into four task areas—dusting, vacuuming, kitchens, and bathrooms—which are in turn divided among the team members. For each task area other than vacuuming, there is a bucket containing rags and the appropriate cleaning fluids, so the biggest decision an employee has to make is which fluid and scrubbing instrument to deploy on which kind of surface; almost everything else has been choreographed in advance. When vacuuming, you begin with the master bedroom; when dusting, with the first room off of the kitchen; then you move through the rooms going left to right. When entering each room, you proceed from left to right and top to bottom, and the same with each surface—top to bottom, left to right. Deviations are subject to rebuke, as I discovered when a team leader caught me moving my arm from right to left, then left to right, while wiping Windex over a French door.

It's not easy for anyone with extensive cleaning experience—and I include myself in this category—to accept this loss of autonomy. But I came to love the system: First, because if you hadn't always been traveling rigorously from left to right it would have been easy to lose your way in some of the larger houses and omit or redo a room. Second, some of the houses were already clean when we started, at least by any normal standards, thanks probably to a housekeeper who kept things up between our

---

1 *Taylorization* Approach to management and workplace psychology initiated by Frederick Winslow Taylor (1856–1915), which involves the creation of a standardized method for completing a task, designed to ensure that the task will be done quickly and uniformly.

visits; but the absence of visible dirt did not mean there was less work to do, for no surface could ever be neglected, so it was important to have "the system" to remind you of where you had been and what you had already "cleaned." No doubt the biggest advantage of the system, though, is that it helps you achieve the speed demanded by the company, which allots only so many minutes per house. After a week or two on the job, I found myself moving robotlike from surface to surface, grateful to have been relieved of the thinking process.

The irony, which I was often exhausted enough to derive a certain malicious satisfaction from, is that "the system" is not very sanitary. When I saw the training videos on "Kitchens" and "Bathrooms," I was at first baffled, and it took me several minutes to realize why: There is no water, or almost no water, involved. I had been taught to clean by my mother, a compulsive housekeeper who employed water so hot you needed rubber gloves to get into it and in such Niagaralike quantities that most microbes were probably crushed by the force of it before the soap suds had a chance to rupture their cell walls. But germs are never mentioned in the videos provided by The Maids. Our antagonists existed entirely in the visible world soap scum, dust, counter crud, dog hair, stains, and smears—and were attacked by damp rag or, in hardcore cases, by a scouring pad. We scrubbed only to remove impurities that might be detectable to a customer by hand or by eye; otherwise our only job was to wipe. Nothing was ever said, in the videos or in person, about the possibility of transporting bacteria, by rag or by hand, from bathroom to kitchen or even from one house to the next. Instead, it is the "cosmetic touches" that the videos emphasize and to which my trainer continually directed my eye. Fluff out all throw pillows and arrange them symmetrically. Brighten up stainless steel sinks with baby oil. Leave all spice jars, shampoos, etc., with their labels facing outward. Comb out the fringes of Persian carpets with a pick. Use the vacuum to create a special, fernlike pattern in the carpets. The loose ends of toilet paper and paper towel rolls have to be given a special fold. Finally, the house is sprayed with the service's signature air freshener—a cloying floral scent in our case, "baby fresh" in the case of the Mini Maids.

When I described the "methods" employed to housecleaning expert Cheryl Mendelson, she was incredulous. A rag moistened with disinfectant will not get a countertop clean, she told me, because most disinfectants are inactivated by contact with organic matter—i.e., dirt—so their effectiveness declines with each swipe of the rag. What you need is a detergent and hot water, followed by a rinse. As for floors, she judged the amount of water we used—one half of a small bucket—to be grossly inadequate, and, in fact, the water I wiped around on floors was often an unsavory gray. I also ran The Maids' cleaning methods by Don Aslett, author of numerous books on cleaning techniques and self-styled "number one cleaner in

America." He was hesitant to criticize The Maids directly, perhaps because he is, or told me he is, a frequent speaker at conventions of cleaning-service franchise holders, but he did tell me how he would clean a countertop: first, spray it thoroughly with an all-purpose cleaner, then let it sit for three to four minutes of "kill time," and finally wipe it dry with a clean cloth. Merely wiping the surface with a damp cloth, he said, just spreads the dirt around. But the point at The Maids, apparently, is not to clean so much as it is to create the appearance of having been cleaned, not to sanitize but to create a kind of stage setting for family life. And the stage setting Americans seem to prefer is sterile only in the metaphorical sense, like a motel room or the fake interiors in which soap operas and sitcoms take place.

30   But even ritual work takes its toll on those assigned to perform it. Turnover is dizzyingly high in the cleaning-service industry, and not only because of the usual challenges that confront the working poor—childcare problems, unreliable transportation, evictions, and prior health problems. As my long-winded interviewer at Merry Maids warned me, and my coworkers at The Maids confirmed, this is a physically punishing occupation, something to tide you over for a few months, not year after year. The hands-and-knees posture damages knees, with or without pads; vacuuming strains the back; constant wiping and scrubbing invite repetitive stress injuries even in the very young. In my three weeks as a maid, I suffered nothing more than a persistent muscle spasm in the right forearm, but the damage would have been far worse if I'd had to go home every day to my own housework and children, as most of my coworkers did, instead of returning to my motel and indulging in a daily after-work regimen of ice packs and stretches. Chores that seem effortless at home, even almost recreational when undertaken at will for twenty minutes or so at a time, quickly turn nasty when performed hour after hour, with few or no breaks and under relentless time pressure.

So far, the independent, entrepreneurial housecleaner is holding her own, but there are reasons to think that corporate cleaning services will eventually dominate the industry. New users often prefer the impersonal, standardized service offered by the chains, and, in a fast-growing industry, new users make up a sizable chunk of the total clientele. Government regulation also favors the corporate chains, whose spokesmen speak gratefully of the "Zoe Baird effect," referring to customers' worries about being caught paying an independent off the books. But the future of housecleaning may depend on the entry of even bigger players into the industry. Merry Maids, the largest of the chains, has the advantage of being a unit within the $6.4 billion ServiceMaster conglomerate, which includes such related businesses as TruGreen-ChemLawn, Terminix, Rescue Rooter, and Furniture Medic. Swisher International, best known as an industrial toilet-cleaning service, operates Swisher Maids in Georgia and North Carolina, and Sears may be feeling its way into the business. If large multinational firms establish a foothold in the industry, mobile professionals will be able to find the same branded and standardized product wherever they relocate. For the actual workers, the change will, in all likelihood, mean a more standardized and speeded-up approach to the work—less freedom of motion and fewer chances to pause.

The trend toward outsourcing the work of the home seems, at the moment, unstoppable. Two hundred years ago women often manufactured soap, candles, cloth, and clothing in their own homes, and the complaints of some women at the turn of the twentieth century that they had been "robbed by the removal of creative work" from the home sound pointlessly reactionary today. Not only have the skilled crafts, like sewing and cooking from scratch, left the home but many of the "white collar" tasks are on their way out, too. For a fee, new firms such as the San Francisco-based Les Concierges and Cross It Off Your List in Manhattan will pick up dry cleaning, baby-sit pets, buy groceries, deliver dinner, even do the Christmas shopping. With other firms and individuals offering to buy your clothes, organize your financial files, straighten out your closets, and wait around in your home for the plumber to show up, why would anyone want to hold on to the toilet cleaning?

Absent a major souring of the economy, there is every reason to think that Americans will become increasingly reliant on paid housekeepers and that this reliance will extend ever further down into the middle class. For one thing, the "time bind" on working parents shows no sign of loosening; people are willing to work longer hours at the office to pay for the people—housecleaners and baby-sitters—who are filling in for them at home. Children, once a handy source of household help, are now off at soccer practice or SAT prep classes; grandmother has relocated to a warmer climate or taken up a second career. Furthermore, despite the fact that people spend less time at home than ever, the square footage of new homes swelled by 33 percent between 1975 and 1998, to include "family rooms," home entertainment rooms, home offices, bedrooms, and often bathrooms for each family member. By the third quarter of 1999, 17 percent of new homes were larger than 3,000 square feet, which is usually considered the size threshold for household help, or the point at which a house becomes unmanageable to the people who live in it.

One more trend impels people to hire outside help, according to cleaning experts such as Aslett and Mendelson: fewer Americans know how to clean or even to "straighten up." I hear this from professional women defending their decision to hire a maid: "I'm just not very good at it myself" or "I wouldn't really know where to begin." Since most of us learn to clean from our parents (usually our mothers), any diminution of cleaning skills is transmitted from one generation to another, like a gene that can, in the appropriate environment, turn out to be disabling or lethal. Upper-middle-class children raised in the servant economy of the Nineties are bound to grow up as domestically incompetent as their parents and no less dependent on people to clean up after them. Mendelson sees this as a metaphysical loss, a "matter of no longer being physically centered in your environment." Having cleaned the rooms of many overly privileged teenagers in my stint with The Maids, I think the problem is a little more urgent than that. The American overclass is raising a generation of young people who will, without constant assistance, suffocate in their own detritus.

35   If there are moral losses, too, as Americans increasingly rely on paid household help, no one has been tactless enough to raise them. Almost everything we buy, after all, is the product of some other person's suffering and miserably underpaid labor. I clean my own house (though—full disclosure—I recently hired someone else to ready it for a short-term tenant), but I can hardly claim purity in any other area of consumption. I buy my jeans at The Gap, which is reputed to subcontract to sweatshops. I tend to favor decorative objects no doubt ripped off, by their purveyors, from scantily paid Third World craftspersons. Like everyone else, I eat salad greens just picked by migrant farm workers, some of them possibly children. And so on. We can try to minimize the pain that goes into feeding, clothing, and otherwise provisioning ourselves—by observing boycotts, checking for a union label, etc.—but there is no way to avoid it altogether without living in the wilderness on berries. Why should housework, among all the goods and services we consume, arouse any special angst?

And it does, as I have found in conversations with liberal-minded employers of maids, perhaps because we all sense that there are ways in which housework is different from other products and services. First, in its inevitable proximity to the activities that compose "private" life. The home that becomes a workplace for other people remains a home, even when that workplace has been minutely regulated by the corporate cleaning chains. Someone who has no qualms about purchasing rugs woven by child slaves in India or coffee picked by impoverished peasants in Guatemala might still hesitate to tell dinner guests that, surprisingly enough, his or her lovely home doubles as a sweatshop during the day. You can eschew the chain cleaning services of course, hire an independent cleaner at a generous hourly wage, and even encourage, at least in spirit, the unionization of the housecleaning industry. But this does not change the fact that someone is working in your home at a job she would almost certainly never have chosen for herself—if she'd had a college education, for example, or a little better luck along the way—and the place where she works, however enthusiastically or resentfully, is the same as the place where you sleep.

It is also the place where your children are raised, and what they learn pretty quickly is that some people are less worthy than others. Even better wages and working conditions won't erase the hierarchy between an employer and his or her domestic help, because the help is usually there only because the employer has "something better" to do with her time, as one report on the growth of cleaning services puts it, not noticing the obvious implication that the cleaning person herself has nothing better to do with her time. In a merely middle-class home, the message may be reinforced by a warning to the children that that's what they'll end up doing if they don't try harder in school. Housework, as radical feminists once proposed, defines a human relationship and, when unequally divided among social groups, reinforces preexisting inequalities. Dirt, in other words, tends to attach to the people who remove it—"garbagemen" and "cleaning ladies." Or, as cleaning entrepreneur Don Aslett told me with some bitterness—and this is a successful man, chairman of the board of an industrial cleaning service and frequent television guest—"The whole mentality out there is that if you clean, you're a scumball."

One of the "better" things employers of maids often want to do with their time is, of course, spend it with their children. But an underlying problem with post-nineteenth-century child-raising, as Deirdre English and I argued in our book *For Her Own Good* years ago, is precisely that it is unmoored in any kind of purposeful pursuit. Once "parenting" meant instructing the children in necessary chores; today it's more likely to center on one-sided conversations beginning with "So how was school today?" No one wants to put the kids to work again weeding and stitching; but in the void that is the modern home, relationships with children are often strained. A little "low-quality time" spent washing dishes or folding clothes together can provide a comfortable space for confidences—and give a child the dignity of knowing that he or she is a participant in, and not just the product of, the work of the home.

There is another lesson the servant economy teaches its beneficiaries and, most troublingly, the children among them. To be cleaned up after is to achieve a certain magical weightlessness and immateriality. Almost everyone complains about violent video games, but paid housecleaning has the same consequence-abolishing effect: you blast the villain into a mist of blood droplets and move right along; you drop the socks knowing they will eventually levitate, laundered and folded, back to their normal dwelling place. The result is a kind of virtual existence, in which the trail of litter that follows you seems to evaporate all by itself. Spill syrup on the floor and the cleaning person will scrub it off when she comes on Wednesday. Leave *The Wall Street Journal* scattered around your airplane seat and the flight attendants will deal with it after you've deplaned. Spray toxins into the atmosphere from your factory's smokestacks and they will be filtered out eventually by the lungs of the breathing public. A servant economy breeds callousness and solipsism in the served, and it does so all the more effectively when the service is performed close up and routinely in the place where they live and reproduce.

40   Individual situations vary, of course, in ways that elude blanket judgment. Some people—the elderly and disabled, parents of new babies, asthmatics who require an allergen-free environment—may well need help performing what nursing-home staff call the "ADLs," or activities of daily living, and no shame should be attached to their dependency. In a more generous social order, housekeeping services would be subsidized for those who have health-related reasons to need them—a measure that would generate a surfeit of new jobs for the low-skilled people who now clean the homes of the affluent. And in a less gender-divided social order, husbands and boyfriends would more readily do their share of the chores.

However we resolve the issue in our individual homes, the moral challenge is, put simply, to make work visible again: not only the scrubbing and vacuuming but all the hoeing, stacking, hammering, drilling, bending, and lifting that goes into creating and maintaining a livable habitat. In an ever more economically unequal culture, where so many of the affluent devote their lives to such ghostly pursuits as stock-trading, image-making, and opinion-polling, real work—in the old-fashioned sense of labor that engages hand as well as eye, that tires the body and directly alters the physical world—tends to vanish from sight. The feminists of my generation tried to bring some of it into the light of day, but, like busy professional women fleeing the house in the morning, they left the project unfinished, the debate broken off in midsentence, the noble intentions unfulfilled. Sooner or later, someone else will have to finish the job.

Questions

1. What arguments does Ehrenreich make for her claim that hiring a domestic cleaner is different from paying for other goods and services? Do you find these arguments persuasive? Why or why not?
2. In the second paragraph Ehrenreich describes "the Joan & David-clad feet and electrolyzed calves" of the typical female homeowner she encountered while working as a cleaner (paragraph 2). Why do you think she uses this particular image? How is this characterization of a person who hires a domestic cleaner important to her essay as a whole?

LAURA ROBINSON

Women's Volleyball

(2002)

Laura Robinson is a sports journalist and former national-level cyclist and Nordic skier. Her books include Crossing the Line: Violence and Sexual Assault in Canada's National Sport *(1998), an investigation of sexual abuse in junior hockey.*

In this passage from Black Tights: Women, Sport, and Sexuality *(2002), Robinson writes about the regulation of uniforms in women's volleyball.*

The International Volleyball Federation—or Fédération internationale de volleyball (FIVB)—is the umbrella organization responsible for beach volleyball; it has been heavily involved with the promotion of the sport, both internationally and at the Olympic level. But this is a sport unlike any other, and its packaging reflects a distinctly American, "Daytona Beach" flavour. Although it now has defined rules of organized play, it maintains its allegiance to rock music, beer, and female skin. And, ironically, the group tasked with overseeing the sport internationally is the aptly named Control Committee.

There are no women on the Control Committee, but its decisions directly affect women athletes, who must abide by them or lose their right to play internationally. It is the Control Committee that decides that women athletes must wear bikinis or high-cut one-piece bathing suits—or not step onto the court. It is the Control Committee that decides that female players can cover their backsides with a slice of Lycra no more than seven centimetres long at the hips. And it is the all-male Control Committee to which women players must appeal if they want to put on a pair of tights and a T-shirt in cold or windy conditions.

Beach volleyball proved to be one of the most popular sports at the Sydney Olympics. Indeed, its television ratings were exceptionally high, given that it is a relatively new sport. Yet the most desirable television sports fan is male, between the ages of 18 and 35, and a follower of male team sports. He tends to like athletic contests with frequent male body contact and bone-crunching injuries. So what is the attraction of a sport with no body contact, where teams of only two players, separated by a net, hug and kiss each other during the match, and then do the same to their opponents at the end of the game?

Easy. This is a sport that keeps women in their place. No matter how strong and athletic they are, no matter how much prize money they earn, they still must do what they are told by the Control Committee. And what they are told to do is to compete in skimpy uniforms. Of course, the women themselves aren't blameless. They willingly accept a physical power imbalance that disadvantages them. And what's most disturbing is that none of them appear to be complaining.

5   I asked Kerri Pottharst, a member of the Australian team that won the gold in Sydney, if she thought women were intelligent enough to decide for themselves what to wear. She bristled. "Of course we are intelligent enough to decide what to wear. There was an issue in Toronto [at a world cup event] when it was really cool—not even 13 degrees—and it was the first time we went to the International Volleyball Federation and they allowed us to wear leggings. I think that they would have allowed us that here [in Sydney] if we'd asked. The health of the athletes is foremost for them—and to sell the sport too. I don't think any of the women have ever complained."

Even after our conversation, I still wasn't sure where Pottharst stood on the issue. She said she felt women were intelligent enough to dress themselves, yet she supports a system that doesn't allow them to exercise that intelligence. Significantly, Pottharst also posed for the book *Sydney Dream*, a collection of black-and-white nude photographs of Australian athletes that was released during the games. She asked her partner, Victor Anfiloff, if he would pose with her because she was "a bit chicken," and she was surprised when she realized there were other people at the sand dune they'd chosen for the shoot. She rationalized her embarrassment by mentioning the skimpy suits women must wear in competition, as if she should have gotten used to that sort of thing by now. "It wasn't as deserted as I thought it would be!" she recalled. "But when you think of what we have to wear in tournaments...."

In fact, plenty of control committees throughout the sporting world are continually dictating the role the female body is to play. In Canada, our national game is overseen by the Canadian Hockey Association, which has a board of directors of 35 people. As of the 2001-02 season, just three of them are women—and only two have a vote. There are no women at all on the powerful seven-member executive committee, and even the CHA's 13-member female council has six men on it. Five men have a vote on this committee, while the other one represents women to the executive committee.

Ironically, the International Volleyball Federation (FIVB) believes it is a governing body that recognizes gender equity because it distributes prize money equally among men and women (though women receive none of the significant amounts of money earned in television revenues). The federation's spokespeople insist they are looking out for the best interests of their female members. After the gold medallists' press conference in Sydney, Allan May, a Toronto promoter and member of the world council for the sport, asked to speak to me. He wanted to talk about the uniform issue. "The FIVB, as an organization, is very sensitive to the uniform issue," he told me. "The players can also wear a one-piece uniform, and I've never seen any of the athletes choose to wear one. It's an evolutionary perspective—I've questioned this a number of times. As a promoter, it was brought to my attention in Toronto that the weather may be hazardous to the athletes. They said, 'We'd prefer to wear cold-weather clothing,' and the Control Committee agreed."

When I asked him why the players should even have to ask for someone else's permission, he made the same excuse as everyone else: Things have to look uniform. The word "uniform," however, seems to be code for revealing attire. Do track and field athletes, triathletes, rowers, or cyclists look bad, I wondered, when they wear slight variations on a theme, depending on how they feel that day? Do they all need control committees of their own to look out for their "best interests"?

I believe this insistence on a "uniform look" really masks a desire for   10 beach volleyball to have a highly gendered appearance. Women are obliged to wear revealing Lycra bathing suits, while men wear baggy cotton shorts and tank tops. There is no mistaking who is who. Clothing acts as a social dividing line.

With its all-male membership and its ridiculous rules, the Control Committee may strike us as funny, but the ideology behind it continues to threaten the autonomy women should have achieved years ago. Whether the issue is reproductive freedom or the freedom to dress as they please, women all over the world can't seem to escape men who feel the need to tell them what they can and cannot do with their own bodies.

Questions

1. Is the author's own opinion on the issue evident in this passage? Provide examples from the text.
2. What evidence does the text provide in making its argument? Is the argument successful? Why or why not?

Law and Politics

MICHEL DE MONTAIGNE

(translated by Tania Therien)

Of a Monstrous Child

(1580)

Michel de Montaigne (1533–92) was a sixteenth-century French thinker and writer, who is generally regarded as the originator of the essay as a literary form. His works were first published in three volumes entitled Essais *(vols. I & II, 1580, vol. III, 1588).*

The following essay is from volume II of Essais.

This account will go simply, for I leave it to the doctors to discuss. The day before yesterday I saw a child that two men and a wet nurse, who said they were the father, uncle and aunt, were leading about trying to attract some money by showing him off because of his strangeness. He was ordinary in all other aspects and was able to stand on his feet, walk, and babble, much like others of the same age. He hadn't yet wanted to eat any food other than at the breast of his nurse and when, after I'd asked, they tried to put something in his mouth, he chewed it a bit and spat it out without swallowing. His cries did seem to be somewhat peculiar. He was just fourteen months old. Below the breast, he was attached and stuck to another child with no head, but a spinal cord protruding and the rest of the body complete. One arm was indeed shorter, but it had been broken by accident at their birth. They were joined facing each other, as though the smaller one had wanted to bind himself to the bigger one. The juncture and space by which they were attached was not more than four digits wide or thereabout, in a manner that if you lifted up the imperfect child you would see the other's navel below, so that the joining took place between the nipples and the navel. The navel of the imperfect child was not visible, but the rest of his stomach was. In this way, whatever of the imperfect child was not attached, like arms, buttocks, thighs and legs, hung and dangled from the other child, and might reach the length of his mid-leg. The nurse noted to us that he urinated from both places, and that the limbs of the other were nourished and living to the same degree as his own, except that they were smaller and thinner. This double body and its various limbs, connected with a single head, could provide a favourable prognostic to the King in maintaining the diverse parts and pieces of our state under the union of his laws, but for fear that the event be refuted, it would be better to leave it alone. For it is better to interpret only things that are past.

Questions

1. Explain in what respects Montaigne likens the child and the state?
2. What is the effect of Montaigne's retreat, at the end of the essay, from this comparison?
3. Compare Montaigne's statement in his first sentence with the tone of his description of the child. Are these consistent? What is the effect of their juxtaposition?

HENRY DAVID THOREAU

Civil Disobedience

(1849)

Henry David Thoreau (1817–62) was an influential American writer known for his individualist and transcendental philosophies, which emphasized the importance of nature, self-reliance, and individual insight as paths to truth. His works include Walden; or, Life in the Woods *(1854), a record of his 26-month retreat to Walden Pond to live by these principles.*

In this essay, written in the wake of his brief imprisonment for refusing to pay a federal poll tax, Thoreau argues for one's right to follow one's own conscience.

I heartily accept the motto, "That government is best which governs least;" and I should like to see it acted up to more rapidly and systematically. Carried out, it finally amounts to this, which also I believe,—"That government is best which governs not at all;" and when men are prepared for it, that will be the kind of government which they will have. Government is at best but an expedient; but most governments are usually, and all governments are sometimes, inexpedient. The objections which have been brought against a standing army, and they are many and weighty, and deserve to prevail, may also at last be brought against a standing government. The standing army is only an arm of the standing government. The government itself, which is only the mode which the people have chosen to execute their will, is equally liable to be abused and perverted before the people can act through it. Witness the present Mexican war,[1] the work of comparatively a few individuals using the standing government as their tool; for, in the outset, the people would not have consented to this measure.

This American government,—what is it but a tradition, though a recent one, endeavoring to transmit itself unimpaired to posterity, but each instant losing some of its integrity? It has not the vitality and force of a single living man; for a single man can bend it to his will. It is a sort of wooden gun to the people themselves. But it is not the less necessary for this; for the peo-

---

1 *Mexican war* The Mexican-American War of 1846–48 was fought over a border dispute. Mexico claimed territory north to the Nueces River, while the Texans claimed that their territory extended south to the Rio Grande.

ple must have some complicated machinery or other, and hear its din, to satisfy that idea of government which they have. Governments show thus how successfully men can be imposed on, even impose on themselves, for their own advantage. It is excellent, we must all allow. Yet this government never of itself furthered any enterprise, but by the alacrity with which it got out of its way. *It* does not keep the country free. *It* does not settle the West. *It* does not educate. The character inherent in the American people has done all that has been accomplished; and it would have done somewhat more, if the government had not sometimes got in its way. For government is an expedient by which men would fain succeed in letting one another alone; and, as has been said, when it is most expedient, the governed are most let alone by it. Trade and commerce, if they were not made of india-rubber, would never manage to bounce over the obstacles which legislators are continually putting in their way; and, if one were to judge these men wholly by the effects of their actions and not partly by their intentions, they would deserve to be classed and punished with those mischievous persons who put obstructions on the railroads.

But, to speak practically and as a citizen, unlike those who call themselves no-government men, I ask for, not at once no government, but at once a better government. Let every man make known what kind of government would command his respect, and that will be one step toward obtaining it.

After all, the practical reason why, when the power is once in the hands of the people, a majority are permitted, and for a long period continue, to rule is not because they are most likely to be in the right, nor because this seems fairest to the minority, but because they are physically the strongest. But a government in which the majority rule in all cases cannot be based on justice, even as far as men understand it. Can there not be a government in which majorities do not virtually decide right and wrong, but conscience?—in which majorities decide only those questions to which the rule of expediency is applicable? Must the citizen ever for a moment, or in the least degree, resign his conscience to the legislator? Why has every man a conscience, then? I think that we should be men first, and subjects afterward. It is not desirable to cultivate a respect for the law, so much as for the right. The only obligation which I have a right to assume is to do at any time what I think right. It is truly enough said that a corporation[1] has no conscience; but a corporation of conscientious men is a corporation *with* a conscience. Law never made men a whit more just; and, by means of their respect for it, even the well-disposed are daily made the agents of injustice. A common and natural result of an undue respect for law is, that you may see a file of soldiers, colonel, captain, corporal, privates, powder-monkeys, and all, marching in admirable order over hill and dale to the wars, against

---

1   *corporation* In the sense of any "body of associated persons" (not formed specifically for business ends).

their wills, ay, against their common sense and consciences, which makes it very steep marching indeed, and produces a palpitation of the heart. They have no doubt that it is a damnable business in which they are concerned; they are all peaceably inclined. Now, what are they? Men at all? or small movable forts and magazines, at the service of some unscrupulous man in power? Visit the Navy-Yard, and behold a marine, such a man as an American government can make, or such as it can make a man with its black arts,—a mere shadow and reminiscence of humanity, a man laid out alive and standing, and already, as one may say, buried under arms with funeral accompaniments, though it may be,—

> "Not a drum was heard, not a funeral note,
>   As his corse to the rampart we hurried;
> Not a soldier discharged his farewell shot
>   O'er the grave where our hero we buried."[1]

5   The mass of men serve the state thus, not as men mainly, but as machines, with their bodies. They are the standing army, and the militia, jailers, constables, *posse comitatus*,[2] etc. In most cases there is no free exercise whatever of the judgment or of the moral sense; but they put themselves on a level with wood and earth and stones; and wooden men can perhaps be manufactured that will serve the purpose as well. Such command no more respect than men of straw or a lump of dirt. They have the same sort of worth only as horses and dogs. Yet such as these even are commonly esteemed good citizens. Others—as most legislators, politicians, lawyers, ministers, and office-holders—serve the state chiefly with their heads; and, as they rarely make any moral distinctions, they are as likely to serve the Devil, without *intending* it, as God. A very few—as heroes, patriots, martyrs, reformers in the great sense, and *men*—serve the state with their consciences also, and so necessarily resist it for the most part; and they are commonly treated as enemies by it. A wise man will only be useful as a man, and will not submit to be "clay," and "stop a hole to keep the wind away,"[3] but leave that office to his dust at least:—

> "I am too high-born to be propertied,
> To be a secondary at control,
> Or useful serving-man and instrument
> To any sovereign state throughout the world."[4]

---

1   *"Not ... buried."* From a poem by Charles Wolfe (1791–1823), "The Burial of Sir John Moore at Corunna."
2   *posse comitatus* Group empowered to uphold the law, i.e., a sheriff's posse.
3   *"stop ... away,"* From Shakespeare's *Hamlet*, V.i.
4   *"I ... world."* From Shakespeare's *King John*, V.ii.

He who gives himself entirely to his fellow-men appears to them useless and selfish; but he who gives himself partially to them is pronounced a benefactor and philanthropist.

How does it become a man to behave toward this American government to-day? I answer, that he cannot without disgrace be associated with it. I cannot for an instant recognize that political organization as *my* government which is the *slave's* government also.

All men recognize the right of revolution; that is, the right to refuse allegiance to, and to resist, the government, when its tyranny or its inefficiency are great and unendurable. But almost all say that such is not the case now. But such was the case, they think, in the Revolution of '75. If one were to tell me that this was a bad government because it taxed certain foreign commodities brought to its ports, it is most probable that I should not make an ado about it, for I can do without them. All machines have their friction; and possibly this does enough good to counterbalance the evil. At any rate, it is a great evil to make a stir about it. But when the friction comes to have its machine, and oppression and robbery are organized, I say, let us not have such a machine any longer. In other words, when a sixth of the population of a nation which has undertaken to be the refuge of liberty are slaves, and a whole country is unjustly overrun and conquered by a foreign army, and subjected to military law, I think that it is not too soon for honest men to rebel and revolutionize. What makes this duty the more urgent is the fact that the country so overrun is not our own, but ours is the invading army.

Paley,[1] a common authority with many on moral questions, in his chapter on the "Duty of Submission to Civil Government," resolves all civil obligation into expediency; and he proceeds to say that "so long as the interest of the whole society requires it, that is, so long as the established government cannot be resisted or changed without public inconveniency, it is the will of God ... that the established government be obeyed,—and no longer. This principle being admitted, the justice of every particular case of resistance is reduced to a computation of the quantity of the danger and grievance on the one side, and of the probability and expense of redressing it on the other." Of this, he says, every man shall judge for himself. But Paley appears never to have contemplated those cases to which the rule of expediency does not apply, in which a people, as well as an individual, must do justice, cost what it may. If I have unjustly wrested a plank from a drowning man, I must restore it to him though I drown myself. This, according to Paley, would be inconvenient. But he that would save his life, in such a case, shall lose it. This people must cease to hold slaves, and to make war on Mexico, though it cost them their existence as a people.

---

1 *Paley* William Paley (1743–1805), English theologian and philosopher.

10   In their practice, nations agree with Paley; but does any one think that Massachusetts does exactly what is right at the present crisis?

> "A drab of state, a cloth-o'-silver slut,
> To have her train borne up, and her soul trail in the dirt."[1]

Practically speaking, the opponents to a reform in Massachusetts are not a hundred thousand politicians at the South, but a hundred thousand merchants and farmers here, who are more interested in commerce and agriculture than they are in humanity, and are not prepared to do justice to the slave and to Mexico, *cost what it may.* I quarrel not with far-off foes, but with those who, near at home, cooperate with, and do the bidding of, those far away, and without whom the latter would be harmless. We are accustomed to say, that the mass of men are unprepared; but improvement is slow, because the few are not materially wiser or better than the many. It is not so important that many should be as good as you, as that there be some absolute goodness somewhere; for that will leaven the whole lump. There are thousands who are *in opinion* opposed to slavery and to the war, who yet in effect do nothing to put an end to them; who, esteeming themselves children of Washington and Franklin, sit down with their hands in their pockets, and say that they know not what to do, and do nothing; who even postpone the question of freedom to the question of free trade, and quietly read the prices-current along with the latest advices from Mexico, after dinner, and, it may be, fall asleep over them both. What is the price-current of an honest man and patriot to-day? They hesitate, and they regret, and sometimes they petition; but they do nothing in earnest and with effect. They will wait, well disposed, for others to remedy the evil, that they may no longer have it to regret. At most, they give only a cheap vote, and a feeble countenance and God-speed, to the right, as it goes by them. There are nine hundred and ninety-nine patrons of virtue to one virtuous man. But it is easier to deal with the real possessor of a thing than with the temporary guardian of it.

All voting is a sort of gaming, like checkers or backgammon, with a slight moral tinge to it, a playing with right and wrong, with moral questions; and betting naturally accompanies it. The character of the voters is not staked. I cast my vote, perchance, as I think right; but I am not vitally concerned that that right should prevail. I am willing to leave it to the majority. Its obligation, therefore, never exceeds that of expediency. Even voting *for the right* is *doing* nothing for it. It is only expressing to men feebly your desire that it should prevail. A wise man will not leave the right to the mercy of chance, nor wish it to prevail through the power of the majority. There is but little virtue in the action of masses of men. When the majority shall at

---

1 *"A drab of state ... dirt"* From Cyril Tourneur (1575?–1626), *The Revengers Tragadie.*

length vote for the abolition of slavery, it will be because they are indifferent to slavery, or because there is but little slavery left to be abolished by their vote. *They* will then be the only slaves. Only *his* vote can hasten the abolition of slavery who asserts his own freedom by his vote.

I hear of a convention to be held in Baltimore, or elsewhere, for the selection of a candidate for the Presidency, made up chiefly of editors, and men who are politicians by profession; but I think, what is it to any independent, intelligent, and respectable man what decision they may come to? Shall we not have the advantage of his wisdom and honesty, nevertheless? Can we not count upon some independent votes? Are there not many individuals in the country who do not attend conventions? But no: I find that the respectable man, so called, has immediately drifted from his position, and despairs of his country, when his country has more reason to despair of him. He forthwith adopts one of the candidates thus selected as the only *available* one, thus proving that he is himself *available* for any purposes of the demagogue. His vote is of no more worth than that of any unprincipled foreigner or hireling native, who may have been bought. O for a man who is a *man*, and, as my neighbor says, has a bone in his back which you cannot pass your hand through! Our statistics are at fault: the population has been returned too large. How many *men* are there to a square thousand miles in this country? Hardly one. Does not America offer any inducement for men to settle here? The American has dwindled into an Odd Fellow,—one who may be known by the development of his organ of gregariousness, and a manifest lack of intellect and cheerful self-reliance; whose first and chief concern, on coming into the world, is to see that the almshouses are in good repair; and, before yet he has lawfully donned the virile garb, to collect a fund for the support of the widows and orphans that may be; who, in short, ventures to live only by the aid of the Mutual Insurance company, which has promised to bury him decently.

It is not a man's duty, as a matter of course, to devote himself to the eradication of any, even the most enormous, wrong; he may still properly have other concerns to engage him; but it is his duty, at least, to wash his hands of it, and, if he gives it no thought longer, not to give it practically his support. If I devote myself to other pursuits and contemplations, I must first see, at least, that I do not pursue them sitting upon another man's shoulders. I must get off him first, that he may pursue his contemplations too. See what gross inconsistency is tolerated. I have heard some of my townsmen say, "I should like to have them order me out to help put down an insurrection of the slaves, or to march to Mexico;—see if I would go;" and yet these very men have each, directly by their allegiance, and so indirectly, at least, by their money, furnished a substitute. The soldier is applauded who refuses to serve in an unjust war by those who do not refuse to sustain the unjust government which makes the war; is applauded by those whose own act and authority he disregards and sets at naught; as if the state were penitent to that degree that it hired one to scourge it while it sinned, but not to that degree that it left off sinning for a moment. Thus, under the name of Order and Civil Government, we are all made at last to pay homage to and support our own meanness. After the first blush of sin comes its indifference; and from immoral it becomes, as it were, *un*moral, and not quite unnecessary to that life which we have made.

15   The broadest and most prevalent error requires the most disinterested virtue to sustain it. The slight reproach to which the virtue of patriotism is commonly liable, the noble are most likely to incur. Those who, while they disapprove of the character and measures of a government, yield to it their allegiance and support are undoubtedly its most conscientious supporters, and so frequently the most serious obstacles to reform. Some are petitioning the State to dissolve the Union, to disregard the requisitions of the President. Why do they not dissolve it themselves,—the union between themselves and the State,—and refuse to pay their quota into its treasury? Do not they stand in the same relation to the state that the State does to the Union? And have not the same reasons prevented the State from resisting the Union which have prevented them from resisting the State?

How can a man be satisfied to entertain an opinion merely, and enjoy *it?* Is there any enjoyment in it, if his opinion is that he is aggrieved? If you are cheated out of a single dollar by your neighbor, you do not rest satisfied with knowing that you are cheated, or with saying that you are cheated, or even with petitioning him to pay you your due; but you take effectual steps at once to obtain the full amount, and see that you are never cheated again. Action from principle, the perception and the performance of right, changes things and relations; it is essentially revolutionary, and does not consist wholly with anything which was. It not only divides States and churches, it divides families; ay, it divides the *individual*, separating the diabolical in him from the divine.

Unjust laws exist: shall we be content to obey them, or shall we endeavor to amend them, and obey them until we have succeeded, or shall we transgress them at once? Men generally, under such a government as this, think that they ought to wait until they have persuaded the majority to alter them. They think that, if they should resist, the remedy would be worse than the evil. But it is the fault of the government itself that the remedy *is* worse than the evil. *It* makes it worse. Why is it not more apt to anticipate and provide for reform? Why does it not cherish its wise minority? Why does it cry and resist before it is hurt? Why does it not encourage its citizens to be on the alert to point out its faults, and *do* better than it would have them? Why does it always crucify Christ, and excommunicate Copernicus and Luther, and pronounce Washington and Franklin rebels?

One would think, that a deliberate and practical denial of its authority was the only offense never contemplated by government; else, why has it not assigned its definite, its suitable and proportionate, penalty? If a man who has no property refuses but once to earn nine shillings for the State, he is put in prison for a period unlimited by any law that I know, and determined only by the discretion of those who placed him there; but if he should steal ninety times nine shillings from the State, he is soon permitted to go at large again.

If the injustice is part of the necessary friction of the machine of government, let it go: perchance it will wear smooth,—certainly the machine will wear out. If the injustice has a spring, or a pulley, or a rope, or a crank, exclusively for itself, then perhaps you may consider whether the remedy will not be worse than the evil; but if it is of such a nature that it requires you to be the agent of injustice to another, then, I say, break the law. Let your life be a counter-friction to stop the machine. What I have to do is to see, at any rate, that I do not lend myself to the wrong which I condemn.

As for adopting the ways which the State has provided for remedying the 20 evil, I know not of such ways. They take too much time, and a man's life will be gone. I have other affairs to attend to. I came into this world, not chiefly to make this a good place to live in, but to live in it, be it good or bad. A man has not everything to do, but something; and because he cannot do *everything*, it is not necessary that he should do *something* wrong. It is not my business to be petitioning the Governor or the Legislature any more than it is theirs to petition me; and if they should not hear my petition, what should I do then? But in this case the State has provided no way: its very Constitution is the evil. This may seem to be harsh and stubborn and unconciliatory; but it is to treat with the utmost kindness and consideration the only spirit that can appreciate or deserves it. So is all change for the better, like birth and death, which convulse the body.

I do not hesitate to say, that those who call themselves Abolitionists should at once effectually withdraw their support, both in person and property, from the government of Massachusetts, and not wait till they constitute a majority of one, before they suffer the right to prevail through them. I think that it is enough if they have God on their side, without waiting for that other one. Moreover, any man more right than his neighbors constitutes a majority of one already.

I meet this American government, or its representative, the State government, directly, and face to face, once a year—no more—in the person of its tax-gatherer; this is the only mode in which a man situated as I am necessarily meets it; and it then says distinctly, Recognize me; and the simplest, the most effectual, and, in the present posture of affairs, the indispensablest mode of treating with it on this head, of expressing your little satisfaction with and love for it, is to deny it then. My civil neighbor, the tax-gatherer, is the very man I have to deal with,—for it is, after all, with men and not with parchment that I quarrel,—and he has voluntarily chosen to be an agent of the government. How shall he ever know well what he is and does as an officer of the government, or as a man, until he is obliged to consider whether he shall treat me, his neighbor, for whom he has respect, as a neighbor and well-disposed man, or as a maniac and disturber of the peace, and see if he can get over this obstruction to his neighborliness without a ruder and more impetuous thought or speech corresponding with his action. I know this well, that if one thousand, if one hundred, if ten men whom I could name,—if ten *honest* men only,—ay, if *one* HONEST man, in this State of Massachusetts, *ceasing to hold slaves*, were actually to withdraw from this copartnership, and be locked up in the county jail therefor, it would be the abolition of slavery in America. For it matters not how small the beginning may seem to be: what is once well done is done forever. But we love better to talk about it: that we say is our mission. Reform keeps many scores of newspapers in its service, but not one man. If my esteemed neighbor, the State's ambassador, who will devote his days to the settlement of the question of human rights in the Council Chamber, instead of being threatened with the prisons of Carolina, were to sit down the prisoner of Massachusetts, that State which is so anxious to foist the sin of slavery upon her sister,— though at present she can discover only an act of inhospitality to be the ground of a quarrel with her,—the Legislature would not wholly waive the subject the following winter.

Under a government which imprisons any unjustly, the true place for a just man is also a prison. The proper place to-day, the only place which Massachusetts has provided for her freer and less desponding spirits, is in her prisons, to be put out and locked out of the State by her own act, as they have already put themselves out by their principles. It is there that the fugitive slave, and the Mexican prisoner on parole, and the Indian come to plead the wrongs of his race should find them; on that separate, but more free and honorable ground, where the State places those who are not *with* her, but *against* her,—the only house in a slave State in which a free man can abide with honor. If any think that their influence would be lost there, and their voices no longer afflict the ear of the State, that they would not be as an enemy within its walls, they do not know by how much truth is stronger than error, nor how much more eloquently and effectively he can combat injustice who has experienced a little in his own person. Cast your whole vote, not a strip of paper merely, but your whole influence. A minority is powerless while it conforms to the majority; it is not even a minority then; but it is irresistible when it clogs by its whole weight. If the alternative is to keep all just men in prison, or give up war and slavery, the State will not hesitate which to choose. If a thousand men were not to pay their tax-bills this year, that would not be a violent and bloody measure, as it would be to pay them, and enable the State to commit violence and shed innocent blood. This is, in fact, the definition of a peaceable revolution, if any such is possible. If the tax-gatherer, or any other public officer, asks me, as one has done, "But what shall I do?" my answer is, "If you really wish to do anything, resign your office." When the subject has refused allegiance, and the officer has resigned his office, then the revolution is accomplished. But even suppose blood should flow. Is there not a sort of blood shed when the conscience is wounded? Through this wound a man's real manhood and immortality flow out, and he bleeds to an everlasting death. I see this blood flowing now.

I have contemplated the imprisonment of the offender, rather than the seizure of his goods,—though both will serve the same purpose,—because they who assert the purest right, and consequently are most dangerous to a corrupt State, commonly have not spent much time in accumulating property. To such the State renders comparatively small service, and a slight tax is wont to appear exorbitant, particularly if they are obliged to earn it by special labor with their hands. If there were one who lived wholly without the use of money, the State itself would hesitate to demand it of him. But the rich man—not to make any invidious comparison—is always sold to the institution which makes him rich. Absolutely speaking, the more money, the less virtue; for money comes between a man and his objects, and obtains them for him; and it was certainly no great virtue to obtain it. It puts to rest many questions which he would otherwise be taxed to answer; while the only new question which it puts is the hard but superfluous one, how to spend it. Thus his moral ground is taken from under his feet. The opportunities of living are diminished in proportion as what are called the "means" are increased. The best thing a man can do for his culture when he is rich is to endeavor to carry out those schemes which he entertained when he was poor. Christ answered the Herodians according to their condition. "Show me the tribute-money," said he;—and one took a penny out of his pocket;—if you use money which has the image of Caesar on it, which he has made current and valuable, that is, *if you are men of the State*, and gladly enjoy the advantages of Caesar's government, then pay him back some of his own when he demands it. "Render therefore to Caesar that which is Caesar's, and to God those things which are God's,"—leaving them no wiser than before as to which was which; for they did not wish to know.

When I converse with the freest of my neighbors, I perceive that, whatever they may say about the magnitude and seriousness of the question, and their regard for the public tranquillity, the long and the short of the matter is, that they cannot spare the protection of the existing government, and they dread the consequences to their property and families of disobedience to it. For my own part, I should not like to think that I ever rely on the protection of the State. But, if I deny the authority of the State when it presents its tax-bill, it will soon take and waste all my property, and so harass me and my children without end. This is hard. This makes it impossible for a man to live honestly, and at the same time comfortably, in outward respects. It will not be worth the while to accumulate property; that would be sure to go again. You must hire or squat somewhere, and raise but a small crop, and eat that soon. You must live within yourself, and depend upon yourself always tucked up and ready for a start, and not have many affairs. A man may grow rich in Turkey even, if he will be in all respects a good subject of the Turkish government. Confucius said: "If a state is governed by the principles of reason, poverty and misery are subjects of shame; if a state is not governed by the principles of reason, riches and honors are the subjects of shame." No: until I want the protection of Massachusetts to be extended to me in some distant Southern port, where my liberty is endangered, or until I am bent solely on building up an estate at home by peaceful enterprise, I can afford to refuse allegiance to Massachusetts, and her right to my property and life. It costs me less in every sense to incur the penalty of disobedience to the State than it would to obey. I should feel as if I were worth less in that case.

Some years ago, the State met me in behalf of the Church, and commanded me to pay a certain sum toward the support of a clergyman whose preaching my father attended, but never I myself. "Pay," it said, "or be locked up in the jail." I declined to pay. But, unfortunately, another man saw fit to pay it. I did not see why the schoolmaster should be taxed to support the priest, and not the priest the schoolmaster; for I was not the State's schoolmaster, but I supported myself by voluntary subscription. I did not see why the lyceum should not present its tax-bill, and have the State to back its demand, as well as the Church. However, at the request of the selectmen, I condescended to make some such statement as this in writing:—"Know all men by these presents, that I, Henry Thoreau, do not wish to be regarded as a member of any incorporated society which I have not joined." This I gave to the town clerk; and he has it. The State, having thus learned that I did not wish to be regarded as a member of that church, has never made a like demand on me since; though it said that it must adhere to its original presumption that time. If I had known how to name them, I should then have signed off in detail from all the societies which I never signed on to; but I did not know where to find a complete list.

I have paid no poll-tax for six years. I was put into a jail on this account, for one night; and, as I stood considering the walls of solid stone, two or three feet thick, the door of wood and iron, a foot thick, and the iron grating which strained the light, I could not help being struck with the foolishness of that institution which treated me as if I were mere flesh and blood and bones, to be locked up. I wondered that it should have concluded at length that this was the best use it could put me to, and had never thought to avail itself of my services in some way. I saw that, if there was a wall of stone between me and my townsmen, there was a still more difficult one to climb or break through before they could get to be as free as I was. I did not for a moment feel confined, and the walls seemed a great waste of stone and mortar. I felt as if I alone of all my townsmen had paid my tax. They plainly did not know how to treat me, but behaved like persons who are underbred. In every threat and in every compliment there was a blunder; for they thought that my chief desire was to stand the other side of that stone wall. I could not but smile to see how industriously they locked the door on my meditations, which followed them out again without let or hindrance, and *they* were really all that was dangerous. As they could not reach me, they had resolved to punish my body; just as boys, if they cannot come at some person against whom they have a spite, will abuse his dog. I saw that the State was halfwitted, that it was timid as a lone woman with her silver spoons, and that it did not know its friends from its foes, and I lost all my remaining respect for it, and pitied it.

Thus the State never intentionally confronts a man's sense, intellectual or moral, but only his body, his senses. It is not armed with superior wit or honesty, but with superior physical strength. I was not born to be forced. I will breathe after my own fashion. Let us see who is the strongest. What force has a multitude? They only can force me who obey a higher law than I. They force me to become like themselves. I do not hear of *men* being *forced* to live this way or that by masses of men. What sort of life were that to live? When I meet a government which says to me, "Your money or your life," why should I be in haste to give it my money? It may be in a great strait, and not know what to do: I cannot help that. It must help itself; do as I do. It is not worth the while to snivel about it. I am not responsible for the successful working of the machinery of society. I am not the son of the engineer. I perceive that, when an acorn and a chestnut fall side by side, the one does not remain inert to make way for the other, but both obey their own laws, and spring and grow and flourish as best they can, till one, perchance, overshadows and destroys the other. If a plant cannot live according to its nature, it dies; and so a man.

The night in prison was novel and interesting enough. The prisoners in their shirt-sleeves were enjoying a chat and the evening air in the doorway, when I entered. But the jailer said, "Come, boys, it is time to lock up;" and so they dispersed, and I heard the sound of their steps returning into the hollow apartments. My room-mate was introduced to me by the jailer as "a first-rate fellow and a clever man." When the door was locked, he showed me where to hang my hat, and how he managed matters there. The rooms were whitewashed once a month; and this one, at least, was the whitest, most simply furnished, and probably the neatest apartment in the town. He naturally wanted to know where I came from, and what brought me there; and, when I had told him, I asked in my turn how he came there, presuming him to be an honest man, of course; and, as the world goes, I believe he was. "Why," said he, "they accuse me of burning a barn; but I never did it." As near as I could discover, he had probably gone to bed in a barn when drunk, and smoked his pipe there; and so a barn was burnt. He had the reputation of being a clever man, been there some three months waiting for his trial to come on, and would have to wait as much longer; but he was quite domesticated and contented, since he got his board for nothing, and thought that he was well treated.

30   He occupied one window, and I the other; and I saw that if one stayed there long, his principal business would be to look out the window. I had soon read all the tracts that were left there, and examined where former prisoners had broken out, and where a grate had been sawed off, and heard the history of the various occupants of that room; for I found that even here there was a history and a gossip which never circulated beyond the walls of the jail. Probably this is the only house in the town where verses are composed, which are afterward printed in a circular form, but not published. I was shown quite a long list of verses which were composed by some young men who had been detected in an attempt to escape, who avenged themselves by singing them.

I pumped my fellow-prisoner as dry as I could, for fear I should never see him again; but at length he showed me which was my bed, and left me to blow out the lamp.

It was like traveling into a far country, such as I had never expected to behold, to lie there for one night. It seemed to me that I never had heard the town clock strike before, nor the evening sounds of the village; for we slept with the windows open, which were inside the grating. It was to see my native village in the light of the Middle Ages, and our Concord was turned into a Rhine stream, and visions of knights and castles passed before me. They were the voices of old burghers that I heard in the streets. I was an involuntary spectator and auditor of whatever was done and said in the kitchen of the adjacent village inn,—a wholly new and rare experience to me. It was a closer view of my native town. I was fairly inside of it. I never had seen its institutions before. This is one of its peculiar institutions; for it is a shire town. I began to comprehend what its inhabitants were about.

In the morning, our breakfasts were put through the hole in the door, in small oblong-square tin pans, made to fit, and holding a pint of chocolate, with brown bread, and an iron spoon. When they called for the vessels again, I was green enough to return what bread I had left; but my comrade seized it, and said that I should lay that up for lunch or dinner. Soon after he was let out to work at haying in a neighboring field, whither he went every day, and would not be back till noon; so he bade me good-day, saying that he doubted if he should see me again.

When I came out of prison,—for some one interfered, and paid that tax,—I did not perceive that great changes had taken place on the common, such as he observed who went in a youth and emerged a tottering and gray-haired man; and yet a change had to my eyes come over the scene,— the town, and State, and country,—greater than any that mere time could effect. I saw yet more distinctly the State in which I lived. I saw to what extent the people among whom I lived could be trusted as good neighbors and friends; that their friendship was for summer weather only; that they did not greatly propose to do right; that they were a distinct race from me by their prejudices and superstitions, as the Chinamen and Malays are; that in their sacrifices to humanity they ran no risks, not even to their property; that after all they were not so noble but they treated the thief as he had treated them, and hoped, by a certain outward observance and a few prayers, and by walking in a particular straight though useless path from time to time, to save their souls. This may be to judge my neighbors harshly; for I believe that many of them are not aware that they have such an institution as the jail in their village.

It was formerly the custom in our village, when a poor debtor came out   35 of jail, for his acquaintances to salute him, looking through their fingers, which were crossed to represent the grating of a jail window, "How do ye do?" My neighbors did not thus salute me, but first looked at me, and then at one another, as if I had returned from a long journey. I was put into jail as I was going to the shoemaker's to get a shoe which was mended. When I was let out the next morning, I proceeded to finish my errand, and, having put on my mended shoe, joined a huckleberry party, who were impatient to put themselves under my conduct; and in half an hour,—for the horse was soon tackled,—was in the midst of a huckleberry field, on one of our highest hills, two miles off, and then the State was nowhere to be seen.

This is the whole history of "My Prisons."

I have never declined paying the highway tax, because I am as desirous of being a good neighbor as I am of being a bad subject; and as for supporting schools, I am doing my part to educate my fellow-countrymen now. It is for no particular item in the tax-bill that I refuse to pay it. I simply wish to refuse allegiance to the State, to withdraw and stand aloof from it effectually. I do not care to trace the course of my dollar, if I could, till it buys a man or a musket to shoot one with,—the dollar is innocent,—but I am concerned to trace the effects of my allegiance. In fact, I quietly declare war with the State, after my fashion, though I will still make what use and get what advantage of her I can, as is usual in such cases.

If others pay the tax which is demanded of me, from a sympathy with the State, they do but what they have already done in their own case, or rather they abet injustice to a greater extent than the State requires. If they pay the tax from a mistaken interest in the individual taxed, to save his property, or prevent his going to jail, it is because they have not considered wisely how far they let their private feelings interfere with the public good.

This, then, is my position at present. But one cannot be too much on his guard in such a case, lest his action be biased by obstinacy or an undue regard for the opinions of men. Let him see that he does only what belongs to himself and to the hour.

I think sometimes, Why, this people mean well, they are only ignorant;   40 they would do better if they knew how: why give your neighbors this pain to treat you as they are not inclined to? But I think again, This is no reason why I should do as they do, or permit others to suffer much greater pain of a different kind. Again I sometimes say to myself, When many millions of men, without heat,[1] without ill will, without personal feeling of any kind, demand of you a few shillings only, without the possibility, such is their constitution, of retracting or altering their present demand, and without the possibility, on your side, of appeal to any other millions, why expose yourself to this overwhelming brute force? You do not resist cold and hunger, the winds and the waves, thus obstinately; you quietly submit to a thousand similar necessities. You do not put your head into the fire. But just in proportion as I regard this as not wholly a brute force, but partly a human force, and consider that I have relations to those millions as to so many millions of men, and not of mere brute or inanimate things, I see that appeal is possible, first and instantaneously, from them to the Maker of them, and, secondly, from them to themselves. But if I put my head deliberately into the fire, there is no appeal to fire or to the Maker of fire, and I have only myself to blame. If I could convince myself that I have any right to be satisfied with men as they are, and to treat them accordingly, and not according, in some respects, to my requisitions and expectations of what they and I ought to be, then, like a good Mussulman and fatalist, I should endeavor to be satisfied with things as they are, and say it is the will of God. And, above all, there is this difference between resisting this and a purely brute or natural force, that I can resist this with some effect; but I cannot expect, like Orpheus, to change the nature of the rocks and trees and beasts.

I do not wish to quarrel with any man or nation. I do not wish to split hairs, to make fine distinctions, or set myself up as better than my neighbors. I seek rather, I may say, even an excuse for conforming to the laws of the land. I am but too ready to conform to them. Indeed, I have reason to suspect myself on this head; and each year, as the tax-gatherer comes round, I find myself disposed to review the acts and position of the general and State governments, and the spirit of the people, to discover a pretext for conformity.

> "We must affect our country as our parents,
> And if at any time we alienate
> Our love or industry from doing it honor,
> We must respect effects and teach the soul
> Matter of conscience and religion,
> And not desire of rule or benefit."

I believe that the State will soon be able to take all my work of this sort out of my hands, and then I shall be no better a patriot than my fellow-countrymen. Seen from a lower point of view, the Constitution, with all its faults, is very good; the law and the courts are very respectable; even this State and

---

1 *heat* Anger.

this American government are, in many respects, very admirable, and rare things, to be thankful for, such as a great many have described them; but seen from a point of view a little higher, they are what I have described them; seen from a higher still, and the highest, who shall say what they are, or that they are worth looking at or thinking of at all?

However, the government does not concern me much, and I shall bestow the fewest possible thoughts on it. It is not many moments that I live under a government, even in this world. If a man is thought-free, fancy-free, imagination-free, that which *is not* never for a long time appearing *to be* to him, unwise rulers or reformers cannot fatally interrupt him.

I know that most men think differently from myself; but those whose lives are by profession devoted to the study of these or kindred subjects content me as little as any. Statesmen and legislators, standing so completely within the institution, never distinctly and nakedly behold it. They speak of moving society, but have no resting-place without it. They may be men of a certain experience and discrimination, and have no doubt invented ingenious and even useful systems, for which we sincerely thank them; but all their wit and usefulness lie within certain not very wide limits. They are wont to forget that the world is not governed by policy and expediency. Webster[1] never goes behind government, and so cannot speak with authority about it. His words are wisdom to those legislators who contemplate no essential reform in the existing government; but for thinkers, and those who legislate for all time, he never once glances at the subject. I know of those whose serene and wise speculations on this theme would soon reveal the limits of his mind's range and hospitality. Yet, compared with the cheap professions of most reformers, and the still cheaper wisdom and eloquence of politicians in general, his are almost the only sensible and valuable words, and we thank Heaven for him. Comparatively, he is always strong, original, and, above all, practical. Still, his quality is not wisdom, but prudence. The lawyer's truth is not Truth, but consistency or a consistent expediency. Truth is always in harmony with herself, and is not concerned chiefly to reveal the justice that may consist with wrong-doing. He well deserves to be called, as he has been called, the Defender of the Constitution. There are really no blows to be given by him but defensive ones. He is not a leader, but a follower. His leaders are the men of '87. "I have never made an effort," he says, "and never propose to make an effort; I have never countenanced an effort, and never mean to countenance an effort, to disturb the arrangement as originally made, by which the various States came into the union." Still thinking of the sanction which the Constitution gives to slavery, he says, "Because it was a part of the original compact,—let it stand." Notwithstanding his special acuteness and ability, he is unable to take a fact out of

---

1   *Webster* Daniel Webster (1782–1852) was one of the great politicians of the mid-nineteenth century.

its merely political relations, and behold it as it lies absolutely to be disposed of by the intellect,—what, for instance, it behooves a man to do here in America to-day with regard to slavery,—but ventures, or is driven, to make some such desperate answer as the following, while professing to speak absolutely, and as a private man,—from which what new and singular code of social duties might be inferred? "The manner," says he, "in which the governments of those States where slavery exists are to regulate it is for their own consideration, under their responsibility to their constituents, to the general laws of propriety, humanity, and justice, and to God. Associations formed elsewhere, springing from a feeling of humanity, or any other cause, have nothing whatever to do with it. They have never received any encouragement from me, and they never will."

45   They who know of no purer sources of truth, who have traced up its stream no higher, stand, and wisely stand, by the Bible and the Constitution, and drink at it there with reverence and humility; but they who behold where it comes trickling into this lake or that pool, gird up their loins once more, and continue their pilgrimage toward its fountain-head.

No man with a genius for legislation has appeared in America. They are rare in the history of the world. There are orators, politicians, and eloquent men, by the thousand; but the speaker has not yet opened his mouth to speak who is capable of settling the much-vexed questions of the day. We love eloquence for its own sake, and not for any truth which it may utter, or any heroism it may inspire. Our legislators have not yet learned the comparative value of free-trade and of freedom, of union, and of rectitude, to a nation. They have no genius or talent for comparatively humble questions of taxation and finance, commerce and manufactures and agriculture. If we were left solely to the wordy wit of legislators in Congress for our guidance, uncorrected by the seasonable experience and the effectual complaints of the people, America would not long retain her rank among the nations. For eighteen hundred years, though perchance I have no right to say it, the New Testament has been written; yet where is the legislator who has wisdom and practical talent enough to avail himself of the light which it sheds on the science of legislation?

The authority of government, even such as I am willing to submit to,—for I will cheerfully obey those who know and can do better than I, and in many things even those who neither know nor can do so well,—is still an impure one: to be strictly just, it must have the sanctions and consent of the governed. It can have no pure right over my person and property but what I concede to it. The progress from an absolute to a limited monarchy, from a limited monarchy to a democracy, is a progress toward a true respect for the individual. Even the Chinese philosopher was wise enough to regard the individual as the basis of the empire. Is a democracy, such as we know it, the last improvement possible in government? Is it not possible to take a step further towards recognizing and organizing the rights of man? There will never be a really free and enlightened State until the State comes to recognize the individual as a higher and independent power, from which all its own power and authority are derived, and treats him accordingly. I please myself with imagining a State at last which can afford to be just to all men, and to treat the individual with respect as a neighbor; which even would not think it inconsistent with its own repose if a few were to live aloof from it, not meddling with it, nor embraced by it, who fulfilled all the duties of neighbors and fellow-men. A State which bore this kind of fruit, and suffered it to drop off as fast as it ripened, would prepare the way for a still more perfect and glorious State, which also I have imagined, but not yet anywhere seen.

Questions

1. Compare "Civil Disobedience" with Martin Luther King's "Letter from Birmingham Jail." Comment on the manner in which the style and the tone of each support the principal ideas.
2. Explain the extended metaphor in paragraph 18. How effective do you find this as a literary device? In what context(s) might an extended metaphor detract from an argument's effectiveness?
3. In paragraph 22, Thoreau appears to equate real and metaphorical violence and bloodshed. Comment on this argumentative strategy.
4. Thoreau often uses personal anecdotes to entice his readers to themselves consider practicing civil disobedience. Using specific examples, explain how this is rhetorically effective or ineffective.

ABRAHAM LINCOLN

The Gettysburg Address

(1863)

Abraham Lincoln (1809–65) was the sixteenth president of the United States, from 1861 to 1865, and the first Republican president. He was elected president on the eve of the secession of the Confederate states and the American Civil War. On 1 January 1863, Lincoln issued the Emancipation Proclamation, which worked toward the abolition of slavery in America. He was assassinated in 1865.

Lincoln delivered the Gettysburg Address on 19 November 1863, during the American Civil War, at the dedication of the Soldiers' National Cemetery in Gettysburg, Pennsylvania.

Fourscore and seven years ago our fathers brought forth upon this continent a new nation, conceived in liberty and dedicated to the proposition that all men are created equal.

Now we are engaged in a great civil war, testing whether that nation or any nation so conceived and so dedicated can long endure. We are met on a great battlefield of that war. We have come to dedicate a portion of that field as a final resting-place for those who here gave their lives that that nation might live. It is altogether fitting and proper that we should do this.

But, in a larger sense, we cannot dedicate, we cannot consecrate, we cannot hallow this ground. The brave men, living and dead who struggled here have consecrated it far above our power to add or detract. The world will little note nor long remember what we say here, but it can never forget what they did here. It is for us the living rather to be dedicated here to the unfinished work which they have thus far so nobly advanced. It is rather for us to be here dedicated to the great task remaining before us—that from these honored dead we take increased devotion to that cause for which they gave the last full measure of devotion—that we here highly resolve that these dead shall not have died in vain, that this nation under God shall have a new birth of freedom, and that government of the people, by the people, for the people shall not perish from the earth.

Questions

1. Where in this speech does Lincoln allude to the main cause of the American Civil War?
2. Explain Lincoln's argument for why the living cannot consecrate the ground.
3. Discuss the implications of the sentence, "The world will little note, nor long remember, what we *say* here, but it can never forget what they *did* here."

RALPH WALDO EMERSON

Politics

(1876)

Poet, philosopher, and essayist Ralph Waldo Emerson (1830–82) was a key figure in the American Transcendentalist movement, which emphasized individualism and the mystical or divine qualities of human souls and nature. Emerson published numerous collections of essays, including Essays *(1841),* Nature *(1849), and* Society and Solitude *(1870).*

In this excerpt from the essay "Politics," Emerson advocates an understanding of law as an evolving structure.

In dealing with the State we ought to remember that its institutions are not aboriginal, though they existed before we were born; that they are not superior to the citizen; that every one of them was once the act of a single man; every law and usage was a man's expedient to meet a particular case; that they all are imitable, all alterable; we may make as good, we may make better. Society is an illusion to the young citizen. It lies before him in rigid repose, with certain names, men and institutions rooted like oak-trees to the centre, round which all arrange themselves the best they can. But the old statesman knows that society is fluid; there are no such roots and centres, but any particle may suddenly become the centre of the movement and compel the system to gyrate round it; as every man of strong will, like Pisistratus[1] or Cromwell,[2] does for a time, and every man of truth, like Plato[3] or Paul,[4] does forever. But politics rest on necessary foundations, and cannot be treated with levity. Republics abound in young civilians who believe that the laws make the city, that grave modifications of the policy and modes of living and employments of the population, that commerce,

---

1 *Pisistratus* Major Athenian ruler (607–528 BCE), who was thought to have created the first welfare state by providing loans to poor farmers.
2 *Cromwell* Oliver Cromwell (1599–1658), who led a rebellion against the British monarchy and became the first prime minister of Britain.
3 *Plato* Influential Greek philosopher (427–347 BCE), who grappled with the problem of how best to govern a nation.
4 *Paul* Paul the Apostle, who hugely influenced the development of Christianity.

education and religion may be voted in or out; and that any measure, though it were absurd, may be imposed on a people if only you can get sufficient voices to make it a law. But the wise know that foolish legislation is a rope of sand which perishes in the twisting; that the State must follow and not lead the character and progress of the citizen; the strongest usurper[1] is quickly got rid of; and they only who build on Ideas, build for eternity; and that the form of government which prevails is the expression of what cultivation exists in the population which permits it. The law is only a memorandum. We are superstitious, and esteem the statute somewhat: so much life as it has in the character of living men is its force. The statute stands there to say, Yesterday we agreed so and so, but how feel ye this article today? Our statute is a currency which we stamp with our own portrait: it soon becomes unrecognizable, and in process of time will return to the mint. Nature is not democratic, nor limited-monarchical,[2] but despotic, and will not be fooled or abated of any jot of her authority by the pertest of her sons; and as fast as the public mind is opened to more intelligence, the code is seen to be brute and stammering. It speaks not articulately, and must be made to. Meantime the education of the general mind never stops. The reveries of the true and simple are prophetic. What the tender poetic youth dreams, and prays, and paints to-day, but shuns the ridicule of saying aloud, shall presently be the resolutions of public bodies; then shall be carried as grievance and bill of rights through conflict and war, and then shall be triumphant law and establishment for a hundred years, until it gives place in turn to new prayers and pictures. The history of the State sketches in coarse outline the progress of thought, and follows at a distance the delicacy of culture and of aspiration.

Questions

1. Emerson writes that Nature is "despotic" and "speaks not articulately, and must be made to." What does he mean by this? What are the implications of this point with regard to Emerson's own argument?
2. Who is both the subject of and the implied audience for this work? Who is excluded from this group by virtue of both Emerson's language and the realities of his time? What is the relationship between Emerson's thesis and this circumstance from the perspective of today's reader?

---

1   *usurper* One who takes control of a government without being elected or appointed.
2   *limited-monarchical* Relating to a form of government in which the monarch rules under conditions prescribed by a constitution.

WINSTON CHURCHILL

Wars Are Not Won by Evacuations

(1940)

Winston Churchill (1874–1965) was the prime minister of Great Britain from 1940–45 and 1951–55. He first became a member of parliament in 1900 and held many posts until 1964, when he did not seek re-election. Churchill was also a writer and an amateur painter. He wrote one novel, two biographies, and numerous volumes of histories of World War I and II.

The following passage is part of a speech Churchill delivered to the House of Commons on 4 June 1940, during World War II. After German troops broke through the Allied line in Belgium, the British Expeditionary Force retreated to the beaches of Dunkirk, France, from which 338,000 troops were subsequently rescued from the advancing German army by the Royal Air Force, the Royal Navy, and an armada of civilian ships. In this speech, Churchill responds to the euphoria in Britain that followed this event.

Turning once again, and this time more generally, to the question of invasion, I would observe that there has never been a period in all these long centuries of which we boast when an absolute guarantee against invasion, still less against serious raids, could have been given to our people. In the days of Napoleon the same wind which would have carried his transports across the Channel might have driven away the blockading fleet. There was always the chance, and it is that chance which has excited and befooled the imaginations of many Continental tyrants. Many are the tales that are told. We are assured that novel methods will be adopted, and when we see the originality of malice, the ingenuity of aggression, which our enemy displays, we may certainly prepare ourselves for every kind of novel stratagem and every kind of brutal and treacherous manoeuvre. I think that no idea is so outlandish that it should not be considered and viewed with a searching, but at the same time, I hope, with a steady eye. We must never forget the solid assurances of sea power and those which belong to air power if it can be locally exercised.

I have, myself, full confidence that if all do their duty, if nothing is neglected, and if the best arrangements are made, as they are being made, we shall prove ourselves once again able to defend our Island home, to ride out the storm of war, and to outlive the menace of tyranny, if necessary for years, if necessary alone. At any rate, that is what we are going to try to do. That is the resolve of His Majesty's Government—every man of them. That is the will of Parliament and the nation. The British Empire and the French Republic, linked together in their cause and in their need, will defend to the death their native soil, aiding each other like good comrades to the utmost of their strength. Even though large tracts of Europe and many old and famous States have fallen or may fall into the grip of the Gestapo and all the odious apparatus of Nazi rule, we shall not flag or fail. We shall go on to the end, we shall fight in France, we shall fight on the seas and oceans, we shall fight with growing confidence and growing strength in the air, we shall defend our Island, whatever the cost may be, we shall fight on the beaches, we shall fight on the landing grounds, we shall fight in the fields and in the streets, we shall fight in the hills; we shall never surrender, and even if, which I do not for a moment believe, this Island or a large part of it were subjugated and starving, then our Empire beyond the seas, armed and guarded by the British Fleet, would carry on the struggle, until, in God's good time, the New World, with all its power and might, steps forth to the rescue and the liberation of the old.

Questions

1. What exactly are Churchill's aims in this speech?
2. Identify both the historical references Churchill makes here and their functions in his speech.
3. Identify and characterize a major shift in tone in this passage. What is its effect?
4. Compare and contrast this passage with comments made by a modern leader of a country at war as reported in a recent newspaper or magazine article.

MARTIN LUTHER KING, JR.

Letter from Birmingham Jail

(1963)

Martin Luther King, Jr. (1929–68) was a Baptist minister and leader of the American civil rights movement in the 1950s and 1960s. He received the 1964 Nobel Peace Prize for his leadership of nonviolent demonstrations for racial equality. King was assassinated in 1968.

The following text was written in response to a statement by eight Alabama clergymen who argued that racial issues were best resolved by the courts rather than by civil disobedience. It is one of the best-known expositions of the principles of the American civil rights movement.

My Dear Fellow Clergymen:

While confined here in the Birmingham city jail, I came across your recent statement calling my present activities "unwise and untimely." Seldom do I pause to answer criticism of my work and ideas. If I sought to answer all the criticisms that cross my desk, my secretaries would have little time for anything other than such correspondence in the course of the day, and I would have no time for constructive work. But since I feel that you are men of genuine good will and that your criticisms are sincerely set forth, I want to try to answer your statement in what I hope will be patient and reasonable terms.

I think I should indicate why I am here in Birmingham, since you have been influenced by the view which argues against "outsiders coming in." I have the honor of serving as president of the Southern Christian Leadership Conference, an organization operating in every southern state, with headquarters in Atlanta, Georgia. We have some eighty-five affiliated organizations across the South, and one of them is the Alabama Christian Movement for Human Rights. Frequently we share staff, educational, and financial resources with our affiliates. Several months ago the affiliate here in Birmingham asked us to be on call to engage in a nonviolent direct-action program if such were deemed necessary. We readily consented, and when the hour came we lived up to our promise. So I, along with several members of my staff, am here because I was invited here. I am here because I have organizational ties here.

But more basically, I am in Birmingham because injustice is here. Just as the prophets of the eighth century B.C. left their villages and carried their "thus saith the Lord" far beyond the boundaries of their home towns, and just as the Apostle Paul left his village of Tarsus and carried the gospel of Jesus Christ to the far corners of the Greco-Roman world, so am I compelled to carry the gospel of freedom beyond my own home town. Like Paul, I must constantly respond to the Macedonian call for aid.

Moreover, I am cognizant of the interrelatedness of all communities and states. I cannot sit idly by in Atlanta and not be concerned about what happens in Birmingham. Injustice anywhere is a threat to justice everywhere. We are caught in an inescapable network of mutuality, tied in a single garment of destiny. Whatever affects one directly, affects all indirectly. Never again can we afford to live with the narrow, provincial "outside agitator" idea. Anyone who lives inside the United States can never be considered an outsider anywhere within its bounds.

You deplore the demonstrations taking place in Birmingham. But your statement, I am sorry to say, fails to express a similar concern for the conditions that brought about the demonstrations. I am sure that none of you would want to rest content with the superficial kind of social analysis that deals merely with effects and does not grapple with underlying causes. It is unfortunate that demonstrations are taking place in Birmingham, but it is even more unfortunate that the city's white power structure left the Negro community with no alternative. 5

In any nonviolent campaign there are four basic steps: collection of the facts to determine whether injustices exist; negotiation; self-purification; and direct action. We have gone through all these steps in Birmingham. There can be no gainsaying the fact that racial injustice engulfs this community. Birmingham is probably the most thoroughly segregated city in the United States. Its ugly record of brutality is widely known. Negroes have experienced grossly unjust treatment in the courts. There have been more unsolved bombings of Negro homes and churches in Birmingham than in any other city in the nation. These are the hard, brutal facts of the case. On the basis of these conditions, Negro leaders sought to negotiate with the city fathers. But the latter consistently refused to engage in good-faith negotiation.

Then, last September, came the opportunity to talk with leaders of Birmingham's economic community. In the course of the negotiations, certain promises were made by the merchants—for example, to remove the stores' humiliating racial signs. On the basis of these promises, the Reverend Fred Shuttlesworth and the leaders of the Alabama Christian Movement for Human Rights agreed to a moratorium on all demonstrations. As the weeks and months went by, we realized that we were the victims of a broken promise. A few signs, briefly removed, returned; the others remained.

As in so many past experiences, our hopes had been blasted, and the shadow of deep disappointment settled upon us. We had no alternative except to prepare for direct action, whereby we could present our very bodies as a means of laying our case before the conscience of the local and the national community. Mindful of the difficulties involved, we decided to undertake a process of self-purification. We began a series of workshops on nonviolence, and we repeatedly asked ourselves: "Are you able to accept blows without retaliating?" "Are you able to endure the ordeal of jail?" We decided to schedule our direct-action program for the Easter season, realizing that except for Christmas, this is the main shopping period of the year. Knowing that a strong economic-withdrawal program would be the by-product of direct action, we felt that this would be the best time to bring pressure to bear on the merchants for the needed change.

Then it occurred to us that Birmingham's mayoral election was coming up in March, and we speedily decided to postpone action until after election day. When we discovered that the Commissioner of Public Safety, Eugene "Bull" Connor, had piled up enough votes to be in the run-off, we decided again to postpone action until the day after the run-off so that the demonstrations could not be used to cloud the issues. Like many others, we wanted to see Mr. Connor defeated, and to this end we endured postponement after postponement. Having aided in this community need, we felt that our direct-action program could be delayed no longer.

10   You may well ask, "Why direct action? Why sit-ins, marches, and so forth? Isn't negotiation a better path?" You are quite right in calling for negotiation. Indeed, this is the very purpose of direct action. Nonviolent direct action seeks so to create such a crisis and foster such tension that a community which has constantly refused to negotiate is forced to confront the issue. It seeks to dramatize the issue that it can no longer be ignored. My citing the creation of tension as part of the work of the nonviolent-resister may sound rather shocking. But I must confess that I am not afraid of the word "tension." I have earnestly opposed violent tension, but there is a type of constructive, nonviolent tension which is necessary for growth. Just as Socrates felt that it was necessary to create a tension in the mind so that individuals could rise from the bondage of myths and half-truths to the unfettered realm of creative analysis and objective appraisal, so must we see the need for nonviolent gadflies to create the kind of tension in society that will help men rise from the dark depths of prejudice and racism to the majestic heights of understanding and brotherhood.

The purpose of our direct-action program is to create a situation so crisis-packed that it will inevitably open the door to negotiation. I therefore concur with you in your call for negotiation. Too long has our beloved Southland been bogged down in a tragic effort to live in monologue rather than dialogue.

One of the basic points in your statement is that the action that I and my associates have taken in Birmingham is untimely. Some have asked: "Why didn't you give the new city administration time to act?" The only answer that I can give to this query is that the new Birmingham administration must be prodded about as much as the outgoing one, before it will act. We are sadly mistaken if we feel that the election of Albert Boutwell as mayor will bring the millennium to Birmingham. While Mr. Boutwell is a much more gentle person than Mr. Connor, they are both segregationists, dedicated to maintenance of the status quo. I have hoped that Mr. Boutwell will be reasonable enough to see the futility of massive resistance to desegregation. But he will not see this without pressure from devotees of civil rights. My friends, I must say to you that we have not made a single gain in civil rights without determined legal and nonviolent pressure. Lamentably, it is an historical fact that privileged groups seldom give up their privileges voluntarily. Individuals may see the moral light and voluntarily give up their unjust posture; but, as Reinhold Niebuhr has reminded us, groups tend to be more immoral than individuals.

We know through painful experience that freedom is never voluntarily given by the oppressor; it must be demanded by the oppressed. Frankly, I have yet to engage in a direct-action campaign that was "well timed" in the view of those who have not suffered unduly from the disease of segregation. For years now I have heard the word "Wait!" It rings in the ear of every Negro with piercing familiarity. This "Wait" has almost always meant "Never." We must come to see, with one of our distinguished jurists, that "justice too long delayed is justice denied."

We have waited for more than 340 years for our constitutional and God-given rights. The nations of Asia and Africa are moving with jetlike speed toward gaining political independence, but we still creep at horse-and-buggy pace toward gaining a cup of coffee at a lunch counter. Perhaps it is easy for those who have never felt the stinging darts of segregation to say, "Wait." But when you have seen vicious mobs lynch your mothers and fathers at will and drown your sisters and brothers at whim; when you have seen hate-filled policemen curse, kick, and even kill your black brothers and sisters; when you see the vast majority of your twenty million Negro brothers smothering in an airtight cage of poverty in the midst of an affluent society; when you suddenly find your tongue twisted and your speech stammering as you seek to explain to your six-year-old daughter why she can't go to the public amusement park that has just been advertised on television, and see tears welling up in her eyes when she is told that Funtown is closed to colored children, and see ominous clouds of inferiority beginning to form in her little mental sky, and see her beginning to distort her personality by developing an unconscious bitterness toward white people; when you have to concoct an answer for a five-year-old son who is asking, "Daddy, why do white people treat colored people so mean?"; when you take a cross-country drive and find it necessary to sleep night after night in the uncomfortable corners of your automobile because no motel will accept you; when you are humiliated day in and day out by nagging signs reading "white" and "colored"; when your first name becomes "nigger," your middle name becomes "boy" (however old you are) and your last name becomes "John," and your wife and mother are never given the respected title "Mrs."; when you are harried by day and haunted by night by the fact that you are a Negro, living constantly at tiptoe stance, never quite knowing what to expect next, and are plagued with inner fears and outer resentments; when you are forever fighting a degenerating sense of "nobodiness"—then you will understand why we find it difficult to wait. There comes a time when the cup of endurance runs over, and men are no longer willing to be plunged into the abyss of despair. I hope, sirs, you can understand our legitimate and unavoidable impatience.

15   You express a great deal of anxiety over our willingness to break laws. This is certainly a legitimate concern. Since we so diligently urge people to obey the Supreme Court's decision of 1954[1] outlawing segregation in the public schools, at first glance it may seem rather paradoxical for us consciously to break laws. One may well ask: "How can you advocate breaking some laws and obeying others?" The answer lies in the fact that there are two types of laws: just and unjust. I would be the first to advocate obeying just laws. One has not only a legal but a moral responsibility to obey just laws. Conversely, one has a moral responsibility to disobey unjust laws. I would agree with St. Augustine that "an unjust law is no law at all."

Now, what is the difference between the two? How does one determine whether a law is just or unjust? A just law is a man-made code that squares with the moral law or the law of God. An unjust law is a code that is out of harmony with the moral law. To put it in the terms of St. Thomas Aquinas: An unjust law is a human law that is not rooted in eternal law and natural law. Any law that uplifts human personality is just. Any law that degrades human personality is unjust. All segregation statutes are unjust because segregation distorts the soul and damages the personality. It gives the segregator a false sense of superiority and the segregated a false sense of inferiority. Segregation, to use the terminology of the Jewish philosopher Martin Buber, substitutes an "I-it" relationship for an "I-thou" relationship and ends up relegating persons to the status of things. Hence segregation is not only politically, economically, and sociologically unsound, it is morally wrong and sinful. Paul Tillich has said that sin is separation. Is not segregation an existential expression of man's tragic separation, his awful estrangement, his terrible sinfulness? Thus it is that I can urge men to obey the 1954 decision of the Supreme Court, for it is morally right; and I can urge them to disobey segregation ordinances, for they are morally wrong.

Let us consider a more concrete example of just and unjust laws. An unjust law is a code that a numerical or power majority group compels a

---

1   *1954* Brown v. Board of Education: prior to 1954 the courts had allowed states to follow policies according to which black and white were supposedly "separate but equal."

minority group to obey but does not make binding on itself. This is *difference* made legal. By the same token, a just law is a code that a majority compels a minority to follow and that it is willing to follow itself. This is *sameness* made legal.

Let me give another explanation. A law is unjust if it is inflicted on a minority that, as a result of being denied the right to vote, had no part in enacting or devising the law. Who can say that the legislature of Alabama which set up that state's segregation laws was democratically elected? Throughout Alabama all sorts of devious methods are used to prevent Negroes from becoming registered voters, and there are some counties in which, even though Negroes constitute a majority of the population, not a single Negro is registered. Can any law enacted under such circumstances be considered democratically structured?

Sometimes a law is just on its face and unjust in its application. For instance, I have been arrested on a charge of parading without a permit. Now, there is nothing wrong in having an ordinance which requires a permit for a parade. But such an ordinance becomes unjust when it is used to maintain segregation and to deny citizens the First-Amendment privilege of peaceful assembly and protest.

I hope you are able to see the distinction I am trying to point out. In no sense do I advocate evading or defying the law, as would the rabid segregationist. That would lead to anarchy. One who breaks an unjust law must do so openly, lovingly, and with a willingness to accept the penalty. I submit that an individual who breaks a law that conscience tells him is unjust, and who willingly accepts the penalty of imprisonment in order to arouse the conscience of the community over its injustice, is in reality expressing the highest respect for law. 20

Of course, there is nothing new about this kind of civil disobedience. It was evidenced sublimely in the refusal of Shadrach, Meshach, and Abednego to obey the laws of Nebuchadnezzar, on the ground that a higher moral law was at stake. It was practiced superbly by the early Christians, who were willing to face hungry lions and the excruciating pain of chopping blocks rather than submit to certain unjust laws of the Roman Empire. To a degree, academic freedom is a reality today because Socrates practiced civil disobedience. In our own nation, the Boston Tea Party represented a massive act of civil disobedience.

We should never forget that everything Adolf Hitler did in Germany was "legal" and everything the Hungarian freedom fighters[1] did in Hungary was "illegal." It was "illegal" to aid and comfort a Jew in Hitler's Germany. Even so, I am sure that, had I lived in Germany at the time, I would have aided and comforted my Jewish brothers. If today I lived in a Communist country

---

1 *freedom fighters* The Hungarian Rebellion in 1956 against an oppressive government was brutally suppressed with the help of the Soviet army.

where certain principles dear to the Christian faith are suppressed, I would openly advocate disobeying that country's anti-religious laws.

I must make two honest confessions to you, my Christian and Jewish brothers. First, I must confess that over the past few years I have been gravely disappointed with the white moderate. I have almost reached the regrettable conclusion that the Negro's great stumbling block in his stride toward freedom is not the White Citizen's Counciler or the Ku Klux Klanner, but the white moderate, who is more devoted to "order" than to justice; who prefers a negative peace which is the absence of tension to a positive peace which is the presence of justice; who constantly says, "I agree with you in the goal you seek, but I cannot agree with your methods of direct action"; who paternalistically believes he can set the timetable for another man's freedom; who lives by a mythical concept of time and who constantly advises the Negro to wait for a "more convenient season." Shallow understanding from people of good will is more frustrating than absolute misunderstanding from people of ill will. Lukewarm acceptance is much more bewildering than outright rejection.

I had hoped that the white moderate would understand that law and order exist for the purpose of establishing justice and that when they fail in this purpose they become the dangerously structured dams that block the flow of social progress. I had hoped that the white moderate would understand that the present tension in the South is a necessary phase of the transition from an obnoxious negative peace, in which the Negro passively accepted his unjust plight, to a substantive and positive peace, in which all men will respect the dignity and worth of human personality. Actually, we who engage in nonviolent direct action are not the creators of tension. We merely bring to the surface the hidden tension that is already alive. We bring it out in the open, where it can be seen and dealt with. Like a boil that can never be cured so long as it is covered up but must be opened with all its ugliness to the natural medicines of air and light, injustice must be exposed, with all the tension its exposure creates, to the light of human conscience and the air of national opinion, before it can be cured.

25   In your statement you assert that our actions, even though peaceful, must be condemned because they precipitate violence. But is this a logical assertion? Isn't this like condemning a robbed man because his possession of money precipitated the evil act of robbery? Isn't this like condemning Socrates because his unswerving commitment to truth and his philosophical inquiries precipitated the act by the misguided populace in which they made him drink hemlock? Isn't this like condemning Jesus because his unique God-consciousness and never-ceasing devotion to God's will precipitated the evil act of crucifixion? We must come to see that, as the federal courts have consistently affirmed, it is wrong to urge an individual to cease his efforts to gain his basic constitutional rights because the quest may precipitate violence. Society must protect the robbed and punish the robber.

I had also hoped that the white moderate would reject the myth concerning time in relation to the struggle for freedom. I have just received a letter from a white brother in Texas. He writes: "All Christians know that the colored people will receive equal rights eventually, but it is possible that you are in too great a religious hurry. It has taken Christianity almost two thousand years to accomplish what it has. The teachings of Christ take time to come to earth." Such an attitude stems from a tragic misconception of time, from the strangely irrational notion that there is something in the very flow of time that will inevitably cure all ills. Actually, time itself is neutral; it can be used either destructively or constructively. More and more I feel that the people of ill will have used time much more effectively than have the people of good will. We will have to repent in this generation not merely for the hateful words and actions of the bad people, but for the appalling silence of the good people. Human progress never rolls in on wheels of inevitability; it comes through the tireless efforts of men willing to be co-workers with God, and without this hard work, time itself becomes an ally of the forces of social stagnation. We must use time creatively, in the knowledge that the time is always ripe to do right. Now is the time to make real the promise of democracy and transform our pending national elegy into a creative psalm of brotherhood. Now is the time to lift our national policy from the quicksand of racial injustice to the solid rock of human dignity.

You speak of our activity in Birmingham as extreme. At first I was rather disappointed that fellow clergymen would see my nonviolent efforts as those of an extremist. I began thinking about the fact that I stand in the middle of two opposing forces in the Negro community. One is a force of complacency, made up in part of Negroes who, as a result of long years of oppression, are so drained of self-respect and a sense of "somebodiness" that they have adjusted to segregation; and in part of a few middle-class Negroes who, because of a degree of academic and economic security and because in some ways they profit by segregation, have become insensitive to the problems of the masses. The other force is one of bitterness and hatred, and it comes perilously close to advocating violence. It is expressed in the various black nationalist groups that are springing up across the nation, the largest and best-known being Elijah Muhammad's Muslim movement. Nourished by the Negro's frustration over the continued existence of racial discrimination, this movement is made up of people who have lost faith in America, who have absolutely repudiated Christianity, and who have concluded that the white man is an incorrigible "devil."

I have tried to stand between these two forces, saying that we need emulate neither the "do-nothingism" of the complacent nor the hatred and despair of the black nationalist. For there is the more excellent way of love and nonviolent protest. I am grateful to God that, through the influence of the Negro church, the way of nonviolence became an integral part of our struggle.

If this philosophy had not emerged, by now many streets of the South would, I am convinced, be flowing with blood. And I am further convinced that if our white brothers dismiss as "rabblerousers" and "outside agitators" those of us who employ nonviolent direct action, and if they refuse to support our nonviolent efforts, millions of Negroes will, out of frustration and despair, seek solace and security in black-nationalist ideologies—a development that would inevitably lead to a frightening racial nightmare.

30   Oppressed people cannot remain oppressed forever. The yearning for freedom eventually manifests itself, and that is what has happened to the American Negro. Something within has reminded him of his birthright of freedom, and something without has reminded him that it can be gained. Consciously or unconsciously, he has been caught up by the *Zeitgeist*, and with his black brothers of Africa and his brown and yellow brothers of Asia, South America, and the Caribbean, the United States Negro is moving with a sense of great urgency toward the promised land of racial justice. If one recognizes this vital urge that has engulfed the Negro community, one should readily understand why public demonstrations are taking place. The Negro has many pent-up resentments and latent frustrations, and he must release them. So let him march; let him make prayer pilgrimages to the city hall; let him go on freedom rides—and try to understand why he must do so. If his repressed emotions are not released in nonviolent ways, they will seek expression through violence; this is not a threat but a fact of history. So I have not said to my people, "Get rid of your discontent." Rather, I have tried to say that this normal and healthy discontent can be channelled into the creative outlet of nonviolent direct action. And now this approach is being termed extremist.

But though I was initially disappointed at being categorized as an extremist, as I continued to think about the matter I gradually gained a measure of satisfaction from the label. Was not Jesus an extremist for love: "Love your enemies, bless them that curse you, do good to them that hate you, and pray for them which despitefully use you, and persecute you." Was not Amos an extremist for justice: "Let justice roll down like waters and righteousness like an ever-flowing stream." Was not Paul an extremist for the Christian gospel: "I bear in my body the marks of the Lord Jesus." Was not Martin Luther an extremist: "Here I stand; I cannot do otherwise, so help me God." And John Bunyan: "I will stay in jail to the end of my days before I make a butchery of my conscience." And Abraham Lincoln: "This nation cannot survive half slave and half free." And Thomas Jefferson: "We hold these truths to be self-evident, that all men are created equal...." So the question is not whether we will be extremists, but what kind of extremists we will be. Will we be extremists for hate or for love? Will we be extremists for the preservation of injustice or for the extension of justice? In that dramatic scene on Calvary's hill three men were crucified. We must never forget that all three were crucified for the same crime—the crime of extremism. Two were extremists for immorality, and thus fell below their environment. The other, Jesus Christ, was an extremist for love, truth, and goodness, and thereby rose above his environment. Perhaps the South, the nation, and the world are in dire need of creative extremists.

I had hoped that the white moderate would see this need. Perhaps I was too optimistic; perhaps I expected too much. I suppose I should have realized that few members of the oppressor race can understand the deep groans and passionate yearnings of the oppressed race, and still fewer have the vision to see that injustice must be rooted out by strong, persistent, and determined action. I am thankful, however, that some of our white brothers in the South have grasped the meaning of this social revolution and committed themselves to it. They are still all too few in quantity, but they are big in quality. Some—such as Ralph McGill, Lillian Smith, Harry Golden, James McBridge Dabbs, Ann Braden, and Sarah Patton Boyle—have written about our struggle in eloquent and prophetic terms. Others have marched with us down nameless streets of the South. They have languished in filthy, roach-infested jails, suffering the abuse and brutality of policemen who view them as "dirty nigger-lovers." Unlike so many of their moderate brothers and sisters, they have recognized the urgency of the moment and sensed the need for powerful "action" antidotes to combat the disease of segregation.

Let me take note of my other major disappointment. I have been so greatly disappointed with the white church and its leadership. Of course, there are some notable exceptions. I am not unmindful of the fact that each of you has taken some significant stands on this issue. I commend you, Reverend Stallings, for your Christian stand on this past Sunday, in welcoming Negroes to your worship service on a nonsegregated basis. I commend the Catholic leaders of this state for integrating Spring Hill College several years ago.

But despite these notable exceptions, I must honestly reiterate that I have been disappointed with the church. I do not say this as one of those negative critics who can always find something wrong with the church. I say this as a minister of the gospel, who loves the church; who was nurtured in its bosom; who has been sustained by its spiritual blessings and who will remain true to it as long as the cord of life shall lengthen.

When I was suddenly catapulted into the leadership of the bus protest in   35
Montgomery, Alabama,[1] a few years ago, I felt we would be supported by the white church. I felt that the white ministers, priests, and rabbis of the South would be among our strongest allies. Instead, some have been outright opponents, refusing to understand the freedom movement and misrepre-

---

1   *Montgomery, Alabama* In December 1955, Rosa Lee Parks, a 42-year-old civil rights activist, refused to give her seat on a local bus to a white man, sparking a year-long boycott by African-Americans of the Montgomery buses.

senting its leaders; all too many others have been more cautious than courageous and have remained silent behind the anesthetizing security of
stained-glass windows.

In spite of my shattered dreams, I came to Birmingham with the hope
that the white religious leadership of this community would see the justice
of our cause and, with deep moral concern, would serve as the channel
through which our just grievances could reach the power structure. I had
hoped that each of you would understand. But again I have been disappointed.

I have heard numerous southern religious leaders admonish their wor-
shippers to comply with a desegregation decision because it is the law, but
I have longed to hear white ministers declare: "Follow this decree because
integration is morally right and because the Negro is your brother." In the
midst of blatant injustices inflicted upon the Negro, I have watched white
churchmen stand on the sideline and mouth pious irrelevancies and sanc-
timonious trivialities. In the midst of a mighty struggle to rid our nation of
racial and economic injustice, I have heard many ministers say: "Those are
social issues, with which the gospel has no real concern." And I have
watched many churches commit themselves to a completely otherworldly
religion which makes a strange un-Biblical distinction between the body
and soul, between the sacred and the secular.

I have traveled the length and breadth of Alabama, Mississippi, and all
the other southern states. On sweltering summer days and crisp autumn
mornings I have looked at the South's beautiful churches with their lofty
spires pointing heavenward. I have beheld the impressive outlines of her
massive religious-education buildings. Over and over I have found myself
asking: "What kind of people worship here? Who is their God? Where were
their voices when the lips of Governor Barnett dripped with words of inter-
position and nullification? Where were they when Governor Wallace gave a
clarion call for defiance and hatred? Where were their voices of support
when bruised and weary Negro men and women decided to rise from the
dark dungeons of complacency to the bright hills of creative protest?"

Yes, these questions are still in my mind. In deep disappointment I have
wept over the laxity of the church. But be assured that my tears have been
tears of love. There can be no deep disappointment where there is not deep
love. Yes, I love the church. How could I do otherwise? I am in the rather
unique position of being the son, the grandson, and the great-grandson of
preachers. Yes, I see the church as the body of Christ. But, oh! How we have
blemished and scarred that body through social neglect and through fear
of being nonconformists.

40   There was a time when the church was very powerful—in the time when
the early Christians rejoiced at being deemed worthy to suffer for what they
believed. In those days the church was not merely a thermometer that
recorded the ideas and principles of popular opinion; it was a thermostat

that transformed the mores of society. Whenever the early Christians entered a town, the people in power became disturbed and immediately sought to convict the Christians of being "disturbers of the peace" and "outside agitators." But the Christians pressed on, in the conviction that they were "a colony of heaven," called to obey God rather than man. Small in number, they were big in commitment. They were too God-intoxicated to be "astronomically intimidated." By their effort and example they brought an end to such ancient evils as infanticide and gladiatorial contests.

Things are different now. So often the contemporary church is a weak, ineffectual voice with an uncertain sound. So often it is an arch-defender of the status quo. Far from being disturbed by the presence of the church, the power structure of the average community is consoled by the church's silent—and often even vocal—sanction of things as they are.

But the judgement of God is upon the church as never before. If today's church does not recapture the sacrificial spirit of the early church, it will lose its authenticity, forfeit the loyalty of millions, and be dismissed as an irrelevant social club with no meaning for the twentieth century. Every day I meet young people whose disappointment with the church has turned into outright disgust.

Perhaps I have once again been too optimistic. Is organized religion too inextricably bound to the status quo to save our nation and the world? Perhaps I must turn my faith to the inner spiritual church, the church within the church, as the true *ekklesia*[1] and the hope of the world. But again I am thankful to God that some noble souls from the ranks of organized religion have broken loose from the paralysing chains of conformity and joined us as active partners in the struggle for freedom. They have left their secure congregations and walked the streets of Albany, Georgia, with us. They have gone down the highways of the South on tortuous rides for freedom. Yes, they have gone to jail with us. Some have been dismissed from their churches, have lost the support of their bishops and fellow ministers. But they have acted in the faith that right defeated is stronger than evil triumphant. Their witness has been the spiritual salt that has preserved the true meaning of the gospel in these troubled times. They have carved a tunnel of hope through the dark mountain of disappointment.

I hope the church as a whole will meet the challenge of this decisive hour. But even if the church does not come to the aid of justice, I have no despair about the future. I have no fear about the outcome of our struggle in Birmingham, even if our motives are at present misunderstood. We will reach the goal of freedom in Birmingham and all over the nation, because the goal of America is freedom. Abused and scorned though we may be, our destiny is tied up with America's destiny. Before the pilgrims landed at Plymouth, we were here. Before the pen of Jefferson etched the majestic

---

1   *ekklesia* The early Christian church.

words of the Declaration of Independence across the pages of history, we were here. For more than two centuries our forebears labored in this country without wages; they made cotton king; they built the homes of their masters while suffering gross injustice and shameful humiliation—and yet out of a bottomless vitality they continued to thrive and develop. If the inexpressible cruelties of slavery could not stop us, the opposition we now face will surely fail. We will win our freedom because the sacred heritage of our nation and the eternal will of God are embodied in our echoing demands.

45   Before closing I feel impelled to mention one other point in your statement that has troubled me profoundly. You warmly commended the Birmingham police for keeping "order" and "preventing violence." I doubt that you would have so warmly commended the police force if you had seen its dogs sinking their teeth into unarmed, nonviolent Negroes. I doubt that you would so quickly commend the policemen if you were to observe their ugly and inhumane treatment of Negroes here in the city jail; if you were to watch them push and curse old Negro women and young Negro girls; if you were to see them slap and kick old Negro men and young boys; if you were to observe them, as they did on two occasions, refuse to give us food because we wanted to sing our grace together. I cannot join you in your praise of the Birmingham police department.

It is true that the police have exercised a degree of discipline in handling the demonstrators. In this sense they have conducted themselves rather "nonviolently" in public. But for what purpose? To preserve the evil system of segregation. Over the past few years I have consistently preached that nonviolence demands that the means we use must be as pure as the ends we seek. I have tried to make clear that it is wrong to use immoral means to attain moral ends. But now I must affirm that it is just as wrong, or perhaps even more so, to use moral means to preserve immoral ends. Perhaps Mr. Connor and his policemen have been rather nonviolent in public, as was Chief Pritchett in Albany, Georgia, but they have used moral means of nonviolence to maintain the immoral end of racial injustice. As T.S. Eliot has said, "The last temptation is the greatest treason: To do the right deed for the wrong reason."[1]

I wish you had commended the Negro sit-inners and demonstrators of Birmingham for their sublime courage, their willingness to suffer, and their amazing discipline in the midst of great provocation. One day the South will recognize its real heroes. They will be the James Merediths,[2] with the noble sense of purpose that enables them to face jeering and hostile mobs, and with the agonizing loneliness that characterizes the life of the pioneer.

---

1   *"The ... reason."* These lines are part of the response of St. Thomas à Becket to the fourth tempter in T.S. Eliot's play *Murder in the Cathedral* (1935).

2   *James Merediths* In 1962 James H. Meredith became the first African-American student at the University of Mississippi.

They will be old, oppressed, battered Negro women, symbolized in a seventy-two-year-old woman in Montgomery, Alabama, who rose up with a sense of dignity and with her people decided not to ride segregated buses, and who responded with ungrammatical profundity to one who inquired about her weariness: "My feets is tired, but my soul is at rest." They will be the young high school and college students, the young ministers of the gospel and a host of their elders, courageously and nonviolently sitting in at lunch counters and willingly going to jail for conscience' sake. One day the South will know that when these disinherited children of God sat down at lunch counters, they were in reality standing up for what is best in the American dream and for the most sacred values in our Judaeo-Christian heritage, thereby bringing our nation back to those great wells of democracy which were dug deep by the founding fathers in their formulation of the Constitution and the Declaration of Independence.

Never before have I written such a long letter. I'm afraid it is much too long to take your precious time. I can assure you that it would have been much shorter if I had been writing from a comfortable desk, but what else can one do when he is alone in a narrow jail cell, other than write long letters, think long thoughts, and pray long prayers?

If I have said anything in this letter that overstates the truth and indicates an unreasonable impatience, I beg you to forgive me. If I have said anything that understates the truth and indicates my having a patience that allows me to settle for anything less than brotherhood, I beg God to forgive me.

I hope this letter finds you strong in the faith. I also hope that circum- 50
stances will soon make it possible for me to meet each of you, not as an integrationist or a civil-rights leader but as a fellow clergyman and a Christian brother. Let us all hope that the dark clouds of racial prejudice will soon pass away and the deep fog of misunderstanding will be lifted from our fear-drenched communities, and in some not too distant tomorrow the radiant stars of love and brotherhood will shine over our great nation with all their scintillating beauty.

Yours for the cause of Peace and Brotherhood,
Martin Luther King, Jr.

Questions

1. Name three elements of King's writing that help make this piece such a striking, powerful, and dramatic work, using examples from the text, and explain their effects on the reader.
2. Find at least three examples of parallel structures in King's writing, involving words, phrases, or clauses. Comment on the effects in each instance of using this structure.

GWYNNE DYER

How People Power Topples the Tyrant

(1999)

Gwynne Dyer (1943–) is a London-based journalist whose articles have been published in 45 countries; he is also a broadcaster, author, lecturer, and filmmaker. Dyer was producer and host of the seven-part televisions series War; *his books include* With Every Mistake *(2005).*

In this article, Dyer traces the roots of upheavals in the 1990s in Europe to earlier events on another continent.

In 15 years, we have gone from a world where two-thirds of the people lived under tyrannies to one where more than two-thirds live in more or less democratic societies. We have done so without the explosions of violence that historically accompany change on this scale.

Ten years ago this weekend, I sat in a stuffy office arguing about the possibility of German unification with Sergei Plekhanov, then a star researcher at the Institute for the Study of the USA and Canada. He thought it might happen in 20 years or so. I said it could well happen before the end of the century. And we both thought ourselves quite daring and far-sighted to be having such a conversation right in the heart of Moscow.

I had been far-sighted, in a sense, for after a 1987 visit to Moscow I had persuaded the CBC[1] (which was both bolder and richer in those days) to give me a travel budget on the grounds that *something* big was going to happen, and I would give them a radio series when it did.

I had spent the summer of 1989 travelling all over the Soviet bloc from Berlin to Baku, talking to everyone from Andrei Sakharov[2] to Boris Yeltsin,[3] and by now I was sure that some kind of democratization was coming soon in the satellites and in the Soviet Union itself.

---

1 *CBC* Canadian Broadcasting Corporation.
2 *Andrei Sakharov* (1921-89), Soviet physicist who helped develop Soviet nuclear arms capability, and then in the 1960s became a vocal political activist, against nuclear proliferation and for human rights.
3 *Boris Yeltsin* (1931-), president of Russia from 1991 to 1999.

But I did not imagine how much, how soon. And then, a couple of weeks   5
later, I got on a plane to Budapest.

You could see that it had started (whatever "it" was going to be) on the
way in from the airport. Trabants, the pathetic two-stroke East German
excuse for a people's car, were abandoned everywhere in the streets.

On Sept. 10, the Hungarian government, which was still formally Communist but with "reformers" in the majority, had abolished exit controls on
its border with Austria. On Sept. 11, East Germans realized they could travel visa-free to the fraternal People's Republic of Hungary, and thence defect
via Austria to West Germany without having to brave the mines and
machine guns of the inter-German border.

On Sept. 12, the hemorrhage began: as many as 10,000 East Germans a
day travelling to Hungary for "holidays" and then fleeing west.

By Sept. 13, when I arrived, the Hungarian government had opened a
refugee camp—with the world's fastest turnover—in a Young Pioneer facility in the hills behind Buda. East Germans mostly arrived by taxi from the
city centre, and convoys of coaches bore them away to West Germany within hours of arrival. I stood outside the gates for a couple of hours, inter-
viewing them as they arrived—they were mostly young couples with good
academic or technical qualifications—and it suddenly became clear that
the jig was up *now*.

I remember writing a piece on the plane back to Canada about how East   10
Germany's Communist regime was like one of those Disney characters that
runs straight off a cliff but doesn't fall until he looks down. As soon as I landed, I booked a ticket back to Berlin. It was frankly a bit frightening, because,
in Europe, revolutions have traditionally been served with buckets of blood.

The question was not whether the Communist regimes of the continent
were finished. They were obviously at the end of their tether, utterly out-
performed economically by the West and politically discredited in the eyes
of their own people. But nobody knew how to get rid of them safely, and as
late as 1956 in Hungary the Communists had shown their willingness to kill
large numbers of people to defend their power.

There was one slightly more hopeful precedent—the "Prague spring"[1] of
1968. But apart from the discouraging fact that it had been easily suppressed by a show of force, you couldn't depend on everybody else to be as
moderate and patient as the Czechs had been. This time, it was going to
start with the Germans, not exactly a historical model of moderation, and
they would be going up against the most unequivocally Stalinist regime left
in Europe. (It came out later that Erich Honecker's Socialist Unity Party
had distributed about half a million weapons to party members to fight off
the counter-revolution, if it came.)

---

1   *"Prague spring"* Brief period of political liberalization in Czechoslovakia in
    1968, ended by Soviet invasion that same year.

There was good reason to worry that the Communists would take a lot of their fellow countrymen with them on the way down—and maybe lots of other people as well, given that this would be happening in a divided and hugely militarized country with six foreign armies on its soil. The Cold War, after all, was still officially on.

I think that's why most of the analysts employed by Western governments simply denied that the wholesale collapse of communism could happen: It seemed unthinkably dangerous. Even those of us who did believe it was coming were thoroughly scared. We were all wrong. It was fast and smooth and almost completely peaceful: The demonstrations against the East German regime in October, the opening of the Berlin Wall followed by the Velvet Revolution in Prague in November, practically all of Eastern Europe free of Communist rule by New Year's Day, and scarcely a life lost in the entire process except in Romania.

15   It was the biggest and best surprise of modern history.

Ten years later, though we know all the details of what happened, there is still no consensus on why it happened as it did: Not just the abrupt collapse of communism in Europe but the overwhelmingly *non-violent* character of the change. It was young East Germans who solved the problem—and I would argue that they did it mostly by watching television pictures from Asia.

A little genealogy here. Non-violent political protest has a long pedigree in the 20th century, and its two most distinguished proponents, Mohandas Gandhi and Martin Luther King, enjoy the status of secular saints. Both Gandhi and King were struggling against essentially democratic and lawbound governments. All discussions of non-violence's potential for effecting real political change down to the 1970s tended to end with the observation that it wouldn't have worked against Hitler or Stalin. But then, in 1986, the Filipinos successfully used it against a dictator.

The Philippines was a good place to start, because it was a media-wise country whose opposition leaders were well aware of both the Asian and the American traditions of non-violence. Moreover, the "people power" revolution in Manila was the first popular uprising where there was television coverage with live satellite up-links, and its leaders brilliantly exploited their direct access to a global audience to deter Ferdinand Marcos from a violent response. If a dictatorship loses its will to resort to force, it is finished: Get on the helicopter quick, and to hell with Imelda's shoes.

The methodology of Manila was broadcast around the world, and other Asians were quick to pick it up. In the next three years, there were successful copycat non-violent revolutions against dictators in Bangladesh, Thailand and South Korea (plus a tragic failure in Burma in 1988, where the media coverage was sparse and the generals were not deterred). And then, in May and June of 1989, the Chinese students tried the same tactics.

20   They failed in the end, but for three weeks they hovered on the brink of

some sort of success while the world watched. Subsequently, I interviewed a number of the students who led the Tiananmen Square occupation, and most confirmed that, in 1988 and early 1989, they were conducting what amounted to clandestine seminars in non-violence at Beijing University. They were deliberately studying Gandhi, King and videotapes of the events in Manila and elsewhere with the idea that the same tactics might work in a Chinese context. Then they took them out and road-tested them.

We will not know how close they came to success until the archives of the Chinese Communist Party are opened, years or even decades from now. For the purposes of the present argument, that doesn't matter. The point is that the whole world saw these tactics apparently coming close to success in a *Communist* capital—including, most important, the East Germans, a majority of whom lived in easy reach of West German television signals.

Less than six months later, having taken note of their own regime's isolation and inability to stop the mass exodus through Hungary, the East Germans got out on the streets of Leipzig and Berlin and used the same tactics with total success. They correctly calculated that local Communists, unlike the Chinese variety, had lost the will to massacre their own citizens—and once that was clear, the game was quickly over, not only in East Germany but all over the Soviet bloc. Three hundred and seventy-five million people in what are now two dozen countries removed their rulers and dismantled an empire with hardly a shot fired.

There have been quite a few shots fired subsequently, mostly in the mountainous and ethnically tangled southern borderlands of the former empire, but that is just the usual post-imperial turmoil. The revolution itself was bloodless almost everywhere, and despite the economic miseries that the transition has brought to many people, the planet is a much better and safer place as a result. No more gulags, no more obsessive discussions of nuclear throw-weight, no more bipolar world where to reject the local orthodoxy was to "defect."

It was the first time that Asia has led the way politically for at least several hundred years, and the expanded scope for non-violent action in a media-saturated world has continued to show its power throughout the past decade in new democratic revolutions from South Africa to Indonesia. In 15 years, we have gone from a world where two-thirds of the people lived under tyrannies to a world where more than two-thirds of the people live in more or less democratic societies, and we have done so without the great explosions of violence that historically accompanied change on this scale.

Even as I write this, I can sense a million lips curling in scorn at my naiveté, a million myopic quibbles being composed about the highly imperfect nature of these new democracies and the wickedness of the new global economy and the thousand other things that are still wrong

25

with the world. If historical ingratitude were a crime, then the entire chattering classes of the West would be serving life sentences at hard labour.

Never mind. It was a miracle created by millions of other people whose imagination and courage triumphed over their natural cynicism. They have given the world a powerful new political strategy that tilts the scales in favour of human rights, and in a sense they have freed us all.

Questions

1. What assumptions does the author make about his audience? What clues can you find as to the nature of the intended audience?
2. In what ways do newspaper articles (such as this one) differ from most of the other essays and articles in this anthology? For each difference you identify, try to come up with a plausible explanation.
3. The author's second last paragraph is devoted to speculating about those who are likely to disagree with him. Discuss the rhetorical strengths or weaknesses of the approach taken in this paragraph. Why do you think Dyer begins this argumentative essay with several paragraphs written in narrative mode?

❧ *History* ❧

JOHN JAY CHAPMAN

Coatesville

(1912)

John Jay Chapman (1862–1933) was born and raised in New York. An essayist, poet, and dramatist, he was educated at Harvard Law School and practiced law for 10 years. Chapman wrote over 25 books and plays during his lifetime, including Emerson and Other Essays *(1898).*

Chapman delivered this speech in Coatesville, Pennsylvania, on 18 August 1912. It commemorated the first anniversary of a mob's torture and murder of a black man suspected to have killed a white police officer. Only two other people attended the meeting where Chapman made this address.

We are met to commemorate the anniversary of one of the most dreadful crimes in history—not for the purpose of condemning it, but to repent of our share in it. We do not start any agitation with regard to that particular crime. I understand that an attempt to prosecute the chief criminals has been made, and has entirely failed; because the whole community, and in a sense our whole people, are really involved in the guilt. The failure of the prosecution in this case, in all such cases, is only a proof of the magnitude of the guilt, and of the awful fact that everyone shares in it.

I will tell you why I am here; I will tell you what happened to me. When I read in the newspapers of August 14, a year ago, about the burning alive of a human being, and of how a few desperate, fiend-minded men had been permitted to torture a man chained to an iron bedstead, burning alive, thrust back by pitchforks when he struggled out of it, while around about stood hundreds of well-dressed American citizens, both from the vicinity and from afar, coming on foot and in wagons, assembling on telephone call, as if by magic, silent, whether from terror or indifference, fascinated and impotent, hundreds of persons watching this awful sight and making no attempt to stay the wickedness, and no one man among them all who was inspired to risk his life in an attempt to stop it, no one man to name the name of Christ, of humanity, of government! As I read the newspaper accounts of the scene enacted here in Coatesville a year ago, I seemed to get a glimpse into the unconscious soul of this country. I saw a seldom revealed picture of the American heart and of the American nature. I seemed to be looking into the heart of the criminal—a cold thing, an awful thing.

I said to myself, "I shall forget this, we shall all forget it; but it will be there. What I have seen is not an illusion. It is the truth. I have seen death in the heart of this people." For to look at the agony of a fellow-being and remain aloof means death in the heart of the onlooker. Religious fanaticism has sometimes lifted men to the frenzy of such cruelty, political passion has sometimes done it, personal hatred might do it, the excitement of the amphitheater in the degenerate days of Roman luxury could do it. But here an audience chosen by chance in America has stood spellbound through an improvised *auto-da-fé*,[1] irregular, illegal, having no religious significance, not sanctioned by custom, having no immediate provocation, the audience standing by merely in cold dislike.

I saw during one moment something beyond all argument in the depth of its significance. You might call it the paralysis of the nerves about the heart in a people habitually and unconsciously given over to selfish aims, an ignorant people who knew not what spectacle they were providing, or what part they were playing in a judgment-play which history was exhibiting on that day.

5   No theories about the race problem, no statistics, legislation, or mere educational endeavor, can quite meet the lack which that day revealed in the American people. For what we saw was death. The people stood like blighted things, like ghosts about Acheron,[2] waiting for someone or something to determine their destiny for them.

Whatever life itself is, that thing must be replenished in us. The opposite of hate is love, the opposite of cold is heat; what we need is the love of God and reverence for human nature. For one moment I knew that I had seen our true need; and I was afraid that I should forget it and that I should go about framing arguments and agitations and starting schemes of education, when the need was deeper than education. And I became filled with one idea, that I must not forget what I had seen, and that I must do something to remember it. And I am here to-day chiefly that I may remember that vision. It seems fitting to come to this town where the crime occurred and hold a prayer-meeting, so that our hearts may be turned to God through whom mercy may flow into us.

---

1   *auto-da-fé* In the Spanish Inquisition, the burning to death of heretics.
2   *Acheron* In ancient Greek mythology, the river across which the dead were ferried into the underworld.

Let me say one thing more about the whole matter. The subject we are dealing with is not local. The act, to be sure, took place at Coatesville and everyone looked to Coatesville to follow it up. Some months ago I asked a friend who lives not far from here something about this case, and about the expected prosecutions, and he replied to me: "It wasn't in my county," and that made me wonder whose county it was in. And it seemed to be in my county. I live on the Hudson River; but I knew that this great wickedness that happened in Coatesville is not the wickedness of Coatesville nor of to-day. It is the wickedness of all America and of three hundred years—the wickedness of the slave trade. All of us are tinctured by it. No special place, no special persons, are to blame. A nation cannot practice a course of inhuman crime for three hundred years and then suddenly throw off the effects of it. Less than fifty years ago domestic slavery was abolished among us; and in one way and another the marks of that vice are in our faces. There is no country in Europe where the Coatesville tragedy or anything remotely like it could have been enacted, probably no country in the world.

On the day of the calamity, those people in the automobiles came by the hundred and watched the torture, and passers-by came in a great multitude and watched it—and did nothing. On the next morning the newspapers spread the news and spread the paralysis until the whole country seemed to be helplessly watching this awful murder, as awful as anything ever done on the earth; and the whole of our people seemed to be looking on helplessly, not able to respond, not knowing what to do next. That spectacle has been in my mind.

The trouble has come down to us out of the past. The only reason that slavery is wrong is that it is cruel and makes men cruel and leaves them cruel. Someone may say that you and I cannot repent because we did not do the act. But we are involved in it. We are still looking on. Do you not see that this whole event is merely the last parable, the most vivid, the most terrible illustration that ever was given by man or imagined by a Jewish prophet, of the relation between good and evil in this world, and of the relation of men to one another?

This whole matter has been an historic episode; but it is a part, not only of our national history, but of the personal history of each one of us. With the great disease (slavery) came the climax (the war), and after the climax gradually began the cure, and in the process of cure comes now the knowledge of what the evil was. I say that our need is new life, and that books and resolutions will not save us, but only such disposition in our hearts and souls as will enable the new life, love, force, hope, virtue, which surround us always, to enter into us.

This is the discovery that each man must make for himself—the discovery that what he really stands in need of he cannot get for himself, but must wait till God gives it to him. I have felt the impulse to come here to-day to testify to this truth.

The occasion is not small; the occasion looks back on three centuries and embraces a hemisphere. Yet the occasion is small compared with the truth it leads us to. For this truth touches all ages and affects every soul in the world.

Questions

1. Chapman says, "I will tell you why I am here; I will tell you what happened to me" (paragraph 2). What is the effect of his use of the first person in this speech?
2. Chapman's ethical perspective is shaped, at least in part, by his belief in God. In what ways would his argument be different if it did not refer to religion?

MARTHA GELLHORN

The Bomber Boys

(1943)

*Martha Gellhorn (1908–98) was a journalist and novelist. She began working as a
foreign correspondent in 1930 when she traveled to Paris. Over the course of her life
she reported on wars and events in Spain, Finland, the Middle East, Vietnam, and
China. She covered the US invasion of Panama when she was 81 years old. In addition to her journalism, Gellhorn was the author of 5 novels, 14 novellas, 2 short story
collections, and a play.*

Gellhorn here describes her visit to a British air force base during World War II.

They were very quiet. There was enough noise going on around them, but
they had no part in it. A truck clanked past with a string of bomb trolleys
behind it. The ground crew was still loading the thousand-pound high-
explosive bombs that look like huge rust-colored sausages. A WAAF's[1] clear
high English voice, relaying orders, mixed with the metal noises. A light on
the open bomb bay made the darkness around the plane even darker. The
moon was skimmed over with cloud, and around the field the great black
Lancasters waited, and men finished the final job of getting them ready. But
the crews who were going to fly seemed to have nothing to do with this
action and haste. Enormous and top-heavy in their Mae Wests[2] or their elec-
trically heated flying suits, these men seemed over-life-size statues. They
stood together near their planes.

   The Group Captain had been driving fast around the perimeter track of
the field in a beetle of a car, checking up. He appeared the way people seem
to, suddenly out of the flat black emptiness of the airdrome, and said,
'Come and meet the boys.' The pilot of this crew was twenty-one and tall
and thin, with a face far too sensitive for this business. He said, 'I was in
Texas for nine months. Smashing place.' This would mean that Texas was
wonderful. The others said how do you do. They were polite and kind and
far away. Talk was nonsense now. Every man went tight and concentrated

---

1 *WAAF* Women's Auxiliary Air Force.
2 *Mae Wests* Inflatable life jackets.

into himself, waiting and ready for the job ahead, and the seven of them who were going together made a solid unit, and anyone who had not done what they did and would never go where they were going could not understand and had no right to intrude. One could only stand in the cold darkness and feel how hard we were all waiting.

We drove to the control station, which looks like a trailer painted in yellow and black checks, and though there was no wind the cold ate into you. The motors were warming up, humming and heavy. Now the big black planes wheeled out and one by one rolled around the perimeter and got into position on the runway. A green light blinked and there was a roar of four motors that beat back in an echo from the sky. Then the first plane was gone into the blackness, not seeming to move very fast, and we saw the taillight lifting, and presently the thirteen planes that were taking off from this field floated against the sky as if the sky were water. Then they changed into distant, slow-moving stars. That was that. The chaps were off. They would be gone all this night. They were going to fly over France, over known and loved cities, cities they would not see and that did not now concern them. They were going south to bomb marshaling yards, to destroy if possible and however briefly one of the two rail connections between France and Italy. If they succeeded, the infantry in southern Italy would have an easier job for a little while.

Several hundreds of planes, thousands of bomber boys, were taking off into the wavering moon from different fields all over this part of England. They were out for the night with the defended coast of France ahead, and the mountain ranges where the peaks go up to ten thousand feet and the winter weather is never a gift; and then of course there would be the target. This trip, however, came under the heading of 'a piece of cake,' which means in the wonderful RAF[1] language a pushover. If you were taking a pessimistic view of this raid you might have called it 'a long stooge,' which means simply a dreary, unsatisfactory bore. No one would have given the mission more importance than that. Still they were very quiet and the airdrome felt bleak when they were gone and the waiting had simply changed its shape. First you wait for them to go and then you wait for them to get back.

5   Perhaps this is a typical bomber station; I do not know. Perhaps every station is different as every man is different. This was an RAF station and the crews flying tonight were English and Canadian, except for one South African and two Australians and an American pilot from Chicago. The youngest pilot was twenty-one and the oldest thirty-two and before the war they had been various things: a commercial artist, a schoolteacher, a detective, a civil servant, a contractor. None of this tells you anything about them. They look tired, and they look older than they are. They fly by night and

---

1   *RAF* Royal Air Force.

sleep somewhat during the day and when they are not flying there is work to do and probably it is exhausting to wait to fly, knowing what the flying is. So they look tired and do not speak of this and if you mention it they say they get plenty of rest and everyone feels very well.

The land where they live is as flat as Kansas and cold now and dun-colored. The land seems unused and almost not lived in, but the air is always busy. At sunset you see a squadron of Spitfires flying back to their station against a tan evening sky, looking like little rowboats and flying home, neat and close. In the thin morning, the day bombers roar over toward the Channel. The air is loud and occupied and the airdrome is noisy too. But the home life of the men is quiet.

They say that if you find all the chaps in the mess reading at teatime, you know there are operations scheduled for that night. This afternoon they sat in the big living room of the country house that has become their mess, and they looked like good tidy children doing their homework. If you read hard enough you can get away from yourself and everyone else and from thinking about the night ahead. That morning they would have made a night flying test, taking the planes up to see that everything was okay. Between the test and the afternoon briefing is the rumor period, during which someone finds out how much gasoline is being loaded on the planes and everyone starts guessing about the target, basing guesses on miles per gallon. The briefing (the instructions about the trip and the target) would normally be finished by late afternoon and then there is an operational meal and then the few bad hours to kill before take-off time. It is a routine they all know and have learned to handle; they have taken on this orderly unshaken quietness as a way of living.

Of course there is relaxation in the nearest village on free nights—the village dance hall and the local girls to dance with, the pubs where you can drink weak war beer, and the movies where you can see the old films. At eleven o'clock all such gaieties stop and the village shuts firmly. No one could say this is a flashing romantic existence; it is somewhere between a boarding school and a monastery. They have their job to do and they take this sort of life as it comes and do not think too much about it or about anything. There is only one clear universal thought and that is: finish it. Win the war and get it over with. There's been enough; there's been too much. The thing to do is win now soon, as fast as possible.

The old life that perhaps seemed flat when they had it becomes beautiful and rare when they remember it. No one who flies could make any detailed plans; there is no sense in counting your bridges as well and safely crossed when you know how many tough bridges are ahead. But vaguely each man thinks of that not-so-distant almost incredible past, when no one did anything much, nothing spectacular, nothing fatal, when a day was quite long and there was an amazing number of agreeable ways to spend it. They want that again, though they want a life that has grown lovelier in their memories. They want a future that is as good as they now imagine the past to have been.

10   It is a long night when you are waiting for the planes from Europe to come back, and it is cold, but it has to end. At four o'clock or around then, the duty officers go to the control tower. The operations officers walk about a certain amount and smoke pipes and say casual things to each other and the waiting gets to be a thing you can touch. Then the first plane calls in to the control tower switchboard. Two WAAFs, who have been up all night and are still looking wide-awake, wonderfully pink-cheeked, perfectly collected and not frozen stiff, begin to direct the planes in. The girls' voices that sound so remarkable to us (it is hard to decide why, perhaps because they seem so poised, so neat) begin: 'Hello George pancake over.' In the glassed-in room you hear the pilots answer. Then the girl again: 'Hello Queen air-drome one thousand over.' The night suddenly becomes weird, with the moon still up and the bright stars and the great searchlights like leaning trees over the runway and the wing lights of the plane far off and then near-er, the noise of the motors circling the field, the ambulances rolling out, and the girls' voices going on and on, cool, efficient, unchanging. 'Hello Uncle airdrome twelve fifty over.' This means that a plane, U for Uncle, is to circle the field at twelve hundred and fifty feet until told to 'pancake' or land. The planes come in slowly at first and then there will be four of them circling and landing. The more planes that come in and are marked up on the blackboard, the worse the waiting gets. None of this shows. No voice changes, no one makes a movement that is in any way unusual, the routine proceeds as normally as if people were waiting in line to buy theater tickets. Nothing shows and nothing is said and it is all there.

Finally all the planes were in except P for Peter and J for Jig. They were late. The job was a piece of cake. They should be in. They would of course be in. Obviously. Any minute now. No one mentioned the delay. We started to go down to the interrogation room and the Group Captain remarked without emphasis that he would stay up here for a bit until the chaps got in.

The crews of the eleven planes that had returned were coming into the basement operations room for questioning. They all had mugs of tea, white china shaving mugs filled with a sweetish ghastly lukewarm drink that seems to mean something to them. They looked tireder around their eyelids and mouths, and slanting lines under their eyes were deeply marked. The inter-rogation again gives the curious impression of being in school. The crews sit on a wooden bench in front of a wooden table, and the intelligence offi-cer, behind the table, asks questions. Both questions and answers are made in such low ordinary voices that the group seems to be discussing some-thing dull and insignificant. No one liked this trip much. It was very long and the weather was terrible; the target was small; there was a lot of smoke; they couldn't see the results well.

The Group Captain in command sat on a table and spoke to the crew members by name, saying, 'Have a good trip?' 'Fairly good, sir.' That was all there was to that. Then he said, 'Anyone get angry with you?' 'No sir,' they said, smiling, 'didn't see a thing.' This is the way they talk and behave and this is the way it is. When it was known that all the planes were back, and all undamaged and no one hurt, there was a visible added jovialness. But everyone was tired, anxious to get through the questioning and back to the mess, back to the famous operational fried egg, and fried potatoes, the margarine and the marmalade and the bread that seems to be partially made of sand, and then to sleep. The bomber crews were standing at the mess bar, which is a closet in the wall, drinking beer and waiting for breakfast. They were talking a little now, making private jokes and laughing easily at them. It was after seven in the morning, a dark cold unfriendly hour. Some of the men had saved their raid rations, a can of American orange juice and a chocolate bar, to eat now. They value them highly. The orange juice is fine, the chocolate bar is a treat. There are those who drink the orange juice and eat the chocolate early on, not wanting to be done out of them, at least, no matter what happens.

The Lancasters looked like enormous deadly black birds going off into the night; somehow they looked different when they came back. The planes carried from this field 117,000 pounds of high explosive and the crews flew all night to drop the load as ordered. Now the trains would not run between France and Italy for a while, not on those bombed tracks anyhow. Here are the men who did it, with mussed hair and weary faces, dirty sweaters under their flying suits, sleep-bright eyes, making humble comradely little jokes, and eating their saved-up chocolate bars.

Questions

1. In what ways do the opening sentences of this essay immediately signal that, although this is war reporting, the piece does not employ classic journalistic style (which focuses on the "who, what, when, where, why" of a story)? What aspects of the situation does this piece seek to make most evident? Using examples from the text, discuss how Gellhorn's diction, tone, and style achieve this.

2. In what ways does Gellhorn's writing style suit or even resemble her subject?

HANNAH ARENDT

Deportations from Western Europe—Denmark

(1963)

Hannah Arendt (1906–75), historian and political thinker, was born in Germany and attended the universities of Marburg and Heidelberg, where she studied philosophy with Martin Heidegger. Upon graduating, she researched anti-Semitic propaganda and was jailed by the Gestapo. Arendt later lived in Paris and spent the 1930s helping Jewish refugees; in 1941 she left France and reached the United States, where she became a citizen in 1951. Arendt was the first woman to become a full professor at Princeton University. She is the author of Origins of Totalitarianism *(1951), among other works.*

This excerpt from the book Eichmann in Jerusalem *(1965) examines the reaction of Danish citizens to the Nazis' attempt to deport the country's Jewish population.*

At the Wannsee Conference,[1] Martin Luther, of the Foreign Office, warned of great difficulties in the Scandinavian countries, notably in Norway and Denmark. (Sweden was never occupied, and Finland, though in the war on the side of the Axis,[2] was the one country the Nazis hardly ever even approached on the Jewish question. This surprising exception of Finland, with some two thousand Jews, may have been due to Hitler's great esteem for the Finns, whom perhaps he did not want to subject to threats and humiliating blackmail.) Luther proposed postponing evacuations from Scandinavia for the time being, and as far as Denmark was concerned, this really went without saying, since the country retained its independent government, and was respected as a neutral state, until the fall of 1943, although it, along with Norway, had been invaded by the German Army in April, 1940. There existed no Fascist or Nazi movement in Denmark worth mentioning, and therefore no collaborators. In NORWAY, however, the Germans had been able to find enthusiastic supporters; indeed, Vidkun Quisling, leader of the pro-Nazi and anti-Semitic Norwegian party, gave his name to what later became known

---

1 *Wannsee Conference* A meeting of the Nazi *Staatssekretäre* (Undersecretaries of State) in January 1942, to deliberate how best to execute the "Final Solution," or the extermination of the Jews.

2 *Axis* The group of countries opposed to the Allies in World War II (primarily Germany, Italy, and Japan).

as a "quisling government." The bulk of Norway's seventeen hundred Jews were stateless, refugees from Germany; they were seized and interned in a few lightning operations in October and November, 1942. When Eichmann's office ordered their deportation to Auschwitz,[1] some of Quisling's own men resigned their government posts. This may not have come as a surprise to Mr. Luther and the Foreign Office, but what was much more serious, and certainly totally unexpected, was that Sweden immediately offered asylum, and sometimes even Swedish nationality, to all who were persecuted. Ernst von Weizsäcker, Undersecretary of State of the Foreign Office, who received the proposal, refused to discuss it, but the offer helped nevertheless. It is always relatively easy to get out of a country illegally, whereas it is nearly impossible to enter the place of refuge without permission and to dodge the immigration authorities. Hence, about nine hundred people, slightly more than half of the small Norwegian community, could be smuggled into Sweden.

It was in DENMARK, however, that the Germans found out how fully justified the Foreign Office's apprehensions had been. The story of the Danish Jews is *sui generis*,[2] and the behavior of the Danish people and their government was unique among all the countries of Europe—whether occupied, or a partner of the Axis, or neutral and truly independent. One is tempted to recommend the story as required reading in political science for all students who wish to learn something about the enormous power potential inherent in non-violent action and in resistance to an opponent possessing vastly superior means of violence. To be sure, a few other countries in Europe lacked proper "understanding of the Jewish question," and actually a majority of them were opposed to "radical" and "final" solutions. Like Denmark, Sweden, Italy, and Bulgaria proved to be nearly immune to anti-Semitism, but of the three that were in the German sphere of influence, only the Danes dared speak out on the subject to their German masters. Italy and Bulgaria sabotaged German orders and indulged in a complicated game of double-dealing and double-crossing, saving their Jews by a tour de force of sheer ingenuity, but they never contested the policy as such. That was totally different from what the Danes did. When the Germans approached them rather cautiously about introducing the yellow badge,[3] they were simply told that the King would be the first to wear it, and the Danish government officials were careful to point out that anti-Jewish measures of any sort would cause their own immediate resignation. It was

---

1 *Auschwitz* A large Nazi concentration camp (with associated smaller camps) in Poland, at which it is estimated, between 1.1 million and 1.6 million people died.
2 *sui generis* Unique or one of a kind.
3 *yellow badge* On 1 September 1941, the Nazi administration passed a law stating that Jews in Germany and Nazi occupied territories must wear an identifying badge, a yellow Star of David inscribed with the word *Jude* ("Jew").

decisive in this whole matter that the Germans did not even succeed in introducing the vitally important distinction between native Danes of Jewish origin, of whom there were about sixty-four hundred, and the fourteen hundred German Jewish refugees who had found asylum in the country prior to the war and who now had been declared stateless by the German government. This refusal must have surprised the Germans no end, since it appeared so "illogical" for a government to protect people to whom it had categorically denied naturalization and even permission to work. (Legally, the prewar situation of refugees in Denmark was not unlike that in France, except that the general corruption in the Third Republic's civil services enabled a few of them to obtain naturalization papers, through bribes or "connections," and most refugees in France could work illegally, without a permit. But Denmark, like Switzerland, was no country *pour se débrouiller.*)[1] The Danes, however, explained to the German officials that because the stateless refugees were no longer German citizens, the Nazis could not claim them without Danish assent. This was one of the few cases in which statelessness turned out to be an asset, although it was of course not statelessness per se that saved the Jews but, on the contrary, the fact that the Danish government had decided to protect them. Thus, none of the preparatory moves, so important for the bureaucracy of murder, could be carried out, and operations were postponed until the fall of 1943.

What happened then was truly amazing; compared with what took place in other European countries, everything went topsy-turvy. In August, 1943—after the German offensive in Russia had failed, the Afrika Korps had surrendered in Tunisia, and the Allies had invaded Italy—the Swedish government canceled its 1940 agreement with Germany which had permitted German troops the right to pass through the country. Thereupon, the Danish workers decided that they could help a bit in hurrying things up; riots broke out in Danish shipyards, where the dock workers refused to repair German ships and then went on strike. The German military commander proclaimed a state of emergency and imposed martial law, and Himmler[2] thought this was the right moment to tackle the Jewish question, whose "solution" was long overdue. What he did not reckon with was that— quite apart from Danish resistance—the German officials who had been living in the country for years were no longer the same. Not only did General von Hannecken, the military commander, refuse to put troops at the disposal of the Reich plenipotentiary, Dr. Werner Best; the special S.S. units (*Einsatzkommandos*)[3] employed in Denmark very frequently objected to "the

---

1   *pour se débrouiller* To find a way out.
2   *Himmler* Heinrich Himmler, commander of the *Schutzstaffel* (or S.S., Nazi military arm) and the *Gestapo* (Nazi secret police).
3   *Einsatzkommandos* Death squads, groups within the S.S. whose special assignment was the execution of the "Final Solution."

measures they were ordered to carry out by the central agencies"—according to Best's testimony at Nuremberg.[1] And Best himself, an old Gestapo man and former legal adviser to Heydrich, author of a then famous book on the police, who had worked for the military government in Paris to the entire satisfaction of his superiors, could no longer be trusted, although it is doubtful that Berlin ever learned the extent of his unreliability. Still, it was clear from the beginning that things were not going well, and Eichmann's office sent one of its best men to Denmark—Rolf Günther, whom no one had ever accused of not possessing the required "ruthless toughness." Günther made no impression on his colleagues in Copenhagen, and now von Hannecken refused even to issue a decree requiring all Jews to report for work.

Best went to Berlin and obtained a promise that all Jews from Denmark would be sent to Theresienstadt[2] regardless of their category—a very important concession, from the Nazis' point of view. The night of October 1 was set for their seizure and immediate departure—ships were ready in the harbor and since neither the Danes nor the Jews nor the German troops stationed in Denmark could be relied on to help, police units arrived from Germany for a door-to-door search. At the last moment, Best told them that they were not permitted to break into apartments, because the Danish police might then interfere, and they were not supposed to fight it out with the Danes. Hence they could seize only those Jews who voluntarily opened their doors. They found exactly 477 people, out of a total of more than 7,800, at home and willing to let them in. A few days before the date of doom, a German shipping agent, Georg F. Duckwitz, having probably been tipped off by Best himself, had revealed the whole plan to Danish government officials, who, in turn, had hurriedly informed the heads of the Jewish community. They, in marked contrast to Jewish leaders in other countries, had then communicated the news openly in the synagogues on the occasion of the New Year services. The Jews had just time enough to leave their apartments and go into hiding, which was very easy in Denmark, because, in the words of the judgment, "all sections of the Danish people, from the King down to simple citizens," stood ready to receive them.

They might have remained in hiding until the end of the war if the Danes   5
had not been blessed with Sweden as a neighbor. It seemed reasonable to ship the Jews to Sweden, and this was done with the help of the Danish fishing fleet. The cost of transportation for people without means—about a hundred dollars per person—was paid largely by wealthy Danish citizens, and that was perhaps the most astounding feat of all, since this was a time when Jews were paying for their own deportation, when the rich among

---

1   *Nuremberg* Nuremberg, Germany, site of the Nuremberg Trials (1945–49) at which Nazis were tried for their roles in World War II.
2   *Theresienstadt* Nazi concentration camp in what is now the Czech Republic.

them were paying fortunes for exit permits (in Holland, Slovakia, and, later, in Hungary) either by bribing the local authorities or by negotiating "legally" with the S.S., who accepted only hard currency and sold exit permits, in Holland, to the tune of five or ten thousand dollars per person. Even in places where Jews met with genuine sympathy and a sincere willingness to help, they had to pay for it, and the chances poor people had of escaping were nil.

It took the better part of October to ferry all the Jews across the five to fifteen miles of water that separates Denmark from Sweden. The Swedes received 5,919 refugees, of whom at least 1,000 were of German origin, 1,310 were half-Jews, and 686 were non-Jews married to Jews. (Almost half the Danish Jews seem to have remained in the country and survived the war in hiding.) The non-Danish Jews were better off than ever before, they all received permission to work. The few hundred Jews whom the German police had been able to arrest were shipped to Theresienstadt. They were old or poor people, who either had not received the news in time or had not been able to comprehend its meaning. In the ghetto, they enjoyed greater privileges than any other group because of the never-ending "fuss" made about them by Danish institutions and private persons. Forty-eight persons died, a figure that was not particularly high, in view of the average age of the group. When everything was over, it was the considered opinion of Eichmann that "for various reasons the action against the Jews in Denmark has been a failure," whereas the curious Dr. Best declared that "the objective of the operation was not to seize a great number of Jews but to clean Denmark of Jews, and this objective has now been achieved."

Politically and psychologically, the most interesting aspect of this incident is perhaps the role played by the German authorities in Denmark, their obvious sabotage of orders from Berlin. It is the only case we know of in which the Nazis met with *open* native resistance, and the result seems to have been that those exposed to it changed their minds. They themselves apparently no longer looked upon the extermination of a whole people as a matter of course. They had met resistance based on principle, and their "toughness" had melted like butter in the sun, they had even been able to show a few timid beginnings of genuine courage. That the ideal of "toughness," except, perhaps, for a few half-demented brutes, was nothing but a myth of self-deception, concealing a ruthless desire for conformity at any price, was clearly revealed at the Nuremberg Trials, where the defendants accused and betrayed each other and assured the world that they "had always been against it" or claimed, as Eichmann was to do, that their best qualities had been "abused" by their superiors. (In Jerusalem, he accused "those in power" of having abused his "obedience." "The subject of a good government is lucky, the subject of a bad government is unlucky. I had no luck.") The atmosphere had changed, and although most of them might have known that they were doomed, not a single one of them had the guts to defend the Nazi ideology. Werner Best claimed at Nuremberg that he had played a complicated double role and that it was thanks to him that the Danish officials had been warned of the impending catastrophe; documentary evidence showed, on the contrary, that he himself had proposed the Danish operation in Berlin, but he explained that this was all part of the game. He was extradited to Denmark and there condemned to death, but he appealed the sentence, with surprising results; because of "new evidence," his sentence was commuted to five years in prison, from which he was released soon afterward. He must have been able to prove to the satisfaction of the Danish court that he really had done his best.

Questions

1. Describe several aspects of how the (attempted) Nazi deportations of Jews from Denmark did not go according to plan—including ways in which Denmark differed from other countries that also "proved to be nearly immune to anti-Semitism."
2. Why does Arendt suggest that this case should be taught in political science courses? What in your view would be the most salient aspects of this case for discussion in the classroom, and beyond?
3. Explain why, for Arendt, "the most interesting aspect of this incident is perhaps the role played by the German authorities in Denmark" (paragraph 7).

ROBERT DARNTON

Workers Revolt: The Great Cat Massacre of the Rue Saint-Séverin

(1984)

Robert Darnton (1939–) is a professor of European history at Princeton University. His books include The Great Cat Massacre: And Other Episodes in French Cultural History *(1984) and* The Forbidden Best-Sellers of Pre-Revolutionary France *(1996).*

In this essay, which describes an incident in a French printing shop, Darnton explores many aspects of eighteenth-century life.

The funniest thing that ever happened in the printing shop of Jacques Vincent, according to a worker who witnessed it, was a riotous massacre of cats. The worker, Nicolas Contat, told the story in an account of his apprenticeship in the shop, rue Saint-Séverin, Paris, during the late 1730s.[1] Life as an apprentice was hard, he explained. There were two of them: Jerome, the somewhat fictionalized version of Contat himself, and Léveillé. They slept in a filthy, freezing room, rose before dawn, ran errands all day while dodging insults from the journeymen and abuse from the master, and received nothing but slops to eat. They found the food especially galling. Instead of dining at the master's table, they had to eat scraps from his plate in the kitchen. Worse still, the cook secretly sold the leftovers and gave the boys cat food—old, rotten bits of meat that they could not stomach and so passed on to the cats, who refused it.

This last injustice brought Contat to the theme of cats. They occupied a special place in his narrative and in the household of the rue Saint-Séverin. The master's wife adored them, especially *la grise* (the gray), her favorite. A passion for cats seemed to have swept through the printing trade, at least at

---

1 Nicolas Contat, *Anecdotes typographiques où l'on voit la description des coutumes, mœurs et usages singuliers des compagnons imprimeurs,* ed. Giles Barber (Oxford, 1980). The original manuscript is dated 1762. Barber provides a thorough description of its background and of Contat's career in his introduction. The account of the cat massacre occurs on pp. 48–56. [Unless otherwise stated, notes are by the author.]

the level of the masters, or *bourgeois* as the workers called them. One bourgeois kept twenty-five cats. He had their portraits painted and fed them on roast fowl. Meanwhile, the apprentices were trying to cope with a profusion of alley cats who also thrived in the printing district and made the boys' lives miserable. The cats howled all night on the roof over the apprentices' dingy bedroom, making it impossible to get a full night's sleep. As Jerome and Léveillé had to stagger out of bed at four or five in the morning to open the gate for the earliest arrivals among the journeymen, they began the day in a state of exhaustion while the bourgeois slept late. The master did not even work with the men, just as he did not eat with them. He let the foreman run the shop and rarely appeared in it, except to vent his violent temper, usually at the expense of the apprentices.

One night the boys resolved to right this inequitable state of affairs. Léveillé, who had an extraordinary talent for mimickry, crawled along the roof until he reached a section near the master's bedroom, and then he took to howling and meowing so horribly that the bourgeois and his wife did not sleep a wink. After several nights of this treatment, they decided they were being bewitched. But instead of calling the curé—the master was exceptionally devout and the mistress exceptionally attached to her confessor—they commanded the apprentices to get rid of the cats. The mistress gave the order, enjoining the boys above all to avoid frightening her *grise.*

Gleefully Jerome and Léveillé set to work, aided by the journeymen. Armed with broom handles, bars of the press, and other tools of their trade, they went after every cat they could find, beginning with *la grise.* Léveillé smashed its spine with an iron bar and Jerome finished it off. Then they stashed it in a gutter while the journeymen drove the other cats across the rooftops, bludgeoning every one within reach and trapping those who tried to escape in strategically placed sacks. They dumped sackloads of half-dead cats in the courtyard. Then the entire workshop gathered round and staged a mock trial, complete with guards, a confessor, and a public executioner. After pronouncing the animals guilty and administering last rites, they strung them up on an improvised gallows. Roused by gales of laughter, the mistress arrived. She let out a shriek as soon as she saw a bloody cat dangling from a noose. Then she realized it might be *la grise.* Certainly not, the men assured her: they had too much respect for the house to do such a thing. At this point the master appeared. He flew into a rage at the general stoppage of work, though his wife tried to explain that they were threatened by a more serious kind of insubordination. Then master and mistress withdrew, leaving the men delirious with "joy," "disorder," and "laughter."[1]

The laughter did not end there. Léveillé reenacted the entire scene in mime at least twenty times during subsequent days when the printers wanted to knock off for some hilarity. Burlesque reenactments of incidents in

1 Contat, *Anecdotes typographiques*, p. 53.

the life of the shop, known as *copies* in printers' slang, provided a major form of entertainment for the men. The idea was to humiliate someone in the shop by satirizing his peculiarities. A successful *copie* would make the butt of the joke fume with rage—*prendre la chèvre* (take the goat) in the shop slang—while his mates razzed him with "rough music." They would run their composing sticks across the tops of the type cases, beat their mallets against the chases, pound on cupboards, and bleat like goats. The bleating (*bais* in the slang) stood for the humiliation heaped on the victims, as in English when someone "gets your goat." Contat emphasized that Léveillé produced the funniest *copies* anyone had ever known and elicited the greatest choruses of rough music. The whole episode, cat massacre compounded by *copies*, stood out as the most hilarious experience in Jerome's entire career.

Yet it strikes the modern reader as unfunny, if not downright repulsive. Where is the humor in a group of grown men bleating like goats and banging with their tools while an adolescent reenacts the ritual slaughter of a defenseless animal? Our own inability to get the joke is an indication of the distance that separates us from the workers of preindustrial Europe. The perception of that distance may serve as the starting point of an investigation, for anthropologists have found that the best points of entry in an attempt to penetrate an alien culture can be those where it seems to be most opaque. When you realize that you are not getting something—a joke, a proverb, a ceremony—that is particularly meaningful to the natives, you can see where to grasp a foreign system of meaning in order to unravel it. By getting the joke of the great cat massacre, it may be possible to "get" a basic ingredient of artisanal culture under the Old Regime.

It should be explained at the outset that we cannot observe the killing of the cats at firsthand. We can study it only through Contat's narrative, written about twenty years after the event. There can be no doubt about the authenticity of Contat's quasi-fictional autobiography, as Giles Barber has demonstrated in his masterful edition of the text. It belongs to the line of autobiographical writing by printers that stretches from Thomas Platter to Thomas Gent, Benjamin Franklin, Nicolas Restif de la Bretonne, and Charles Manby Smith. Because printers, or at least compositors, had to be reasonably literate in order to do their work, they were among the few artisans who could give their own accounts of life in the working classes two, three, and four centuries ago. With all its misspellings and grammatical flaws, Contat's is perhaps the richest of these accounts. But it cannot be regarded as a mirror-image of what actually happened. It should be read as Contat's version of a happening, as his attempt to tell a story. Like all story telling, it sets the action in a frame of reference; it assumes a certain repertory of associations and responses on the part of its audience; and it provides meaningful shape to the raw stuff of experience. But since we are attempting to get at its meaning in the first place, we should not be put off by its fabricated character. On the contrary, by treating the narrative as fiction or meaningful fabrication we can use it to develop an ethnological *explication de texte*.

The first explanation that probably would occur to most readers of Contat's story is that the cat massacre served as an oblique attack on the master and his wife. Contat set the event in the context of remarks about the disparity between the lot of workers and the bourgeois—a matter of the basic elements in life: work, food, and sleep. The injustice seemed especially flagrant in the case of the apprentices, who were treated like animals while the animals were promoted over their heads to the position the boys should have occupied, the place at the master's table. Although the apprentices seem most abused, the text makes it clear that the killing of the cats expressed a hatred for the bourgeois that had spread among all the workers: "The masters love cats; consequently [the workers] hate them." After masterminding the massacre, Léveillé became the hero of the shop, because "all the workers are in league against the masters. It is enough to speak badly of them [the masters] to be esteemed by the whole assembly of typographers."[1]

Historians have tended to treat the era of artisanal manufacturing as an idyllic period before the onset of industrialization. Some even portray the workshop as a kind of extended family in which master and journeymen labored at the same tasks, ate at the same table, and sometimes slept under the same roof.[2] Had anything happened to poison the atmosphere of the printing shops in Paris by 1740?

During the second half of the seventeenth century, the large printing houses, backed by the government, eliminated most of the smaller shops, and an oligarchy of masters seized control of the industry.[3] At the same time, the situation of the journeymen deteriorated. Although estimates vary and statistics cannot be trusted, it seems that their number remained stable: approximately 335 in 1666, 339 in 1701, and 340 in 1721. Meanwhile the number of masters declined by more than half, from eighty-three to thirty-six, the limit fixed by an edict of 1686. That meant fewer shops with larger work forces, as one can see from statistics on the density of presses: in 1644

10

---

1 Ibid., pp. 52 and 53.
2 See, for example, Albert Soboul, *La France à la veille de la Révolution* (Paris, 1966), p. 140; and Edward Shorter, "The History of Work in the West: An Overview" in *Work and Community in the West*, ed. Edward Shorter (New York, 1973).
3 The following discussion is derived from Henri-Jean Martin, *Livre, pouvoirs et société à Paris au XVIIe siècle (1598–1701)* (Geneva, 1969); and Paul Chauvet, *Les Ouvriers du livre en France, des origines à la Révolution de 1789* (Paris, 1959). The statistics come from investigations by the authorities of the Old Regime as reported by Martin (II, 699–700) and Chauvet (pp. 126 and 154).

Paris had seventy-five printing shops with a total of 180 presses; in 1701 it had fifty-one shops with 195 presses. This trend made it virtually impossible for journeymen to rise into the ranks of the masters. About the only way for a worker to get ahead in the craft was to marry a master's widow, for masterships had become hereditary privileges, passed on from husband to wife and from father to son.

The journeymen also felt threatened from below because the masters tended increasingly to hire *alloués*, or underqualified printers, who had not undergone the apprenticeship that made a journeyman eligible, in principle, to advance to a mastership. The *alloués* were merely a source of cheap labor, excluded from the upper ranks of the trade and fixed, in their inferior status, by an edict of 1723. Their degradation stood out in their name: they were *à louer* (for hire), not *compagnons* (journeymen) of the master. They personified the tendency of labor to become a commodity instead of a partnership. Thus Contat served his apprenticeship and wrote his memoirs when times were hard for journeymen printers, when the men in the shop in the rue Saint-Séverin stood in danger of being cut off from the top of the trade and swamped from the bottom.

How this general tendency became manifest in an actual workshop may be seen from the papers of the Société typographique de Neuchâtel (STN). To be sure, the STN was Swiss, and it did not begin business until seven years after Contat wrote his memoirs (1762). But printing practices were essentially the same everywhere in the eighteenth century. The STN's archives conform in dozens of details to Contat's account of his experience. (They even mention the same shop foreman, Colas, who supervised Jerome for a while at the Imprimerie Royale and took charge of the STN's shop for a brief stint in 1779.) And they provide the only surviving record of the way masters hired, managed, and fired printers in the early modern era.

The STN's wage book shows that workers usually stayed in the shop for only a few months.[1] They left because they quarreled with the master, they got in fights, they wanted to pursue their fortune in shops further down the road, or they ran out of work. Compositors were hired by the job, *labeur* or *ouvrage* in printer's slang. When they finished a job, they frequently were fired, and a few pressmen had to be fired as well in order to maintain the balance between the two halves of the shop, the *casse* or composing sector and the *presse* or pressroom (two compositors usually set enough type to occupy a team of two pressmen.) When the foreman took on new jobs, he hired new hands. The hiring and firing went on at such a fierce pace that the work force was rarely the same from one week to the next. Jerome's fellow workers in the rue Saint-Séverin seem to have been equally volatile.

---

1 For a more detailed discussion of this material, see Robert Darnton, "Work and Culture in an Eighteenth-Century Printing Shop," an Englehard lecture at the Library of Congress to be published by the Library of Congress.

They, too, were hired for specific *labeurs,* and they sometimes walked off the job after quarrels with the bourgeois—a practice common enough to have its own entry in the glossary of their slang which Contat appended to his narrative: *emporter son Saint Jean* (to carry off your set of tools or quit). A man was known as an *ancien* if he remained in the shop for only a year. Other slang terms suggest the atmosphere in which the work took place: *une chèvre capitale* (a fit of rage), *se donner la grate* (to get in a fight), *prendre la barbe* (to get drunk), *faire la déroute* (to go pub crawling), *promener sa chape* (to knock off work), *faire des loups* (to pile up debts).[1]

The violence, drunkenness, and absenteeism show up in the statistics of income and output one can compile from the STN's wage book. Printers worked in erratic spurts—twice as much in one week as in another, the weeks varying from four to six days and the days beginning anywhere from four in the morning until nearly noon. In order to keep the irregularity within bounds, the masters sought men with two supreme traits: assiduousness and sobriety. If they also happened to be skilled, so much the better. A recruiting agent in Geneva recommended a compositor who was willing to set out for Neuchâtel in typical terms: "He is a good worker, capable of doing any job he gets, not at all a drunkard and assiduous at his labor."[2]

The STN relied on recruiters because it did not have an adequate labor pool in Neuchâtel and the streams of printers on the typographical *tours de France* sometimes ran dry. The recruiters and employers exchanged letters that reveal a common set of assumptions about eighteenth-century artisans: they were lazy, flighty, dissolute, and unreliable. They could not be trusted, so the recruiter should not loan them money for travel expenses and the employer could keep their belongings as a kind of security deposit in case they skipped off after collecting their pay. It followed that they could be discarded without compunction, whether or not they had worked diligently, had families to support, or fell sick. The STN ordered them in "assortments" just as it ordered paper and type. It complained that a recruiter in Lyon "sent us a couple in such a bad state that we were obliged to ship them off"[3] and lectured him about failing to inspect the goods. "Two of those whom you have sent to us have arrived all right, but so sick that they could infect all the rest; so we haven't been able to hire them. No one in town wanted to give them lodging. They have therefore left again and took the route for Besançon, in order to turn themselves in at the *hôpital.*"[4] A bookseller in Lyon advised them to fire most of their men during a slack period in their printing in order to flood the labor supply in eastern France and

15

---

1   Contat, *Anecdotes typographiques,* pp. 68–73.
2   Christ to STN, Jan. 8, 1773, papers of the Société typographique de Neuchâtel, Bibliothèque de la Ville de Neuchâtel, Switzerland, hereafter cited as STN.
3   STN to Joseph Duplain, July 2, 1777.
4   STN to Louis Vernange, June 26, 1777.

"give us more power over a wild and undisciplinable race, which we cannot control."[1] Journeymen and masters may have lived together as members of a happy family at some time somewhere in Europe, but not in the printing houses of eighteenth-century France and Switzerland.

Contat himself believed that such a state had once existed. He began his description of Jerome's apprenticeship by invoking a golden age when printing was first invented and printers lived as free and equal members of a "republic," governed by its own laws and traditions in a spirit of fraternal "union and friendship."[2] He claimed that the republic still survived in the form of the *chapelle* or workers' association in each shop. But the government had broken up general associations; the ranks had been thinned by *alloués*; the journeymen had been excluded from masterships; and the masters had withdrawn into a separate world of *haute cuisine* and *grasses matinées*. The master in the rue Saint-Séverin ate different food, kept different hours, and talked a different language. His wife and daughters dallied with worldly abbés. They kept pets. Clearly, the bourgeois belonged to a different subculture—one which meant above all that he did not work. In introducing his account of the cat massacre, Contat made explicit the contrast between the worlds of worker and master that ran throughout the narrative: "Workers, apprentices, everyone works. Only the masters and mistresses enjoy the sweetness of sleep. That makes Jerome and Léveillé resentful. They resolve not to be the only wretched ones. They want their master and mistress as associates (associés)."[3] That is, the boys wanted to restore a mythical past when masters and men worked in friendly association. They also may have had in mind the more recent extinction of the smaller printing shops. So they killed the cats.

But why cats? And why was the killing so funny? Those questions take us beyond the consideration of early modern labor relations and into the obscure subject of popular ceremonies and symbolism.

Folklorists have made historians familiar with the ceremonial cycles that marked off the calendar year for early modern man.[4] The most important of these was the cycle of carnival and Lent, a period of revelry followed by a period of abstinence. During carnival the common people suspended the

---

1 Joseph Duplain to STN, Dec. 10, 1778.
2 Contat, *Anecdotes typographiques*, pp. 30–31.
3 Ibid., p. 52.
4 For a recent overview of the vast literature on folklore and French history and bibliographic references, see Nicole Belmont, *Mythes et croyances dans l'ancienne France* (Paris, 1973). The following discussion is based primarily on the material collected in Eugène Rolland, *Faune populaire de la France* (Paris, 1881), IV; Paul Sébillot, *Le Folk-lore de France* (Paris, 1904–7), 4 vols., especially III, 72–155 and IV, 90–98; and to a lesser extent Arnold Van Gennep, *Manuel de folklore français contemporain* (Paris, 1937–58), 9 vols.

normal rules of behavior and ceremoniously reversed the social order or turned it upside down in riotous procession. Carnival was a time for cutting up by youth groups, particularly apprentices, who organized themselves in "abbeys" ruled by a mock abbot or king and who staged charivaris or burlesque processions with rough music in order to humiliate cuckolds, husbands who had been beaten by their wives, brides who had married below their age group, or someone else who personified the infringement of traditional norms. Carnival was high season for hilarity, sexuality, and youth run riot—a time when young people tested social boundaries by limited outbursts of deviance, before being reassimilated in the world of order, submission, and Lentine seriousness. It came to an end on Shrove Tuesday or Mardi Gras, when a straw mannequin, King Carnival or Caramantran, was given a ritual trial and execution. Cats played an important part in some charivaris. In Burgundy, the crowd incorporated cat torture into its rough music. While mocking a cuckold or some other victim, the youths passed around a cat, tearing its fur to make it howl. *Faire le chat,* they called it. The Germans called charivaris *Katzenmusik,* a term that may have been derived from the howls of tortured cats.[1]

Cats also figured in the cycle of Saint John the Baptist, which took place on June 24, at the time of the summer solstice. Crowds made bonfires, jumped over them, danced around them, and threw into them objects with magical power, hoping to avoid disaster and obtain good fortune during the rest of the year. A favorite object was cats—cats tied up in bags, cats suspended from ropes, or cats burned at the stake. Parisians liked to incinerate cats by the sackful, while the Courimauds (*cour à miaud* or cat chasers) of Saint Chamond preferred to chase a flaming cat through the streets. In parts of Burgundy and Lorraine they danced around a kind of burning May pole with a cat tied to it. In the Metz region they burned a dozen cats at a time in a basket on top of a bonfire. The ceremony took place with great pomp in Metz itself, until it was abolished in 1765. The town dignitaries arrived in procession at the Place du Grand-Saulcy, lit the pyre, and a ring of riflemen from the garrison fired off volleys while the cats disappeared screaming in the flames. Although the practice varied from place to place, the ingredients were everywhere the same: a *feu de joie* (bonfire), cats, and an aura of hilarious witch-hunting.[2]

1   In Germany and Switzerland, *Katzenmusik* sometimes included mock trials and executions. The etymology of the term is not clear. See E. Hoffman-Krayer and Hans Bächtold-Stäubli, *Handwörterbuch des deutschen Aberglaubens* (Berlin and Leipzig, 1931–32), IV, 1125–32 and Paul Grebe et al., *Duden Etymologie: Herkunftwörterbuch der deutschen Sprache* (Mannheim, 1963), p. 317.

2   Information on the cat burning in Saint Chamond comes from a letter kindly sent to me by Elinor Accampo of Colorado College. The Metz ceremony is described in A. Benoist, "Traditions et anciennes coutumes du pays messin," *Revue des traditions populaires,* XV (1900), 14.

20   In addition to these general ceremonies, which involved entire communities, artisans celebrated ceremonies peculiar to their craft. Printers processed and feasted in honor of their patron, Saint John the Evangelist, both on his saint's day, December 27, and on the anniversary of his martyrdom, May 6, the festival of Saint Jean Porte Latine. By the eighteenth century, the masters had excluded the journeymen from the confraternity devoted to the saint, but the journeymen continued to hold ceremonies in their chapels.[1] On Saint Martin's day, November 11, they held a mock trial followed by a feast. Contat explained that the chapel was a tiny "republic," which governed itself according to its own code of conduct. When a worker violated the code, the foreman, who was the head of the chapel and not part of the management, entered a fine in a register: leaving a candle lit, five sous; brawling, three livres; insulting the good name of the chapel, three livres; and so on. On Saint Martin's, the foreman read out the fines and collected them. The workers sometimes appealed their cases before a burlesque tribunal composed of the chapel's "ancients," but in the end they had to pay up amidst more bleating, banging of tools, and riotous laughter. The fines went for food and drink in the chapel's favorite tavern, where the hell-raising continued until late in the night.[2]

Taxation and commensality characterized all the other ceremonies of the chapel. Special dues and feasts marked a man's entry into the shop (*bienvenue*), his exit (*conduite*), and even his marriage (*droit de chevet*). Above all, they punctuated a youth's progress from apprentice to journeyman. Contat described four of these rites, the most important being the first, called the taking of the apron, and the last, Jerome's initiation as a full-fledged *compagnon*.

The taking of the apron (*la prise de tablier*) occurred soon after Jerome joined the shop. He had to pay six livres (about three days' wages for an ordinary journeyman) into a kitty, which the journeymen supplemented by small payments of their own (*faire la reconnaissance*). Then the chapel repaired to its favorite tavern, Le Panier Fleury in the rue de la Huchette. Emissaries were dispatched to procure provisions and returned loaded down with bread and meat, having lectured the shopkeepers of the neighborhood on which cuts were worthy of typographers and which could be left for cobblers. Silent and glass in hand, the journeymen gathered around Jerome in a special room on the second floor of the tavern. The subforeman approached, carrying the apron and followed by two "ancients," one from each of the "estates" of the shop, the *casse* and the *presse*. He handed the apron, newly made from close-woven linen, to the foreman, who took Jerome by the hand and led him to the center of the room, the subforeman

---

1   Contat, *Anecdotes typographiques*, pp. 30 and 66–67; and Chauvet, *Les Ouvriers du livre*, pp. 7–12.

2   Contat, *Anecdotes typographiques*, pp. 65–67.

and "ancients" falling behind. The foreman made a short speech, placed the apron over Jerome's head and tied the strings behind him, as everyone drank to the health of the initiate. Jerome was then given a seat with the chapel dignitaries at the head of the table. The rest rushed for the best places they could find and fell on the food. They gobbled and guzzled and called out for more. After several Gargantuan rounds, they settled down to shop talk—and Contat lets us listen in:

> "Isn't it true," says one of them, "that printers know how to shovel it in? I am sure that if someone presented us with a roast mutton, as big as you like, we would leave nothing but the bones behind...." They don't talk about theology nor philosophy and still less of politics. Each speaks of his job: one will talk to you about the *casse*, another the *presse*, this one of the tympan, another of the ink ball leathers. They all speak at the same time, whether they can be heard or not.

At last, early in the morning after hours of swilling and shouting, the workers separated—sotted but ceremonial to the end: "Bonsoir, Monsieur notre prote [foreman]"; "Bonsoir, Messieurs les compositeurs"; "Bonsoir, Messieurs les imprimeurs"; "Bonsoir Jerome." The text explains that Jerome will be called by his first name until he is received as a journeyman.[1]

That moment came four years later, after two intermediary ceremonies (the *admission à l'ouvrage* and the *admission à la banque*) and a vast amount of hazing. Not only did the men torment Jerome, mocking his ignorance, sending him on wild goose chases, making him the butt of practical jokes, and overwhelming him with nasty chores; they also refused to teach him anything. They did not want another journeyman in their over-flooded labor pool, so Jerome had to pick up the tricks of the trade by himself. The work, the food, the lodging, the lack of sleep, it was enough to drive a boy mad, or at least out of the shop. In fact, however, it was standard treatment and should not be taken too seriously. Contat recounted the catalogue of Jerome's troubles in a light-hearted manner, which suggested a stock comic genre, the *misère des apprentis*.[2] The *misères* provided farcical accounts, in doggerel verse or broadsides, of a stage in life that was familiar and funny to everyone in the artisanate. It was a transitional stage, which marked the passage from childhood to adulthood. A young man had to sweat his way through it so that he would have paid his dues—the printers demanded actual payments, called *bienvenues* or *quatre heures*, in addition to razzing the

---

1   Ibid., pp. 37–41, quotation from pp. 39–40.
2   A good example of the genre, *La Misère des apprentis imprimeurs* (1710) is printed as an appendix to Contat, *Anecdotes typographiques*, pp. 101–10. For other examples, see A.C. Cailleau, *Les Misères de ce monde, ou complaints facétieuses sur les apprentissages des différents arts et métiers de la ville et faubourgs de Paris* (Paris, 1783).

apprentices—when he reached full membership in a vocational group. Until he arrived at that point, he lived in a fluid or liminal state, trying out adult conventions by subjecting them to some hell-raising of his own. His elders tolerated his pranks, called *copies* and *joberies* in the printing trade, because they saw them as wild oats, which needed to be sown before he could settle down. Once settled, he would have internalized the conventions of his craft and acquired a new identity, which was often symbolized by a change in his name.[1]

25   Jerome became a journeyman by passing through the final rite, *compagnonnage*. It took the same form as the other ceremonies, a celebration over food and drink after the candidate paid an initiation fee and the journeymen chipped in with *reconnaissance*. But this time Contat gave a summary of the foreman's speech:[2]

> The newcomer is indoctrinated. He is told never to betray his colleagues and to maintain the wage rate. If a worker doesn't accept a price [for a job] and leaves the shop, no one in the house should do the job for a smaller price. Those are the laws among the workers. Faithfulness and probity are recommended to him. Any worker who betrays the others,

---

1 The classic study of this process is Arnold Van Gennep, *Les Rites de passage* (Paris, 1908). It has been extended by subsequent ethnographic research, notably that of Victor Turner: *The Forest of Symbols: Aspects of Ndembu Ritual* (Ithaca, N.Y., 1967) and *The Ritual Process* (Chicago, 1969). Jerome's experience fits the Van Gennep-Turner model very well, except in a few respects. He was not considered sacred and dangerous, although the chapel could fine journeymen for drinking with him. He did not live outside adult society, although he left his home for a makeshift room at the edge of the master's household. And he was not exposed to secret *sacra*, although he had to acquire an esoteric lingo and to assimilate a craft ethos after a great deal of tribulation climaxed by a communal meal. Joseph Moxon, Thomas Gent, and Benjamin Franklin mention similar practices in England. In Germany the initiation rite was much more elaborate and had structural similarities to the rites of tribes in Africa, New Guinea, and North America. The apprentice wore a filthy headdress adorned with goat's horns and a fox's tail, indicating that he had reverted to an animal state. As a *Cornut* or *Mittelding*, part man, part beast, he underwent ritual tortures, including the filing of his fingertips. At the final ceremony, the head of the shop knocked off the hat and slapped him in the face. He then emerged newborn—sometimes newly named and even baptized—as a full-fledged journeyman. Such at least was the practice described in German typographical manuals, notably Christian Gottlob Täubel, *Praktisches Handbuch der Buchdruckerkunst für Anfänger* (Leipzig, 1791); Wilhelm Gottlieb Kircher, *Anweisung in der Buchdruckerkunst so viel davon das Drucken betrifft* (Brunswick, 1793); and Johann Christoph Hildebrand, *Handbuch für Buchdrucker-Lehrlinge* (Eisenach, 1835). The rite was related to an ancient popular play, the *Depositio Cornuti typographici*, which was printed by Jacob Redinger in his *Neu aufgesetztes Format Büchlein* (Frankfurt-am-Main, 1679).

2 Contat, *Anecdotes typographiques*, pp. 65–66.

when something forbidden, called *marron* [chestnut], is being printed, must be expelled ignominiously from the shop. The workers blacklist him by circular letters sent around all the shops of Paris and the provinces.... Aside from that, anything is permitted: excessive drinking is considered a good quality, gallantry and debauchery as youthful feats, indebtedness as a sign of wit, irreligion as sincerity. It's a free and republican territory in which everything is permitted. Live as you like but be an *honnête homme*, no hypocrisy.

Hypocrisy turned out in the rest of the narrative to be the main characteristic of the bourgeois, a superstitious religious bigot. He occupied a separate world of pharasaical bourgeois morality. The workers defined their "republic" against that world and against other journeyman's groups as well—the cobblers, who ate inferior cuts of meat, and the masons or carpenters who were always good for a brawl when the printers, divided into "estates" (the *casse* and the *presse*) toured country taverns on Sundays. In entering an "estate," Jerome assimilated an ethos. He identified himself with a craft; and as a full-fledged journeyman compositor, he received a new name. Having gone through a rite of passage in the full, anthropological sense of the term, he became a *Monsieur*.[1]

So much for ceremonies. What about cats? It should be said at the outset that there is an indefinable *je ne sais quoi* about cats, a mysterious something that has fascinated mankind since the time of the ancient Egyptians. One can sense a quasi-human intelligence behind a cat's eyes. One can mistake a cat's howl at night for a human scream, torn from some deep, visceral part of man's animal nature. Cats appealed to poets like Baudelaire and painters like Manet, who wanted to express the humanity in animals along with the animality of men—and especially of women.[2]

This ambiguous ontological position, a straddling of conceptual categories, gives certain animals—pigs, dogs, and cassowaries as well as cats—in certain cultures an occult power associated with the taboo. That is why Jews do not eat pigs, according to Mary Douglas, and why Englishmen can insult

---

1   The text does not give Jerome's last name, but it stresses the name change and the acquisition of the "Monsieur": "It is only after the end of the apprenticeship that one is called Monsieur; this quality belongs only to journeymen and not to apprentices" (p. 41). In the wage book of the STN, the journeymen always appear with their "Monsieur," even when they were called by nicknames, such as "Monsieur Bonnemain."

2   The black cat in Manet's *Olympia* represents a common motif, the animal "familiar" of a nude. On Baudelaire's cats, see Roman Jakobson and Claude Lévi-Strauss, "*Les Chats* de Charles Baudelaire," *L'Homme*, II (1962), 5–21; and Michel Riffaterre, "Describing Poetic Structures: Two Approaches to Baudelaire's *Les Chats*," in *Structuralism*, ed. Jacques Ehrmann (New Haven, 1966).

one another by saying "son-of-a-bitch" rather than "son-of-a-cow," according to Edmund Leach.[1] Certain animals are good for swearing, just as they are "good for thinking" in Lévi-Strauss's famous formula. I would add that others—cats in particular—are good for staging ceremonies. They have ritual value. You cannot make a charivari with a cow. You do it with cats: you decide to *faire le chat*, to make *Katzenmusik*.

The torture of animals, especially cats, was a popular amusement throughout early modern Europe. You have only to look at Hogarth's *Stages of Cruelty* to see its importance, and once you start looking you see people torturing animals everywhere. Cat killings provided a common theme in literature, from *Don Quixote* in early seventeenth-century Spain to *Germinal* in late nineteenth-century France.[2] Far from being a sadistic fantasy on the part of a few half-crazed authors, the literary versions of cruelty to animals expressed a deep current of popular culture, as Mikhail Bakhtin has shown in his study of Rabelais.[3] All sorts of ethnographic reports confirm that view. On the *dimanche des brandons* in Semur, for example, children used to attach cats to poles and roast them over bonfires. In the *jeu du chat* at the Fete-Dieu in Aix-en-Provence, they threw cats high in the air and smashed them on the ground. They used expressions like "patient as a cat whose claws are being pulled out" or "patient as a cat whose paws are being grilled." The English were just as cruel. During the Reformation in London, a Protestant crowd shaved a cat to look like a priest, dressed it in mock vestments, and hanged it on the gallows at

---

1   Mary Douglas, *Purity and Danger: An Analysis of Concepts of Pollution and Taboo* (London, 1966); and E.R. Leach, "Anthropological Aspects of Language: Animal Categories and Verbal Abuse," in *New Directions in the Study of Language*, ed. E.H. Lenneberg (Cambridge, Mass., 1964).

2   Cervantes and Zola adapted traditional cat lore to the themes of their novels. In *Don Quixote* (part II, chap. 46), a sack full of howling cats interrupts the hero's serenade to Altisidora. Taking them for devils, he tries to mow them down with his sword, only to be bested by one of them in single combat. In *Germinal* (part V, chap. 6), the symbolism works in the opposite way. A mob of workers pursues Maigrat, their class enemy, as if he were a cat trying to escape across the rooftops. Screaming "Get the cat! Get the cat!" they castrate his body "like a tomcat" after he falls from the roof. For an example of cat killing as a satire on French legalism, see Friar John's plan to massacre the Furry Lawcats in Rabelais' *Gargantua and Pantagruel*, book V, chap. 15.

3   Mikhail Bakhtin, *Rabelais and His World*, trans. Helene Iswolsky (Cambridge, Mass., 1968). The most important literary version of cat lore to appear in Contat's time was *Les Chats* (Rotterdam, 1728) by François Augustin Paradis de Moncrif. Although it was a mock treatise aimed at a sophisticated audience, it drew on a vast array of popular superstitions and proverbs, many of which appeared in the collections of folklorists a century and a half later.

Cheapside.[1] It would be possible to string out many other examples, but the point should be clear: there was nothing unusual about the ritual killing of cats. On the contrary, when Jerome and his fellow workers tried and hanged all the cats they could find in the rue Saint-Séverin, they drew on a common element in their culture. But what significance did that culture attribute to cats?

To get a grip on that question, one must rummage through collections of folktales, superstitions, proverbs, and popular medicine. The material is rich, varied, and vast but extremely hard to handle. Although much of it goes back to the Middle Ages, little can be dated. It was gathered for the most part by folklorists in the late nineteenth and early twentieth centuries, when sturdy strains of folklore still resisted the influence of the printed word. But the collections do not make it possible to claim that this or that practice existed in the printing houses of mid-eighteenth-century Paris. One can only assert that printers lived and breathed in an atmosphere of traditional customs and beliefs which permeated everything. It was not everywhere the same—France remained a patchwork of *pays* rather than a unified nation until late in the nineteenth century—but everywhere some common motifs could be found. The commonest were attached to cats. Early modern Frenchmen probably made more symbolic use of cats than any other animal, and they used them in distinct ways, which can be grouped together for the purposes of discussion, despite the regional peculiarities.

First and foremost, cats suggested witchcraft. To cross one at night in virtually any corner of France was to risk running into the devil or one of his agents or a witch abroad on an evil errand. White cats could be as satanic as the black, in the daytime as well as at night. In a typical encounter, a peasant woman of Bigorre met a pretty white house cat who had strayed in the fields. She carried it back to the village in her apron, and just as they came to the house of a woman suspected of witchcraft, the cat jumped out, saying "Merci, Jeanne."[2] Witches transformed themselves into cats in order to cast spells on their victims. Sometimes, especially on Mardi Gras, they gathered for hideous sabbaths at night. They howled, fought, and copulated horribly under the direction of the devil himself in the form of a huge tomcat. To protect yourself from sorcery by cats there was one, classic remedy: maim it. Cut its tail, clip its ears, smash one of its legs, tear or burn its fur,

30

---

1   C.S.L. Davies, *Peace, Print and Protestantism* (St. Albans, Herts, 1977). The other references come from the sources cited in note 4, p. 216. Among the many dictionaries of proverbs and slang, see André-Joseph Panckoucke, *Dictionaire des proverbs françois et des façons de parler comiques, burlesques, et familières* (Paris, 1748) and Gaston Esnault, *Dictionnaire historique des argots français* (Paris, 1965).

2   Rolland, *Faune populaire*, p. 118. See note 4, p. 216, for the other sources on which this account is based.

and you would break its malevolent power. A maimed cat could not attend sabbath or wander abroad to cast spells. Peasants frequently cudgeled cats who crossed their paths at night and discovered the next day that bruises had appeared on women believed to be witches—or so it was said in the lore of their village. Villagers also told stories of farmers who found strange cats in barns and broke their limbs to save the cattle. Invariably a broken limb would appear on a suspicious woman the following morning.

Cats possessed occult power independently of their association with witchcraft and deviltry. They could prevent the bread from rising if they entered bakeries in Anjou. They could spoil the catch if they crossed the path of fishermen in Brittany. If buried alive in Béarn, they could clear a field of weeds. They figured as staple ingredients in all kinds of folk medicine aside from witches' brews. To recover from a bad fall, you sucked the blood out of a freshly amputated tail of a tomcat. To cure yourself from pneumonia, you drank blood from a cat's ear in red wine. To get over colic, you mixed your wine with cat excrement. You could even make yourself invisible, at least in Brittany, by eating the brain of a newly killed cat, provided it was still hot.

There was a specific field for the exercise of cat power: the household and particularly the person of the master or mistress of the house. Folktales like "Puss 'n Boots" emphasized the identification of master and cat, and so did superstitions such as the practice of tying a black ribbon around the neck of a cat whose mistress had died. To kill a cat was to bring misfortune upon its owner or its house. If a cat left a house or stopped jumping on the sickbed of its master or mistress, the person was likely to die. But a cat lying on the bed of a dying man might be the devil, waiting to carry his soul off to hell. According to a sixteenth-century tale, a girl from Quintin sold her soul to the devil in exchange for some pretty clothes. When she died, the pallbearers could not lift her coffin; they opened the lid, and a black cat jumped out. Cats could harm a house. They often smothered babies. They understood gossip and would repeat it out of doors. But their power could be contained or turned to your advantage if you followed the right procedures, such as greasing their paws with butter or maiming them when they first arrived. To protect a new house, Frenchmen enclosed live cats within its walls—a very old rite, judging from cat skeletons that have been exhumed from the walls of medieval buildings.

Finally, the power of cats was concentrated on the most intimate aspect of domestic life: sex. *Le chat, la chatte, le minet* mean the same thing in French slang as "pussy" does in English, and they have served as obscenities for centuries.[1] French folklore attaches special importance to the cat as a

---

1   Emile Chautard, *La Vie étrange de l'argot* (Paris, 1931), pp. 367–68. The following expressions come from Panckoucke, *Dictionnaire des proverbs français;* Esnault, *Dictionnaire historique des argots français*; and *Dictionnaire de l'Académie*

sexual metaphor or metonym. As far back as the fifteenth century, the petting of cats was recommended for success in courting women. Proverbial wisdom identified women with cats: "He who takes good care of cats will have a pretty wife." If a man loved cats, he would love women; and vice versa: "As he loves his cat, he loves his wife," went another proverb. If he did not care for his wife, you could say of him, "He has other cats to whip." A woman who wanted to get a man should avoid treading on a cat's tail. She might postpone marriage for a year—or for seven years in Quimper and for as many years as the cat meowed in parts of the Loire Valley. Cats connoted fertility and female sexuality everywhere. Girls were commonly said to be "in love like a cat"; and if they became pregnant, they had "let the cat go to the cheese." Eating cats could bring on pregnancy in itself. Girls who consumed them in stews gave birth to kittens in several folktales. Cats could even make diseased apple trees bear fruit, if buried in the correct manner in upper Brittany.

It was an easy jump from the sexuality of women to the cuckolding of men. Caterwauling could come from a satanic orgy, but it might just as well be toms howling defiance at each other when their mates were in heat. They did not call as cats, however. They issued challenges in their masters' names, along with sexual taunts about their mistresses: "Reno! Francois!" "Où allez-vous?—Voir la femme à vous.—Voir la femme à moi! Rouah!" (Where are you going?—To see your wife.—To see my wife! Ha!) Then the toms would fly at each other like the cats of Kilkenny, and their sabbath would end in a massacre. The dialogue differed according to the imaginations of the listeners and the onomatopoetic power of their dialect, but it usually emphasized predatory sexuality.[1] "At night all cats are gray," went the proverb, and the gloss in an eighteenth-century proverb collection made the sexual hint explicit: "That is to say that all women are beautiful enough at night."[2] Enough for what? Seduction, rape, and murder echoed in the air when the cats howled at night in early modern France. Cat calls summoned up *Katzenmusik*, for charivaris often took the form of howling under a cuckold's window on the eve of Mardi Gras, the favorite time for cat sabbaths.

Witchcraft, orgy, cuckoldry, charivari, and massacre, the men of the Old Regime could hear a great deal in the wail of a cat. What the men of the rue Saint-Séverin actually heard is impossible to say. One can only assert that cats bore enormous symbolic weight in the folklore of France and that the

35

---

française (Paris, 1762), which contains a surprising amount of polite cat lore. The impolite lore was transmitted in large measure by children's games and rhymes, some of them dating from the sixteenth century; Claude Gaignebet, *Le Folklore obscène des enfants* (Paris, 1980), p. 260.

1   Sébillot, *Le Folk-lore de France*, III, 93–94.
2   Panckoucke, *Dictionnaire des proverbes français*, p. 66.

lore was rich, ancient, and widespread enough to have penetrated the printing shop. In order to determine whether the printers actually drew on the ceremonial and symbolic themes available to them, it is necessary to take another look at Contat's text.

The text made the theme of sorcery explicit from the beginning. Jerome and Léveillé could not sleep because "some bedeviled cats make a sabbath all night long."[1] After Léveillé added his cat calls to the general caterwauling, "the whole neighborhood is alarmed. It is decided that the cats must be agents of someone casting a spell." The master and mistress considered summoning the curé to exorcise the place. In deciding instead to commission the cat hunt, they fell back on the classic remedy for witchcraft: maiming. The bourgeois—a superstitious, priest-ridden fool—took the whole business seriously. To the apprentices it was a joke. Léveillé in particular functioned as a joker, a mock "sorcerer" staging a fake "sabbath," according to the terms chosen by Contat. Not only did the apprentices exploit their master's superstition in order to run riot at his expense, but they also turned their rioting against their mistress. By bludgeoning her familiar, *la grise*, they in effect accused her of being the witch. The double joke would not be lost on anyone who could read the traditional language of gesture.

The theme of charivari provided an additional dimension to the fun. Although it never says so explicitly, the text indicates that the mistress was having an affair with her priest, a "lascivious youth," who had memorized obscene passages from the classics of pornography—Aretino and *L'Académie des dames*—and quoted them to her, while her husband droned on about his favorite subjects, money and religion. During a lavish dinner with the family, the priest defended the thesis "that it is a feat of wit to cuckold one's husband and that cuckolding is not a vice." Later, he and the wife spent the night together in a country house. They fit perfectly into the typical triangle of printing shops: a doddering old master, a middle-aged mistress, and her youthful lover.[2] The intrigue cast the master in the role of a stock comic figure: the cuckold. So the revelry of the workers took the form of a charivari. The apprentices managed it, operating within the liminal area where novitiates traditionally mocked their superiors, and the journeymen

---

1   This and the following quotations come from Contat's account of the cat massacre, *Anecdotes typographiques*, pp. 48–56.
2   According to Giles Barber (ibid., pp. 7 and 60), the actual Jacques Vincent for whom Contat worked began his own apprenticeship in 1690; so he probably was born about 1675. His wife was born in 1684. Thus when Contat entered the shop, the master was about 62, the mistress about 53, and the bawdy young priest in his twenties. That pattern was common enough in the printing industry, where old masters often left their businesses to younger wives, who in turn took up with still younger journeymen. It was a classic pattern for charivaris, which often mocked disparities in age among newlyweds as well as humiliating cuckolds.

responded to their antics in the traditional way, with rough music. A riotous, festival atmosphere runs through the whole episode, which Contat described as a *fête*. "Léveillé and his comrade Jerome preside over the *fête*," he wrote, as if they were kings of a carnival and the cat bashing corresponded to the torturing of cats on Mardi Gras or the *fête* of Saint John the Baptist.

As in many Mardi Gras, the carnival ended in a mock trial and execution. The burlesque legalism came naturally to the printers because they staged their own mock trials every year at the *fête* of Saint Martin, when the chapel squared accounts with its boss and succeeded spectacularly in getting his goat. The chapel could not condemn him explicitly without moving into open insubordination and risking dismissal. (All the sources, including the papers of the STN, indicate that masters often fired workers for insolence and misbehavior. Indeed, Léveillé was later fired for a prank that attacked the bourgeois more openly.) So the workers tried the bourgeois in absentia, using a symbol that would let their meaning show through without being explicit enough to justify retaliation. They tried and hanged the cats. It would be going too far to hang *la grise* under the master's nose after being ordered to spare it; but they made the favorite pet of the house their first victim, and in doing so they knew they were attacking the house itself, in accordance with the traditions of cat lore. When the mistress accused them of killing *la grise*, they replied with mock deference that "nobody would be capable of such an outrage and that they have too much respect for that house." By executing the cats with such elaborate ceremony, they condemned the house and declared the bourgeois guilty—guilty of overworking and underfeeding his apprentices, guilty of living in luxury while his journeymen did all the work, guilty of withdrawing from the shop and swamping it with *alloués* instead of laboring and eating with the men, as masters were said to have done a generation or two earlier, or in the primitive "republic" that existed at the beginning of the printing industry. The guilt extended from the boss to the house to the whole system. Perhaps in trying, confessing, and hanging a collection of half-dead cats, the workers meant to ridicule the entire legal and social order.

They certainly felt debased and had accumulated enough resentment to explode in an orgy of killing. A half-century later, the artisans of Paris would run riot in a similar manner, combining indiscriminate slaughter with improvised popular tribunals.[1] It would be absurd to view the cat massacre as a dress rehearsal for the September Massacres of the French Revolution, but the earlier outburst of violence did suggest a popular rebellion, though it remained restricted to the level of symbolism.

Cats as symbols conjured up sex as well as violence, a combination per-

40

---

1 Pierre Caron, *Les Massacres de septembre* (Paris, 1935).

fectly suited for an attack on the mistress. The narrative identified her with *la grise*, her *chatte favorite*. In killing it, the boys struck at her: "It was a matter of consequence, a murder, which had to be hidden." The mistress reacted as if she had been assaulted: "They ravished from her a cat without an equal, a cat that she loved to madness." The text described her as lascivious and "impassioned for cats" as if she were a she-cat in heat during a wild cat's sabbath of howling, killing, and rape. An explicit reference to rape would violate the proprieties that were generally observed in eighteenth-century writing. Indeed, the symbolism would work only if it remained veiled— ambivalent enough to dupe the master and sharp enough to hit the mistress in the quick. But Contat used strong language. As soon as the mistress saw the cat execution she let out a scream. Then the scream was smothered in the realization that she had lost her *grise*. The workers assured her with feigned sincerity of their respect and the master arrived. "'Ah! the scoundrels,' he says. 'Instead of working they are killing cats.' Madame to Monsieur: 'These wicked men can't kill the masters; they have killed my cat.' ... It seems to her that all the blood of the workers would not be sufficient to redeem the insult."

It was metonymic insult, the eighteenth-century equivalent of the modern schoolboy's taunt: "Ah, your mother's girdle!" But it was stronger, and more obscene. By assaulting her pet, the workers ravished the mistress symbolically. At the same time, they delivered the supreme insult to their master. His wife was his most precious possession, just as her *chatte* was hers. In killing the cat, the men violated the most intimate treasure of the bourgeois household and escaped unharmed. That was the beauty of it. The symbolism disguised the insult well enough for them to get away with it. While the bourgeois fumed over the loss of work, his wife, less obtuse, virtually told him that the workers had attacked her sexually and would like to murder him. Then both left the scene in humiliation and defeat. "Monsieur and Madame retire, leaving the workers in liberty. The printers, who love disorder, are in a state of great joy. Here is an ample subject for their laughter, a beautiful *copie*, which will keep them amused for a long time."

This was Rabelaisian laughter. The text insists upon its importance: "The printers know how to laugh, it is their sole occupation." Mikhail Bakhtin has shown how the laughter of Rabelais expressed a strain of popular culture in which the riotously funny could turn to riot, a carnival culture of sexuality and sedition in which the revolutionary element might be contained within symbols and metaphors or might explode in a general uprising, as in 1789. The question remains, however, what precisely was so funny about the cat massacre? There is no better way to ruin a joke than to analyze it or to overload it with social comment. But this joke cries out for commentary—not because one can use it to prove that artisans hated their bosses (a truism that may apply to all periods of labor history, although it has not been appreciated adequately by eighteenth-century historians), but because it can help one to see how workers made their experience meaningful by playing with themes of their culture.

The only version of the cat massacre available to us was put into writing, long after the fact, by Nicolas Contat. He selected details, ordered events, and framed the story in such a way as to bring out what was meaningful for him. But he derived his notions of meaning from his culture just as naturally as he drew in air from the atmosphere around him. And he wrote down what he had helped to enact with his mates. The subjective character of the writing does not vitiate its collective frame of reference, even though the written account must be thin compared with the action it describes. The workers' mode of expression was a kind of popular theater. It involved pantomime, rough music, and a dramatic "theater of violence" improvised in the work place, in the street, and on the rooftops. It included a play within a play, because Léveillé reenacted the whole farce several times as *copies* in the shop. In fact, the original massacre involved the burlesque of other ceremonies, such as trials and charivaris. So Contat wrote about a burlesque of a burlesque, and in reading it one should make allowances for the refraction of cultural forms across genres and over time.

Those allowances made, it seems clear that the workers found the mas- 45
sacre funny because it gave them a way to turn the tables on the bourgeois. By goading him with cat calls, they provoked him to authorize the massacre of cats, then they used the massacre to put him symbolically on trial for unjust management of the shop. They also used it as a witch hunt, which provided an excuse to kill his wife's familiar and to insinuate that she herself was the witch. Finally, they transformed it into a charivari, which served as a means to insult her sexually while mocking him as a cuckold. The bourgeois made an excellent butt of the joke. Not only did he become the victim of a procedure he himself had set in motion, he did not understand how badly he had been had. The men had subjected his wife to symbolic aggression of the most intimate kind, but he did not get it. He was too thickheaded, a classic cuckold. The printers ridiculed him in splendid Boccaccian style and got off scot-free.

The joke worked so well because the workers played so skillfully with a repertory of ceremonies and symbols. Cats suited their purposes perfectly. By smashing the spine of *la grise* they called the master's wife a witch and a slut, while at the same time making the master into a cuckold and a fool. It was metonymic insult, delivered by actions, not words, and it struck home because cats occupied a soft spot in the bourgeois way of life. Keeping pets was as alien to the workers as torturing animals was to the bourgeois. Trapped between incompatible sensitivities, the cats had the worst of both worlds.

The workers also punned with ceremonies. They made a roundup of cats into a witch hunt, a festival, a charivari, a mock trial, and a dirty joke. Then they redid the whole thing in pantomime. Whenever they got tired of working, they transformed the shop into a theater and produced *copies*—their kind of copy, not the authors'. Shop theater and ritual punning suited the traditions of their craft. Although printers made books, they did not use written words to convey their meaning. They used gestures, drawing on the culture of their craft to inscribe statements in the air.

Insubstantial as it may seem today, this joking was a risky business in the eighteenth century. The risk was part of the joke, as in many forms of humor, which toy with violence and tease repressed passions. The workers pushed their symbolic horseplay to the brink of reification, the point at which the killing of cats would turn into an open rebellion. They played on ambiguities, using symbols that would hide their full meaning while letting enough of it show through to make a fool of the bourgeois without giving him a pretext to fire them. They tweaked his nose and prevented him from protesting against it. To pull off such a feat required great dexterity. It showed that workers could manipulate symbols in their idiom as effectively as poets did in print.

The boundaries within which this jesting had to be contained suggest the limits to working-class militancy under the Old Regime. The printers identified with their craft rather than their class. Although they organized in chapels, staged strikes, and sometimes forced up wages, they remained subordinate to the bourgeois. The master hired and fired men as casually as he ordered paper, and he turned them out into the road when he sniffed insubordination. So until the onset of proletarianization in the late nineteenth century, they generally kept their protests on a symbolic level. A *copie*, like a carnival, helped to let off steam; but it also produced laughter, a vital ingredient in early artisanal culture and one that has been lost in labor history. By seeing the way a joke worked in the horseplay of a printing shop two centuries ago, we may be able to recapture that missing element— laughter, sheer laughter, the thigh-slapping, rib-cracking Rabelaisian kind, rather than the Voltairian smirk with which we are familiar.

Appendix: Contat's Account of the Cat Massacre

50   The following account comes from Nicolas Contat, *Anecdotes typographiques où l'on voit la description des coutumes, moeurs et usages singuliers des compagnons imprimeurs*, ed. Giles Barber (Oxford, 1980), pp. 51–53. After a day of exhausting work and disgusting food, the two apprentices retire to their bedroom, a damp and draughty lean-to in a corner of the courtyard. The episode is recounted in the third person, from the viewpoint of Jerome:

He is so tired and needs rest so desperately that the shack looks like a palace to him. At last the persecution and misery he has suffered throughout the day have come to an end, and he can relax. But no, some bedeviled cats celebrate a witches' sabbath all night long, making so much noise that they rob him of the brief period of rest allotted to the apprentices before the journeymen arrive for work early the next morning and demand admission by constant ringing of an infernal bell. Then the boys have to get up and cross the courtyard, shivering under their nightshirts, in order to open the door. Those journeymen never let up. No matter what you do, you always make them lose their time and they always treat you as a lazy good-for-nothing. They call for Léveillé. Light the fire under the cauldron! Fetch water for the dunking-troughs! True, those jobs are supposed to be done by the beginner apprentices, who live at home, but they don't arrive until six or seven. Thus everyone is soon at work— apprentices, journeymen, everyone but the master and the mistress: they alone enjoy the sweetness of sleep. That makes Jerome and Léveillé jealous. They resolve that they will not be the only ones to suffer; they want this master and mistress as associates. But how to turn the trick?

Léveillé has an extraordinary talent for imitating the voices and the smallest gestures of everyone around him. He is a perfect actor; that's the real profession that he has picked up in the printing shop. He also can produce perfect imitations of the cries of dogs and cats. He decides to climb from roof to roof until he reaches a gutter next to the bedroom of the bourgeois and the bourgeoise. From there he can ambush them with a volley of meows. It's an easy job for him: he is the son of a roofer and can scramble across roofs like a cat.

Our sniper succeeds so well that the whole neighborhood is alarmed. The word spreads that there is witchcraft afoot and that the cats must be the agents of someone casting a spell. It is a case for the curé, who is an intimate of the household and the confessor of Madame. No one can sleep any more.

Léveillé stages a sabbath the next night and the night after that. If you didn't know him, you would be convinced he was a witch. Finally, the master and the mistress cannot stand it any longer. "We'd better tell the boys to get rid of those malevolent animals," they declare. Madame gives them the order, exhorting them to avoid frightening la grise. That is the name of her pet pussy.

This lady is impassioned for cats. Many master printers are also. One of them has twenty-five. He has had their portraits painted and feeds them on roast fowl. [55]

The hunt is soon organized. The apprentices resolve to make a clean sweep of it, and they are joined by the journeymen. The masters love cats, so consequently they must hate them. This man arms himself with the bar of a press, that one with a stick from the drying-room, others with broom handles. They hang sacks at the windows of the attic and the storerooms to catch the cats who attempt to escape by leaping outdoors. The beaters are named, everything is organized. Léveillé and his comrade Jerome preside over the fête, each of them armed with an iron bar from the shop. The first thing they go for is la grise, Madame's pussy. Léveillé stuns it with a quick blow on the kidneys, and Jerome finishes it off. Then Léveillé stuffs the body in a gutter, for they don't want to get caught: it is a matter of consequence, a murder, which must be kept hidden. The men produce terror on the rooftops. Seized by panic, the cats throw themselves into the sacks. Some are killed on the spot. Others are condemned to be hanged for the amusement of the entire printing shop.

Printers know how to laugh; it is their sole occupation.

The execution is about to begin. They name a hangman, a troop of guards, even a confessor. Then they pronounce the sentence.

In the midst of it all, the mistress arrives. What is her surprise, when she sees the bloody execution! She lets out a scream; then her voice is cut, because she thinks she sees la grise, and she is certain that such a fate has been reserved for her favorite puss. The workers assure her that no one would be capable of such a crime: they have too much respect for the house.

60   The bourgeois arrives. "Ah! The scoundrels," he says. "Instead of working, they are killing cats." Madame to Monsieur: "These wicked men can't kill the masters, so they have killed my pussy. She can't be found. I have called la grise everywhere. They must have hanged her." It seems to her that all the workers' blood would not be sufficient to redeem the insult. The poor grise, a pussy without a peer!

Monsieur and Madame retire, leaving the workers in liberty. The printers delight in the disorder; they are beside themselves with joy.

What a splendid subject for their laughter, for a *belle copie!* They will amuse themselves with it for a long time. Léveillé will take the leading role and will stage the play at least twenty times. He will mime the master, the mistress, the whole house, heaping ridicule on them all. He will spare nothing in his satire. Among printers, those who excel in this entertainment are called *jobeurs*; they provide *joberie.*

Léveillé receives many rounds of applause.

It should be noted that all the workers are in league against the masters. It is enough to speak badly of them [the masters] to be esteemed by the whole assembly of typographers. Léveillé is one of those. In recognition of his merit, he will be pardoned for some previous satires against the workers.

Questions

1. Darnton describes the attack as a "metonymic insult." Explain what is meant by this.
2. With reference to specific passages, discuss how Darnton's essay seeks to animate an historical event. What is the purpose of such a technique? Is it successful in this essay? Why or why not?
3. Find evidence in this essay that indicates the author's own attitude toward the printers, "Monsieur and Madame," and the killing of the cats. Discuss the relationships between the author's attitudes, the general conclusions of his essay, and your own expectations of historical writing.

PHILIP GOUREVITCH

We Wish to Inform You That Tomorrow We Will Be Killed with Our Families

(1998)

A staff writer for The New Yorker, *Philip Gourevitch (1961–) was initially sent by that magazine to Rwanda in 1995 to study the aftermath of the genocide of the Tutsi minority. He stayed nine months in Rwanda and in neighbouring Congo, and published the book* We Wish to Inform You That Tomorrow We Will Be Killed with Our Families: Stories from Rwanda *(1998).*

In this excerpt from the book, the author inquires into how ordinary people can be capable of extraordinary crimes.

In the Province of Kibungo, in eastern Rwanda, in the swamp and pasture-land near the Tanzanian border, there's a rocky hill called Nyarubuye with a church where many Tutsis were slaughtered in mid-April of 1994. A year after the killing I went to Nyarubuye with two Canadian military officers. We flew in a United Nations helicopter, traveling low over the hills in the morning mists, with the banana trees like green starbursts dense over the slopes. The uncut grass blew back as we dropped into the center of the parish schoolyard. A lone soldier materialized with his Kalashnikov, and shook our hands with stiff, shy formality. The Canadians presented the paperwork for our visit, and I stepped up into the open doorway of a classroom.

At least fifty mostly decomposed cadavers covered the floor, wadded in clothing, their belongings strewn about and smashed. Macheted skulls had rolled here and there.

The dead looked like pictures of the dead. They did not smell. They did not buzz with flies. They had been killed thirteen months earlier, and they hadn't been moved. Skin stuck here and there over the bones, many of which lay scattered away from the bodies, dismembered by the killers, or by scavengers—birds, dogs, bugs. The more complete figures looked a lot like people, which they were once. A woman in a cloth wrap printed with flowers lay near the door. Her fleshless hip bones were high and her legs slightly spread, and a child's skeleton extended between them. Her torso was hollowed out. Her ribs and spinal column poked through the rotting cloth.

Her head was tipped back and her mouth was open: a strange image—half agony, half repose.

I had never been among the dead before. What to do? Look? Yes. I wanted to see them, I suppose; I had come to see them—the dead had been left unburied at Nyarubuye for memorial purposes—and there they were, so intimately exposed. I didn't need to see them. I already knew, and believed, what had happened in Rwanda. Yet looking at the buildings and the bodies, and hearing the silence of the place, with the grand Italianate basilica standing there deserted, and beds of exquisite, decadent, death-fertilized flowers blooming over the corpses, it was still strangely unimaginable. I mean one still had to imagine it.

5   Those dead Rwandans will be with me forever, I expect. That was why I had felt compelled to come to Nyarubuye: to be stuck with them—not with their experience, but with the experience of looking at them. They had been killed there, and they were dead there. What else could you really see at first? The Bible bloated with rain lying on top of one corpse or, littered about, the little woven wreaths of thatch which Rwandan women wear as crowns to balance the enormous loads they carry on their heads, and the water gourds, and the Converse tennis sneaker stuck somehow in a pelvis.

The soldier with the Kalashnikov—Sergeant Francis of the Rwandese Patriotic Army, a Tutsi whose parents had fled to Uganda with him when he was a boy, after similar but less extensive massacres in the early 1960s, and who had fought his way home in 1994 and found it like this—said that the dead in this room were mostly women who had been raped before being murdered. Sergeant Francis had high, rolling girlish hips, and he walked and stood with his butt stuck out behind him, an oddly purposeful posture, tipped forward, driven. He was, at once, candid and briskly official. His English had the punctilious clip of military drill, and after he told me what I was looking at I looked instead at my feet. The rusty head of a hatchet lay beside them in the dirt.

A few weeks earlier, in Bukavu, Zaire, in the giant market of a refugee camp that was home to many Rwandan Hutu militiamen, I had watched a man butchering a cow with a machete. He was quite expert at his work, taking big precise strokes that made a sharp hacking noise. The rallying cry to the killers during the genocide was "Do your work!" And I saw that it *was* work, this butchery; hard work. It took many hacks—two, three, four, five hard hacks—to chop through the cow's leg. How many hacks to dismember a person?

Considering the enormity of the task, it is tempting to play with theories of collective madness, mob mania, a fever of hatred erupted into a mass crime of passion, and to imagine the blind orgy of the mob, with each member killing one or two people. But at Nyarubuye, and at thousands of other sites in this tiny country, on the same days of a few months in 1994, hundreds of thousands of Hutus had worked as killers in regular shifts. There was always the next victim, and the next. What sustained them, beyond the frenzy of the first attack, through the plain physical exhaustion and mess of it?

The pygmy in Gikongoro said that humanity is part of nature and that we must go against nature to get along and have peace. But mass violence, too, must be organized; it does not occur aimlessly. Even mobs and riots have a design, and great and sustained destruction requires great ambition. It must be conceived as the means toward achieving a new order, and although the idea behind that new order may be criminal and objectively very stupid, it must also be compellingly simple and at the same time absolute. The ideology of genocide is all of those things, and in Rwanda it went by the bald name of Hutu Power. For those who set about systematically exterminating an entire people—even a fairly small and unresisting subpopulation of perhaps a million and a quarter men, women, and children, like the Tutsis in Rwanda—blood lust surely helps. But the engineers and perpetrators of a slaughter like the one just inside the door where I stood need not enjoy killing, and they may even find it unpleasant. What is required above all is that they want their victims dead. They have to want it so badly that they consider it a necessity.

So I still had much to imagine as I entered the classroom and stepped   10
carefully between the remains. These dead and their killers had been neighbors, schoolmates, colleagues, sometimes friends, even in-laws. The dead had seen their killers training as militias in the weeks before the end, and it was well known that they were training to kill Tutsis; it was announced on the radio, it was in the newspapers, people spoke of it openly. The week before the massacre at Nyarubuye, the killing began in Rwanda's capital, Kigali. Hutus who opposed the Hutu Power ideology were publicly denounced as "accomplices" of the Tutsis and were among the first to be killed as the extermination got under way. In Nyarubuye, when Tutsis asked the Hutu Power mayor how they might be spared, he suggested that they seek sanctuary at the church. They did, and a few days later the mayor came to kill them. He came at the head of a pack of soldiers, policemen, militiamen, and villagers; he gave out arms and orders to complete the job well. No more was required of the mayor, but he was also said to have killed a few Tutsis himself.

The killers killed all day at Nyarubuye. At night they cut the Achilles tendons of survivors and went off to feast behind the church, roasting cattle looted from their victims in big fires, and drinking beer. (Bottled beer, banana beer—Rwandans may not drink more beer than other Africans, but they drink prodigious quantities of it around the clock.) And, in the morning, still drunk after whatever sleep they could find beneath the cries of their prey, the killers at Nyarubuye went back and killed again. Day after day, minute to minute, Tutsi by Tutsi: all across Rwanda, they worked like that. "It was a process," Sergeant Francis said. I can see that it happened, I can be told how, and after nearly three years of looking around Rwanda and listening to Rwandans, I can tell you how, and I will. But the horror of it—the idiocy, the waste, the sheer wrongness—remains uncircumscribable.

Like Leontius, the young Athenian in Plato, I presume that you are reading this because you desire a closer look, and that you, too, are properly disturbed by your curiosity. Perhaps, in examining this extremity with me, you hope for some understanding, some insight, some flicker of self-knowledge—a moral, or a lesson, or a clue about how to behave in this world: some such information. I don't discount the possibility, but when it comes to genocide, you already know right from wrong. The best reason I have come up with for looking closely into Rwanda's stories is that ignoring them makes me even more uncomfortable about existence and my place in it. The horror, as horror, interests me only insofar as a precise memory of the offense is necessary to understand its legacy.

The dead at Nyarubuye were, I'm afraid, beautiful. There was no getting around it. The skeleton is a beautiful thing. The randomness of the fallen forms, the strange tranquillity of their rude exposure, the skull here, the arm bent in some uninterpretable gesture there—these things were beautiful, and their beauty only added to the affront of the place. I couldn't settle on any meaningful response: revulsion, alarm, sorrow, grief, shame, incomprehension, sure, but nothing truly meaningful. I just looked, and I took photographs, because I wondered whether I could really see what I was seeing while I saw it, and I wanted also an excuse to look a bit more closely.

We went on through the first room and out the far side. There was another room and another and another and another. They were all full of bodies, and more bodies were scattered in the grass and there were stray skulls in the grass, which was thick and wonderfully green. Standing outside, I heard a crunch. The old Canadian colonel stumbled in front of me, and I saw, though he did not notice, that his foot had rolled on a skull and broken it. For the first time at Nyarubuye my feelings focused, and what I felt was a small but keen anger at this man. Then I heard another crunch, and felt a vibration underfoot. I had stepped on one, too.

15   Rwanda is spectacular to behold. Throughout its center, a winding succession of steep, tightly terraced slopes radiates out from small roadside settlements and solitary compounds. Gashes of red clay and black loam mark fresh hoe work; eucalyptus trees flash silver against brilliant green tea plantations; banana trees are everywhere. On the theme of hills, Rwanda produces countless variations: jagged rain forests, round-shouldered buttes, undulating moors, broad swells of savanna, volcanic peaks sharp as filed teeth. During the rainy season, the clouds are huge and low and fast, mists

cling in highland hollows, lightning flickers through the nights, and by day the land is lustrous. After the rains, the skies lift, the terrain takes on a ragged look beneath the flat unvarying haze of the dry season, and in the savannas of the Akagera Park wildfire blackens the hills.

One day, when I was returning to Kigali from the south, the car mounted a rise between two winding valleys, the windshield filled with purple-bellied clouds, and I asked Joseph, the man who was giving me a ride, whether Rwandans realize what a beautiful country they have. "Beautiful?" he said. "You think so? After the things that happened here? The people aren't good. If the people were good, the country might be OK." Joseph told me that his brother and sister had been killed, and he made a soft hissing click with his tongue against his teeth. "The country is empty," he said. "Empty!"

It was not just the dead who were missing. The genocide had been brought to a halt by the Rwandese Patriotic Front, a rebel army led by Tutsi refugees from past persecutions, and as the RPF advanced through the country in the summer of 1994, some two million Hutus had fled into exile at the behest of the same leaders who had urged them to kill. Yet except in some rural areas in the south, where the desertion of Hutus had left nothing but bush to reclaim the fields around crumbling adobe houses, I, as a newcomer, could not see the emptiness that blinded Joseph to Rwanda's beauty. Yes, there were grenade-flattened buildings, burnt homesteads, shot-up facades, and mortar-pitted roads. But these were the ravages of war, not of genocide, and by the summer of 1995, most of the dead had been buried. Fifteen months earlier, Rwanda had been the most densely populated country in Africa. Now the work of the killers looked just as they had intended: invisible.

From time to time, mass graves were discovered and excavated, and the remains would be transferred to new, properly consecrated mass graves. Yet even the occasionally exposed bones, the conspicuous number of amputees and people with deforming scars, and the superabundance of packed orphanages could not be taken as evidence that what had happened to Rwanda was an attempt to eliminate a people. There were only people's stories.

"Every survivor wonders why he is alive," Abbé Modeste, a priest at the cathedral in Butare, Rwanda's second-largest city, told me. Abbé Modeste had hidden for weeks in his sacristy, eating communion wafers, before moving under the desk in his study, and finally into the rafters at the home of some neighboring nuns. The obvious explanation of his survival was that the RPF had come to the rescue. But the RPF didn't reach Butare till early July, and roughly seventy-five percent of the Tutsis in Rwanda had been killed by early May. In this regard, at least, the genocide had been entirely successful: to those who were targeted, it was not death but life that seemed an accident of fate.

"I had eighteen people killed at my house," said Etienne Niyonzima, a 20 former businessman who had become a deputy in the National Assembly.

"Everything was totally destroyed—a place of fifty-five meters by fifty meters. In my neighborhood they killed six hundred and forty-seven people. They tortured them, too. You had to see how they killed them. They had the number of everyone's house, and they went through with red paint and marked the homes of all the Tutsis and of the Hutu moderates. My wife was at a friend's, shot with two bullets. She is still alive, only"—he fell quiet for a moment—"she has no arms. The others with her were killed. The militia left her for dead. Her whole family of sixty-five in Gitarama were killed." Niyonzima was in hiding at the time. Only after he had been separated from his wife for three months did he learn that she and four of their children had survived. "Well," he said, "one son was cut in the head with a machete. I don't know where he went." His voice weakened, and caught. "He disappeared." Niyonzima clicked his tongue, and said, "But the others are still alive. Quite honestly, I don't understand at all how I was saved."

Laurent Nkongoli attributed his survival to "Providence, and also good neighbors, an old woman who said, 'Run away, we don't want to see your corpse.'" Nkongoli, a lawyer, who had become the vice president of the National Assembly after the genocide, was a robust man, with a taste for double-breasted suit jackets and lively ties, and he moved, as he spoke, with a brisk determination. But before taking his neighbor's advice, and fleeing Kigali in late April of 1994, he said, "I had accepted death. At a certain moment this happens. One hopes not to die cruelly, but one expects to die anyway. Not death by machete, one hopes, but with a bullet. If you were willing to pay for it, you could often ask for a bullet. Death was more or less normal, a resignation. You lose the will to fight. There were four thousand Tutsis killed here at Kacyiru"—a neighborhood of Kigali. "The soldiers brought them here, and told them to sit down because they were going to throw grenades. And they sat."

"Rwandan culture is a culture of fear," Nkongoli went on. "I remember what people said." He adopted a pipey voice, and his face took on a look of disgust: "'Just let us pray, then kill us,' or 'I don't want to die in the street, I want to die at home.'" He resumed his normal voice. "When you're that resigned and oppressed you're already dead. It shows the genocide was prepared for too long. I detest this fear. These victims of genocide had been psychologically prepared to expect death just for being Tutsi. They were being killed for so long that they were already dead."

I reminded Nkongoli that, for all his hatred of fear, he had himself accepted death before his neighbor urged him to run away. "Yes," he said. "I got tired in the genocide. You struggle so long, then you get tired."

Every Rwandan I spoke with seemed to have a favorite, unanswerable question. For Nkongoli, it was how so many Tutsis had allowed themselves to be killed. For François Xavier Nkurunziza, a Kigali lawyer, whose father was Hutu and whose mother and wife were Tutsi, the question was how so many Hutus had allowed themselves to kill. Nkurunziza had escaped death only by chance as he moved around the country from one hiding place to another, and he had lost many family members. "Conformity is very deep, very developed here," he told me. "In Rwandan history, everyone obeys authority. People revere power, and there isn't enough education. You take a poor, ignorant population, and give them arms, and say, 'It's yours. Kill.' They'll obey. The peasants, who were paid or forced to kill, were looking up to people of higher socio-economic standing to see how to behave. So the people of influence, or the big financiers, are often the big men in the genocide. They may think they didn't kill because they didn't take life with their own hands, but the people were looking to them for their orders. And, in Rwanda, an order can be given very quietly."

As I traveled around the country, collecting accounts of the killing, it   25
almost seemed as if, with the machete, the *masu*—a club studded with nails—a few well-placed grenades, and a few bursts of automatic-rifle fire, the quiet orders of Hutu Power had made the neutron bomb obsolete.

"Everyone was called to hunt the enemy," said Theodore Nyilinkwaya, a survivor of the massacres in his home village of Kimbogo, in the southwestern province of Cyangugu. "But let's say someone is reluctant. Say that guy comes with a stick. They tell him, 'No, get a *masu*.' So, OK, he does, and he runs along with the rest, but he doesn't kill. They say, 'Hey, he might denounce us later. He must kill. Everyone must help to kill at least one person.' So this person who is not a killer is made to do it. And the next day it's become a game for him. You don't need to keep pushing him."

At Nyarubuye, even the little terracotta votive statues in the sacristy had been methodically decapitated. "They were associated with Tutsis," Sergeant Francis explained.

Questions

1. What is the author's conclusion at the end of his journey? What message is Gourevitch trying to convey to the reader about the events in Rwanda?
2. How can you explain Gourevitch's use of the word "beautiful" in reference to the massacred bodies he sees (paragraph 13)? Why does he use it, and what effect does it have on the reader?
3. The first part of the essay details how Gourevitch dealt personally with confronting the facts of the massacre. The second part deals in a more theoretical way with the politics underlying the massacre. How does the first part of the essay affect your reading of the second part? Suggest other effective ways Gourevitch could have arranged his argument.

JOAN DIDION

History Lesson

(2003)

Joan Didion (1934–), essayist and novelist, worked as a feature editor at Vogue
Magazine *for 8 years before moving into freelance journalism, fiction, and screen-
writing. Her works of fiction include* Play It As It Lays *(1970); her nonfiction works
include* The White Album *(1979) and* The Year of Magical Thinking *(2005).*

*This essay, describing Didion's visit to a Paris museum, explores the interplay between
artifact and meaning, past and present.*

There is in the collection of the E.G. Bührle Foundation in Zurich an 1880
Renoir portrait of a gravely beautiful French child, eight or nine years old,
her long hair tied back, her small hands folded in her lap. The name of the
child was Irène Cahen d'Anvers, and at age eighteen she married Moïse de
Camondo, the thirty-one-year-old heir to much of the wealth of a
Sephardic[1] banking family that had migrated from Spain in the fifteenth
century to Constantinople to Trieste and finally, in the nineteenth century,
to Paris. Before running away with the Italian who trained her husband's
horses, this gravely beautiful French child bore Moïse de Camondo one son
and one daughter, Nissim and Béatrice. Nissim de Camondo volunteered to
fly for the French in World War I and was killed in combat, leaving his
father and sister alone in the house on the Rue de Monceau that the father
had built after the mother defected. The sister married in 1918. The father
died in 1935. In accordance with his wish, the house on the Rue de Monceau, and the perfect examples of eighteenth-century French furniture
with which he had filled it, were given to France, to be maintained as a
museum named for the lost son, Nissim. Only a small plaque at the
entrance to the courtyard of the Musée Nissim de Camondo now gives us
the fate of the sister: "Mme. Léon Reinach, born Béatrice de Camondo, her
children, Fanny and Bertrand, the last descendants of the founder, and M.
Léon Reinach, deported by the Germans in 1943-44, died at Auschwitz."

I paid a visit to this house on the Rue de Monceau late last November,
during a week in Paris when the dark was already stretching late into the

---

1 *Sephardic* The branch of European Jews that settled in Spain and Portugal.

day and falling back over the city not long after lunch. I felt the weight of the copper pots in the pristine kitchen. I counted the places set at the long table in the servants' dining room, and already forget how many there were. Twelve, fourteen? More? I counted the place settings in the wall of Sèvres[1] off the main dining room, and lost track. I stood at the windows and watched the rain blow the branches in the Parc Monceau, its lawns and follies largely deserted, none of the small children for which the park is famous, only an occasional jogger sufficiently determined to ignore the rain. Just one thing had changed since I first visited this house, several years before: at that time there had been, hanging from the racks in an upstairs bathroom, monogrammed towels, the monograms threadbare and the toweling itself worn thin by repeated laundering, a sharp reminder of the life once lived there.

It had been the towels, on that first visit to the house on the Rue de Monceau, that brought tears to my eyes. This November it was something else. There is upstairs a dressing room in which glass cases have been placed, for the display of letters and documents in one way or another meaningful to those who had lived there. There are many documents from the Louvre, of which Moïse de Camondo was a director and to which his cousin Isaac bequeathed his Fragonards and Watteaus and Monets and Cézannes and some thirty works by Degas. There is a letter of condolence from Marcel Proust, delivered to Moïse de Camondo after the death of his son. There are medals, honors, accountings of expenses. There is also, and this is what stopped me in November, an engraved invitation to a weekend shooting party at the country estate of the Camondo family—just a card, one such invitation of what must have been many, yet it spoke to me that day in a way I did not immediately understand.

I did nothing much else, that November week in Paris. I watched CNN and the BBC. War in Iraq, and whatever might follow, was by then a foregone conclusion to all but the most wishful. A worldwide disruption seemed for the first time since my childhood a distinct possibility. My husband and I had dinner with friends whose sense of foreboding matched our own, an American reporter and his wife who were leaving the next day for Amman. The imminence of war was very much with the four of us that night: the reporter's son was an Army officer already serving in the Middle East, and my husband's nephew was a Marine officer due to leave for Kuwait in January.

Days passed. We started out to see a Modigliani exhibition and ended up 5 walking instead in the Jardin de Luxembourg, the wet leaves underfoot, the only greenery remote behind the glass of the locked greenhouses. We started out to see the Monets at the Musée Marmottan and ended up sitting instead in the Ranelagh gardens, watching the children play soccer. We lit

---

1 *Sèvres* Porcelain depicting court opulence, made at Sèvres (south-west of Paris) since 1738.

candles at Saint-Sulpice. We walked through a flea market behind the École Militaire,[1] one stall after another filled with monogrammed coffee spoons, amateur watercolors, faded table linens folded in pale tissue, the detritus of comfortable bourgeois lives. The dark, wet days allowed a sadness, a gravity that offered relief from what had come to seem through the fall in New York and Washington an increasingly histrionic enthusiasm for confrontation and its collateral damage, "security." It did not escape my attention that there was at the entrance to the Élysée Palace an absence of the kind of visibly brandished security we in the United States had come to take for granted. To enter the Élysée Palace one rings the bell, and someone answers the door, yet I do not imagine the official residence of the president of France to be unprotected.

I had gone to Paris to think about what I should be writing, to think where the world was going, but when I tried that week to contemplate fundamentalism and tribalism, confrontation and "security," it was the Camondo family that kept coming back to me. There was the glory of the Sèvres, there was the sweet thrift of the worn towels on the bathroom racks, there was the engraved card with the invitation to the shooting party. The Sèvres and the towels and the engraved card all told the same story: This was a family with reason to believe that it had managed over the centuries to obtain the right visas, negotiate an escape from the woes of tribalism, arrive in a place where its members would be honored. This was a family that had thought itself exempt from history. This was a family that had been wrong.

Questions

1. "History Lesson" opens with a description of a portrait by Renoir. Discuss the role and significance of artwork in this essay.
2. Why does Didion place quotation marks around the word "security" in some cases and not in others?
3. What parallel is Didion drawing between the fate of the Camondo family and her perception of American politics that November?

---

1   *École Militaire* Military School.

JONATHAN VANCE

The Soldier as Novelist

Literature, History, and the Great War
(2003)

Jonathan Vance is an historian who teaches at the Department of History at the University of Western Ontario. He studies the relationship between war and national identity and culture. His books include Death So Noble: Memory, Meaning, and the First World War *(1997).*

In this article, Vance discusses the controversial relationships between history and memory in literature about World War I.

We have become accustomed to disagreements over the nature of collective memory, and in few places have these disputes been so bitter as in the record of past wars. In January 1995, the Smithsonian Institution in Washington reconsidered elaborate plans for an exhibit discussing the necessity and morality of the atomic bombings of Hiroshima and Nagasaki after veterans' groups protested that it did a disservice to the memory of the war. This incident probably seemed tame to Canadians, who witnessed a prolonged and frequently acrimonious battle involving veterans, historians, the Canadian Broadcasting Corporation, and documentary filmmakers Terence and Brian McKenna over the interpretation of certain events of World War II depicted in the McKennas' 1992 television production *The Valour and the Horror.*

This was not the first time, however, that Canadian veterans have led a spirited and very public campaign to protect their past. In the 1920s and 1930s, veterans of the Great War went to considerable lengths to ensure that their war retained a prominent and proper place in the nation's collective memory. In particular, they were determined to protect the image of their comrades, living and dead, from threats posed by a genre of literature which began to appear in the late 1920s. The veterans' case, however, was complicated by the fact that the authors of this competing memory were also ex-soldiers. In this sense, the struggle differed from modern examples in one very important respect: in the interwar years, the bitterest battles were not between veterans and non-veterans (or people with no personal knowledge of the events under dispute), but between ex-soldiers, all of whom had first-hand experience of life at the front. The ensuing struggle between two contradictory strands of memory saw one group of veterans stake out their role, not simply as defenders of their comrades' image, but as the sole proprietors of historical truth.

Such struggles characterize the construction of a community's perception of its past; most often, a variety of interest groups, usually differentiated by class, gender, ethnicity, or political orientation, champion different versions of the past as a way to advance specific goals in the present and future. The Canadian veterans who took up their pens to defend the image of their comrades, however, were a very heterogeneous group. They were not linked by any economic or social factors, so it is impossible to describe them as members of a particular class. Nor were they a highly politicized body, like other groups (such as the *Stahlhelm* in Germany) which sought to fashion a certain image of the Great War soldier for political reasons. On the contrary, those veterans who became the staunchest defenders of the average soldier had little in common beyond their service at the front. It was a common past, rather than anything in the present, which motivated them.

This is not to say that all veterans remembered the war in exactly the same way. The private in the ranks did not experience the same war as his divisional commander, so the two could not possibly construct the same memory. Nevertheless, both versions were built on the same assumption: that the war possessed certain positive features which offered some compensation for its horrors. The most important of these was the comradeship of soldiers. The notion of comradeship was central to the veterans' memory of the war, and the deep and enduring bond between ex-soldiers was the dominant element of veteran culture in the 1920s and 1930s (Mosse 79; Vance 126-34). As one prominent veteran leader said, soldiers were forever bound "by ties that cannot be broken but are written in blood, ties that we formed in days of trial that cannot be broken now by anything else, ties that are sacred to those who have gone and to those who still live" (*Proceedings of the 4th Convention* 102). Respect for these ties dominated the activities of veterans, who celebrated comradeship as an "equalizing treasure," to use Will Bird's phrase, that compensated for the horrors they had endured at the front (343). Comradeship was not only shared by the living, however. The communion between the survivor of the war and the fallen soldier endured, the bonds between them only strengthened by death. The survivors were determined to ensure that the fallen were not forgotten, and gradually adopted the role of custodians of the memory of their dead comrades (Leed 212). Because the fallen could not speak for themselves, the survivors had to speak for them, to ensure that their memory was not impugned or their reputation tarnished.

They were drawn to battle in 1928, by a burst of publishing activity that 5
has since become known as the war book boom. Over the next few years,
there appeared the works which have become classics of Great War literature: in 1928, Edmund Blunden's *Undertones of War*, Arnold Zweig's *The Case
of Sergeant Grischa*, R.C. Sherriff's *Journey's End*; in 1929, Erich Maria Remarque's *All Quiet on the Western Front*, Richard Aldington's *Death of a Hero*,
Robert Graves's *Good-bye to All That*; and in 1930, Siegfried Sassoon's *Memoirs of an Infantry Officer*, Henry Tomlinson's *All Our Yesterdays*, and Henry
Williamson's *A Patriot's Progress*, to name but a few.

The boom encompassed a variety of responses, from the bucolic musings
of Blunden to the stridency of Aldington to the horror of Remarque. Some
were clearly fictional, others obviously autobiographical, but all were
lumped together into the canon of anti-war literature, which contemporary
observers and later scholars, most notably Paul Fussell (whose brilliant 1975
study *The Great War and Modern Memory* re-energized the debate), characterized by its negativity. The characters are victims, trapped in a war they do
not understand and dominated by forces they cannot control. Their suffering is at once monumental and insignificant. The war strips them of everything, including the dignity to suffer as individuals: instead of identity, the
war gives them anonymity. They lack even the consoling hope that good will
emerge from their agony, and must exist in the horrific circumstances of
the trenches until death or madness releases them. Any who survive can
look forward only to a life of bitterness, regret, and painful memories.

Veterans around the world reacted to the anti-war books in various ways.
Many of them approved of the vision they conveyed, for it fed their disillu-
sionment with the postwar world (Eksteins 361). However, others reacted
negatively, seeing the anti-war memory as a perversion of their experience.
Britain's major newspapers were deluged with complaints from enraged veterans, and Douglas Jerrold, who had served with the Royal Naval Division
at Gallipoli and in France, published a stinging pamphlet entitled *The Lie
About the War* which attacked them for their pretensions to historical accuracy. In New Zealand, film versions of *All Quiet on the Western Front* and *Journey's End* were banned, and there was widespread sympathy for veterans,
who viewed such works as a "foul libel" on their comrades. In Australia, the
Returned Soldiers' League advocated censoring war books which were
deemed to defame Australian soldiers (M. Sharpe 10; Gerster 118). In the
United States, the poet Archibald MacLeish (a former infantry officer
whose brother had been killed in action with the Royal Flying Corps) railed
against the canon for lacking totality and balance. Life at the front did
mean discomfort, agony, and death, but it also meant heroism, friendship,
and humour. To emphasize the former at the expense of the latter was to
distort the reality of the war (Cooperman 189).

MacLeish's response identified what was at the heart of the veterans' campaign to defend the memory of their comrades. They judged any account, be it Canadian, British, or German, on the degree to which it captured the balance of the war experience as they remembered it. When Reverend Ephram McKegney, wounded in 1918 while serving as chaplain to a Canadian infantry battalion, reminded his listeners at a 1928 Armistice Day service that to recall the terrible life at the front was also to recall the wonderful spirit of fellowship that prevailed there, he was merely expressing what many veterans had accepted as the only criterion for evaluating any memory of the war ("C.N.R. Shopmen"). Those versions which gave equal emphasis to the harrowing artillery bombardments and the rollicking evenings drinking *vin blanc* were acceptable; those which dwelt only on the horrors were invalid.

This simple formula was implicit in the judgement that Canadian veterans passed on any personal account of the war, autobiographical (like Graves's) or fictional (like Remarque's). *Shrieks and Crashes*, a memoir published in 1929 by historian and ex-artilleryman W.B. Kerr, is a case in point. Kerr is no Remarque, and the soldiers he describes are nowhere near as bleak as those in *All Quiet*. Indeed, he took pains to point out that he was not writing to "shock readers by descriptions of horrors of a length and intensity disproportionate to the actual place these filled in the minds of soldiers" (Foreword). Yet Major J.F. Cummins, who served in the Canadian Expeditionary Force (CEF) throughout the war, criticized Kerr for not moving far enough away from the anti-war school and being overly "sombre and serious" instead of giving "a reflection of the joyous hours off duty in the villages and towns behind the guns" (262). The same criterion was applied to another memoir, James Pedley's *Only This: A War Retrospect*, a fine book that captures the totality of the war experience in unusually realistic tones. But Pedley, too, missed the mark, at least in the eyes of some veterans. He had not committed Kerr's sin of being too gloomy, but rather had stepped beyond good, clean fun into an inappropriate bawdiness. Kerr himself lamented Pedley's lack of imagination which led him "to see so much of the flesh, and miss so much of the spirit, of the Canadian Corps" (Kerr, "Historical Literature" 420), while Major Hamilton Warren, formerly of the 38th Battalion, thought that Pedley "showed wretched taste in the brutal frankness and perhaps prejudice" with which he handled his subject. Major Cummins also found *Only This* a bit too fleshly, and questioned the author's judgement in relating "the intimate wartime details of carousals, flirtations, and courts martial" (250).

10   Peregrine Acland was another soldier-novelist who fell into this trap. Acland had sailed to Europe in 1914 as a lieutenant with the 15th Battalion, serving at the front until October 1916, when he was badly wounded and invalided home. In 1929 he published *All Else Is Folly*, the semi-autobiographical tale of an eastern Canadian university student and his ruination

by war. Despite a number of ringing celebrity endorsements, critical commentary was mixed. The New York *Herald Tribune* and *Evening Post* and the *Times Literary Supplement* praised the battle scenes, but felt that the love scenes were ineptly handled. The *New York Times*, however, lauded it for "showing that the men who fought ... were occasionally able to find some hilarity in their calling" (*Book Review Digest*, 1929). For some Canadian veterans, there was a little too much hilarity. Colonel Cy Peck, the Victoria Cross winner who had commanded the 16th Battalion at the front for over two years, also praised the book's descriptions of the battlefields but lambasted Acland for having his protagonist Falcon consort with prostitutes (the subtitle was, after all, "A Tale of War and Passion"). This, felt Peck, put the author "on a level with the filth-purveyors of other nations" (7).

But Peck did not stop with Peregrine Acland, and launched a general broadside in the pages of *The Brazier*, the newsletter of the 16th Battalion Association. After considering the modern war book as a genre, Peck was discouraged by what he found: they were shot through with "morbidity and hopelessness," and said nothing about the sterling qualities exhibited by the troops in France. He insisted that their authors were "ten minute warriors" who had only a superficial knowledge of conditions at the front, and for that reason dismissed virtually every work that is now recognized as a classic of the Great War. Sherriff's *Journey's End* was a libellous slander for including a scene in which an officer has to be driven into action at gunpoint. Graves's *Good-bye to All That*, which claimed that Canadian soldiers occasionally murdered prisoners, was "the product of an unstable and degenerate mind"; interestingly, Graves himself later referred to his own book as "a reckless autobiography ... written with small consideration for anyone's feelings" (Graves and Hodge 217). *All Quiet on the Western Front* was worse still. Canadian soldiers fought just as hard as the characters created by Remarque, claimed Peck, "but it did not lower their spirits or throw them into a state of agonizing gruesomeness." Mocking the book as something that was loved by the "smart set" who talk about its naughtiness and "think themselves quite the wickedest things that ever were," he found nothing whatsoever redeeming in it. It was "printed putridness," he snorted.

The most revealing comments on anti-war literature, however, came not from former officers but from two rankers. F.W. Bagnall, a native of Hazel Grove, Prince Edward Island, had enlisted in September 1914, rose to the rank of sergeant, and was wounded and invalided home before the end of the war. In a bitter and confused memoir which he published privately in 1933, he lashed out at the "continual calumnies and a succession of lies [*sic*]" contained in films about the war (he was likely referring to the screen version of *All Quiet on the Western Front*, released in 1930) (54). Bagnall felt aggrieved that he had fought "doggedly against every form of discomfort living in ditches, only to be held up to the eyes of even your own people as belonging to a group who were as pictured on the screen horribly depraved" (70). This point, if expressed rather clumsily, was central to the veterans' argument. For Bagnall, it was not a matter of interpretation. The anti-war memory was not just a different perception of events; it was simply a series of malicious falsehoods that constituted a personal attack on the individual soldier. Each time *All Quiet on the Western Front* was sold or its film version screened, it was a libel upon Bagnall, and upon every Canadian veteran. There was no question of competing but equally valid memories; there was a right memory, and anything which did not conform to it was vicious, hurtful, and false.

Will R. Bird, who was decorated for gallantry as a member of the 42nd Battalion, felt the same frustration as Bagnall. Now known primarily as a folklorist, Bird had a thriving career in the interwar period as the unofficial bard of the CEF. He published five books and hundreds of short stories, articles, and poems about his wartime experiences, and his work shares some similarities with Pedley's. He does not gloss over the horrors of war, nor does he suggest that his comrades were saints in khaki. He describes the abject terror of enduring an artillery bombardment and the bitterness of seeing officers dine from china and starched tablecloths while the soldiers ate cold, greasy stew from battered tins, yet he also recalls hilarious evenings spent in local *estaminets* and the idealism of soldiers who emerged from the inferno with spirit and soul intact. The immense popularity of Bird's works among veterans suggests that he came closest to capturing the proper balance.

Like Bagnall, Bird had no time for anti-war books, which he claimed were "putrid with so-called 'realism.'" Such books, Bird wrote in his memoir *And We Go On*, portrayed the soldier

> as a coarse-minded, profane creature, seeking only the solace of loose women or the courage of strong liquor. Vulgar language and indelicacy of incident are often their substitute for lack of knowledge, and their distorted pictures of battle action are especially repugnant. On the whole, such literature, offered to our avid youth, is an irrevocable insult to those gallant men who lie in French and Belgian graves. (5)

15 His own book strove for a more balanced picture. It showed that "the private in the trenches had other thoughts than of the flesh, had often finer vision and strength of soul than those who would fit him to their sordid, sensation-seeking fiction" (5).

In asserting that vulgarity was a substitute for knowledge, Bird made an explicit claim for the veracity of his own memory: because he had seen action himself, his memory of the trenches was accurate. When conflicting memories emerged, there was only one possible explanation: their authors had not experienced life in the trenches, so their memory must be fabricated. Bird also introduced the notion that there was only one memory of the war that could honour the dead. His book, because it was true, was a fitting tribute to Canada's fallen. The memory contained in anti-war novels, because it was fabricated, was akin to spitting on their graves. If that was not enough, this memory was fabricated for commercial reasons; its authors were "sensation-seekers" willing to defile the name of the dead for fame and fortune, an accusation that may have had some merit (Bance). In contrast, Bird's memory was the truth, and truth, not profit, must be the real goal of any writer.

The various threads of the veterans' critique of anti-war literature came together in the response to the novel *Generals Die in Bed*, written by an obscure Jewish American novelist named Charles Yale Harrison. The novel is widely regarded as the finest Canadian example of the genre, and is often cited as an authentic and evocative description of the trench experience (Novak 60-70). Yet when it first appeared in 1930, it immediately became a lightning rod that drew Canadian veterans into a bitter debate over the relationship between literature and history.

Since the book's first publication, some confusion has surrounded the background of its author, confusion that has been perpetuated by recent publicity materials. A native of Philadelphia, Harrison emigrated to Canada before the beginning of the war; the biographical sketch that has long accompanied the novel claimed that he joined the staff of a Montreal newspaper, but on his enlistment papers, he gave his occupation as student. In January 1917, Harrison volunteered for the 244th Battalion, proceeding overseas in March. He was posted to the 14th Battalion in France in December 1917. Reviews have also noted that Harrison was decorated for gallantry; he was not, although he did have a few brushes with military police over minor infractions before being wounded at Amiens in August 1918 and returning to Montreal. Harrison spent only a short time in Canada after the war, before moving to New York City in the early 1920s. He then began a manuscript which he entitled *Generals Die in Bed*. Extracts from it were serialized in various magazines as early as 1928, but the entire manuscript was rejected when Harrison first offered it to New York publishers. It was eventually accepted by Williams and Norgate, a small English publisher, which released it on 13 May 1930. The American edition, published by William Morrow, appeared on 12 June 1930.

The novel begins in a Montreal barrack room, where the narrator and his fellow recruits are recuperating from a bender before embarking for Britain. The scene then shifts immediately to the trenches, where the characters undergo a succession of ordeals, each more brutalizing than the last—an artillery bombardment, a trench raid, and finally the major offensive in which the narrator is wounded, and thereby escapes from the trenches.

Along the way, the narrator watches his pals die in horrific circumstances, joins in a looting spree in the deserted city of Arras, and bayonets a German soldier, only to discover that he cannot dislodge the blade from his victim's chest. Through it all, Harrison writes in uncompromising prose—sharp, staccato sentences, visceral descriptors, and powerful imagery.

20   But these were the characteristics of much of the anti-war canon, and some critics believed that Harrison said nothing that had not already been said by more capable authors. The *New Statesman* called *Generals Die in Bed* "a poison memory which the author had to expel from his system," while *Outlook* decided that it suffered from "constant literary explosiveness" (*Book Review Digest*, 1931). Henry Williamson, who had himself contributed a better book to the canon, called it a "hotch-potch ... which out-farted the curtain pole to such an extent that the *Daily Mail* in a leading article called for its withdrawal"; Williamson admitted that he did not quite understand his own phraseology, which he had borrowed from elsewhere (qtd. in Onions, 50). The book, however, was guaranteed a rougher ride in Canada. Because it alleged that members of the 14th Battalion had pillaged Arras and often murdered prisoners, *Generals Die in Bed* was bound to raise the ire of Canadian veterans.

Many of them took Bird's lead and denounced Harrison's divergent memory as complete fabrication, while other ex-soldiers took up Bagnall's argument that the book's falsehoods constituted a kind of libel. Veterans' groups deluged politicians with complaints and demanded that the government ban the book on account of its "many libellous statements" about Canadian soldiers; distribution of the book in Canada was indeed delayed after the Minister of National Revenue, W.D. Euler, agreed to launch an enquiry into allegations that it slandered Canadian soldiers. Sir Archibald Macdonell, a former divisional commander, became almost apoplectic with rage when he read it. "I hope to live long enough to have the opportunity of (in good trench language) shoving my fist into that s— of a b— Harrison's tummy until his guts hang out of his mouth!!!" Macdonell fumed to Sir Arthur Currie, the former commander of the Canadian Corps.[1]

Currie's initial reaction was a little calmer. Shortly before the book appeared in Canada, he had won a libel judgement against an Ontario newspaper, an action he had pursued in part because he believed that allegations about his conduct of operations around Mons in November 1918 reflected badly upon the men who had served under him in the Canadian Corps. The trial took a toll on his health, yet Currie considered it worthwhile because it put to rest decade-old insinuations that had cast a cloud over the CEF's achievements. When Harrison's book appeared and threatened to tarnish the reputations he had struggled to defend, he must have

---

1   I have engaged in a more detailed discussion of the reaction of ex-soldiers to Harrison's work in *Death So Noble* (193–96). [Vance's note]

been much distressed. However, Currie usually declined to respond to allegations contained in novels. Earlier, the editor of the *Presbyterian Witness* had requested an article refuting the charges made in Graves's *Good-bye to All That*, but Currie replied that "the reputation of the Canadian soldier stands too high for me to rush into print to defend them, not from charges, but from certain insinuations made in a novel." When *Generals Die in Bed* burst on the scene, Currie refused a similar invitation from a Toronto newspaper, observing that Harrison "most probably wrote the book for the sole purpose of making money and therefore has provided sensational chapters, knowing that that is what appeals to the public, who prefer always to hear the evil rather than the good" (Letter to Oliver).

Currie's reply was evidently written before he had actually read *Generals Die in Bed*. Having done so, the general could scarcely contain his anger. It was "a mass of filth, lies and appeals to everything base and mean and nasty," he raged to Macdonell. "A more scurrilous thing was never published ... It appeals to the worst appetite that can be found.... The book is badly titled, has a weak style, no worth while matter, is full of vile and misrepresentation, and cannot have any lasting influence." While Currie was perhaps not the soundest authority on literary style, he certainly had a right to comment on the title, and was likely thinking of two old friends and fellow commanders who had not died in bed: Major-General Malcolm Mercer, killed in action at Mount Sorrel in June 1916 while leading the 3rd Division; and Major-General Louis Lipsett, killed in action in September 1918 shortly after leaving the 3rd Division. This may explain the personal edge to Currie's bitter comments on *Generals Die in Bed*. "There is not a single line in it worth reading, nor a single incident worthy of record," he wrote. "I have never read, nor do I hope ever to read, a meaner, nastier and more foul book" (qtd. in R. Sharpe 76).

Why did Canadian veterans, from the lowly ranker to his Corps Commander, react so strongly against *Generals Die in Bed*, and against all those books which comprised the canon of anti-war literature, even those which made no reference to Canada? It seems unlikely that they united to defend establishment values or the social hierarchy against threats posed by these books. It would be difficult to find any social, political, or economic factors that could have drawn together such diverse individuals as the bitter ex-sergeant F.W. Bagnall, the small-town cleric Ephram McKegney, and the revered old soldier Sir Arthur Currie. Nevertheless, these veterans, regardless of their social status or economic situation, criticized the anti-war canon in strikingly similar terms.

In the first place, they invariably dismissed the books as falsifications of history: because anti-war books failed to recount the good times along with the bad, their vision of the war experience was untrue. The fact that their authors had, in general, as much experience in the trenches as their strongest critics was irrelevant; because it was divergent, their memory could only be fabricated. In this regard, Harrison's book, which so riled Canadian veterans, can serve as a useful case study. Ex-soldiers alleged that much of the book was complete fabrication. To what degree were they right? Did the incidents that Harrison described so vividly spring from his own experience, or were they invented, perhaps inspired (as alleged by some European critics who dismissed Harrison's work as derivative) by other war novels he had read?

Fortunately, Harrison's service record and the war diaries of the 244th and 14th Battalions allow us to answer these questions by comparing the historical record to the events described by the narrator. Clearly, portions of the book do correspond with what Harrison experienced. The general description of the 244th Battalion's departure from Montreal rings true, given the unit's history. It was not an especially successful battalion, and the officers may well have had difficulty rounding up the men for embarkation; when it left Montreal, it was only about sixty per cent of its authorized strength. And, while the novel's chronology does not match Harrison's (the narrator reaches the trenches in September 1917, but Harrison did not enter the lines until 15 December 1917), it is certain that he did experience a number of the events he describes, including the trench raid, the bombardment, and the major offensive. All of these occurred while Harrison was with the 14th Battalion, and his descriptions have a vividness that is ultimately convincing, even if we admit that Harrison actually spent very little time (forty-three days) in the front lines.

However, a number of other elements are clearly invented. Although the relevant chapter is plausible enough, Harrison never enjoyed leave to London from the trenches; he simply did not put in enough service in the lines to merit leave. It is also worth noting that, while he used the real names of men from his unit in the novel, he changed their identities, probably to open up dramatic possibilities by filling his fictional platoon with a broader range of personalities. Furthermore, there is no evidence to support two of the most contentious elements of the book: the description of the looting of Arras by Canadian troops, and the accusation that the hospital ship *Llandovery Castle*, torpedoed in June 1918 with a full complement of medical personnel on board, was carrying military cargo in contravention of international law. These elements of the novel, it must be admitted, are completely fabricated. Finally, the narrator's wound that puts him out of action is rather more serious than the wound which knocked Harrison out of the war. As the narrator describes it, "My right foot feels numb. I look at it; it is spurting a ruby fountain ... an artery must be cut" (259-60). Harrison did take a bullet in the foot at Amiens in August 1918, but his medical records characterize it as merely a minor flesh wound; "slight" and "superficial" are the adjectives used.

But so what? This exercise merely confirms that Harrison wrote like a novelist, combining his own experience with the products of his imagination to produce a dramatic narrative; indeed, condemning novels like *Generals Die in Bed* for not adhering to historical fact seems to be missing the point. But within the contemporary debate as it was structured by veterans on all sides, this was precisely the point. On the one hand, the novelists and their publishers claimed that these works were historically accurate. They purported to tell "the truth about the war," something the press generally took at face value. The reviewer for the *New York Times*, for example, was non-committal about the enduring literary merit of *Generals Die in Bed*, but was certain that it would live on as "a burning, breathing historical document" (Woodman 55). Indeed, when the novel first appeared in the paper's "Latest Books Received" section, it was listed under History and Biography, not Fiction ("Latest"). The book's most recent publisher has continued this trend: its website offers suggestions for using the novel in history classes as historical document ("Teachers Guides").

Yet the war novelists did not see themselves as constrained by the conventions of history, feeling at liberty to exercise, in the words of one modern critic, "fiction's teleological right to exclude ordinary everyday elements which are redundant to its theme" (Onions 64-66). Joyous nights in Belgian *estaminets* undoubtedly occurred but were irrelevant to a novel dedicated, as Harrison's was, to the "bewildered youth" of all armies. So, he felt warranted in omitting them. For many veterans, such omissions were unacceptable. Because this genre of literature pretended to be history, they felt quite justified in judging it as such. The literary merit of the books became irrelevant; they were simply bad history. Furthermore, suggestions in the press that "people prefer to take their histories of the war in the form of fiction" made the veterans' choice appear all the more sensible (McAree). Since novelists were going to claim their works were history and since readers were going to use fiction as history, veterans felt justified in criticizing fiction as history.

The other common thread in the veterans' critique was the assertion that the anti-war books were libellous. They offended Canadian veterans for the same reason that they impressed later critics: because they universalized the experience of the trenches. Harrison's Broadbent and Remarque's Paul Baumer might have served in any army, for they represented the suffering of millions of soldiers from all nations, including Canada. This, of course, was precisely the objection. As Bagnall had argued, universalization was in fact defamation: these books tarred Canadian soldiers with the sins of others by claiming that, like all soldiers, the men of the CEF had been brutalized and dehumanized by war. The anti-war vision suggested that the war stripped soldiers of their identity, transforming them into pawns whose life, suffering, and death were of little consequence to anyone. Many veterans

30

found this vision unpalatable. Instead of rational, purposeful human beings, it made them dupes of forces they could not hope to understand, much less control. They did not want to be identified as anonymous victims sacrificed in a pointless slaughter, nor did they want to share guilt by association in crimes committed by their semi-fictional counterparts.

Moreover, the anti-war books cast doubt on the very thing that many soldiers valued most highly from their wartime odyssey: the gift of comradeship. Especially as the interwar years passed, when the material rewards for service were few and society seemed to have little concern for the values that the war had ostensibly been fought to defend, the soldier could look upon the comradeship of the trenches as a reward in itself. However, by averring that the soldier took nothing of value from his trench experience, the anti-war books threatened to deny that one bit of comfort that remained. Instead of characterizing veterans as a band of brothers whose comradeship and courage triumphed over war and death, Harrison's narrator observed sourly that "*camaraderie—esprit de corps*—good fellowship— these are the words for journalists to use, not for us. Here in the line they do not exist" (91). Instead of recognizing the "equalizing treasure" of friendship, to use Bird's phrase (343), the anti-war books spoke of "a generation of men who, even though they may have escaped its shells, were destroyed by the war" (Remarque, dedication). In this vision, there could be no happy evenings spent in Belgian *estaminets*, no days passed lounging in the sun as they rested in a rear-area billet, none of those memories which dominated the culture of the veteran movement in the interwar era. For denying everything that they celebrated, many ex-soldiers considered the anti-war vision to be beyond the pale.

In May 1930, at the height of the storm over *Generals Die in Bed*, Charles Yale Harrison was asked to comment on the backlash against his book. When the Toronto *Daily Star* located Harrison, he was working for the *Bronx Home News* in New York City, "as a newspaperman, not a journalist," he said revealingly. The "youthful author" denied that he had slandered Canadian soldiers, insisting that to do so "would be to smear at myself." On the contrary, he wanted it noted that the Canadian Corps was the finest fighting unit in the field: "Vimy Ridge, Passchendaele, Ypres, the Somme, Cambrai and Mons speak for themselves." As for the allegations that Canadian troops had looted Arras, Harrison stood by his story, but added a significant caveat: "realizing the circumstances under which the town was looted, I did not consider that this in any way reflects upon the heroism and courage of the Canadian troops" ("Denies New War Book").

In this interview, Harrison implicitly conceded what his harshest critics had been arguing all along: that there was a balance missing from his book, and by extension from anti-war literature generally. No one, least of all a veteran, denied that the soldier at the front had endured horrors which surpassed the imagination. But, they insisted, the war had not been without positive features; the success of the Canadian Corps in battle was one, the heroism and courage of Canadian soldiers was another. Although his novel contains no hint of these compensating factors, Harrison recognized them in this short interview, using phrases that would never have been uttered by the characters he created.

Harrison's admission did little to quell the outrage, but he and the other authors who wrote in the same genre had the last laugh. Were they alive today, Will Bird, Cy Peck, and Arthur Currie would be dismayed by the literary landscape of the Great War. Bird's *And We Go On*, widely regarded by veterans as the most authentic of Great War memoirs, virtually disappeared after it was first published in 1930. Clarke Irwin released a much less interesting version, entitled *Ghosts Have Warm Hands*, in 1968, but the original remains all but unobtainable. The anti-war books, on the other hand, have held sway for more than seventy years. *All Quiet on the Western Front* and *Goodbye to All That* are enshrined as modern classics, and *Generals Die in Bed* has become a staple of undergraduate literature, and indeed history, courses. More notably, it has recently been released in a new edition for teenagers, and has been favourably reviewed as a powerful, evocative, and informative work for young readers.[1] Debates over the veracity of these books now seem quaint and outdated, rendered irrelevant by the recognition of their literary qualities. And yet the story of the Great War novel is a cautionary tale, reminding us that the relationship between literature, history, and memory is far more complicated than it often appears.

Works Cited

Bagnall, F.W. *Not Mentioned in Despatches*. Vancouver: North Shore, 1933.

Bance, A.F. "*Im Westen Nichts Neues:* A Bestseller in Context." *Modern Language Review* 72 (1977): 359–73.

Bird, Will. *And We Go On*. Toronto: Hunter Rose, 1930.

The Book Review Digest: Books of 1929. New York: H.W. Wilson, 1930.

The Book Review Digest: Books of 1930. New York: H.W. Wilson, 1931.

"C.N.R. Shopmen Hold Memorial." *Free Press* [London] 9 Nov. 1928: 4.

Cooperman, Stanley. *World War I and the American Novel*. Baltimore: Johns Hopkins UP, 1967.

Cummins, J.F. Rev. of *Shrieks and Crashes*, by W.B. Kerr. *Canadian Defence Quarterly* 7 (1930): 262.

Currie, Sir Arthur. Letter to Douglas Oliver. 7 June 1930. Sir Arthur Currie Papers, vol. 12, f. 37. National Archives of Canada.

1   The Annick Press website (www.annickpress.com) quotes from various reviews praising *Generals Die in Bed*. [Vance's note]

—. Letter to *Presbyterian Witness*. 14 January 1930. Sir Arthur Currie Papers, vol. 8, f. 23. National Archives of Canada.

—. Letter to A.C. Macdonell. 25 June 1930. Sir Arthur Currie Papers, vol. 11, f. 33. National Archives of Canada.

"Denies New War Book Slanders Canadians." *Daily Star* [Toronto] 31 May 1930: 3.

Eksteins, Modris. "*All Quiet on the Western Front* and the Fate of a War." *Journal of Contemporary History* 15 (1980): 345-66.

Fussell, Paul. *The Great War and Modern Memory*. New York: Oxford UP, 1975.

Gerster, Robin. *Big-noting: The Heroic Theme in Australian War Writing*. Melbourne: Melbourne UP, 1987.

Graves, Robert, and Alan Hodge. *The Long Week-End: A Social History of Great Britain, 1918–1939*. London: Faber, 1940.

Harrison, Charles Yale. *Generals Die in Bed*. 1930. Waterdown, ON: Potlatch Publications, 1975.

Jerrold, Douglas. *The Lie About the War*. London: Faber, 1930.

Kerr, W.B. *Shrieks and Crashes: Being Memories of Canada's Corps, 1917*. Toronto: Hunter Rose, 1929.

—. "Historical Literature on Canada's Participation in the Great War." *Canadian Historical Review* 14 (1933): 412-36.

—. "Latest Books Received." *New York Times* 15 June 1930: BR11.

Leed, Eric. *No Man's Land: Combat and Identity in World War I*. Cambridge: Cambridge UP, 1979.

Macdonell, A.C. "The Canadian Soldier—As I Knew Him on the Western Front." *Queen's Quarterly* 28 (1921): 339-50.

—. Letter to Sir Arthur Currie. 26 June 1930. Sir Arthur Currie Papers, vol. 11, f. 33. National Archives of Canada.

McAree, J.V. "Recalling Exploits of Canada's Army." *Globe and Mail* 15 July 1938: 6.

Mosse, George. *Fallen Soldiers: Reshaping the Memory of the World Wars*. Oxford: Oxford UP, 1990.

Novak, Dagmar. *Dubious Glory: The Two World Wars and the Canadian Novel*. New York: Peter Lang, 2000.

Oliver, Douglas. Letter to Sir Arthur Currie. 4 June 1930. Sir Arthur Currie Papers, vol. 12, f. 37. National Archives of Canada.

Onions, John. *English Fiction and Drama of the Great War, 1918-39*. London: Macmillan, 1990.

Peck, Cyrus. "Modern War Books." *The Brazier* 18 (1930): 7.

Pedley, James. *Only This: A War Retrospect*. Ottawa, ON: Graphic, 1927.

Proceedings of the 4th Convention of the Army and Navy Veterans in Canada, Toronto, Ontario. October 25th to 29th, 1921. [Toronto, 1921?].

Remarque, Erich Maria. *All Quiet on the Western Front*. Trans. A.W. Wheen. Boston: Little, Brown, 1929.

Sharpe, Maureen. "Anzac Day in New Zealand: 1916 to 1939." *New Zealand Journal of History* 15 (1981): 97-114.

Sharpe, Robert. *The Last Day, The Last Hour: The Currie Libel Trial.* Toronto: Carswell, 1988.

"Teachers Guides." *Annick Press.* 28 May 2003. <http://annickpress.com/ forteachers/generalsdieinbed.html>.

Vance, Jonathan F. *Death So Noble: Memory, Meaning and the First World War.* Vancouver: U of British Columbia P, 1997.

Warren, Hamilton. Letter to R.B. Viets. 14 December 1927. R.B. Viets Papers, f. 5. National Archives of Canada.

Woodman, Lawrence. "And Still the Great War Thunders in Literature." Rev. of *Generals Die in Bed*, by Charles Yale Harrison. *New York Times* 30 Aug. 1930: 55.

Questions

1. Why were novelists of World War I such as Charles Yale Harrison expected to adhere closely to historical fact, though they were writing fiction?
2. Describe in detail the structure of this essay. How does this structure lend itself to the writer's aim in this work?
3. Is there evidence in this essay of the author's own point of view on the relationship between historical events and their representation in literature? Does the essay offer an argument that sustains this point of view?

❧ *Science and Technology* ❧

STEPHEN JAY GOULD

Entropic Homogeneity Isn't Why No One Hits .400 Any More

(1986)

Stephen Jay Gould (1941–2002) was a palaeontologist, professor of geology, and author of several books, including Ever Since Darwin: Reflections in Natural History *(1980) and* The Structure of Evolutionary Theory *(2002).*

To hit .400 in baseball means that out of every 1000 chances at bat, a player registers a hit 400 times. Since 1941, no one has ever hit .400 over the course of a major league baseball season, and in this essay Gould asks why.

Comparisons may be odious, but we cannot avoid them in a world that prizes excellence and yearns to know whether current pathways lead to progress or destruction. We are driven to contrast past with present and use the result to predict an uncertain future. But how can we make fair comparison since we gaze backward through the rose-colored lenses of our most powerful myth—the idea of a former golden age?

Nostalgia for an unknown past can elevate hovels to castles, dung heaps to snow-clad peaks. I had always conceived Calvary, the site of Christ's martyrdom, as a lofty mountain, covered with foliage and located far from the hustle and bustle of Jerusalem. But I stood on its paltry peak last year. Calvary lies inside the walls of old Jerusalem (just barely beyond the city borders of Christ's time). The great hill is but one staircase high: its summit lies *within* the Church of the Holy Sepulchre.

I had long read of Ragusa, the great maritime power of the medieval Adriatic. I viewed it at grand scale in my mind's eye, a vast fleet balancing the powers of Islam and Christendom, sending forth its élite to the vanguard of the "invincible" Spanish Armada. Medieval Ragusa has survived intact—as Dubrovnik in Yugoslavia. No town (but Jerusalem) can match its charm, but I circled the battlements of its city walls in 15 minutes. Ragusa, by modern standards, is a modest village at most.

The world is so much bigger now, so much faster, so much more complex. Must our myths of ancient heroes expire on this altar of technological progress? We might dismiss our deep-seated tendency to aggrandize older heroes as mere sentimentalism—and plainly false by the argument just presented for Calvary and Ragusa. And yet, numbers proclaim a sense of truth in our persistent image of past giants as literally outstanding. Their legitimate claims are relative, not absolute. Great cities of the past may be villages today, and Goliath would barely qualify for the NBA. But, compared with modern counterparts, our legendary heroes often soar much farther above their own contemporaries. The distance between commonplace and extraordinary has contracted dramatically in field after field.

Baseball provides my favorite examples. Our national pastime may strike readers as an odd topic for this magazine, but few systems offer better data for a scientific problem that evokes as much interest, and sparks as much debate, as any other: the meaning of trends in history as expressed by measurable differences between past and present. This article uses baseball to address the general question of how we may compare an elusive past with a different present. How can we know whether past deeds matched or exceeded current prowess? In particular, was Moses right in his early pronouncement (Genesis 6:4): "There were giants in the earth in those days"?

Baseball has been a bastion of constancy in a tumultuously changing world, a contest waged to the same purpose and with the same basic rules for 100 years. It has also generated an unparalleled flood of hard numbers about achievement measured every which way that human cleverness can devise. Most other systems have changed so profoundly that we cannot meaningfully mix the numbers of past and present. How can we compare the antics of Larry Bird with basketball as played before the 24-second rule[1] or, going further back, the center jump after every basket, the two-hand dribble, and finally nine-man teams tossing a lopsided ball into Dr. Naismith's peach basket?[2] Yet while styles of play and dimensions of ball parks have altered substantially, baseball today is the same game that Wee Willie Keeler and Nap Lajoie played in the 1890s. Bill James, our premier guru of baseball stats, writes that "the rules attained essentially their modern form after 1893" (when the pitching mound retreated to its current distance of 60 feet 6 inches). The numbers of baseball can be compared meaningfully for a century of play.

When we contrast these numbers of past and present, we encounter the well known and curious phenomenon that inspired this article: great players of the past often stand further apart from their teammates. Consider

---

1   *the 24-second rule* According to the rules of modern basketball, once a team has possession of the ball it must attempt a shot within twenty-four seconds.

2   *peach basket* Canadian James Naismith (1861–1939) developed the game of basketball while working at the YMCA in Springfield, MA, in 1891; the first baskets were round fruit baskets with the bottoms cut out.

only the principal measures of hitting and pitching: batting average and earned run average. No one has hit .400 since Ted Williams reached .406 nearly half a century ago in 1941; yet eight players exceeded .410 in the 50 years before then. Bob Gibson had an earned run average of 1.12 in 1968. Ten other pitchers have achieved a single season E.R.A. below 1.30, but before Gibson we must go back a full 50 years to Walter Johnson's 1.27 in 1918. Could the myths be true after all? Were the old guys really better? Are we heading towards entropic homogeneity and robotic sameness?

These past achievements are paradoxical because we know perfectly well that all historical trends point to a near assurance that modern athletes must be better than their predecessors. Training has become an industry and obsession, an upscale profession filled with engineers of body and equipment, and a separate branch of medicine for the ills of excess zeal. Few men now make it to the majors just by tossing balls against a barn door during their youth. We live better, eat better, provide more opportunity across all social classes. Moreover, the pool of potential recruits has increased fivefold in 100 years by simple growth of the American population.

Numbers affirm this ineluctable improvement for sports that run against the absolute standard of a clock. The Olympian powers-that-be finally allowed women to run the marathon in 1984. Joan Benoit won it in 2:24:54. In 1896, Spiridon Loues had won in just a minute under three hours; Benoit ran faster than any male Olympic champion until Emil Zatopek's victory at 2:23:03 in 1952. Or consider two of America's greatest swimmers of the 1920s and '30s, men later recruited to play Tarzan (and faring far better than Mark Spitz in his abortive commercial career). Johnny Weissmuller won the 100-meter freestyle in 59.0 in 1924 and 58.6 in 1928. The women's record then stood at 1:12.4 and 1:11.0, but Jane had bested Tarzan by 1972 and the women's record has now been lowered to 54.79. Weissmuller also won the 400-meter freestyle in 5:04.2 in 1924, but Buster Crabbe had cut off more than 15 seconds by 1932 (4:48.4). Female champions in those years swam the distance in 6:02.2 and 5:28.5. The women beat Johnny in 1956, Buster in 1964, and have now (1984) reached 4:07.10, half a minute quicker than Crabbe.

10   Baseball, by comparison, pits batter against pitcher and neither against a constant clock. If everyone improves as the general stature of athletes rises, then why do we note any trends at all in baseball records? Why do the best old-timers stand out above their modern counterparts? Why don't hitting and pitching continue to balance?

The disappearance of .400 hitting becomes even more puzzling when we recognize that *average* batting has remained relatively stable since the beginning of modern baseball in 1876. The chart [below] displays the history of mean batting averages since 1876. (We only included men with an average of at least two at-bats per game since we wish to gauge trends of regular players. Nineteenth-century figures [National League only] include 80 to 100 players for most years [a low of 54 to a high of 147]. The American League began in 1901 and raised the average to 175 players or so during the long reign of two eight-team leagues, and to above 300 for more recent division-al play.) Note the constancy of mean values: the average ballplayer hit about .260 in the 1870s, and he hits about .260 today. Moreover, this stability has been actively promoted by judicious modifications in rules whenever hitting or pitching threatened to gain the upper hand and provoke a runaway trend of batting averages either up or down. Consider all the major fluctuations:

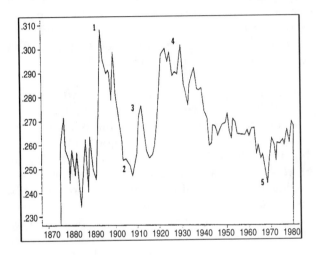

Mean Batting Average By Year

Averages rose after the pitching mound was moved back (1); declined after adoption of the foul-strike rule (2); rose again after the invention of the cork-center ball (3) and during the "lively ball" era (4). The dip in the '60s (5) was corrected in 1969 by lowering the pitching mound and decreasing the strike zone.

After beginning around .260, averages began to drift downwards, reaching the .240s during the late 1880s and early 1890s. Then, during the 1893 sea-son, the pitching mound was moved back to its current 60 feet 6 inches from home plate (it had begun at 45 feet, with pitchers delivering the ball underhand, and had moved steadily back during baseball's early days). The mean soared to its all-time high of .307 in 1894 and remained high (too high, by my argument) until 1901, when adoption of the foul-strike rule promoted a rapid down-turn. (Previously, foul balls hadn't influenced the count.[1]) But averages went down too far during the 1900s until the intro-duction of the cork-center ball sent them abruptly up in 1911. Pitchers

---

1   *the count* Since 1901, a foul ball has counted as a strike (except that a batter cannot go out on a foul).

accommodated, and within two years, averages returned to their .260 level—until Babe Ruth wreaked personal havoc upon the game by belting 29 homers in 1919 (more than entire teams had hit many times before). Threatened by the Black Sox scandal,[1] and buoyed by the Babe's performance (and the public's obvious delight in his free-swinging style), the moguls introduced—whether by conscious collusion or simple acquiescence we do not know—the greatest of all changes in 1920. Scrappy one-run, savvy-baserunning, pitcher's baseball was out; big offense and swinging for the fences was in. Averages rose abruptly, and this time they stayed high for a full 20 years, even breaking .300 for the second (and only other) time in 1930. Then in the early 1940s, after war had siphoned off the best players, averages declined again to their traditional .260 level.

The causes behind this 20-year excursion have provoked one of the greatest unresolved debates in baseball history. Conventional wisdom attributes these rises to introduction of a "lively ball." But Bill James, in his masterly *Historical Baseball Abstract*, argues that no major fiddling with baseballs can be proved in 1920. He attributes the rise to coordinated changes in rules (and pervasive alteration of attitudes) that imposed multiple and simultaneous impediments upon pitching, upsetting the traditional balance for a full 20 years. Trick pitches—the spitball, shine ball, and emery ball—were all banned. More important, umpires now supplied shiny new balls any time the slightest scruff or spot appeared. Previously, soft, scratched, and darkened balls remained in play as long as possible (fans were even expected to throw back "souvenir" fouls). The replacement of discolored and scratched with shiny and new, according to James, would be just as effective for improving hitting as any mythical "lively ball." In any case averages returned to the .260s by the 1940s and remained quite stable until their marked decline in the mid-1960s. When Carl Yastrzemski won the American League batting title with a paltry .301 in 1968, the time for redress had come again. The moguls lowered the mound, restricted the strike zone, and averages promptly rose again—right back to their time-honored .260 level, where they have remained ever since.

This exegetical detail shows how baseball has been maintained, carefully and consistently, in unchanging balance since its inception. Is it not, then, all the more puzzling that downward trends in best performances go hand in hand with constancy of average achievement? Why, to choose the premier example, has .400 hitting disappeared, and what does this erasure teach us about the nature of trends and the differences between past and present?

---

1   *Black Sox Scandal* Eight players on the 1919 Chicago White Sox were accused of throwing that year's World Series against the Cincinnati Reds, and were banned from professional baseball.

We can now finally explicate the myth of ancient heroes—or, rather, we   15
can understand its partial truth. Consider the two ingredients of our puzzle
and paradox: (1) admitting the profound and general improvement of athletes (as measured in clock sports with absolute standards), star baseball
players of the past probably didn't match today's leaders (or, at least,
weren't notably better); (2) nonetheless, top baseball performances have
declined while averages are actively maintained at a fairly constant level. In
short, the old-timers did soar farther above their contemporaries, but must
have been worse (or at least no better) than modern leaders. The .400 hitters of old were relatively better, but absolutely worse (or equal).

How can we get a numerical handle on this trend? I've argued several
times in various articles for *Discover* that students of biological evolution (I
am one) approach the world with a vision different from time-honored
Western perspectives. Our general culture still remains bound to its Pla-
tonic heritage of pigeonholes and essences. We divide the world into a set
of definite "things" and view variation and subtle shadings as nuisances that
block the distinctness of real entities. At best, variation becomes a device for
calculating an average value seen as a proper estimate of the true thing
itself. But variation *is* the irreducible reality; nature provides nothing else.
Averages are often meaningless (mean height of a family with parents and
young children). There is no quintessential human being—only black
folks, white folks, skinny people, little people, Manute Bol and Eddie
Gaedel. Copious and continuous variation is us.

But enough general pontification. The necessary item for this study is
practical, not ideological. The tools for resolving the paradox of ancient
heroes lie in the direct study of variation, not in exclusive attention to stellar achievements. We've failed to grasp this simple solution because we
don't view variation as reality itself, and therefore don't usually study it
directly.

I can now state, in a few sentences, my theory about trends in general and
.400 hitting in particular (sorry for the long cranking up, and the slow
revving down to come, but simple ideas with unconventional contexts
require some exposition if they hope to become reader-friendly). Athletes
have gotten better (the world in general has become bigger, faster, and
more efficient—this may not be a good thing at all; I merely point out that
it has happened). We resist this evident trend by taking refuge in the myth
of ancient heroes. The myth can be exploded directly for sports with
absolute clock standards. In a system with relative standards (person against
person)—especially when rules are subtly adjusted to maintain constancy in
measures of average performance—this general improvement is masked
and cannot be recovered when we follow our usual traditions and interpret
figures for average performances as measures of real things. We can, how-

ever, grasp the general improvement of systems with relative standards by a direct study of variation—recognizing that variation itself is the irreducible reality. This improvement manifests itself as a *decline in variation*. Paradoxically, this decline produces a decrease in the difference between average and stellar performance. Therefore, modern leaders don't stand so far above their contemporaries. The "myth" of ancient heroes—the greater distance between average and best in the past—actually records the improvement of play through time.

Declining variation is the key to our puzzle. Hitting .400 isn't a thing in itself, but an extreme value in the distribution of batting averages (I shall present the data for this contention below). As variation shrinks around a constant mean batting average, .400 hitting disappears. It is, I think, as simple as that.

20   Reason One for Declining Variation: *Approach to the outer limits of human capacity.*

Well-off people in developed nations are getting taller and living longer, but the trend won't go on forever. All creatures have outer limits set by evolutionary histories. We're already witnessing the approach to limits in many areas. Maximum life span isn't increasing (although more and more people live long enough to get a crack at the unchanging heights). Racehorses have hardly speeded up, despite enormous efforts of breeders and the unparalleled economic incentive for shaving even a second off top performance (Kentucky Derby winners averaged 2:06.4 during the 1910s and 2:02.0 for the past ten years). Increase in human height has finally begun to level off (daughters of Radcliffe women are now no taller than their mothers). Women's sports records are declining rapidly as opportunity opens up, but some male records are stabilizing.

We can assess all these trends, and the inevitable decline in improvement as we reach the outer limits, because they're measured by absolute clock standards. Baseball players must also be improving, but the relative standard of batting averages, maintained at a mean of about .260, masks the advance. Let's assume that the wall at the right in the top diagram [below] represents the outer limit, and the bell-shaped curve well to its left marks variation in batting prowess 100 years ago. I suspect that all eras boast a few extraordinary individuals, people near the limits of body and endurance, however lower the general average. So, a few players resided near the right wall in 1880—but the average Joe stood far to their left, and variation among all players was great. Since then, everyone has improved. The best may have inched a bit towards the right wall, but average players have moved substantially in that direction. Meanwhile, increasing competition and higher standards have eliminated very weak hitters (once tolerated for their superior fielding and other skills).

The Extinction of .400 Hitting

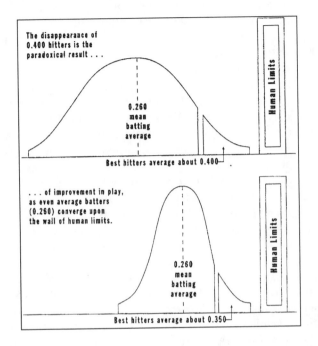

The disappearance of
0.400 hitters is the
paradoxical result . . .

0.260
mean
batting
average

Human Limits

Best hitters average about 0.400

. . . of improvement in play,
as even average batters
(0.260) converge upon
the wall of human limits.

0.260
mean
batting
average

Human Limits

Best hitters average about 0.350

So as average players approach the limiting right wall, variation decreases strongly on both flanks—at the high end for simple decline in space between the average and the limit, and at the low end by decreasing tolerance as general play improves. The relative standards of baseball have masked this trend; hitting has greatly improved, but we still measure its average as .260 because pitching has gained in concert. We can, however, assess this improvement in a different way—by inevitable decline in variation as the average converges upon the limiting wall. Modern stars may be an inch or two closer to the wall—they're absolutely better (or at least no worse) than ancient heroes. But the average has moved several feet closer—and the distance between ordinary (kept at .260) and best has decreased. In short, no more .400 hitters. Ironically, the disappearance of .400 hitting is a sign of improvement, not decline.

Reason Two (really the same point stated differently): *Systems equilibrate as they improve.*

Baseball was feeling its way during the early days of major league play. Its rules were our rules, but scores of subtleties hadn't yet been developed or discovered; rough edges careered out in all directions from a stable center. To cite just a few examples (again from Bill James): pitchers began to cover first base in the 1890s; during the same decade, Brooklyn invented the cut-

25

off play, while the Boston Beaneaters developed the hit-and-run and signals from runner to batter. Gloves were a joke in those early days—just a little leather over the hand, not a basket for trapping balls. In 1896 the Phillies actually experimented for 73 games with a lefty shortstop. Traditional wisdom applied. He stank; he had the worst fielding average and the fewest assists in the league among regular shortstops.

In an era of such experiment and indifference, truly great players could take advantage in ways foreclosed ever since. As I wrote in a previous article (*Vanity Fair*, March 1983), Wee Willie Keeler could "hit 'em where they ain't" (and bat .432 in 1897) because fielders didn't yet know where they should be. Consider the predicament of a modern Wade Boggs or a Rod Carew. Every pitch is charted, every hit mapped to the nearest square inch. Fielding and relaying have improved dramatically. Boggs and Keeler probably stood in the same place, just a few inches from the right wall of human limits, but average play has so crept up on Boggs that he lacks the space for taking advantage of suboptimality in others. All these improvements must rob great batters of 10 or 20 hits a year—more than enough to convert our modern best into .400 hitters.

To summarize, variation in batting averages must decrease as improving play eliminates the rough edges that great players could exploit, and as average performance moves towards the limits of human possibility and compresses great players into an ever decreasing space between average play and the unmovable right wall.

In my *Vanity Fair* article, I measured this decline of variation about a constant average on the cheap. I simply took the five highest and five lowest averages for regular players in each year and compared them with the league average. I found that differences between both average and highest and between average and lowest have decreased steadily through the years (*see chart, page 267*). The disappearance of .400 hitting—the most discussed and disputed trend in the history of baseball—isn't a reflection of generally higher averages in the past (for no one hit over .400 during the second decade of exalted averages, from 1931 to 1940, and most .400 hitting in our century occurred between 1900 and 1920, when averages stood at their canonical [and current] .260 level). Nor can this eclipse of high hitting be entirely attributed to the panoply of conventional explanations that view .400 averages as a former "thing" now extinct—more grueling schedules, too many night games, better fielding, invention of the slider and relief pitching. For .400 hitting isn't a thing to be extirpated, but an extreme value in a distribution of variation for batting averages. The reasons for declining variation, as presented above, are different from the causes for disappearance of an entity. Declining variation is a general property of systems that stabilize and improve while maintaining constant rules of performance through time. The extinction of .400 hitting is, paradoxically, a mark of increasingly *better* play.

We have now calculated the decline of variation properly, and at vastly more labor (with thanks to my research assistant Ned Young for weeks of work, and to Ed Purcell, Nobel laureate and one of the world's great physicists—but also just a fan with good ideas). The standard deviation is a statistician's basic measure of variation. To compute the standard deviation, you take (in this case) each individual batting average and subtract from it the league average for that year. You then square each value (multiply it by itself) in order to eliminate negative numbers for batting averages below the mean (a negative times a negative gives a positive number). You then add up all these values and divide them by the total number of players—giving an average squared deviation of individual players from the mean. Finally, you take the square root of this number to obtain the average, or standard, deviation itself. The higher the value, the more extensive, or spread out, the variation.

We calculated the standard deviation of batting averages for each year (an improvement from my former high and low five, but much more work). The chart on page 267 plots the trend of standard deviations in batting averages year by year. Our hypothesis is clearly confirmed. Standard deviations have been dropping steadily and irreversibly. The decline itself has decelerated over the years as baseball stabilizes—rapidly during the nineteenth century, more slowly through the twentieth, and reaching a stable plateau by about 1940.

30

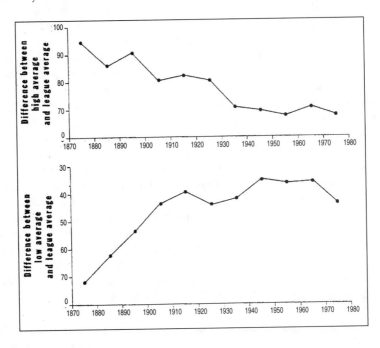

The Decline in Extremes
Batting averages are neither as high nor as low as they used to be.

If I may make a personal and subjective comment. I was stunned and delighted (beyond all measure) by the elegance and clarity of this result. I pretty well knew what the general pattern would be because standard deviations are so strongly influenced by extreme values (a consequence of squaring each individual deviation in the calculation)—so my original cheap method of five highest and lowest produced a fair estimate. But I never dreamed that the decline would be so regular, so devoid of exception or anomaly for even a single year—so unvarying that we could even pick out such subtleties as the deceleration in decline. I've spent my entire professional career studying such statistical distributions, and I know how rarely one obtains such clean results in better behaved data of controlled experiments or natural growth in simple systems. We usually encounter some glitch, some anomaly, some funny years. But the decline of standard deviation for batting averages is so regular that it looks like a plot for a law of nature. I find this all the more remarkable because the graph of averages themselves through time (*page 269*) shows all the noise and fluctuation expected in natural systems. Yet mean batting averages have been constantly manipulated by the moguls of baseball to maintain a general constancy, while no one has tried to monkey with the standard deviation. Thus, while mean batting averages have gone up and down to follow the whims of history and the vagaries of invention, the standard deviation has marched steadily down at a decreasing pace, apparently perturbed by nothing of note. I regard this regularity of decline as further evidence that decreasing variation through time is the primary predictable feature of stabilizing systems.

The details are impressive in their regularity. All four beginning years of the 1870s sport high values of standard deviation greater then 0.050, while the last reading in excess of 0.050 occurs in 1886. Values between 0.04 and 0.05 mark the rest of the nineteenth century, with three years just below, at 0.038 to 0.040. The last reading in excess of 0.040 occurs in 1911. Subsequently, decline within the 0.03 and 0.04 range shows the same precision of detail by even decrease with years. The last reading as high as 0.037 occurs in 1937, and of 0.035 in 1941. Only two years have exceeded 0.034 since 1957. Between 1942 and 1980, values remained entirely within the restricted range of 0.0285 to 0.0348. I'd thought that at least one unusual year would upset the pattern—that one nineteenth-century value would achieve late twentieth-century lows, or one more recent year soar to ancient highs—but we find no such thing. All measures from 1906 back to the beginning are higher than every reading from 1938 to 1980. We find no overlap at all. This—take it from an old trooper—is regularity with a vengeance. Something general is going on here, and I think I know what.

The decadal averages are listed on page 269, and show continuous decline before stabilization in the 1940s. (A note for statistically minded readers: standard deviations are expressed in their own units of measurement— mouse tails in millimeters, mountains in megatons. Thus, as mean values rise and fall, standard deviations may go up and down to track the mean rather than record exclusively the amount of spread. This poses no problem for most of our chart, because averages have been so stable through time at about .260. But the 20-point rise in averages during the 1920s and 1930s might entail artificially elevated standard deviations. We can correct for this effect by computing the coefficient of variation—100 times the standard deviation divided by the mean—for each year. Also listed are decadal averages for coefficients of variation—and we now see that apparent stabilization between the 1910s and 1920s was masking a continuing decline in coefficient of variation, as the 1920s rise in averages canceled out decline in variation when measured by the standard deviation.)

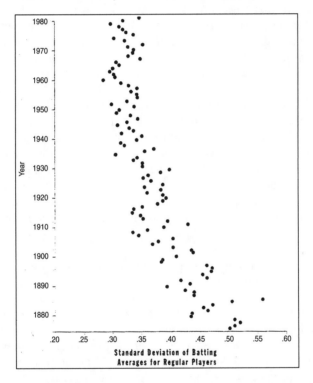

If my editors were more indulgent, I could wax at distressing length about more details and different measures. Just one final hint of more interesting pattern revealed by finer dissection: the chart above amalgamates the two leagues, but their trends are somewhat different. In the National League, variation declined during the nineteenth century, but stabilized early in the twentieth. In the American League, founded in 1901, variation dropped steadily right through the 1940s. Thus, each league followed the same pattern—time of origin setting pattern of decline for decades to come. Can we use existence or stabilization of declining variation as a mark of maturity? Did the leagues differ fundamentally during the early years of our century—the National already mature, the American still facing a few decades of honing and trimming the edges?

35 No one has invested more time and energy in the study of numbers than baseball aficionados. We have measures and indices for everything imaginable—from simple lists of at-bats to number of times a black shortstop under six feet tall has been caught stealing third on pitchouts by righties to left-handed catchers. Yet I don't think that this most basic pattern in the standard deviation of batting averages has been properly noted, or its significance assessed. As I argued above, the biases of our upbringing force a focus on averages treated as things, and virtually preclude proper attention to variation considered as irreducible reality. The standard deviation is our base-level tool for studying variation—as fundamental as milk for babies and cockroaches for New York apartments. Yet, after decades of loving attention to minutiae of averages, we can still gain insights from an unexplored pattern in the very simplest kiddie measure of variation. What better illustration for my claim that our culture undervalues variation at its peril?

After this detail, I've earned the right to end with a bit of philosophical musing, ostensibly in the great decline-of-civilization tradition, but really a sneaky bit of optimism from the depth of my sanguine soul.

The message of this study in variation might seem glum, almost cosmically depressing in its paradox—that general improvement clips the wings of true greatness. No one soars above the commonplace any more. General advance brings declining variation in its wake; heroes are extinct. The small population of Europe yielded both a Bach and a Mozart in just 100 years; where shall we find such transcendent geniuses to guide (or at least enlighten) our uncertain and perilous present?

I wish to propose, in closing, a more general framework for understanding trends in time as an interaction between the location of bell-shaped curves in variation and the position (and potential for mobility) of the limiting right wall for human excellence. This theme transcends sports (or any particular example), and our model should include mind work as well as body work. I suggest three rough categories, with a fundamental example for each, ranging from high to low potential for future accomplishment.

Consider science as a system of knowledge. In most areas, our ignorance is abysmal compared with our sense of what we might learn and know. The curve of knowledge, in other words, stands far from the right wall. Moreover, the wall itself (or at least our perception of it) seems flexible before the growth of knowledge, as new theories suggest pathways to insight never considered previously. Science seems progressive since current ignorance provides so much space to its right, and since the wall itself can be pushed back by the very process that signals our approach. Still, one cannot avoid—with that special sadness reserved for recognizing a wonderful thing gone forever—the conviction that certain seminal discoveries established truths so central and so broad in import that we cannot hope to win insight in such great gulps again, for the right wall moves slowly and with limits, and we may never again open up space for jumps so big. Plate tectonics has revolutionized geology, but we cannot match the thrill of those who discovered that time comes in billions, not thousands—for deep time, once discovered, set the root of a profession forever. These are exciting days for biology, but no one will taste the intellectual power of a man alone at Downe—Charles Darwin reformulating all nature with the passkey of evolution.

I would place most sports, as well as musical performance, in a second category, where the best have long stood near an inflexible right wall. When we remove impediments imposed by custom (women's sports) or technology (certain musical instruments), improvement may be rapid. But progress comes in inches or milliseconds for goals long sought and unimpeded (I doubt that Stern plays notably better than Paganini, Horowitz than Liszt, E. Power Biggs than Bach—and neither horse nor human male is shaving much off the mile run these days). The small contribution of this article lies in this second domain—in showing that decline in variation will measure improvement when relative standards mask progress measured against such absolute criteria as clocks.

Lest we lament this second category for its limited licenses in improvement, consider the painful plight of a third domain where success in striving depletes the system itself. The right wall of our first domain was far away and somewhat flexible, near and rigid (but still stable) in our second. In this third domain, success hits the wall and consumes it—as if the mile run had disappeared as a competitive sport as soon as 100 people ran the distance in less than four minutes. Given an ethic that exalts perennial originality in artistic composition, the history of music (and many other arts) may fall into this domain. One composer may exploit a basic style for much of a career, but successors may not follow this style in much detail, or for very long. Such striving for newness may grant us joy forever if a limitless array of potential styles awaits discovery and exploitation. But perhaps the world is not so bounteous; perhaps we've already explored most of what even a highly sophisticated audience can deem accessible. Perhaps the wall of an intelligible vanguard has been largely consumed. Perhaps there is a simple solution to the paradox of why we now generate no Bach or Mozart in a world far larger, with musical training provided for millions more. Perhaps they reside among us, but we've consumed all styles of expression so deeply tuned to the human soul. If so, I might timidly advance a truly reactionary proposal. The death of Mozart at 35 may have been the deepest tragedy of our cultural history (great scientists have died even younger, but their work can be done by others). We perform his handful of operas over and over again. We might be enjoying a dozen more—some counted as the most sublime of all musical works—if he had survived even to 50. Suppose a composer now lived who could master his style and write every bit as well. The ethic of originality forbids it absolutely, but would the integrity of art collapse forever if this person wrote just a

40

few more great pieces in that genre? Not a hundred, just three or four to supplement *Don Giovanni* and *Die Zauberflöte*. Would this not be esteemed a public service beyond all others?

Enough. I'm waxing lugubrious, despite promises to the contrary. For while I may yearn to hear Beethoven's tenth symphony, I don't lament a lost past or decry a soft present. In sports, and art, and science (how I wish it were so in politics as well), we live in the best world we've ever known, though not in the best of all possible worlds. So be it that improvement must bury in its wake the myth of ancient heroes. We've exposed the extinction of .400 hitting as a sign of progress, not degradation—the paradoxical effect of declining variation as play improves and stabilizes, and as average contestants also approach the right wall of human limits.

Do not lament the loss of literally outstanding performance (largely a figment, in any case, of failings among the ordinary, not a mark of greater prowess among the best). Celebrate instead the immense improvement of average play. (I rather suspect that we would regard most operatic performances of 1850, and most baseball games of 1900, as sloppy and amateurish—not to mention the village squabbles that enter history as epic battles.) Do not lament our past ease in distinguishing the truly great. Celebrate instead the general excellence that makes professional sport so exciting today. And appreciate the need for subtlety and discernment that modern fans must develop to make proper assessments: we must all now be connoisseurs to appreciate our favorite games fully. Above all, remember that the possibility for transcendence never dies. We live for that moment, the truly unpredictable performance that shatters all expectation. We delight all the more in Dwight Gooden and Larry Bird because they stand out among a panoply of true stars. Besides, I really wrote this article only because I have a hunch that I want to share (and we professor types need to set context before we go out on a limb): Wade Boggs is gonna hit .400 this year.[1]

Questions

1. What effect does the introduction of gender have (paragraph 9) on Gould's thesis?
2. Do you agree that Gould's argument about improvement (paragraph 27) follows logically and effectively from the points that precede it?

---

1 *this year* Wade Boggs hit .356 in 1986. The closest that a modern hitter has come to hitting .400 was Tony Gwynn of the San Diego Padres hitting .394 in the strike-shortened season of 1994.

JAY INGRAM

This Chapter is a Yawner

(1989)

Science broadcaster and writer Jay Ingram co-hosts Discovery Channel's science show, Daily Planet. *He hosted CBC Radio's* Quirks and Quarks *from 1979–92. His books include* The Barmaid's Brain *(1998) and* The Velocity of Honey *(2003).*

This essay examines the mystery of yawning.

You'd think there would be only two important questions to ask about yawning: why do we do it, and why, when one person starts yawning, do others immediately follow? But scientists are much more cautious than that: they want to make sure they know what a yawn *is* first. And it is "a stereotyped and often repetitive motor act characterized by gaping of the mouth and accompanied by a long inspiration followed by a short expiration." That may be a long and accurate definition, but it makes yawning sound like breathing, and other than the fact that they both involve air going in and out, they couldn't feel more dissimilar. One gets the feeling that if that's the definition, then we're still barely out of the starting gates on this one.

How often do we yawn? Students sitting alone in a room for half an hour, pushing a button whenever they start to yawn and releasing it when they finish, have established the length of an average yawn to be six seconds, give or take two seconds. But amazingly, the frequency of yawning varies from only one in half an hour to *seventy-six*. If those seventy-six yawns each lasted six seconds, then that individual spent an entire half-hour yawning, with an average break of only seventeen seconds between yawns.

There's a popular idea that we yawn to get more oxygen to our brains, or conversely, to rid our blood of excess carbon dioxide. The more oxygen in the blood, the more glucose we can burn for energy. Carbon dioxide is a waste product that takes up space in our red blood cells that could be used for oxygen, and it could conceivably build up if we're breathing shallowly for long periods of time. This theory would explain why we yawn when we're tired or sitting in a stuffy overheated lecture hall at three o'clock in the afternoon—not enough fresh air.

But one of the few psychologists researching yawns, Robert Provine at the

University of Maryland, has found that changing the levels of carbon dioxide or oxygen seems not to affect yawning. Breathing *pure* oxygen didn't make subjects yawn less, and breathing air high in carbon dioxide didn't make them yawn more. Now it may be that setting this up in a laboratory situation somehow misses a critical factor, but if the cause of yawning were simply the levels of gases in the blood, experiments like this should show some effect. And they don't.

5 But these experiments don't completely kill the idea that yawning might refresh an oxygen-deprived brain. It's possible that by forcing your mouth wide open as you yawn, and stretching at the same time, you constrict some blood vessels while dilating others, with the net effect of forcing more blood to the brain. More blood means more oxygen, and presumably heightened alertness. It is true that opening your mouth wide is an important part of yawning: volunteers who yawned with clenched teeth reported it to be a highly abnormal experience that did nothing to satisfy the urge to yawn. If you try this yourself you'll see how incredibly unfulfilling it is, and the difficulty of explaining why that should be so just underlines how little yawning is understood. After all, you can still breathe in and out when your teeth are clenched, so it can't be lack of fresh air that leaves you dissatisfied. Maybe it's true that the wide-open stretching of your jaws and the resulting contraction of the facial muscles really do cause changes in blood flow to the brain. But does that mean that instead of yawning, you could just open your mouth as wide as possible for a few seconds, breathe in and out and get the same effects and the same satisfaction? No, it wouldn't be the same.

Medical doctors have collected evidence which suggests that yawning is controlled in a very primitive part of the brain, an area that runs for the most part on automatic pilot, beyond the reach of our conscious mind. Anencephaly is a tragic birth defect in which a newborn is missing most of the brain. Such children (who don't usually live long) have no cerebral hemispheres, the convoluted upper parts of the brain where most of our thinking takes place. But they have no trouble yawning. This must mean that the control of yawning is in one of the few brain parts they have—a lower, more "primitive" area like the medulla oblongata, a structure at the bottom of the brain that's responsible for normal breathing. It seems reasonable that yawning would be pretty well out of reach of your conscious mind; not only can a yawn start without a thought from you, it's also so difficult to stifle one once it's started—a powerful yawn can easily override your conscious efforts to stop it.[1]

---

1 There have also been cases where a patient with an arm paralyzed by a stroke or other brain damage has miraculously moved that paralyzed limb while yawning! They have no control over the movement: the arm just stretches on its own as it would normally do to accompany yawning. This strange occurrence suggests a link between yawning and stretching that completely bypasses the normal voluntary control of movement. [Ingram's note]

This yawning centre must have a complicated set of connections within the brain, because it has to trigger yawns in response to all kinds of different stimuli, ranging from the sight of other people yawning, through fatigue to boredom. In fact the absence of yawning may indicate a problem not with the yawning centre itself, but with another part of the brain to which it is connected. Psychiatrist Hans Lehmann at McGill University noted that he almost never saw mental patients yawn—on the wards, on buses, at public gatherings or in restaurants. It made perfect sense to Lehmann that these patients, most of whom were schizophrenics, didn't yawn because they were so emotionally flat that they had little interest in what was going on around them. He reasoned that to be bored enough by what's going on around you to yawn, you have to be aware there *is* something going on. These patients were too withdrawn to know what was going on around them, so they couldn't be bored, and didn't yawn. It is said to be a positive sign when some mental patients yawn, because it suggests they're trying to establish contact with reality.

The biggest mystery of all about yawning is its infectiousness. You see somebody yawn, you yawn yourself. This is sometimes explained as coincidence—everyone is yawning at the same time because there's too little air circulation or too little oxygen in the air, and therefore it only appears to be contagious. But as I've already pointed out, experiments have shown that breathing air that's too high in carbon dioxide has no effect on the frequency of yawning. More to the point, you don't even have to be in the same room as the yawner to feel the yawning urge. Students in Robert Provine's lab who watched videotapes of an actor yawned much more often if the actor was yawning than if he were smiling (55 percent versus 24 percent).

Actually you will be prompted to yawn if you just read about yawning. (As you've probably already noticed.) The sound of yawning even provokes blind people to do it. We proved the power of this contagiousness on our program "Quirks and Quarks" in December 1988, when after making a few brief comments on some yawning research, I suggested that any listener who had felt the urge to yawn while I had been talking should write to us. I expected at most a couple of dozen letters (we weren't giving away T-shirts or promising to mention anyone on air), but we were all stunned by the avalanche of letters. The final count was close to three hundred, and the picture that emerged was that of thousands of Canadians yawning uncontrollably at about 12:50 P.M. on December 17, 1988, as they listened to the radio.

Why would we respond to the yawns of others with one of our own? The   10
most popular suggestion is that yawning might be a hangover from our ancestral animal past, something called a "stereotyped action pattern." This is an automatic response to a signal that is common among birds and animals—for example, a frog will lunge hungrily, and unthinkingly, at any small dark moving object—but why would we yawn simply because other humans are yawning? In the early sixties, anthropologist Ashley Montagu,

who was one of the believers in the idea that yawning heightened alertness by shunting fresh blood to the brain, speculated that group yawning would, by this mechanism, increase everyone's alertness. On the other hand, in a beautiful example of how any theory fits if you have very little data, an English doctor named Malcolm Weller had recently suggested the exact reverse—that the infectiousness of yawning might have originated as a signal among social animals to go to sleep, not to revive. Weller thinks that if one animal were to signal his weariness by yawning, the pack would imitate him and soon settle for the night.

This picture of our distant ancestors engaging in communal yawning for the good of the group is fine, and if that behaviour became automatic, we might well still be doing it today, long after it had outlived its usefulness. But this is a tricky business, using what anthropologists *think* our ancestors were doing to explain why we do it today.

If our primitive ancestors used yawning as a signal, at what point did we start covering our mouths when we yawn? Obviously it would have been counterproductive for those animals which were signalling each other with their yawns to have been hiding those same yawns with their hands or paws. You can argue that covering the mouth is a recent human cultural invention superimposed on the ancient habit of yawning openly. But by doing so, you're ignoring some intriguing observations of our closest living relatives.

By studying the habits of modern apes and monkeys, scientists believe they can infer some of the ways our ancient ape-like ancestors behaved millions of years ago. Yawning is a social signal among animals like monkeys and baboons, but an aggressive one. Dominant male baboons engage in "threat yawns," a gesture some scientists interpret as being more threatening than a raised eyebrow or a stare. Anthropologist John Hadidian spent seven hundred hours watching black apes yawn, and he concluded that the ones doing the yawning are the dominant males: the number one male averaged three yawns an hour, while number four yawned only once every three hours. These apes, and many other related species, have especially long canine teeth which a yawn displays to great advantage.

Some biologists have even reported seeing subordinate animals cover their yawning mouths with their paws, apparently to prevent those yawns from being interpreted as threats they couldn't back up. We claim that we cover our mouths because to do otherwise would be "rude", but maybe that's just our civilized way of saying that it's somehow threatening. An open-mouthed yawn directed at you may not actually be a physical threat, but it can convey an unflattering, even unfriendly message (even without prominent canines).[1] What is really needed here is a study of human

---

1   Just to add another twist to the story, Robert Provine's research has shown that people will yawn in response to a yawning face with the mouth blanked out— the eyes and forehead are enough to stimulate yawns. So covering your mouth when you yawn does not interfere with its contagiousness. [Ingram's note]

groups to see if the dominant individuals don't bother covering their mouths, while the submissive ones do. The Godfather's henchmen always laughed when he did, and stopped laughing when he did. What did they do when he yawned?

And when all the research falls into place, and we know exactly why we   15 yawn, and especially why we yawn when others are yawning, where will the rat data fit in? The rat data? A variety of studies have established that certain drugs will quickly bring on two responses in rats: yawning and erections.

Questions

1. Why do you think Ingram makes frequent use of rhetorical questions in this piece?
2. Explain the theory that yawning provides more oxygen to the brain, and the experiments which disprove this theory.

WITOLD RYBCZYNSKI

One Good Turn

Why the Robertson Screwdriver is the Biggest Little Invention
of the Twentieth Century
(2000)

*Witold Rybczynski (1943–) is an architect, a leading writer on cultural and archi-
tectural history, and a professor in the School of Architecture at the University of
Pennsylvania. He has written numerous works on the subject of architecture, urban-
ism and design, including the books* Home: A Short History of an Idea *(1986)
and* The Most Beautiful House in the World *(1989).*

This article grew out of an assignment for New York Times Magazine *to write an
essay about the best tool of the millennium.*

Take a close look at a modern screw. It is a remarkable little object. The
thread begins at a gimlet point, sharp as a pin. This point gently tapers into
the body of the screw, whose core is cylindrical. At the top, the core tapers
into a smooth shank, the thread running out to nothing.

From the time of their invention in the Middle Ages until the beginning
of the twentieth century, all screws had either square or octagonal heads, or
slots. The former were turned by a wrench, the latter by a screwdriver.
There is no mystery as to the origin of the slot. A square head had to be
accurate to fit the wrench; a slot was a shape that could be roughly filed or
cut by hand. Screws with slotted heads could also be countersunk so that
they would not protrude beyond the surface.

Yet a slotted screw has several drawbacks. It is easy to "cam out," that is,
to push the screwdriver out of the slot; the result is often damage to the
material that is being fastened or injury to one's fingers—or both. The slot
offers a tenuous purchase on the screw, and it is not uncommon to strip the
slot when trying to tighten a new screw or loosen an old one. Finally, there
are awkward situations—balancing on a stepladder, for example, or working in confined quarters—when one has to drive the screw with one hand.
This is almost impossible to do with a slotted screw. The screw wobbles, the
screwdriver slips, the screw falls to the ground and rolls away, the handyman
curses—not for the first time—the inventor of this maddening device.

American screw manufacturers were well aware of these shortcomings. Between 1860 and 1890, there was a flurry of patents for magnetic screwdrivers, screw-holding gadgets, slots that did not extend across the face of the screw, double slots, and a variety of square, triangular, and hexagonal sockets or recesses. The last held the most promise. Replacing the slot by a socket held the screwdriver snugly and prevented cam-out. The difficulty— once more—lay in manufacturing. Screw heads are formed by mechanically stamping a cold-steel rod; punching a socket sufficiently deep to hold the screwdriver tended to either weaken the screw or deform the head.

The solution was discovered by a twenty-seven-year-old Canadian, Peter 5 L. Robertson. Robertson was a so-called "high-pitch man" for a Philadelphia tool company, a travelling salesman who plied his wares on street corners and at country fairs in eastern Canada. He spent his spare time in his workshop, dabbling in mechanical inventions. He invented and promoted "Robertson's 20th Century Wrench-Brace," a combination tool that could be used as a brace, a monkey wrench, a screwdriver, a bench vise, and a rivet-maker. He vainly patented an improved corkscrew, a new type of cufflink, even a better mousetrap. Then, in 1906, he applied for a patent for a socket-head screw.

Robertson later said that he got the idea for the socket head while demonstrating a spring-loaded screwdriver to a group of sidewalk gawkers in Montreal—the blade slipped out of the slot and injured his hand. The secret of his invention was the exact shape of the recess, which was square with chamfered edges, slightly tapering sides, and a pyramidal bottom. Later, he rather grandly explained his invention: "It was discovered early by the use of this form of punch, constructed with the exact angles indicated, cold metal would flow to the sides, and not be driven ahead of the tools, resulting beneficially in knitting the atoms into greater strength, and also assisting in the work of lateral extension, and without a waste or cutting away of any of the metal so treated, as is the case in the manufacture of the ordinary slotted head screw."

An enthusiastic promoter, Robertson found financial backers, talked a small Ontario town, Milton, into giving him a loan and other concessions, and established his own screw factory. "The big fortunes are in the small inventions," he trumpeted to prospective investors. "This is considered by many as the biggest little invention of the twentieth century so far." In truth, the square socket really was a big improvement. The special square-headed screwdriver fitted snugly—Robertson claimed an accuracy within one one-thousandth of an inch—and never cammed out. Craftsmen, especially furniture-makers and boat builders, appreciated the convenience of screws that were self-centring and could be driven with one hand. Industry liked socket-head screws, too, since they reduced product damage and speeded up production. The Fisher Body Company, which made wood bodies in Canada for Ford cars, became a large Robertson customer; so did the new

Ford Model T plant in Windsor, Ontario, which soon accounted for a third of Robertson's output. Within five years, he was employing seventy-five workers and had built his own powerhouse and a plant to draw the cold-steel rod used in making the screws.

In 1913, Robertson decided to expand his business outside Canada. His father had been a Scottish immigrant, so Robertson turned his attention to Britain. He established an independent English company to serve as a base for exporting to Germany and Russia. The venture was not a success. He was thwarted by a combination of undercapitalization, World War I, the defeat of Germany, and the Russian Revolution. Moreover, it proved difficult to run businesses on two continents. After seven years, unhappy English shareholders replaced Robertson as managing director. The English company struggled along until it was liquidated in 1926.

Meanwhile, Robertson turned to the United States. Negotiations with a large screw manufacturer in Buffalo broke down after it became clear that Robertson was unwilling to share control over production decisions. Henry Ford was interested, since his Canadian plants were reputedly saving as much as $2.60 per car using Robertson screws. However, Ford, too, wanted a measure of control that the stubborn Robertson was unwilling to grant. They met, but no deal was struck. It was Robertson's last attempt to export his product. A life-long bachelor, he spent the rest of his life in Milton, a big fish in a decidedly small pond.

10   Meanwhile, American automobile manufacturers followed Ford's lead and stuck to slotted screws. Yet the success of the new Robertson screw did not go unnoticed. In 1936 alone, there were more than twenty American patents for improved screws and screwdrivers.

Several of these were granted to Henry F. Phillips, a forty-six-year-old businessman in Portland, Oregon. Like Robertson, Phillips had been a travelling salesman. He was also a promoter of new inventions and acquired patents from a Portland inventor, John P. Thompson, for a socket screw. Thompson's socket was too deep to be practicable, but Phillips incorporated its distinctive shape—a cruciform—into an improved design of his own. Like Robertson, Phillips claimed that the socket was "particularly adapted for firm engagement with a correspondingly shaped driving tool or screwdriver, and in such a way that there will be no tendency of the driver to cam out of the recess." Unlike Robertson, however, Phillips did not start his own company but planned to license his patent to screw manufacturers.

All the major screw companies turned him down. "The manufacture and marketing of these articles do not promise sufficient commercial success," was a typical response. Phillips did not give up. Several years later the president of the giant American Screw Company agreed to undertake the industrial development of the innovative socket screw. In his patents, Phillips emphasized that the screw was particularly suited to power-driven operations, which at the time chiefly meant automobile assembly lines. The American Screw Company convinced General Motors to test the new screw; it was used first in the 1936 Cadillac. The trial proved so effective that within two years all automobile companies save one had switched to socket screws, and by 1939 most screw manufacturers produced what were now called Phillips screws.

The Phillips screw has many of the same benefits as the Robertson screw (and the added advantage that it can be driven with a slotted screwdriver if necessary). "We estimate that our operators save between thirty and sixty percent of their time by using Phillips screws," wrote a satisfied builder of boats and gliders. "Our men claim they can accomplish at least seventy-five percent more work than with the old-fashioned type," maintained a manufacturer of garden furniture. Phillips screws—and the familiar cross-tipped screwdrivers—were now everywhere. World War I had stymied Robertson; World War II ensured that the Phillips screw became an industry standard as it was widely adopted by wartime manufacturers. By the mid-1960s, when Phillips's patents expired, there were more than 160 domestic, and eighty foreign, licensees.

The Phillips screw became the international socket screw; the Robertson screw is used only in Canada and by a select number of American woodworkers. (Starting in the 1950s, Robertson screws began to be used by some American furniture manufacturers, by the mobile-home industry, and eventually by a growing number of craftsmen and hobbyists. The Robertson company itself was purchased by an American conglomerate in 1968.) A few years ago, *Consumer Reports* tested Robertson and Phillips screwdrivers. "After driving hundreds of screws by hand and with a cordless drill fitted with a Robertson tip, we're convinced. Compared with slotted and Phillips-head screwdrivers, the Robertson worked faster, with less cam-out."

The explanation is simple. Although Phillips designed his screw to have   15
"firm engagement" with the screwdriver, in fact a cruciform recess is a less perfect fit than a square socket. Paradoxically, this very quality is what attracted automobile manufacturers to the Phillips screw; the point of an automated driver turning the screw with increasing force would pop out of the recess when the screw was fully set, preventing overscrewing. Thus, a certain degree of cam-out was incorporated into the design from the beginning. However, what worked on the assembly line has bedevilled handymen ever since. Phillips screws are notorious for slippage, cam-out, and stripped sockets (especially if the screw or the screwdriver is improperly made).

Here I must confess myself to be a confirmed Robertson user. The square-headed screwdriver sits snugly in the socket; you can shake a Robertson screwdriver, and the screw on the end will not fall off; drive a Robertson screw with a power drill and the fully set screw simply stops the drill dead; no matter how old, rusty, or painted over, a Robertson screw can always be unscrewed. The "biggest little invention of the twentieth century"? Why not.

Questions

1. Although Rybczynski claims that the Robertson is a superior screw to the Phillips, it has not had the commercial success of the Phillips. What role did the differing business philosophies of the two inventors play in this result?
2. At what moments does Rybczynski give clues to Robertson's character (or to his own attitude toward Robertson)? What do these moments reveal about the author himself?
3. Rybczynski is often described as an "engaging" writer. Identify a few of the ways by which he effectively engages the interest of his readers.

Why the Fries Taste Good

(2001)

Eric Schlosser (1959–) has worked as a correspondent for The Atlantic Monthly. *He is the author of* Fast Food Nation: The Dark Side of the All-American Meal *(2001) and* Reefer Madness: Sex, Drugs, and Cheap Labor in the American Black Market *(2003).*

In this excerpt from Fast Food Nation, *Schlosser investigates the "flavor" industry.*

The taste of McDonald's french fries has long been praised by customers, competitors, and even food critics. James Beard[1] loved McDonald's fries. Their distinctive taste does not stem from the type of potatoes that McDonald's buys, the technology that processes them, or the restaurant equipment that fries them. Other chains buy their french fries from the same large processing companies, use Russet Burbanks, and have similar fryers in their restaurant kitchens. The taste of a fast food fry is largely determined by the cooking oil. For decades, McDonald's cooked its french fries in a mixture of about 7 percent cottonseed oil and 93 percent beef tallow. The mix gave the fries their unique flavor—and more saturated beef fat per ounce than a McDonald's hamburger.

Amid a barrage of criticism over the amount of cholesterol in their fries, McDonald's switched to pure vegetable oil in 1990. The switch presented the company with an enormous challenge: how to make fries that subtly taste like beef without cooking them in tallow. A look at the ingredients now used in the preparation of McDonald's french fries suggests how the problem was solved. Toward the end of the list is a seemingly innocuous, yet oddly mysterious phrase: "natural flavor." That ingredient helps to explain not only why the fries taste so good, but also why most fast food—indeed, most of the food Americans eat today—tastes the way it does.

Open your refrigerator, your freezer, your kitchen cupboards, and look at the labels on your food. You'll find "natural flavor" or "artificial flavor" in just about every list of ingredients. The similarities between these two broad categories of flavor are far more significant than their differences. Both are

---

1 *James Beard* (1903–85), American food writer and chef.

man-made additives that give most processed food most of its taste. The initial purchase of a food item may be driven by its packaging or appearance, but subsequent purchases are determined mainly by its taste. About 90 percent of the money that Americans spend on food is used to buy processed food. But the canning, freezing, and dehydrating techniques used to process food destroy most of its flavor. Since the end of World War II, a vast industry has arisen in the United States to make processed food palatable. Without this flavor industry, today's fast food industry could not exist. The names of the leading American fast food chains and their best-selling menu items have become famous worldwide, embedded in our popular culture. Few people, however, can name the companies that manufacture fast food's taste.

The flavor industry is highly secretive. Its leading companies will not divulge the precise formulas of flavor compounds or the identities of clients. The secrecy is deemed essential for protecting the reputation of beloved brands. The fast food chains, understandably, would like the public to believe that the flavors of their food somehow originate in their restaurant kitchens, not in distant factories run by other firms.

5 The New Jersey Turnpike runs through the heart of the flavor industry, an industrial corridor dotted with refineries and chemical plants. International Flavors & Fragrances (IFF), the world's largest flavor company, has a manufacturing facility off Exit 8A in Dayton, New Jersey; Givaudan, the world's second-largest flavor company, has a plant in East Hanover. Haarmann & Reimer, the largest German flavor company, has a plant in Teterboro, as does Takasago, the largest Japanese flavor company. Flavor Dynamics has a plant in South Plainfield; Frutarom is in North Bergen; Elan Chemical is in Newark. Dozens of companies manufacture flavors in the corridor between Teaneck and South Brunswick. Indeed, the area produces about two-thirds of the flavor additives sold in the United States.

The IFF plant in Dayton is a huge pale blue building with a modern office complex attached to the front. It sits in an industrial park, not far from a BASF plastics factory, a Jolly French Toast factory, and a plant that manufactures Liz Claiborne cosmetics. Dozens of tractor-trailers were parked at the IFF loading dock the afternoon I visited, and a thin cloud of steam floated from the chimney. Before entering the plant, I signed a nondisclosure form, promising not to reveal the brand names of products that contain IFF flavors. The place reminded me of Willy Wonka's chocolate factory. Wonderful smells drifted through the hallways, men and women in neat white lab coats cheerfully went about their work, and hundreds of little glass bottles sat on laboratory tables and shelves. The bottles contained powerful but fragile flavor chemicals, shielded from light by the brown glass and the round plastic caps shut tight. The long chemical names on the little white labels were as mystifying to me as medieval Latin. They were the odd-sounding names of things that would be mixed and poured and turned into new substances, like magic potions.

I was not invited to see the manufacturing areas of the IFF plant, where it was thought I might discover trade secrets. Instead, I toured various laboratories and pilot kitchens, where the flavors of well-established brands are tested or adjusted, and where whole new flavors are created. IFF's snack and savory lab is responsible for the flavor of potato chips, corn chips, breads, crackers, breakfast cereals, and pet food. The confectionery lab devises the flavor for ice cream, cookies, candies, toothpastes, mouthwashes, and antacids. Everywhere I looked, I saw famous, widely advertised products sitting on laboratory desks and tables. The beverage lab is full of brightly colored liquids in clear bottles. It comes up with the flavor for popular soft drinks, sport drinks, bottled teas, and wine coolers, for all-natural juice drinks, organic soy drinks, beers, and malt liquors. In one pilot kitchen I saw a dapper food technologist, a middle-aged man with an elegant tie beneath his lab coat, carefully preparing a batch of cookies with white frosting and pink-and-white sprinkles. In another pilot kitchen I saw a pizza oven, a grill, a milk-shake machine, and a french fryer identical to those I'd seen behind the counter at countless fast food restaurants.

In addition to being the world's largest flavor company, IFF manufactures the smell of six of the ten best-selling fine perfumes in the United States, including Estée Lauder's Beautiful, Clinique's Happy, Lancôme's Trésor, and Calvin Klein's Eternity. It also makes the smell of household products such as deodorant, dishwashing detergent, bath soap, shampoo, furniture polish, and floor wax. All of these aromas are made through the same basic process: the manipulation of volatile chemicals to create a particular smell. The basic science behind the scent of your shaving cream is the same as that governing the flavor of your TV dinner.

The aroma of a food can be responsible for as much as 90 percent of its flavor. Scientists now believe that human beings acquired the sense of taste as a way to avoid being poisoned. Edible plants generally taste sweet; deadly ones, bitter. Taste is supposed to help us differentiate food that's good for us from food that's not. The taste buds on our tongues can detect the presence of half a dozen or so basic tastes, including: sweet, sour, bitter, salty, astringent, and umami (a taste discovered by Japanese researchers, a rich and full sense of deliciousness triggered by amino acids in foods such as shellfish, mushrooms, potatoes, and seaweed). Taste buds offer a relatively limited means of detection, however, compared to the human olfactory system, which can perceive thousands of different chemical aromas. Indeed "flavor" is primarily the smell of gases being released by the chemicals you've just put in your mouth.

The act of drinking, sucking, or chewing a substance releases its volatile 10 gases. They flow out of the mouth and up the nostrils, or up the passageway in the back of the mouth, to a thin layer of nerve cells called the olfactory epithelium, located at the base of the nose, right between the eyes. The brain combines the complex smell signals from the epithelium with the simple taste signals from the tongue, assigns a flavor to what's in your mouth, and decides if it's something you want to eat.

Babies like sweet tastes and reject bitter ones; we know this because scientists have rubbed various flavors inside the mouths of infants and then recorded their facial reactions. A person's food preferences, like his or her personality, are formed during the first few years of life, through a process of socialization. Toddlers can learn to enjoy hot and spicy food, bland health food, or fast food, depending upon what the people around them eat. The human sense of smell is still not fully understood and can be greatly affected by psychological factors and expectations. The color of a food can determine the perception of its taste. The mind filters out the overwhelming majority of chemical aromas that surround us, focusing intently on some, ignoring others. People can grow accustomed to bad smells or good smells; they stop noticing what once seemed overpowering. Aroma and memory are somehow inextricably linked. A smell can suddenly evoke a long-forgotten moment. The flavors of childhood foods seem to leave an indelible mark, and adults often return to them, without always knowing why. These "comfort foods" become a source of pleasure and reassurance, a fact that fast food chains work hard to promote. Childhood memories of Happy Meals can translate into frequent adult visits to McDonald's, like those of the chain's "heavy users," the customers who eat there four or five times a week.

The human craving for flavor has been a largely unacknowledged and unexamined force in history. Royal empires have been built, unexplored lands have been traversed, great religions and philosophies have been forever changed by the spice trade. In 1492 Christopher Columbus set sail to find seasoning. Today the influence of flavor in the world marketplace is no less decisive. The rise and fall of corporate empires—of soft drink companies, snack food companies, and fast food chains—is frequently determined by how their products taste.

The flavor industry emerged in the mid-nineteenth century, as processed foods began to be manufactured on a large scale. Recognizing the need for flavor additives, the early food processors turned to perfume companies that had years of experience working with essential oils and volatile aromas. The great perfume houses of England, France, and the Netherlands produced many of the first flavor compounds. In the early part of the twentieth century, Germany's powerful chemical industry assumed the technological lead in flavor production. Legend has it that a German scientist discovered methyl anthranilate, one of the first artificial flavors, by accident while mixing chemicals in his laboratory. Suddenly the lab was filled with the sweet smell of grapes. Methyl anthranilate later became the chief flavoring compound of grape Kool-Aid. After World War II, much of the perfume industry shifted from Europe to the United States, settling in New York City near the garment district and the fashion houses. The flavor industry came with it, subsequently moving to New Jersey to gain more plant capacity. Man-made flavor additives were used mainly in baked goods, candies, and sodas until the 1950s, when sales of processed food began to soar. The invention of gas chromatographs and mass spectrometers—machines capable of detecting volatile gases at low levels—vastly increased the number of flavors that could be synthesized. By the mid-1960s the American flavor industry was churning out compounds to supply the taste of Pop Tarts, Bac-Os, Tab, Tang, Filet-O-Fish sandwiches, and literally thousands of other new foods.

The American flavor industry now has annual revenues of about $1.4 billion. Approximately ten thousand new processed food products are introduced every year in the United States. Almost all of them require flavor additives. And about nine out of every ten of these new food products fail. The latest flavor innovations and corporate realignments are heralded in publications such as *Food Chemical News, Food Engineering, Chemical Market Reporter,* and *Food Product Design.* The growth of IFF has mirrored that of the flavor industry as a whole. IFF was formed in 1958, through the merger of two small companies. Its annual revenues have grown almost fifteenfold since the early 1970s, and it now has manufacturing facilities in twenty countries.

The quality that people seek most of all in a food, its flavor, is usually present in a quantity too infinitesimal to be measured by any traditional culinary terms such as ounces or teaspoons. Today's sophisticated spectrometers, gas chromatographs, and headspace vapor analyzers provide a detailed map of a food's flavor components, detecting chemical aromas in amounts as low as one part per billion. The human nose, however, is still more sensitive than any machine yet invented. A nose can detect aromas present in quantities of a few parts per trillion—an amount equivalent to 0.000000000003 percent. Complex aromas, like those of coffee or roasted meat, may be composed of volatile gases from nearly a thousand different chemicals. The smell of a strawberry arises from the interaction of at least 350 different chemicals that are present in minute amounts. The chemical that provides the dominant flavor of bell pepper can be tasted in amounts as low as .02 parts per billion; one drop is sufficient to add flavor to five average size swimming pools. The flavor additive usually comes last, or second to last, in a processed food's list of ingredients. As a result, the flavor of a processed food often costs less than its packaging. Soft drinks contain a larger proportion of flavor additives than most products. The flavor in a twelve-ounce can of Coke costs about half a cent.

The color additives in processed foods are usually present in even smaller amounts than the flavor compounds. Many of New Jersey's flavor com-

15

panies also manufacture these color additives, which are used to make processed foods look appealing. Food coloring serves many of the same purposes as lipstick, eye shadow, mascara—and is often made from the same pigments. Titanium dioxide, for example, has proved to be an especially versatile mineral. It gives many processed candies, frosting, and icing their bright white color; it is a common ingredient in women's cosmetics; and it is the pigment used in many white oil paints and house paints. At Burger King, Wendy's, and McDonald's, coloring agents have been added to many of the soft drinks, salad dressings, cookies, condiments, chicken dishes, and sandwich buns.

Studies have found that the color of a food can greatly affect how its taste is perceived. Brightly colored foods frequently seem to taste better than bland-looking foods, even when the flavor compounds are identical. Foods that somehow look off-color often seem to have off tastes. For thousands of years, human beings have relied on visual cues to help determine what is edible. The color of fruit suggests whether it is ripe, the color of meat whether it is rancid. Flavor researchers sometimes use colored lights to modify the influence of visual cues during taste tests. During one experiment in the early 1970s, people were served an oddly tinted meal of steak and French fries that appeared normal beneath colored lights. Everyone thought the meal tasted fine until the lighting was changed. Once it became apparent that the steak was actually blue and the fries were green, some people became ill.

The Food and Drug Administration does not require flavor companies to disclose the ingredients of their additives, so long as all the chemicals are considered by the agency to be GRAS (Generally Regarded As Safe). This lack of public disclosure enables the companies to maintain the secrecy of their formulas. It also hides the fact that flavor compounds sometimes contain more ingredients than the foods being given their taste. The ubiquitous phrase "artificial strawberry flavor" gives little hint of the chemical wizardry and manufacturing skill that can make a highly processed food taste like a strawberry.

A typical artificial strawberry flavor, like the kind found in a Burger King strawberry milk shake, contains the following ingredients: amyl acetate, amyl butyrate, amyl valerate, anethol, anisyl formate, benzyl acetate, benzyl isobutyrate, butyric acid, cinnamyl isobutyrate, cinnamyl valerate, cognac essential oil, diacetyl, dipropyl ketone, ethyl acetate, ethyl amylketone, ethyl butyrate, ethyl cinnamate, ethyl heptanoate, ethyl heptylate, ethyl lactate, ethyl methylphenylglycidate, ethyl nitrate, ethyl propionate, ethyl valerate, heliotropin, hydroxyphenyl-2-butanone (10 percent solution in alcohol), (α-ionone, isobutyl anthranilate, isobutyl butyrate, lemon essential oil, maltol, 4-methylacetophenone, methyl anthranilate, methyl benzoate, methyl cinnamate, methyl heptine carbonate, methyl naphthyl ketone, methyl salicylate, mint essential oil, neroli essential oil, nerolin, neryl isobutyrate, orris butter, phenethyl alcohol, rose, rum ether, γ-undecalactone, vanillin, and solvent.

Although flavors usually arise from a mixture of many different volatile chemicals, a single compound often supplies the dominant aroma. Smelled alone, that chemical provides an unmistakable sense of the food. Ethyl-2-methyl butyrate, for example, smells just like an apple. Today's highly processed foods offer a blank palette: whatever chemicals you add to them will give them specific tastes. Adding methyl-2-peridylketone makes something taste like popcorn. Adding ethyl-3-hydroxybutanoate makes it taste like marshmallow. The possibilities are now almost limitless. Without affecting the appearance or nutritional value, processed foods could even be made with aroma chemicals such as hexanal (the smell of freshly cut grass) or 3-methyl butanoic acid (the smell of body odor). 20

The 1960s were the heyday of artificial flavors. The synthetic versions of flavor compounds were not subtle, but they did not need to be, given the nature of most processed food. For the past twenty years food processors have tried hard to use only "natural flavors" in their products. According to the FDA, these must be derived entirely from natural sources—from herbs, spices, fruits, vegetables, beef, chicken, yeast, bark, roots, etc. Consumers prefer to see natural flavors on a label, out of a belief that they are healthier. The distinction between artificial and natural flavors can be somewhat arbitrary and absurd, based more on how the flavor has been made than on what it actually contains. "A natural flavor," says Terry Acree, a professor of food science at Cornell University, "is a flavor that's been derived with an out-of-date technology." Natural flavors and artificial flavors sometimes contain exactly the same chemicals, produced through different methods. Amyl acetate, for example, provides the dominant note of banana flavor. When you distill it from bananas with a solvent, amyl acetate is a natural flavor. When you produce it by mixing vinegar with amyl alcohol, adding sulfuric acid as a catalyst, amyl acetate is an artificial flavor. Either way it smells and tastes the same. The phrase "natural flavor" is now listed among the ingredients of everything from Stonyfield Farm Organic Strawberry Yogurt to Taco Bell Hot Taco Sauce.

A natural flavor is not necessarily healthier or purer than an artificial one. When almond flavor (benzaldehyde) is derived from natural sources, such as peach and apricot pits, it contains traces of hydrogen cyanide, a deadly poison. Benzaldehyde derived through a different process—by mixing oil of clove and the banana flavor, amyl acetate—does not contain any cyanide. Nevertheless, it is legally considered an artificial flavor and sells at a much lower price. Natural and artificial flavors are now manufactured at the same chemical plants, places that few people would associate with Mother Nature. Calling any of these flavors "natural" requires a flexible attitude toward the English language and a fair amount of irony.

The small and elite group of scientists who create most of the flavor in most of the food now consumed in the United States are called "flavorists."

They draw upon a number of disciplines in their work: biology, psychology, physiology, and organic chemistry. A flavorist is a chemist with a trained nose and a poetic sensibility. Flavors are created by blending scores of different chemicals in tiny amounts, a process governed by scientific principles but demanding a fair amount of art. In an age when delicate aromas, subtle flavors, and microwave ovens do not easily coexist, the job of the flavorist is to conjure illusions about processed food and, in the words of one flavor company's literature, to ensure "consumer likeability." The flavorists with whom I spoke were charming, cosmopolitan, and ironic. They were also discreet, in keeping with the dictates of their trade. They were the sort of scientist who not only enjoyed fine wine, but could also tell you the chemicals that gave each vintage its unique aroma. One flavorist compared his work to composing music. A well-made flavor compound will have a "top note," followed by a "dry-down," and a "leveling-off," with different chemicals responsible for each stage. The taste of a food can be radically altered by minute changes in the flavoring mix. "A little odor goes a long way," one flavorist said.

In order to give a processed food the proper taste, a flavorist must always consider the food's "mouthfeel"—the unique combination of textures and chemical interactions that affects how the flavor is perceived. The mouthfeel can be adjusted through the use of various fats, gums, starches, emulsifiers, and stabilizers. The aroma chemicals of a food can be precisely analyzed, but mouthfeel is much harder to measure. How does one quantify a french fry's crispness? Food technologists are now conducting basic research in rheology, a branch of physics that examines the flow and deformation of materials. A number of companies sell sophisticated devices that attempt to measure mouthfeel. The TA.XT2i Texture Analyzer, produced by the Texture Technologies Corporation, performs calculations based on data derived from as many as 250 separate probes. It is essentially a mechanical mouth. It gauges the most important rheological properties of a food— the bounce, creep, breaking point, density, crunchiness, chewiness, gumminess, lumpiness, rubberiness, springiness, slipperiness, smoothness, softness, wetness, juiciness, spreadability, springback, and tackiness.

25   Some of the most important advances in flavor manufacturing are now occurring in the field of biotechnology. Complex flavors are being made through fermentation, enzyme reactions, fungal cultures, and tissue cultures. All of the flavors being created through these methods—including the ones being synthesized by funguses—are considered natural flavors by the FDA. The new enzyme-based processes are responsible for extremely lifelike dairy flavors. One company now offers not just butter flavor, but also fresh creamy butter, cheesy butter, milky butter, savory melted butter, and super-concentrated butter flavor, in liquid or powder form. The development of new fermentation techniques, as well as new techniques for heating mixtures of sugar and amino acids, have led to the creation of much more realistic meat flavors. The McDonald's Corporation will not reveal the

exact origin of the natural flavor added to its french fries. In response to inquiries from *Vegetarian Journal*, however, McDonald's did acknowledge that its fries derive some of their characteristic flavor from "animal products."

Other popular fast foods derive their flavor from unexpected sources. Wendy's Grilled Chicken Sandwich, for example, contains beef extracts. Burger King's BK Broiler Chicken Breast Patty contains "natural smoke flavor." A firm called Red Arrow Products Company specializes in smoke flavor, which is added to barbecue sauces and processed meats. Red Arrow manufactures natural smoke flavor by charring sawdust and capturing the aroma chemicals released into the air. The smoke is captured in water and then bottled, so that other companies can sell food which seems to have been cooked over a fire.

The Vegetarian Legal Action Network recently petitioned the FDA to issue new food labeling requirements for foods that contain natural flavors. The group wants food processors to list the basic origins of their flavors on their labels. At the moment, vegetarians often have no way of knowing whether a flavor additive contains beef, pork, poultry, or shellfish. One of the most widely used color additives—whose presence is often hidden by the phrase "color added"—violates a number of religious dietary restrictions, may cause allergic reactions in susceptible people, and comes from an unusual source. Cochineal extract (also known as carmine or carminic acid) is made from the desiccated bodies of female Dactlyopius coccus Costa, a small insect harvested mainly in Peru and the Canary Islands. The bug feeds on red cactus berries and color from the berries accumulated in the females and their unhatched larvae. The insects are collected, dried, and ground into pigment. It takes about 70,000 of them to produce one pound of carmine, which is used to make processed foods look pink, red, or purple. Dannon strawberry yogurt gets its color from carmine, as do many frozen fruit bars, candies, fruit fillings, and Ocean Spray pink-grapefruit juice drink.

In a meeting room at IFF, Brian Grainger let me sample some of the company's flavors. It was an unusual taste test; there wasn't any food to taste. Grainger is a senior flavorist at IFF, a soft-spoken chemist with graying hair, an English accent, and a fondness for understatement. He could easily be mistaken for a British diplomat or the owner of a West End brasserie[1] with two Michelin[2] stars. Like many in the flavor industry, he has an Old World, old-fashioned sensibility which seems out of step with our brand-conscious, egocentric age. When I suggested that IFF should put its own logo on the products that contain its flavors—instead of allowing other brands to enjoy

---

1 *brasserie* Coffeehouse where food as well as alcoholic and nonalcoholic beverages are served.
2 *Michelin* Popular guidebook for travelers.

the consumer loyalty and affection inspired by those flavors—Grainger politely disagreed, assuring me such a thing would never be done. In the absence of public credit or acclaim, the small and secretive fraternity of flavor chemists praises one another's work. Grainger can often tell, by analyzing the flavor formula of a product, which of his counterparts at a rival firm devised it. And he enjoys walking down supermarket aisles, looking at the many products that contain his flavors, even if no one else knows it.

Grainger had brought a dozen small glass bottles from the lab. After he opened each bottle, I dipped a fragrance testing filter into it. The filters were long white strips of paper designed to absorb aroma chemicals without producing off-notes. Before placing the strips of paper before my nose, I closed my eyes. Then I inhaled deeply, and one food after another was conjured from the glass bottles. I smelled fresh cherries, black olives, sautéed onions, and shrimp. Grainger's most remarkable creation took me by surprise. After closing my eyes, I suddenly smelled a grilled hamburger. The aroma was uncanny, almost miraculous. It smelled like someone in the room was flipping burgers on a hot grill. But when I opened my eyes, there was just a narrow strip of white paper and a smiling flavorist.

Questions

1. Who is Schlosser's audience? How does he reach this audience? Is he successful?
2. Compare and contrast the style, diction, and rhetorical strategies and aims of this essay with those of Naomi Klein's "The Swoosh."

MEENAKSHI WADHWA

(as told to Calvin Fussman)

In Her Own Words

(2004)

Meenakshi Wadhwa was born and raised in India, and studied geology at Panjab University near Chandigarh. She later studied in the United States and earned a doctorate from Washington University. Wadwha's fascination with rocks that fall from space led her to work as the Assistant Curator of Meteorites in the Geology Department of the Field Museum in Chicago. Her research focuses on meteorite formation and composition. She is especially interested in samples from Mars.

In this interview, Wadhwa muses on her education, career, family, and being a woman in an often male-dominated field.

When I was 8 years old, the science teacher in my school taught us that we breathe in oxygen and let out carbon dioxide. I sat there thinking: "There must be all this carbon dioxide building up in the atmosphere. Are we going to be out of oxygen pretty soon?" I got really worried about it and ran home to my mother. "Did you know this?" I asked. "Is the world coming to an end?" My mother laughed and explained the cycles in nature that keep Earth systems in balance. So I learned at a young age that we don't understand how much we don't understand.

My father was a logistics officer in the Indian Air Force, and we moved every two years or so. At one point we lived in the south of the country in a house surrounded by mango groves. I'd climb the trees and pick the fruits—even before they were ripe. I just loved to bite into them. But the juice of raw mangoes can be pretty nasty. It's corrosive and causes sores wherever it touches the skin. My mom would always say: "Don't be impatient! Wait until those mangoes ripen!" The next day, the rash would show up on my face.

I learned a big lesson about patience when my mother died. I was 15 at the time, the oldest daughter, and I had to step into a motherly role with my younger sister. I also felt I had to take care of my dad. It was a big responsibility, and I had to learn to deal with the world from a completely different perspective. I realized I couldn't always get things my way. I had to take other people into consideration.

You know, a lot of science is not exciting stuff. It's a day-to-day thing that you have to do methodically and carefully until you get to the end product. My mother's death made me look at the big picture—not the here and now. That was important to me down the road because impatience is just not how science works.

5 In India you pretty much have to decide out of high school what track you're going to take. At age 17, you have to choose whether you're going to be a doctor or an engineer or go for a liberal arts degree. That's good if you know what you want to do. But if you don't, you are forced into a discipline, and you have to follow that course. And if you flunk out, you might not get a second chance because there are age limits for admissions. It's a one-shot deal.

I had always been interested in the sciences, but at that time I had just read *The Fountainhead* by Ayn Rand. The book inspired in me a glorified image of an architect. That image was not based on reality, but I was in love with it, which is part of the danger implicit in having to make such a big decision at 17. I wanted to be an architect, and I shut out everything else from my radar screen.

I applied to architecture school and did not get admitted. What now? There are certain jobs—doctor, teacher, nurse—that are considered acceptable for a woman in India, jobs that allow her to raise a family at the same time. I started to look at options, but all I really had to do was open the door.

At that time, we were living in Chandigarh, in the foothills of the Himalayas. Just looking at these mountain ranges is inspirational. It makes you feel that there are forces that are much bigger than we human beings. It makes you want to understand them.

I started to think about majoring in geology. "What's that?" some people asked. I'm serious. But I went to visit the geology department of nearby Panjab University. There weren't many women. At the time, it seemed like a haven for guys who couldn't get into engineering or physics or whatever it was that they really wanted to do. So they were all looking at me, wondering, "What kind of loser are you?" For a little while I wondered if I should try to enroll in something that would be more acceptable in my social environment, but I'm glad I followed my instincts. I just wanted to better understand the world in which I lived. I guess it all goes back to oxygen and carbon dioxide.

10 Let's say the length of your arms stretched out is the history of Earth. Then you take a nail file and rub your furthest fingernail. You've just removed all of human history. That's one of writer John McPhee's analogies for geologic time that I use when I'm teaching. But the truth is that the scale of

geology is so much bigger than the human experience that it's hard to wrap your mind around it. And at the time I was first introduced to it, there were distractions.

There was only one other girl in my class. I wasn't dating anyone in particular and didn't really want to. It soon became clear to me that it was considered weird to be a single woman who wanted to study rock formations, of all things. I felt like I was on the defensive at a time when I wanted to be open to all that I was learning.

It was stressful, so on geology field trips to the mountains around Chandigarh, I often went off on my own and sketched. The hardest part of sketching mountains, especially the Himalayas, is getting a sense of scale. You can put on paper only little vistas of what you see here and there. And what you see from one vantage point changes completely when you go to another.

That was a good thing to grasp. So I thought: "I should go to graduate school in the United States. The ratio of women to men there has got to be better." Sure enough, I arrive at Washington University in St. Louis, and I'm the only woman in my class.

There I was, in the fall of 1989, plopped down in the middle of this country, where there are no mountains. It was a bit of a shock, but it probably didn't matter where I lived because I always seemed to be up for three nights in a row, studying to catch up. I hadn't had access to the latest textbooks in India. There was so much I didn't have a clue about. One day, a faculty member, Ghislaine Crozaz, asked me, "Would you like to see a piece of Mars?"

It may be hard for you to imagine what it was like for me to hear those 15 words at that time. I was 21. I knew about the manned *Apollo 11* moon landing in 1969, but I didn't know how many there had been after that, or that hundreds of kilograms of moon rocks were available to be studied. So my reaction was, "Whoa! You actually have a piece of Mars?"

She explained that some large impacts had most likely occurred there and chucked pieces of Mars's crust into space, and that they eventually fell to Earth. The first piece of Mars I saw was a very thin slice that we looked at under a microscope. Most scientists who study meteorites believe that this sample came from Mars because the gases trapped in it have the exact same composition as the Mars atmosphere—a very distinctive composition that was determined by the *Viking* spacecraft in 1976. The section must have been about 30 microns thick—a micron is one thousandth of a millimeter—and at that level the minerals are essentially transparent. When polarized light is passed through them, you can see brilliant colors—reds and greens and yellows and blues that are diagnostic of the different minerals.

It was beautiful, but it was strange because it wasn't *weird*. In fact, it was a little disappointing because the sample looked so much like Earth rocks that I'd seen. Then I thought, "What can you learn about the history of this other planet that's supposed to have evolved so differently from ours, yet was able to produce this rock that looks so familiar?"

From that moment on, there was no pulling me away.

Professor Crozaz was using state-of-the-art equipment to analyze the sample's formation. Working with mass spectrometers, where you can apply physics and chemistry to try to understand rocks from Earth and other planets, brought together everything I wanted to do and to learn about.

20   Then Professor Crozaz mentioned that she was going to hunt for meteorites in Antarctica ...

A couple of years later, in December 1992, I was on a snowmobile. Six of us had been dropped by plane on an ice field roughly 100 miles from McMurdo Base, the largest camp in Antarctica.

There are no more meteorites falling on Antarctica than anywhere else in the world. But it's easier to spot a dark rock atop light-colored ice. There's no vegetation, nothing to confuse you. So any rocks you see on the surface of these thick ice sheets in Antarctica have to come from space.

Also, there's a unique conveyer belt–like mechanism that operates in Antarctica. These ice sheets move very slowly from the interior of the continent out toward the shoreline. They've been around for hundreds of thousands of years. During that time, meteorites have fallen on them, become embedded, and gotten carried along. The deep freeze within the ice sheets keeps the meteorites virtually pristine. Sometimes a moving ice sheet gets blocked by a mountain where high velocity winds ablate the surface, eventually exposing the meteorites. As soon as they come up, these meteorites do begin to get weathered and oxidized, but it's much less severe than the weathering that occurs in meteorites found in hotter or wetter environments. So, in many cases, Antarctic meteorites are the better samples to study.

You might find hundreds of meteorites in a zone the size of a football field. What you do is map out the field, then space the members of your team 20 feet apart and systematically drive your snowmobiles up and down the field. When you find the first one, you holler, everybody speeds over, and you jump up and down. Then you find 10 others, and you get sort of used to it.

25   I was in Antarctica for more than two months of that continent's summer. Your sense of time gets warped when there's constant light: The days just slip by. But then the wind would start gusting, and it'd get down to −70 with the windchill, and we'd have to stay in our double-walled tents. Try that for 10 straight days and you'll know time at the other extreme. My best advice for when time becomes interminable is: read.

Every two or three weeks we'd get a mail drop. I'd open a letter from

India and think about boundaries. You know, Indian families can be pretty governing. Parents often make important life decisions for their children regarding career and marriage. I was very lucky that my family supported my decisions. Because they did, I was able to stand in places where only a handful of people have ever been. My boundaries were evolving—they still are. If there's one thing you learn as a scientist, it's never close your mind off to things that seem far-fetched.

I went to grad school in St. Louis, so I know about Mark McGwire. I work at the Field Museum in Chicago, so I know about Sammy Sosa. I've seen how the crowd reacts after home runs, especially record-breaking runs. I would never dive over anyone's back to try to grab a home-run ball. But in the spring of 2003, I got an idea of what the scramble must feel like.

Around midnight on March 26, a meteorite shower pelted houses and streets in Park Forest, a suburb south of Chicago. This was the most densely populated urban area ever hit by a meteorite shower. People reported objects falling through their roofs, and police took a lot of the meteorites as evidence. I headed over to the police station as soon as I heard. They had 15 or 20 pieces all laid out on a table like suspects in a lineup: a rogues' gallery of meteorites! Freshest stuff I've ever seen. To see and hold a meteorite that has been in space only a few hours ago is amazing. And these were chondrites, a class of meteorites that were formed early in the history of our solar system.

I started out thinking that $1 a gram would be a reasonable price to offer. But dealers and collectors descended upon Park Forest, and it became a feeding frenzy. Meteorites that break through windows and roofs are actually worth more on the dealer-collector market. There's nothing more scientifically interesting about the house smashers than any other pieces of meteorite, but their value rises when there's a good story attached. If they crash through your roof, you may have hit the jackpot.

People were trying to sell them for $5 to $25 a gram, so many of the pieces that weighed hundreds of grams were worth a considerable amount. There were times when I felt totally helpless. I tried to explain how much the rocks meant to science, to the museum, to me, but it's hard for someone to be civic-minded when a lot of money is involved. People received offers that were incredibly high. What's more, there was no assigned value. It could change the next day. So it was wild. You'd get a call from someone who'd say: "Don't deal with my sister! She stole the meteorite from me."

I was nervous that the Field was not going to end up with *any* of the meteorites. When you're in a situation like that you can't say to yourself, "I'm a scientist who is above this sort of stuff." There is no high road. If you want samples, you've got to dive in.

We eventually got about three kilograms.

There are actually ways of figuring out through the geochemistry of rocks how long it took to build this planet, what kind of components went into it, and how it was built. These are some of the fundamental questions we're trying to answer. Ultimately, the answers will help us understand how our solar system originated.

We've built a lab at the museum that is able to get at these questions by measuring very, very small quantities of material. It's pretty unusual for a museum to have a laboratory of this sort.

35   Now there are mass spectrometers, and there are *mass spectrometers*. Ours arrived in a several-ton FedEx package on a pallet that was 10 feet by 10 feet. I call it the Beast—not just because of the size, but because it takes some taming to get good results. It's very versatile in terms of the different elements it can analyze, from elements as light as lithium all the way up to uranium. We measure not just meteorites but all kinds of rock samples. The front end has a plasma torch that gets up to many thousands of degrees Celsius, as hot as the sun's surface. It strips electrons off the atoms to make ions. Then we pull the ionized sample into the mass spectrometer, where we can measure elements that may be present in one part in a billion—or less.

We can separate these elements from the rock matrix and look at their exact chemical makeup, their isotope ratios. We can measure radioactive elements so precisely that we can determine how old a particular rock sample is. Examining the nonradioactive elements, we can look at how heavy isotopes or light isotopes are favored and learn something about the process by which they formed. So our lab focuses on timescales and processes.

We also hope to analyze samples that will be returned from future spacecraft missions to other planets and asteroids. Right now there's actually a NASA spacecraft, *Genesis*, sitting between the sun and Earth collecting solar wind, that will deliver a sample to us in September. Basically, it will tell us the exact composition of the outer skin of the sun. Did you know that the sun makes up more than 99.8 percent of the mass of our solar system? That's another one of those mind-boggling facts. Earth is really nothing in comparison. Trying to wrap your mind around the scale of objects in the universe is a constant challenge.

Sometimes it amazes me that I get to try to answer huge questions about our solar system with sophisticated, expensive laboratory equipment. I can remember a time when I couldn't afford a simple camera to photograph the Himalayas.

The very first solid grains formed within the solar system have been very precisely aged at 4,567 million years. I think of it as coincidence that I met the guy who became my husband at a specific moment in that time span.

It happened when I was traveling back to St. Louis from Antarctica in   40
1993. On a whim, I decided to stop off in Hawaii to thaw out for a while.
There was a professor at the University of Hawaii I thought I might want to
work with as a postdoc. Mark was a graduate student there at the time—and
that's how we met.

He's a planetary geologist. As a research professor at Northwestern University, he attends some of the same conferences I go to, but those conferences sometimes host thousands of people. There's no knowing whether we
ever would have crossed paths had I not stopped in Hawaii.

If a third person were to hear our dinner conversations, it would probably be amusing. Or not amusing at all. He might ask, "What's the range of
iron content in the ordinary chondrites?" After dinner, it's "Oh, I down-
loaded this really neat set of *Mars Global Surveyor* images. Wanna take a
look?"

When you think of what happened to the space shuttle *Columbia* last year,
it's hard to get past the enormity of the blow to the families of the astronauts and the rest of us. For me, there was more involved. I'd known one
of the astronauts, Kalpana Chawla, since I was 11. Her family lived in Kar-
nal, a small town between Delhi and Chandigarh. She was about five years
older than me and attended aeronautical engineering school. That was an
unusual choice for a woman. She was interested in learning to fly. I remember being a little in awe of her.

The last time I saw her was in India in the early '80s. I had the opportunity to catch up with her because I go to Houston every year for a planetary
science conference. Many times I thought about getting in touch with her.
But you get so busy, and I never did. It's sad. There I was trying to wrap my
mind around concepts like the depth of geologic time, and I didn't take the
5 or 10 minutes to call her and see how she was doing.

The last year or so I've wondered about having kids. There's work in the   45
lab—teaching, communicating with the public at the museum. It's a challenge. I know women who always knew they wanted children. And I also
know women who have not had them and have no regrets. I don't have any
desire right now. But when I see other women with children, I wonder, "Am
I missing out on something important?" One thing everybody tells me:
There's no perfect time to have children. I'm 36. The unfortunate part is I
don't have too much time to figure it out.

I would love to have, within my lifetime, actual rocks picked up from the
surface of Mars to examine in my laboratory. There's a chance that the
meteorites I've looked at from Mars are samples of atypical rocks on that
planet. At the moment, there are no plans to bring back samples. The cost

of such a mission is likely to be high—certainly higher than NASA's *Discovery* class missions and also the *New Frontiers* missions that are planned. But I remain the eternal optimist.

There are questions that we'll never have the answers to in our lifetime. But we can keep trying and lay down steps for those with that same sense of wonder who come after us.

The simple act of gazing at the stars allows us to see the universe back in time. I remember staring up at the sky with amazement the night after I'd learned that. I must have been 13. It's hard to believe that there is now an asteroid named after that girl.

Astronomers have the prerogative of naming asteroids they discover. They nominate people based on research and accomplishments, and the nominations must be approved by the International Astronomical Union.

50   Carolyn Shoemaker and her husband, Gene, discovered this asteroid. The largest known asteroid is about 600 miles across, but many are much smaller. This particular one is not very big—a few tens of miles perhaps. In 1999 it was named Wadhwa. I've never seen it, and it's unlikely that I ever will. But the great part is that it's a Mars-crossing asteroid. So you never know, one day I just might have an impact on Mars.

Questions

1. Who is the intended audience (or audiences) for this text? What evidence supports your answer?
2. In what ways does this text show evidence of having originated in an interview? In what ways does it show evidence of having been edited? Explain why the text might have been arranged in this manner.

Human Nature

WILLIAM HAZLITT

On the Pleasure of Hating

(1826)

An influential British literary critic and political satirist, William Hazlitt (1778–1830) was part of a circle of politically radical writers in London that included Percy Bysshe Shelley and Lord Byron. Hazlitt published numerous works of both political writing and literary criticism, establishing himself as the period's foremost Shakespearean scholar.

In this passage from the essay "On the Pleasure of Hating," Hazlitt analyzes the psychology of hatred.

Nature seems (the more we look into it) made up of antipathies: without something to hate, we should lose the very spring of thought and action. Life would turn to a stagnant pool, were it not ruffled by the jarring interests, the unruly passions, of men. The white streak in our own fortunes is brightened (or just rendered visible) by making all around it as dark as possible; so the rainbow paints its form upon the cloud. Is it pride? Is it envy? Is it the force of contrast? Is it weakness or malice? But so it is, that there is a secret affinity, a *hankering* after, evil in the human mind, and that it takes a perverse, but a fortunate delight in mischief, since it is a never-failing source of satisfaction. Pure good soon grows insipid, wants variety and spirit. Pain is a bittersweet; which never surfeits. Love turns, with a little indulgence, to indifference or disgust: hatred alone is immortal. Do we not see this principle at work everywhere? Animals torment and worry one another without mercy: children kill flies for sport: every one reads accidents and offences in a newspaper as the cream of the jest: a whole town runs to be present at a fire, and the spectator by no means exults to see it extinguished. It is better to have it so, but it diminishes the interest; and our feelings take part with our passions rather than with our understandings. Men assemble in crowds, with eager enthusiasm, to witness a tragedy: but if there were an execution going forward in the next street, as Mr. Burke[1] observes, the theatre would be left empty. A strange cur in a village, an idiot, a crazy woman, are set upon and baited by the whole community. Public nuisances are in the nature of public benefits. How long did the Pope, the Bourbons,[2] and the Inquisition keep the people of England in breath, and supply them with nicknames to vent their spleen[3] upon! Had they done us any harm of late? No: but we have always a quantity of superfluous bile upon the stomach, and we wanted an object to let it out upon. How loth were we to give up our pious belief in ghosts and witches, because we liked to persecute the one, and frighten ourselves to death with the other! It is not the quality so much as the quantity of excitement that we are anxious about: we cannot bear a state of indifference and *ennui:*[4] the mind seems to abhor a *vacuum* as much as ever matter was supposed to.

Questions

1. What judgment does Hazlitt make about human nature?
2. Describe Hazlitt's tone in this passage, providing examples from the work. In what way does this tone affect his argument?

---

1   *but if ... empty* Cf. Edmund Burke, *A Philosophical Enquiry into the Origin Of Our Ideas of the Sublime and Beautiful* (1757), 1.15 "Chuse a day on which to represent the most sublime and affecting tragedy we have; ... and when you have collected your audience, ... let it be reported that a state criminal of high rank is on the point of being executed in the adjoining square; in a moment the emptiness of the theatre would demonstrate the comparative weakness of the imitative arts."
2   *Bourbons* House of Bourbon, a French royal house that ruled from the sixteenth century until the French Revolution.
3   *vent their spleen* To express anger. In this period the spleen was thought to be the center of human emotion.
4   *ennui* Boredom.

GEORGE ELIOT

Only Temper

(1860)

George Eliot (1819–80), born Mary Ann Evans, was an English writer now famous as an important novelist. Amongst her works are the novels Adam Bede *(1859),* The Mill on the Floss *(1860),* Silas Marner *(1861),* Felix Holt *(1866), and* Middlemarch *(1871). Eliot was also a distinguished essayist.*

In this excerpt from the essay "Only Temper," Eliot discusses society's attitude towards expressions of bad temper.

What is temper? Its primary meaning, the proportion and mode in which qualities are mingled, is much neglected in popular speech, yet even here the word often carries a reference to an habitual state or general tendency of the organism in distinction from what are held to be specific virtues and vices. As people confess to bad memory without expecting to sink in mental reputation, so we hear a man declared to have a bad temper and yet glorified as the possessor of every high quality. When he errs or in any way commits himself, his temper is accused, not his character, and it is understood that but for a brutal bearish mood he is kindness itself. If he kicks small animals, swears violently at a servant who mistakes orders, or is grossly rude to his wife, it is remarked apologetically that these things mean nothing— they are all temper.

Certainly there is a limit to this form of apology, and the forgery of a bill, or the ordering of goods without any prospect of paying for them, has never been set down to an unfortunate habit of sulkiness or of irascibility. But on the whole there is a peculiar exercise of indulgence towards the manifestations of bad temper which tends to encourage them, so that we are in danger of having among us a number of virtuous persons who conduct themselves detestably, just as we have hysterical patients who, with sound organs, are apparently labouring under many sorts of organic disease. Let it be admitted however, that a man may be "a good fellow" and yet have a bad temper, so bad that we recognise his merits with reluctance, and are inclined to resent his occasionally amiable behaviour as an unfair demand on our admiration.

[Dion] Touchwood is that kind of good fellow. He is by turns insolent, quarrelsome, repulsively haughty to innocent people who approach him with respect, neglectful of his friends, angry in face of legitimate demands, procrastinating in the fulfilment of such demands, prompted to rude words and harsh looks by a moody disgust with his fellow-men in general—and yet, as everybody will assure you, the soul of honour, a steadfast friend, a defender of the oppressed, an affectionate-hearted creature. Pity that, after a certain experience of his moods, his intimacy becomes insupportable! A man who uses his balmorals to tread on your toes with much frequency and an unmistakeable emphasis may prove a fast friend in adversity, but meanwhile your adversity has not arrived and your toes are tender. The daily sneer or growl at your remarks is not to be made amends for by a possible eulogy or defence of your understanding against depreciators who may not present themselves, and on an occasion which may never arise. I cannot submit to a chronic state of blue and green bruise as a form of insurance against an accident.

Touchwood's bad temper is of the contradicting pugnacious sort. He is the honourable gentleman in opposition, whatever proposal or proposition may be broached, and when others join him he secretly damns their superfluous agreement, quickly discovering that his way of stating the case is not exactly theirs. An invitation or any sign of expectation throws him into an attitude of refusal. Ask his concurrence in a benevolent measure: he will not decline to give it, because he has a real sympathy with good aims; but he complies resentfully, though where he is let alone he will do much more than any one would have thought of asking for. No man would shrink with greater sensitiveness from the imputation of not paying his debts, yet when a bill is sent in with any promptitude he is inclined to make the tradesman wait for the money he is in such a hurry to get. One sees that this antagonistic temper must be much relieved by finding a particular object, and that its worst moments must be those where the mood is that of vague resistance, there being nothing specific to oppose. Touchwood is never so little engaging as when he comes down to breakfast with a cloud on his brow, after parting from you the night before with an affectionate effusiveness at the end of a confidential conversation which has assured you of mutual understanding. Impossible that you can have committed any offence. If mice have disturbed him, that is not your fault; but, nevertheless, your cheerful greeting had better not convey any reference to the weather, else it will be met by a sneer which, taking you unawares, may give you a crushing sense that you make a poor figure with your cheerfulness, which was not asked for. Some daring person perhaps introduces another topic, and uses the delicate flattery of appealing to Touchwood for his opinion, the topic being included in his favourite studies. An indistinct muttering, with a look at the carving-knife in reply, teaches that daring person how ill he has chosen a

market for his deference. If Touchwood's behaviour affects you very closely you had better break your leg in the course of the day: his bad temper
will then vanish at once: he will take a painful journey on your behalf; he
will sit up with you night after night; he will do all the work of your department so as to save you from any loss in consequence of your accident; he
will be even uniformly tender to you till you are well on your legs again,
when he will some fine morning insult you without provocation, and make
you wish that his generous goodness to you had not closed your lips against
retort.

It is not always necessary that a friend should break his leg for Touch-   5
wood to feel compunction and endeavour to make amends for his bearish-
ness or insolence. He becomes spontaneously conscious that he has misbe-
haved, and he is not only ashamed of himself, but has the better prompting
to try and heal any wound he has inflicted. Unhappily the habit of being
offensive "without meaning it" leads usually to a way of making amends
which the injured person cannot but regard as a being amiable without
meaning it. The kindnesses, the complimentary indications or assurances,
are apt to appear in the light of a penance adjusted to the foregoing laps-
es, and by the very contrast they offer call up a keener memory of the wrong
they atone for. They are not a spontaneous prompting of good will, but an
elaborate compensation. And, in fact, Dion's atoning friendliness has a ring
of artificiality. Because he formerly disguised his good feeling towards you
he now expresses more than he quite feels. It is in vain. Having made you
extremely uncomfortable last week he has absolutely diminished his power
of making you happy to-day: he struggles against this result by excessive
effort, but he has taught you to observe his fitfulness rather than to be
warmed by his episodic show of regard.

Questions

1. What exactly does Eliot argue here?
2. Here, as in her novels, Eliot has a tendency towards long sentences.
   Choose one long sentence that you feel works well and try to explain
   why. Also, choose one long sentence that seems to you to be too long
   or confusing, and again, try to explain why.
3. Do you agree that there is a distinction between "character" and "temper" as Eliot uses these words? Provide evidence for your argument.

MARK TWAIN

Corn-Pone Opinions

(1923)

Born Samuel Langhorne Clemens, Mark Twain (1835–1910) grew up in Missouri, and at 22 became a Mississippi river pilot. Five years later he began writing for a living, and was soon publishing humorous tales and delivering public lectures. The works for which he is now most famous include The Adventures of Tom Sawyer *(1876),* Life on the Mississippi *(1883), and* The Adventures of Huckleberry Finn *(1884).*

In this essay, published posthumously, Twain explores the human urge to conform to public opinion.

Fifty years ago, when I was a boy of fifteen and helping to inhabit a Missourian village on the banks of the Mississippi, I had a friend whose society was very dear to me because I was forbidden by my mother to partake of it. He was a gay and impudent and satirical and delightful young black man— a slave—who daily preached sermons from the top of his master's woodpile, with me for sole audience. He imitated the pulpit style of the several clergymen of the village, and did it well, and with fine passion and energy. To me he was a wonder. I believed he was the greatest orator in the United States and would some day be heard from. But it did not happen; in the distribution of rewards he was overlooked. It is the way, in this world.

He interrupted his preaching, now and then, to saw a stick of wood; but the sawing was a pretense—he did it with his mouth; exactly imitating the sound the bucksaw makes in shrieking its way through the wood. But it served its purpose; it kept his master from coming out to see how the work was getting along. I listened to the sermons from the open window of a lumber room at the back of the house. One of his texts was this:

"You tell me whar a man gits his corn pone,[1] en I'll tell you what his 'pinions is."

I can never forget it. It was deeply impressed upon me. By my mother. Not upon my memory, but elsewhere. She had slipped in upon me while I was absorbed and not watching. The black philosopher's idea was that a

---

1 *corn pone* Corn bread made with salt, water, and corn meal.

man is not independent, and cannot afford views which might interfere with his bread and butter. If he would prosper, he must train with the majority; in matters of large moment, like politics and religion, he must think and feel with the bulk of his neighbors, or suffer damage in his social standing and in his business prosperities. He must restrict himself to corn-pone opinions—at least on the surface. He must get his opinions from other people; he must reason out none for himself; he must have no first-hand views.

I think Jerry was right, in the main, but I think he did not go far enough.   5

1. It was his idea that a man conforms to the majority view of his locality by calculation and intention.

This happens, but I think it is not the rule.

2. It was his idea that there is such a thing as a first-hand opinion; an original opinion; an opinion which is coldly reasoned out in a man's head, by a searching analysis of the facts involved, with the heart unconsulted, and the jury room closed against outside influences. It may be that such an opinion has been born somewhere, at some time or other, but I suppose it got away before they could catch it and stuff it and put it in the museum.

I am persuaded that a coldly-thought-out and independent verdict upon a fashion in clothes, or manners, or literature, or politics, or religion, or any other matter that is projected into the field of our notice and interest, is a most rare thing—if it has indeed ever existed.

A new thing in costume appears—the flaring hoopskirt,[1] for example—   10 and the passers-by are shocked, and the irreverent laugh. Six months later everybody is reconciled; the fashion has established itself; it is admired, now, and no one laughs. Public opinion resented it before, public opinion accepts it now, and is happy in it. Why? Was the resentment reasoned out? Was the acceptance reasoned out? No. The instinct that moves to conformity did the work. It is our nature to conform; it is a force which not many can successfully resist. What is its seat? The inborn requirement of self-approval. We all have to bow to that; there are no exceptions. Even the woman who refuses from first to last to wear the hoopskirt comes under that law and is its slave; she could not wear the skirt and have her own approval; and that she *must* have, she cannot help herself. But as a rule our self-approval has its source in but one place and not elsewhere—the approval of other people. A person of vast consequences can introduce any kind of novelty in dress and the general world will presently adopt it— moved to do it, in the first place, by the natural instinct to passively yield to that vague something recognized as authority, and in the second place by the human instinct to train with the multitude and have its approval. An empress introduced the hoopskirt, and we know the result. A nobody intro-

---

1   *hoopskirt* Popularized by Empress Eugenie, wife of France's Napoleon III, the fashionably wide skirts of the 1850s and 1860s required an underskirt with sewn-in hoops to support its bell-like shape.

duced the bloomer,[1] and we know the result. If Eve should come again, in her ripe renown, and reintroduce her quaint styles—well, we know what would happen. And we should be cruelly embarrassed, along at first.

The hoopskirt runs its course and disappears. Nobody reasons about it. One woman abandons the fashion; her neighbor notices this and follows her lead; this influences the next woman; and so on and so on, and presently the skirt has vanished out of the world, no one knows how nor why; nor cares, for that matter. It will come again, by and by; and in due course will go again.

Twenty-five years ago, in England, six or eight wine glasses stood grouped by each person's plate at a dinner party, and they were used, not left idle and empty; today there are but three or four in the group, and the average guest sparingly uses about two of them. We have not adopted this new fashion yet, but we shall do it presently. We shall not think it out; we shall merely conform, and let it go at that. We get our notions and habits and opinions from outside influences; we do not have to study them out.

Our table manners, and company manners, and street manners change from time to time, but the changes are not reasoned out; we merely notice and conform. We are creatures of outside influences; as a rule we do not think, we only imitate. We cannot invent standards that will stick; what we mistake for standards are only fashions, and perishable. We may continue to admire them, but we drop the use of them. We notice this in literature. Shakespeare is a standard, and fifty years ago we used to write tragedies which we couldn't tell from—from somebody else's; but we don't do it any more, now. Our prose standard, three quarters of a century ago, was ornate and diffuse; some authority or other changed it in the direction of compactness and simplicity, and conformity followed, without argument. The historical novel starts up suddenly, and sweeps the land. Everybody writes one, and the nation is glad. We had historical novels before; but nobody read them, and the rest of us conformed—without reasoning it out. We are conforming in the other way, now, because it is another case of everybody.

The outside influences are always pouring in upon us, and we are always obeying their orders and accepting their verdicts. The Smiths like the new play; the Joneses go to see it, and they copy the Smith verdict. Morals, religions, politics, get their following from surrounding influences and atmospheres, almost entirely; not from study, not from thinking. A man must and will have his own approval first of all, in each and every moment and circumstance of his life—even if he must repent of a self-approved act the

---

1   *bloomer* Amelia Bloomer (1818–94), American editor of the feminist periodical *The Lily*, urged women to reject the restrictive fashions of the 1850s as unhealthy symbols of their inferior status. Despite national ridicule, Bloomer wore an unusual costume that consisted of long pantaloons gathered at the ankle and a knee-length skirt for nearly six years during the 1850s.

moment after its commission, in order to get his self-approval *again*: but, speaking in general terms, a man's self-approval in the large concerns of life has its source in the approval of the peoples about him, and not in a searching personal examination of the matter. Mohammedans are Mohammedans because they are born and reared among that sect, not because they have thought it out and can furnish sound reasons for being Mohammedans; we know why Catholics are Catholics; why Presbyterians are Presbyterians; why Baptists are Baptists; why Mormons are Mormons; why thieves are thieves; why monarchists are monarchists; why Republicans are Republicans and Democrats, Democrats. We know it is a matter of association and sympathy, not reasoning and examination; that hardly a man in the world has an opinion upon morals, politics, or religion which he got otherwise than through his associations and sympathies. Broadly speaking, there are none but corn-pone opinions. And broadly speaking, corn-pone stands for self-approval. Self-approval is acquired mainly from the approval of other people. The result is conformity. Sometimes conformity has a sordid business interest—the bread-and-butter interest—but not in most cases, I think. I think that in the majority of cases it is unconscious and not calculated; that it is born of the human being's natural yearning to stand well with his fellows and have their inspiring approval and praise—a yearning which is commonly so strong and so insistent that it cannot be effectually resisted, and must have its way.

A political emergency brings out the corn-pone opinion in fine force in its two chief varieties—the pocketbook variety, which has its origin in self-interest, and the bigger variety, the sentimental variety—the one which can't bear to be outside the pale; can't bear to be in disfavor; can't endure the averted face and the cold shoulder; wants to stand well with his friends, wants to be smiled upon, wants to be welcome, wants to hear the precious words, "*He's* on the right track!" Uttered, perhaps by an ass, but still an ass of high degree, an ass whose approval is gold and diamonds to a smaller ass, and confers glory and honor and happiness, and membership in the herd. For these gauds[1] many a man will dump his life-long principles into the street, and his conscience along with them. We have seen it happen. In some millions of instances.

Men think they think upon great political questions, and they do; but they think with their party, not independently; they read its literature, but not that of the other side; they arrive at convictions, but they are drawn from a partial view of the matter in hand and are of no particular value. They swarm with their party, they feel with their party, they are happy in their party's approval; and where the party leads they will follow, whether for right and honor, or through blood and dirt and a mush of mutilated morals.

15

---

1 *gauds* Showy ornaments.

In our late canvass half of the nation passionately believed that in silver lay salvation,[1] the other half as passionately believed that that way lay destruction. Do you believe that a tenth part of the people, on either side, had any rational excuse for having an opinion about the matter at all? I studied that mighty question to the bottom—came out empty. Half of our people passionately believe in high tariff,[2] the other half believe otherwise. Does this mean study and examination, or only feeling? The latter, I think. I have deeply studied that question, too—and didn't arrive. We all do no end of feeling, and we mistake it for thinking. And out of it we get an aggregation which we consider a boon. Its name is Public Opinion. It is held in reverence. It settles everything. Some think it the Voice of God.

Questions

1. Twain's essay opens with a humorous account of his friend, Jerry. How does this anecdote establish the essay's tone?
2. How does Twain's view of public opinion differ from Jerry's?
3. According to Twain, "a coldly-thought-out and independent verdict ... is a most rare thing—if it has indeed ever existed" (paragraph 9). How does such an assertion affect Twain's authority as a writer?

---

1 *In our late canvass ... lay salvation* One of the major issues of the American presidential election of 1896 was the debate over free silver. Strongly endorsing the gold standard, Republican William McKinley earned half of the popular vote to defeat Democrat William Jennings Bryan, a proponent of the unlimited coinage of silver.

2 *high tariff* McKinley supported high taxes on imported goods to protect American industry.

STANLEY MILGRAM

Behavioral Study of Obedience

(1963)

Stanley Milgram (1933–84) is regarded as one of the most important social psychologists of the twentieth century. He is best known for his human obedience experiments, his study of the effects of televised antisocial behaviour, and his experiments using the "six-degrees of separation" theory.

In the following excerpts from the article "Behavioral Study of Obedience," Milgram reports the results of an experiment on obedience to authority conducted at Yale University.

Obedience is as basic an element in the structure of social life as one can point to. Some system of authority is a requirement of all communal living, and it is only the man dwelling in isolation who is not forced to respond, through defiance or submission, to the commands of others. Obedience, as a determinant of behavior, is of particular relevance to our time. It has been reliably established that from 1933–45 millions of innocent persons were systematically slaughtered on command. Gas chambers were built, death camps were guarded, daily quotas of corpses were produced with the same efficiency as the manufacture of appliances. These inhumane policies may have originated in the mind of a single person, but they could only be carried out on a massive scale if a very large number of persons obeyed orders....

General Procedure

A procedure was devised which seems useful as a tool for studying obedience (Milgram, 1961). It consists of ordering a naive subject to administer electric shock to a victim. A simulated shock generator is used, with 30 clearly marked voltage levels that range from 15 to 450 volts. The instrument bears verbal designations that range from Slight Shock to Danger: Severe Shock. The responses of the victim, who is a trained confederate of the experimenter, are standardized. The orders to administer shocks are given to the naive subject in the context of a "learning experiment" ostensibly set up to study the effects of punishment on memory. As the experiment proceeds the naive subject is commanded to administer increasingly more intense shocks to the victim, even to a point of reaching the level marked Danger: Severe Shock. Internal resistances become stronger, and at a certain point the subject refuses to go on with the experiment. Behavior prior to this rupture is considered "obedience," in that the subject complies with the commands of the experimenter. The point of rupture is the act of disobedience. A quantitative value is assigned to the subject's performance based on the maximum intensity shock he is willing to administer before he refuses to participate further. Thus for any particular subject and for any particular experimental condition the degree of obedience may be specified with a numerical value. The crux of the study is to systematically vary the factors believed to alter the degree of obedience to the experimental commands....

METHOD

Subjects

The subjects were 40 males between the ages of 20 and 50, drawn from New Haven and surrounding communities. Subjects were obtained by a newspaper advertisement and direct mail solicitations. Those who responded to the appeal believed they were to participate in a study of memory and learning at Yale University. A wide range of occupations is represented in the sample. Typical subjects were postal clerks, high school teachers, salesmen, engineers, and laborers. Subjects ranged in educational level from one who had not finished elementary school, to those who had doctorate and other professional degrees. They were paid $4.50 for their participation in the experiment. However, subjects were told that payment was simply for coming to the laboratory, and that the money was theirs no matter what happened after they arrived....

Personnel and Locale

The experiment was conducted on the grounds of Yale University in the elegant interaction laboratory. (This detail is relevant to the perceived legitimacy of the experiment. In further variations, the experiment was dissociated from the university, with consequences for performance.) The role of experimenter was played by a 31-year-old high school teacher of biology. His manner was impassive, and his appearance somewhat stern throughout the experiment. He was dressed in a gray technician's coat. The victim was played by a 47-year-old accountant, trained for the role; he was of Irish-American stock, whom most observers found mild-mannered and likeable.

Procedure

5   One naive subject and one victim (an accomplice) performed in each experiment. A pretext had to be devised that would justify the administra-

tion of electric shock by the naive subject. This was effectively accomplished by the cover story. After a general introduction on the presumed relation between punishment and learning, subjects were told:

> But actually, we know *very little* about the effect of punishment on learning, because almost no truly scientific studies have been made of it in human beings.
>
> For instance, we don't know how *much* punishment is best for learning—and we don't know how much difference it makes as to who is giving the punishment, whether an adult learns best from a younger or an older person than himself—or many things of that sort.
>
> So in this study we are bringing together a number of adults of different occupations and ages. And we're asking some of them to be teachers and some of them to be learners.
>
> We want to find out just what effect different people have on each other as teachers and learners, and also what effect *punishment* will have on learning in this situation.
>
> Therefore, I'm going to ask one of you to be the teacher here tonight and the other one to be the learner.
>
> Does either of you have a preference?

Subjects then drew slips of paper from a hat to determine who would be the teacher and who would be the learner in the experiment. The drawing was rigged so that the naive subject was always the teacher and the accomplice always the learner. (Both slips contained the word "Teacher.") Immediately after the drawing, the teacher and learner were taken to an adjacent room and the learner was strapped into an "electric chair" apparatus.

The experimenter explained that the straps were to prevent excessive movement while the learner was being shocked. The effect was to make it impossible of him to escape from the situation. An electrode was attached to the learner's wrist, and electrode paste was applied "to avoid blisters and burns." Subjects were told that the electrode was attached to the shock generator in the adjoining room.

In order to improve credibility the experimenter declared, in response to a question by the learner: "Although shocks can be extremely painful, they cause no permanent tissue damage."

Learning task. The lesson administered by the subject was a paired-associate learning task. The subject read a series of word pairs to the learner, and then read the first word of the pair along with four terms. The learner was to indicate which of the four terms had originally been paired with the first word. He communicated his answer by pressing one of four switches in front of him, which in turn lit up one of four numbered quadrants in an answer-box located atop the shock generator.

10   *Shock generator.* The instrument panel consists of 30 lever switches set in a horizontal line. Each switch is clearly labeled with a voltage designation that ranges from 15 to 450 volts. There is a 15-volt increment from one switch to the next going from left to right. In addition, the following verbal designations are clearly indicated for groups of four switches going from left to right: Slight Shock, Moderate Shock, Strong Shock, Intense Shock, Extremely Intense Shock, Danger: Severe Shock. (Two switches after this last designation are simply marked XXX.)

Upon depressing a switch: a pilot light corresponding to each switch is illuminated in bright red; an electric buzzing is heard; an electric blue light, labeled "voltage energizer," flashes; the dial on the voltage meter swings to the right; various relay clicks are sounded.

The upper left-hand corner of the generator is labeled Shock generator, Type ZLB, Dyson Instrument Company, Waltham, Mass. Output 15 volts–450 volts.

Details of the instrument were carefully handled to insure an appearance of authenticity. The panel was engraved by precision industrial engravers, and all components were of high quality. No subject in the experiment suspected that the instrument was merely a simulated shock generator.

Sample shock. Each naive subject is given a sample shock on the shock generator, prior to beginning his run as teacher. This shock is always 45 volts, and is applied by pressing the third switch of the generator. The shock is applied to the wrist of the naive subject, and has its source in a 45-volt battery wired to the generator. This further convinces the subject of the authenticity of the generator.

15   *Shock instructions.* The subject is told to administer a shock to the learner each time he gives a wrong response. Moreover—and this is the key command—the subject is instructed to "move one level higher on the shock generator each time the learner flashes a wrong answer." He is also instructed to announce the voltage level before administering a shock. This serves to continually remind subjects of the increasing intensity of shocks administered to the learner.

Preliminary and regular run. Pretests revealed that the procedure of reading words and administering shocks requires some practice before it can be handled smoothly. Therefore, immediately preceding the regular run, the teacher is given a preliminary series of 10 words to read to the learner. There are 3 neutral words in the practice series (i.e., words that the learner answers correctly), so that the shocks are administered for 7 of the words, with the maximum shock of 105 volts (moderate shock). Almost all subjects master the procedure by the time the preliminary run is over.

Subjects are then presented with a second list, and are told that the procedure is the same as for the first list; the experimenter adds however:

When you get to the bottom of the list, repeat it over again, and continue giving shocks, until the learner has learned all the pairs correctly.

The experimenter instructs the subject to,

start from 15 volts and increase the shock level one step each time the learner gives a wrong answer.

Feedback from the victim. In all conditions the learner gives a predetermined set of responses to the word pair test, based on a schedule of approximately three wrong answers to one correct answer. In the present experimental condition no vocal response or other sign of protest is heard from the learner until Shock Level 300 is reached. When the 300-volt shock is administered, the learner pounds on the wall of the room in which he is bound to the electric chair. The pounding can be heard by the subject. From this point on, the learner's answers no longer appear on the four-way panel.

At this juncture, subjects ordinarily turn to the experimenter for guidance. The experimenter instructs the subject to treat absence of a response as a wrong answer, and to shock the subject according to the usual schedule. He advises the subject to allow 5–10 seconds before considering no response as a wrong answer, and to increase the shock level one step each time the learner fails to respond correctly. The learner's pounding is repeated after the 315-volt shock is administered; afterwards he is not heard from, nor do his answers reappear on the four-way signal box.   20

Experimenter feedback. At various points in the experiment the subject may turn to the experimenter for advice on whether he should continue to administer shocks. Or he may indicate that he does not wish to go on. It was important to standardize the experimenter's responses to these inquiries and reactions.

If the subject indicated his unwillingness to go on, the experimenter responded with a sequence of "prods," using as many as necessary to bring the subject into line.

Prod 1: Please continue. *or* Please go on.

Prod 2: The experiment requires that you continue.

Prod 3: It is absolutely essential that you continue.

Prod 4: You have no other choice, you *must* go on.

The prods were always made in sequence: Only if Prod 1 had been unsuccessful, could Prod 2 be used. If the subject still refused to obey the experimenter after Prod 4, the experiment was terminated. The experimenter's tone of voice was at all times firm, but not impolite. The sequence was begun anew on each occasion that the subject balked or showed reluctance to follow orders.

Special prods. If the subject asked if the learner was liable to suffer permanent physical injury, the experimenter said:

Although the shocks may be painful, there is no permanent tissue damage, so please go on. [Followed by Prods 2, 3, and 4 if necessary.]

If the subject said that the learner did not want to go on, the experimenter replied:

Whether the learner likes it or not, you must go on until he has learned all the word pairs correctly. So please go on. [Followed by Prods 2, 3, and 4 if necessary.]

Dependent Measures

25 The primary dependent measure for any subject is the maximum shock he administers before he refuses to go any further. In principle this may vary from 0 (for a subject who refuses to administer even the first shock) to 30 (for a subject who administers the highest shock on the generator). A subject who breaks off the experiment at any point prior to administering the thirtieth shock level is termed a *defiant subject*. One who complies with experimental command fully, and proceeds to administer all shock levels commanded, is termed an *obedient* subject....

Interview and dehoax. Following the experiment, subjects were interviewed; open-ended questions, projective measures, and attitude scales were employed. After the interview, procedures were undertaken to assure that the subject would leave the laboratory in a state of well being. A friendly reconciliation was arranged between the subject and the victim, and an effort was made to reduce any tensions that arose as a result of the experiment.

RESULTS

Preliminary Notions

Before giving an account of the experimental results, it is instructive to consider how persons predict others will perform when commanded to administer powerful shocks to another person. Fourteen Yale seniors, all psychology majors, were provided with a detailed description of the experimental situation. They were asked to reflect carefully on it, and to predict the behavior of 100 hypothetical subjects. More specifically, they were instructed to plot the distribution of obedience of "100 Americans of diverse occupations, and ranging in age from 20 to 50 years," who were placed in the experimental situation.

There was considerable agreement among the respondents on the expected behavior of hypothetical subjects. All respondents predicted that only an insignificant minority would go through to the end of the shock series. (The estimates ranged from 0 to 3%; i.e., the most "pessimistic" member of the class predicted that of 100 persons, 3 would continue through to the most potent shock available on the shock generator—450 volts.) The class mean was 1.2%. The question was also posed informally to colleagues of the author, and the most general feeling was that few if any subjects would go beyond the designation Very Strong Shock.

Result of Experiment 1

Subjects accept situation. With few exceptions subjects were convinced of the reality of the experimental situation, that they were administering shocks to another person, and the most potent shocks were extremely painful. In the post-experimental interview subjects were asked: "How painful to the learner were the last few shocks that you administered to him?" Subjects were instructed to indicate their answers on a printed 14-point scale ranging from "Not at all painful" to "Extremely painful." The modal response was 14 (Extremely painful) with the mean at 13.42.

Signs of extreme tension. Many subjects showed signs of nervousness in the 30 experimental situation, and especially upon administering the more powerful shocks. In a large number of cases the degree of tension reached extremes that are rarely seen in sociopsychological laboratory studies. Subjects were observed to sweat, tremble, stutter, bite their lips, groan, and dig their fingernails into their flesh. These were characteristic rather than exceptional responses to the experiment.

One sign of tension was the regular occurrence of nervous laughing fits. Fourteen of the 40 subjects showed definite signs of nervous laughter and smiling. The laughter seemed entirely out of place, even bizarre. Full-blown, uncontrollable seizures were observed for 3 subjects. On one occasion we observed a seizure so violently convulsive that it was necessary to call a halt to the experiment. The subject, a 46-year old encyclopedia salesman, was seriously embarrassed by his untoward and uncontrollable behavior. In the post-experimental interviews subjects took such pains to point out that they were not sadistic types, and that the laughter did not mean they enjoyed shocking the victim.

Table 1: Distribution of Breakoff Points

Verbal designation and voltage indication	Number of subjects for whom this was maximum shock
Slight Shock	
15	0
30	0
45	0
60	0
Moderate Shock	
75	0
90	0
105	0
120	0
Strong Shock	
135	0
150	0
165	0
180	0
Very Strong Shock	
195	0
210	0
225	0
240	0
Intense Shock	
255	0
270	0
285	0
300	5
Extreme Intensity Shock	
315	4
330	2
345	1
360	1
Danger: Severe Shock	
375	1
390	0
405	0
420	0
XXX	
435	0
450	26

Distribution of scores. It had been conjectured that persons would not, in general, agree to administer shocks beyond the level designated Very Strong Shock. The distribution of maximum shocks for this experiment is shown in Table 1. The obtained distribution of scores deviates radically from the prediction.

Upon command of the experimenter, each of the 40 subjects went beyond the expected breakoff point. No subject stopped prior to administering Shock Level 20. (At this level—300 volts—the victim kicks on the wall and no longer provides answers to the teacher's multiple-choice questions.)

Of the 40 subjects, 5 refused to obey the experimental commands beyond the 300-volt level. Four more subjects administered one further shock, and then refused to go on. Two broke off at the 330-volt level, and 1 each at 345, 360, and 375 volts. Thus a total of 14 subjects defied the experimenter. It is instructive to reprint their remarks at the point of defiance, as transcribed from the tape recordings:

[0124] I think he's trying to communicate, he's knocking.... Well it's not fair to shock the guy ... these are terrific volts. I don't think this is very humane.... Oh, I can't go on with this; no this isn't right. It's a hell of an experiment. The guy is suffering in there. No, I don't want to go on. This is crazy. [Subject refused to administer more shocks.]

[0123] He's banging in there. I'm gonna chicken out. I'd like to continue, but I can't do that to a man.... I'm sorry I can't do that to a man. I'll hurt his heart. You take your check.... No really, I couldn't do it.

These subjects were frequently in a highly agitated and even angered state. Sometimes, verbal protest was at a minimum, and the subject simply got up from his chair in front of the shock generator, and indicated that he wished to leave the laboratory.   35

Of the 40 subjects, 26 obeyed the orders of the experimenter to the end, proceeding to punish the victim until they reached the most potent shock available on the shock generator. At that point, the experimenter called a halt to the sessions. (The maximum shock is labeled 450 volts, and is two steps beyond the designation: Danger: Severe Shock.) Although obedient subjects continued to administer shocks, they often did so under extreme stress. Some expressed reluctance to administer shocks beyond the 300-volt level, and displayed fears similar to those who defied the experimenter; yet they obeyed.

After the maximum shocks had been delivered, and the experimenter called a halt to the proceedings, many obedient subjects heaved sighs of relief, mopped their brows, rubbed their fingers over their eyes, or nervously fumbled cigarettes. Some shook their heads, apparently in regret.

Some subjects had remained calm throughout the experiment, and displayed only minimal signs of tension from beginning to end.

DISCUSSION

The experiment yielded two findings that were surprising. The first finding concerns the sheer strength of obedient tendencies manifested in this situation. Subjects have learned from childhood that it is a fundamental breach of moral conduct to hurt another person against his will. Yet, 26 subjects abandon this tenet in following the instructions of an authority who has no special powers to enforce his commands. To disobey would bring no material loss to the subject; no punishment would ensue. It is clear from the remarks and outward behavior of many participants that in punishing the victim they are often acting against their own values. Subjects often expressed deep disapproval of shocking a man in the face of his objections, and others denounced it as stupid and senseless. Yet the majority complied with the experimental commands. This outcome was surprising from two perspectives: first, from the standpoint of predictions made in the questionnaire described earlier. (Here, however, it is possible that the remoteness of the respondents from the actual situation, and the difficulty of conveying to them the concrete details of the experiment, could account for the serious underestimation of obedience.)

But the results were also unexpected to persons who observed the experiment in progress, through one-way mirrors. Observers often uttered expressions of disbelief upon seeing a subject administrate more powerful shocks to the victim. These persons had a full acquaintance with the details of the situation, and yet systematically underestimated the amount of obedience that subjects would display.

40   The second unanticipated effect was the extraordinary tension generated by the procedures. One might suppose that a subject would simply break off or continue as his conscience dictated. Yet, this is very far from what happened. There were striking reactions of tension and emotional strain.

Questions

1. What was the purpose of the experiment conducted at Yale?
2. What elements were included to make the experiment seem authentic? How did the experimenters signify authority to the naive subjects?
3. What is the effect of the very scientific style in which this paper is written?
4. What does the term "naive subject" refer to, literally? What does it seem to imply figuratively?

Changes of Mind

(1982)

Nicholson Baker (1957–) is an American novelist and essayist. His novels include The Mezzanine *(1988),* Vox *(1992),* The Fermata *(1994), and* Checkpoint *(2004). In 1999 he established a non-profit organization, the American Newspaper Repository, to rescue library newspaper archives planned for destruction.*

This essay examines the generally overlooked process of changing one's mind.

If your life is like my life, there are within it brief stretches, usually a week to ten days long, when your mind achieves a polished and freestanding coherence. The chanting tapeloops of poetry anthologies, the crumbly pieces of philosophy, the unsmelted barbarisms, the litter torn from huge collisions of abandoned theories—all this nomadic suborbital junk suddenly, like a milling street crowd in a movie-musical, re-forms itself into a proud, pinstriped, top-hatted commonwealth. Your opinions become neat and unruffleable. Every new toy design, every abuse of privilege or gesture of philanthropy, every witnessed squabble at the supermarket checkout counter, is smoothly remade into evidence for five or six sociological truths. Puffed up enough to be charitable, you stop urging your point with twisting jabs of your fork; you happily concede winnable arguments to avoid injuring the feelings of your friends; your stock of proverbs from Samuel Johnson[1] seems elegant and apt in every context; you are firm, you think fast, you offer delicately phrased advice.

Then one Thursday, out on a minor errand, you inexplicably come to a new conclusion ("Keynesian economics[2] is spent"), and it—like the fetching plastic egg that cruel experimenters have discovered will cause a mother bird to thrust her own warm, speckled ones from the nest—upsets your equilibrium. The community of convictions flies apart, you sense unguessed contradictions,

---

1 *Samuel Johnson* Dr. Johnson (1709–84), English lexicographer, writer, and critic.
2 *Keynesian economics* Economic theory based on the work of John Maynard Keynes (1883–1946), English economist who believed that government spending on public works is necessary for economic stability and growth.

there are disavowals, frictions, second thoughts, pleas for further study; you stare in renewed perplexity out the laundromat's plate-glass window, while your pulped library card dries in a tumbling shirt pocket behind you.

Such alert intermissions happen only infrequently: most of the time we are in some inconclusive phase of changing our minds about many, if not all, things. We have no choice. Our opinions, gently nudged by circumstance, revise themselves under cover of inattention. We tell them, in a steady voice, No, I'm not interested in a change at present. But there is no stopping opinions. They don't care about whether we want to hold them or not; they do what they have to do.

And graver still, we are sometimes only minimally aware of just which new beliefs we have adopted. If one of the wire services were able to supply each subscriber with a Personal Opinion Printout, delivered with the paper every morning, it would be a real help: then we could monitor our feelings about Pre-Raphaelite[1] furniture, or the influences of urbanization on politeness, or the wearing of sunglasses indoors, or the effect of tort[2] language on traditions of trust, as we adjusted our thoughts about them week by week, the way we keep an eye on lightly traded over-the-counter stocks. Instead, we stride into a discussion with our squads of unexamined opinions innocently at our heels—and, discovering that, yes, we do feel strongly about watertable rights, or unmanned space exploration, or the harvesting of undersea sponges, say, we grab the relevant opinion and, without dress rehearsals, fling it out into audibility (*"Fly*, you mother"), only to discover, seconds later, its radical inadequacy.

5   Let me now share with you something about which I changed my mind. Once I was riding the bus between New York City and Rochester. At the Binghamton stop, the driver noticed a shoe sitting on the ledge below the front windshield. The sight of it bothered him. He held it up to us and said, "Is this anybody's?" There was no response, so he left the bus for a moment and threw the shoe in a nearby trash can. We drove on toward Rochester. Idle, I became caught up in a little plan to furnish my future apartment: I would buy yellow forklifts and orange backhoes, *rows* of them, upholstered so that my guests might sit if they wished in the scoops or on the slings slung between the forks. I had begun to calculate how many forklifts a typical floor would sustain when a man with disorderly hair walked to the front of the bus wearing two socks and one shoe. "Did you by any chance see a shoe?" he asked the driver. The driver said: "I asked about that shoe in Binghamton. It's gone now." The man apologized for having been asleep and returned to his seat.

---

1 *Pre-Raphaelite* Adhering to the principles and aesthetics of the Pre-Raphaelite Brotherhood, a group of nineteenth-century English artists who admired the work of Italian artists before Raphael.

2 *tort* Breach of a legal duty which allows the injured party to sue for damages.

Since that bus trip, five years ago, I find that, without my knowledge, I have changed my mind. I no longer want to live in an apartment furnished with forklifts and backhoes. Somewhere I jettisoned that interest *as irrevocably as the bus driver tossed out the strange sad man's right shoe.* Yet I did not experience during the intervening time a single uncertainty or pensive moment in regard to a backhoe. Five years of walking around cities, flipping through seed catalogs, and saying "Oho!" to statements I disagreed with—the effect of which has been to leave me with a disinclination to apply heavy machinery to interior design.

Multiply this example by a thousand, a hundred thousand, unannounced reversals: a mad flux is splashing around the pilings of our personalities. For a while I tried to make home movies of my opinions in their native element, undisturbed, as they grazed and romped in fields of inquiry, gradually altering in emphasis and coloration, mating, burrowing, and dying, like prairie dogs, but the presence of my camera made their behavior stilted and self-conscious—which brings us to what I can't help thinking is a relevant point about the passage of time. Changes of mind should be distinguished from decisions, for decisions seem to reside pertly in the present, while changes of mind imply habits of thought, a slow settling-out of truth, a partially felt, dense past. I may decide, for instance, that when I take off my pants I should not leave them draped over the loudspeakers, as I normally do, but contrive to suspend them on some sort of hook or hanger. I may decide to ask that person sitting across from me at the table to refrain from ripping out the spongy inside of her dinner roll and working it into small balls between her palms. We are bound to make lots of such future-directed choices: they are the reason for risk-benefit analysis. But at the same time, on the outskirts of our attention, hosts of gray-eyed, bright-speared opinions have been rustling, shifting, skirmishing. "What I think about Piaget"[1] is out there, growing wiser, moodier, more cynical, along with some sort of answer to "What constitutes a virtuous life?" Unless I am being unusually calculating, I don't *decide* to befriend someone, and it is the same way with a conviction: I slowly come to enjoy its company, to respect its counsel, to depend on it for reassurance; I find myself ignoring its weaknesses or excesses—and if the friendship later ends, it is probably owing not to a sudden rift, but to a barnacling-over of nearly insignificant complaints.

Seldom, then, will any single argument change our minds about anything really interesting or important. In fact, reasoning and argument count for surprisingly little in the alluvial triumph of a thought—no more than 12 to 15 percent. Those reasons we do cite are often only a last flourish of bright plumage, a bit of ceremony to commemorate the result of a rabblement of tendencies too cross-purposed to recapitulate. A haphazard flare of memo-

---

1   *Piaget* Jean Piaget (1896–1980), Swiss scientist and psychologist famous for his research on children's cognitive development.

ry; an irrelevant grief; an anecdote in the newspaper; a turn of conversation that stings into motion a tiny doubt: from such incessant percussions the rational soul reorganizes itself—we change our minds as we change our character. Years go by and the movement remains unrecognized: "I wasn't aware of it, but my whole feeling about car-pool lanes (or planned communities, or slippery-slope arguments, or rhyme, or Shostakovich,[1] or whether things are getting better or worse) was undergoing a major overhaul back then." We must not overlook sudden conversions and wrenching insights, but usually we fasten on to these only in hindsight, and exaggerate them for the sake of narrative—a tool perfected by the great nineteenth-century novelists, who sit their heroines down and have them deduce the intolerability of their situation in one unhappy night, as the fire burns itself into embers in the grate.

Consider "whether things are getting better or worse" at closer range. Impossibly vague and huge as it is, most of us nonetheless believe it to be a question that merits a periodical self-harvest of opinion. Here are some of the marginally rational things that from one season to the next may contribute to my feelings concerning progress: There is more static in long-distance calls than there was a while ago. The Wonder Bread concrete they now use for sidewalks is a real step down from the darker, pebblier substance they used to use, and that in turn was a decline from the undulant slabs of weathered blue slate, thrust into gradients and peaks by the roots of a nearby tree, that were on my street as a child. Progresso artichoke hearts frequently have sharp, thistly pieces left on them now, as they never used to. When I tip the paper boy these days, he doesn't say thank you. Cemetery statues suffer increasing vandalism. On the other hand, there is Teflon II. Reflective street signs. The wah-wah pedal. Free libraries for everyone. Central heating. Fire codes. Federal Express. Stevie Wonder. Vladimir Nabokov.[2] Lake Ontario is cleaner. My friends like my new blue coat. Somehow the mind arrives at a moving weighted average of these apples and oranges.

10   Occasionally a change of mind follows alternate routes. One belief, about which initially I would admit of no doubt, gradually came to seem more porous and intricate in its structure, but instead of moderating my opinion correspondingly, and conceding the justice of several objections, I simply lost interest in it, and now I nod absently if the topic comes up over lunch. Another time a cherished opinion weakened as I became too familiar with the three examples that advocates used over and over to support it. Under the glare of this repetition, the secondary details, the richer underthrumming of the opinion, faded; I seemed to have held it once too often; I tried

---

1   *Shostakovich* Dmitri Shostakovich (1906–75), Soviet musician and composer.
2   *Vladimir Nabokov* Russian-born author (1899–1977), best known for his novel *Lolita*.

but failed to find the rhetorical or figurative twist that would revive it for me. I crept insensibly toward the opposing view.

How is it that whole cultures and civilizations can change their "minds" in ways that seem so susceptible to synoptic explanation? From the distance of the historian of ideas, things blur nicely: one sees a dogma and its vocabulary seeping from discipline to disciplines, from class to class; if you squint away specificity you can make out splinter groups, groundswells of opposition, rival and revival schools of thought. The smoothness and sweep is breathtaking; the metaphors are all ready-made.

But when I am at the laundromat, trying to reconstitute for myself the collaboration of influences, disgusts, mistakes, and passions that swept me toward a simple change of heart about forklifts, the variables press in, description stammers and drowns in detail, and imagination hops up and down on one shoe to little purpose. I consult more successful attempts by the major intellectual autobiographers—Saint Augustine,[1] Gibbon,[2] Mill,[3] Newman,[4] and men of similar kidney—but even their brilliant accounts fail to satisfy: I don't want the story of the feared-but-loved teacher, the book that hit like a thunderclap, the years of severe study followed by a visionary breakdown, the clench of repentance; I want each sequential change of mind in its true, knotted, clotted, viny multifariousness, with all of the colorful streamers of intelligence still taped on and flapping in the wind.

Questions

1. Baker asks, "How is it that whole cultures and civilizations can change their 'minds'?" Does Baker answer this question satisfactorily?
2. How would you characterize the relationship between the style of Baker's essay and its subject?
3. In what ways, do you imagine, is Baker's style similar to and different from that of the other writers he mentions?

1　*Saint Augustine* Aurelius Augustinus (354–430 CE), author of *Confessions*, whose many writings played a major role in the development of Western theology.

2　*Gibbon* Edward Gibbon (1737–94), English historian best known for *The History of the Decline and Fall of the Roman Empire* (1776–88).

3　*Mill* John Stuart Mill (1806–73), English philosopher and economist, author of such works as *On Liberty* and *Utilitarianism* (1861).

4　*Newman* Cardinal John Henry Newman (1801–91), English theologian and priest, one of the founders of the Oxford Movement and famous convert to Roman Catholicism.

RICHARD WRANGHAM

Killer Species

(2004)

Richard Wrangham is a professor of biological anthropology at Harvard University specializing in the study of primate social behaviour. In his book Demonic Males: Apes and the Origins of Human Violence *(1996) (co-written with Dale Peterson) he draws parallels between human and chimpanzee sexual and violent behaviour.*

In this excerpt from the longer essay, Wrangham analyzes patterns of violent behaviour in several types of carnivorous mammals: chimpanzees, wolves, and humans.

With chimpanzees, wolves, and humans the big picture is consistent: in typical populations of these three species, it can be mortally dangerous to meet the neighbors.

That's why they all have war zones.

War zones are the border areas where territories abut, danger lurks, and parties rarely go. Low rates of foraging mean that war zones can become lands of plenty—rich in tempting resources.

The Upper Missouri War Zone, a corridor five hundred kilometers long and two hundred forty kilometers wide, was a focal area for the intertribal aggression of numerous indigenous groups, including the Nez Perce, Crow, and Shoshone. Lewis and Clark[1] described the presence there of "immence [sic] quantities of buffalo in every direction";[2] the herbivores benefited from the low human predation pressure resulting from the dangers of hunting in these contested ranges. So the feared war zone became a game sink.[3] Territorial tension sometimes works the same way today. The Demilitarized Zone (DMZ) separating North and South Korea is so empty of people that it has particularly high biodiversity, and supports large populations

---

1 *Lewis and Clark* Meriwether Lewis (1774–1809) and William Clark (1770–1838) led an expedition of American exploration from 1804–06. They studied the flora, fauna, and peoples of unsettled areas in the United States.
2 Paul S. Martin and Christine R. Szuter, "War Zones and Game Sinks in Lewis and Clark's West," *Conservation Biology* 13 (1999): 36–45. [Wrangham's note]
3 *game sink* An area rich in plant and animal species.

of rare and endangered species extinct on the rest of the Korean peninsula. (Conservationists should be worried about the prospect of peace. When peace came to the Upper Missouri War Zone, prey animals were hunted to extinction.)

War zones occurred among hunter-gatherers also. Anthropologist Bion   5
Griffin reports, for example, that the Agta of the Philippines knew where the danger lay. "Hunters are especially aware of the chance of illegal trespassers and assume that they may be bent on raiding," Griffin writes. "In the remotest forest hunting zones, where hunters from more than one dialect group may range, precautions are taken and one would seldom hunt alone."[1]

In Australia, expeditions outside the core of the territory were likewise viewed as dangerous: "The red ochre gathering expeditions ... were normally all-male parties, and although cordial relationships between groups were sought, fighting appears to have been a common hazard faced by traveling parties. One entire party, with the exception of one man, is recorded as having been ambushed and killed in about 1870, whilst in about 1874 all but one of a group of 30 men were 'entombed in the excavations.'"[2]

Among chimpanzees, evidence of a game sink in war zones comes from the group size of their favorite prey species, red colobus monkeys. Groups averaged 46 percent smaller in the core of the territory than in the border area, according to primatologist Craig Stanford. He attributed the difference to the lower hunting pressure in the border areas, where chimpanzees feared to go.

Meanwhile, David Mech describes how except during periods of extreme food shortage, the threat of encountering hostile neighbors keeps packs of wolves out of border areas. White-tailed deer therefore occur at particularly high density in the zones of wolf-pack territorial overlap. Mech believes that these war-zone populations of deer are critical for the long-term relationship between predator and prey, since they provide the stock for recolonizing the over-hunted areas in the core of the wolf territories. Wolf war zones, in other words, provide conservation areas rather in the style of the Korean DMZ.

It's not the abutment of territories that makes a war zone. Redtail monkeys in Kibale[3] also live within territories, but they do not kill members of

---

1   P. Bion Griffin, "Forager Resource and Land Use in the Humid Tropics: The Agta of Northeastern Luzon, the Philippines," in Carmel Schrire, ed., *Past and Present in Hunter-Gatherer Studies* (New York: Academic Press, 1984), 106. [Wrangham's note.]

2   The quotation is from R.G. Kimber, "Hunter-Gatherer Demography: The Recent Past in Central Australia," in Betty Meehan and Neville White, eds., *Hunter-Gatherer Demography Past and Present* (Sydney: University of Sydney Press, 1990), 160–70. [Wrangham's note.]

3   *Kibale* District in western Uganda.

neighboring communities and they do not avoid the territorial borders.
They use the territory fully, right up to the border, and merely defend their
ranges with chases when they meet neighbors. What makes a war zone is not
a territory, but the risk of being victimized at its edge.

War zones also aren't known among bonobos,[1] or, for that matter, among
most primates or most mammals or most animals. In the great majority of
species, territorial encounters involve display, chases, and occasional grap-
pling, but not outright killing. There are only a select few species whose territorial boundaries are places of death and avoidance. The question is why
this selection should include chimpanzees, wolves, and humans.

A strong evolutionary rationale for killing derives from the harsh logic of
natural selection. Every homicide shifts the power balance in favor of the
killers. So the killers have an increased chance of outnumbering their
opponents in future territorial battles, and therefore of winning them. Bigger territories mean more food, and therefore more babies.

This unpleasant formula implies that killing is favored by two conditions.
It pays whenever resource competition is intense, and whenever killing can
be carried out at low risk to the aggressors.

All animals face resource competition. In the wild, for example, female
chimpanzees lose weight during poor seasons and are often so short of food
that they must wait for an abundant fruiting season before they can conceive. All hunter-gatherer populations show similar evidence of intermit-
tent food scarcity, such as reduced growth during poor seasons.

Persistent food shortages suggest that a larger territory will always pay,
and long-term data from Gombe[2] confirm it. During two decades the territory of the Kasekela chimpanzee community varied in size. Shifts in the balance of power with neighboring communities may have been responsible
for these oscillations. When the territory was small, the chimpanzees had
inadequate food. Individuals lost body weight and tended to travel in the
small parties typical of periods of low food supply. Females then had long
intervals between births, and offspring survival was low. When the territory
was larger, everything changed. Male efforts at expanding the territory led
to gains for both sexes. With a better food supply, all adults gained weight,
females reproduced faster, and the young survived better.[3]

The Gombe study nicely shows the importance of a larger territory. But
it doesn't show anything special about the killer species. Any territory-
holding group can be expected to fare better if its neighbors' power

---

1 *bonobos* Type of chimpanzee, often referred to as the "Pygmy Chimpanzee."

2 *Gombe* Gombe National Park, Tanzania, the site of primatologist Jane Goodall's
   famous study of chimpanzees.

3 Jennifer M. Williams, Anne E. Pusey, John V. Carlis, B.P. Farm, and Jane
   Goodall, "Female Competition and Male Territorial Behavior Influence Female
   Chimpanzees' Ranging Patterns," *Animal Behaviour* 63 (2002): 347–60. [Wrang-
   ham's note.]

declines, allowing its territory to expand. By the same process seen in Gombe, a group of any species that gets a larger territory can be expected to have improved food and better reproduction. This principle should apply as much to bonobos and redtail monkeys as to chimpanzees, wolves, and humans. But bonobos and monkeys don't kill.

So resource competition is a necessary condition for war-zone killing, but it's not enough on its own. The second condition is the sufficient one. Killing must be cheap.

The special feature of the killer species is that when parties from neighboring territories meet, there is sometimes an imbalance of power so great that one party can kill a victim without any significant risk of any of them getting hurt themselves. For chimpanzees and wolves, the imbalances of power come entirely from their protean grouping patterns. For hunter-gatherers, the same applies, but there is an extra twist from human inventiveness. For modern humans, imbalances of power come not only from being able to form a larger subgroup than the enemy's, but also from striking the first lethal blow—such as by throwing a spear, flaming a hut, or flying an airplane into a building.

Among chimpanzees, the most likely victims of homicide are adults found alone or immediately abandoned by their friends after being cornered by members of a hostile community. Among wolves, the evidence is less direct, but 90 percent of kills in Denali[1] occurred in winter. At that time, the probability of a lone individual meeting a party of at least three other wolves is 40 times higher than in the summer.

Support for the supposed importance of power imbalances comes from the species that don't kill. Bonobos and monkeys live in relatively stable groups, with individuals rarely in parties so small that they might be overwhelmed by neighbors. Those species have diets that allow parties the luxury of permanent association.

But among humans, power imbalances are routine in intercommunity conflict, and the predominant tactic of war for small-scale societies is unambiguous. It's hit-and-run or ambush. Anthropologist A.R. Radcliffe-Brown recorded the attitude of the Andaman Islanders, hunter-gatherers living east of India. "The whole art of fighting," he wrote, "was to come upon your enemies by surprise, kill one or two of them and then retreat.... They would not venture to attack the enemy's camp unless they were certain of taking it by surprise.... If they met with any serious resistance or lost one of their own number, they would immediately retire. Though the aim of the attacking party was to kill the men, it often happened that women or children were killed."[2]

20

---

1   *Denali* Denali National Park, Alaska.

2   A.R. Radcliffe-Brown, *The Andaman Islanders: A Study in Social Anthropology* (Cambridge: Cambridge University Press, 1948), 85. [Wrangham's note.]

Similar tactics have been described for hunter-gatherers around the world. In Australia, Walbiri men who surprised enemy camps were said to have killed or driven off the enemy males, and to have carried away any women they could find. In the Arctic, by contrast, raiders would normally kill everyone, though they might spare young girls. Raids typically involved 15 to 20 men, and could take 10 days to complete.[1]

That hunter-gatherers would have raided each other may seem surprising in view of the reputation of forager societies like the Kalahari Bushmen for living peacefully. Scrutiny of early records of contact with hunter-gatherers, however, shows widespread evidence of primitive violence, even in the Kalahari. And material culture supports the picture. Archaeologist Steven LeBlanc has recently drawn attention to the shields of Eskimos that attest to the occurrence of battles. Australian Aborigines also had shields as well as weapons used exclusively for warfare, such as a hooked boomerang and a heavy spear. Both in the Arctic and in Australia there is clear historical evidence for a combination of raids and battles.[2]

The principle that underlies the mayhem is simple, then. When the killing is cheap, kill. In any particular instance it may or may not lead to a bigger territory, but from the perspective of natural selection, the specific case is less important than the average benefit. The integrating effect of selective pressures on emotional systems requires only that killing should lead to benefits sufficiently often. Just as the first male fig wasp that emerges from pupation will immediately attempt to kill any other males he finds in the same fig, so the defenders of territory benefit by taking advantage of opportunity. The killers don't have to think through the logic. They may think of their action as revenge, or placating the gods, or a rite of manhood—or they may not think about it at all. They may do it because it's exciting, as seems the case for chimpanzees. The rationale doesn't matter to natural selection.[3]

What matters, it seems, is that in future battles the neighbors will have one less warrior. So those who killed will become a little more powerful as a result.

25   Why, then, do humans, chimpanzees, and wolves share the unusual practice of deliberately and frequently killing neighbors? In each species the violence makes sense. Protean grouping patterns allow individuals to attack

1 Azar Gat, "The Human Motivational Complex: Evolutionary Theory and the Causes of Hunter-Gatherer Fighting, Part I: Primary Somatic and Reproductive Causes," *Anthropological Quarterly* 73 (2000): 20–34. [Wrangham's note.]
2 Steven A. LeBlanc, *Constant Battles* (New York: St. Martin's Press, 2003). [Wrangham's note.]
3 Klaus Reinhold, "Influence of Male Relatedness on Lethal Combat in Fig Wasps: A Theoretical Analysis," *Proceedings of the Royal Society of London* B 270 (2003): 1171–75. [Wrangham's note.]

only when they have overwhelming power. Such tactical success allows them to kill safely and cheaply, and thereby win a likely increase in resources over the succeeding months or years. Killing thus emerges as a consequence of having territories, dispersed groups, and unpredictable power relations. These driving variables, in turn, appear to result from ecological adaptations, whether to a scattered fruit supply or to the challenges of hunting vertebrate prey. The implication is that because of our particular evolutionary ecology, natural selection has favored in the brains of humans, chimpanzees, and wolves a tendency to take advantage of opportunities to kill enemies.

This doesn't condemn us to be violent in general. Indeed, within our communities humans are markedly less violent than most other primates, and in some ways humans are specially peaceful. Nor does it mean that intergroup aggression is inevitable: rather, it predicts little violence when power is balanced between neighboring communities. Nor, again, does it mean that gang attacks on members of other tribes or religions or clubs or countries are necessarily adaptive: in evolutionary terms, they may or may not be. Nor does it mean that women are incapable of violence, or are inherently less aggressive than men: it suggests instead why the circumstances that favor aggression are not identical for men and women.

What it does imply, however, is that selection has favored a human tendency to identify enemies, draw moral divides, and exploit weaknesses pitilessly across boundaries. As a result, our species remains specially predisposed to certain types of violent emotion. That selection operated in the context of a hunter-gatherer world that has all but disappeared. But if its legacy is that we are biologically prepared by natural selection to be killers, an understanding of the neural basis of intergroup violence should be a research priority.

Questions

1. What are the implications of Wrangham's findings for each of the species involved?
2. What do you think Wrangham wants to achieve with this article? Who is his implied audience?
3. What insights into human violence does Wrangham gain by comparing humans to animals? What are the potential problems with his approach?
4. Wrangham concludes "our species remains specially predisposed to certain types of violent emotion" (paragraph 27). Comment on the usefulness of Wrangham's findings in preventing violence among humans.

❧ *Languages and Culture* ❧

ERNEST HEMINGWAY

Pamplona in July

(1923)

Ernest Hemingway (1898–1961) was an American journalist, short-story writer, and novelist famous for his prose style. A Nobel Prize winner in 1954, Hemingway was one of the most influential writers of the twentieth century. His many novels and collections of short stories include In Our Time *(1925),* The Sun Also Rises *(1926),* A Farewell to Arms *(1929),* The Old Man and the Sea *(1952), and* The Snows of Kilimanjaro and Other Stories *(1963).*

This essay, published in The Toronto Star Weekly, *27 October 1923, describes a Spanish bullfighting festival.*

In Pamplona,[1] a white-walled, sun-baked town high up in the hills of Navarre, is held in the first two weeks of July each year the world series of bullfighting.

Bullfight fans from all Spain jam into the little town. Hotels double their prices and fill every room. The cafés under the wide arcades that run around the Plaza de la Constitución have every table crowded, the tall Pilgrim Father sombreros of Andalusia sitting over the same table with straw hats from Madrid and the flat blue Basque caps of Navarre and the Basque country.

Really beautiful girls, gorgeous, bright shawls over their shoulders, dark, dark-eyed, black lace mantillas over their hair, walk with their escorts in the crowds that pass from morning until night along the narrow walk that runs between inner and outer belts of café tables under the shade of the arcade out of the white glare of the Plaza de la Constitución. All day and all night there is dancing in the streets. Bands of blue-shirted peasants whirl and lift and swing behind a drum, fife and reed instruments in the ancient Basque

---

1 *Pamplona* Capital city of Navarre, a region in northern Spain.

Riau-Riau dances.[1] And at night there is the throb of the big drums and the military band as the whole town dances in the great open square of the Plaza.

We landed at Pamplona at night. The streets were solid with people dancing. Music was pounding and throbbing. Fireworks were being set off from the big public square. All the carnivals I have ever seen paled in comparison. A rocket exploded over our heads with a blinding burst and the stick came swirling and whishing down. Dancers, snapping their fingers and whirling in perfect time through the crowd, bumped into us before we could get our bags down from the top of the station bus. Finally I got the bags through the crowd to the hotel.

We had wired and written for rooms two weeks ahead. Nothing had been   5 saved. We were offered a single room with a single bed opening onto the kitchen ventilator shaft for seven dollars a day apiece. There was a big row with the landlady, who stood in front of her desk with her hands on her hips, and her broad Indian face perfectly placid, and told us in a few words of French and much Basque Spanish that she had to make all her money for the whole year in the next ten days. That people would come and that people would have to pay what she asked. She could show us a better room for ten dollars apiece. We said it would be preferable to sleep in the streets with the pigs. The landlady agreed that might be possible. We said we preferred it to such a hotel. All perfectly amicable. The landlady considered. We stood our ground. Mrs. Hemingway sat down on our rucksacks.

"I can get you a room in a house in the town. You can eat here," said the landlady.

"How much?"

"Five dollars."

We started off through the dark, narrow, carnival-mad streets with a boy carrying our rucksacks. It was a lovely big room in an old Spanish house with walls thick as a fortress. A cool, pleasant room, with a red tile floor and two big, comfortable beds set back in an alcove. A window opened on to an iron-grilled porch out over the street. We were very comfortable.

All night long the wild music kept up in the street below. Several times in   10 the night there was a wild roll of drumming, and I got out of bed and across the tiled floor to the balcony. But it was always the same. Men, blue-shirted, bareheaded, whirling and floating in a wild fantastic dance down the street behind the rolling drums and shrill fifes.

Just at daylight there was a crash of music in the street below. Real military music. Herself was up, dressed, at the window.

---

1 *Riau-Riau dances* Traditionally, local youths attempted to block a vespers procession by town officials by dancing and singing in a large crowd.

"Come on," she said. "They're all going somewhere." Down below the street was full of people. It was five o'clock in the morning. They were all going in one direction. I dressed in a hurry and we started after them.

The crowd was all going toward the great public square. People were pouring into it from every street and moving out of it toward the open country we could see through the narrow gaps in the high walls.

"Let's get some coffee," said Herself.

15 "Do you think we've got time? Hey, what's going to happen?" I asked a newsboy.

"Encierro," he said scornfully. "The encierro commences at six o'clock."

"What's the encierro?" I asked him.

"Oh, ask me tomorrow," he said, and started to run. The entire crowd was running now.

"I've got to have my coffee. No matter what it is," Herself said.

20 The waiter poured two streams of coffee and milk into the glass out of his big kettles. The crowd were still running, coming from all the streets that fed into the Plaza.

"What is this encierro anyway?" Herself asked, gulping the coffee.

"All I know is that they let the bulls out into the streets."

We started out after the crowd. Out of a narrow gate into a great yellow open space of country with the new concrete bullring standing high and white and black with people. The yellow and red Spanish flag blowing in the early-morning breeze. Across the open and once inside the bullring, we mounted to the top looking toward the town. It cost a peseta[1] to go up to the top. All the other levels were free. There were easily twenty thousand people there. Everyone jammed on the outside of the big concrete amphitheatre, looking toward the yellow town with the bright red roofs, where a long wooden pen ran from the entrance of the city gate across the open, bare ground to the bullring.

It was really a double wooden fence, making a long entry from the main street of the town into the bullring itself. It made a runway about two hundred and fifty yards long. People were jammed solid on each side of it. Looking up it toward the main street.

25 Then far away there was a dull report.

"They're off," everybody shouted.

"What is it?" I asked a man next to me who was leaning far out over the concrete rail.

"The bulls! They have released them from the corrals on the far side of the city. They are racing through the city."

---

1 *peseta* Until the adoption of the euro, the peseta was Spain's standard currency, equal to 100 céntimos.

"Whew," said Herself. "What do they do that for?"

Then down the narrow fenced-in runway came a crowd of men and boys   30
running. Running as hard as they could go. The gate feeding into the bullring was opened and they all ran pell-mell under the entrance levels into
the ring. Then there came another crowd. Running even harder. Straight
up the long pen from the town.

"Where are the bulls?" asked Herself.

Then they came in sight. Eight bulls galloping along, full tilt, heavyset,
black, glistening, sinister, their horns bare, tossing their heads. And running with them, three steers with bells on their necks. They ran in a solid
mass, and ahead of them sprinted, tore, ran and bolted the rear guard of
the men and boys of Pamplona who had allowed themselves to be chased
through the streets for a morning's pleasure.

A boy in his blue shirt, red sash, white canvas shoes, with the inevitable
leather wine bottle hung from his shoulders, stumbled as he sprinted down
the straightaway. The first bull lowered his head and made a jerky, sideways
toss. The boy crashed up against the fence and lay there limp, the herd running solidly together passed him up. The crowd roared.

Everybody made a dash for the inside of the ring, and we got into a box
just in time to see the bulls come into the ring filled with men. The men
ran in a panic to each side. The bulls, still bunched solidly together, ran
straight with the trained steers across the ring and into the entrance that
led to the pens.

That was the entry. Every morning during the bullfighting festival of San   35
Fermin[1] at Pamplona, the bulls that are to fight in the afternoon are
released from their corrals at six o'clock in the morning and race through
the main street of the town for a mile and a half to the pen. The men who
run ahead of them do it for the fun of the thing. It has been going on each
year since a couple of hundred years before Columbus had his historic
interview with Queen Isabella in the camp outside of Granada.[2]

There are two things in favor of there being no accidents. First, that fighting bulls are not aroused and vicious when they are together. Second, that
the steers are relied upon to keep them moving.

Sometimes things go wrong, a bull will be detached from the herd as
they pile through into the pen and with his crest up, a ton of speed and
viciousness, his needle-sharp horns lowered, will charge again and again
into the packed mass of men and boys in the bullring. There is no place
for the men to get out of the ring. It is too jammed for them to climb over

---

1   *San Fermin* Pamplona's week-long festival in July held in honour of Saint Fer-
    min, the patron saint of Pamplona and Navarre.

2   *Columbus ... Granada* After defeating the Muslims in Granada in 1492, Queen
    Isabella of Spain finally agreed to fund Christopher Columbus's voyage to the
    Indies.

the barrera or red fence that rims the field. They have to stay in and take it. Eventually the steers get the bull out of the ring and into the pen. He may wound or kill thirty men before they can get him out. No armed men are allowed to oppose him. That is the chance the Pamplona bullfight fans take every morning during the Feria.[1] It is the Pamplona tradition of giving the bulls a final shot at everyone in town before they enter the pens. They will not leave until they come out into the glare of the arena to die in the afternoon.

Consequently Pamplona is the toughest bullfight town in the world. The amateur fight that comes immediately after the bulls have entered the pens proves that. Every seat in the great amphitheatre is packed. About three hundred men, with capes, odd pieces of cloth, old shirts, anything that will imitate a bullfighter's cape, are singing and dancing in the arena. There is a shout, and the bullpen opens. Out comes a young bull just as fast as he can come. On his horns are leather knobs to prevent his goring anyone. He charges and hits a man. Tosses him high in the air, and the crowd roars. The man comes down on the ground, and the bull goes for him, bumping him with his head. Worrying him with his horns. Several amateur bullfighters are flopping their capes in his face to make the bull charge and leave the man on the ground. The bull charges and bags another man. The crowd roars with delight.

Then the bull will turn like a cat and get somebody who has been acting very brave about ten feet behind him. Then he will toss a man over the fence. Then he picks out one man and follows him in a wild twisting charge through the entire crowd until he bags him. The barrera is packed with men and boys sitting along the top, and the bull decides to clear them all off. He goes along, hooking carefully with his horn and dropping them off with a toss of his horns like a man pitching hay.

40   Each time the bull bags someone the crowd roars with joy. Most of it is home-talent stuff. The braver the man has been or the more elegant pass he has attempted with his cape before the bull gets him, the more the crowd roars. No one is armed. No one hurts or plagues the bull in any way. A man who grabbed the bull by the tail and tried to hang on was hissed and booed by the crowd and the next time he tried it was knocked down by another man in the bullring. No one enjoys it more than the bull.

As soon as he shows signs of tiring from his charges, the two old steers, one brown and the other looking like a big Holstein, come trotting in and alongside the young bull, who falls in behind them like a dog and follows them meekly on a tour of the arena and then out.

---

1   *Feria* Festival.

Another comes right in, and the charging and tossing, the ineffectual cape-waving, and wonderful music are repeated right over again. But always different. Some of the animals in this morning amateur fight are steers. Fighting bulls from the best strain who had some imperfection or other in build so they could never command the high prices paid for combat animals, $2,000 to $3,000 apiece. But there is nothing lacking in their fighting spirit.

The show comes off every morning. Everybody in town turns out at five thirty when the military bands go through the streets. Many of them stay up all night for it. We didn't miss one, and it is *quelque*[1] sporting event that will get us both up at five thirty o'clock in the morning for six days running.

As far as I know, we were the only English-speaking people in Pamplona during the Feria of last year.

There were three minor earthquakes while we were there. Terrific cloud-bursts in the mountains and the Ebro River flooded out Zaragoza.[2] For two days the bullring was under water and the corrida[3] had to be suspended for the first time in over a hundred years. That was during the middle of the fair. Everyone was desperate. On the third day it looked gloomier than ever, poured rain all morning, and then at noon the clouds rolled away up across the valley, the sun came out bright and hot and baking and that afternoon there was the greatest bullfight I will perhaps ever see.

There were rockets going up into the air and the arena was nearly full when we got into our regular seats. The sun was hot and baking. Over on the other side we could see the bullfighters standing ready to come in. All wearing their oldest clothes because of the heavy, muddy going in the arena. We picked out the three matadors of the afternoon with our glasses. Only one of them was new. Olmos, a chubby-faced, jolly-looking man, something like Tris Speaker.[4] The others we had seen often before. Maera, dark, spare and deadly looking, one of the very greatest toreros[5] of all time. The third, young Algabeno, the son of a famous bullfighter, a slim young Andalusian with a charming Indian-looking face. All were wearing the suits they had probably started bullfighting with, too tight, old fashioned, outmoded.

There was the procession of entrance, the wild bullfight music played, the preliminaries were quickly over, the picadors[6] retired along the red

45

---

1   *quelque* Some.
2   *Zaragoza* Capital city of Aragón, a region, and former kingdom, of Spain.
3   *corrida* Bullfight.
4   *Tris Speaker* Tristram E. Speaker (1888–1958), American baseball player known for his outstanding defensive skills.
5   *toreros* Bullfighters on foot.
6   *picadors* Mounted bullfighters who provoke the bull with lances.

fence with their horses, the heralds sounded their trumpets and the door of the bullpen swung open. The bull came out in a rush, saw a man standing near the barrera and charged him. The man vaulted over the fence and the bull charged the barrera. He crashed into the fence in full charge and ripped a two-by-eight plank solidly out in a splintering smash. He broke his horn doing it and the crowd called for a new bull. The trained steers trotted in, the bull fell in meekly behind them, and the three of them trotted out of the arena.

The next bull came in with the same rush. He was Maera's bull and, after perfect cape play, Maera planted the banderillos.[1] Maera is Herself's favorite bullfighter. And if you want to keep any conception of yourself as a brave, hard, perfectly balanced, thoroughly competent man in your wife's mind, never take her to a real bullfight. I used to go into the amateur fights in the morning to try and win back a small amount of her esteem but the more I discovered that bullfighting required a great quantity of a certain type of courage of which I had an almost complete lack, the more it became apparent that any admiration she might ever redevelop for me would have to be simply an antidote to the real admiration for Maera and Villalta. You cannot compete with bullfighters on their own ground. If anywhere. The only way most husbands are able to keep any drag with their wives at all is that, first there are only a limited number of bullfighters, second there are only a limited number of wives who have ever seen bullfights.

Maera planted his first pair of banderillos sitting down on the edge of the little step-up that runs around the barrera. He snarled at the bull and as the animal charged, leaned back tight against the fence and as the horns struck on either side of him, swung forward over the brute's head and planted the two darts in his hump. He planted the next pair, same way, so near to us we could have leaned over and touched him. Then he went out to kill the bull and, after he had made absolutely unbelievable passes with the little red cloth of the muleta,[2] drew up his sword and as the bull charged, Maera thrust. The sword shot out of his hand and the bull caught him. He went up in the air on the horns of the bull and then came down. Young Algabeno flopped his cape in the bull's face. The bull charged him and Maera staggered to his feet. But his wrist was sprained.

50   With his wrist sprained, so that every time he raised it to sight for a thrust it brought beads of sweat out on his face, Maera tried again and again to make his death thrust. He lost his sword again and again, picked it up with his left hand from the mud floor of the arena and transferred it to the right for the thrust. Finally he made it and the bull went over. The bull nearly got him twenty times. As he came in to stand up under us at the barrera side,

---

1   *banderillos* Darts with streamers that are jabbed into the bull's neck and shoulders.

2   *muleta* Stick covered with red cloth.

his wrist was swollen to twice normal size. I thought of prizefighters I had seen quit because they had hurt their hands.

There was almost no pause while the mules galloped in and hitched on to the first bull and dragged him out and the second came in with a rush. The picadors took the first shock of him with their bull lances. There was the snort and charge, the shock and the mass against the sky, the wonderful defense by the picador with his lance that held off the bull, and then Rosario Olmos stepped out with his cape.

Once he flopped the cape at the bull and floated it around in an easy graceful swing. Then he tried the same swing, the classic "veronica,"[1] and the bull caught him at the end of it. Instead of stopping at the finish, the bull charged on in. He caught Olmos squarely with his horn, hoisted him high in the air. He fell heavily and the bull was on top of him, driving his horns again and again into him. Olmos lay on the sand, his head on his arms. One of his teammates was flopping his cape madly in the bull's face. The bull lifted his head for an instant and charged and got his man. Just one terrific toss. Then he whirled and chased a man just in back of him toward the barrera. The man was running full tilt and as he put his hand on the fence to vault it the bull had him and caught him with his horn, shooting him way up into the crowd. He rushed toward the fallen man he had tossed who was getting to his feet and all alone Algabeno met him with the cape. Once, twice, three times he made the perfect, floating, slow swing with the cape, perfectly, graceful, debonair, back on his heels, baffling the bull. And he had command of the situation. There never was such a scene at any world series game.

There are no substitute matadors allowed. Maera was finished. His wrist could not lift a sword for weeks. Olmos had been gored badly through the body. It was Algabeno's bull. This one and the next five.

He handled them all. Did it all. Cape play easy, graceful, confident. Beautiful work with the muleta. And serious, deadly killing. Five bulls he killed, one after the other, and each one was a separate problem to be worked out with death. At the end there was nothing debonair about him. It was only a question if he would last through or if the bulls would get him. They were all very wonderful bulls.

"He is a very great kid," said Herself. "He is only twenty."

"I wish we knew him," I said.

"Maybe we will some day," she said. Then considered a moment. "He will probably be spoiled by then."

They make twenty thousand a year.

That was just three months ago. It seems in a different century now, working in an office. It is a very long way from the sunbaked town of Pamplona,

55

---

1   *veronica* Matador's pass made by sweeping the cape slowly away from the bull without moving the feet.

where the men race through the streets in the mornings ahead of the bulls to the morning ride to work on a Bay-Caledonia car.[1] But it is only fourteen days by water to Spain and there is no need for a castle. There is always that room at 5 Calle de Eslava, and a son, if he is to redeem the family reputation as a bullfighter, must start very early.

Questions

1. What is the role of "Herself" in the article? Why do you think Hemingway never refers to her by name?
2. What effect does Hemingway produce by using sentence fragments? Does it enrich your reading? If yes, how exactly does this style advance the essay as a whole? If no, what changes would improve it?
3. In what ways does Hemingway's writing in this essay particularly suit its subject?

---

1 *Bay-Caledonia car* Streetcar route in Toronto.

GEORGE ORWELL

Shooting an Elephant

(1950)

Born Eric Arthur Blair, English writer George Orwell (1903–50) was a novelist, essayist, and journalist. He is most famous for his novels Animal Farm *(1945) and* Nineteen Eighty-Four *(1949). Orwell was born in India but moved to England at a young age. Returning to India in 1922, he served briefly with the Indian Imperial Police in Burma, until his growing distaste for the effects of colonial rule caused him to resign his post.*

This essay, based on Orwell's experiences as an Imperial Police Officer, charts his growing dissatisfaction with England's imperialist role.

In Moulmein, in Lower Burma, I was hated by large numbers of people—the only time in my life that I have been important enough for this to happen to me. I was sub-divisional police officer of the town, and in an aimless, petty kind of way anti-European feeling was very bitter. No one had the guts to raise a riot, but if a European woman went through the bazaars alone somebody would probably spit betel[1] juice over her dress. As a police officer I was an obvious target and was baited whenever it seemed safe to do so. When a nimble Burman tripped me up on the football field and the referee (another Burman) looked the other way, the crowd yelled with hideous laughter. This happened more than once. In the end the sneering yellow faces of young men that met me everywhere, the insults hooted after me when I was at a safe distance, got badly on my nerves. The young Buddhist priests were the worst of all. There were several thousands of them in the town and none of them seemed to have anything to do except stand on street corners and jeer at Europeans.

All this was perplexing and upsetting. For at that time I had already made up my mind that imperialism was an evil thing and the sooner I chucked up my job and got out of it the better. Theoretically—and secretly, of course—I was all for the Burmese and all against their oppressors, the British. As for the job I was doing, I hated it more bitterly than I can perhaps make clear.

---

1 *betel* Green plant leaf that is wrapped around slivers of the Areca Palm nut and chewed for its invigorating and aphrodisiac properties.

In a job like that you see the dirty work of Empire at close quarters. The wretched prisoners huddling in the stinking cages of the lock-ups, the grey, cowed faces of the long-term convicts, the scarred buttocks of the men who had been flogged with bamboos—all these oppressed me with an intolerable sense of guilt. But I could get nothing into perspective. I was young and ill-educated and I had had to think out my problems in the utter silence that is imposed on every Englishman in the East. I did not even know that the British Empire is dying, still less did I know that it is a great deal better than the younger empires that are going to supplant it. All I knew was that I was stuck between my hatred of the empire I served and my rage against the evil-spirited little beasts who tried to make my job impossible. With one part of my mind I thought of the British Raj[1] as an unbreakable tyranny, as something clamped down, *in saecula saeculorum,*[2] upon the will of prostrate peoples; with another part I thought that the greatest joy in the world would be to drive a bayonet into a Buddhist priest's guts. Feelings like these are the normal by-products of imperialism; ask any Anglo-Indian official, if you can catch him off duty.

One day something happened which in a roundabout way was enlightening. It was a tiny incident in itself, but it gave me a better glimpse than I had had before of the real nature of imperialism—the real motives for which despotic governments act. Early one morning the sub-inspector at a police station the other end of the town rang me up on the 'phone and said that an elephant was ravaging the bazaar. Would I please come and do something about it? I did not know what I could do, but I wanted to see what was happening and I got on to a pony and started out. I took my rifle, an old .44 Winchester and much too small to kill an elephant, but I thought the noise might be useful *in terrorem.*[3] Various Burmans stopped me on the way and told me about the elephant's doings. It was not, of course, a wild elephant, but a tame one which had gone "must."[4] It had been chained up, as tame elephants always are when their attack of "must" is due, but on the previous night it had broken its chain and escaped. Its mahout,[5] the only person who could manage it when it was in that state, had set out in pursuit, but had taken the wrong direction and was now twelve hours' journey away, and in the morning the elephant had suddenly reappeared in the town. The Burmese population had no weapons and were quite helpless against it. It had already destroyed somebody's bamboo hut, killed a cow and raided some fruit-stalls and devoured the stock; also it had met the

---

1 *British Raj* Informal term for the era of British Colonial rule over the Indian subcontinent.

2 *in saecula saeculorum* "For centuries upon centuries; forever" (Latin).

3 *in terrorem* "In fright, terror, or alarm" (Latin).

4 *must* An annual frenzy that afflicts male elephants.

5 *mahout* Elephant trainer or keeper.

municipal rubbish van, and, when the driver jumped out and took to his heels, had turned the van over and inflicted violences upon it.

The Burmese sub-inspector and some Indian constables were waiting for me in the quarter where the elephant had been seen. It was a very poor quarter, a labyrinth of squalid bamboo huts, thatched with palm-leaf, winding all over a steep hillside. I remember that it was a cloudy, stuffy morning at the beginning of the rains. We began questioning the people as to where the elephant had gone, and, as usual, failed to get any definite information. That is invariably the case in the East; a story always sounds clear enough at a distance, but the nearer you get to the scene of events the vaguer it becomes. Some of the people said that the elephant had gone in one direction, some said that he had gone in another, some professed not even to have heard of any elephant. I had almost made up my mind that the whole story was a pack of lies, when we heard yells a little distance away. There was a loud, scandalized cry of "Go away, child! Go away this instant!" and an old woman with a switch in her hand came round the corner of a hut, violently shooing away a crowd of naked children. Some more women followed, clicking their tongues and exclaiming; evidently there was something that the children ought not to have seen. I rounded the hut and saw a man's dead body sprawling in the mud. He was an Indian, a black Dravidian coolie,[1] almost naked, and he could not have been dead many minutes. The people said that the elephant had come suddenly upon him round the corner of the hut, caught him with its trunk, put its foot on his back and ground him into the earth. This was the rainy season and the ground was soft, and his face had scored a trench a foot deep and a couple of yards long. He was lying on his belly with arms crucified and head sharply twisted to one side. His face was coated with mud, the eyes wide open, the teeth bared and grinning with an expression of unendurable agony. (Never tell me, by the way, that the dead look peaceful. Most of the corpses I have seen looked devilish.) The friction of the great beast's foot had stripped the skin from his back as neatly as one skins a rabbit. As soon as I saw the dead man I sent an orderly to a friend's house nearby to borrow an elephant rifle. I had already sent back the pony, not wanting it to go mad with fright and throw me if it smelt the elephant.

The orderly came back in a few minutes with a rifle and five cartridges, and meanwhile some Burmans had arrived and told us that the elephant was in the paddy fields below, only a few hundred yards away. As I started forward practically the whole population of the quarter flocked out of the houses and followed me. They had seen the rifle and were all shouting excitedly that I was going to shoot the elephant. They had not shown much interest in the elephant when he was merely ravaging their homes, but it

5

---

1   *coolie* Derogatory word for an unskilled Asian laborer.

was different now that he was going to be shot. It was a bit of fun to them, as it would be to an English crowd; besides they wanted the meat. It made me vaguely uneasy. I had no intention of shooting the elephant—I had merely sent for the rifle to defend myself if necessary—and it is always unnerving to have a crowd following you. I marched down the hill, looking and feeling a fool, with the rifle over my shoulder and an ever-growing army of people jostling at my heels. At the bottom, when you got away from the huts, there was a metalled road and beyond that a miry waste of paddy fields a thousand yards across, not yet ploughed but soggy from the first rains and dotted with coarse grass. The elephant was standing eight yards from the road, his left side towards us. He took not the slightest notice of the crowd's approach. He was tearing up bunches of grass, beating them against his knees to clean them and stuffing them into his mouth.

I had halted on the road. As soon as I saw the elephant I knew with perfect certainty that I ought not to shoot him. It is a serious matter to shoot a working elephant—it is comparable to destroying a huge and costly piece of machinery—and obviously one ought not to do it if it can possibly be avoided. And at that distance, peacefully eating, the elephant looked no more dangerous than a cow. I thought then and I think now that his attack of "must" was already passing off; in which case he would merely wander harmlessly about until the mahout came back and caught him. Moreover, I did not in the least want to shoot him. I decided that I would watch him for a little while to make sure that he did not turn savage again, and then go home.

But at that moment I glanced round at the crowd that had followed me. It was an immense crowd, two thousand at the least and growing every minute. It blocked the road for a long distance on either side. I looked at the sea of yellow faces above the garish clothes—faces all happy and excited over this bit of fun, all certain that the elephant was going to be shot. They were watching me as they would watch a conjurer about to perform a trick. They did not like me, but with the magical rifle in my hands I was momentarily worth watching. And suddenly I realized that I should have to shoot the elephant after all. The people expected it of me and I had got to do it; I could feel their two thousand wills pressing me forward, irresistibly. And it was at this moment, as I stood there with the rifle in my hands, that I first grasped the hollowness, the futility of the white man's dominion in the East. Here was I, the white man with his gun, standing in front of the unarmed native crowd—seemingly the leading actor of the piece; but in reality I was only an absurd puppet pushed to and fro by the will of those yellow faces behind. I perceived in this moment that when the white man turns tyrant it is his own freedom that he destroys. He becomes a sort of hollow, posing dummy, the conventionalized figure of a sahib.[1] For it is the condition of his rule that he shall spend his life in trying to impress the

---

1 *sahib* European in position of power in India.

"natives," and so in every crisis he has got to do what the "natives" expect of him. He wears a mask, and his face grows to fit it. I had got to shoot the elephant. I had committed myself to doing it when I sent for the rifle. A sahib has got to act like a sahib; he has got to appear resolute, to know his own mind and do definite things. To come all that way, rifle in hand, with two thousand people marching at my heels, and then to trail feebly away, having done nothing—no, that was impossible. The crowd would laugh at me. And my whole life, every white man's life in the East, was one long struggle not to be laughed at.

But I did not want to shoot the elephant. I watched him beating his bunch of grass against his knees, with that preoccupied grandmotherly air that elephants have. It seemed to me that it would be murder to shoot him. At that age I was not squeamish about killing animals, but I had never shot an elephant and never wanted to. (Somehow it always seems worse to kill a *large* animal.) Besides, there was the beast's owner to be considered. Alive, the elephant was worth at least a hundred pounds; dead, he would only be worth the value of his tusks, five pounds, possibly. But I had got to act quickly. I turned to some experienced-looking Burmans who had been there when we arrived, and asked them how the elephant had been behaving. They all said the same thing: he took no notice of you if you left him alone, but he might charge if you went too close to him.

It was perfectly clear to me what I ought to do. I ought to walk up to within, say, twenty-five yards of the elephant and test his behaviour. If he charged I could shoot, if he took no notice of me it would be safe to leave him until the mahout came back. But also I knew that I was going to do no such thing. I was a poor shot with a rifle and the ground was soft mud into which one would sink at every step. If the elephant charged and I missed him, I should have about as much chance as a toad under a steam-roller. But even then I was not thinking particularly of my own skin, only of the watchful yellow faces behind. For at that moment, with the crowd watching me, I was not afraid in the ordinary sense, as I would have been if I had been alone. A white man mustn't be frightened in front of "natives"; and so, in general, he isn't frightened. The sole thought in my mind was that if anything went wrong those two thousand Burmans would see me pursued, caught, trampled on and reduced to a grinning corpse like that Indian up the hill. And if that happened it was quite probable that some of them would laugh. That would never do. There was only one alternative. I shoved the cartridges into the magazine[1] and lay down on the road to get a better aim.

The crowd grew very still, and a deep, low, happy sigh, as of people who see the theatre curtain go up at last, breathed from innumerable throats. They were going to have their bit of fun after all. The rifle was a beautiful German thing with cross-hair sights. I did not then know that in shooting

10

---

1 *magazine* An ammunition storage device within a firearm.

an elephant one would shoot to cut an imaginary bar running from ear-hole to ear-hole. I ought, therefore, as the elephant was sideways on, to have aimed straight at his ear-hole; actually I aimed several inches in front of this, thinking the brain would be further forward.

When I pulled the trigger I did not hear the bang or feel the kick—one never does when a shot goes home—but I heard the devilish roar of glee that went up from the crowd. In that instant, in too short a time, one would have thought, even for the bullet to get there, a mysterious, terrible change had come over the elephant. He neither stirred nor fell, but every line of his body had altered. He looked suddenly stricken, shrunken, immensely old, as though the frightful impact of the bullet had paralysed him without knocking him down. At last, after what seemed a long time—it might have been five seconds, I dare say—he sagged flabbily to his knees. His mouth slobbered. An enormous senility seemed to have settled upon him. One could have imagined him thousands of years old. I fired again into the same spot. At the second shot he did not collapse but climbed with desperate slowness to his feet and stood weakly upright, with legs sagging and head drooping. I fired a third time. That was the shot that did for him. You could see the agony of it jolt his whole body and knock the last remnant of strength from his legs. But in falling he seemed for a moment to rise, for as his hind legs collapsed beneath him he seemed to tower upwards like a huge rock toppling, his trunk reaching skywards like a tree. He trumpeted, for the first and only time. And then down he came, his belly towards me, with a crash that seemed to shake the ground even where I lay.

I got up. The Burmans were already racing past me across the mud. It was obvious that the elephant would never rise again, but he was not dead. He was breathing very rhythmically with long rattling gasps, his great mound of a side painfully rising and falling. His mouth was wide open—I could see far down into caverns of pale pink throat. I waited a long time for him to die, but his breathing did not weaken. Finally I fired my two remaining shots into the spot where I thought his heart must be. The thick blood welled out of him like red velvet, but still he did not die. His body did not even jerk when the shots hit him, the tortured breathing continued without a pause. He was dying, very slowly and in great agony, but in some world remote from me where not even a bullet could damage him further. I felt that I had got to put an end to that dreadful noise. It seemed dreadful to see the great beast lying there, powerless to move and yet powerless to die, and not even to be able to finish him. I sent back for my small rifle and poured shot after shot into his heart and down his throat. They seemed to make no impression. The tortured gasps continued as steadily as the ticking of a clock.

In the end I could not stand it any longer and went away. I heard later that it took him half an hour to die. Burmans were bringing dahs[1] and baskets even before I left, and I was told they had stripped his body almost to the bones by the afternoon.

Afterwards, of course, there were endless discussions about the shooting of the elephant. The owner was furious, but he was only an Indian and could do nothing. Besides, legally I had done the right thing, for a mad elephant has to be killed, like a mad dog, if its owner fails to control it. Among the Europeans opinion was divided. The older men said I was right, the younger men said it was a damn shame to shoot an elephant for killing a coolie, because an elephant was worth more than any damn Coringhee coolie. And afterwards I was very glad that the coolie had been killed; it put me legally in the right and it gave me a sufficient pretext for shooting the elephant. I often wondered whether any of the others grasped that I had done it solely to avoid looking a fool.

Questions

1. This essay, first published in 1936, relates an incident that happened in 1926. What changes in Orwell's views have occurred during that span?
2. Analyze Orwell's use of theatrical metaphors and their effects, using evidence from the text.
3. The long death of the elephant is described in graphic detail. Why? What literary devices does Orwell use to drag out the death scene? What is the effect?
4. Orwell says, "when the white man turns tyrant it is his own freedom he destroys" (paragraph 7). Explain.
5. In what ways does the "incident" give Orwell insight into "the real nature of imperialism" (paragraph 3)?

---

1   *dahs* Short swords or knives.

N. SCOTT MOMADAY

The Way to Rainy Mountain

(1969)

N. Scott Momaday (1934–) is a poet, novelist, painter, playwright, and Professor Emeritus at the University of Arizona. His novel House Made of Dawn *(1968) won the Pulitzer Prize.*

The following passage is an excerpt from his book The Way to Rainy Mountain *(1969), which is both a memoir and a retelling of the Kiowa myths Momaday learned from his grandmother.*

A single knoll rises out of the plain in Oklahoma, north and west of the Wichita Range. For my people, the Kiowas, it is an old landmark, and they gave it the name Rainy Mountain. The hardest weather in the world is there. Winter brings blizzards, hot tornadic winds arise in the spring, and in summer the prairie is an anvil's edge. The grass turns brittle and brown, and it cracks beneath your feet. There are green belts along the rivers and creeks, linear groves of hickory and pecan, willow and witch hazel. At a distance in July or August the steaming foliage seems almost to writhe in fire. Great green and yellow grasshoppers are everywhere in the tall grass, popping up like corn to sting the flesh, and tortoises crawl about on the red earth, going nowhere in the plenty of time. Loneliness is an aspect of the land. All things in the plain are isolate; there is no confusion of objects in the eye, but *one* hill or *one* tree or *one* man. To look upon that landscape in the early morning, with the sun at your back, is to lose the sense of proportion. Your imagination comes to life, and this, you think, is where Creation was begun.

I returned to Rainy Mountain in July. My grandmother had died in the spring, and I wanted to be at her grave. She had lived to be very old and at last infirm. Her only living daughter was with her when she died, and I was told that in death her face was that of a child.

I like to think of her as a child. When she was born, the Kiowas were living the last great moment of their history. For more than a hundred years they had controlled the open range from the Smoky Hill River to the Red, from the headwaters of the Canadian to the fork of the Arkansas and

Cimarron. In alliance with the Comanches, they had ruled the whole of the southern Plains. War was their sacred business, and they were among the finest horsemen the world has ever known. But warfare for the Kiowas was preeminently a matter of disposition rather than of survival, and they never understood the grim, unrelenting advance of the U.S. Cavalry. When at last, divided and ill-provisioned, they were driven onto the Staked Plains in the cold rains of autumn, they fell into panic. In Palo Duro Canyon they abandoned their crucial stores to pillage and had nothing then but their lives. In order to save themselves, they surrendered to the soldiers at Fort Sill and were imprisoned in the old stone corral that now stands as a military museum. My grandmother was spared the humiliation of those high gray walls by eight or ten years, but she must have known from birth the affliction of defeat, the dark brooding of old warriors.

Her name was Aho, and she belonged to the last culture to evolve in North America. Her forebears came down from the high country in western Montana nearly three centuries ago. They were a mountain people, a mysterious tribe of hunters whose language has never been positively classified in any major group. In the late seventeenth century they began a long migration to the south and east. It was a journey toward the dawn, and it led to a golden age. Along the way the Kiowas were befriended by the Crows, who gave them the culture and religion of the Plains. They acquired horses, and their ancient nomadic spirit was suddenly free of the ground. They acquired Tai-me, the sacred Sun Dance doll, from that moment the object and symbol of their worship, and so shared in the divinity of the sun. Not least, they acquired the sense of destiny, therefore courage and pride. When they entered upon the southern Plains they had been transformed. No longer were they slaves to the simple necessity of survival; they were a lordly and dangerous society of fighters and thieves, hunters and priests of the sun. According to their origin myth, they entered the world through a hollow log. From one point of view, their migration was the fruit of an old prophecy, for indeed they emerged from a sunless world.

Although my grandmother lived out her long life in the shadow of Rainy Mountain, the immense landscape of the continental interior lay like memory in her blood. She could tell of the Crows, whom she had never seen, and of the Black Hills, where she had never been. I wanted to see in reality what she had seen more perfectly in the mind's eye, and traveled fifteen hundred miles to begin my pilgrimage.

Yellowstone, it seemed to me, was the top of the world, a region of deep lakes and dark timber, canyons and waterfalls. But, beautiful as it is, one might have the sense of confinement there. The skyline in all directions is close at hand, the high wall of the woods and deep cleavages of shade. There is a perfect freedom in the mountains, but it belongs to the eagle and the elk, the badger and the bear. The Kiowas reckoned their stature by the distance they could see, and they were bent and blind in the wilderness.

Descending eastward, the highland meadows are a stairway to the plain. In July the inland slope of the Rockies is luxuriant with flax and buckwheat, stonecrop and larkspur. The earth unfolds and the limit of the land recedes. Clusters of trees, and animals grazing far in the distance, cause the vision to reach away and wonder to build upon the mind. The sun follows a longer course in the day, and the sky is immense beyond all comparison. The great billowing clouds that sail upon it are the shadows that move upon the grain like water, dividing light. Farther down, in the land of the Crows and Black-feet, the plain is yellow. Sweet clover takes hold of the hills and bends upon itself to cover and seal the soil. There the Kiowas paused on their way; they had come to the place where they must change their lives. The sun is at home on the plains. Precisely there does it have the certain character of a god. When the Kiowas came to the land of the Crows, they could see the dark lees of the hills at dawn across the Bighorn River, the profusion of light on the grain shelves, the oldest deity ranging after the solstices. Not yet would they veer southward to the caldron of the land that lay below; they must wean their blood from the northern winter and hold the mountains a while longer in their view. They bore Tai-me in procession to the east.

A dark mist lay over the Black Hills, and the land was like iron. At the top of a ridge I caught sight of Devil's Tower upthrust against the gray sky as if in the birth of time the core of the earth had broken through its crust and the motion of the world was begun. There are things in nature that engender an awful quiet in the heart of man; Devil's Tower is one of them. Two centuries ago, because they could not do otherwise, the Kiowas made a legend at the base of the rock. My grandmother said:

Eight children were there at play, seven sisters and their brother. Suddenly the boy was struck dumb; he trembled and began to run upon his hands and feet. His fingers became claws, and his body was covered with fur. Directly there was a bear where the boy had been. The sisters were terrified; they ran, and the bear after them. They came to the stump of a great tree, and the tree spoke to them. It bade them climb upon it, and as they did so it began to rise into the air. The bear came to kill them, but they were just beyond its reach. It reared against the tree and scored the bark all around with its claws. The seven sisters were borne into the sky, and they became the stars of the Big Dipper.

From that moment, and so long as the legend lives, the Kiowas have kinsmen in the night sky. Whatever they were in the mountains, they could be no more. However tenuous their well-being, however much they had suffered and would suffer again, they had found a way out of the wilderness.

My grandmother had a reverence for the sun, a holy regard that now is   10
all but gone out of mankind. There was a wariness in her, and an ancient
awe. She was a Christian in her later years, but she had come a long way
about, and she never forgot her birthright. As a child she had been to the
Sun Dances; she had taken part in those annual rites, and by them she had
learned the restoration of her people in the presence of Tai-me. She was
about seven when the last Kiowa Sun Dance was held in 1887 on the
Washita River above Rainy Mountain Creek. The buffalo were gone. In
order to consummate the ancient sacrifice—to impale the head of a buffalo bull upon the medicine tree—a delegation of old men journeyed into
Texas, there to beg and barter for an animal from the Goodnight herd. She
was ten when the Kiowas came together for the last time as a living Sun
Dance culture. They could find no buffalo; they had to hang an old hide
from the sacred tree. Before the dance could begin, a company of soldiers
rode out from Fort Sill under orders to disperse the tribe. Forbidden without cause the essential act of their faith, having seen the wild herds slaughtered and left to rot upon the ground, the Kiowas backed away forever from
the medicine tree. That was July 20, 1890, at the great bend of the Washita.
My grandmother was there. Without bitterness, and for as long as she lived,
she bore a vision of deicide.

Now that I can have her only in memory, I see my grandmother in the several postures that were peculiar to her: standing at the wood stove on a winter morning and turning meat in a great iron skillet; sitting at the south window, bent above her beadwork, and afterwards, when her vision failed,
looking down for a long time into the fold of her hands; going out upon a
cane, very slowly as she did when the weight of age came upon her; praying.
I remember her most often at prayer. She made long, rambling prayers out
of suffering and hope, having seen many things. I was never sure that I had
the right to hear, so exclusive were they all mere custom and company.
The last time I saw her she prayed standing by the side of her bed at night,
naked to the waist, the light of a kerosene lamp moving upon her dark skin.
Her long, black hair, always drawn and braided in the day, lay upon her
shoulders and against her breasts like a shawl. I do not speak Kiowa, and I
never understood her prayers, but there was something inherently sad in the
sound, some merest hesitation upon the syllables of sorrow. She began in a
high and descending pitch, exhausting her breath to silence; then again and
again—and always the same intensity of effort, of something that is, and is
not, like urgency in the human voice. Transported so in the dancing light
among the shadows of her room, she seemed beyond the reach of time. But
that was illusion; I think I knew then that I should not see her again.

Houses are like sentinels in the plain, old keepers of the weather watch.
There, in a very little while, wood takes on the appearance of great age. All
colors wear soon away in the wind and rain, and then the wood is burned

gray and the grain appears and the nails turn red with rust. The window-panes are black and opaque; you imagine there is nothing within, and indeed there are many ghosts, bones given up to the land. They stand here and there against the sky, and you approach them for a longer time than you expect. They belong in the distance; it is their domain.

Once there was a lot of sound in my grandmother's house, a lot of coming and going, feasting and talk. The summers there were full of excitement and reunion. The Kiowas are a summer people; they abide the cold and keep to themselves, but when the season turns and the land becomes warm and vital they cannot hold still; an old love of going returns upon them. The aged visitors who came to my grandmother's house when I was a child were made of lean and leather, and they bore themselves upright. They wore great black hats and bright ample shirts that shook in the wind. They rubbed fat upon their hair and wound their braids with strips of colored cloth. Some of them painted their faces and carried the scars of old and cherished enmities. They were an old council of warlords, come to remind and be reminded of who they were. Their wives and daughters served them well. The women might indulge themselves; gossip was at once the mark and compensation of their servitude. They made loud and elaborate talk among themselves, full of jest and gesture, fright and false alarm. They went abroad in fringed and flowered shawls, bright beadwork and German silver. They were at home in the kitchen, and they prepared meals that were banquets.

There were frequent prayer meetings, and great nocturnal feasts. When I was a child I played with my cousins outside, where the lamplight fell upon the ground and the singing of the old people rose up around us and carried away into the darkness. There were a lot of good things to eat, a lot of laughter and surprise. And afterwards, when the quiet returned, I lay down with my grandmother and could hear the frogs away by the river and feel the motion of the air.

15   Now there is a funeral silence in the rooms, the endless wake of some final word. The walls have closed in upon my grandmother's house. When I returned to it in mourning, I saw for the first time in my life how small it was. It was late at night, and there was a white moon, nearly full. I sat for a long time on the stone steps by the kitchen door. From there I could see out across the land; I could see the long row of trees by the creek, the low light upon the rolling plains, and the stars of the Big Dipper. Once I looked at the moon and caught sight of a strange thing. A cricket had perched upon the handrail, only a few inches away from me. My line of vision was such that the creature filled the moon like a fossil. It had gone there, I thought, to live and die, for there, of all places, was its small definition made whole and eternal. A warm wind rose up and purled like the longing within me.

The next morning I awoke at dawn and went out on the dirt road to Rainy Mountain. It was already hot, and the grasshoppers began to fill the air. Still, it was early in the morning, and the birds sang out of the shadows. The long yellow grass on the mountain shone in the bright light, and a scissortail hied above the land. There, where it ought to be, at the end of a long and legendary way, was my grandmother's grave. Here and there on the dark stones were ancestral names. Looking back once, I saw the mountain and came away.

Questions

1. With reference to paragraph 4 and paragraph 7, discuss the relationship of Kiowas to their mythology as Momaday presents it.
2. Momaday's first paragraph includes both physically vivid descriptions and a reference to loneliness. In what ways does this juxtaposition inform the logic and style of the piece as a whole?
3. Find instances in the essay where Momaday uses words in an odd or atypical manner. How does this affect the reader?

NGUGI WA THIONG'O

Decolonising the Mind

(1986)

Ngugi wa Thiong'o (1938–) is East Africa's leading novelist and social critic. Originally named James Thiong'o Ngugi, the author changed his name as an act of resistance against the effects of colonialism in Africa. His works include the novels Weep Not, Child *(1964),* The River Between *(1965), and* Petals of Blood *(1977), and the essay collections* Homecoming *(1972) and* Moving the Centre *(1993).*

In this excerpt from Decolonising the Mind: The Politics of Language in African Literature *(1986), Ngugi discusses some of the connections between language and culture.*

III

I was born into a large peasant family: father, four wives and about twenty-eight children. I also belonged, as we all did in those days, to a wider extended family and to the community as a whole.

We spoke Gīkūyū as we worked in the fields. We spoke Gīkūyū in and outside the home. I can vividly recall those evenings of storytelling around the fireside. It was mostly the grown-ups telling the children but everybody was interested and involved. We children would re-tell the stories the following day to other children who worked in the fields picking the pyrethrum flowers, tea-leaves or coffee beans of our European and African landlords.

The stories, with mostly animals as the main characters, were all told in Gīkūyū. Hare, being small, weak but full of innovative wit and cunning, was our hero. We identified with him as he struggled against the brutes of prey like lion, leopard, hyena. His victories were our victories and we learnt that the apparently weak can outwit the strong. We followed the animals in their struggle against hostile nature—drought, rain, sun, wind—a confrontation often forcing them to search for forms of co-operation. But we were also interested in their struggles amongst themselves, and particularly between the beasts and the victims of prey. These twin struggles, against nature and other animals, reflected real-life struggles in the human world.

Not that we neglected stories with human beings as the main characters. There were two types of characters in such human-centred narratives: the species of truly human beings with qualities of courage, kindness, mercy, hatred of evil, concern for others; and a man-eat-man two-mouthed species with qualities of greed, selfishness, individualism and hatred of what was good for the larger co-operative community. Co-operation as the ultimate good in a community was a constant theme. It could unite human beings with animals against ogres and beasts of prey, as in the story of how dove, after being fed with castor-oil seeds, was sent to fetch a smith working far away from home and whose pregnant wife was being threatened by these man-eating two-mouthed ogres.

There were good and bad story-tellers. A good one could tell the same   5
story over and over again, and it would always be fresh to us, the listeners. He or she could tell a story told by someone else and make it more alive and dramatic. The differences really were in the use of words and images and the inflexion of voices to effect different tones.

We therefore learnt to value words for their meaning and nuances. Language was not a mere string of words. It had a suggestive power well beyond the immediate and lexical meaning. Our appreciation of the suggestive magical power of language was reinforced by the games we played with words through riddles, proverbs, transpositions of syllables, or through nonsensical but musically arranged words. So we learnt the music of our language on top of the content. The language, through images and symbols, gave us a view of the world, but it had a beauty of its own. The home and the field were then our pre-primary school but what is important, for this discussion, is that the language of our evening teach-ins, and the language of our immediate and wider community, and the language of our work in the fields were one.

And then I went to school, a colonial school, and this harmony was broken. The language of my education was no longer the language of my culture. I first went to Kamaandura, missionary run, and then to another called Maanguū run by nationalists grouped around the Gīkūyū Independent and Karinga Schools Association. Our language of education was still Gīkūyū. The very first time I was ever given an ovation for my writing was over a composition in Gīkūyū. So for my first four years there was still harmony between the language of my formal education and that of the Limuru peasant community.

It was after the declaration of a state of emergency over Kenya in 1952 that all the schools run by patriotic nationalists were taken over by the colonial regime and were placed under District Education Boards chaired by Englishmen. English became the language of my formal education. In Kenya, English became more than a language: it was *the* language, and all the others had to bow before it in deference.

Thus one of the most humiliating experiences was to be caught speaking Gīkūyū in the vicinity of the school. The culprit was given corporal punishment—three to five strokes of the cane on bare buttocks—or was made to carry a metal plate around the neck with inscriptions such as I AM STUPID or I AM A DONKEY. Sometimes the culprits were fined money they could hardly afford. And how did the teachers catch the culprits? A button was initially given to one pupil who was supposed to hand it over to whoever was caught speaking his mother tongue. Whoever had the button at the end of the day would sing who had given it to him and the ensuing process would bring out all the culprits of the day. Thus children were turned into witch-hunters and in the process were being taught the lucrative value of being a traitor to one's immediate community.

10   The attitude to English was the exact opposite: any achievement in spoken or written English was highly rewarded; prizes, prestige, applause; the ticket to higher realms. English became the measure of intelligence and ability in the arts, the sciences, and all the other branches of learning. English became *the* main determinant of a child's progress up the ladder of formal education.

As you may know, the colonial system of education in addition to its apartheid racial demarcation had the structure of a pyramid: a broad primary base, a narrowing secondary middle, and an even narrower university apex. Selections from primary into secondary were through an examination, in my time called Kenya African Preliminary Examination, in which one had to pass six subjects ranging from Maths to Nature Study and Kiswahili. All the papers were written in English. Nobody could pass the exam who failed the English language paper no matter how brilliantly he had done in the other subjects. I remember one boy in my class of 1954 who had distinctions in all subjects except English, which he had failed. He was made to fail the entire exam. He went on to become a turn boy in a bus company. I who had only passes but a credit in English got a place at the Alliance High School, one of the most elitist institutions for Africans in colonial Kenya. The requirements for a place at the University, Makerere University College, were broadly the same: nobody could go on to wear the undergraduate red gown, no matter how brilliantly they had performed in all the other subjects unless they had a credit—not even a simple pass!—in English. Thus the most coveted place in the pyramid and in the system was only available to the holder of an English language credit card. English was the official vehicle and the magic formula to colonial elitedom.

Literary education was now determined by the dominant language while also reinforcing that dominance. Orature (oral literature) in Kenyan languages stopped. In primary school I now read simplified Dickens and Stevenson alongside Rider Haggard.[1] Jim Hawkins, Oliver Twist, Tom Brown—not Hare, Leopard and Lion—were now my daily companions in the world of

---

1 *Rider Haggard* H. Rider Haggard (1856–1925), a British author of adventure novels, many set in Africa.

imagination. In secondary school, Scott and G.B. Shaw vied with more Rider Haggard, John Buchan, Alan Paton, Captain W.E. Johns. At Makerere I read English: from Chaucer to T.S. Eliot with a touch of Grahame Greene.

Thus language and literature were taking us further and further from ourselves to other selves, from our world to other worlds.

What was the colonial system doing to us Kenyan children? What were the consequences of, on the one hand, this systematic suppression of our languages and the literature they carried, and on the other the elevation of English and the literature it carried? To answer those questions, let me first examine the relationship of language to human experience, human culture, and the human perception of reality.

IV

Language, any language, has a dual character: it is both a means of communication and a carrier of culture. Take English. It is spoken in Britain and in Sweden and Denmark. But for Swedish and Danish people English is only a means of communication with non-Scandinavians. It is not a carrier of their culture. For the British, and particularly the English, it is additionally, and inseparably from its use as a tool of communication, a carrier of their culture and history. Or take Swahili in East and Central Africa. It is widely used as a means of communication across many nationalities. But it is not the carrier of a culture and history of many of those nationalities. However in parts of Kenya and Tanzania, and particularly in Zanzibar, Swahili is inseparably both a means of communication and a carrier of the culture of those people to whom it is a mother-tongue.

Language as communication has three aspects or elements. There is first what Karl Marx once called the language of real life, the element basic to the whole notion of language, its origins and development: that is, the relations people enter into with one another in the labour process, the links they necessarily establish among themselves in the act of a people, a community of human beings, producing wealth or means of life like food, clothing, houses. A human community really starts its historical being as a community of co-operation in production through the division of labour; the simplest is between man, woman and child within a household; the more complex divisions are between branches of production such as those who are sole hunters, sole gatherers of fruits or sole workers in metal. Then there are the most complex divisions such as those in modern factories where a single product, say a shirt or a shoe, is the result of many hands and minds. Production is co-operation, is communication, is language, is expression of a relation between human beings and it is specifically human.

The second aspect of language as communication is speech and it imitates the language of real life, that is communication in production. The

15

verbal signposts both reflect and aid communication or the relation established between human beings in the production of their means of life. Language as a system of verbal signposts makes that production possible. The spoken word is to relations between human beings what the hand is to the relations between human beings and nature. The hand through tools mediates between human beings and nature and forms the language of real life: spoken words mediate between human beings and form the language of speech.

The third aspect is the written signs. The written word imitates the spoken. Where the first two aspects of language as communication through the hand and the spoken word historically evolved more or less simultaneously, the written aspect is a much later historical development. Writing is representation of sounds with visual symbols, from the simplest knot among shepherds to tell the number in a herd or the hieroglyphics among the Agĩkũyũ gicaandi singers and poets of Kenya, to the most complicated and different letter and picture writing systems of the world today.

In most societies the written and the spoken languages are the same, in that they represent each other: what is on paper can be read to another person and be received as that language, which the recipient has grown up speaking. In such a society there is broad harmony for a child between the three aspects of language as communication. His interaction with nature and with other men is expressed in written and spoken symbols or signs which are both a result of that double interaction and a reflection of it. The association of the child's sensibility is with the language of his experience of life.

20   But there is more to it: communication between human beings is also the basis and process of evolving culture. In doing similar kinds of things and actions over and over again under similar circumstances, similar even in their mutability, certain patterns, moves, rhythms, habits, attitudes, experiences and knowledge emerge. Those experiences are handed over to the next generation and become the inherited basis for their further actions on nature and on themselves. There is a gradual accumulation of values which in time become almost self-evident truths governing their conception of what is right and wrong, good and bad, beautiful and ugly, courageous and cowardly, generous and mean in their internal and external relations. Over a time this becomes a way of life distinguishable from other ways of life. They develop a distinctive culture and history. Culture embodies those moral, ethical and aesthetic values, the set of spiritual eyeglasses, through which they come to view themselves and their place in the universe. Values are the basis of a people's identity, their sense of particularity as members of the human race. All this is carried by language. Language as culture is the collective memory bank of a people's experience in history. Culture is almost indistinguishable from the language that makes possible its genesis, growth, banking, articulation and indeed its transmission from one generation to the next.

Language as culture also has three important aspects. Culture is a product of the history which it in turn reflects. Culture in other words is a product and a reflection of human beings communicating with one another in the very struggle to create wealth and to control it. But culture does not merely reflect that history, or rather it does so by actually forming images or pictures of the world of nature and nurture. Thus the second aspect of language as culture is as an image-forming agent in the mind of a child. Our whole conception of ourselves as a people, individually and collectively, is based on those pictures and images which may or may not correctly correspond to the actual reality of the struggles with nature and nurture which produced them in the first place. But our capacity to confront the world creatively is dependent on how those images correspond or not to that reality, how they distort or clarify the reality of our struggles. Language as culture is thus mediating between me and my own self; between my own self and other selves; between me and nature. Language is mediating in my very being. And this brings us to the third aspect of language as culture. Culture transmits or imparts those images of the world and reality through the spoken and the written language, that is through a specific language. In other words, the capacity to speak, the capacity to order sounds in a manner that makes for mutual comprehension between human beings is universal. This is the universality of language, a quality specific to human beings. It corresponds to the universality of the struggle against nature and that between human beings. But the particularity of the sounds, the words, the word order into phrases and sentences, and the specific manner, or laws, of their ordering is what distinguishes one language from another. Thus a specific culture is not transmitted through language in its universality but in its particularity as the language of a specific community with a specific history. Written literature and orature are the main means by which a particular language transmits the images of the world contained in the culture it carries.

Language as communication and as culture are then products of each other. Communication creates culture: culture is a means of communication. Language carries culture, and culture carries, particularly through orature and literature, the entire body of values by which we come to perceive ourselves and our place in the world. How people perceive themselves affects how they look at their culture, at their politics and at the social production of wealth, at their entire relationship to nature and to other beings. Language is thus inseparable from ourselves as a community of human beings with a specific form and character, a specific history, a specific relationship to the world.

V

So what was the colonialist imposition of a foreign language doing to us children?

The real aim of colonialism was to control the people's wealth: what they produced, how they produced it, and how it was distributed; to control, in other words, the entire realm of the language of real life. Colonialism imposed its control of the social production of wealth through military conquest and subsequent political dictatorship. But its most important area of domination was the mental universe of the colonised, the control, through culture, of how people perceived themselves and their relationship to the world. Economic and political control can never be complete or effective without mental control. To control a people's culture is to control their tools of self-definition in relationship to others.

25   For colonialism this involved two aspects of the same process: the destruction or the deliberate undervaluing of a people's culture, their art, dances, religions, history, geography, education, orature and literature, and the conscious elevation of the language of the coloniser. The domination of a people's language by the languages of the colonising nations was crucial to the domination of the mental universe of the colonised.

Take language as communication. Imposing a foreign language, and suppressing the native languages as spoken and written, were already breaking the harmony previously existing between the African child and the three aspects of language. Since the new language as a means of communication was a product of and was reflecting the "real language of life" elsewhere, it could never as spoken or written properly reflect or imitate the real life of that community. This may in part explain why technology always appears to us as slightly external, *their* product and not *ours*. The word "missile" used to hold an alien far-away sound until I recently learnt its equivalent in Gĩkũyũ, *ngurukuhĩ* and it made me apprehend it differently. Learning, for a colonial child, became a cerebral activity and not an emotionally felt experience.

But since the new, imposed languages could never completely break the native languages as spoken, their most effective area of domination was the third aspect of language as communication, the written. The language of an African child's formal education was foreign. The language of the books he read was foreign. The language of his conceptualisation was foreign. Thought, in him, took the visible form of a foreign language. So the written language of a child's upbringing in the school (even his spoken language within the school compound) became divorced from his spoken language at home. There was often not the slightest relationship between the child's written world, which was also the language of his schooling, and the world of his immediate environment in the family and the community. For a colonial child, the harmony existing between the three aspects of language as communication was irrevocably broken. This resulted in the disassociation of the sensibility of that child from his natural and social environment, what we might call colonial alienation. The alienation became reinforced in the teaching of history, geography, music, where bourgeois Europe was always the centre of the universe.

This disassociation, divorce, or alienation from the immediate environment becomes clearer when you look at colonial language as a carrier of culture.

Since culture is a product of the history of a people which it in turn reflects, the child was now being exposed exclusively to a culture that was a product of a world external to himself. He was being made to stand outside himself to look at himself. *Catching Them Young* is the title of a book on racism, class, sex, and politics in children's literature by Bob Dixon. "Catching them young" as an aim was even more true of a colonial child. The images of his world and his place in it implanted in a child take years to eradicate, if they ever can be.

Since culture does not just reflect the world in images but actually, through those images, conditions a child to see that world a certain way, the colonial child was made to see the world and where he stands in it as seen and defined by or reflected in the culture of the language of imposition.

And since those images are mostly passed on through orature and literature it meant the child would now only see the world as seen in the literature of his language of adoption. From the point of view of alienation, that is of seeing oneself from outside oneself as if one was another self, it does not matter that the imported literature carried the great humanist tradition of the best Shakespeare, Goethe, Balzac, Tolstoy, Gorky, Brecht, Sholokhov, Dickens. The location of this great mirror of imagination was necessarily Europe and its history and culture and the rest of the universe was seen from that centre.

But obviously it was worse when the colonial child was exposed to images of his world as mirrored in the written languages of his coloniser. Where his own native languages were associated in his impressionable mind with low status, humiliation, corporal punishment, slow-footed intelligence and ability or downright stupidity, non-intelligibility and barbarism, this was reinforced by the world he met in the works of such geniuses of racism as a Rider Haggard or a Nicholas Monsarrat;[1] not to mention the pronouncement of some of the giants of western intellectual and political establishment, such as Hume[2] ("... The negro is naturally inferior to the whites ..."), Thomas Jefferson ("... The blacks ... are inferior to the whites on the endowments of both body and mind ..."), or Hegel[3] with his Africa comparable to a land of childhood still enveloped in the dark mantle of the night as far as the development of self-conscious history was concerned. Hegel's statement

30

---

1   *Nicholas Monsarrat* (1910–79) British novelist, some of whose writings are set in South Africa.
2   *Hume* David Hume (1711–76), Scottish philosopher.
3   *Hegel* Georg Wilhelm Friedrich Hegel (1770–1831), German philosopher.

that there was nothing harmonious with humanity to be found in the African character is representative of the racist images of Africans and Africa such a colonial child was bound to encounter in the literature of the colonial languages. The results could be disastrous.

Questions

1. Why do you think Ngugi chose this opening sentence? How does the autobiographical character of the beginning of this text evolve throughout the work? What is the effect of that evolution?
2. Discuss both the effectiveness and the limitations of writing in a language while simultaneously writing "against" that language.

PERRI KLASS

Learning the Language

(1987)

Perri Klass (1958–) is an American paediatrician, writer, and children's literacy advocate whose short stories have received five O. Henry awards. An author of both fiction and non-fiction, Klass has written on such diverse topics as parenting, mother-daughter relationships, women in the medical profession, diet and nutrition, and knitting.

In the following essay, Klass recounts her introduction to medical jargon.

"Mrs. Tolstoy is your basic LOL in NAD, admitted for a soft rule-out MI," the intern announces. I scribble that on my patient list. In other words, Mrs. Tolstoy is a Little Old Lady in No Apparent Distress who is in the hospital to make sure she hasn't had a heart attack (rule out a Myocardial Infarction). And we think it's unlikely that she has had a heart attack (a *soft* rule-out).

If I learned nothing else during my first three months of working in the hospital as a medical student, I learned endless jargon and abbreviations. I started out in a state of primeval innocence, in which I didn't even know that "s̄ CP, SOB, N/V" meant "without chest pain, shortness of breath, or nausea and vomiting." By the end I took the abbreviations so much for granted that I would complain to my mother the English professor, "And can you believe I had to put down *three* NG tubes last night?"

"You'll have to tell me what an NG tube is if you want me to sympathize properly," my mother said. NG, nasogastric—isn't it obvious?

I picked up not only the specific expressions but also the patterns of speech and the grammatical conventions; for example, you never say that a patient's blood pressure fell or that his cardiac enzymes rose. Instead, the patient is always the subject of the verb: "He dropped his pressure." "He bumped his enzymes." This sort of construction probably reflects the profound irritation of the intern when the nurses come in the middle of the night to say that Mr. Dickinson has disturbingly low blood pressure. "Oh, he's gonna hurt me bad tonight," the intern might say, inevitably angry at Mr. Dickinson for dropping his pressure and creating a problem.

5   When chemotherapy fails to cure Mrs. Bacon's cancer, what we say is, "Mrs. Bacon failed chemotherapy."

"Well, we've already had one hit today, and we're up next, but at least we've got mostly stable players on our team." This means that our team (group of doctors and medical students) has already gotten one new admission today, and it is our turn again, so we'll get whoever is admitted next in emergency, but at least most of the patients we already have are fairly stable, that is, unlikely to drop their pressures or in any other way get suddenly sicker and hurt us bad. Baseball metaphor is pervasive. A no-hitter is a night without any new admissions. A player is always a patient—a nitrate player is a patient on nitrates, a unit player is a patient in the intensive care unit, and so on, until you reach the terminal player.

It is interesting to consider what it means to be winning, or doing well, in this perennial baseball game. When the intern hangs up the phone and announces, "I got a hit," that is not the cause for congratulations. The team is not scoring points; rather, it is getting hit, being bombarded with new patients. The object of the game from the point of view of the doctors, considering the players for whom they are already responsible, is to get as few new hits as possible.

This special language contributes to a sense of closeness and professional spirit among people who are under a great deal of stress. As a medical student, I found it exciting to discover that I'd finally cracked the code, that I could understand what doctors said and wrote, and could use the same formulations myself. Some people seem to become enamored of the jargon for its own sake, perhaps because they are so deeply thrilled with the idea of medicine, with the idea of themselves as doctors.

I knew a medical student who was referred to by the interns on the team as Mr. Eponym[1] because he was so infatuated with eponymous terminology, the more obscure the better. He never said "capillary pulsations" if he could say "Quincke's pulses." He would lovingly tell over the multinamed syndromes—Wolff-Parkinson-White,[2] Lown-Ganong-Levine,[3] Schönlein-Henoch[4]—until the temptation to suggest Schleswig-Holstein[5] or Stevenson-Kefauver[6] or Baskin-Robbins became irresistible to his less reverent colleagues.

1 *Eponym* Real or fictional person associated with an activity or object.
2 *Wolff-Parkinson-White* Heart condition resulting from an abnormal electrical system.
3 *Lown-Ganong-Levine* Another heart condition due to an abnormal electrical system.
4 *Schönlein-Henoch* Inflammation of the blood vessels.
5 *Schleswig-Holstein* Northernmost state in Germany bordering Denmark.
6 *Stevenson-Kefauver* Partnership of Adlai Stevenson and Carey Estes Kefauver, unsuccessful Democratic presidential and vice-presidential candidates respectively against Dwight Eisenhower in the 1956 election.

And there is the jargon that you don't ever want to hear yourself using.   10
You know that your training is changing you, but there are certain changes
you think would be going a little too far.

The resident was describing a man with devastating terminal pancreatic
cancer. "Basically he's CTD," the resident concluded. I reminded myself
that I had resolved not to be shy about asking when I didn't understand
things. "CTD?" I asked timidly.

The resident smirked at me. "Circling The Drain."

The images are vivid and terrible. "What happened to Mrs. Melville?"

"Oh, she boxed last night." To box is to die, of course.

Then there are the more pompous locutions that can make the begin-   15
ning medical student nervous about the effects of medical training. A
friend of mine was told by his resident, "A pregnant woman with sickle-cell[1]
represents a failure of genetic counseling."

Mr. Eponym, who tried hard to talk like the doctors, once explained to
me, "An infant is basically a brainstem preparation." The term "brainstem
preparation," as used in neurological research, refers to an animal whose
higher brain functions have been destroyed so that only the most primitive
reflexes remain, like the sucking reflex, the startle reflex, and the rooting
reflex.

And yet at other times the harshness dissipates into a strangely elusive
euphemism. "As you know, this is a not entirely benign procedure," some
doctor will say, and that will be understood to imply agony, risk of compli-
cations, and maybe even a significant mortality rate.

The more extreme forms aside, one most important function of medical
jargon is to help doctors maintain some distance from their patients. By
reformulating a patient's pain and problems into a language that the
patient doesn't even speak, I suppose we are in some sense taking those
pains and problems under our jurisdiction and also reducing their emotional impact. This linguistic separation between doctors and patients
allows conversations to go on at the bedside that are unintelligible to the
patient. "Naturally, we're worried about adeno-CA,"[2] the intern can say to
the medical student, and lung cancer need never be mentioned.

I learned a new language this past summer. At times it thrills me to hear
myself using it. It enables me to understand my colleagues, to communicate
effectively in the hospital. Yet I am uncomfortably aware that I will never
again notice the peculiarities and even atrocities of medical language as
keenly as I did this summer. There may be specific expressions I manage to
avoid, but even as I remark them, promising myself I will never use them, I
find that this language is becoming my professional speech. It no longer

---

1   *sickle-cell* Inherited disorder of the blood resulting in anemia; sickle cell disease
    requires both parents to pass on the gene.
2   *adeno-CA* Form of lung cancer (adenocarcinoma).

sounds strange in my ears—or coming from my mouth. And I am afraid that as with any new language, to use it properly you must absorb not only the vocabulary but also the structure, the logic, the attitudes. At first you may notice these new and alien assumptions every time you put together a sentence, but with time and increased fluency you stop being aware of them at all. And as you lose that awareness, for better or for worse, you move closer and closer to being a doctor instead of just talking like one.

Questions

1. Klass comments on the grammatical conventions used by doctors, in particular how the "patient is always the subject of the verb," and suggests that such a construction may indicate a doctor's irritation when something goes wrong. What other attitudes might this construction reflect?
2. What is the significance of the patients' names in this essay?
3. Discuss the significance of the prevalent "baseball metaphor" described by Klass (paragraph 6). What attitudes emerge from such usage?

AMY TAN

Mother Tongue

(1991)

Amy Tan (1952–) is the author of five novels including The Joy Luck Club *(1989) and* Saving Fish from Drowning *(2005), two books for children, and a collection of essays,* The Opposite of Fate: A Book of Musings *(2003).*

In this essay, Tan writes about her mother's Chinese American English, and about how her mother's language has shaped her own relationships to language and identity.

I am not a scholar of English or literature. I cannot give you much more than personal opinions on the English language and its variations in this country or others.

I am a writer. And by that definition, I am someone who has always loved language. I am fascinated by language in daily life. I spend a great deal of my time thinking about the power of language—the way it can evoke an emotion, a visual image, a complex idea, or a simple truth. Language is the tool of my trade. And I use them all—all the Englishes I grew up with.

Recently, I was made keenly aware of the different Englishes I do use. I was giving a talk to a large group of people, the same talk I had already given to half a dozen other groups. The nature of the talk was about my writing, my life, and my book, *The Joy Luck Club.* The talk was going along well enough, until I remembered one major difference that made the whole talk sound wrong. My mother was in the room. And it was perhaps the first time she had heard me give a lengthy speech, using the kind of English I have never used with her. I was saying things like, "The intersection of memory upon imagination" and "There is an aspect of my fiction that relates to thus-and-thus"—a speech filled with carefully wrought grammatical phrases, burdened, it suddenly seemed to me, with nominalized forms, past perfect tenses, conditional phrases, all the forms of standard English that I had learned in school and through books, the forms of English I did not use at home with my mother.

Just last week, I was walking down the street with my mother, and I again found myself conscious of the English I was using, the English I do use with her. We were talking about the price of new and used furniture and I heard myself saying this: "Not waste money that way." My husband was with us as well, and he didn't notice any switch in my English. And then I realized why. It's because over the twenty years we've been together I've often used that same kind of English with him, and sometimes he even uses it with me. It has become our language of intimacy, a different sort of English that relates to family talk, the language I grew up with.

5   So you'll have some idea of what this family talk I heard sounds like, I'll quote what my mother said during a recent conversation which I video-taped and then transcribed. During this conversation, my mother was talking about a political gangster in Shang-hai who had the same last name as her family's, Du, and how the gangster in his early years wanted to be adopted by her family, which was rich by comparison. Later, the gangster became more powerful, far richer than my mother's family, and one day showed up at my mother's wedding to pay his respects. Here's what she said in part:

"Du Yusong having business like fruit stand. Like off the street kind. He is Du like Du Zong—but not Tsung-ming Island people. The local people call putong, the river east side, he belong to that side local people. That man want to ask Du Zong father take him in like become own family. Du Zong father wasn't look down on him, but didn't take seriously, until that man big like become a mafia. Now important person, very hard to inviting him. Chinese way, came only to show respect, don't stay for dinner. Respect for making big celebration, he shows up. Mean gives lots of respect. Chinese custom. Chinese social life that way. If too important won't have to stay too long. He come to my wedding. I didn't see, I heard it. I gone to boy's side, they have YMCA dinner. Chinese age I was nineteen."

You should know that my mother's expressive command of English belies how much she actually understands. She reads the *Forbes* report, listens to *Wall Street Week*, converses daily with her stockbroker, reads all of Shirley MacLaine's books with ease—all kinds of things I can't begin to understand. Yet some of my friends tell me they understand 50 percent of what my mother says. Some say they understand 80 to 90 percent. Some say they understand none of it, as if she were speaking pure Chinese. But to me, my mother's English is perfectly clear, perfectly natural. It's my mother tongue. Her language, as I hear it, is vivid, direct, full of observation and imagery. That was the language that helped shape the way I saw things, expressed things, made sense of the world.

Lately, I've been giving more thought to the kind of English my mother speaks. Like others, I have described it to people as "broken" or "fractured" English. But I wince when I say that. It has always bothered me that I can think of no way to describe it other than "broken," as if it were damaged and needed to be fixed, as if it lacked a certain wholeness and soundness. I've heard other terms used, "limited English," for example. But they seem just as bad, as if everything is limited, including people's perceptions of the limited English speaker.

I know this for a fact, because when I was growing up, my mother's "limited" English limited *my* perception of her. I was ashamed of her English. I believed that her English reflected the quality of what she had to say. That is, because she expressed them imperfectly her thoughts were imperfect. And I had plenty of empirical evidence to support me: the fact that people in department stores, at banks, and at restaurants did not take her seriously, did not give her good service, pretended not to understand her, or even acted as if they did not hear her.

My mother has long realized the limitations of her English as well. When   10
I was fifteen, she used to have me call people on the phone to pretend I was she. In this guise, I was forced to ask for information or even to complain and yell at people who had been rude to her. One time it was a call to her stockbroker in New York. She had cashed out her small portfolio and it just so happened we were going to go to New York the next week, our very first trip outside California. I had to get on the phone and say in an adolescent voice that was not very convincing, "This is Mrs. Tan."

And my mother was standing in the back whispering loudly, "Why he don't send me check, already two weeks late. So mad he lie to me, losing me money."

And then I said in perfect English, "Yes, I'm getting rather concerned. You had agreed to send the check two weeks ago, but it hasn't arrived."

Then she began to talk more loudly. "What he want, I come to New York tell him front of his boss, you cheating me?" And I was trying to calm her down, make her be quiet, while telling the stockbroker, "I can't tolerate any more excuses. If I don't receive the check immediately, I am going to have to speak to your manager when I'm in New York next week." And sure enough, the following week there we were in front of this astonished stockbroker, and I was sitting there red-faced and quiet, and my mother, the real Mrs. Tan, was shouting at his boss in her impeccable broken English.

We used a similar routine just five days ago, for a situation that was far less humorous. My mother had gone to the hospital for an appointment, to find out about a benign brain tumor a CAT scan had revealed a month ago. She said she had spoken very good English, her best English, no mistakes. Still, she said, the hospital did not apologize when they said they had lost the CAT scan and she had come for nothing. She said they did not seem to have any sympathy when she told them she was anxious to know the exact diagnosis, since her husband and son had both died of brain tumors. She said they would not give her any more information until the next time and she would have to make another appointment for that. So she said she would not leave until the doctor called her daughter. She wouldn't budge. And when the doctor finally called her daughter, me, who spoke in perfect English—lo and behold—we had assurances the CAT scan would be found, promises that a conference call on Monday would be held, and apologies for any suffering my mother had gone through for a most regrettable mistake.

15   I think my mother's English almost had an effect on limiting my possibilities in life as well. Sociologists and linguists probably will tell you that a person's developing language skills are more influenced by peers. But I do think that the language spoken in the family, especially in immigrant families which are more insular, plays a large role in shaping the language of the child. And I believe that it affected my results on achievement tests, IQ tests, and the SAT. While my English skills were never judged as poor, compared to math, English could not be considered my strong suit. In grade school I did moderately well, getting perhaps B's, sometimes B-pluses, in English and scoring perhaps in the sixtieth or seventieth percentile on achievement tests. But those scores were not good enough the override the opinion that my true abilities lay in math and science, because in those areas I achieved A's and scored in the ninetieth percentile or higher.

This was understandable. Math is precise; there is only one correct answer. Whereas, for me at least, the answers on English tests were always a judgment call, a matter of opinion and personal experience. Those tests were constructed around items like fill-in-the-blank sentence completion, such as, "Even though Tom was _____, Mary thought he was _____." And the correct answer always seemed to be the most bland combinations of thoughts, for example, "Even though Tom was shy, Mary thought he was charming," with the grammatical structure "even though" limiting the correct answer to some sort of semantic opposites, so you wouldn't get answers like, "Even though Tom was foolish, Mary thought he was ridiculous." Well, according to my mother, there were very few limitations as to what Tom could have been and what Mary might have thought of him. So I never did well on tests like that.

The same was true with word analogies, pairs of words in which you were supposed to find some sort of logical, semantic relationship—for example, "*Sunset* is to *nightfall* as _____ is to _____." And here you would be presented with a list of four possible pairs, one of which showed the same kind of relationship: *red* is to *stoplight, bus* is to *arrival, chills* is to *fever, yawns* is to *boring*. Well, I could never think that way. I knew what the tests were asking, but I could not block out of my mind the images already created by the first pair, "*sunset* is to *nightfall*"—and I would see a burst of colors against a darkening sky, the moon rising, the lowering of a curtain of stars. And all the other pairs of words—red, bus, stoplight, boring—just threw up a mass of confusing images, making it impossible for me to sort out something as logical as saying: "A sunset precedes nightfall" is the same as "a chill precedes a fever." The only way I would have gotten that answer right would have been to imagine an associative situation, for example, my being disobedient and staying out past sunset, catching a chill at night, which turns into a feverish pneumonia as punishment, which indeed did happen to me.

I have been thinking about all this lately, about my mother's English, about achievement tests. Because lately I've been asked, as a writer, why there are not more Asian Americans represented in American literature. Why are there few Asian Americans enrolled in creative writing programs? Why do so many Chinese students go into engineering? Well, these are broad sociological questions I can't begin to answer. But I have noticed in surveys—in fact, just last week—that Asian students, as a whole, always do significantly better on math achievement tests than in English. And this makes me think that there are other Asian-American students whose English spoken in the home might also be described as "broken" or "limited." And perhaps they also have teachers who are steering them away from writing and into math and science, which is what happened to me.

Fortunately, I happen to be rebellious in nature and enjoy the challenge of disproving assumptions made about me. I became an English major my first year in college, after being enrolled as pre-med. I started writing nonfiction as a freelancer the week after I was told by my former boss that writing was my worst skill and I should hone my talents toward account management.

But it wasn't until 1985 that I finally began to write fiction. And at first I wrote using what I thought to be wittily crafted sentences, sentences that would finally prove I had mastery over the English language. Here's an example from the first draft of a story that later made its way into *The Joy Luck Club,* but without this line: "That was my mental quandary in its nascent state." A terrible line, which I can barely pronounce.

Fortunately, for reasons I won't get into today, I later decided I should envision a reader for the stories I would write. And the reader I decided upon was my mother, because these were stories about mothers. So with this reader in mind—and in fact she did read my early drafts—I began to write stories using all the Englishes I grew up with: the English I spoke to my mother, which for lack of a better term might be described as "simple"; the English she used with me, which for lack of a better term might be described as "broken"; my translation of her Chinese, which could certainly be described as "watered down"; and what I imagined to be her translation of her Chinese if she could speak in perfect English, her internal language, and for that I sought to preserve the essence, but neither an English nor a Chinese structure. I wanted to capture what language ability tests can never reveal: her intent, her passion, her imagery, the rhythms of her speech and the nature of her thoughts.

20

Apart from what any critic had to say about my writing, I knew I had succeeded where it counted when my mother finished reading my book and gave me her verdict: "So easy to read."

Questions

1. What does Tan mean by the term "Englishes," and what are the implications of her use of this term?
2. Identify three places in Tan's essay where she describes or implies the senses of meaning (besides dictionary meaning) that language can carry.
3. How exactly does Tan's own writing in this essay embody or complement the arguments she makes about language?

Literature and Other Arts

GILBERT HIGHET

The Gettysburg Address

(1954)

Gilbert Highet (1906–78) taught at Oxford University before becoming a professor of Greek and Latin at Columbia University in 1938, a position he held until 1972. Highet wrote and edited books of poetry, history, criticism, and classicism, including The Classical Tradition: Greek and Roman Influences on Western Literature *(1949).*

In this essay, Highet analyzes Abraham Lincoln's Gettysburg Address *(1863).*

Fourscore and seven years ago ...
These five words stand at the entrance to the best-known monument of American prose, one of the finest utterances in the entire language and surely one of the greatest speeches in all history. Greatness is like granite: it is molded in fire, and it lasts for many centuries.

Fourscore and seven years ago.... It is strange to think that President Lincoln was looking back to the 4th of July 1776, and that he and his speech are now further removed from us than he himself was from George Washington and the Declaration of Independence. Fourscore and seven years before the Gettysburg Address, a small group of patriots signed the Declaration. Fourscore and seven years after the Gettysburg Address, it was the year 1950,[1] and that date is already receding rapidly into our troubled, adventurous, and valiant past.

Inadequately prepared and at first scarcely realized in its full importance, the dedication of the graveyard at Gettysburg was one of the supreme moments of American history. The battle itself had been a turning point of the war. On the 4th of July 1863, General Meade repelled Lee's invasion of Pennsylvania. Although he did not follow up his victory, he had broken one of the most formidable aggressive enterprises of the Confederate armies.

---

1 In November 1950 the Chinese had just entered the war in Korea. [Highet's note.]

Losses were heavy on both sides. Thousands of dead were left on the field, and thousands of wounded died in the hot days following the battle. At first, their burial was more or less haphazard; but thoughtful men gradually came to feel that an adequate burying place and memorial were required. These were established by an interstate commission that autumn, and the finest speaker in the North was invited to dedicate them. This was the scholar and statesman Edward Everett of Harvard. He made a good speech—which is still extant: not at all academic, it is full of close strategic analysis and deep historical understanding.

Lincoln was not invited to speak, at first. Although people knew him as an effective debater, they were not sure whether he was capable of making a serious speech on such a solemn occasion. But one of the impressive things about Lincoln's career is that he constantly strove to *grow*. He was anxious to appear on that occasion and to say something worthy of it. (Also, it has been suggested, he was anxious to remove the impression that he did not know how to behave properly—an impression which had been strengthened by a shocking story about his clowning on the battlefield of Antietam the previous year.) Therefore when he was invited he took considerable care with his speech. He drafted rather more than half of it in the White House before leaving, finished it in the hotel at Gettysburg the night before the ceremony (not in the train, as sometimes reported), and wrote out a fair copy next morning.

5   There are many accounts of the day itself, 19 November 1863. There are many descriptions of Lincoln, all showing the same curious blend of grandeur and awkwardness, or lack of dignity, or—it would be best to call it humility. In the procession he rode horseback: a tall lean man in a high plug hat, straddling a short horse, with his feet too near the ground. He arrived before the chief speaker, and had to wait patiently for half an hour or more. His own speech came right at the end of a long and exhausting ceremony, lasted less than three minutes, and made little impression on the audience. In part this was because they were tired, in part because (as eyewitnesses said) he ended almost before they knew he had begun, and in part because he did not speak the Address, but read it, very slowly, in a thin high voice, with a marked Kentucky accent, pronouncing "to" as "toe" and dropping his final R's.

Some people of course were alert enough to be impressed. Everett congratulated him at once. But most of the newspapers paid little attention to the speech, and some sneered at it. The *Patriot and Union* of Harrisburg wrote, "We pass over the silly remarks of the President; for the credit of the nation we are willing ... that they shall no more be repeated or thought of"; and the London *Times* said, "The ceremony was rendered ludicrous by some of the sallies of that poor President Lincoln," calling his remarks "dull and commonplace." The first commendation of the Address came in a single sentence of the Chicago *Tribune*, and the first discriminating and detailed praise of it appeared in the Springfield *Republican*, the Providence *Journal*, and the Philadelphia *Bulletin*. However, three weeks after the ceremony and then again the following spring, the editor of *Harper's Weekly* published a sincere and thorough eulogy of the Address, and soon it was attaining recognition as a masterpiece.

At the time, Lincoln could not care much about the reception of his words. He was exhausted and ill. In the train back to Washington, he lay down with a wet towel on his head. He had caught smallpox. At that moment he was incubating it, and he was stricken down soon after he reentered the White House. Fortunately it was a mild attack, and it evoked one of his best jokes: he told his visitors, "At last I have something I can give to everybody."

He had more than that to give to everybody. He was a unique person, far greater than most people realize until they read his life with care. The wisdom of his policy, the sources of his statesmanship—these were things too complex to be discussed in a brief essay. But we can say something about the Gettysburg Address as a work of art.

A work of art. Yes: for Lincoln was a literary artist, trained both by others and by himself. The textbooks he used as a boy were full of difficult exercises and skillful devices in formal rhetoric, stressing the qualities he practiced in his own speaking: antithesis, parallelism, and verbal harmony. Then he read and reread many admirable models of thought and expression: the King James Bible, the essays of Bacon, the best plays of Shakespeare. His favorites were *Hamlet, Lear, Macbeth, Richard III*, and *Henry VIII*, which he had read dozens of times. He loved reading aloud, too, and spent hours reading poetry to his friends. (He told his partner Herndon that he preferred getting the sense of any document by reading it aloud.) Therefore his serious speeches are important parts of the long and noble classical tradition of oratory which begins in Greece, runs through Rome to the modem world, and is still capable (if we do not neglect it) of producing masterpieces.

The first proof of this is that the Gettysburg Address is full of quotations—or rather of adaptations—which give it strength. It is partly religious, partly (in the highest sense) political: therefore it is interwoven with memories of the Bible and memories of American history. The first and the last words are Biblical cadences. Normally Lincoln did not say "fourscore" when he meant eighty; but on this solemn occasion he recalled the important dates in the Bible—such as the age of Abram when his first son was born to him, and he was "fourscore and six years old."[1] Similarly he did not say there was a chance that democracy might die out: he recalled the somber

10

---

1 Genesis 16:16; and Exodus 7:7. [Highet's note.]

phrasing of the Book of Job—where Bildad speaks of the destruction of one who shall vanish without a trace, and says that "his branch shall be cut off: his remembrance shall perish from the earth."[1] Then again, the famous description of our State as "government of the people, by the people, for the people" was adumbrated by Daniel Webster in 1830 (he spoke of "the people's government, made for the people, made by the people, and answerable to the people") and then elaborated in 1854 by the abolitionist Theodore Parker (as "government of all the people, by all the people, for all the people"). There is good reason to think that Lincoln took the important phrase "under God" (which he interpolated at the last moment) from Weems, the biographer of Washington; and we know that it had been used at least once by Washington himself.

Analyzing the address further, we find that it is based on a highly imaginative theme, or group of themes. The subject is—how can we put it so as not to disfigure it?—the subject is the kinship of life and death, that mysterious linkage which we see sometimes as the physical succession of birth and death in our world, sometimes as the contrast, which is perhaps a unity, between death and immortality. The first sentence is concerned with birth:

> Our *fathers brought forth* a *new* nation, *conceived* in liberty.

The final phrase but one expresses the hope that

> this nation, under God, shall have a *new birth* of freedom.

And the last phrase of all speaks of continuing life as the triumph over death. Again and again throughout the speech, this mystical contrast and kinship reappear: "those who *gave their lives* that that nation might *live*," "the brave men *living* and *dead*," and so in the central assertion that the dead have already consecrated their own burial place, while "it is for us, the *living*, rather to be dedicated ... to the great task remaining." The Gettysburg Address is a prose poem; it belongs to the same world as the great elegies, and the adagios of Beethoven.

Its structure, however, is that of a skillfully contrived speech. The oratorical pattern is perfectly clear. Lincoln describes the occasion, dedicates the ground, and then draws a larger conclusion by calling on his hearers to dedicate themselves to the preservation of the Union. But within that, we can trace his constant use of at least two important rhetorical devices.

15   The first of these is *antithesis*: opposition, contrast. The speech is full of it. Listen:

---

1   Job 18:16–17; Jeremiah 10:11; Micah 7:2. [Highet's note.]

The world will little *note*
nor long *remember* what *we say* here
but   it can never *forget* what *they did* here.

And so in nearly every sentence: "brave men, *living* and *dead*"; "to *add* or *detract*." There is the antithesis of the Founding Fathers and the men of Lincoln's own time:

Our *fathers brought forth* a new nation ...
now *we* are testing whether that nation ... can *long endure*.

And there is the more terrible antithesis of those who have already died and those who still live to do their duty. Now, antithesis is the figure of contrast and conflict. Lincoln was speaking in the midst of a great civil war.

The other important pattern is different. It is technically called *tricolon*— the division of an idea into three harmonious parts, usually of increasing power. The most famous phrase of the Address is a tricolon:

government of the people
by the people
and   for the people.

The most solemn sentence is a tricolon:

we cannot dedicate
we cannot consecrate
we cannot hallow   this ground.

And above all, the last sentence (which has sometimes been criticized as too   20
complex) is essentially two parallel phrases, with a tricolon growing out of the second and then producing another tricolon: a trunk, three branches, and a cluster of flowers. Lincoln says that it is for his hearers to be dedicated to the great task remaining before them. Then he goes on,

that from these honored dead

—apparently he means "in such a way that from these honored dead"—

we take increased devotion to that cause.

Next, he restates this more briefly:

that we here highly resolve....

And now the actual resolution follows, in three parts of growing intensity:

> that these dead shall not have died in vain
> that this nation, under God, shall have a new birth of freedom

and that (one more tricolon)

> government of the people
>   by the people
>   and   for the people.
> shall not perish from the earth.

25   Now, the tricolon is the figure which, through division, emphasizes basic harmony and unity. Lincoln used antithesis because he was speaking to a people at war. He used the tricolon because he was hoping, planning, praying for peace.

No one thinks that when he was drafting the Gettysburg Address, Lincoln deliberately looked up these quotations and consciously chose these particular patterns of thought. No, he chose the theme. From its development and from the emotional tone of the entire occasion, all the rest followed, or grew—by that marvelous process of choice and rejection which is essential to artistic creation. It does not spoil such a work of art to analyze it as closely as we have done; it is altogether fitting and proper that we should do this: for it helps us to penetrate more deeply into the rich meaning of the Gettysburg Address, and it allows us the very rare privilege of watching the workings of a great man's mind.

Sources

W.E. Barton. *Lincoln at Gettysburg.* Bobbs-Merrill. 1930.
R.P. Basler. "Abraham Lincoln's Rhetoric." *American Literature.* 11:1939–40, 167–82.
L.E. Robinson. *Abraham Lincoln as a Man of Letters.* Chicago. 1918.

Questions

1. Identify some of the arguments Highet makes in this essay. What evidence does he provide for these arguments? Do you agree with these points?
2. What analogies does Highet make between the Gettysburg Address and other forms of created works—that is, with works more conventionally considered as art? In what ways are these analogies apt? In what ways are they not?
3. In what ways does Highet's essay mimic the rhetoric of its subject, the Gettysburg Address?

LAWRENCE WESCHLER

Comedy of Values

(2000)

Lawrence Weschler (1952–) is a prominent journalist whose books include Vermeer in Bosnia: Cultural Comedies and Political Tragedies *(2004) and* Everything That Rises: A Book of Convergences *(2006). He was a staff writer for* The New Yorker *for over twenty years, and has been a faculty member in the Department of Journalism at New York University.*

In this article, adapted from the book Boggs: A Comedy of Values *(1999), Weschler introduces the artist J.S.G. Boggs, whose works challenge assumptions about money and material culture.*

J.S.G. Boggs draws money. Then he tries to spend the drawings. His transactions bring him to the fault line where art and money meet and overlap.

J.S.G. Boggs is a young artist with a certain flair, a certain panache, a certain *je ne paye pas*. What he likes to do, for example, is to invite you out to dinner at some fancy restaurant, to run up a tab of, say, $87, and then, while sipping coffee after dessert, to reach into his satchel and pull out a drawing that he has worked on for several hours before the meal. The drawing, on a small sheet of high-quality paper, might consist, in this instance, of a virtually perfect rendition of the face-side of a $100 bill. He then pulls out a couple of precision pens from his satchel—one green ink, the other black—and proceeds to apply the finishing touches to his drawing. This activity invariably causes a stir. Guests at neighbouring tables crane their necks. Passing waiters stop to gawk. The maitre d' eventually drifts over, stares for a while, and then praises the young man on the excellence of his art. "That's good," says Boggs. "I'm glad you like this drawing, because I intend to use it as payment for our meal."

At this point, a vertiginous chill descends upon the room—or, more precisely, upon the maitre d'. He blanches. You can see his mind reeling ("Oh no, not another nutcase") as he begins to plot strategy. (Should he call the police? How is he going to avoid a scene?) But Boggs almost immediately re-establishes a measure of equilibrium by reaching into his satchel, pulling out a real $100 bill—indeed, the model for the very drawing he has just completed—and saying: "Of course, if you want you can take this regular $100 bill instead." Colour is already returning to the maitre d's face. "But, as you can see," Boggs continues, "I'm an artist, and I drew this; it took me many hours to do it, and it's certainly worth something. I'm assigning it an arbitrary price that just happens to coincide with its face value—$100. That means, if you decide to accept it as full payment for our meal, you're going to have to give me $13 in change.

"So you have to make up your mind whether you think this piece of art is worth more or less than this regular $100 bill. It's entirely up to you." Boggs smiles and, once again, the maitre d' blanches, because now he's into serious vertigo: the free-fall of worth and values.

5   Boggs has been perpetrating variations on this formula (and the initial transaction, when successful, turns out to constitute only the first phase of a compounding, confounding philoso-comic chase) for more than 15 years now, to the tune of several million dollars' worth of successful transactions (for everything from chocolate bars to rent, first-class air fare, nights in luxury hotels and fully souped-up motorcycles). In the process, he has provoked the successively less bemused ire of treasury police all over the world, who regularly attempt to nail him on counterfeiting and reproduction charges or the like (including a celebrated case brought against him by the Bank of England at the Old Bailey[1] in 1987), although no jury has ever returned a guilty verdict. He is currently involved in a marathon legal struggle with the US Secret Service.

It all began innocently enough in a Chicago diner, back in 1984, when a curious waitress offered to accept the napkin doodle of a $1 bill in exchange for his coffee tab, and then even (to his astonishment) returned a dime's change. Boggs had almost accidentally stumbled upon the terrain, but then decided, quite deliberately, to pitch his tent there along the fault line where art and money abut and overlap. And his work has definite ramifications in both directions. The questions it raises start out as small perturbations: How is this drawing different from its model (this dollar bill)? Would you accept it in lieu of this bill? If so, why? If not, why not? But, as you think about and savour such questions, they quickly expand into true tremblers: What is art? What is money? What is the one worth, and what the other? What is worth worth? How does value itself arise, and live, and gutter out?

In 1900, Georg Simmel, the great German-Jewish philosopher and sociologist, published his *Philosophy of Money*. In its final pages, Simmel concludes that "there is no more striking symbol of the completely dynamic character of the world than money. The meaning of money lies in the fact that it will be given away. When money stands still, it is no longer money

---

1   *Old Bailey* Central criminal court for United Kingdom.

according to its specific value and significance. The effect that it occasionally exerts in a state of repose arises out of an anticipation of its further motion. Money is nothing but the vehicle for a movement in which everything else that is not in motion is completely extinguished." But if, in one of its aspects, Simmel saw pure motion in money, in another he located an absolute stillness: "As a tangible item, money is the most ephemeral thing in the external-practical world; yet its content is the most stable, since it stands at the point of indifference and balance between all other phenomena in the world ..."

Reading Simmel recently, it occurred to me that Boggs's work operates in the space between those two absolute characterisations. He momentarily slows the mindless frenzy of exchange, forcing us to mind it; and in so doing, he briefly forces the age-old monolithic stasis to budge and shudder. It is a sort of magic. But then, all art is magic (we knew that), and so is all money.

Jackson Pollock[1] is said to have settled his drinks bills with paintings (lucky bartender!), and Kurt Schwitters[2] merrily included everyday receipts in his collages (*Merzzeichnungen* and *Merzbilder*, he called them, those framed jumbles, words he derived from *Kommerz*, a German word for commerce). Boggs is by no means the first artist to have stumbled upon these precincts. Picasso,[3] the story is told, used to go out shopping: he would sign his cheques and then dash off smart little doodles on the back—the cheques were seldom cashed. Years later, the Swedish artist Carl Fredrik Reutersward made a three-dimensional bronze of Picasso's signature, stood it on a tottering pedestal and called it *The Great Fetish*. He also printed stretched-out versions of Salvador Dali's[4] signature and sold them by the centimetre. Marcel Duchamp[5] went to his dentist one day, couldn't pay, or didn't want to, and instead drew an ornate cheque, filled it in and signed it—and the dentist accepted it. (Years later, when Jurgen Harten was trying to procure the cheque for inclusion in his "Money" show at the Dusseldorf *Kunsthalle*,[6] the Italian dealer who then owned it demanded $3,000 just for the loan of the picture.)

The mad artist-brut Adolf Wolfi, holed up in a Berne asylum for schizo-   10
phrenics for the last 35 years of his life (he died in 1930), did a series of large, wild drawings of bill-like entities, covered over with elaborate calculations and tabulations: he kept his endless delusional accounts. Years later, the Romanian-Swiss artist Daniel Spoerri (born 1930) opened his cheque-

---

1 *Jackson Pollock* (1912–56) American abstract painter.
2 *Kurt Schwitters* (1887–48) German collage artist.
3 *Picasso* Pablo Picasso (1881–1973), Spanish painter.
4 *Salvador Dali* (1904–1989) Spanish Surrealist artist.
5 *Marcel Duchamp* (1887–1968) French Dada artist.
6 *Kunsthalle* German: art gallery.

book and wrote out a series of cheques, payable to cash at ten Deutschmarks each, and sold them as art for DM20 apiece. ("In exchanging art for money," he explained, "we exchange one abstraction for another.") Timm Ulrichs, a young German artist, went to court and had his name declared a trademark. On 1 March 1971, Pieter Engels went on lifelong strike as a visual artist and proposed that the Dutch government pay him 25 million forms for a stone marker ("a visualisation") commemorating the ongoing event.

In 1932, during Germany's terrifying bout with hyperinflation, a Munich cabaret artist called Karl Valentin papered over a park bench with worthless DM100,000 notes. The German word for bench is Bank; he called his piece "Deutsche Bank". (My grandmother, who lived through those days, used to tell amazing stories. She described, for instance, how café waiters would take your order on improvised pads of stapled-together DM100,000 notes: the bills literally were not worth the paper they were printed on; it would have cost the establishment more to buy fresh pads than to bundle the used notes.) Yves Klein used gold leaf in some of his monochrome series, which in turn gave him the idea for his *Zones Sensibles Immaterielles.*

Accompanied by a collector, he would take a small glass box filled with gold flakes to the bank of the Seine, open the box and toss the flakes to the wind. The collector would gain "possession" of the piece by purchasing the receipt for the gold at face value, plus a minor profit for the artist.

Larry Rivers[1] created a famous sequence of paintings based on slapdash renditions of French money, which in turn feature engraved versions of Jacques-Louis David's[2] portrait of the dashing young Napoleon. (This around the time that Jasper Johns[3] was painting his American flag; both artists were bringing expressionistic energy to bear on the flattest of surfaces and imagery.) Andy Warhol,[4] early on, created a silk screen that consisted of a sheet of two-dollar bills, as if fresh off the presses. The French artist Arman filled a transparent polyester mannequin torso with suspended dollar bills and called her Venus. In 1969, the Canadian Les Levine purchased 500 common shares of the Cassette Cartridge corporation at $4.75 per share. As he declared in the press release that accompanied (and, in a sense, was) his piece: "After a period of one year, or at any time which it is deemed profitable prior to that, the Cassette Cartridge shares will be resold. The profit or loss of the transaction will become the work of art." Robert Morris,[5] as his contribution to that year's "Anti-Illusion" show at the Whitney Museum, New York, undertook a

1 *Larry Rivers* (1923–2002) American pop artist and sculptor.
2 *Jacques-Louis David* (1748–1825) French artist.
3 *Jasper Johns* (born 1930) American painter. His most famous painting, *Flag*, is an American flag created by dripping thick paint over a collage of found objects such as newspapers.
4 *Andy Warhol* (1928–87) American pop artist.
5 *Robert Morris* (born 1931) American minimalist sculptor.

more convoluted but less risky transaction, which he titled *Money*. He arranged for the Whitney to solicit a $100,000 loan at 5 per cent interest, for the duration of the show, from a stockbroker-collector; that money was in turn invested with the Morgan Guarantee Trust in the Whitney's name at 5 per cent return. At the conclusion of the show, the Whitney withdrew the money and interest from the bank and returned all of it to the collector, who then made a tax-deductible contribution to the museum in the amount of the 5 per cent interest, which the museum then paid to Morris for having come up with the whole brilliant scheme. All of this was documented on the walls of the museum during the show in the form of the three-way exchange of letters in which it had all been agreed to in advance. Rafael Ferrer,[1] as his contribution to the same show, spread out 15 large cakes of melting ice strewn with autumn leaves and declared, Klein-like: "If anyone complains that it's not collectible art, I'll send them the bill for the ice as a drawing."

In the early 1970s, during a time of stringent military repression and wide-ranging media censorship in Brazil, the artist Cildo Meireles launched an anonymous project, "Insertions into Ideological Circuits", in which he momentarily extracted paper bills from circulation, stencilled political slogans and contraband news accounts on their faces, and then reintroduced them into circulation. (In a sly homage to the contemporaneous pop tradition, he did the same thing with Coke bottles, printing slogans and despatches on the pale-greenish glass in a white ink that proved virtually invisible when he returned the bottles for deposit, but presently divulged secret subversive messages when the recycled bottles, emerging from the bottling plant, had once again been filled up with the dark drink.)

So yes, Boggs was by no means first to stumble upon these precincts. Although he had known relatively little about most of these other sorts of work before he started with his own drawings, he had been hearing of them with some regularity ever since. Far from feeling threatened, he seemed positively to celebrate each new instance, largely because he was genuinely fascinated by the issues that such works raised—fascinated and still at something of a loss himself as to the ultimate significance and meaning of his own work.

Furthermore, for all the similarities, there were profound differences. Most of these other kinds of work had focused principally on internal issues of art and money: how money skews the workings of the art world, how fame skews money, what people value in art and how they express that value, and so on. Boggs's work, by contrast, was chiefly about the world outside galleries and museums: his work takes place at a three-way intersection, that of art, money and the everyday world. If anything, a more apt sort of precursor to Boggs's vocation might be found in the work of the young Charles Simonds, back in the early Seventies. The artist set up shop, as it were, on the sidewalks of dilapidated neighbourhoods, and fashioned his

15

---

1 *Rafael Ferrer* (born 1933) Puerto Rican artist.

miniature-brick archaeo-fantastical ruins in the hollowed-out flanks of crumbling tenements. Simonds would invariably draw a crowd of onlookers, but would leave the question hanging as to just what sort of activity was going on. Art? Play? Madness? And indeed, that confusion was part of what the work was about.

In a similar sort of way, Boggs is engaged in philosophical disruptions, in provoking brief, momentary tears in the ordinarily seamless fabric of taken-for-granted mundanity. The people he addresses (at least those he involves in the early stages of his enactments) are cruising along on autopilot—and hey, he confronts them: Wake up, wake up, look down there, what's holding this thing up, there are no visible means of support, how is it that we fly at all?

Questions

1. Why, according to Weschler, is Boggs's work different from that of other artists who incorporate aspects of money into their work?
2. Weschler says Boggs provokes "brief, momentary tears in the ordinarily seamless fabric of taken-for-granted mundanity." What does this mean? Do you agree?
3. What does Boggs's work say about money? About art? About values? Do you think his work succeeds in its aim?
4. What is the importance of humour in Boggs's work? In Weschler's essay?
5. Why is art that plays with the idea of money and its value so controversial?

MAYA LIN

Vietnam Veterans Memorial

(2000)

In 1981, Maya Lin's design for the national Vietnam Veterans Memorial was chosen from more than 1,400 submissions. At the time, she was a 21-year-old undergraduate student at Yale. Since then, Lin's architecture and art have won many awards, and have been exhibited at numerous museums and galleries throughout the United States.

In this essay, Lin reflects on the process of designing the memorial, the controversy that surrounded its selection, and its eventual execution in Washington, D.C.

It's taken me years to be able to discuss the making of the Vietnam Veterans Memorial, partly because I needed to move past it and partly because I had forgotten the process of getting it built. I would not discuss the controversy surrounding its construction and it wasn't until I saw the documentary *Maya Lin: A Strong Clear Vision* that I was able to remember that time in my life. But I wrote the body of this essay just as the memorial was being completed—in the fall of 1982. Then I put it away ... until now. –M.L.

I think the most important aspect of the design of the Vietnam Veterans Memorial was that I had originally designed it for a class I was taking at Yale and not for the competition. In that sense, I had designed it for me—or, more exactly, for what I believed it should be. I never tried to second-guess a jury. And it wasn't until after I had completed the design that I decided to enter it in the competition.

The design emerged from an architectural seminar I was taking during my senior year. The initial idea of a memorial had come from a notice posted at the school announcing a competition for a Vietnam veterans memorial. The class, which was on funereal architecture, had spent the semester studying how people, through the built form, express their attitudes on death. As a class, we thought the memorial was an appropriate design idea for our program, so we adopted it as our final design project.

At that point, not much was known about the actual competition, so for the first half of the assignment we were left without concrete directions for what "they" were looking for or even who "they" were. Instead, we had to determine for ourselves what a Vietnam memorial should be. Since a previous project had been to design a memorial for World War III, I had already begun to ask the simple questions: What exactly is a memorial? What should it do?

5   My design for a World War III memorial was a tomblike underground structure that I deliberately made to be a very futile and frustrating experience. I remember the professor of the class, Andrus Burr, coming up to me afterward, saying quite angrily, "If I had a brother who died in that war, I would never want to visit this memorial." I was somewhat puzzled that he didn't quite understand that World War III would be of such devastation that none of us would be around to visit any memorial, and that my design was instead a pre-war commentary. In asking myself what a memorial to a third world war would be, I came up with a political statement that was meant as a deterrent.

I had studied earlier monuments and memorials while designing that memorial and I continued this research for the design of the Vietnam memorial. As I did more research on monuments, I realized most carried larger, more general messages about a leader's victory or accomplishments rather than the lives lost. In fact, at the national level, individual lives were very seldom dealt with, until you arrived at the memorials for World War I. Many of these memorials included the names of those killed. Partly it was a practical need to list those whose bodies could not be identified—since dog tags as identification had not yet been adopted and, due to the nature of the warfare, many killed were not identifiable—but I think as well the listing of names reflected a response by these designers to the horrors of World War I, to the immense loss of life.

The images of these monuments were extremely moving. They captured emotionally what I felt memorials should be: honest about the reality of war, about the loss of life in war, and about remembering those who served and especially those who died.

I made a conscious decision not to do any specific research on the Vietnam War and the political turmoil surrounding it. I felt that the politics had eclipsed the veterans, their service, and their lives. I wanted to create a memorial that everyone would be able to respond to, regardless of whether one thought our country should or should not have participated in the war. The power of a name was very much with me at the time, partly because of the Memorial Rotunda at Yale. In Woolsey Hall, the walls are inscribed with the names of all the Yale alumni who have been killed in wars. I had never been able to resist touching the names cut into these marble walls, and no matter how busy or crowded the place is, a sense of quiet, a reverence, always surrounds those names. Throughout my freshman and sophomore years, the stonecutters were carving in by hand the names of those killed in the Vietnam War, and I think it left a lasting impression on me ... the sense of the power of a name.

One memorial I came across also made a strong impression on me. It was a monument to the missing soldiers of the World War I Battle of the Somme by Sir Edwin Lutyens in Thiepval, France. The monument includes more than 100,000 names of people who were listed as missing because, without ID tags, it was impossible to identify the dead. (The cemetery contains the bodies of 70,000 dead.) To walk past those names and realize those lost lives—the effect of that is the strength of the design. This memorial acknowledged those lives without focusing on the war or on creating a political statement of victory or loss. This apolitical approach became the essential aim of my design; I did not want to civilize war by glorifying it or by forgetting the sacrifices involved. The price of human life in war should always be clearly remembered.

But on a personal level, I wanted to focus on the nature of accepting and   10
coming to terms with a loved one's death. Simple as it may seem, I remember feeling that accepting a person's death is the first step in being able to overcome that loss.

I felt that as a culture we were extremely youth-oriented and not willing or able to accept death or dying as a part of life. The rites of mourning, which in more primitive and older cultures were very much a part of life, have been suppressed in our modern times. In the design of the memorial, a fundamental goal was to be honest about death, since we must accept that loss in order to begin to overcome it. The pain of the loss will always be there, it will always hurt, but we must acknowledge the death in order to move on.

What then would bring back the memory of a person? A specific object or image would be limiting. A realistic sculpture would be only one interpretation of that time. I wanted something that all people could relate to on a personal level. At this time I had as yet no form, no specific artistic image.

The use of names was a way to bring back everything someone could remember about a person. The strength in a name is something that has always made me wonder at the "abstraction" of the design; the ability of a name to bring back every single memory you have of that person is far more realistic and specific and much more comprehensive than a still photograph, which captures a specific moment in time or a single event or a generalized image that may or may not be moving for all who have connections to that time.

Then someone in the class received the design program, which stated the basic philosophy of the memorial's design and also its requirements: all the names of those missing and killed (57,000) must be a part of the memorial; the design must be apolitical, harmonious with the site, and conciliatory.

15   These were all the thoughts that were in my mind before I went to see the site.

Without having seen it, I couldn't design the memorial, so a few of us traveled to Washington, D.C., and it was at the site that the idea for the design took shape. The site was a beautiful park surrounded by trees, with traffic and noise coming from one side—Constitution Avenue.

I had a simple impulse to cut into the earth.

I imagined taking a knife and cutting into the earth, opening it up, an initial violence and pain that in time would heal. The grass would grow back, but the initial cut would remain a pure flat surface in the earth with a polished, mirrored surface, much like the surface on a geode when you cut it and polish the edge. The need for the names to be on the memorial would become the memorial; there was no need to embellish the design further. The people and their names would allow everyone to respond and remember.

It would be an interface, between our world and the quieter, darker, more peaceful world beyond. I chose black granite in order to make the surface reflective and peaceful. I never looked at the memorial as a wall, an object, but as an edge to the earth, an opened side. The mirrored effect would double the size of the park, creating two worlds, one we are a part of and one we cannot enter. The two walls were positioned so that one pointed to the Lincoln Memorial and the other pointed to the Washington Monument. By linking these two strong symbols for the country, I wanted to create a unity between the nation's past and present.

20   The idea of destroying the park to create something that by its very nature should commemorate life seemed hypocritical, nor was it in my nature. I wanted my design to work with the land, to make something with the site, not to fight it or dominate it. I see my works and their relationship to the landscape as being an additive rather than a combative process.

On our return to Yale, I quickly sketched my idea up, and it almost seemed too simple, too little. I toyed with adding some large flat slabs that would appear to lead into the memorial, but they didn't belong. The image was so simple that anything added to it began to detract from it.

I always wanted the names to be chronological, to make it so that those who served and returned from the war could find their place in the memorial. I initially had the names beginning on the left side and ending on the right. In a preliminary critique, a professor asked what importance that left for the apex, and I, too, thought it was a weak point, so I changed the design for the final critique. Now the chronological sequence began and ended at the apex so that the time line would circle back to itself and close the sequence. A progression in time is memorialized. The design is not just a list of the dead. To find one name, chances are you will see the others close by, and you will see yourself reflected through them.

The memorial was designed before I decided to enter the competition. I didn't even consider that it might win. When I submitted the project, I had the greatest difficulty trying to describe it in just one page. It took longer, in fact, to write the statement that I felt was needed to accompany the required drawings than to design the memorial. The description was critical to understanding the design since the memorial worked more on an emotional level than a formal level.

Coincidentally, at the time, I was taking a course with Professor Vincent Scully, in which he focused, just happened to focus, on the same memorial I had been so moved by—the Lutyens memorial to the missing. Professor Scully described one's experience of that piece as a passage or journey through a yawning archway. As he described it, it resembled a gaping scream, which after you passed through, you were left looking out on a simple graveyard with the crosses and tombstones of the French and the English. It was a journey to an awareness of immeasurable loss, with the names of the missing carved on every surface of this immense archway.

I started writing furiously in Scully's class. I think he has always been puzzled by my connection to the Lutyens memorial. Formally the two memorials could not be more different. But for me, the experiences of these two memorials describe a similar passage to an awareness about loss. 25

The competition required drawings, along with the option to include a written description. As the deadline for submission approached, I created a series of simple drawings. The only thing left was to complete the essay, which I instinctively knew was the only way to get anyone to understand the design, the form of which was deceptively simple. I kept reworking and reediting the final description. I actually never quite finished it. I ended up at the last minute writing freehand directly onto the presentation boards (you can see a few misprints on the actual page), and then I sent the project in, never expecting to hear about it again.

The drawings were in soft pastels, very mysterious, very painterly, and not at all typical of architectural drawings. One of the comments made by a juror was "*He* must really know what he is doing to dare to do something so naive" (italics mine). But ultimately, I think it was the written description that convinced the jurors to select my design.

On my last day of classes my roommate, Liz Perry, came to retrieve me from one of my classes, telling me a call from Washington had come in and that it was from the *Vietnam Veterans Memorial* Fund; they needed to talk to me and would call back with a few questions about the design. When they called back, they merely said they needed to ask me a few questions and wanted to fly up to New Haven to talk to me. I was convinced that I was number 100 and they were only going to question me about drainage and other technical issues. It never occurred to me that I might have won the competition. It was still, in my mind, an exercise—as competitions customarily are for architecture students.

And even after three officers of the fund were seated in my college dorm room, explaining to me that it was the largest competition of its kind, with more than fourteen hundred entries, and Colonel Schaet, who was talking, without missing a beat calmly added that I had won (I think my roommate's face showed more emotion than mine did at the time), it still hadn't registered. I don't think it did for almost a year. Having studied the nature of competitions, especially in Washington (for instance, the FDR Memorial, still unbuilt in 1981, nearly forty years after it was first proposed, or the artwork Robert Venturi and Richard Serra collaborated on for L'Enfant Plaza, which was completely modified as it went through the required Washington design process of approvals), my attitude about unusual projects getting built in Washington was not optimistic. Partly it's my nature— I never get my hopes up—and partly I assumed the simplicity of the design, and its atypical form and color, would afford it a difficult time through the various governmental-approval agencies.

30   After the design had been chosen, it was subject to approval by various governmental agencies at both the conceptual and design development phases. I moved to Washington and stayed there throughout these phases. I expected the design to be debated within the design-approval agencies; I never expected the politics that constantly surrounded its development and fabrication.

I was driven down to D.C. the day of my college graduation, and I immediately became part of an internal struggle for control of the design. I think my age made it seem apparent to some that I was too young to understand what I had done or to see it through to completion. To bring the design into reality would require that I associate with an architect of record, a qualified firm that would work with me to realize the design. I had a very difficult time convincing the fund in charge of the memorial, the VVMF, of the importance of selecting a qualified firm that had experience both in architecture and landscape-integrated solutions, and that would be sympathetic to the design.

I had gone to Cesar Pelli, then dean of Yale's School of Architecture, for the names of some firms that could handle the job. A firm by the name of Cooper-Lecky was the one he recommended, and I presented its name to the fund, unaware that the competition's adviser was the fund's choice as architect of record. I was told by the fund that this person was the architect of record, and that was that.

After a few weeks of tense and hostile negotiations (in which at one point I was warned that I would regret these actions, and that I would "come crawling back on my hands and knees"), I was finally able to convince the fund to go through a legitimate process of selecting a firm to become the architect of record. The then architecture critic for *The Washington Post*, Wolf Von Eckardt, was instrumental in pressing the fund to listen to me. But the struggle left a considerable amount of ill will and mistrust between the veterans and myself.

Through the remaining phases of the project I worked with the Cooper-Lecky architectural firm. We worked on the practical details of the design, from the addition of a safety curb to a sidewalk to the problems in inscribing the names. Many of the issues we dealt with were connected to the text and my decision to list the names chronologically. People felt it would be an inconvenience to have to search out a name in a book and then find its panel location and thought that an alphabetical listing would be more convenient—until a tally of how many Smiths had died made it clear that an alphabetical listing wouldn't be feasible. The MIA[1] groups wanted their list of the missing separated out and listed alphabetically. I knew this would break the strength of the time line, interrupting the real-time experience of the piece, so I fought hard to maintain the chronological listing. I ended up convincing the groups that the time in which an individual was noted as missing was the emotionally compelling time for family members. A system of noting these names with a symbol[2] that could be modified to signify if the veteran was later found alive or officially declared dead would appease the concerns of the MIA groups without breaking the time line. I knew the time line was key to the experience of the memorial: a returning veteran would be able to find his or her time of service when finding a friend's name.

The text of the memorial and the fact that I had left out everything 35 except the names led to a fight about what else needed to be said about the war. The apex is the memorial's strongest point; I argued against the addition of text at that point for fear that a politically charged statement, one that would force a specific reading, would destroy the apolitical nature of the design. Throughout this time I was very careful not to discuss my beliefs in terms of politics; I played it extremely naive about politics, instead turning the issue into a strictly aesthetic one. Text could be added, but whatever was said needed to fit in three lines—to match the height of the dates "1959" and "1975" that it would be adjacent to. The veterans approved this

1 *MIA* Missing in action.
2 Each name is preceded (on the west wall) or followed (on the east wall) by one of two symbols: a diamond or a cross. The diamond denotes that the serviceman's or servicewoman's death was confirmed. The cross symbolized those who were missing in action or prisoners at the end of the war. When a serviceperson's remains were returned, the diamond symbol is superimposed over the cross. If a serviceman or woman returns alive, a circle will be inscribed around the cross. [Lin's note.]

graphic parameter, and the statements became a simple prologue and epilogue.

The memorial is analogous to a book in many ways. Note that on the right-hand panels the pages are set ragged right and on the left they are set ragged left, creating a spine at the apex as in a book. Another issue was scale; the text type is the smallest that we had come across, less than half an inch, which is unheard of in monument type sizing. What it does is create a very intimate reading in a very public space, the difference in intimacy between reading a billboard and reading a book.

The only other issue was the polished black granite and how it should be detailed, over which I remember having a few arguments with the architects of record. The architects could not understand my choice of a reflective, highly polished black granite. One of them felt I was making a mistake and the polished surface would be "too *feminine*." Also puzzling to them was my choice of detailing the monument as a thin veneer with barely any thickness at its top edge. They wanted to make the monument's walls read as a massive, thick stone wall, which was not my intention at all. I always saw the wall as pure surface, an interface between light and dark, where I cut the earth and polished its open edge. The wall dematerializes as a form and allows the names to become the object, a pure and reflective surface that would allow visitors the chance to see themselves with the names. I do not think I thought of the color black as a color, more as the idea of a dark mirror into a shadowed mirrored image of the space, a space we cannot enter and from which the names separate us, an interface between the world of the living and the world of the dead.

One aspect that made the project unusual was its politicized building process. For instance, the granite could not come from Canada or Sweden. Though those countries had beautiful black granites, draft evaders went to both countries, so the veterans felt that we could not consider their granites as options. (The stone finally selected came from India.) The actual building process went smoothly for the most part, and the memorial was built very close to my original intentions.

As far as all of the controversy is concerned, I really never wanted to go into it too much. The memorial's starkness, its being below grade, being black, and how much my age, gender, and race played a part in the controversy, we'll never quite know. I think it is actually a miracle that the piece ever got built. From the very beginning I often wondered, If it had not been an anonymous entry 1026 but rather an entry by Maya Lin, would I have been selected?

40   I remember at the very first press conference a reporter asking me if I did not find it ironic that the memorial was for the Vietnam War and that I was of Asian descent. I was so righteous in my response that my race was com-

pletely irrelevant. It took me almost nine months to ask the VVMF, in charge of building the memorial, if my race was at all an issue. It had never occurred to me that it would be, and I think they had taken all the measures they could to shield me from such comments about a "gook" designing the memorial.

I remember reading the article that appeared in *The Washington Post* referring to "An Asian Memorial for an Asian War" and I knew we were in trouble. The controversy exploded in Washington after that article. Ironically, one side attacked the design for being "too Asian," while others saw its simplicity and understatement, not as an intention to create a more Eastern, meditative space, but as a minimalist statement which they interpreted as being non-referential and disconnected from human experience.

This left the opinion in many that the piece emanated from a series of intellectualized aesthetic decisions, which automatically pitted artist against veterans. The fact that I was from an Ivy League college and had hair down to my knees further fueled this distrust of the design and suspicions of a hippie college liberal or aesthetic elitist forcing her art and commentary upon them.

Perhaps it was an empathetic response to the idea about war that had led me to cut open the earth—an initial violence that heals in time but leaves a memory, like a scar. But this imagery, which some detractors would later describe as "a black gash of shame and sorrow" in which the color black was called the "universal color of shame and dishonor," would prove incredibly difficult to defend. The misreading of the design as a negative political statement that in some way was meant to reflect upon the service of the veterans was in part fueled by a cultural prejudice against the color black as well as by the misreading or misinformation that led some veterans to imagine the design as a ditch or a hole. It took a prominent four-star general, Brigadier General George Price, who happened to be black, testifying before one of the countless subcommittee hearings and defending the color black, before the design could move forward.

But the distrust, the fact that no veterans had been on the jury, the unconventionality of the design and the designer, and a very radical requirement made by the Vietnam veterans to include all the names of those killed made it inevitable that the project would become controversial. I think ultimately that much of the negative response goes back to the very natural response to cover up or not acknowledge that which is painful or unpleasant. The very fact that the veterans themselves had required the listing and therefore the acknowledgment of the more than 57,000 casualties, which is a landmark in our country in terms of seeing a war through the individual lives lost, was very hard for many to face. I remember Ross Perot when he was trying to persuade the veterans that it was an inappropriate design, asking me if I truly didn't feel that the veterans would prefer a parade instead, something happy or uplifting, and I can remember thinking that a parade would not in the long term help them to overcome the enormous trauma of the politics of that war.

45   I do not think I fully realized until the dedication and homecoming parade that the veterans needed both. In effect the veterans gave themselves their own homecoming. In November 1982, I was in tears watching these men welcoming themselves home after almost ten years of not being acknowledged by their country for their service, their sacrifice.

But until the memorial was built I don't think they realized that the design was experiential and cathartic, and, most importantly, designed not for me, but for them. They didn't see that the chronology of the names allowed a returning veteran the ability to find his or her own time frame on the wall and created a psychological space for them that directly focused on human response and feeling. I remember one of the veterans asking me before the wall was built what I thought people's reaction to it would be. I realized then that these veterans were willing to defend a design they really didn't quite understand. I was too afraid to tell him what I was thinking, that I knew a returning veteran would cry.

An architect once told me to look always at what was originally envisioned and try to keep it. I left Washington before ground breaking. I had to. The fund and I knew that we had to accept a compromise. The closer you watch something grow, the less able you are to notice changes in it. When I saw the site again, the granite panels were being put up and the place was frighteningly close to what I thought it should be. It terrified me. It was a strange feeling, to have had an idea that was solely yours be no longer a part of your mind but totally public, no longer yours.

There was always the expectation that since the war had been controversial, the memorial must be also. It wasn't so much an artistic dispute as a political one. The choice to make an apolitical memorial was in itself political to those who felt only a positive statement about the war would make up for the earlier antiwar days, a past swing to the left now to be balanced. It was extremely naive of me to think that I could produce a neutral statement that would not become politically controversial simply because it chose not to take sides.

Anyway, the push, as one congressman put it, to "politicize" the design didn't really affect the memorial in this way. The addition of the statue of infantrymen and then the addition of the female statue to make them equal are to me sad indicators that some politicians believe that you can please all of the people all of the time by compromise and conglomerate works. These statues leave only the false reading that the wall is for the dead and they are for the living, when the design I made was for the returning veterans and equally names all who served regardless of race, creed, or sex. I am only glad that the three infantrymen are not where they had been originally intended to be, right in the center of the memorial, heads sticking up higher than the walls, converting the walls to a backdrop and violating that private contemplative space. Ironically, the compromise memorializes the conflict in the building of the piece.

People cannot resolve that war, nor can they separate the issues, the politics, from it. As for me, the first time I visited the memorial after it was completed I found myself searching out the name of a friend's father and touching it. It was strange to realize that I was another visitor and I was reacting to it as I had designed it. 50

Questions

1. Lin writes that, "As far as all of the controversy is concerned, I really never wanted to go into it too much" (paragraph 39). Why might she have decided to address the controversy in this piece, published almost twenty years later? How does the structure and tone of this essay compare to Lin's descriptions of her design of the Vietnam Veteran's Memorial?
2. What differences do you notice in Lin's diction and tone when she is describing her conception of the memorial and when she is relating historical and personal events?
3. Why do you think Lin chooses to end the piece with her own first visit to the memorial?

DOUGLAS COUPLAND

Group of Seven

(2002)

Douglas Coupland (1961–) studied art and design at the Emily Carr Institute, and has published many novels and short story collections. His novels include Generation X: Tales for an Accelerated Culture *(1991), the book that popularized the term "generation X," and* Eleanor Rigby *(2005).*

Coupland has also published two volumes of short non-fiction works, Souvenir of Canada *(2002), from which this piece is taken, and* Souvenir of Canada 2 *(2004).*

Canada officially became a country at roughly the same time that the camera became a consumer item. Thus, the Canadian landscape is richly photo-documented. But the late nineteenth-century triumph of the camera also caused a crisis in the art world that continues to this day. Painters, released from the burden of faithful rendering, were creatively liberated. They quickly devised new ways to view the world—Impressionism and cubism and surrealism being the three that most people are familiar with. Cubism and surrealism had little or no effect on Canadian landscape painting, while Impressionism did ... but only slightly. Dots and washes of colour were great for evoking the mood of the European garden or Parisian picnics, but when it came to a landscape as raw and cataclysmic as Canada's, Impressionism was simply not up to the task.

In the 1920s a group of young painters set out across the Canadian wilderness, quite literally in canoes, hiking boots and snowshoes, in an attempt to create a form of painterly gesture worthy and capable of evoking Canada's rugged and often brutal wonder. These men were the Group of Seven (although a few others were their equals, and some were not men). With an elemental intensity not found in European or even American painting, they brought Canada alive. They developed a set of lush, forceful painted gestures new to the world. It is possibly the one truly Canadian painting style, and their works are the nation's jewels.

After writing the above words, I sat here at my desk quite drained. And then I had this flash ... this *moment* ... that lasted maybe two minutes. I'd been thinking about the Canadian landscape, and then suddenly—

craaaack!—in my head I was racing across Canada at a thousand kilometres a second: over the mountains that made the pioneers despair, across the prairies that will remain flat until our sun goes supernova, over the rock and roots of Ontario and Quebec—and then down into the lunar gorges of Newfoundland. My arms flew up to my sides as though they were trying to get as far away from my body as possible, and my breathing grew short—I was unable to move and saw a lucid flashing sequence of my life in this country: the weather, the soil, the plant life and animals. My upper body stretched upward as though drawn by a magnet, and my eyeballs got hot and began to tear. I was connecting with something vast—connecting with all the people with whom I've ever shared the land.

After the visitation (for lack of a better word) had passed, I sat here at my desk, not knowing what to make of it. So I phoned my mother. She once believed in the supernatural, but I'd always thought she'd surrendered her dreams of messages years ago. When I told her what had just happened, she admitted that she still believed in the profound, too, but she also said that it got somehow harder with the years. She was speaking on a cell phone, and while audible, her voice came through sounding slightly processed—like these old reel-to-reel tapes she had of her parents sending tape-recorded letters to her when our family was stationed in Germany. We started talking about summer, and my mother remembered that her own mother used to take her and her sisters to Lake Winnipeg each August, and that at the end of the day she'd peel off their sunburned skin. "But the sun was different back then. We didn't have lotions or anything, but they weren't as necessary. It wasn't the same sun."

When I hung up the phone, it rang, and it was my nephew who'd just learned my phone number. He's five. I'd given him a bar magnet the day before, and he'd figured out that Canada's two-dollar coins are magnetic, so I promised that we'd go to the beach beside the Pacific and that I'd hide coins, and if he found them he could keep them.

And that was that. Whatever it was, it had passed.

Does this sound nuts? How could it not? But it was real. I think we all have moments like this—*the peace that passeth all understanding*—and they do get fewer and more far between as we grow older. And that's why we have painters and all kinds of artists, because through their work, their eyes and souls and understanding, they can animate others long after they themselves are dead and bring to us a sense of intimacy with life that will support us once life begins to fail us.

Question

1. Compare the visual artistic techniques (and effects) that Coupland describes with his own writerly techniques (and effects) in this piece.

SUSAN SONTAG

Looking at War

(2002)

Susan Sontag (1933–2004) was the author of four novels, eight non-fiction works, several plays, and numerous essays. Among her books are On Photography *(1977),* Illness as Metaphor *(1978), and* Regarding the Pain of Others *(2003), as well as the novel* The Volcano Lover *(1992). Sontag was also a well-known human rights activist who won many international awards for her writing and activism.*

In these excerpts from a longer article first published in The New Yorker, *Sontag examines the art and effects of war photography.*

I

There are many uses of the innumerable opportunities that a modern life supplies for regarding—at a distance, through the medium of photography—other people's pain. Photographs of an atrocity may give rise to opposing responses: a call for peace; a cry for revenge; or simply the bemused awareness, continually restocked by photographic information, that terrible things happen. Who can forget the three color pictures by Tyler Hicks that the *New York Times* ran on November 13, 2001, across the upper half of the first page of its daily section devoted to America's new war? The triptych depicted the fate of a wounded Taliban soldier who had been found in a ditch by some Northern Alliance soldiers advancing toward Kabul. First panel: the soldier is being dragged on his back by two of his captors—one has grabbed an arm, the other a leg—along a rocky road. Second panel: he is surrounded, gazing up in terror as he is pulled to his feet. Third panel: he is supine with arms outstretched and knees bent, naked from the waist down, a bloodied heap left on the road by the dispersing military mob that has just finished butchering him. A good deal of stoicism is needed to get through the newspaper each morning, given the likelihood of seeing pictures that could make you cry. And the disgust and pity that pictures like Hicks's inspire should not distract from asking what pictures, whose cruelties, whose deaths you are *not* being shown.

II

Photography has kept company with death ever since cameras were invented, in 1839. Because an image produced with a camera is, literally, a trace of something brought before the lens, photographs had an advantage over any painting as a memento of the vanished past and the dear departed. To seize death in the making was another matter: the camera's reach remained limited as long as it had to be lugged about, set down, steadied. But, once the camera was emancipated from the tripod, truly portable, and equipped with a range finder and a variety of lenses that permitted unprecedented feats of close observation from a distant vantage point, picture-taking acquired an immediacy and authority greater than any verbal account in conveying the horror of mass-produced death. If there was one year when the power of photographs to define, not merely record, the most abominable realities trumped all the complex narratives, surely it was 1945, with the pictures taken in April and early May in Bergen-Belsen, Buchenwald, and Dachau, in the first days after the camps were liberated, and those taken by Japanese witnesses such as Yosuke Yamahata in the days following the incineration of the populations of Hiroshima and Nagasaki, in early August.

Photographs had the advantage of uniting two contradictory features. Their credentials of objectivity were inbuilt, yet they always had, necessarily, a point of view. They were a record of the real—incontrovertible, as no verbal account, however impartial, could be (assuming that they showed what they purported to show)—since a machine was doing the recording. And they bore witness to the real, since a person had been there to take them.

III

It seems that the appetite for pictures showing bodies in pain is almost as keen as the desire for ones that show bodies naked. For a long time, in Christian art, depictions of Hell offered both of these elemental satisfactions. On occasion, the pretext might be a Biblical decapitation story (Holofernes, John the Baptist) or massacre yarn (the newborn Hebrew boys, the eleven thousand virgins) or some such, with the status of a real historical event and of an implacable fate. There was also the repertoire of hard-to-look-at cruelties from classical antiquity—the pagan myths, even more than the Christian stories, offer something for every taste. No moral charge attaches to the representation of these cruelties. Just the provocation: Can you look at this? There is the satisfaction at being able to look at the image without flinching. There is the pleasure of flinching.

5   Not surprisingly, many of the canonical images of early war photography turn out to have been staged, or to have had their subjects tampered with. Roger Fenton,[1] after reaching the much shelled valley near Sebastopol[2] in his horse-drawn darkroom, made two exposures from the same tripod position: in the first version of the celebrated photograph he was to call "The Valley of the Shadow of Death" (despite the title, it was not across this landscape that the Light Brigade made its doomed charge), the cannonballs are thick on the ground to the left of the road; before taking the second picture—the one that is always reproduced—he oversaw the scattering of cannonballs on the road itself. A picture of a desolate site where a great deal of dying had indeed recently taken place, Beato's "Ruins of Sikandarbagh Palace," involved a more thorough theatricalization of its subject, and was one of the first attempts to suggest with a camera the horrific in war. The attack occurred in November, 1857, after which the victorious British troops and loyal Indian units searched the palace room by room, bayoneting the eighteen hundred surviving Sepoy[3] defenders who were now their prisoners and throwing their bodies into the courtyard; vultures and dogs did the rest. For the photograph he took in March or April, 1858, Beato constructed the courtyard as a deathscape, stationing some natives by two pillars in the rear and distributing human bones about the foreground.

  At least they were old bones. It's now known that the Brady[4] team rearranged and displaced some of the recently dead at Gettysburg; the picture titled "The Home of a Rebel Sharpshooter, Gettysburg" in fact shows a dead Confederate soldier who was moved from where he had fallen on the field to a more photogenic site, a cove formed by several boulders flanking a barricade of rocks, and includes a prop rifle that Gardner[5] leaned against the barricade beside the corpse. (It seems not to have been the special rifle a sharpshooter would have used, but a common infantryman's rifle; Gardner didn't know this or didn't care.)

  Only starting with the Vietnam War can we be virtually certain that none of the best-known photographs were setups. And this is essential to the moral authority of these images. The signature Vietnam War horror photograph, from 1972, taken by Huynh Cong Ut, of children from a village that has just been doused with American napalm running down the highway, shrieking with pain, belongs to the universe of photographs that can-

---

1 *Roger Fenton* Pioneering nineteenth-century photographer known for his images of war.

2 *Sebastopol* City in what is now Ukraine and the scene of a key battle in the Crimean War.

3 *Sepoy* A British soldier who is also a native of India.

4 *Brady* Mathew Brady (1822–96), a photographer famous for his images of the American Civil War.

5 *Gardner* Alexander Gardner (1821-82), prominent photographer who was first the assistant and then the colleague of Matthew Brady (see note 4).

not possibly be posed. The same is true of the well-known pictures from the most widely photographed wars since.

That there have been so few staged war photographs since the Vietnam War probably should not be attributed to higher standards of journalistic probity. One part of the explanation is that it was in Vietnam that television became the defining medium for showing images of war, and the intrepid lone photographer, Nikon or Leica in hand, operating out of sight much of the time, now had to compete with, and endure the proximity of, TV crews. There are always witnesses to a filming. Technically, the possibilities for doctoring or electronically manipulating pictures are greater than ever—almost unlimited. But the practice of inventing dramatic news pictures, staging them for the camera, seems on its way to becoming a lost art.

IV

That a gory battlescape could be beautiful—in the sublime or awesome or tragic register of the beautiful—is a commonplace about images of war made by artists. The idea does not sit well when applied to images taken by cameras: to find beauty in war photographs seems heartless. But the landscape of devastation is still a landscape. There is beauty in ruins. To acknowledge the beauty of photographs of the World Trade Center ruins in the months following the attack seemed frivolous, sacrilegious. The most people dared say was that the photographs were "surreal," a hectic euphemism behind which the disgraced notion of beauty cowered. But they were beautiful, many of them—by veteran photographers such as Gilles Peress, Susan Meiselas, and Joel Meyerowitz and by many little-known and nonprofessional photographers. The site itself, the mass graveyard that had received the name Ground Zero, was, of course, anything but beautiful. Photographs tend to transform, whatever their subject; and as an image something may be beautiful—or terrifying, or unbearable, or quite bearable—as it is not in real life.

Transforming is what art does, but photography that bears witness to the   10
calamitous and the reprehensible is much criticized if it seems "aesthetic"; that is, too much like art. The dual powers of photography—to generate documents and to create works of visual art—have produced some remarkable exaggerations about what photographers ought or ought not to do. These days, most exaggeration is of the puritanical kind. Photographs that depict suffering shouldn't be beautiful, as captions shouldn't moralize. In this view, a beautiful photograph drains attention from the sobering subject and turns it toward the medium itself, inviting the viewer to look "aesthetically," and thereby compromising the picture's status as a document. The photograph gives mixed signals. Stop this, it urges. But it also exclaims, What a spectacle!

The problem is not that people remember through photographs but that they remember only the photographs. This remembering through photographs eclipses other forms of understanding and remembering. The concentration camps—that is, the photographs taken when the camps were liberated, in 1945—are most of what people associate with Nazism and the miseries of World War II. Hideous deaths (by genocide, starvation, and epidemic) are most of what people retain of the clutch of iniquities and failures that have taken place in postcolonial Africa.

To remember is, more and more, not to recall a story but to be able to call up a picture. Even a writer as steeped in nineteenth-century and early-modern literary solemnities as W.G. Sebald was moved to seed his lamentation-narratives of lost lives, lost nature, lost cityscapes with photographs. Sebald was not just an elegist;[1] he was a militant elegist. Remembering, he wanted the reader to remember, too.

Harrowing photographs do not inevitably lose their power to shock. But they don't help us much to understand. Narratives can make us understand. Photographs do something else: they haunt us. Consider one of the most unforgettable images of the war in Bosnia, a photograph of which the *New York Times* foreign correspondent John Kifner wrote, "The image is stark, one of the most enduring of the Balkan wars: a Serb militiaman casually kicking a dying Muslim woman in the head. It tells you everything you need to know." But of course it doesn't tell us everything we need know.

From the identification supplied by the photographer, Ron Haviv, we learn that the photograph was taken in the town of Bijeljina in April, 1992, the first month of the Serb rampage through Bosnia. From behind, we see a uniformed Serb soldier, a youthful figure with sunglasses perched on the top of his head, a cigarette between the second and third fingers of his raised left hand, rifle dangling in his right hand, right leg poised to kick a woman lying face down on the sidewalk between two other bodies. The photograph doesn't tell us that she is Muslim, but she is not likely to have been labeled in any other way, or why would she and the two others be lying there, as if dead (why "dying"?), under the gaze of some Serb soldiers? In fact, the photograph tells us very little—except that war is hell, and that graceful young men with guns are capable of kicking in the head overweight older women lying helpless, or already killed.

The pictures of Bosnian atrocities were seen soon after they took place. Like pictures from the Vietnam War, such as Ron Haberle's documents of the massacre by a company of American soldiers of some five hundred unarmed civilians in the village of My Lai in March, 1968, they became important in bolstering indignation at this war which had been far from inevitable, far from intractable; and could have been stopped much sooner. Therefore one could feel an obligation to look at these pictures, grue-

---

1   *elegist* A poet who laments the dead.

some as they were, because there was something to be done, right now, about what they depicted. Other issues are raised when the public is invited to respond to a dossier of hitherto unknown pictures of horrors long past.

An example: a trove of photographs of black victims of lynching in small   15
towns in the United States between the eighteen-nineties and the nineteen-thirties, which provided a shattering, revelatory experience for the thousands who saw them in a gallery in New York in 2000. The lynching pictures tell us about human wickedness. About inhumanity. They force us to think about the extent of the evil unleashed specifically by racism. Intrinsic to the perpetration of this evil is the shamelessness of photographing it. The pictures were taken as souvenirs and made, some of them, into postcards; more than a few show grinning spectators, good churchgoing citizens, as most of them had to be, posing for a camera with the backdrop of a naked, charred, mutilated body hanging from a tree. The display of the pictures makes us spectators, too.

What is the point of exhibiting these pictures? To awaken indignation? To make us feel "bad"; that is, to appall and sadden? To help us mourn? Is looking at such pictures really necessary, given that these horrors lie in a past remote enough to be beyond punishment? Are we the better for seeing these images? Do they actually teach us anything? Don't they rather just confirm what we already know (or want to know)?

All these questions were raised at the time of the exhibition and afterward when a book of the photographs, *Without Sanctuary*,[1] was published. Some people, it was said, might dispute the need for this grisly photographic display, lest it cater to voyeuristic appetites and perpetuate images of black victimization or simply numb the mind. Nevertheless, it was argued, there is an obligation to "examine"—the more clinical "examine" is substituted for "look at"—the pictures. It was further argued that submitting to the ordeal should help us understand such atrocities not as the acts of "barbarians" but as the reflection of a belief system, racism, that by defining one people as less human than another legitimatizes torture and murder. But maybe they *were* barbarians. Maybe *this* is what barbarians look like. (They look like everybody else.)

That being said, whom do we wish to blame? More precisely, whom do we believe we have the right to blame? The children of Hiroshima and Nagasaki were no less innocent than the young African-American men (and a few women) who were butchered and hanged from trees in small-town America. More than a hundred thousand German civilians, three-fourths of them women, were incinerated in the R.A.F. fire bombing of Dresden on the night of February 13, 1945; seventy-two thousand civilians were killed by the

1   Als, Hilton, Jon Lewis, Leon F. Litwack, and James Allen. *Without Sanctuary: Lynching Photography in America.* Santa Fe, NM: Twin Palms Publishers, 2000.

American bomb dropped on Hiroshima. The roll call could be much longer. Again, whom do we wish to blame? What atrocities from the incurable past do we think we are obliged to see?

Probably, if we are Americans, we think that it would be "morbid" to go out of our way to look at pictures of burned victims of atomic bombing or the napalmed flesh of the civilian victims of the American war on Vietnam but that we have some kind of duty to look at the lynching pictures—if we belong to the party of the right-thinking, which on this issue is now large. A stepped-up recognition of the monstrousness of the slave system that once existed, unquestioned by most, in the United States is a national project of recent decades that many Euro-Americans feel some tug of obligation to join. This ongoing project is a great achievement, a benchmark of civic virtue. But acknowledgment of American use of disproportionate firepower in war (in violation of one of the cardinal laws of war) is very much not a national project. A museum devoted to the history of America's wars that included the vicious war the United States fought against guerrillas in the Philippines from 1899 to 1902 (expertly excoriated by Mark Twain), and that fairly presented the arguments for and against using the atomic bomb in 1945 on the Japanese cities, with photographic evidence that showed what those weapons did, would be regarded—now more than ever—as an unpatriotic endeavor.

Questions

1. What does Sontag mean when she writes about the power of photography to "define, not merely record, the most abominable realities" (paragraph 2)? What are the implications of her argument with regard to the powers (and limitations) of writing?
2. What two special features make photographs a uniquely powerful method of recording atrocities, according to Sontag? Compare and contrast Sontag's writing (about the photography of atrocities) with the characteristics she attributes to the photography of atrocities.
3. Both Sontag (paragraph 9) and Philip Gourevitch (paragraph 13 in "We Wish to Inform You That Tomorrow We Will be Killed with Our Families") use the word "beautiful" in relation to atrocities. Compare their uses of this word and their explanations for using it.

HENRY LOUIS GATES, JR.

Phillis Wheatley on Trial

(2003)

Henry Louis Gates, Jr. (1950–) is chair of the Department of African and African-American Studies at Harvard University. His books include Figures in Black: Signs and the "Racial" Self *(1987),* The Signifying Monkey: A Theory of Afro-American Literary Criticism *(1988),* Loose Canons: Notes on the Culture Wars *(1992), and* Thirteen Ways of Looking at a Black Man *(1997).*

This article provides an historical overview of Phillis Wheatley's life and status as a poet.

It was the primal scene of African-American letters. Sometime before October 8, 1772, Phillis Wheatley, a slim African slave in her late teens who was a published poet, met with eighteen of the most influential thinkers and politicians of the Massachusetts Colony. The panel had been assembled to verify the authorship of her poems and to answer a much larger question: Was a Negro capable of producing literature? The details of the meeting have been lost to history, but I've often imagined how it all might have happened. Phillis walks into a room—perhaps in Boston's Town Hall, the Old Colony House—and stands before these New England illuminati with a manuscript consisting of twenty-odd poems that she claims to have written. She is on trial, and so is her race.

Wheatley's poems had been appearing in periodicals and newspapers in New England and Britain since she was fourteen. One of her adolescent works, "On Being Brought from Africa to America," displays her typical subject matter and the hallmarks of her early style—religious piety wrapped in heroic couplets. The eight-line poem has been widely anthologized in collections of African-American literature in this century, most recently in James G. Basker's "Amazing Grace: An Anthology of Poems About Slavery, 1660-1810" (Yale; $45). It is a modest and not particularly sophisticated paean to her Christian education, and expresses a forgiving, even grateful attitude toward human trafficking:

'Twas mercy brought me from my *Pagan* land,
Taught my benighted soul to understand
That there's a God, that there's a *Saviour* too:
Once I redemption neither sought nor knew.
Some view our sable race with scornful eye,
"Their colour is a diabolic die."
Remember, *Christians*, *Negros*, black as *Cain*,
May be refin'd, and join th' angelic train.

She had arrived in Boston on July 11, 1761, on board the Phillis, a slaver that was returning from Senegal, Sierra Leone, and the Isles de Los, off the coast of Guinea. Most likely a native Wolof speaker from the Senegambian coast, she was "a slender, frail, female child," naked except for a kilt made from "a quantity of dirty carpet," as a descendant of her owners wrote in 1834. She had lost her front teeth, and so was thought to be about seven or eight years old. Susanna Wheatley, the wife of a prosperous tailor and merchant, John Wheatley, acquired her as a house servant, and named her after the slave ship.

John and Susanna Wheatley had teen-aged twins, Nathaniel and Mary, who were living at home when Phillis arrived. Phillis spoke no English, and Mary, apparently with her mother's encouragement, began to teach her to read, tutoring her in English, Latin, and the Bible. By 1765, Wheatley had written her first poem; in 1767, when she was thirteen or fourteen, the Newport *Mercury* published a poem that Susanna Wheatley submitted on her behalf. In 1770, when she was about seventeen, an elegy she wrote on the death of the Reverend George Whitefield, a popular English preacher who was a leader of the evangelical movement in England and America, was published in newspapers in Boston, Newport, New York, and Philadelphia. Whitefield had been the personal chaplain of an English philanthropist, Selina Hastings, the Countess of Huntingdon. Wheatley shrewdly apostrophized[1] the Countess in the Whitefield elegy and sent her a letter of condolence with the poem enclosed. With the poem's publication in London, in 1771, Wheatley suddenly had a wide readership on both sides of the Atlantic.

5   As her literary reputation grew, however, so did doubts about her authenticity, and the Wheatleys, attempting to publish her manuscript, were unable to elicit the number of book orders that printers in those days required. Eighteenth-century philosophers like David Hume[2] believed that blacks were a different species, and there was widespread incredulity at the idea of a black litterateur. It was John Wheatley who assembled the illustrious group of interrogators, hoping that they would support Phillis's claim of authorship, and that the opinion of the general public would follow.

---

1 *apostrophized* Addressed in an exclamatory manner.
2 *David Hume* (1711–76), Scottish philosopher, historian, and sceptic.

Picture the eighteen men gathered in a semicircle. At the center was, no doubt, His Excellency Thomas Hutchinson, the governor of Massachusetts. Hutchinson, a Colonial historian and a royal official, was born into a wealthy merchant family in Boston. He entered Harvard College at the age of twelve, where, because of his family's social position, he was ranked third in his class. (Even back then, grade inflation loomed on the Charles.) Following the Boston Tea Party,[1] he went to London, "for consultations," and never returned.

Andrew Oliver, the colony's lieutenant governor, would have been seated on one side of Hutchinson. Oliver imprudently allowed himself to be publicly identified as a supporter of the Stamp Act of 1765,[2] prompting angry crowds to ransack his house and uproot his garden. When, in 1774, Oliver had a stroke and died, commentators assumed that it was related to the political turmoil.

Quite a few men of the cloth were present. The Reverend Mather Byles was the minister of the Hollis Street Congregational Church, in Boston; he was the grandson of Increase Mather and the nephew of Cotton Mather.[3] As a young man, he had corresponded with Alexander Pope and Isaac Watts,[4] and in 1744 he had published a book of verse, "Poems on Several Occasions." Like Hutchinson and Oliver, Byles was a Tory loyalist, and he lost his pulpit when Massachusetts finally rebelled. He was sentenced to banishment, later commuted to house arrest, for his loyalist views. (Byles called the sentry stationed just outside the house his "Observe-a-Tory.")

Others of the Wheatley witnesses, though, were to become prominent figures in the newly founded republic. Among them was John Hancock, the head of the House of Hancock, which had grown rich by trading in whale oil and real estate. Hancock was later the president of the Second Continental Congress[5] and the first governor of the Commonwealth of Massachusetts.

---

1 *Boston Tea Party* On 16 December 1773, the Sons of Liberty boarded three English ships and dumped forty-five tons of tea into Boston Harbor.

2 *Stamp Act of 1765* British tax resulting from the mandatory use of stamped, or embossed, paper for such items as legal documents, newspapers, and playing cards; the stamp meant that the tax had been paid.

3 *Increase Mather* (1639–1723) American clergyman and strict Puritan who held considerable influence in the affairs of Colonial Massachusetts; *Cotton Mather* (1663–1728) Son of Increase Mather, American clergyman and writer who helped to found Yale University.

4 *Alexander Pope* (1688–1744) English poet and satirist; *Isaac Watts* (1674–1748) English hymn-writer and Nonconformist clergyman.

5 *Second Continental Congress* Colonial delegates initially formed the First Continental Congress in 1774 to protest against Britain's unpopular colonial policies; the Second Congress (1775–81) advocated independence from Britain, creating a Continental army with George Washington as commander in chief, and adopting the Declaration of Independence in 1776.

10   Nearly all the men present were Harvard graduates and a majority were slaveholders. One, Thomas Hubbard, had been a dealer in slaves; another, the Reverend Charles Chauncy, had attacked the Great Awakening, an evangelical movement that threatened the established religious order, because it allowed "women and girls; yea Negroes ... to do the business of preachers." The group that Wheatley faced was not exactly an association for the advancement of colored people.

There is no transcript of what took place in that room. Was Wheatley given scansion tests? Quizzed on the Latin subjunctive? Asked to recite the Psalms? We'll never know. Whatever the nature of the exam, she passed it, and earned the letter of support that she and her master had hoped for:

> We whose Names are under-written, do assure the World, that the Poems specified in the following Page, were (as we verily believe) written by Phillis, a young Negro Girl, who was but a few Years since, brought an uncultivated Barbarian from *Africa*, and has ever since been, and now is, under the Disadvantage of serving as a Slave in a Family in this Town. She has been examined by some of the best Judges, and is thought qualified to write them.

Even after the validation of the esteemed Bostonians, no American publisher was willing to take on Wheatley's manuscript, and so Susanna Wheatley turned to English friends for help. The publishing climate in England was more receptive to black authors. The Countess of Huntingdon, though a slaveholder herself (she had inherited slaves in Georgia), had already, in 1772, shepherded into print one of the earliest slave narratives, by James Gronniosaw.[1] Vincent Carretta, a leading scholar of eighteenth-century black transatlantic literature and an expert on Wheatley, has observed that the British market for black literature may have been indirectly created by a court ruling, in 1772, that made it illegal for slaves who had come to England to be forcibly returned to the colonies. Although the ruling stopped short of outlawing slavery in England, it encouraged an atmosphere of sympathy toward blacks.

Through the captain of the commercial ship that John Wheatley used for trade with England, Susanna engaged a London publisher, Archibald Bell, to bring out the manuscript. The Countess agreed to let Wheatley dedicate the book to her. An engraving of Wheatley appeared as the book's frontispiece, at the Countess's request.

"Poems on Various Subjects, Religious and Moral, by Phillis Wheatley, Negro Servant to Mr. John Wheatley of Boston" was published in Septem-

---

1 *James Gronniosaw* Author of *A Narrative of the Most Remarkable Particulars in the Life of James Albert Ukawsaw Gronniosaw, an African Prince* (1772), former African slave who lived in England.

ber, 1773. Five advertisements that ran in the London *Morning Post* & *Daily Advertiser* the month before pointed to the statement of the Boston panel as proof that Wheatley was the "real Author." The book's publication represented a significant moment in black literary achievement. Various black authors had published individual poems, but even these instances were rare. Jupiter Hammon,[1] a slave from Long Island, had published the first of several poems in 1760. Francis Williams,[2] a Jamaican who is said to have studied at Cambridge University, had caused a minor sensation when it was posthumously revealed that he had written an ode in Latin in 1759. Wheatley's book was widely reviewed and discussed in England and in America, where it became available in 1774. Voltaire[3] wrote to a correspondent that Phillis Wheatley had proved blacks could write poetry.

While Phillis was in London, where she had been sent with Nathaniel   15
Wheatley in the spring of 1773 to oversee the book's publication, she met the Earl of Dartmouth, who gave her five guineas to buy the works of Alexander Pope; Granville Sharp, the scholar and anti-slavery activist, who took her to the Tower of London; and Brook Watson, a future Lord Mayor of London, who gave her a folio edition of "Paradise Lost." Benjamin Franklin paid her a visit, which he mentions in a letter to his nephew Jonathan Williams, Sr. "Upon your Recommendation I went to see the black Poetess and offer'd her any Services I could do her," he wrote. "And I have heard nothing since of her." On the strength of this seemingly perfunctory visit, Wheatley decided to dedicate her second volume of poetry to Franklin. Even an audience with King George was arranged, although she had to cancel it when Susanna Wheatley suddenly fell ill and needed her care.

Within a month of the book's publication and Phillis's return to America, the Wheatleys freed her. (English reviewers, using Wheatley's book as a point of departure, had condemned the hypocrisy of a colony that insisted on liberty and equality when it came to its relationship to England but did not extend those principles to its own population.) Freedom meant that she became fully responsible for her literary career, and for her finances. In mid-October, she wrote a letter to David Wooster, the customs collector in New Haven, alerting him that a shipment of her books would soon arrive from England, and urging him to canvass among his friends for orders.

---

1   *Jupiter Hammon* African-American poet and slave (1711–1806?), author of "An Evening Thought: Salvation by Christ, With Penitential Cries" (c. 1760) and the first published African-American writer in America.

2   *Francis Williams* Jamaican poet (c. 1702–c. 1770), protégé of the Duke of Montagu, who was sent to England for private education.

3   *Voltaire* François-Marie Arouet (1694–1778), influential French enlightenment philosopher, dramatist, and essayist.

"Use your interest with Gentlemen & Ladies of your acquaintance to subscribe also, for the more subscribers there are, the more it will be for my advantage as I am to have half the Sale of the Books." She continued, "This I am the more solicitous for, as I am now upon my own footing and whatever I get by this is entirely mine, & it is the Chief I have to depend upon. I must also request you would desire the Printers in New Haven, not to reprint that Book, as it will be a great hurt to me, preventing any further Benefit that I might receive from the Sale of my Copies from England."

In the spring of 1774, the British occupied Boston. Susanna Wheatley died the same year, and when John Wheatley fled the city Phillis moved to Providence, where John Wheatley's daughter, Mary, and her husband lived. With the outbreak of war, in April of 1775, Phillis's prospects dimmed considerably. A number of the people who had signed the attestation were dead, and the others who had earlier supported her, both Tories and Patriots, were more concerned with winning the war than with the African prodigy. But Wheatley lost no opportunity to cultivate powerful friends, and on October 26, 1775, she wrote to General George Washington at his headquarters in Cambridge, aligning herself with the Revolutionary cause:

SIR

I Have taken the freedom to address your Excellency in the enclosed poem, and entreat your acceptance, though I am not insensible of its inaccuracies. Your being appointed by the Grand Continental Congress to be Generalissimo of the armies of North America, together with the fame of your virtues, excite sensations not easy to suppress. Your generosity, therefore, I presume, will pardon the attempt. Wishing your Excellency all possible success in the great cause you are so generously engaged in, I am,

Your Excellency's most obedient humble servant,

PHILLIS WHEATLEY

The accompanying poem was nothing if not flattering:

One century scarce perform'd its destined round,
When Gallic powers Columbia's fury found;
And so may you, whoever dares disgrace
The land of freedom's heaven-defended race! ...
Proceed, great chief, with virtue on thy side,
Thy ev'ry action let the goddess guide.
A crown, a mansion, and a throne that shine,
With gold unfading, WASHINGTON! be thine.

On February 28, 1776, Washington responded:

MISS PHILLIS,

Your favor of the 26th of October did not reach my hands, till the middle of December. Time enough, you will say, to have given an answer ere this. Granted. But a variety of important occurrences, continually interposing to distract the mind and withdraw the attention, I hope will apologize for the delay, and plead my excuse for the seeming but not real neglect. I thank you most sincerely for your polite notice of me, in the elegant lines you enclosed; and however undeserving I may be of such encomium and panegyric, the style and manner exhibit a striking proof of your poetical talents; in honor of which, and as a tribute justly due to you, I would have published the poem, had I not been apprehensive, that, while I only meant to give the world this new instance of your genius, I might have incurred the imputation of vanity. This, and nothing else, determined me not to give it place in the public prints.

If you should ever come to Cambridge, or near headquarters, I shall be happy to see a person so favored by the Muses, and to whom nature has been so liberal and beneficent in her dispensations. I am, with great respect, your obedient humble servant.

GEORGE WASHINGTON

In the event, Washington overcame his fear of the imputation of vanity and, by means of an intermediary, secured publication of Wheatley's pentametric praise in the *Virginia Gazette*, in March of 1776.

By late 1776, Wheatley had moved back to Boston. In 1778, she married a black man named John Peters. Peters was a small-time grocer and a sometime lawyer about whom very little is known—only that he successfully applied for the right to sell spirits in his store, and that a Wheatley relative remembered him as someone who affected the airs of a gentleman. Meanwhile, the poet continued her efforts to publish a second volume. In 1779, she advertised six times in the Boston *Evening Post* & *General Advertiser*, mentioning that she intended to dedicate the book to Benjamin Franklin. The advertisements failed to generate the necessary number of subscribers, and the book was never published.

Wheatley's freedom had enslaved her to a life of hardship. Peters abandoned her soon after she gave birth to their third child (the first two died in infancy). She placed her last advertisement in the September, 1784, issue of *The Boston Magazine* and died in December, at the age of thirty, poor and alone. Her baby died with her. Peters is thought to have sold the only copy of the second manuscript. A few years ago, one of the poems surfaced at Christie's, and sold for nearly seventy thousand dollars, but the full manuscript has never been recovered. 20

To her black contemporaries, Wheatley was a heroine. Jupiter Hammon published a laudatory poem entitled "An Address to Miss Phillis Wheatley

Ethiopian Poetess, in Boston," in 1778. Hammon's poem echoed and approved of the sentiments expressed in "On Being Brought from Africa to America": "Thou hast left the heathen shore, / Thro' mercy of the Lord, / Among the heathen live no more, / Come magnify thy God." Wheatley encouraged the work of other black artists, such as Hammon and Scipio Moorhead,[1] a well-known painter to whom she dedicated a poem. In letters to her best friend, Obour Tanner, a black woman she had met in Providence, Wheatley argued for the inherent right of blacks to be free. She corresponded with the English philanthropist John Thornton, a wealthy merchant and a friend of the Countess of Huntingdon. She used her fame and her acquaintance with political figures to complain bitterly about the human costs of the slave trade, as in a famous poem called "To the Right Honourable William, Earl of Dartmouth":

> I, young in life, by seeming cruel fate
> Was snatch'd from *Afric's* fancy'd happy seat:
> What pangs excruciating must molest,
> What sorrows labour in my parent's breast?
> Steel'd was that soul and by no misery mov'd
> That from a father seiz'd his babe belov'd:
> Such, such my case. And can I then but pray
> Others may never feel tyrannic sway?

And there is a letter Wheatley wrote about the evils of slavery to the Reverend Samson Occom, a Mohegan Indian minister in the Countess's circle. The letter was published several months after her manumission.[2] It appeared in *The Connecticut Gazette* on March 11, 1774, and reads, in part:

> In every human Breast, God has implanted a Principle, which we call Love of Freedom; it is impatient of Oppression, and pants for Deliverance; and by the Leave of our Modern Egyptians I will assert, that the same Principle lives in us.

In the half century following her death, Wheatley remained something of an icon in the abolitionist movement, and was frequently cited as proof of Africans' innate intellectual equality with whites.

At the same time, her popularity among the abolitionists brought her some formidable detractors. In "Notes on the State of Virginia," which was published in America in 1787, Thomas Jefferson dismissed Wheatley's poetry as undeserving of the name:

---

1 *Scipio Moorhead* African-American engraver and slave (c. 1750–?) whose portrait of Wheatley appeared on the cover page of her book.

2 *manumission* Freedom from slavery.

Misery is often the parent of the most affecting touches in poetry. Among the blacks is misery enough, God knows, but no poetry. Love is the peculiar oestrum[1] of the poet. Their love is ardent, but it kindles the senses only, not the imagination. Religion, indeed, has produced a Phillis Wheatley; but it could not produce a poet. The compositions composed under her name are below the dignity of criticism.

Phillis had plenty of experience—"misery enough"—and, thanks to the   25
Wheatleys, training in spelling and composition. What she lacked, Jefferson wrote, was an animating intellect. "Epictetus, Terence, and Phaedrus,[2] were slaves. But they were of the race of whites. It is not [the blacks'] condition then, but nature, which has produced the distinction." The authentication of Wheatley's authorship in 1772 missed the point, in Jefferson's view. The issue wasn't whether she was the genuine author but whether what she produced was genuine poetry.

The emergence, in the mid-eighteen-forties, of fugitive-slave authors, such as Frederick Douglass,[3] rendered Wheatley's stylized rhymes passé. Under the leadership of William Lloyd Garrison, the abolitionist movement was assuming an urgency and a stridency consonant with the angry realism of Douglass's voice. Wheatley disappeared from view, and when she reappeared, in the late nineteenth century, it was as a version of what Jefferson had made of her—a symbol of artificiality, of spiritless and rote convention. Unlike Douglass, who was embraced by the black literary community, she was a pariah, reviled for "On Being Brought from Africa to America," even though the poem belongs among her juvenilia. In 1887, Edward Wilmot Blyden, one of the fathers of black nationalism, wrote about her contemptuously, and the tone was set for the century to come.

"One looks in vain for some outburst or even complaint against the bondage of her people, for some agonizing cry about her native land," James Weldon Johnson[4] wrote about "On Being Brought from Africa to America," in 1922. Instead, one finds a "smug contentment at her own

---

1   *oestrum* Motivation or force that incites a person into doing something.
2   *Epictetus* Greek Stoic philosopher (c. 55–c. 135 CE) born into slavery but later freed; *Terence* North African dramatist (c. 190–159 BCE) brought to Rome as a slave, but was later freed by his master, a Roman senator; *Phaedrus* Thracian slave (c. 15 BCE–50 CE), freed in the household of Augustus, author of Latin verse fables modeled on Aesop.
3   *Frederick Douglass* American abolitionist and writer (c. 1817–95) who escaped from slavery in 1838, author of *Narrative of the Life of Frederick Douglass* (1845), and editor of the *North Star*, an abolitionist periodical.
4   *James Weldon Johnson* African-American poet, novelist, critic, journalist, songwriter, librettist, and educator (1871–1938).

escape therefrom." Wallace Thurman,[1] in 1928, called her "a third-rate imitation" of Alexander Pope: "Phillis in her day was a museum figure who would have caused more of a sensation if some contemporary Barnum had exploited her." Another black critic described her as "a clever imitator, nothing more."

By the nineteen-sixties, criticism of Wheatley had risen to a high pitch of disdain. Amiri Baraka, a founder of the Black Arts Movement, wrote in 1962 that Wheatley's "pleasant imitations of eighteenth-century English poetry are far and, finally, ludicrous departures from the huge black voices that splintered southern nights with their hollers, chants, arwhoolies, and ballits." In "Images of the Negro in American Literature" (1966), Seymour Gross wrote, "This Negro poetess so well fits the Uncle Tom syndrome.... She is pious, grateful, retiring, and civil." A few years later, the critic Addison Gayle, Jr., issued his own bill of indictment: Wheatley, he wrote, was the first among black writers "to accept the images and symbols of degradation passed down from the South's most intellectual lights and the first to speak with a sensibility finely tuned by close approximation to [her] oppressors." She had, in sum, "surrendered the right to self-definition to others." Phillis Wheatley, who had once been cast as the great paragon of Negro achievement, was now given a new role: race traitor.

The examples could be multiplied, as versions of the Jeffersonian critique have been taken up by successive generations of black writers and critics. Too black to be taken seriously by white critics in the eighteenth century, Wheatley was now considered too white to interest black critics in the twentieth. She was an impostor, a fraud, an avatar of inauthenticity. It's striking that Jefferson and Amiri Baraka, two figures in American letters who agreed on little else, could concur in the terms of their condemnation of Phillis Wheatley.

30   For Wheatley's critics, her sacrifices, her courage, her humiliations, her trials could never be enough. And so things came full circle: the sorts of racist suspicions and anxieties that first greeted Wheatley's writing were now directed at forms of black expression that failed the new test of cultural affirmation. The critics of the Black Arts Movement and after were convening their own interrogators, and they were a rather more hostile group than met that day in 1772. We can almost imagine Wheatley being frog-marched through another hall in the nineteen-sixties or seventies, surrounded by dashiki-clad[2] figures of "the Revolution": "What is Ogun's relation to Esu?"[3] "What are the seven principles of Kwanzaa?"[4]

---

1   *Wallace Thurman* African-American writer, editor, and journalist (1902–34), member of the Harlem Renaissance.
2   *dashiki* Brightly-patterned, loose, pull-over shirt.
3   *Ogun ... Esu* Deities of the Yoruba religion of West Africa.
4   *Kwanzaa* African-American festival, held between 26 December to 1 January.

"Santeria[1] is derived from which African culture?" And, finally, "Where you gonna be when the revolution comes, *sista?*"

If Wheatley stood for anything, of course, it was the creed that culture did, or could, belong equally to everyone. That's an ideal that has been arraigned, interrogated, and prosecuted with unremitting zeal, but it remains worth defending. The republic of letters that Wheatley so yearned to join—one that might embrace the writing of both Jefferson and his African-American descendants—was based on common expression, not common experience. What would happen, then, if we ceased to stereotype Wheatley, to cast her in this role or that, but, instead, read her, with all the resourcefulness that she herself brought to her craft? That's the only way to let Phillis Wheatley take the stand.

Questions

1. How does Gates compare Wheatley's hostile critics in the eighteenth century with those in the twentieth century? How is this comparison important to his argument?
2. Explain the distinction between "common expression" and "common experience" that Gates makes in the final paragraph of this essay.

---

1   *Santeria* Afro-Cuban religion melding aspects of Yoruba worship with Catholicism.

SOURCES

Arendt, Hannah. "Deportations from Western Europe," from *Eichmann in Jerusalem*. Copyright © 1963, 1964 by Hannah Arendt. Reprinted by permission of Viking Penguin, a division of Penguin Group (USA) Inc.

Baker, Nicholson. "Changes of Mind," from *The Size of Thoughts*. Copyright © 1996 by Nicholson Baker. Reprinted by permission of Random House, Inc.

Baldwin, James. "Notes of a Native Son," from *Notes of a Native Son*. New York: Literary Classics of the United States, 1998. Copyright © 1949, 1950, 1951, 1953, 1954, 1955 by James Baldwin.

Coupland, Douglas. "Cigs" and "Group of Seven," from *Souvenir of Canada*. Copyright © 2002 by Douglas Coupland. Reprinted by permission of Douglas & McIntyre Ltd.

Darnton, Robert. "Workers Revolt: The Great Cat Massacre of the Rue Saint-Séverin," from *The Great Cat Massacre and Other Essays in French Cultural History*. Copyright © 1984 by Robert Darnton. Reprinted by permission of Basic Books, a member of Perseus Books, LLC.

Didion, Joan. "History Lesson," from *Travel + Leisure Magazine*. Copyright © 2003 by Joan Didion. Reprinted by permission of Janklow and Nesbit Associates.

Dillard, Annie. "Terwilliger Bunts One," from *An American Childhood*. Copyright © 1987 by Annie Dillard. Reprinted by permission of HarperCollins Publishers Inc.

Dyer, Gwynne. "How People Power Topples the Tyrant," from *The Globe and Mail*. Copyright © 1999 by Gwynne Dyer. Reprinted by permission of Gwynne Dyer.

Ehrenreich, Barbara. "Maid to Order," from *Harper's Magazine*. Copyright © 2000 by Barbara Ehrenreich. Reprinted by permission of International Creative Management, Inc.

Franklin, Nancy. "Model Citizens," from *The New Yorker*. Copyright © 2003 by Nancy Franklin. Reprinted by permission of the author.

Freedman, David H. "The Aggressive Egg," from *Discover Magazine*. Copyright © 1992 by David H. Freedman. Reprinted by permission of the author.

Fussman, Cal. "In Her Own Words: Meenakshi Wadhwa," from *Discover Magazine*. Copyright © 2004 by Cal Fussman. Reprinted by permission of the author.

Gates Jr., Henry Louis. "Phillis Wheatley on Trial," from *The New Yorker*. Copyright © 2003 by Henry Louis Gates, Jr. Reprinted by permission of the author.

Gayton, Don. "A Cautionary Tale," from *Alternatives Journal*. Copyright © 2003 by Don Gayton. Reprinted by permission of the author

Gellhorn, Martha."The Bomber Boys," from *The Face of War*. Copyright © 1993 by Dr. Sandy Matthews. Reprinted by permission of Dr. Sandy Matthews.

Gladwell, Malcolm. "Brain Candy," from *The New Yorker*. Copyright © 2005 by Malcolm Gladwell. Reprinted by permission of the author.

Gould, Stephen Jay. "Entropic Homogeneity Isn't Why No One Hits .400 Any More," from *Discover Magazine*. Copyright © 1986 by Stephen Jay Gould. Reprinted by permission of Rhonda R. Shearer.

Gourevitch, Phillip. "We Wish to Inform You That Tomorrow We Will Be Killed with Our Families," from *We Wish to Inform You That Tomorrow We Will Be Killed With Our Families*. Copyright © 1998 by Philip Gourevitch. Reprinted by permission of Farrar, Strauss and Giroux, LLC.

Grandin, Temple. "My Story," from *Animals in Translation: Using the Mysteries of Autism to Decode Animal Behavior*. Copyright © 2005 by Temple Grandin. Reprinted by permission of the author.

Grealy, Lucy. "Pony Party," from *Autobiography of a Face*. Copyright © 1994 by Lucy Grealy. Reprinted by permission of Houghton Mifflin Company. All rights reserved.

Hemingway, Ernest. "Pamplona in July," from *By-Line: Ernest Hemingway*. Edited by William White. Copyright © 1967 By-Line Ernest Hemingway, Inc. Copyright renewed © 1995 by Patrick Hemingway and John H. Hemingway. Reprinted by permission of Scribner, an imprint of Simon & Schuster Adult Publishing Group.

Highet, Gilbert. "The Gettysburg Address," from *A Clerk of Oxenford: Essays on Literature and Life*. Copyright © 1954 by Gilbert Highet. Reprinted by permission of Curtis Brown, Ltd.

Hoagland, Edward. "The Courage of Turtles," from *The Village Voice*. Copyright © 1971 by Edward Hoagland. Reprinted by permission of Lescher & Lescher Ltd.

Ingram, Jay. "This Chapter is a Yawner," from *The Science of Everyday Life*. Copyright © 1989 by Jay Ingram. Reprinted by permission of the author

King Jr., Martin Luther. "Letter From Birmingham Jail," from *Why We Can't Wait*. Copyright © 1963 Martin Luther King Jr., copyright © renewed 1991 Coretta Scott King. Reprinted by arrangement with the Estate of Martin Luther King Jr., c/o Writers House as agent for the proprietor New York, NY.

Klass, Perri. "Learning the Language," *from A Not Entirely Benign Procedure: Four Years as a Medical Student*. Copyright © 1987 by Perri Klass. Reprinted by permission of Elaine Markson Literary Agency.

Klein, Naomi. "The Swoosh," from *No Logo*. Copyright © by Naomi Klein. Reprinted by permission of Knopf Canada.

Lin, Maya. "Vietnam Veterans Memorial," from *Boundaries*. Copyright ©

2002 by Maya Lin Studio, Inc. Reprinted by permission of Simon & Schuster Adult Publishing Group.

Lopez, Barry. "The Passing Wisdom of Birds," from *Crossing Open Ground.* Copyright © 1988 by Barry Lopez. Reprinted by permission of Sterling Lord Literistic, Inc.

Milgram, Stanley. "Behavioural Study of Obedience," from *Journal of Abnormal and Social Psychology.* Copyright © renewal 1991 by Alexandra Milgram. Reprinted by permission.

Momaday, N. Scott. "The Way to Rainy Mountain" from *The Way to Rainy Mountain.* Copyright © 1969 by the University of New Mexico Press. First Published in *The Reporter,* January 26, 1967. Reprinted by permission of New Mexico Press.

Murray, Robert W. "It's Not Like Falling Asleep." Originally published in *Harper's Magazine.* November 2000. Excerpted from "Chapter 11: It's Not Like Falling Asleep," from *Life on Death Row.* Reprinted by permission of Robert W. Murray.

Orwell, George. "Shooting An Elephant" from *Shooting An Elephant and Other Essays.* Copyright © 1950 by Harcourt, Inc., and renewed 1979 by Sonia Brownell Orwell. Reprinted by permission of the publisher.

Robinson, Laura. "Gender Testing by Any Other Name," from *Black Tights: Women, Sport and Sexuality.* Copyright © 2002 by Laura Robinson. Reprinted by permission of the author.

Rodriguez, Richard. "Profession (Section I)," from *Hunger of Memory.* Boston: David Godine, 1981. Copyright © 1981 by Richard Rodriguez. Reprinted by permission of Georges Borchardt Inc., on behalf of the author.

Rybczynski, Witold. "One Good Turn," from *One Good Turn: A Natural History of the Screwdriver and the Screw.* Copyright © 2000 by Witold Rybczynski. Reprinted by permission of Witold Rybczynski.

Schlosser, Eric. "Why McDonald's French Fries Taste So Good," from *Fast Food Nation: The Dark Side Of The All American Meal.* Copyright © 2001 by Eric Schlosser. First published in *The Atlantic Monthly,* January 2001. Excerpted and reprinted by permission of Houghton Mifflin Company. All rights reserved.

Sedaris, David. "Old Faithful," from *The New Yorker.* Copyright © 2004 by David Sedaris. Reprinted by permission of Don Congdon Associates, Inc.

Singer, Peter. "Speciesism," from *Animal Liberation.* Copyright © 2002 by Peter Singer. Reprinted by permission of Peter Singer.

Sontag, Susan. "Looking at War," from *The New Yorker,* first published December 9, 2002. Copyright © 2002 by Susan Sontag. Reprinted by permission of The Wylie Agency.

Steinem, Gloria. "Supremacy Crimes," from *Ms. Magazine.* Copyright © 1999 by Ms. Magazine. Reprinted by permission of *Ms. Magazine.*

GLOSSARY OF TERMS

Abstraction See **rhetorical pattern**.

Allegory (Greek, "speaking otherwise") A form of extended metaphor in which the elements of a story (its characters, actions, objects, etc.) can be understood to represent abstract ideas or principles outside of the story itself. (See **metaphor, symbol**.)

Alliteration (Latin, "repeating the same letter") A figure of speech in which the initial consonant or vowel sounds of a word are repeated in successive (or proximate) syllables within a given phrase or line of writing. Though more often employed in poetry, alliterative constructions in prose can help to emphasize key elements of argument or description. (See **assonance, consonance**.)

Allusion A brief reference to another work of literature or art, or to an historical or literary figure or event. Allusions attempt to draw upon a body of knowledge that is shared between the writer and his or her intended audience in order to enrich, through association, a particular passage, or the reading experience in general.

Ambiguity The quality in a word, statement, or entire piece of writing of having more than one possible meaning. Most frequently, the writer of an essay is best advised to avoid ambiguity, as it can lead to confusing or misleading writing. Occasionally, however, ambiguity can be employed in a provocative manner, prompting further reflection on hazy or thorny issues, or guiding the reader to probe the facets of a given argument more deeply.

Analepsis (Greek, "a taking back") In analeptic writing, more commonly called "flashbacks," descriptions of events or experiences from an earlier time are inserted into a narrative, taking the narrative back in time from the point it has reached, or has been assumed to have reached. (See **prolepsis**.)

Analogy (Greek, "proportion") A comparison of two parallel things or situations by which the less familiar is clarified by comparing it to something more familiar.

Anaphora (Greek, "a carrying up or back") The repetition of a word or group of words at the beginning of two or more successive clauses or sentences.

Anastrophe (Greek, "a turning back") The transposition of the normal word order of a sentence to place emphasis on certain words or clauses.

Antithesis (Greek, "opposition") A figure of speech in which sharply contrasting words, phrases, or ideas are employed in close proximity to one another in a balanced or parallel structure.

Aphorism (Greek, "distinction, definition") A concise, sometimes terse statement of a truth or principle. An aphorism both expands and condenses at the same time, in that it encapsulates a lofty idea in just a few words.

Apostrophe (Greek, "a turning away") A figure of speech in which a person, a place, a thing, or an idea is directly addressed as if present and capable of understanding.

Argumentation One of the four main modes of composition. Argumentation aims to convince a reader of the truth or falseness of an idea by making appeals to emotion or to reason. (See **description**, **exposition**, **narration**.)

Assonance The repetition of similar vowel sounds close together, usually in order to achieve a pleasing, harmonious effect. (See **alliteration**, **consonance**, **euphony**.)

Asyndeton (Greek, "unconnected") A means of achieving compact expression by omitting conjunctions in a sequence in which one might normally expect them to appear. Caesar's "I came, I saw, I conquered" is a common example. (See **polysyndeton**.)

Audience The actual or intended readers of a piece of writing. A writer's choice of audience will influence the tone and diction of a piece of work. Whereas a diary entry may give rise to idiosyncratic or colloquial writing, an essay for class will most likely require a much more formal approach.

Bathos (Greek, "depth") An unintentional, abrupt fall from the exalted to the banal or commonplace, either in style or content. Bathos produces an anti-climactic effect that makes a piece of writing sound ridiculous.

Cacophony (Greek, "harshness of sound") A harsh, unpleasant combination of sounds. (See **euphony**.)

Cause and Effect See **rhetorical pattern**.

Classification See **rhetorical pattern**.

Cliché A trite, overused expression or idea.

Comparison and Contrast See **rhetorical pattern**.

Conciseness Crispness or succinctness in writing and speaking achieved by expressing ideas meticulously and economically.

Conclusion The closing section of a piece of writing. Customarily, conclusions provide a succinct summary of the essay's main point or points. More complex conclusions may also offer the following:
1. Comments or suggestions on the broader implications of one's argument.
2. An illustrative quotation or anecdote that complements the preceding argumentation.
3. Suggestions regarding the future development of the issue.

Connotation The set of associations suggested by a word or phrase above and beyond the literal meaning. (See **denotation**.)

Consonance The repetition of similar consonant sounds close together, before or after different vowel sounds. Consonance is often used to reinforce meaning or to link related words. (See **alliteration, assonance**.)

Deduction A method of reasoning by which one examines general principles in order to arrive at a specific conclusion. (See **induction**.)

Definition See **rhetorical pattern**.

Denotation The literal meaning of a word, regardless of the emotional associations it may have. (See **connotation**.)

Description One of the four main modes of composition. Description aims to bring something to life so that a reader might better picture a scene or setting or mood; description is usually used in conjunction with other modes of discourse. (See **argumentation, exposition, narration**.)

Diction A writer's word choice; the vocabulary he or she uses. Diction involves the arrangement of words; determining one's audience; evaluating one's purpose; and, often, deciding on a particular form of writing or principal mode of discourse.

Didacticism (Greek, "teaching") The inclination in writing to instruct or give guidance, usually but not always toward some moral purpose. Strictly speaking, all writing is didactic in that all writing attempts to communicate something; didacticism, however, is more often used in a pejorative sense to describe writing that comes across as self-righteous, smug, or overzealous.

Digression A deviation from the subject; any discussion of material not strictly relevant to the main subject of a work.

Emphasis The stressing of important words, ideas, themes, or arguments in order to make them stand out. There are a variety of ways in which this can be accomplished: proportion (devoting more or less space to major and minor arguments); position (the arrangement of a key point at the beginning or end of a paragraph, or key arguments at the beginning or end of an essay); repetition (e.g., restated words or the rephrasing of ideas); and various literary devices, as well, such as **anastrophe, alliteration, polysyndeton**, and **hyperbole**, can be used to emphasize key words or ideas.

Euphony (Greek, "sweetness of sound") A harmonious, pleasant combination of sounds. (See **cacophony**.)

Exposition One of the four main modes of composition. Exposition aims to present information and, accordingly, is the primary mode of composition employed by students in their own writing. A wide variety of techniques are available to the writer of expository prose, including classifying, defining, drawing analogies, comparing and contrasting, etc. (See **argumentation, description, narration**.)

Figurative Language Language that departs from the literal meaning of words in order to achieve a special effect or association. This is accomplished by employing figures of speech, e.g., **imagery, metaphor, simile, hyperbole**, and **metonymy**.

Generalization See **rhetorical pattern**.

Hyperbole (Greek, "excess") A figure of speech in which exaggeration is used, usually for humorous or ironic effect. (See **irony, litotes, meiosis**.)

Imagery The use of language to represent objects, ideas, feelings, experiences, sensory perceptions, etc. Also, figurative illustrations of these things. (See **figurative language, metaphor, simile, symbol**.)

Induction A method of reasoning by which one examines specific details in order to arrive at a general conclusion. (See **deduction**.)

Introduction The opening section of a piece of writing. An introduction establishes the topic to be discussed, the writer's attitude toward it, and, possibly, the ideas or arguments that will follow.

Irony (Greek, "dissimulation") There are three kinds of irony used by writers, all of which involve some form of dissembling for effect, rather than to deceive or misinform. **Verbal** irony is the use of words to imply one thing while saying something entirely different; the writer's control of his or her tone thus becomes critical in distinguishing meaning. In **situational** irony there is a discrepancy between appearance and reality or between actions and their results; what might normally be expected to occur in a given situation does not. In **dramatic** irony (found in plays, novels, and other fiction), readers are privy to information that the characters lack, thus often plainly revealing their wisdom or folly. (See **hyperbole**, **litotes**, **meiosis**, **sarcasm**.)

Litotes (Greek, "small, plain, meagre") A form of understatement, or **meiosis**, in which a positive statement is expressed through the negation of a contrary statement. Examples include the statements "not bad" (meaning "good") and "not smart" (meaning "stupid"). (See **hyperbole**, **irony**, **meiosis**.)

Logical Fallacies Errors in reasoning. Some of the more common examples follow.

Ad hominem (Latin, "directed at the person")
A personal attack on an opponent rather than on his or her ideas or opinions.

Straw man argument
Ascribing to an opponent an extreme view that has in fact never been put forward; then, assuming a winning position in the argument by having dismantled that extreme view.

Begging the question
Taking for granted the very thing to be argued about, and implying or directly asserting its truth from the start.

Hasty generalization
A generalization based on limited or biased evidence.

Slippery slope argument
The assumption that one development in a certain direction will give rise to further developments in that same direction.

False analogy
Assuming the likeness of two things based on comparing only their similarities, while overlooking differences that may weaken the argument.

False dichotomy
An argument that insists on only two alternatives when in fact its complexity suggests more possibilities exist. This is sometimes referred to as "either/or reasoning." (Related to this is *oversimplification*, which implies a single cause or solution for an issue that is in reality much more complex.)

Missing premises
Taking shortcuts by not acknowledging all the underlying premises of an argument.

Post hoc, propter hoc (Latin, "after this, because of this")
Assuming that if one thing happens after another, then the first thing caused the second to happen. Confusing cause and effect.

Non sequitur (Latin, "it does not follow")
A conclusion that does not follow logically from the premise or premises one has outlined.

Meiosis (Greek, "lessening") An intentional understatement, used for emphasis or for ironic or dramatic effect. (See **hyperbole, irony, litotes**.)

Metaphor A figure of speech in which one thing is described by making use of the terms or qualities of another, thus drawing an implicit comparison (as opposed to the explicit comparison made by a simile). (See **imagery, simile**.)

Metonymy (Greek, "change of name") A figure of speech in which one thing is represented by one of its attributes, or by something else that is associated with it. (See **synecdoche**.)

Narration One of the four main modes of composition. Narration is the recounting of an event or series of events. (See **argumentation, description, exposition**.)

Objectivity The quality or state of being uninfluenced by emotion, assumption, or personal opinion. (See **subjectivity**.)

Onomatopoeia (Greek, "word-making") A word that imitates a certain sound (for example, "zoom" or "whoosh") or whose sound suggests its meaning. Also, the formation and use of such words. (See **cacophony, euphony**.)

Oxymoron (Greek, "pointedly foolish") A figure of speech that combines apparently contradictory words to achieve a particular effect.

Paradox (Greek, "beyond opinion") A statement that may seem contradictory or absurd but that, on closer inspection, reveals a certain truthfulness.

Paragraph A unified group of sentences that deals with a single idea or episode.

Parallelism The arrangement of two or more phrases or clauses of equal importance in a similar grammatical form.

Parody (Greek, "burlesque poem or song") A work that imitates aspects of another, ridiculing it either playfully or critically, often by means of exaggeration.

Pathos (Greek, "suffering, emotion") The quality in art or literature that arouses feelings of pity, sympathy, tenderness, or sorrow.

Periphrasis (Greek, "roundabout speech") Speaking or writing in an indirect, roundabout manner; circumlocution. The use of meandering prose and long words where a few simple sentences would suffice.

Person A grammatical distinction among three groups of pronoun forms: the speaker, or first person (I, we); the individual addressed, or second person (you); and the individual spoken about, or third person (he, she, it, they).

Point of View Refers to a writer's attitude toward his or her subject, and the position from which this attitude is considered and conveyed. (See **objectivity**, **subjectivity**.)

Polysyndeton (Greek, "bound together many times") The repetition of conjunctions (often "and" or "or") in a series of coordinate words, phrases, or clauses in which they would not normally be expected to appear, thus forcing the reader to "slow down." (See **asyndeton**.)

Prolepsis (Greek, "preconception, anticipation") An anachronism in which something is presumed to have happened before it does (that is, a future event is treated as if past), or an attribute is applied before it properly should be, in anticipation of some event (e.g., referring to a man on death row as a "dead man"). The term can also refer to the anticipating—and answering—of a potential counter-argument before an opponent has had the opportunity to present it. (See **analepsis**.)

Revision The process of reading over a piece of writing in order to identify errors and inconsistencies, and then of changing or reorganizing text from draft to draft with an eye to improving it, possibly through changes in focus, tone, structure, organization, attention to audience, emphasis, mechanics, and spelling.

Rhetoric The art of using language for persuasion, including all the techniques that may be used to sway someone's opinion, such as the employment of figures of speech, the emphasis of words and ideas, argumentation, the particular diction and organization used, etc.

Rhetorical Pattern The general manner in which an essay is organized; the method by which it presents its topic to the reader. Rarely will an essay incorporate one method to the exclusion of all others.

> **Narration** The recounting of an event or series of events. Narration is also one of the four main modes of composition.
>
> **Classification**
>> Compare/Contrast. A method that aims to show the similarities and differences between two or more things or ideas.
>>
>> Description. A method that aims to bring something to life so that a reader might better picture a scene or setting or mood. Description is also one of the four main modes of composition.
>>
>> Definition. An explanation of the essential properties of a thing or idea. In an essay, a writer will often extend or qualify a definition in order to elaborate upon an argument.
>
> **Generalization** and **Abstraction**
>> Generalization is the process of using observations or conclusions about a single member or a few members of a group to form a conclusion about all or most of that group. Abstraction is the consideration of some particular quality or attribute of a thing independently of the rest of its properties.
>
> **Cause and Effect**
>> A method that aims to show the *why* and *what* of an issue, event, idea or incident, whether real or fictional.

Rhetorical Question A question put forward for effect, without the expectation of a reply, or one for which the answer is more or less self-evident.

Sarcasm (Greek, "tearing of flesh") An insult spoken as apparent praise, or a cutting remark designed to mock through obvious understatement or exaggeration. (See **irony.**)

Satire (Latin, "medley") A disapproving and sometimes contemptuous work which, by utilizing wit and humour, aims to improve or reform human folly or wickedness.

Simile (Latin, "like") A figure of speech in which one thing is explicitly compared to another, essentially unlike thing, most often in a phrase introduced by *like* or *as.* (See **imagery, metaphor.**)

Style A writer's characteristic manner of expression. Assessing style involves studying how the writer uses language—e.g., the choice of words (diction); the extent to which figurative language might be used; the arrangement and shape or length of sentences (syntax); and the methods of emphasis.

Subjectivity The condition of being absorbed in, or concerned with, personal experiences and feelings; the quality of viewing things exclusively through one's own experience. (See **objectivity, point of view**.)

Symbol (Greek, "mark, token") An object that stands in for or represents something else, beyond itself (usually something abstract, such as an idea or quality—for example, the dove, symbolizing peace). (See **allegory, imagery, metonymy, synecdoche**.)

Synecdoche (Greek, "a taking up with something else") A figure of speech in which a part of something stands in for, or is used to represent, the whole. A common example is the biblical reference to "bread," meaning meals in general (as in "Give us this day our daily bread"). The term also occasionally refers to the reverse process, in which the whole of something stands in for a part. (See **metonymy, symbol**.)

Tautology (Greek, "repetition of what has been said") The repetition of words or ideas that do not add either force or clarity.

Thesis A proposition to be proved or a position on an issue to be clarified.

Tone The writer's attitude toward the subject. A writer's tone helps a reader determine how to react to the writing; for example, a writer's tone may be serious and formal, or humorous and informal, to use just two opposing possibilities. Tone's differentiation from style can be illustrated by observing their parallels in speech. A parent's *tone* of voice when punishing a child may be stern and severe, but later on at the dinner table it may perhaps be kind and agreeable. However, the *style* of the parent's speech may not show any significant change; that is, his or her style of speaking—the diction and syntax—can remain the same while the tone alters. (See **style**.)

Topic Sentence A sentence, usually placed at the beginning of a paragraph, that communicates the main idea of that paragraph.

Transition A word, phrase, sentence, or series of sentences that connects one section of writing with another.

Unity An organizing principle relating to the overall coherence of a work, according to which all parts work together toward a single, consistent goal.

A piece of writing with perfect unity would suffer if any one part were omitted or any additional part added.

Verisimilitude The degree to which a work maintains the semblance of truth, regardless of whether or not it is based on reality. In order to maintain such an appearance of reality, the work must follow an internal logic and present its reality as plausible.

INDEX
AUTHOR AND TITLE